HALF BITTER, HALF SWEET

**An Excursion into
Italian-American History**

Alexander DeConde

HALF BITTER,

HALF SWEET

An Excursion into
Italian-American History

CHARLES SCRIBNER'S SONS
New York

1971

Acknowledgment

The idea for this book came to me while I was a Fulbright scholar at the *Centro di Studi Americani* in Palazzo Antici-Mattei, Rome, in 1965. Since that time my thinking on the subject has gone through numerous changes, profiting from the help of friends, scholars, colleagues, and others. Lynne Cantlay read the manuscript with a critical eye, making perceptive suggestions for intellectual and stylistic improvement; the manuscript also had the benefit of the skilled editorial eye of Gillian M. Burdett. Three graduate students, Perry Kaufman, Alberta Sanders, and Rolfe Buzzell worked with me as research assistants, contributing invaluable support. The John Simon Guggenheim Memorial Foundation granted me a fellowship in 1968 for travel to and research in Italy and the Research Council of the University of California, Santa Barbara, also financed research and writing. To these and all others who helped, especially the gracious librarians scattered over the country, I offer thanks.

A.D.

Table of Contents

HALF BITTER, HALF SWEET

**An Excursion into
Italian-American History**

Early
Encounters

1

Although an Italian, Cristoforo Colombo, discovered America and
another, Amerigo Vespucci, gave it his name, neither Italians as a
people nor Italy as a country had a significant place in the early history of the United States. During the colonial period, a few men from
the Italian peninsula settled in the cities along the Atlantic seaboard,
but this sprinkling of Italians left no noteworthy mark on the life of
the English colonies. In 1621, a small group of Italian glassmakers at
Jamestown did make an impression, but a negative one. According to
the secretary of that colony, "a more damned crew hell never
vomited."

The largest group of Italians to settle in North America consisted
of about 200 Protestants from the valleys of Piedmont. Usually called
"Waldensians" after Peter Waldo of Lyon, the merchant who founded
their sect, they suffered persecution and massacre at home, and fled
to Holland. From there they sought refuge in the New World, arriving in New Amsterdam in the spring of 1657. A few weeks after their
arrival, they moved on to Delaware, where, on land purchased for
them by Dutch Protestants, they organized the first government of the
colony of New Amstel, later called New Castle. Historians know little
about these settlers and their movements except that they were Italians who spoke and kept their records in French, and that a small
band of them also established a settlement at Stony Brook, New
York.

Since few Italians lived in the colonies and English navigation laws
restricted trade between the colonials and the states of the Italian
peninsula, the people of British North America had little reason for
interesting themselves in Italy or in her politics. Those few colonists
of wealth and education who knew something about Italy admired
her art and literature but had practically no concern for her people.

Only a handful of colonists visited Italy, among them Robert Child and Henry Saltonstall, members of the first class of Harvard College. Both studied medicine at the University at Padua, Child receiving his doctorate in 1639 and Saltonstall in 1649. John Winthrop, Jr., a friend of Child's who later became governor of Connecticut, also traveled in Italy in these years.

Later, when the English colonists became stirred by the Corsican struggle for independence, knowledge of Italy and her problems gained some prominence in North America. Over a period of two centuries, the Corsicans had tried several times to break away from Genoa, the state that controlled their island. In 1755, when Pasquale Paoli, a fiery leader and able fighter, landed on the island from the Italian mainland to lead them, their struggle took a dramatic turn. For fourteen years, Paoli fought desperately, arousing wide admiration for his cause, particularly in England and in North America. His battles ended in 1768 when Genoa sold Corsica to France. Then Paoli and 400 of his followers left the island and sought refuge at Leghorn. Eventually he moved to London, where he died in 1804. In North America, Paoli's name became a symbol of heroism and freedom. Benjamin Franklin and others admired him, and at public banquets colonists drank toasts to Paoli and his Corsicans. A town just outside Philadelphia was named after him. Later, as the colonists began to take up arms against England, his chief admirers became the Sons of Liberty, men who themselves used violence to overthrow British rule.

Although limited in their knowledge of Italy, the English colonists probably knew more about Italians than even educated Italians knew about North Americans. Aside from Franklin, whose writings were well known in Italy, colonial America produced few cultural or scientific leaders of sufficient international distinction to arouse Italian interest in colonial life and thought. Books about the New World published in eighteenth-century Italy usually described the land before the coming of the European, the early voyages of discovery, and society in Spanish America. Italians also wrote poems, novels, and dramas extolling the qualities of the American Indians which supported the concept of the noble savage. Only in the second half of the century did literate Italians begin to shift their interest to life in the colonies of British North America. This interest, in part at least, grew out of a high regard for everything English—a viewpoint that had become the vogue in Italy.

Books giving a glimpse into the life of the people in North America now began appearing in Italy to help satisfy the desire of cultured Italians for accurate information about the New World. In 1763, a publisher in Leghorn brought out an Italian translation of *The American Gazetteer,* published the previous year in London. In Venice in that same year, there appeared an Italian version of Edmund Burke's *An Account of the European Settlements in America.* Italians, so the translator said, were the only people without a colony in that new world that Italians had discovered. He wanted his countrymen to know something about America and urged the poor among them to go to North America, suggesting that the British authorities would gladly provide land there for an Italian settlement. Concern over the lack of Italian colonization in America became a recurring lament of many of those Italians who wrote about the New World. At the time, the sorrow may have been unrealistic. The laws of the various Italian states, particularly of those in the south, barred emigration. In the eighteenth century, the Italians, unlike the English, were not considered a migrating people. Alfred Legoyt, a French student of emigration, wrote that Italy is "the land in which love of country had the deepest roots in the hearts of its inhabitants." History has not, he pointed out in a book published in 1861, "recorded in Italy any important outward movement of population." The peasants worked the soil and were unwilling to leave it. Italians, it was said, were rooted in the ground like trees.

The few Italians who made their way to British or Spanish North America in the colonial era usually did so as individuals, not as part of a group migration. There were, of course, the usual exceptions. In 1768 about 100 Italians, indentured laborers, took part in the unsuccessful effort to establish a colony at New Smyrna in Florida to raise indigo plants. Those who settled in the English colonies were often artists or adventurers. Several of the early Italians stood out because of some unique quality. Giovanni Gualdo, "a wine merchant from Italy, but late from London," who was also a composer and conductor, arrived in Philadelphia in 1767. Within four years, he presented a series of concerts that gave him the reputation of being one of colonial America's most versatile musicians.

By far the best-known Italian in North America of the late colonial period was Filippo Mazzei, a Tuscan physician from a small town near Florence. In London, where he lived for more than seventeen years, Mazzei had met a number of important men—among them Benjamin Franklin—from the North American colonies. In 1771 George Washington, Thomas Jefferson, and some other planters put up about $10,000 to bring Mazzei and a group of Tuscan farm workers to America to conduct agricultural experiments in Virginia on grapevines, olive trees, and other plants. The Italian farmers arrived in Virginia in November, 1773, and went ahead with the planting as planned. But the experiment failed, partly because Mazzei became involved in the growing colonial agitation against England. He did, nonetheless, introduce a number of vegetables to America's farmers that they had not previously known.

While participating in colonial politics, Mazzei helped draft some laws and reforms, including possibly the first version of Virginia's constitution of 1776. Under the pen name "Furioso," he wrote an article for the *Virginia Gazette* which was translated from the Italian into English by Jefferson, containing phrases similar to those later used in the preamble of the Declaration of Independence. While Jefferson was working on the Declaration of Independence, he sent one of his first drafts to Mazzei. A few years later, in January, 1779, Governor Patrick Henry, acting for the state of Virginia, commissioned Mazzei for a special mission to Italy. He was instructed to negotiate a loan and to obtain military supplies from the Grand Duke of Tuscany, and also to encourage more people from Latin Europe to immigrate to Virginia. The Grand Duke was known to be sympathetic to the struggling Americans. He had followed affairs in North America with considerable interest, boasting that he knew the situation there "better than anyone else in Europe."

Arriving in Florence in October, 1780, Mazzei interviewed the Grand Duke a number of times and began a correspondence with him. While in Europe, Mazzei also kept in touch with John Adams and other American diplomats stationed in various capitals there. During the more than four years of his mission, the Tuscan doctor could not persuade the Grand Duke to aid the Americans, and he raised no money. But Mazzei published propaganda pamphlets in Florence and in other ways publicized what he called in one of his essays "The Justice of the American Cause."

In November, 1783, after the Americans had made good their independence, Mazzei returned to the United States, where he established a "Society of the Constitution" designed to guard the fundamental rights of the people. Its members included Virginia's most prominent leaders. While in America, he also took an active interest in religious freedom. But, as he recalled in his memoirs, the people of Virginia never fully trusted him because he came from a Catholic country. Yet he had become a naturalized Virginian. In 1785 Mazzei sailed for France, never to return to his home in Virginia. While living in poverty in Paris, he wrote in Italian a rambling commentary on American institutions, politics, and social conditions. He had the work translated into French and then published it in four volumes.* Although superficial as history, it offered Europeans one of the more serious and accurate views of America then available to them.

In 1774, not long after Mazzei's arrival in Virginia, Carlo Bellini, a friend from Florence, joined him. Four years later, with the help of Jefferson, Bellini obtained a professorship of languages at the College of William and Mary, holding the position for twenty-four years. In this post he became the first teacher of Italian, along with other languages, in an American college. Later, as an ability to read Italian came to be considered a desirable accomplishment for the well-educated young American, other teachers of Italian appeared in various cities.

While Bellini was establishing himself in Williamsburg, another Italian, Giuseppe Maria Francesco Vigo, a Piedmontese who had served in the Spanish army, was settling in New Orleans. Later Vigo moved to St. Louis, where he became an Indian trader and successful merchant. He gained a noteworthy reputation as an explorer, because he helped to open the Old Northwest to settlement. During the revolution, he fought under General George Rogers Clark, to wrest the Northwest from the British.

Although in these years, during the course of the American Revolution, Italian interest in North America picked up, Italians did not at first grasp the full significance of the fighting in the English colonies. Like other Europeans, they at first considered the quarrel between England and her colonies a small family fight that would be smoothed over quickly. Italians practically ignored the Declaration of Independence when the colonists announced it, but they followed the course of the revolution itself with great interest. Italian newspapers regularly carried accounts of battles and other events in North America. Italian writers and others sympathized with the Americans, expressing admiration for a people who would defy the might of Britain. The Abbé Ferdinando Galiani, a thoughtful and witty man, said, "I would bet in favor of America." Other Italians, some of whom wrote books on the war in America, expressed similar sentiments.

In 1776, Vincenzo Martinelli, a Florentine writer and friend of

* *Recherches historiques et politiques sur les États-Unis de l'Amérique septentrionale* (4 vols., Paris, 1788).

Franklin, brought out a small book on the British colonies in India and North America.* Devoting more than half of his pages to North America, he too lamented the absence of Italian settlements in the New World. The outcome of the American Revolution, he wrote, rested in the hands of God, but he suggested that circumstances favored the rebelling colonists. Several other books on the Revolution published in Italy at this time were translated from works in French; but in 1781 in Venice, Vincenzo Formaleoni published an original account of the war.** Within the next two years, Gian Rinaldo Carli, an economist and a professor at the University of Padua, produced a widely acclaimed comparative study in three volumes of the peoples of the Old and New Worlds called *American Letters.* Viewing the American Revolution as a clash between European decadence, exemplified by England, and American liberty and tolerance, he said that the "spirit of America" would show the Europeans the way to that happiness promised by the Enlightenment.

Another who interpreted the American Revolution as a struggle for liberty was the Piedmontese poet Vittorio Alfieri, one of the first Italian intellectuals to conceive of the idea of a unified Italy and to see similarities between her plight and that of the thirteen American colonies. In 1784, in the first of five odes published under the title *L'America liberata* (Free America), he analyzed the causes of the revolution and described America before the fighting had broken out as a place

> Where 'neath the shade of laws inviolate
> A folk, though rich, grew free,
> From whom a fortunate wind doth blow away
> That evil which o'er Europe holds full sway

Alfieri contrasted "sad Italy," a land "bound in her hated chains" which she "must drag on," to America, a land of liberty. In his fourth ode, he praised George Washington and invoked Franklin, that "ravisher of lightnings empyreal;" and in his fifth, he celebrated the prowess of American arms, the peace, and the freedom Americans had won for themselves. A few years later, while still a passionate admirer of the United States, he dedicated his tragedy, *Brutus the First,* to Washington. "No name but that of America's liberator," Alfieri wrote in 1788, "may precede the tragedy of the liberator of Rome."

---

* *Istoria del governo d'Inghilterra e delle sue colonie in India, e nell' America settentrionale.*
** *Teatro della guerra . . . fra la Gran Brettagna. . . .*

After the Revolution, information on the United States in foreign works on history, commerce, and industry was reprinted by Italian publishers. It was in order to satisfy this interest in America that publishers at Cremona and Padua, in 1785 (two years after its American appearance), put out separate editions of Franklin's pamphlet, *Information to Those Who Would Remove to America,* written to discourage artists, office seekers, soldiers, parasitic noblemen, and various misfits from going to the United States. The New World, Franklin made clear, was a "land of labor" with no place for the luxuries, privileges, and vices of Europe.

A number of Italians then came to see for themselves that land of liberty that Alfieri had praised. One of the first Italian travelers of distinction, the Milanese botanist Count Luigi Castiglioni, visited the United States in 1785. The American Revolution, he wrote, "is one of the most memorable events of this century." So, he explained, "I . . . was moved by curiosity to behold the political birth of a republic composed of diverse nationalities, spread over vast provinces. . . ." He remained for two years, traveling in every one of the thirteen states. Distinguished Americans such as Washington and Ezra Stiles, the president of Yale College, entertained him; and while he lingered in Philadelphia, the American Philosophical Society elected him to membership. In 1790, after he had returned to Milan, he published an account of his American experiences, giving also a brief history of the new nation, of each state, comments on the Constitution and the government, and descriptions of many of the plants he had seen.*

Several years after Castiglioni had left, a naturalist and physicist from Milan, Count Paolo Andreani, traveled in the United States. Known as one of the pioneers of aeronautics, and the first Italian to climb the sky in a balloon, Andreani won election to the American Philosophical Society. On good terms with prominent Americans such as Jefferson and Madison, he brought President Washington a copy of Alfieri's odes on America. In 1791, Andreani explored the region around Lake Superior, noting his observations in a journal.

Castiglioni, Andreani, and other educated Italian visitors were usually impressed by the degree of personal freedom they found in the new nation. This liberty seemed especially striking when contrasted with the atmosphere of petty despotism prevalent in their own states. The belief that such freedom sprang from the success of the war for

* *Viaggio negli Stati Uniti dell'America settentrionale fatto negli anni 1785, 1786 e 1787. Con alcune osservazioni sui vegetabili piu utili di quel paese* (2 vols., Milan, 1790).

American independence, combined with the example of the French Revolution, helped to awaken Italian nationalism. Eighteenth-century Italian historians of the American Revolution were among the first to perceive nationalist motives in the colonial rebellion, mainly because they reacted more sensitively to such issues than did other historians. For example, a Milanese economist and political thinker, Melchiorre Gioia, in a piece entitled *Which of the Free Governments Is Most Suitable for the Happiness of Italy,* pleaded for a united Italian republic and called on the spirit that brought independence to Americans to inspire Italians.

In these years of budding nationalism in Italy, shipping connections between North American and Mediterranean ports increased, bringing a few more Italians to the United States. They were not ordinary settlers, but mostly entertainers—actors, musicians, ballet dancers, and operators of puppet shows. Some had other special talents, such as the marble cutters that Jefferson brought from Italy to work on the buildings of the University of Virginia at Charlottesville. A few, such as Giuseppe Ceracchi, a Roman and the first noteworthy Italian sculptor to visit the United States, were artists. Franklin had told Ceracchi that a sculptor could not expect to do well in the United States, but the Italian ignored the advice, visiting the country twice in the early 1790's. While in the United States, Ceracchi made portrait busts of a number of the Founding Fathers, such as Washington and Adams, apparently intending to use the figures in a grandiose monument to American liberty.

Another Italian, Filippo Traetta, a composer, singer, and musician from Venice, brought with him a concern for classical music. In Boston in 1801, two years after his arrival, Traetta became a cofounder of what has been considered the new nation's first conservatory of music. In the following years, through his singing, composing, writing, and concerts, he made other contributions to the development of serious music in the United States. He achieved a measure of contemporary fame for his composition "Washington's Death March". As a result of the coming of the entertainers and musicians, downtown Broadway in New York City, by 1805, had an "Italian Theater." Even Cleveland, then only a village, had an "Italian Hall."

At this time, in June, 1805, Lorenzo Da Ponte, formerly the librettist for Mozart and himself a dramatist, poet, and musical impressario, arrived in Philadelphia. Now fifty-six years old, this exiled Venetian Jew turned Catholic, and a man of international reputation, started a new life in a new country. He was appalled by the lack of knowledge about Italian culture among Americans. "To the shame of our country," he wrote, "there is not in the whole of America a bookshop kept by an Italian." So he opened a small bookstore where he sold Italian books and other items from Italy, and tried to earn a living from it. Da Ponte also taught the Italian language to hundreds of Americans, wrote and lectured on Italian culture, defended the Italian character, and in various ways spread knowledge of Italy in the United States. When he started teaching Italian in New York, he said, "it was no better known than Turkish or Chinese." In 1825, he became the first professor of Italian literature at Columbia College, really a private tutorship he held without salary from the college itself. At the age of eighty-four, he formed an opera company and opened an Italian Opera House in New York City.

In the same year that Da Ponte obtained his position at Columbia, Harvard College established a post in Italian and Spanish. Pietro Bacchi, a recent arrival from Italy, a Sicilian who had obtained a law degree from the University of Palermo and had been exiled because of revolutionary activities, got the appointment. Bacchi taught at Harvard for more than twenty years. During these years, while Da Ponte and Bacchi were stimulating an American appreciation of Italian culture, Italians were beginning to receive more substantial accounts of affairs in the United States than they had in the past. In 1809 Carlo Botta, a Piedmontese scholar and patriot who had written a popular though ponderous history of Italy, published at his own expense a *History of the American Revolution* in four volumes. This history grew out of a conversation he had had one evening three years earlier in the home of Alessandro Manzoni's mother, who was also the daughter of the criminologist Cesare Beccaria. When talking about what modern event would make the most suitable theme for a heroic poem, the guests all agreed on the American Revolution. So Botta wrote his history, modeling it on grandiloquent, poetic examples.

Botta's book, the first history of the Revolution written in Europe or elsewhere, achieved such success that its fame quickly spread to the United States, something unusual for an Italian book because Americans knew hardly any of the works of contemporary Italian writers. Before 1800, few Italian books were translated into English and published in the United States. Bookstores, however, did sell volumes brought from Italy as well as Italian grammars, and travel books about the Italian peninsula that had been published in England. In the early years of the nineteenth century, as educated Americans studied major Italian poets such as Dante, Petrarca, and Ariosto, and sought a broader acquaintance with Italian literature, the demand for Italian books grew. Americans of this kind read Botta's history and gave it such a warm welcome that George Alexander Otis translated the work into English and in 1820 published it in Philadelphia, the first of many editions of "Otis's *Botta*."

Adams, Jefferson, and others praised Botta's history. Adams said, with some exaggeration, that it "will be in demand as long as the American Revolution is an object of curiosity." Despite such praise, the work had serious flaws. Like Thucydides, Botta frequently invented the speeches he put in his narrative. While this practice may have appealed to his readers, it did nothing for the accuracy of his history. Yet for Italians, Botta's history served an important cause. It suggested analogies between Italy's distant past and contemporary history as Americans were making it. The book helped to arouse nationalistic aspirations in Italian readers.

In Milan in 1812, a few years after Botta's work appeared, Carlo Giuseppe Londonio published another history of the American nation in three volumes.* He, too, tried to use the United States as a model for the nationalist aspirations of Italians. But Londonio differed from Botta in basing his work on a more solid foundation of documentation. Six years later, another important book on American society appeared in Rome.** The author, Giovanni Grassi, a Jesuit from Bergamo, had lived in the United States. He had taught at Georgetown College and then had become its president. Grassi used nearly half of his book to discuss the state of the various churches in America. He also advised his fellow Italians not to settle in the United States, warning those who were thinking about emigrating to "consider the proverb that he who fares well should stay at home."

Regardless of this advice, the idea of immigrating to the United States now became more attractive to Italians than it had been in the past. In September 1816, the American consul at Leghorn reported that "the number of applicants to go to the United States has become incalculable; from professors of the highest services down to the labouring peasant; and had they the means, as they have the will, Italy would be half depopulated." James Sloan, an American in Italy, observed that "an insatiable curiosity exists in Italy relative to the gov-

---

* *Storia delle colonie inglesi in America della loro fondazione fino allo stabilimento della loro independenza.*
** *Notizie varie sullo stato presente della repubblica degli Stati Uniti dell' America settentrionale.*

ernment of the United States," and that the example of American self-government stirred unrest among thinking Italians. Two years later, William Berrian, a clergyman from New York who also visited Italy, wrote a perceptive book about conditions there, noting that America was "the common subject of conversation at the coffee houses" in Milan.

Despite all this talk about the United States and of immigration to it, no one really knew much about the flow of Italian immigrants. State governments dealt with those who entered their ports, and each state handled immigration records in its own way. Not until 1819 did Congress provide, as part of a law regulating the carriage of steerage passengers at sea, for the collection of statistics on immigration. Beginning in 1820, therefore, the federal government began keeping records, based on passenger lists of ships from foreign ports, on those who entered the United States. Although an improvement over what the states had done, federal record keeping did not for many years give a reliable account of Italian immigration. Federal officials had difficulty in keeping accurate records because of Italy's political divisions and because foreigners controlled parts of the peninsula. For example, American officials could list a native of Venice either as an Italian or an Austrian, for Austria ruled in Venetia. According to federal immigration statistics, only thirty Italians arrived in the United States in 1820, but more probably came. Elsewhere Italians were already on the move; in that year, nearly half of all immigrants who went to Brazil were Italian. After that date, a few hundred Italians trickled into the United States each year.

Most cultivated Italians, like other Europeans, still thought of America as the land of the noble savage and had only the haziest of ideas about the United States itself. In 1821, for instance, a bookseller in Rome asked young George Bancroft, who later became a noted historian, what his nationality was. "An American from Boston," Bancroft replied. "Ah," the bookseller sighed, "I have a large book in my shop about Boston." It turned out to be a history of Hindustan. "Forgive me," the bookseller said, "a little mistake. I took Hindustan to be Boston."

Yet Italians kept alive their curiosity and a special interest in the United States. Those few who knew something about the country generally came to have a favorable attitude toward it, even an affinity for it. Intellectuals saw it as the model for Italy of the future. According to Theodore Dwight, who traveled in Italy in 1821, Italians considered the United States the happiest country on earth, a place where men were "born and educated among political privileges and blessings far, very far superior to those at which they were aspiring."

At this time, from 1820 to 1822, Giuseppe Campagnoni, a prolific writer of books on various subjects, who hailed from Lombardy, catered to the appetite for information on American life. He published in Milan a history of America in fourteen volumes.* Caleb Cushing, the New England politician, reviewed the work, saying that at the time "no other nation but Italy possessed a full and methodical account of events in America from the first discovery of the new world by Columbus down to the present day." Campagnoni, too, held up the United States as an example for his own countrymen to follow in building a unified Italian nation.

Curiosity attracted Italian adventurers, as well as writers, to the United States. In 1822, a forty-four-year-old former judge and political conspirator, Giacomo Constantino Beltrami, arrived from Italy looking for adventure and glory. Outfitted as a frontiersman with buckskins, moccasins, and a soft felt hat, he plunged into the wilderness of Minnesota in August of the following year. After a number of adventures and misadventures, he came out claiming he had discovered the source of the Mississippi River, a feat historians usually attribute to the geologist, Indian agent, and writer Henry R. Schoolcraft. The Italian had apparently approached the source from the wrong side of the watershed. First Beltrami extravagantly described his adventures in a book published in New Orleans in 1824.** Then, four years later in London, he published his observations on North America in two volumes called *A Pilgrimage*. The dispute over his claims more than the quality of his books made the colorful Beltrami one of the best known of the early Italian travelers in the United States.

In April, 1825, shortly after Beltrami's adventures, Count Carlo Vidua, another inquisitive traveler, landed in New York. This Piedmontese nobleman spent almost a year touring all parts of the United States except the Southeast. He talked to such prominent men as Jefferson, Madison, Monroe, and President John Quincy Adams, all of whom he admired. Although Vidua kept notes and diaries, all that has survived concerning his American experiences are the observations in his posthumously published letters, which created no stir in Italy. These letters show that he was impressed by the industriousness

* *Storia dell'America in continuazione del compendio della Storia universale del sig. conte de Segur.*
** *La découverte des sources du Mississippi et de la Rivière Sanglante.*

of Americans, their law-abiding qualities, and the way they lived in "unlimited personal safety" having "no fear of arbitrary powers" as many did in Europe. Among the traits he disliked were money grubbing and rudeness, and he detested slavery. The spectacle, he wrote, "of two million human beings whipped, sold, loaned like beasts because their skin is not white, saddened constantly my sojourn in the boasted *land of liberty.*"

While Vidua was observing American culture, Americans themselves were reading more and more books, magazines, essays, and newspaper articles on Italian art and society. Books on travel in Italy gained a special popularity. Americans now also became increasingly interested in Italian opera. Although audiences in Baltimore and New York had seen Italian operas sung either in English or French as early as 1790, Americans did not hear their first opera sung in Italian until November, 1825. At that time, a Spanish company presented Rossini's *Barber of Seville* at the Park Theater in New York City.

The next noteworthy operatic troupe to appear in the United States came from Italy, opening at the Richmond Hill Theater in New York City in October, 1832, with Rossini's *La cenerentola* and closing the following February in Philadelphia. New Yorkers, led by Da Ponte, now formed an association for financing an opera house which they built and called the Italian Opera House. It opened in November, 1833, with a performance of Rossini's *La gazza ladra.* Although this company failed, others were started elsewhere and Italian opera could now be heard in a number of American cities. In 1847, the Astor Place Opera House, built especially for Italian opera, opened its doors; and in that same year, the Havana Opera Company, staffed with Italian singers, brought opera of top quality to the United States. Seven years later, the Academy of Music, at Irving Place and Fourteenth Street, became the home of opera in New York City. There fine singers performed Italian grand opera regularly, year in and year out, for over thirty years. In 1859, Adelina Patti, the "Queen of Song," not yet seventeen, made her operatic debut as Lucia in Donizetti's *Lucia di Lammermoor* in New York. For years, this brilliant soprano reigned as the best-known Italian singer in America.

Enthusiastic support for opera came from Americans who had visited Italy and had seen performances there. They often responded with a passionate devotion to this form of musical spectacle. In journals, letters, and travel accounts these Americans repeatedly expressed their enthusiasm for what had come to them as a new experience.

The spreading appreciation of various aspects of Italian culture, such as opera, pleased Count Francesco Arese, a nobleman from Lombardy who came to the United States in 1837 to be with his homesick friend, Louis Napoleon. The French prince soon returned to Europe, but Arese remained, making a tour of the Atlantic seaboard and traveling in the West, all the while keeping a journal on what he saw. Although not striking in content or ideas, this journal, which he modestly called "Notes," was unique because no other highly cultivated, much traveled, and observant Italian left a similar commentary on the United States in this period. In Boston, Arese visited the Athenaeum, where the librarian showed him the holdings. "My national pride," the Count wrote, "was so much stirred by the pompous eulogies which he made on the work of Italy and on the Italians that I could not refrain from telling him that I belonged to that beautiful and unhappy country."

While Arese was finding pleasure in what he heard about Italy from representatives of a cultivated minority of Americans who appreciated Italian achievements, a far less complimentary image of his country and countrymen was taking shape in the United States. The American who read popular accounts about Italy quickly learned that it was a land of beautiful scenery, ancient ruins, and old churches, and also of ragged beggars, rampant *banditti,* and violent feuds. The ordinary American of these days had little interest in cultural matters at home, and far less in the literature and arts of Italy. Italians were commonly viewed as a people whose distinguished achievements in the arts went along with an unsound character. The individual Italian immigrants and the pockets of Italian settlement that were now spreading slowly across the United States did not help in building a more favorable image of Italy.

Only in California did Italian settlers shape a different, almost unique, image—that of pioneers who contributed to the state's early growth. Elsewhere in the United States, the Italians had not been part of the pioneer movement. A few Italian missionaries, seamen, and travelers had gone to the Pacific Coast before 1830, but it took the discovery of gold in California in 1849 to draw a substantial number of Italians. They came mostly by sea around Cape Horn, and some by land; they came from Italy, from the East Coast, and from places of earlier migration such as South America. The Italian influx led the Kingdom of Sardinia in 1850 to open a consulate in San Francisco, headed by Colonel Leonetto Cipriani, a fighter for unification, to care for Italians on the West Coast.

Several of the Italian gold seekers amassed small fortunes, but they were part of only a handful who actually found gold. Most of the Italian forty-niners turned almost at once into merchants, small shopkeepers, owners of taverns, growers of grapes, makers of wine, and truck gardeners. One of the most successful of these, Domenico Ghirardelli, found prosperity by traveling through the mining towns selling sweets. He brought together enough capital to found the Ghirardelli Chocolate Company of San Francisco, a successful firm. Giuseppe Lobero, another Italian gold seeker, was a musician who ran a saloon at first; later, he built a fine theater in Santa Barbara that bore his name. Within a decade, the Italian community in and around San Francisco had become large enough to have a weekly newspaper called *La voce del popolo,* a mutual-benefit society, a hospital of its own, and several opera companies and theaters.

Elsewhere the Italian immigrants, though few in number, encountered various prejudices. Poor and friendless, they clung together in the slums of eastern cities, fearing to settle in the hostile countryside of rural America. In the early 1850's, when cities such as New York saw a swift rise in their Italian populations, reformers and social workers began expressing deep concern over the living conditions of these newcomers. In December 1855, the Children's Aid Society of New York City, a philanthropic agency inspired by Charles Loring Brace's work among slum children, opened an Italian Industrial School in an old dilapidated frame house at Five Points. This elementary school, just a "stone's throw" from Broadway in an area notorious as the haunt of thieves, murderers, and prostitutes, tried to help the poor youths of the growing Italian population in the city. In its first years, the school carried on a vigorous campaign against the "*padrone* traffic." Men called *padroni* collected children from Italy's countryside and carried them to the United States, practically in the condition of slaves, to be employed in various ways, often as wandering musicians and street acrobats. As a result of this practice, many Americans came to look upon Italians as enslavers of children.

Americans fixed another stereotype concerning Italians in their minds at this time: that Italians were all Papists and therefore undesirable as neighbors. Yet, because there were few in the country at the time, Italians escaped most of the ire of the nativist anti-Catholic agitation of the 1840's. In the fifties, nativists revived the agitation on a national scale, first with the founding of the secret Order of the Star-Spangled Banner, then with its successor, the American party, popularly called the Know-Nothing party. At this time, the small number of Italian settlers in the country, contrary to the views of writers who maintain that Italians did not suffer from discrimination until they came in great numbers decades later, felt the sting and cruelty of an inescapable bigotry. Men such as the New England intellectual George Ticknor, who disliked the German immigrants ("active red republicans") and the Irish ("prone to brute violence"), were already talking about restricting immigration to preserve America's homogeneity of blood and conviction.

In view of their anti-Catholic, anti-foreign prejudices, the Know-Nothings acted logically in showing hostility toward the Italians. From Rome, the seat of the Catholic church, had come Italian missionaries and priests who had helped to establish Catholicism in the United States.

The earliest Italian missionaries came to the United States to convert Indians, not to minister to the religious needs of their fellow countrymen who had emigrated. These missionaries laid the foundations of the Catholic church west of the Mississippi River; only a few of the early Italian priests organized parishes in the eastern states. The first of these priests, according to known records, was Father Nicholas Zucchi, a Jesuit who arrived in Maryland in 1803. Italian priests coming in groups first reached the United States in the 1820's. They were mainly Lazarist Fathers, or members of the Congregation of the Mission, who labored in the trans-Mississippi West, in Philadelphia, and in Baltimore. The second group, made up mostly of Jesuits with a few Franciscan, Passionist, Servite, and Capuchin Fathers scattered among them, began arriving in the 1840's.

Only a handful of Italian secular priests served in the United States in these years. In the fifties, two Italian priests served New York's small Italian community. About half of all the Italian priests were educators—teachers of theology, languages, and science in colleges. Italian missionary priests headed by Giovanni Nobili and Michael Accolti established their first college for the education of young Americans in March, 1851, at Santa Clara, California. Although open to all, Catholics as well as Protestants, the College of Santa Clara was for years run by Italian Jesuits. Four years later, another Piedmontese Jesuit, Anthony Maraschi, after teaching in Catholic colleges in Baltimore, founded Saint Ignatius College, later the University of San Francisco.

Although the activities of Italian priests, and of Italian immigrants in general, aroused the ire of nativists, the problems Italians faced in the United States in the forties and fifties were few in comparison to what would come later. The Italians who immigrated in these years and before were usually people who desired permanent settlement. The voyage from the Mediterranean and across the Atlantic to America in a crowded sailing ship was long (anywhere from one to three months), arduous, and expensive. Any immigrant family that made the trip did not easily decide to return.

These early immigrants, about 14,000 of them between 1820 and 1860 according to official records, but probably more, came mostly from the central and northern regions of the Italian peninsula. They settled in various parts of the United States, but mostly in eastern cities, although California had more Italians than New York. Many were small shopkeepers, street vendors, entertainers, and truck gardeners. Those with an education often taught languages—Italian, French, and Spanish. Some of these immigrants were political refugees, men without a trade or technical knowledge, who possessed university degrees in the humanities that proved useless in helping them to earn a living in the United States. Through their political agitation, these men brought Italy into the consciousness of the American mind. They aroused an American interest in the Italian struggle for unification.

Wanderers
in Arcadia

2

Throughout most of the eighteenth century, wealthy young Englishmen followed the custom of spending two or three years wandering over Europe in fashionable carriages, each accompanied by one or more servants and usually also a young companion who at least acted the part of a tutor. This period of travel, known as the grand tour, was intended somehow to add to a young gentleman's education, but more often it became an extended pleasure jaunt, especially satisfying to the intellectually curious. Although the grand tour had no fixed itinerary, it usually took in France, Germany, the Low Countries, and almost always Italy, which generally provided the high point, "the finishing part of a polite education." Often the grand tour amounted to nothing more than an Italian trip.

In the middle of the eighteenth century, North Americans of genteel taste and wealth who came increasingly into contact with the gentry of England also took up the grand tour. Some of these young North Americans, especially the sons of prosperous merchants, journeyed to England for their college and graduate studies. A few of them followed this experience with a shortened version of the grand tour, usually consisting of a year of travel on the continent, much of it in Italy, to add a cultural polish to their education.

In the English colonies, the marked interest in Italian travel began early in 1760 when William Allen, the Chief Justice of Pennsylvania, arranged letters of credit for his son John, then twenty-one, to spend "a few months in Italy" before going on to London through Switzerland and France. John Allen sailed for Leghorn on a ship carrying wheat and flour. With him, as companions, went his cousin Joseph Shippen and Benjamin West, "a young ingenious Painter" from Philadelphia anxious to improve his skills by visiting Florence and Rome, the fountainheads of art.

Young Allen and Shippen had suggested that they might achieve some practical benefits from their tour by making trading connections at Leghorn. Judge Allen was not deceived; he realized that what they desired most was "to have the pleasure of visiting the different parts of Italy." West, too, had a practical side. He had saved the money he earned as a painter of portraits to make the trip. This young Quaker was the first artist to travel from the North American shore to study the fine arts in Italy.

To these curious young Philadelphians, life in eighteenth-century Italy seemed inferior to what they had known at home. But what they saw of Italy's heritage impressed them as magnificent. They wrote that "as to the grandeur of the ancients, from what we can see of their remains, it is most extraordinary. Arts with them seem to have been in a perfection . . . which could not be imagined. Their palaces, temples, aqueducts, baths, theatres, amphitheatres, statues, sculptures, were most amazing." In Milan, Venice, Naples, and Rome, the travelers gazed at art and monuments, taking careful notes and copying inscriptions. Several of the touring North Americans in these years became members of a group of English and Italian *cognoscenti,* the Arcadian Society of Belles Lettres of Rome.

West, who remained in Italy, mostly in Rome, for about four years, also visited various other cities to study and copy paintings before going on to London. He was elected to the academies of Parma, Florence, and Bologna. In Rome, where he became a general favorite, he made drawings of the best classical subjects. Like other visitors, this influential American painter linked artistic and social decay. "The country was covered with ruins," he wrote, "and the human character was in ashes." Later he took a more favorable attitude, saying he considered the Italians "a calm, persuasive and pensive people."

In 1763, while West was still in Rome, another young Philadelphian, Dr. John Morgan, who had gone to Europe, mainly Edinburgh, London, and Paris, for education, ideas, and scientific models, also traveled in Italy. Morgan, who later became known as "the founder of American medicine" for his part in establishing the first medical college in America, had just taken a degree at the Edinburgh College of Physicians. In Italy he visited various hospitals, medical schools, art galleries, and churches, keeping a record of his impressions. At Padua, Parma, and Bologna he listened to lectures by distinguished Italian doctors and scientists, and talked to several of them. He met the aging Giovanni Battista Morgagni, the leader of Italian medicine and the father of pathological anatomy, who gave him a set of his works. Morgan presented the Italian professor with a copy of his doctoral dissertation. Educated men in various countries read the works of Morgagni and other Italian scientists, for in science and medicine Italian universities had retained their distinguished international reputation. Yet young Morgan, who in Rome was made a member of the *Accademia degli Arcadi,* considered medical education in Italy "deplorable."

A few Americans read the works of the Italian scholars and even corresponded with them. A number of these scholars and other well-informed Italians admired Benjamin Franklin, mainly for his experiments with electricity, for the stove he invented (which was used in Italy), and for his various writings. As early as 1755, an Italian *philosophe,* Francesco Algarotti, wrote that "from Philadelphia a Quaker [*sic*] has sent us the most beautiful reasonings in the world on electricity; and all our European electricians must doff their hats to this American." Italians everywhere associated Franklin's name with the lightning rod, which they widely used. Franklin, who for years had studied Italian and could read it, corresponded with several Italian scholars and scientists, among them Giovanni Battista Beccaria, an eminent physicist, philosopher, and university professor, and the man who introduced the American's scientific theories into Italy, popularized them, and defended them. Other Italian intellectuals who exchanged ideas with Franklin were the Marchese Cesare Beccaria and Gaetano Filangieri. The Philadelphian was also elected to several Italian academies of learning.

Filangieri, a Neopolitan political philosopher with a reputation as one of the finest representatives of the Italian Enlightenment, admired not only Franklin but also Americans as a people. "Free citizens of independent America," he wrote in exaggerated admiration, "you are too virtuous and too enlightened not to know that by winning the right to govern yourselves you have contracted in the eyes of the universe the sacred duty of being wiser, more moderate, and happier than all other peoples." Franklin had started corresponding with Filangieri while representing the newly independent United States in Paris. Filangieri gave him copies of his influential work, published in several volumes, *The Science of Legislation,* which Franklin praised. Later Franklin sent Filangieri a copy of a book on the state constitutions in the United States. Filangieri returned it with his own comments, and Franklin responded with comments on Filangieri's commentaries. Their correspondence continued until Franklin's death.

Cesare Beccaria, through his book *Dei delitti e delle pene (Of*

Crimes and Punishment) which was published in 1761, passed through six editions in eighteen months, and appeared in an English version in 1768, had a wider influence in North America than did Filangieri. In his writing, Beccaria urged a fair balance between crimes and their punishment, the elimination of secret grounds for accusations, the suppression of torture in police work, and other penal reforms. He wanted to do away with the death penalty and to put order into criminal procedure and the administration of prisons.

Those in North America who were interested in penology accepted Beccaria's views as though they had the force of laws. William Bradford, Pennsylvania's Attorney General, wrote in 1786 that "the name *Beccaria* has become familiar in *Pennsylvania*. His authority has become great and his principles are spread in every class of persons and have become deeply engraved in the hearts of our citizens." Beccaria's ideas formed the basis of Pennsylvania's penal code, enacted in the 1790's and considered one of the most advanced in the world. Jefferson copied about twenty-six passages from Beccaria's book in the original Italian.

A year after Beccaria had published his book, Henry Benbridge, a Philadelphian of twenty-one, arrived in Rome to study art, the second American painter of note to do so. In 1768, with a commission from James Boswell, he went to Corsica to paint a full-length portrait of Pasquale Paoli. Benbridge stayed five years in Italy and England, and then spent the rest of his days as a painter of portraits in Virginia and Charleston. In part, he had followed a pattern set by Benjamin West.

West himself advised one of his pupils, John Singleton Copley, to go to Italy to study the Renaissance painters—Michelangelo, Correggio, and Titian—as a source of taste. Copley also wanted to acquire that "bold, free and graceful style" found in the Italian paintings. So in 1775, he went on a tour of Italy to study art and copy paintings. Although he did not mix with Italians, he fell in love with their country. In Naples he met Ralph Izard, a South Carolinian who had visited Italy in 1774 to satisfy his passion for art and music and who three years later had been named American Commissioner to the Tuscan court. The Continental Congress appointed him after it had voted to send commissioners to the courts of Tuscany and Vienna "to cultivate the friendship of those princes and to form such treaties of commerce as may be beneficial to those countries and the United States."

Izard thought the Italian states would want to lend money to the new American nation, for if England lost the war, the Italians might be able then to free themselves from English supremacy in the Mediterranean. "A very advantageous connexion may unquestionably be formed between us—and the commercial parts of Italy," he wrote. "It is very much their interest to promote the success of our cause." Despite his optimism, Izard failed to obtain the loan he sought or to establish commercial realtions with Tuscany, a country he never succeeded in reaching. Yet he did take consolation in the knowledge that many Italians, and the Grand Duke of Tuscany himself, sympathized with America's revolutionary cause.

In Rome, at this time, Copley painted Izard's portrait. Izard had become his patron. Later Copley returned to England, where he spent the rest of his life.

Unlike West, Benbridge, and Copley, Americans who went to Italy after independence did not visit there as a stopping place to or from England. They traveled directly to the Italian peninsula and returned home with souvenirs and works of art, retaining the flavor of Italy fresh and undiluted. Almost everyone who lingered in Italy, it seemed, brought back sketches by the engraver Giovanni Battista Piranesi. The soft Piranesi etchings of classical scenes, of the Roman Forum, of the great piazzas, and of the elegant palazzos could be seen in homes in New York, Boston, Charleston, and elsewhere, providing evidence and personal reminders of Italian antiquity, of a pilgrimage to Arcadia.

Now, as the eighteenth century slipped away, Americans in increasing numbers began visiting Italy for practical reasons—to study art, architecture, and agriculture. Others went just to absorb culture. Izard, for example investigated soil conditions and fruit growing in Italy. In Lombardy and Piedmont, where the best silk was produced, he studied the soil with the idea of planting white mulberry trees on his plantation at home and of producing good quality silk there. He also loved music and regretted the lack of opera in Rome. His curiosity led him to look carefully at political and social conditions, too, and to conclude that there was "no freedom in any state in Italy."

At this time, in 1786, Charles Bulfinch, the first American-born architect of note, visited Italy at Thomas Jefferson's suggestion to study classical architecture there, for Jefferson, who could read Italian, had made himself familiar with Italian art and literature. Bulfinch spent only a short time in Italy, but what he saw there had a lasting influence on his style. When he first entered St. Peter's in Rome, it was said, he "was moved to tears" by the magnificence of that great church.

In the following year, Jefferson himself visited Italy. His "peep into Elysium," as he called his trip, was brief and utilitarian in purpose. "Italy is a field where the inhabitants of the southern states may see much to copy in agriculture," he told a governor of South Carolina, "and a country with which we shall carry on a considerable trade." Entering Italy by land from Marseilles and Nice, he spent three weeks touring the countryside around Genoa, Milan, and Turin and studying agriculture. He investigated the making of Parmesan cheese and took careful notes on soils, cultivation, and various problems of farming. Especially interested in the cultivation of rice, the Virginian hoped to bring back to the United States ideas or techniques from the northern Italian rice fields that would work in North Carolina. Even though the Sardinian kingdom prohibited the export of rice in the rough state, he smuggled some out of the country.

Although Jefferson found "much amusement" in the "architecture, painting, and sculpture" he did see, he did not have time to visit Italy's great art collections and monuments. He did stop to look at the magnificent Carthusian monastery, the *Certosa di Pavia,* gaining from it important architectural ideas. Many of his ventures in architecture reflected ancient Roman or more modern Italian models. He was deeply influenced by the Renaissance architect Andrea Palladio. Jefferson designed the first version of his own home, Monticello, a name selected from Italian usage, from prints of Palladio's work.

Jefferson also sent William Short, who served as his secretary while he was Minister to France, on a tour of the Italian cities that he had not been able to see for himself. Along with several other young Americans, Short spent three months in Italy studying architecture, visiting ruins, discovering art, and all the time keeping a record of what he saw. In his letters to Jefferson, he commented on everything from the making of wine and macaroni to the beauty of Rome's Pantheon.

Americans who could not go to Italy to study her art now had some of that art brought to them. In 1786, 130 Italian paintings arrived in Philadelphia, the first so-called old masters to be seen there. They were shown and offered for sale in Charles Willson Peale's exhibition room. His son, Rembrandt Peale, rushed home from school when they arrived so he could watch his father stretch the canvases and mend the paintings. Father and son then thumbed through a biographical dictionary to learn about the lives of the artists. Taken by the colors, sights, and designs in the paintings, and fascinated by what he read of the painters, Rembrandt Peale now longed to see Italy.

Within the next few decades, other Americans, especially artists and writers, also experienced the desire to visit Italy. By the early part of the nineteenth century, cultivated Americans who had the time and money, as well as the desire, made a visit to Italy a significant aspect of American cultural life. A trip to Italy, for many, had become something of a cultural tradition.

Washington Irving, America's first full-time professional writer, was one of the first of these Americans to wander in Arcadia. His elder brothers sent him on the grand tour, hoping he would improve both his health and education. Irving arrived in Genoa in 1804, a young man of twenty-two. He sailed to Naples in a ship sent to pick up a cargo of wines for the American market. Near the island of Elba, a privateer stopped the ship. Brandishing pistols, stilettoes, and cutlasses, crewmen from the privateer then swarmed aboard. They took nothing from young Irving and caused him no injury, but the experience frightened him, predisposing him for a while to see *banditti* everywhere in Italy.

Soon, Irving's wandering over the countryside and his study of the Italian language and literature inspired in him a warmth for Italy. He acquired a love for Italian music, which he heard everywhere, a love that remained with him for the rest of his life. Whenever and wherever he could, he attended opera "with the eagerness of an Italian." Irving noted in his journal that "men discover taste and fancy in Italy." Italians and Italy, he concluded, were quite different from America and the Americans. Italians, he observed, "place gay flowers in their hats," and live in "poetic fields" that were not the same as "our honest American hills and dales, where stubborn fact presides." He even changed his views on Italian *banditti,* portraying them sympathetically in his writings, often as lovers of liberty who fought despots.

While in Rome, Irving might have encountered another young American visitor there, John Izard Middleton of South Carolina, known as America's first archaeologist. Middleton roamed the Italian peninsula, studying the ruins of antiquity and making accurate water-color drawings of what he saw. He published the results of his investigations in 1812 in a book, *Grecian Remains in Italy.* This was the first American contribution to the study of classical antiquity.

In Rome, Washington Irving did meet Washington Allston, a romantic artist with whom he had much in common. A tall, slender South Carolinian in his middle twenties, Allston spent nearly four years, from 1804 to 1808, rambling among Italy's ruins, olive groves, and art galleries, frequently with companions such as Irving or the English poet Samuel Taylor Coleridge. Italy's scenery, especially the regions around Rome, deeply influenced Allston's paintings. These paintings, in turn, had an effect on America's cultural ties with Italy, for American contemporaries regarded Allston as the greatest painter their country had yet produced. As the first American artist to paint the Italian landscape with genuine interest, he did more than others to make his countrymen familiar with Italy. He started a trend followed by American intellectuals, of visiting Italy for stimulus to the mind and imagination.

These were the years of the Napoleonic Wars, and as those wars surged through Italy and across Europe, travel to Italy almost stopped. After the wars ended, the artists, poets, scholars, clergymen, and just ordinary tourists again started roaming over Italy, but now in ever-increasing numbers. Rome in the 1830's took the place of London as the mecca for Americans touring Europe. In Rome on a spring day in 1833, Ralph Waldo Emerson, the Concord philosopher, took delight in counting "fifteen persons from Boston alone." By the middle of the next decade, scholars have estimated, about a thousand Americans were arriving in Italy each year. Many of these visitors contributed to the stream of travel books that rushed on to the American market in the 1850's. These books stimulated still more travel to Italy.

As had the earliest of American visitors, these nineteenth-century travelers found the contrasts between prosperous America and Italy's fallen splendor so striking that they commented on it time after time. Everything in Italy seemed neglected, rotting, decaying. "The moral and intellectual grandeur of Italy," an American tourist observed in 1817, was "mutilated and faded." He also saw "her civil and political institutions" as "exhausted and decrepit" and her agriculture as having made no progress since the days of the Roman Republic. Another traveler explained the change from the United States to Italy as from movement to repose, from hope to memory. Italy, he felt, had "sunk into a state" of "half slumber and half despair."

Italy's political and social backwardness did not matter to young scholars from Massachusetts, such as the historian William Hickling Prescott; the cultural journalist, historian, and linguist George Ticknor; and the writer and politician Edward Everett. Steeped in the history and literature of Rome, they plunged into the Italian peninsula to see and study her ruins, not her politics and people. In 1817, Prescott spent six weeks in Rome, and traveled in other parts of Italy.

Despite his initial concern with the past only, Italy gripped him. He took up the study of Italian and thoroughly explored Dante's *Divine Comedy*. Later he wrote two long essays on Italian poetry for the *North American Review*. Ticknor, too, studied the Italian language and literature, carrying a copy of the *Divine Comedy* with him all over Europe, discussing it, and corresponding about it with his friend Prescott. Later, as a professor of languages, Ticknor introduced the study of Dante at Harvard. He spent the winter of 1817-1818 in Rome, saying he enjoyed himself "more in Italy than in all the rest of Europe, and . . . Rome is worth all the other cities in the world." Everett also saw the usual sights in Italy, but he wandered far from the routes tourists ordinarily traveled. In 1818, on his way to Greece, he went overland from Naples to Bari and through other parts of Italy's south, a region other visitors seldom saw.

Another young scholar, the nationalistic historian George Bancroft, toured Europe in these years after studying in Germany. Like Ticknor, who believed that the cultural level of contemporary Italians had sunk to a low point, Bancroft had an ambivalent attitude toward Italy and Italians. He wrote to his father shortly after his arrival in Naples in 1822 that the people were "so corrupt, the nation so cowardly, dishonest and degenerate" that these faults counterbalanced the attractions of climate. But he also said a little later that "everything conspires to make a journey in Italy the most interesting in the world." Italy's attractions apparently outweighed her vices, for all these scholars found themselves compelled somehow to return to her shores as older, more mature, men.

For those who made up America's cultural elite in the first half of the nineteenth century, art represented Italy's glowing attraction. She, more than any other land, they realized, embodied Western civilization's soaring achievements in the fine arts. But these Americans often held contemporary Italian art in low repute, as though to emphasize the gap between modern decay and the glories of the past. In the first two decades of the nineteenth century, therefore, American painters continued to go to England for training and enlightenment. Gradually Italy attracted more and more of the artists. By the second half of the century, many of America's major painters and sculptors were spending some time on the Italian peninsula, studying, traveling, or merely seeking inspiration.

The first American sculptor to work in Italy, Horatio Greenough, arrived in Rome in 1825, but did not stay long because he fell sick and went back to Boston. Three years later he returned, living first in

Carrara and then in Florence, where he made his home for twenty-five years. Sculptors often settled in Florence and Carrara because marble was cheap there. His studio on the Piazza Maria Antonia attracted a parade of visiting Americans, and he became the best-known American artist of his day in Italy. He spoke Italian, and, unlike other American artists, participated extensively in Italian life. He even dabbled in politics, taking up the cause of Italian liberalism. Greenough obtained his first commission from James Fenimore Cooper, who spent nearly two years in Italy, from 1828 to 1829. Cooper's fame had preceded him, many of his novels having been translated into Italian. Even in small towns and country inns, people knew of him; and throughout the century, Italians continued to read his works. His historical novel of ruthless political power, *The Bravo,* set in Venice, aroused bitter criticism among Italian writers but went through several Italian editions. Cooper spent a winter in Florence and while there twice saw the Grand Duke of Tuscany, Leopold II. The ruler said he had heard good things about Cooper's books and asked him about the United States, its towns, people, and customs.

Americans, Cooper felt, were much too critical of Italy and Italians, and much too apt to exaggerate the virtues of their own country. "If it be patriotism to deem all our geese swans," he wrote, "I am no patriot, nor ever was." He admitted having arrived in Italy "with too many of the prejudices that had got abroad concerning the Italian," but through association and observation he came to admire even the "common Italians." Unlike Ticknor, he thought upper-class Italians possessed a graciousness, simplicity, and sincerity that made the cultivated Italian "the nearest true standard of any gentleman of Europe." He also discounted the stories about *banditti* and assassins circulated by Americans such as Irving, saying those tales too were "enormously exaggerated." "Italy is the land to love," Cooper wrote. He regretted leaving Italy more than he had any other country. Envying Italians for their apparent contentment, he felt that far more than Americans they knew how to make the most of what they had, how to squeeze enjoyment out of the passing moment. The departure from Italy, he wrote, was like "quitting his own home."

Samuel F. B. Morse, the painter, inventor, and bigot whom Cooper met in Rome, was far more critical of Italians. Hating Catholicism, his experiences in Rome brought his prejudices foaming to the surface. He even saw evils in the opera, saying the oppressive regimes in the Italian states encouraged the theater in order to distract men's minds from religion and politics. While in Venice on July 4, 1831, he expressed joy for having been born an American, indicating that what he saw in Italy made him realize how fortunate Americans were. Nonetheless, he proposed a toast to "the political and religious regeneration of Italy."

The young poet Henry Wadsworth Longfellow, who visited Italy in these years, also at first reacted critically to what he saw, though he said the effect on him of Rome's ruins was "almost delirious." A gifted linguist, he studied Dante's writings practically every night; eventually he translated *The Divine Comedy* into English. He also studied other Italian writers and gained inspiration from them; in time he acquired a love for Italy, returning to her in later years. "The mind resolutely refuses to associate anything disagreeable with Italy," Longfellow announced in a lecture at Harvard in 1851. "Say what ill of it you may, it still remains to the poet the land of his predilection, to the artist the land of his necessity, and to all the land of dreams and visions of delight." Later, his writings became popular in Italy partly because he had a deep knowledge of Italian scholarship and because his interest in things Italian flattered Italians.

In Rome, Longfellow lived with George Washington Greene, the historian from Rhode Island who was to spend twenty years in Italy, marry an Italian girl, and serve as the American consul in Rome from 1837 to 1845. Americans in Rome came to know Greene well, but he also mingled with Italians, becoming a particularly close friend of the historian Carlo Botta. Greene spoke Italian with "an exquisite Roman accent," delved into Italian life and culture, and knew Italian literature.

To Rembrandt Peale, now a grown man and established painter, a pilgrimage to Italy seemed a necessity. "Italy," he wrote while fearing he might never get there, "which was my reverie by day, became the torment of my dreams at night." In 1829, at the age of fifty-one, he finally got to Rome.

Two years later, Thomas Cole, the father of American landscape painting and a founder of the Hudson River school, arrived in Italy to spend four years in Rome and Florence, which he called "a painter's paradise." In the *campagna romana,* he painted *The Dream of Arcadia* that embodied a conception similar to Peale's reverie, and was, as the literary historian Van Wyck Brooks has pointed out, "really the dream for a hundred years of all the travelling American artists and writers." The most important American artist of his generation to visit Italy, Cole returned again a decade after his first arrival.

Long before his first tour of Italy in 1833, Ralph Waldo Emerson had dreamed his own dream of Arcadia, of a picturesque countryside filled with "broken columns and fallen friezes." This philosopher of democracy found the reality quite unlike the dream, took a narrow view of Italy, and spoke bitterly of Italians and Italian society. So did the poet and editor William Cullen Bryant, who visited Italy in the same year. In Emerson's estimation, the streets of Naples, littered with diseased and maimed beggars, looked like the wards of a hospital. In his first encounter with Venice, he found that city "not at all attractive," but he considered Rome a "grand town," saying it "works mightily upon the senses and upon the soul. It fashions my dreams even. . . ." He also liked Florence; it had "good streets, industrious population, spacious, well-furnished lodgings, elegant and cheap caffès," and no beggars.

Attractions such as these brought many Americans to Florence. In the 1830's, it already had a sizeable American colony. Americans also visited Milan, where some sought out the novelist Alessandro Manzoni. Andrews Norton of Harvard, the "Unitarian Pope," had translated his *I promessi sposi* into English, helping to make Manzoni known to Americans. Manzoni himself knew something of conditions in the United States. With considerable feeling, he told George Ticknor in 1837 that the United States must work toward the abolition of slavery. Two years later, Manzoni expressed gratitude to the novelist Maria Sedgwick for the generous treatment Italian exiles had received in the United States.

In Florence, American society swirled around Hiram Powers, a Yankee from Vermont who arrived in 1837, became the most fashionable sculptor of his day, and remained for the rest of his life. Although most of the visiting Americans called on Powers, either at his studio or home, neither he nor his family were as open with Italians. They seemed hermetically sealed against the human part of their environment, practically never participating in Italian affairs.

Even though he did not plunge into the turbulent stream of Italian life, Charles Sumner, another New Englander who later became a powerful member of the U.S. Senate, did go to Italy in 1839 to study the language; and he made himself familiar with art, literature, and thought there. He spent three years in Europe studying continental jurisprudence. From Venice he wrote, "I now find myself in the midst of some of the most remarkable works of our age," several of them in the field of law. The legal scholar Giovanni Domenico Romagnosi's introduction to the " 'Diritto Publico' is a specimen of masterly analysis, and strength of conception; his 'Genesi del Diritto Penale' is the most remarkable work I know on 'Criminal Law.' " Then Sumner added a broad, exaggerated evaluation to his comments, saying, "I know no country that within a few years has produced such great regenerating writers as this despised Italy."

Now, in the forties and fifties, well-to-do Americans, especially from Boston, made a winter in Rome something fashionable and socially desirable. The Eternal City became a refuge for American expatriates. These men, and other American visitors, sent home books, news, and pictures of the Italian scene. More Americans than ever were becoming familiar with paintings, drawings, reproductions of Italian towns and countryside, and Italian architecture. In these decades, for those who could afford them, houses in the formal Italian style became a fashion.

Margaret Fuller, the sensitive journalist and literary critic, recalled of her home in New York in the early forties that "our walls were hung with prints of the Sistine frescoes; we were all petty collectors; and prints of Correggio and Guercino took the place, for the time, of epics and philosophy." In 1847, a writer in the *American Whig Review* said there was a glut of Italian pictures. "People have their houses full of Italian views, and their libraries full of Italian travels," he observed, "and boarding school misses are twaddling *nelle parole Tuscane.*" Better homes of every kind also often contained another Italian feature, the mantel in the parlor and in other rooms. This usually came from Italy, or stonecutters of Italian extraction in America had made it.

Rome's visitors from Boston and elsewhere often acquired works of art created by American artists in Italy and sent the paintings and statues home. These travelers, probably motivated largely by vanity, were particularly anxious to have American sculptors carve portrait busts of them. One of the most popular of these sculptors with the American visitors was Thomas Crawford, a young man from New York who had studied architecture and had cut marble. Although Crawford arrived in Rome in 1835, his days of glory came in the forties and fifties. For a span of twenty years, his studio served as the nucleus of American artistic life in Rome. It and his home also became fashionable social centers for visiting Americans. Like Greenough, he responded to the aspirations of the people around him, becoming a supporter of Italian liberalism. He even joined Rome's Civic Guard and often walked through the Piazza di Spagna with his friends while wearing his uniform.

Another familiar American figure in Florence in the early fifties was the art critic, collector, and art historian James Jackson Jarves. He warned his countrymen against fraudulent Italian art. Although they might find good original paintings at reasonable prices, they could not expect to pick up works by the great masters, as some hoped they could. Dishonest dealers sold bad pictures to gullible visitors and also shipped old paintings, bought in wholesale lots and touched up a bit, to the United States to be sold as neglected masterpieces. So much art, fragments of ruins, medieval seals, and other objects of interest to American tourists was available in Florence that he called it "the world's capital of Bric-a-bracdom." Jarves searched everywhere for good paintings—in monasteries, churches, and palazzi—bringing back to the United States an important collection of Italian primitives. He traveled through remote small towns in the Apennines and acquired a feeling of appreciation for the peasants, saying that in them, rather than in her quarries and vineyards, lay Italy's promise. He sympathized with the *Risorgimento* and followed the deeds of its leaders.

Despite warnings from men such as Jarves, many Americans went to Italy intent on buying pictures and sculptures. Since numerous American artists lived in Rome and Florence, the visitors from the New World searched out their studios and now turned to contemporary art as a diversion from museums filled with old masters. Most of the American painters working in Italy were undistinguished and remained so; but a few, such as George Inness, who spent two years there in the fifties, and Christopher Cranch later attained some eminence. The American painter who attracted the greatest attention in Rome in these years was William Page, a young man from Albany. Contemporaries considered him practically a genius and his work wondrous, but his technique caused his paintings to darken and become obscure.

The search for health, not art, drew Francis Parkman, the future historian of British and French North America, to Italy. During his senior year at Harvard College he became dreadfully sick. After graduation in 1844, he sailed on a small ship to the Mediterranean. He traveled through Sicily and the Italian mainland, observing and assessing Italian life. Wishing to gain a close view of Catholic practices that would help him in writing his future history of French Canada, Parkman spent a week in a Passionist monastery in Rome, near the Coliseum. He disliked the monks, members of "the strictest order in Rome," and much of what he saw in Italy. But in Rome on a festival day, this austere young Bostonian found that joining the crowd and tossing flowers at young ladies on balconies could be fun. He also observed that the Italians disliked the 4,000 Englishmen in Rome because they were trying "to turn Rome into England." But "we sixty or seventy Americans," he wrote, "seem, I am happy to say, liked and esteemed everywhere."

Another Bostonian, the reformer and educator Samuel Gridley Howe, also looked at Italy of the 1840's, particularly her schools, through critical eyes. "There is not a school in Rome," he wrote, "which must not be considered as a beacon to warn rather than a light to guide the inquirer." The indifference of the rich toward the plight of the poor appalled him. To help the unfortunate, he opened a school in Rome for blind children of kindergarten age.

Few Americans were less critical of Italy and Italians than the versatile and talented William Wetmore Story. Lawyer, sculptor, musician, painter, and poet, he claimed since childhood to have been haunted by "dreams of art and Italy." Of Rome, he wrote, "the soil and stain that many call dirt, I call colour." Story first traveled to Italy in 1847 to study sculpture so that he could complete a monument for the grave of his father, Supreme Court Justice Joseph Story. After returning to New England, young Story decided that Italy must be his home. In 1856, he gave up a successful law practice and settled his family in Palazzo Barberini, where he lived for forty-five years, becoming Rome's best-known American artist and the leader of American society there. His home became a center for visiting Americans, but he did not shut himself off from Italian life. Italians admired him and his many talents, and he took part in Italian society.

In the same year that Story established himself in Rome, Dorothea Lynde Dix, the reformer from Boston, stopped there while on a tour of Europe inspecting mental hospitals. The conditions in Rome's hospitals shocked her. In an audience with Pope Pius IX, she persuaded him to investigate. He did, and was also shocked. Then he thanked her for informing him of the abuses, promised to carry out reforms, and bought land for a new hospital to be run according to enlightened practices.

Whether reformers like Dorothea Dix, artists or students of art, or just plain tourists, several thousand Americans by the end of the fifties were visiting Italy each year. "My countrymen," Emerson wrote in 1860, "are . . . infatuated with the *rococo* toy of Italy." According to their journals, diaries, letters, and books, among the countries they saw, Italy was usually the most interesting and satisfying place. Many looked back on their Italian tours as one of the most important events in their lives. A Boston clergyman, Ephraim Peabody, spoke for the many when he commented, "Till a man has seen Italy and breathed it . . . he cannot be said to have lived."

Despite this enthusiasm for the country, these visiting Americans, even when they lived there for years, did not truly get to know Italy and Italians. Oblivious to Italy's economic and social problems, these Americans saw only a distorted image of her and carried away an ambivalent attitude toward her. Many went to Italy with prejudices already formed. They took with them a stereotyped impression of Italians, generally so negative that it barred any effective steps toward friendship. This attitude pictures Italy as a land of widespread poverty that had tumbled into degeneracy from the heights of Roman antiquity and Renaissance brilliance.

Americans usually became convinced of the validity of this attitude from the contacts they had with the Italians who served them or worked for them. Because some of the baggage hustlers, innkeepers, carriage drivers, especially in the south in places such as Naples, cheated travelers, Americans frequently concluded that all Italians were liars and cheats. Dishonesty, some Americans said, was bred in the Italian character. Of course, many people have commonly reacted to other people of different customs in the same way.

Americans based their estimate of Italian character on preconceived notions and on what they saw of Italians in the mass. Because few of the Americans spoke Italian and only a limited number of Italians could converse in English, meaningful contacts between individuals seldom took place. Americans, even the expatriates who lived for years in Rome and Florence, mingled mainly with other Americans and Englishmen. They made no real effort to meet Italian intellectuals, had few Italian friends, generally remained outside the mainstream of Italian social life, and seldom knew its meaning. Longfellow, despite his love of Italy, rarely met truly noteworthy Italians, nor did Washington Irving, James Fenimore Cooper, and other writers; but all were influenced deeply by their Italian experience. To many an American wanderer in Arcadia, life in Italy was "like lovely scenery to a blind man."

The few curious visitors who made an effort to probe beneath the surface of what they saw discovered that Italians differed markedly from the stereotype image familiar to Americans. Usually the longer a perceptive American stayed in Italy and the more Italians he met, the more favorable became his estimate of Italian character. When the American found that his experiences did not match his preconceptions, he sometimes suffered a psychological conflict he could not easily resolve. "This wavering between the traditional judgment, which so many things confirmed, and a far more positive view," as the historian Paul R. Baker has pointed out, "remains a dominant theme in the American response to the Italian people."

This wavering response was evident in various passing judgments. Seeing numerous beggars and idle men in the streets, many Americans concluded that Italians were basically lazy and indolent. Yet other Americans rightly pointed out that the masses were idle because they could not get work. Most Italians had to sweat day in and day out merely to eat. They were, perceptive visitors said, a toiling, frugal, and patient people, if not "the most industrious people in the world," as one American claimed.

Americans frequently made contradictory assessments. Italians, some visitors remarked, were backward because they were deficient intellectually. Yet most Americans credited them with remarkable wit. If the American considered the Italian as clannish, he also viewed him as friendly and social; if the American saw the Italian as devious, he also said he was courteous. Most Americans who went to Italy agreed, however, that Italians had taste and an eye for beauty that their own countrymen lacked. Some Americans even seemed to envy the poorer Italian because of his seeming ability to find happiness in small things.

If visiting Americans disliked one aspect of Italian life more than any other, it was religion. Protestant Americans blamed much of Italy's backwardness on the Roman Catholic church and its practices. In the forties, as the stream of American visitors increased, American Protestant groups became interested in Italy. The American Philo-Italian Society, founded in 1842, had a far-fetched objective—to make Italy, the world center of Catholicism, a Protestant republic. Americans argued that through dissemination of the Scriptures they would aid the Italian people in freeing themselves from religious superstition and a grasping priesthood, help them to throw off their chains, and reform their society.

A few Americans condemned Italian life because it got in the way of their enjoyment of Italy's colorful and impressive monuments of the past. They had, after all, gone to Italy to see ruins and art, not to meet the people. They considered Italy one vast theater. "Every thing here has a kind of stage effect," one American said. "It seems," another commented, "as if the world has indeed turned into a stage, and the men and women into players."

Understandably, Italians did not like the attitude that reduced them to mere actors in a spectacle, or to custodians in a huge museum maintained for the enjoyment of foreigners. They resented the contempt that foreigners showed for them in the present while lauding their achievements in the past. Italians felt that Americans who sought out only the picturesque, the galleries, and the museums were missing much that was vital in Italy. These Italians, although critical, were also often eager to meet Americans because they admired what they knew of American institutions. To many of them, Americans stood out above other foreigners; they were representatives from a country that served as a model for Italy's own national awakening.

Risorgimento
3

The expanding cultural connections between Italy and the United States were not matched by a similar growth in political and economic relations. Since the time of the American Revolution when the Kingdom of the Two Sicilies had invited American ships to make use of the ports of southern Italy (an invitation they accepted) there had been friendly but limited and isolated relations between the new United States and the Italian states. The government of the new American nation had few interests that clashed with those of the various Italian states or that required close cooperation with their governments.

Americans trading in the Mediterranean, on the other hand, constantly ran into Italians and had to deal with them in business transactions. These traders had to have some knowledge of the Italian language, as well as Italian business methods, for in the early years of the American republic, all along the eastern and African shores of the Mediterranean, and on the coasts of the Red and Black seas, too, merchants, travelers, and others used Italian as the language of international communication. These Americans, as commerce in the Mediterranean picked up, asked their government to establish consular posts on the Italian peninsula.

Since, in their practical way, the men in the American government were interested in the Mediterranean trade and in the possibility of commerce with the Italian states, they went along with these requests. The American government appointed its first consuls in Italy in the 1790's—at Leghorn in 1794, Naples in 1796, Rome in 1797, and Genoa in 1799. Although American officials had considered the making of treaties of amity and commerce with the Kingdom of the Two Sicilies and the Grand Duchy of Tuscany as early as 1783, and with the Papal States in 1784, the United States did not establish regular diplomatic relations with any of the Italian states until after Napoleon's downfall several years later. Formal diplomatic relations with the Kingdom of the Two Sicilies went into effect in 1816, mainly, as Secretary of State James Monroe said, for the purpose of enhancing trade with the "powers bordering on the Mediterranean." The United States, however, did not have a consul in Florence until 1819, and never did establish the usual diplomatic relations with the Grand Duchy of Tuscany.

Various Americans who had visited the area urged their government to encourage and support traders in Italy and the Mediterranean. In April, 1796, for example, Joel Barlow, a poet and diplomat from Massachusetts, after spending six weeks in Algiers on a special mission for the American government, advised Secretary of State Timothy Pickering on how the United States should conduct its affairs in the Mediterranean. Small trading vessels from New England used to go to ports in Sicily and on the Italian mainland with cargoes of dried fish, salt meat, and corn. They usually picked up fruit or wine. But this trade was small, most of it carried on by foreign ships. Barlow believed the Italian states could offer a substantial market for American products. He suggested, therefore, that the United States make commercial treaties with as many of the Italian and Levantine states as possible and then appoint resident consuls in the various Mediterranean cities. Competition in trade would be stiff, he warned. "It is well known," he wrote, "that Naples, Genoa and most of the Italian States can navigate cheaper than we can. Their seamen live on nothing except a little dried fruit and coarse bread and their wages are a dollar a month . . . [so] the Italians would do all their own navigations and a good deal more."

There were also other obstacles to trade in the Mediterranean. In order to get in and out of that sea at the Strait of Gibraltar, American traders paid tribute to the pirates of North Africa's Barbary States. In May, 1801, the Pasha of Tripoli demanded heavier tribute than in the past; when he did not receive it, he declared war against the United States. During this Tripolitan War, the Kingdom of the Two Sicilies allowed the United States Navy to use the port of Syracuse as its base. Italians helped outfit American ships and took part in some of the fighting. Six Italian gunboats and bomb vessels fought under Commodore Edward Preble in his attack on Tripoli in 1804, the biggest engagement of the war. This was the first time that Americans and Italians fought side by side, conducting a kind of "joint operation against a common enemy."

In the following year, after the war had ended, American trade with several of the Italian states, especially with the kingdoms of the Two Sicilies and Sardinia, expanded. According to one report, 145 ships of American registry arrived in Leghorn in 1807, 85 of them directly from the United States. In 1815, in part to protect this growing commerce, the United States deployed a naval squadron on a regular basis in the Mediterranean. Four years later, the King of Sardinia told James Schee, the first American consul at Genoa, that he desired more commerce with the United States. Then as trade increased, so did the need for official relations with the Sardinians and other Italians.

In October, 1832, the United States negotiated its first treaty with an Italian state, an agreement of indemnity with the Kingdom of the Two Sicilies. For twenty years, the government of that state had owed money for American ships and cargoes seized by Joachim Murat, Napoleon's brother-in-law and former King of Naples. Early in 1832, John Nelson, the American *chargé* at Naples, after prolonged efforts to collect the money, told the Secretary of State that only coercive measures would bring payment. President Andrew Jackson therefore ordered a naval squadron of four ships to the Bay of Naples. Two of the frigates arrived in July and anchored so that the royal palace stood within range of their guns. "Great uneasiness was felt upon the occasion," Nelson wrote, "and vigorous preparations were made for the defense of the City, which its Inhabitants had the weakness to suppose, was about to be attacked." The Americans used no force, but the show of strength led King Ferdinand II to negotiate the treaty. In it he promised to pay slightly more than 2 million ducats for the old spoliations on American commerce. Commodore Matthew C. Perry, in command of the warships, reported that the "appearance of the Squadron in this bay had had great effect in producing so favorable a result." He had assisted the negotiations by entertaining members of the Neapolitan aristocracy on board his flagship, the newest frigate in the Navy, the U.S.S. *Brandywine*.

Sardinia's king, still eager for more trade with the United States, also wanted to open diplomatic relations. The American government agreed and in 1838 concluded a treaty of general commerce with his kingdom. Two years later, the United States established formal diplomatic relations with Sardinia, sending a *chargé d'affaires* to Turin. This man, however, showed signs of insanity and could understand only English. Five years after that, the United States completed its first commercial treaty with the Two Sicilies.

Americans who traveled in Italy in the first half of the nineteenth century found that their country's lack of diplomatic representation in the areas they visited most—Rome, Florence, and the northern regions—meant that they were usually on their own in dealing with Italian society and officialdom. Sometimes one of the expatriates living in Rome or Florence would perform the small duties which were usually a part of diplomatic or consular routine. For years, Americans in Florence looked upon the sculptor Hiram Powers as something of an official representative of their homeland. He found housing and servants for visitors, stored their goods and personal possessions in his own home, arranged for the burial of Americans who died in Florence, or shipped their bodies back to the United States. But Powers, who avoided anything that would involve him in Italian politics, could not and would not represent Americans before the Tuscan government.

As the more politically minded Americans in Italy, and at home, became involved in various problems of the *Risorgimento,* and as the Italian struggle for unification intensified, American policy makers became increasingly interested in official connections with the more important Italian states. Stories of Habsburg and Bourbon tyrannies aroused the humanitarian feelings of liberal Americans. These tales came from returned travelers in Italy, from newspapermen in Europe, and from a new kind of Italian in the United States—the political refugee who had escaped tyranny and sought a haven. Many Americans previously disinterested in Italy now became aroused by her struggle for liberation from foreign rule and for unification. Although also sympathizing with Italian national aspirations, American businessmen and government officials were hardheaded. They saw in a unified Italy not only the fulfillment of a liberal ideal but also opportunities for greater trade than in the past.

Even though most American visitors to Italy gave little thought to her political struggles, some of them, such as the sculptors Horatio Greenough and Thomas Crawford, developed a passion for Italy's liberation. James Jackson Jarves expressed an open dislike for "papal misrule" and "the ruthless tyranny and dirty state-craft of Austria in Italy." Visitors, such as George Ticknor, sought out leaders of the *Risorgimento.* Among Americans in Italy, Ticknor stood out as an exception; he mingled with Italians, spoke their language, learned their customs and habits, and built friendships with their intellectuals. Other Americans, too, when in Florence, talked to the aging patriot Marchese Gino Capponi. Edward Everett, editor of the *North Ameri-*

can Review, began an exchange of his magazine and Capponi's *Antologia.* In 1840, as a gesture of respect, Horatio Greenough modeled a bust of the Italian.

This American appreciation for leaders of the *Risorgimento* had its counterpart among Italian patriots. They became more intensely interested in the idea of the American Revolution as offering parallels, if not a model, for their *Risorgimento.* Earlier, the French Revolution had seemed to provide the ideals most appealing to Italian intellectuals; but as disappointment set in over its results, they turned more and more to the American model. They envisioned the American uprising as the beginning of a movement for the liberation of all mankind from tyranny.

Established authorities in Italy, on the other hand, saw danger in the American ideals. In the mid-forties when Robert Wickliffe, Jr., the American *chargé* at Turin, sought publication for an Italian translation of George Bancroft's history of the United States, Piedmontese officials blocked him. They denounced Bancroft's views on religion and government as "utterly radical and subversive of all order and government." Nonetheless, within a few years, as interest in the American Revolution increased and as Piedmont became more and more concerned with Italian unification, the Italian version of the history came out.*

Italians now regularly praised the United States, saying it had inherited the virtues of ancient Rome which modern Italy must recover. Both countries, the intellectuals pointed out, had begun as a group of separate states, each dominated by foreign powers and weakened by internal dissent. Even though forced, the parallel seemed pertinent. "America," the writer Cesare Correnti told fellow Italians, ". . . perhaps more than your country . . . is the country of all those who look for one." Carlo Cattaneo, a believer in federalism, argued that unity and liberty could come only in a United States of Italy patterned after the American model. Another thinker, Vincenzo Gioberti, concluded that the United States would lead Europe, not just Italy, to republican forms of government. What the Italian historians implied was clear enough; Italy would achieve progress and independence through the revival of ideals exemplified by the ancient Romans and now by the Americans. Yet well-informed Italians, like other Europeans, wondered if Americans had not also acquired some of the less-admirable qualities of the old Romans. In looking at the annexation

* George Bancroft, *Storia degli Stati Uniti dalla scoperta del continente americano* (2 vols., Turin, 1847).

of Texas and the war with Mexico, these Italians saw in the American national character evidence of an expansionist greed.

Ironically, some American expansionists found themselves attracted to Italian nationalist ideas. Intellectuals, especially, admired Giuseppe Mazzini and his Young Italy movement, mainly because he wanted to remake Italy under a republican government similar to their own, one that would form the nucleus for a kind of United States of Europe. "We content ourselves, as free Americans, and brethren to the friends of freedom everywhere," the *Democratic Review* announced in 1841, to hope "that the *Giovine Italia*, may before no very distant day, triumph over its enemies. . . ."

Led by Eleutario Felice Foresti, an exile who had been active in the *Carboneria*, Italians and others in New York in 1841 organized the *Congrega Centrale*, an American branch of the Young Italy organization. This organizational bridge between Italian nationalists and American intellectuals gained much from the activities of refugees such as Foresti, himself an intellectual, who succeeded Da Ponte as professor of Italian at Columbia College.

These refugees had started coming, usually alone or in small groups, after the European revolutions of the 1830's when reactionary governments dumped their political undesirables on the United States under the assumption that the plotting of these exiles against their home governments would be ineffective on the other side of the Atlantic. When Ferdinand I ascended the Austrian throne in 1835, for example, he commuted the sentences of some Italian prisoners in the Spielberg fortress, a notorious prison, on the condition that they accept deportation to the United States. Foresti, among others, agreed to this condition. This system, if it can be called that, continued for the next two decades, with political prisoners from Lombardy, Tuscany, the Papal States, the Kingdom of the Two Sicilies, and elsewhere being deported to New York.

These exiles, often destitute and bewildered but usually educated and intelligent men, some of them scholars with superior talents, were welcomed by kindred intellectuals in the United States. A few of the refugees came because American liberals had encouraged them to do so, and others sought the trans-Atlantic sanctuary because they had been influenced by the utopian impressions of the United States then current in Italy. A number of the exiles quickly discovered that the reality differed from the utopian image. In 1842, one of them, Pietro D'Alessandro, was so grateful to reach the United States that on landing at Boston "with tearful eyes," he said, "I stooped reverently to kiss the land sacred to liberty, and felt then for the first time, that I too was a *man*." Within two months, he became so disillusioned by what he encountered that he urged a friend not to follow him. Americans, he said, had an aversion to foreigners.

Some of these refugees, working within the Young Italy movement or a mutual-aid organization such as the *Società di Unione e Benovolenza Italiana,* set up schools in New York, Boston, and elsewhere where poor Italian children could gain some instruction. The schools were patterned after one that Mazzini had started in London. In New York, sympathetic native Americans gave a building, free of charge, for the use of the school. In December 1842 Protestants in New York, among them Samuel F. B. Morse, organized the American Philo-Italian Society, later called the Christian Alliance, to help finance these schools and others. This Christian Alliance was more an anti-Catholic than a pro-Italian organization; and in 1844 Pope Gregory XVI condemned it. When the Alliance sent agents into Italy "to promote religious freedom, and to diffuse useful religious knowledge," Mazzini, who desired their help, called them men "sent from America to biblicize and protestantize or reform Italy."

As for the Italian refugees, whether engaged in revolutionary, religious, or military activities (such as forming an Italian Guard to train soldiers for a future war of Italian independence), it was mainly in the intellectual circles of the eastern cities that they found a degree of happiness. There some of them had an important effect on influential members of America's cultural elite through their ideas and lively personalities. These exiles often supported themselves by teaching Italian language and literature in New York, Cambridge, Massachusetts, and elsewhere. They had as pupils or friends sensitive young women such as the writer and critic Margaret Fuller, the novelist Catherine Maria Sedgwick, and the reformer's wife Julia Ward Howe. These women all visited Italy or lived there, and being politically minded, they threw themselves into the turmoil of the *Risorgimento.* Miss Sedgwick, who knew the Italian exiles intimately and had along with her brothers been among the first to welcome them to the United States, was shocked by the oppressive measures imposed on the people by the alien governments in Italy, and particularly the treatment of civilians by the omnipresent Austrian soldiers. Julia Ward Howe, who had studied Dante under Foresti and who wrote poems in Italian, had a special feeling for the Italian patriots. In 1843, when she visited Milan, she exerted herself to call on some of Foresti's relatives.

These Americans, and liberal-minded intellectuals everywhere, were delighted when Giovanni Mastai Ferretti, who became Pope Pius IX in 1846, launched some liberal reforms in the States of the Church. Henry T. Tuckerman, an essayist and literary critic, addressed two sonnets to the Pope, the "Benign Reformer," saying in one:

> The world with benedictions breathes thy name,
> And hails the Vatican as Freedom's home.

Italians, Americans, and others uncritically assumed that Pius might become the regenerator of a united Italy. An editorial in the New York *Herald* described him as the only pontiff in 1,000 years who discovered that "religion and democracy can go hand in hand through the world, to heaven. . . ." A few skeptics such as George Perkins Marsh worried, "Do not, for heaven's sake, commit yourself to the belief in a liberal Pope! It is a contradiction in terms—an impossibility in the very nature of things." In cities such as New York and Philadelphia, where clergymen and other leaders followed the events of the *Risorgimento,* most people expressed approval of the Pope's program and sympathy for a united Italy.

A meeting of Italian sympathizers in New York, held in November, 1847, received a message from former President Martin Van Buren, saying he ardently prayed for the success of Italy's struggle for unification. "When it becomes known to the people of Italy and their patriotic head," he asserted, "that the hearts of a great nation [the United States] are with them, it cannot but give hope to their cause and energy to their exertions." Van Buren's words contained more than mere political wind. Italian liberals translated the issue of the New York *Herald* which carried full accounts of the New York meeting into their own language and distributed it throughout their peninsula. The reports of the speeches and resolutions, carried also by Italian newspapers, created a great stir. Grateful Italians declared the American people their friends and brothers, and some of these Italians wrote poems honoring America's institutions and heroes. In Genoa, a crowd marched by torchlight to the American consulate, shouting praise for the United States.

So enthusiastic were some Americans about the Pope's reforms that they wanted their government to establish diplomatic relations with the States of the Church. In December, 1847, after Pius IX had made official overtures, President James K. Polk told Congress he favored such a step. The political developments in those states as well as American commercial interests, he said, made the measure expedient. Finally, in March, 1848, after spirited debate in Congress filled with anti-Catholic emotion, the American government decided to establish regular diplomatic relations with the Papal government by sending a *chargé d'affaires* to Rome. Secretary of State James Buchanan instructed the first *chargé,* Dr. Jacob L. Martin, who unfortunately died of Roman fever just a week after presenting his credentials, to confine his activities to civil and commercial matters, and to avoid anything concerning religion.

When the Italian enthusiasm for reform spread from the Papal States to the other parts of the peninsula, sparking the revolt that led the people in the Kingdom of the Two Sicilies to delcare themselves independent of their Bourbon king, many Americans rejoiced. James Roosevelt, the father of Franklin Delano Roosevelt, joined Garibaldi's army and for a month or two wore the red shirt. Then he resumed his walking tour of Italy. Another American, Dr. Valentine Mott, Jr., took part in the uprising in Palermo. He contributed money to the rebel cause and served as surgeon general and colonel of cavalry. Fighting broke out at Messina in February, 1848. There revolutionaries, after seizing a fort, celebrated the victory by saluting the American flag. A month later, the new Sicilian government offered the American navy the right to use the harbor at Syracuse as a base. Wishing to remain officially neutral, the American government turned down the offer, at least until the revolutionary regime proved itself sufficiently stable to warrant recognition.

Italians in New York City organized a militia unit to help the Sicilian revolutionaries. In May, when the brig *Carolina* arrived from Sicily flying the tricolor of Italy, these Italians greeted her with special enthusiasm. For the first time since the days of the Roman Empire, the New York *Herald* declared, a national flag of Italy, the emblem of a revived Italian nationality, floated in the breezes. Italian residents of New York presented the captain of the *Carolina* with a new republican tricolor, as a token of friendship between Italians and Americans, in exchange for the flag he had brought with him.

This feeling of kinship with the United States expressed itself in a number of the other Italian uprisings of 1848. In March, when Venice proclaimed itself a republic and established a provisional government, the people immediately converged on the American consulate yelling, "Long live the United States; long live our sister republic." William A. Sparks, the consul, then joined the celebrating crowd in Piazza San Marco with an American flag in one hand and the Italian tricolor in the other, and thanked the people for their good will toward the United States. A few days later Daniele Manin, the President of the Venetian Republic, expressed the feeling of kinship with Americans that many Italians felt. "The ocean divides us, but we are not divided by bonds of sympathy," he wrote in a special message to the United States. Liberty, "like the electric current traversing the seas," he said, "will bring us your examples, and maintain the communion of thought and feeling. . . . We have much to learn from you; and, though your elders in civilization, we blush not to acknowledge it."

Several months later Nathaniel Niles, the *chargé* at Turin, urged the stationing of "an American ship of war" in the harbor at Venice to break an Austrian blockade of the city. "The presence of a war Steamer under the American flag in the waters of Venice," he explained, "would certainly give a moral strength to the struggling cause of freedom and independence without subjecting us to the charge of illegal interference." Nothing came of the suggestion.

In Tuscany, in the autumn, when an uprising forced the Grand Duke to flee, a provisional government took over. Among the crowds cheering the change, only one foreign flag could be seen, that of the United States.

Such sentimentality appealed strongly to American idealists, and particularly to the dynamic Margaret Fuller. In 1846, she had gone to Europe as a correspondent for the New York *Tribune*. First she visited England, where she met the exiled Mazzini, becoming one of his passionate admirers. She described Mazzini as "by far the most beauteous person I have seen," and at another time said that "he is as beauteous as pure music." He won her to his program of Young Italy and to the idea of a United Italy. Early in the following year, she made her way to Italy, traveling through various parts of the peninsula and finally settling in Rome. "Italy," she wrote, "receives me as a long lost child."

Miss Fuller arrived in Rome when everyone was rejoicing over the reforms of *Pio Nono*, as the Italians called the Pope, and she, too, joined in the general feeling that the spirit of the *Risorgimento* would take hold everywhere. Her attachment to the liberal cause became stronger when she met the Marchese Giovanni Angelo Ossoli, a handsome, gentle, but poor Roman nobleman, ten years younger than she, who had committed himself to the cause of unification and the ideals of Mazzini. She lived with Ossoli and may have married him, but in any case, they considered themselves married and in September,

1848, she bore his child. By this time, Margaret Fuller Ossoli not only spoke Italian with ease but also boasted that she had begun to think in Italian.

In the following April, *Pio Nono* repudiated his political reforms, precipitating a revolution that forced him to flee Rome. Then in February, 1849, the people proclaimed a Roman Republic. Margaret Fuller Ossoli tried to promote American aid to the republic through Horace Greeley, but failed. Marchese Ossoli, as a captain in the insurgent Civic Guard, fought in defense of Rome against French troops. His wife stood by him, tending the wounded in a military hospital, and bringing together materials for a history of the brief Roman Republic. In May, 1850, the Ossolis embarked for the United States. On July 19, their ship foundered off Fire Island, practically within sight of the American shore, and all three were drowned. Margaret's manuscript of her history was lost too. Other Americans in Rome, with much less drama, also supported the republic; some contributed money to it.

The agony of the Romans led John Greenleaf Whittier, the American poet most interested in the *Risorgimento* and the one who wrote most often about it in his poetry, to attack the Pope as a cowardly tyrant, "the Nero of our time." In his poem "To Pius IX," written in 1849, Whittier also said

> Stand where Rome's blood was freest shed,
>   Mock Heaven with impious thanks and call
> Its curses on the patriot dead,
>   Its blessing on the Gaul!

Even though Whittier himself claimed to be "no enemy of Catholics," merely of the political activities of the Pope, within the United States religious feelings clouded the attitudes of Americans toward the Roman Republic and the other uprisings of 1848. The Pope, of course, claimed temporal power in the States of the Church. Protestant Americans, welcoming anything that could destroy that power, hailed the Roman Republic; many demanded that their government grant it official recognition. Catholic leaders, clergy and laity, opposed such action; they sympathized with the Pope and condemned the Roman rebels.

Secretary of State Buchanan and Lewis Cass, Jr., the *chargé* in Rome, also opposed recognition, mainly because they felt the republic would not last. So the Polk administration, despite pressure for recognition from friends of the republicans, such as the American consul at Rome, Nicholas Browne, followed a policy of non-interference toward the Roman Republic. Cass himself came to admire Rome's republicans. "It is difficult," he wrote, "to remain an indifferent spectator of such a struggle." Those Americans who believed that their government's moral support could be a determining factor in the fate of the republic protested Polk's policy. They felt that somehow America's own liberal ideals were being betrayed.

When French troops crushed the Roman Republic, most Americans newspapers denounced France. The New York *Herald* called the French action "a reactionary movement that entitled its author and abettors to everlasting infamy and disgrace." Napoleon III, another newspaper said, was the "Benedict Arnold of the old world"; and a poet wrote that "France hath stooped to shame, selling her birthright for a tyrant's name."

Some Americans saw the Roman defeat as evidence of Italian unfitness for a democratic republic. Italians, these critics said, needed more preparation for it. Margaret Fuller had condemned this bitter attitude as stemming from a prejudiced and ignorant view of the Italians. Those critical visiting Americans, "ignorant of Italian literature and Italian life," she said, "talk about the corrupt and degenerate state of Italy as they do about that of our slaves at home. They come ready trained to that mode of reasoning which affirms, that, because men are degraded by bad institutions, they are not fit for better."

Like Fuller in the thick of action, liberal Americans everywhere felt sorrow over the failure of the revolutions of 1848 in Italy. William Ware, a Unitarian clergyman from Massachusetts who had been in Italy during the uprisings, commented that modern Italians were "too amiable a people, and too averse to war, to be ever able to secure their rights." The Roman Republic itself long remained a special object of sympathy, with liberals arguing that American recognition could have saved it. After the failures of 1848, quite a few of these Americans, even though still moved by the republican ideals of Mazzini, began to place their faith in the Kingdom of Sardinia, as she took over the leadership of the *Risorgimento,* as the most likely instrument for Italy's unification.

Now, too, in the wake of the Italian defeats at the hands of the Austrians and others, more Italian refugees made their way to the United States. Two of the most distinguished of these were Giuseppe Avezzana and Giuseppe Garibaldi. Avezzana had been a revolutionary in the Young Italy movement, had fought for liberal causes in Spain and Mexico, and had been minister of war in the Roman Republic. When the republic fell, Avezzana, who had earlier lived in the United States as a political exile and had left his family in New York, gained the protection of the American consul at Civitavecchia, obtained an American passport, and made his way to New York City, where he arrived in August, 1849. The Italians in the city gave him a hero's welcome, complete with a reception by the mayor and the common council at City Hall.

Garibaldi arrived in the following July, and although more distinguished than Avezzana, received no public welcome. He, too, had profited from American friendship. He had received an American passport and had had an American corvette, which he did not use, placed at his disposal at Civitavecchia. His friends and admirers wished to arrange a large public ceremony welcoming him, but he refused to participate, pleading ill health. Fearing violence, local authorities and Catholic leaders in New York City also opposed the plan, forcing its abandonment. Nonetheless, according to the New York *Herald*, Americans showered him with "an ardour of feeling" and "republican enthusiasm" and other unofficial expressions of sympathy. Senator Lewis Cass of Michigan wrote a letter of welcome. "Your glorious exertions, followed by misfortunes, borne with equanimity," Cass said, "are a passport to the hearts and homes of my countrymen." During his stay, Garibaldi received frequent visits from distinguished foreigners and Americans of all ranks and took an active part in the life of New York's Italian colony. His presence also caused difficulties between the United States and one of the Italian states. The government of the Two Sicilies feared that Garibaldi was recruiting men and money in the United States so that he could raise an expedition against Sicily. The Sicilian monarchy complained to the American government about Garibaldi's activities.

Garibaldi lived on Staten Island among other Italians and worked in a small candle factory on Bleecker Street, in New York City; the factory belonged to Antonio Meucci, a Florentine friend. Even though Garibaldi took out his first citizenship papers he never became, as he sometimes claimed, an American citizen. From the first, the United States impressed him. "This nation," he wrote prophetically soon after his arrival, "is certainly living up to its reputation and will soon become the first among the great nations." After spending nine months working in New York, he grew restless and sailed off in April, 1851, for Central America.

At this time, influenced by the new influx of refugees, Americans built up a new enthusiasm for Mazzini. His Young Italy movement branched out into various parts of the United States, and numerous Americans hailed him as one of the most distinguished men of the age. He also had detractors, Americans who considered him a red republican, a Socialist, even a Communist. These charges could not possibly be true, his defenders argued, because he used George Washington as his model, and American institutions—republicanism and democracy—rested on his doctrines. He wanted to plant those institutions in Europe.

In 1851, as a result of visits to the United States by Hugh Forbes, an English military man who had fought against monarchy in the uprisings in Venetia, Palermo, and Rome, and Louis Kossuth, the dynamic leader of a republican revolution in Hungary in 1848, enthusiasm for Mazzini's kind of revolutionary republicanism reached a high point. Americans praised him and Kossuth in song and verse, as in these lines.

> Hail! hero-martyrs of Humanity!
> Twin stars upon the sky of Europe's night
> Bright heralds of the broad, advancing light
> The surging glory of the coming day!

Such sentiments led radicals within the Democratic party in 1852 to organize themselves under the banner of Young America. Forbes and Kossuth, meanwhile, traveled over the country giving lectures on the revolutionary movement in Europe, the spirit of republicanism, and on conditions in Italy. Forbes' lectures on Italy, widely advertised in the newspapers, were especially popular in New York. Those he gave at New York University were printed and distributed as a pamphlet. Kossuth made frequent reference to "fair, but unfortunate, Italy." "We have a common enemy," he said of Italian republicans; "so we are brothers in arms for freedom and independence." Mazzini himself believed that Americans would give him aid when the proper time arrived.

The activities of Forbes, Kossuth, and other political refugees brought to the attention of the American public, in a personal and dramatic way, the repressions in Italy following the collapse of the uprisings of 1848. Prominent Americans, Horace Greeley, the crusading editor of the New York *Tribune* among them, protested the new tyrannies. When Greeley visited Italy in 1851, what he saw depressed him. "It is too true," he said, "that ages of subjugation have demoralized the Italian people to a fearful extent." Italy, he feared, would never gain freedom solely through the efforts of her own people.

John Hughes, New York's first Catholic archbishop, also visited Italy at this time, but he returned expressing views quite unlike those of Greeley. From the pulpit of St. Patrick's Cathedral, he denounced the Italians, especially the Romans, as corrupt and ungrateful. They were, in his judgment, unfit for self-government. The outspoken prelate's views infuriated the Italian republicans in the United States, with whom he feuded. He was particularly harsh toward Giovanni Francesco Secchi de Casali, a Protestant exile from Piacenza who had founded in 1849 a weekly newspaper in New York City called *L'Europeo-Americano*. Printed in Italian and English, it attempted to maintain "among the Italian residents in the United States, their love of their country and to inform them in their own language of the events in Europe in general, and of those of Italy in particular." It supported the Roman Republic and attacked the Catholic church.

When the republic fell, the paper had collapsed, but Secchi de Casali, even though virtually without money or subscribers, quickly started another weekly, *L'eco d'Italia*, the first Italian-language paper published in the United States. In it he continued his attacks on church and state in Italy. As before, he aroused resentment among Italians, some of whom started an opposition paper called *Il proscritto*. In 1851, Secchi de Casali launched another paper in English, the *Crusader,* and dedicated it to "waging war against the Papacy and Jesuitism." Hughes contemptuously dismissed the journalist as a "renegade both to creed and country." Many Americans, with their deeply ingrained anti-Catholic feelings, took the accusations of men such as Secchi de Casali, who published *L'eco* into the 1880's, quite seriously.

Although few of the political refugees were as truculent as Secchi de Casali, a number of them became storm centers. All through the fifties, the exiles continued to trickle into the United States. At first they usually received kind treatment; but like Garibaldi, they were frequently unhappy and had to rely on their own limited resources to eke out a living. Most of them remained in the large cities along the Atlantic seaboard among the few clusters of Italians who had already settled there. The refugees arrived by various means. In one instance, in 1851, the Papal government agreed to allow thirteen young Roman political prisoners to go into exile in any country that would accept them. Lewis Cass, Jr., the *chargé* in Rome, then paid their passage to the United States. Americans welcomed them and praised Cass for his humanitarian action.

In May, 1853, another group of eighty-two refugees became the center of a squabble. These exiles, including three women and members of some of Italy's finest families, arrived in New York City aboard the Sardinian frigate *San Giovanni*. The Sardinian government had imprisoned and then deported them for aiding Mazzini when he had tried to overthrow monarchical rule in Lombardy. The *San Giovanni* received a mixed reception. Many New Yorkers welcomed her enthusiastically as the first warship to enter an American port flying the Italian tricolor with the cross of Savoy in the middle. Ardent supporters of Mazzini, on the other hand, sympathized only with the refugees. To show their feelings, the Mazzinians attacked the crew of the *San Giovanni*.

Such squabbling by Italians over the issue of politics across the sea upset American observers, particularly those who resented having political prisoners of any kind dumped on their shores. Some of the men deported, critics pointed out, were not political exiles at all, but criminals of the worst type. Even those Americans who sympathized with Italy's exiles and the cause they had fought for expressed concern over the character of the deportees, and also over their means of earning a living in a strange land. They did not want foreign governments to ship their undesirables to the United States.

To the dismay of some people and to the delight of others, the Italian refugees sometimes became involved in the heated religious controversies of the time. One of these tempests swirled around Monsignore Gaetano Bedini, who visited the United States in June, 1853, as a diplomatic representative of the Pope. Bedini called on President Franklin Pierce and other government officials, all of whom received him cordially. From the first, his visit stimulated fears that foreign Catholics would influence the government, but his presence did not provoke a violent reaction until several Italian refugees denounced him. Alessandro Gavazzi, an apostate priest, ardent republican, and political exile from Italy, accused Bedini, unjustly, of having been responsible for the flaying alive, scalping, and execution at Bologna of Ugo Bassi, a chaplain in Garibaldi's army. Tall, well-knit, graceful, fast in movement, and eloquent in speech (in both Italian and English), Gavazzi was an impressive figure. When he lectured against the Pope, for instance, his words flashed with an "almost savage physical energy." So his attack on Bedini, made with more than his usual fervor, struck the raw emotions of Italian patriots and anti-Catholic Americans.

In January, 1854, a group of Italians in New York City issued a manifesto corroborating Gavazzi's charges against Bedini. Secchi de

Casali said "it was the duty of Italians to expose the wolf who had crept in dressed in sheep's clothing, and that Gavazzi has done, and done well." Now, when Bedini appeared in public, people insulted him and mobs rioted. The Catholic press defended him and senators made speeches condemning the rioters. Many of those who demonstrated against Bedini merely let loose their anti-Catholic prejudices. Others denounced him because they resented the repressive politics in the Papal States.

American indignation against Ferdinand II of the Two Sicilies was even stronger than against the Papal government because of his brutal rule and his bombardment of Messina in 1848, which earned him the epithet of "King Bomba." Yet the growing importance of commercial relations with this kingdom prompted the American government to raise the level of its diplomatic mission at Naples by replacing the *chargé d'affaires* there with a minister resident. More than 300 American ships a year were now entering the ports of the Two Sicilies. Commerce with the northern Italian states was also increasing and so was naval activity to protect it. In 1848, the United States asked the Sardinian government for permission to use Spezia, on the Ligurian coast, as a depot for its Mediterranean squadron. The Sardinians said yes, and the American navy used the depot for twenty years, or until the Italian kingdom took it over for its own expanding navy. With the Kingdom of Sardinia in the decade from 1848 to 1858, American commerce jumped from $300,000 to $3,000,000 annually. Sardinian statesmen wanted to promote greater trade, mainly with a line of steamers running between Genoa and New York. Nothing came of the plan until after the Crimean War, when ships that had carried supplies to the Crimea took up the peacetime American trade.

The quality of American diplomatic representation in Sardinia at this time did little to improve commercial or any other relations between the two countries. In February, 1854, the *chargé* in Turin, John M. Daniel, a young Virginian, sent a letter to a Richmond newspaper denouncing the Sardinian court as little better than a collection of *lazzaroni* ("loafers"). The whole country, even the nobility, he wrote, "stank of onions and garlic." Understandably, when these comments got back to the people of Turin, they became infuriated; several wanted to settle the score with Daniel in duels.

Despite the gaucheries of men such as Daniel, American liberals, and especially American diplomats in Italy, more and more realized that only the Kingdom of Sardinia offered some hope for the future of

Italy as a unified nation stretching the length of the peninsula. They were pleased, too, because the Sardinian government looked to the United States for models in its political and social reforms, particularly in the field of public education. Sardinian diplomats in the United States sent home all kinds of information on education, including full reports on the free public schools of New York and Massachusetts.

Italians everywhere, as well as other Europeans, continued to see the United States as the hope of things to come for their own country. Cavour himself admired Americans, and the American example inspired him in his fight for unification. Since Americans enjoyed a political freedom and prosperity that all envied, the mere existence of the United States had become an unsettling factor among Europeans. Italians often told visiting Americans that political and social conditions in the United States, according to reports, approached a way of life that they could realize only in dreams. Often, too, they expressed a desire to immigrate to what seemed to them a utopia of plenty.

Most Italians, nonetheless, looked to Sardinia for the leadership that would improve life at home. When Sardinia entered the Crimean War, some sympathetic Americans considered the action a mistake, a betrayal of Italian hopes. The war, they felt, would weaken her and make her an easy prey for Austria. Others approved, believing that participation in the war would bring Sardinia such international prestige that she would enhance her leadership in Italian affairs and bring new hope to Italians throughout the peninsula.

These and similar observations came mostly from Americans in Italy, whose reports on political conditions there stimulated the interest of their countrymen at home in the progress and setbacks of the *Risorgimento*. One of these prominent visitors, the Harvard art and literary historian Charles Eliot Norton, had been brought up with a deep feeling for the *Risorgimento*. His father had translated Manzoni's *I promessi sposi* into English and his mother had done the same with Silvio Pellico's *Le mie prigioni* (My Prisons), a personal and dramatic account of Austrian political tyranny. Young Norton cared deeply for the future of Italy, but found conditions there in the fifties disheartening, especially in Rome and the Papal States. In December, 1857, he wrote to James Russell Lowell, the writer and poet, that "there is no change in Italian politics; the people are oppressed, restless, divided, and impotent. . . ." Yet Norton found considerable attractions in the Italians as a people. Like Norton, Lowell, who traveled in Italy in the fifties, believed that Papal rule was suffocating. "The Papacy lies dead in the Vatican," he wrote, "but the secret is kept for the present, and government is carried on in its name."

Harriet Beecher Stowe, well known to Italians through translations and numerous printings of her *Uncle Tom's Cabin*, a book they found more moving than any other from America, also considered the political atmosphere of Rome of the fifties oppressive. An incident in the shop of a goldsmith moved her to tears. One of the owners who recognized her, handed her a small, beautifully made head of an Egyptian slave, fashioned in black onyx. "Madam, we know what you have been to the poor slave," he said. "We ourselves are but poor slaves still in Italy. You feel for us. Will you keep this gem as a slight recognition for what you have done?" Deeply moved, she did.

Other American writers, including Herman Melville and Nathaniel Hawthorne, wandered through Italy in these years, observing social conditions as well as the ruins and picture galleries. Arriving in Rome in the winter of 1858 and catching a bad cold, Hawthorne was at first miserable there. He condemned practically everything in the city, writing that without French soldiers to keep order it "would very likely be a den of *banditti.*" Later, he acquired an affection for the city, saying "the intellect finds a home there, more than in any other spot in the world, and wins the heart to stay with it, in spite of a great many things strewn all about to disgust us." He also liked Florence, where he began *The Marble Faun*, with its Italian background and atmosphere of art, antiquity, corruption, and decay, and where he called life "delicious for its own simple sake." Even his estimate of Italian character changed. Like many American travelers, he had, as his *Marble Faun* indicates, expected Italians to be dishonest. When Hawthorne carelessly lost a leather bag containing a manuscript in a Tuscan railroad station and it was promptly returned, he revised his estimate of Italian integrity. He was aware of what he called "Papal despotism," but took no great interest in the *Risorgimento,* apparently not seeing in it anything that would cure Italy of the evils he disliked.

Various other American men of letters actively promoted the cause of Italian nationalism. Articles on political conditions in Italy now appeared with some frequency in American magazines, thereby making the *Risorgimento* the subject of frequent thought and comment among literate Americans.

Among liberals, interest in Mazzini remained strong; but with others, it was on the wane. In November, 1858, Signora Meriton White Mario, better known as Jessie White, a young English writer and an eloquent spokesman for Italian republicanism, came to the United States to boost Mazzini's sagging cause. While she appealed to native Americans, her husband, Alberto Mario, lectured to Italian residents in the cities they visited. In their lectures, delivered over a period of six months, they stressed the common ideals of Italian and American republicanism. Jessie's speeches dripped with sentimentality. She told her first audience in New York City that she had seen nothing but love and affection in the eyes of Italians as they gazed at the Star-Spangled Banner. They believed that Americans sympathized with their national aspirations, a conviction that in their struggles gave Italians hope and courage.

Some of Italy's well-wishers, among them the *New York Times*, admitted sympathy with Signora White's theme but opposed her mission. The *Times* felt that all Italians, including republicans, should rally behind the Kingdom of Sardinia. It was the only Italian power on bad terms with Austria and with a good army. Apparently many Americans agreed with the *Times*, for the lecture tour of the Marios ended in financial failure.

The advice of the *New York Times* was meaningful, for Sardinia and Austria were on the verge of war. American newspaper correspondents planted themselves at the scene, sending home accounts of the military preparations. The approach of hostilities split the Italian community in the United States into two factions. Those sympathetic to Sardinia favored war; those loyal to Mazzini's republicanism, seemingly a majority, considered the coming war as nothing more than a contest to see if Italy would change oppressive masters. Among those Italians who supported the Kingdom of Sardinia, the question of returning to Italy to fight arose immediately. The question even got to Cavour, who answered it in February, 1859, in a letter to *L'eco d'Italia*. Sardinia, he said, needed contributions of money more than the return of men from overseas. "The greater part of our countrymen now in America," he explained, "can as effectually serve the Italian cause by remaining in the United States and using their influence in favor of our efforts as by returning to Italy." Yet when hostilities began, many Italians in the United States returned to fight. Others sent money to Sardinia. In New York, and later in other cities, too, they organized a General Italian Committee to raise funds as Cavour desired. They sponsored various functions, such as special performances of operas where Italian artists donated their services, that brought in modest amounts.

American opinion on the war was divided. Most Americans fa-

vored Sardinia and France. American correspondents followed the
Italian troops into battle and vividly described the various engage-
ments. Newspapers paid special attention to Garibaldi's movements.
The Catholic hierarchy, and apparently American Catholics in gen-
eral, sided with Austria. They saw in a united Italy an anticlerical
Italy that would destroy the temporal sovereignty of the Pope.

The historian Henry Adams appeared, however, to reflect widespread feeling when he called Austria an "evil spirit," as did a San
Francisco newspaper that condemned her "scorpion rule" in Italy.
"Every friend of free institutions," the Portland *Transcript* claimed,
"will ardently desire that Austria may be soundly thrashed and
forever driven out of Italy." President James Buchanan sensed the
general mood. "The sympathy for poor, down-trodden Italy," he told
the Earl of Clarendon, "is very strong in this country and our people
would hail her deliverer with enthusiastic applause." When France
and Sardinia won, American policy makers, as well as the people,
were pleased. In the following year, the American government raised
the level of its diplomatic mission to Sardinia by replacing the *chargé*
in Turin with a minister plenipotentiary.

In July, 1859, after the war had ended, Cavour thanked the presi-
dent of the General Italian Committee for the help that it and the
Italians in the United States had given. "The country of George
Washington," Cavour wrote, "was ever among the first to give us
effectual and practical proof of its benevolence." American help for
Italian nationalism did not stop with the end of the Austrian war. In
November, 1859, New Yorkers organized two committees to collect
money for Garibaldi and his Red Shirts. One of these, the New York
Garibaldi Fund Committee, appealed for contributions to buy a mil-
ion rifles.

Seen as a patriot, a fighter against great odds, a doer, and a man of
action, Garibaldi was an appealing figure to many Americans. To
young Henry Adams, who interviewed him at Palermo in 1860, Garibaldi looked like and was "the very essence and genius of revolution."
Americans therefore responded to pleas as in the New York *Herald*
asking "all friends of human progress" to contribute money to the
"Italian patriots." "If there is one nation more than another that is
bound to sympathize with them," the *Herald* observed, "it is this, for
we have had to fight the same fight, under the same difficulties, for
political independence."

Through fund-raising meetings and other devices, American sympathizers in New York City collected about $100,000 in arms, provi-

sions, and cash and sent it all to Garibaldi. Various Americans, including sailors from warships in Italian harbors, aided him in his Sicilian campaign in 1860; and some served as volunteers in his army. William DeRohan (the assumed name of William Dahlgren), a sea captain and soldier of fortune from Philadelphia who became an admiral in the Italian navy, was the most prominent of these. He brought three steamships, which he had purchased at Marseilles and paid for with his own money, to Sicily for Garibaldi's use as troop transports. These steamers carried American papers obtained from the consul at Genoa and flew the American flag. DeRohan gave all three ships American names. The wooden side-wheeler that carried Garibaldi across the Strait of Messina was called the *Franklin*; the others were named the *Washington* and the *Oregon*.

This American help proved decisive. Only the ammunition and troops that DeRohan brought him enabled Garibaldi to continue his campaign, extend his control over Sicily, and confine the Neapolitans to their garrison towns. Even in July, two months after the sailing of the "thousand," more than three-fourths of the reinforcements that left the mainland for Sicily were carried by DeRohan's ships. The American volunteers who crossed the Atlantic to join Garibaldi's forces contributed little more than sympathy; they arrived after the fighting had ended. In November, when Vittorio Emmanuele entered Naples in triumph, of all the foreign warships that crowded the bay, only the U.S.S. *Iroquois* joined the Piedmontese in a gun-for-gun salute.

In the United States at this time, some Fourth of July orators extolled Garibaldi as much as they did the Founding Fathers, calling him "the George Washington of Italy." After he won his war against the Two Sicilies, the acclaim became more lavish. "No such feat," the New York *Herald* announced, "is recorded in history, nor even amongst the deeds of mythological heroes."

Such praise was realistic only as an expression of American rejoicing. Yet even more conservative observers, such as Charles Eliot Norton, could pull out the stopper. "History was never more interesting than now," he wrote in September, 1860. "The new birth of Italy is already the grandest event of the modern period." In December, about 3,000 people gathered at New York's Cooper Institute "to give expression to the sympathy felt by the American nation" for Italian liberty and Garibaldi. Even though the new Italy was not the republic that many American liberals had hoped she would be, several months later, when Vittorio Emmanuele became King of the united

Italy, these Americans could still rejoice over what seemed for them the triumph of the liberal nationalism they had long supported.

All during the years of the *Risorgimento*, these Americans of liberal leanings, as well as others, had a special passion for the cause of Italian nationalism. Poets such as Whittier, Bryant, and James Russell Lowell all wrote hymns to Italian liberty and the *Risorgimento*. Whittier never visited Italy, but Bryant and Lowell knew her firsthand. Knowledgeable Americans paid far more attention to what was happening in Italy than to developments in any other European country where their own immediate national interests were not involved.

This interest did not always spring from affection for Italy or Italians. Many Americans saw Italy as the friend of the United States, the home of Garibaldi, Mazzini, and Cavour, the birthplace of Dante, the fountainhead of the arts, and an important battleground where Italians had been martyrs for nineteenth-century liberal nationalism. But this view represented only one part of the American image of Italy. The other part of the image was less complimentary. It pictured Italians as shallow, immoral, and decadent, a people ignorant and incapable of self-government. In New York City in 1857, for example, when an Italian was charged with murdering a police officer, mobs attacked and insulted all the Italians they could find, showing a feeling of indiscriminate hatred. Although the two parts of the image contradicted each other, this twisted view of Italians, persisted in the American mind. During the *Risorgimento*, the first and more favorable half of the image seemed to make the deepest impression on Americans. Later in the century, as old fears intensified, Americans would more readily accept the unfavorable image of Italians.

Unification
and Emigration

4

Even though in 1861 an Italian nation had come into existence, all Italy was not yet unified. It would take almost a decade of struggle for unification to be complete. During this time, Americans fought each other in a great civil war, in large part to preserve the unity their country had achieved many years before.

The United States and the new Kingdom of Italy had exchanged diplomats just as the civil conflict erupted. Almost from the outset, the Italian government expressed sympathy for the Union cause, saying that Abraham Lincoln was seeking to preserve the principle of nationality which Italians, too, were struggling to uphold. "We shall be the friend of Italy," Secretary of State William H. Seward told the Italians, "and Italy, we are sure, cannot be otherwise than friendly to us." Although these sentiments were more than the usual exchange of diplomatic courtesies, they were still only official expressions of friendship. In Italy the masses knew little about the American war and the issues at stake, just as the American man in the street understood only vaguely the problems of the *Risorgimento*. Nonetheless a few newspapers and periodicals reaching educated readers sent correspondents to the United States to report on developments there or published serious articles about the rebellion, thereby making the war known in Italy. So, despite their limited communication and the agony of their own problems, knowledgeable Americans and Italians sympathized with each other's struggles.

As a result of these attitudes, during the course of the Civil War, the Italian government, and many of the people also, gave moral support and limited material aid to the Union side, but the support fluctuated with the fortunes of the Union armies. The government forbade the sale of munitions to Confederate cruisers and would not permit them to touch any of its ports. Even though the textile industries of

Piedmont suffered from an embargo—enforced by the Union navy—against cotton grown in the American South, most Italians who followed the progress of the Civil War favored the North. The liberal nationalists, and other Italians, too, detested slavery; they viewed the war as a crusade for the freedom of slaves. This feeling became stronger in 1863 after Lincoln issued his Emancipation Proclamation and Italian liberals had a chance to use it as propaganda.

Prominent among the liberals who favored the Union was Giuseppe Mazzini. He admired the abolitionists and considered the fiery John Brown one of the world's great martyrs for truth and justice, along with Socrates and Christ. On the eve of the Civil War, Mazzini expressed his feelings to Theodore Weld, another passionate antislavery leader. "We are fighting the same sacred battle for freedom and the emancipation of the oppressed," Mazzini wrote, "you, Sir, against *negro,* we against *white* slavery."

Like Mazzini, Giuseppe Garibaldi considered the Civil War a crusade against slavery and not necessarily a struggle to preserve the Union. Sulking in seclusion on the island of Caprera, he talked about shaking the dust of Italy off his feet and going to the United States to fight for the Union cause. Over a period of several months in 1861, therefore, American diplomats approached him. In September, Henry S. Sanford, the American minister in Brussels, in the name of President Lincoln offered him a commission of major general in the Union army; Sanford also assured the Red Shirt leader that he would have considerable freedom in his conduct of military operations, "and a hearty welcome of the American People." Garibaldi declined because he wanted supreme command of the Union army and authority to abolish slavery in occupied territory. Since Lincoln could not meet these terms, Sanford could discuss the matter no further. Later Garibaldi reluctantly turned down another feeler to fight in America.

Even though the Americans negotiated with Garibaldi in secrecy, news of the talks leaked to the newspapers and upset Italian liberals. *La nazione,* a Florence paper, expressed their feelings by saying that "the arm of Garibaldi certainly could not serve a nobler cause, were it not that the supreme interest of his own country demanded his presence here." Liberals circulated hundreds of petitions all over the country urging Garibaldi to remain in Italy and help to complete her unification. Garibaldi himself assured Lincoln that his heart as well as his mind sided with the Union cause. In October, 1862, he even suggested that he might, when he recovered from a sickness, go to America, his "second country," and fight in her "holy battle." Nothing came of this offer, but in the following year the old soldier took the initiative in gaining a public expression of sympathy in Italy for the North.

A number of those who had fought in Garibaldi's forces crossed the Atlantic to volunteer for service in the Union armies. Far more Italians volunteered than ever left Italy's ports, for they could not on their own raise expenses for the trip to the United States. One officer offered to form an Italian legion for North America. Italian political exiles also fought for the Union. One of the volunteers, a former Piedmontese soldier who had fought in the wars of 1848 and the Crimean War, Count Luigi Palma di Cesnola, became a colonel in a New York cavalry regiment, ultimately reaching the rank of general and winning the Congressional Medal of Honor. Eduardo Ferrero, also from New York, fought in various engagements, commanded a division of black troops, and was brevetted a major general. Francis B. Spinola, a native New Yorker prominent in pre-war Democratic politics, raised the Empire Brigade of New York, served as a brigadier general, and twice suffered wounds in action. Another regiment, the Thirty-ninth New York Infantry, composed of international volunteers, about fifty of whom were Italians, took the name "Garibaldi Guard." A hard-fighting outfit, which according to the New York *Herald* included "all the organ grinders of the city," it took heavy casualties in various battles. Some Italians, mainly from New Orleans, fought on the Confederate side.

Those people in Italy who sympathized with the Confederacy, and there were a number, argued that their countrymen, especially the liberals, were illogical in claiming for Italians the right of revolution against oppression and the right to settle national questions by popular vote while favoring the North and denying such rights to the Confederate states. Vincenzo Botta, the New York correspondent of the *Gazzetta ufficiale* of Turin, who had been living in the United States since 1853, answered this argument in articles in the *Rivista contemporanea,* the finest literary periodical in Italy. Botta said that the position of the Confederacy could not be compared with that of Italy. The Confederate states were rebelling to perpetuate slavery, a thoroughly unworthy institution. They were trying to destroy the political unity of a people and nation, the ideal that Italians wanted to achieve. He considered the Union cause just and had confidence in its ultimate victory.

Regardless of such arguments, anti-republicans in Italy found considerable comfort in the Civil War. They claimed it revealed the fatal weakness of republicanism. Italians should, therefore, profit from the bad example and shun republicanism. On the whole, however, whether Italians considered the example good or bad, neither Italy nor her people became heavily involved in the conflict. Italy was not capable of affecting it decisively, and Italians in the United States were too few to make much of an impact on the course of the war. Yet Lincoln expressed gratitude for Italy's good will throughout, saying in July, 1864, that "at no stage in this unhappy fraternal war . . . has the king or the people of Italy faltered in addressing to us the language of respect, confidence and friendship." In keeping with these sentiments, Italy expressed pleasure over the Union's victory. In 1866, almost before the smoke of battle had cleared, Augusto Pau reflected this feeling in a history of the Civil War for Italians that showed a bias for the Union throughout.

During the conflict, liberals everywhere in Europe had sympathized with the Union; some had urged Lincoln to forge an alliance between the United States and European republicans. When the war ended, Mazzini revived the idea, believing that the United States had, as a nation, a special mission to uphold the republican principle not only at home but also everywhere else in the world. For example, he urged American leaders to take strong action against the "imperialism at their own door," meaning the troops Napoleon III of France had sent to Mexico to uphold a monarchy there.

"You have become a Nation-Guide," Mazzini said of the United States at this time, "and you must act as such. You must aid your republican brethren everywhere the sacred battle is fought. . . . This is your mission; this is your glory and safety; this is your future!" Despite such grand sentiments, nothing ever came of this idea taken up by many under the name Universal Republican Alliance. By the summer of 1867, even though early converts remained enthusiastic, Mazzini's scheme had collapsed.

By this time, too, American liberals had lost much of their old faith in Mazzini and his revolutionary ideas. Italy had become a major nation not as a republic but as a monarchy. Yet most Americans still saw her as a great museum or art gallery, a source of cultural, not political, inspiration. As a reflection of this attitude, several of the important consular and diplomatic posts in Italy, such as those at Rome and Venice, usually went to artists, writers, or scholars. George Perkins Marsh, the New Englander who in 1861 became the first American minister to the Kingdom of Italy, was one of these, a lawyer and politician, but also a philologist and scholar of great breadth.

Marsh spent twenty years in Italy as minister, a term unmatched by any other American diplomat, making himself an important influence there. Even though he sometimes criticized Italian policy, he liked Italy and enjoyed life there as he did nowhere else. "The people of Italy," his wife wrote, "excited his liveliest interest and he lost no opportunity of studying their character and condition." When the Italians were framing their new constitution, they often consulted him, accepting a number of his suggestions before completing their work. After 1864, when his pioneering book on conservation, *Man and Nature,* was translated into Italian, he influenced the policy of the Italian government in matters of reforestation. He showed how the denuding of mountains brought flood, drought, and calamity to the countryside and its people. His writings helped persuade the Italian government to plant trees on the mountainsides in a reforestation campaign. He died at Vallombrosa, Tuscany, in July, 1882, while spending the summer at the school of forestry established in a mountain monastery there.

Like Marsh, William J. Stillman, the American consul in Rome during the Civil War years, concerned himself more with cultural matters than with politics. Yet Stillman, a journalist and painter, had earlier been involved with Mazzini and Kossuth. He also had a romantic admiration for Garibaldi, and later wrote a good history of Italian unification. Still, he spent much of his time as minister on the *campagna* painting.

In Venice, during these years, the consulship had gone to the journalist, future novelist, and poet from Ohio, William Dean Howells, as a reward for a campaign biography he had written of Lincoln. When Howells took over as consul, he was only twenty-four. His duties, all of them slight, included the making of the usual reports on the commerce of the city. He also had to keep an eye out for Confederate raiders, such as the *Alabama,* that might use Venetian waters, and to discourage the various European exiles who were seeking posts of honor in the Union army or navy. In his first year, only four American ships called at Venice, and three sailed away in ballast, fearing capture by Confederate raiders.

Unlike many other Americans in Italy, Howells mingled with all classes of people—workers, fishermen, and others—and became fluent in Italian. He found the Italians cheerful, prudent, temperate, and frugal, seeing in them none of the laziness and sloth that others spoke about. Since Austrian soldiers occupied Venice and an American could not be seen talking with Austrian officers for fear of losing his Italian friends, Howells found himself caught up in the emotions of Italian nationalism. Venice, he recorded, has a "suppressed look," and to nationalists Garibaldi "was still a god, and the gondoliers expected him as in a second coming." Howells quickly gained an appreciation for Italian cultural life. One of the first books he read in Venice was the memoirs of the distinguished eighteenth-century dramatist, Carlo Goldoni; Howells later translated it into English. For years Howells talked about writing a history of Venice. He never wrote it, but he did get documents in Venice copied for the historian John Lothrop Motley, who was then the American minister to Austria.

Not many Americans traveled to Venice while Howells worked there. But after the Civil War, the American tourists again invaded Italy in large numbers to gape at the ruins and the art. Among these, Mark Twain made a special impact. He arrived in Italy in 1867 as a journalist for New York and California newspapers on the first American cruise ship (*Quaker City*) traveling to Europe and the Middle East, a trip he described in his popular book, *The Innocents Abroad*. Twain called Italy "one vast museum of magnificence and misery," poked fun at her monuments, ridiculed the singing of Venetian gondoliers as "caterwauling," and spoke scathingly of the culture seekers there. He also claimed that only with extreme difficulty might a bar of soap be found in Milan. On a later visit, however, he confessed an infatuation with Italy.

Regardless of Twain's criticism, American culture seekers crowded the museums and historic places. In March, 1868, Bayard Taylor, America's first professional traveler and travel writer, reported a count of some 1,200 Americans in Rome alone. Among these Americans were some new types, such as the practical man from the world of business and the educated, socially conscious visitor who was interested as much in Italy's people and institutions as in her art. The older types also continued to come. For instance, Henry James, the novelist, arrived in Rome in September, 1869, a youth of twenty-six. On his day of arrival, he immediately roamed through most of the city in high anticipation of pleasure. The sights and sounds of Rome did not disappoint him. "At last—for the first time—I live!" he wrote in summing up that day. "It beats everything. . . . I went reeling and moaning through the streets in a fever of enjoyment." He became a lover of Italy, returning again and again, and wrote several novels and many short stories while there, the most important of these being *The Portrait of a Lady*. Everywhere in Italy, James found bustling American visitors, many of them homespun tourists weighted down with guidebooks and opera glasses, poor artists shuffling through the galleries, and businessmen in the restaurants commanding service. To him the most striking quality of these new traveling Americans was their lack of culture, a quality he analyzed many times in his books. Yet even they could not spoil the Italy he loved for the rest of his life. "As I grow older," he later wrote to Charles Eliot Norton, "many things come and go, but Italy remains."

Norton, who made his second visit to Italy in 1870, shared James's feeling. Unlike his other friend, the English writer John Ruskin, who had no sympathy for the *Risorgimento* and despised Italians, Norton remained deeply drawn to them. "If one knows how to live with them, they are the sweetest people on earth," he said. "If I ever come back, may I be born an Italian." Augustus Saint-Gaudens, America's greatest sculptor, also made a pilgrimage to Italy in 1870 in the manner of the earlier visitors to Arcadia. He remained for three years and modeled *Hiawatha*, his first statue, there.

Another of the new types of Americans who were now visiting Italy were the Protestant missionaries who came to proselytize. As one result of their activities, Naples by the end of the sixties had two well-stocked Protestant bookstores. Elsewhere, Protestants established and ran several schools, set up missions, and distributed religious tracts and the Bible. Protestantism now gained some ground among Italians, especially in Florence. This Protestant activity became possible because the Italian kingdom, or its various provinces, had passed anticlerical laws but had officially endorsed religious toleration. Although Protestantism seemed to have no chance of gaining a large hold on the country, it did appear capable to some of shaking the temporal power of the Papacy in Italy. So the Catholic church opposed freedom of religion. This opposition, particularly in Rome and the adjacent territory (known as the Patrimony of St. Peter), where the Pope still exercised temporal as well as religious authority, annoyed Protestant Americans.

In clinging to his remnant of temporal power, Pope Pius IX also resisted all efforts of the Italian government to bring Rome into the new nation. "Those, who are trying to destroy the Temporal Power," he said, "have for their object the entire overthrow of our holy religion." Italian patriots wanted to complete the struggle for unification by making Rome and Venetia integral parts of the new nation. Of the two territories, Rome aroused the greatest passion. "Without Rome, Italy is nothing," Count Bettino Ricasoli, the prime minister from Tuscany said; "for Venice we must wait, the day will come; for Rome we cannot wait." Yet the Italians could do little more than yearn for Rome. French troops protected the papal territory; any effort to take it could bring war with France. Italian statesmen realized that their country could not fight France alone. They also knew that the Pope's authority there could not last a week once the French troops left. They had no choice; they had to wait impatiently.

Venetia appeared almost as elusive as Rome. Some Italian statesmen thought they might be able to buy the territory, but Austria would not sell. The Austrians even tried to smother Italian life there, filling government positions with Germans and publishing the laws in German. Deeply resentful, Venetians defied the Austrians with a passive rebellion. Since peaceful acquisition seemed out of the question, Italian statesmen concluded that they could gain Venice only through war. But Italy lacked the strength to take on Austria alone, so they turned to Prussia as a logical ally. In April, 1866, the Italians and the Prussians signed a secret treaty binding them to fight Austria, a country considered a barrier to both Italian and German nationalist aspirations.

In June, Prussia's chancellor, Otto von Bismarck, provoked war with Austria, and within four days, Italy joined the conflict. Since their army and navy were stronger than Austria's on the Italian front, the Italians expected to conquer Venetia, and even the Trentino, another territory with an Italian population still held by the Austrians. Instead, the Austrians defeated the Italian army near the village of Custozza and the navy, whose ironclad ships were American-built, off the Adriatic island of Lissa. Neither was a crushing defeat, but together they gave a terrible blow to Italian morale.

To everyone's amazement, the Prussians quickly beat the Austrians; and contrary to his treaty with Italy, Bismarck made a separate peace with them. The settlement permitted Austria to concentrate all her forces against Italy, forcing the Italians to choose between peace terms they detested or a terrible war they probably could not win. They chose the distasteful peace. From it Italy gained Venetia, but not Trentino, which was known henceforth as *terre irredente* ("unredeemed Italian land"). Venetia came secondhand, as a gift from a foreigner, not as something Italians had gained for themselves. Austria ceded Venetia to France, who then retroceded it to Italy. The

Austrians yielded Venice because Prussia, not Italy, had defeated them. George Perkins Marsh, for one, considered the manner of turning over Venetia to Italy insulting. So, even though the Seven Weeks' War had brought Italy another step closer to full unification, it left her discredited by defeats, shaken economically, injured in pride, and isolated and friendless.

Nowhere did Italy's weakness seem more frustrating than in her position with regard to the papal territory. Earlier, in September, 1864, Napoleon III had promised to withdraw the French troops from Rome in exchange for a promise from the Italian government to protect the Pope from attack. As agreed, by the end of 1866 the last French troops pulled out, leaving the Pope under the protection of a private army made up of volunteers from all over the world. In the following year, Garibaldi called on the people in the papal territory to revolt and led a band of volunteers into Rome to wrench it from the Pope's forces. Garibaldi not only failed; he also brought French troops back into Rome. He next involved the American government in a small controversy with the papal government. After being arrested, he appealed for help to George Perkins Marsh, who obtained his release.

Despite Garibaldi's failure, the American government sympathized with Italy's desire to gain Rome. In 1867, the United States broke off diplomatic relations with the Holy See by withdrawing its minister in Rome, but an American consul to the Papal States remained. Congress refused to continue appropriations for the diplomatic mission, according to public reports, because the Pope would not permit Protestant worship within the city's walls. More important, leading figures in Congress such as Charles Sumner, a powerful senator from Massachusetts, wanted to express sympathy for the aspirations of the Italians who wished to complete their country's unification. This mixture of political and religious motives ended the diplomatic connection to the Vatican.

The final steps in Italian unification, watched by American statesmen with intense interest and official neutrality, came almost accidentally in 1870 after France and Prussia had gone to war. Napoleon III asked the Italians for help, and they were willing to give it, but only if he pulled the French troops out of Rome. The French emperor refused to desert the Pope. "Better the Prussians at Paris than the Piedmontese at Rome," his empress was reported to have said.

After the Prussians won a number of stunning victories, Napoleon had to recall the garrison in Rome. Now he begged for Italian troops.

Vittorio Emmanuele II wanted to help, but his advisers restrained him. Then in September, after the French Empire fell, to be succeeded by a republic, Italian troops marched into Rome. They encountered no resistance. "Events did everything for us," an Italian journalist wrote, "and we ourselves did little or nothing." Vittorio Emmanuele arrived by train on the last day of December to annex the city officially. As he stepped down from his carriage, he muttered in his Piedmontese dialect, "Here we are at last." Finally the Eternal City became the capital of a unified Italy.

Most Americans hailed this last act in the political drama of the *Risorgimento* with considerable pleasure, believing that the Italians had finally achieved their just aspirations. In a "Hymn for the celebration of Italian Unity" written in January, 1871, Julia Ward Howe said:

> Let one joy illume the heavens and the earthly paradise,
>   Since Italy is one!

In cities across the country, Americans held public meetings to rejoice and congratulate the people of Italy on the unification of their country. Newspapers everywhere expressed similar sentiments. "Even liberal Catholics," the *New York Times* said, "support secularization of the state."

Devout Catholics and conservatives offered no such support; some demonstrated against the taking of Rome, and from various pulpits, priests denounced Vittorio Emmanuele, that "excommunicated usurper." Unhappy, too, were the small number of American artists and writers who were concerned that the fall of papal Rome and the unification of Italy had ended a unique cultural era and that the romantic arts and the picturesque ways in Italy would fade away. Actually, they did not disappear, though the attitude toward ruins became one of scientific examination rather than romantic contemplation. Rome and Florence had just lost their attractions for American painters who, at the end of the Civil War, started to settle in studios in Paris, Dusseldorf, and elsewhere. But George Inness, who had become one of America's most popular artists, returned to Italy in 1871 to spend almost four years near Rome painting landscapes.

Now, too, with the abolition of the civil authority of the Pope, the American government quickly recognized Italy's occupation of Rome and severed its relations with the Vatican. They remained severed despite efforts in Congress to revive them. Then in February, 1871, after negotiations had dragged on for seven years, the United States concluded a comprehensive Treaty of Commerce and Navigation with the Italian kingdom that embodied traditional American principles on neutral rights and on the privileges of the most-favored nation. The treaty also gave Americans and Italians free access to all ports in each other's countries that were normally open to foreign commerce.

This new Italy entered the community of nations as the weakest of the great powers and the greatest of the minor nations. She could not in her relations with the United States, or any other powerful nation, carry on as though she were a great power, but she tried. She planned a big army and a large navy, and the cost of building them drained her economy. This military establishment, the costs of running the centralized system of government imposed by the Piedmontese, and the pressures of an increasing population made Italy's ecomomic situation worse than it had been before unification. Many Italians, particularly in the south, now came to look upon emigration as an alternative to economic strangulation. Before unification, the south had been an independent region of low taxes and a small public debt; after unification, taxes, the debt, and, worst of all, the cost of living all zoomed upward.

Before unification, there had been a notable emigration from the Italian peninsula, but it had usually been on an individual basis, seasonal, and mostly to neighboring countries. Workers from northern Italy migrated each year to France, Switzerland, and Germany to get jobs. Some went to North Africa, especially to Tunis. They labored on the Alpine tunnels, on the railroads of central Europe, on the Suez Canal, and on the farms and railroads of Tunis and Algiers. They worked as stonecutters, masons, and unskilled laborers. Those who remained in the foreign lands often became merchants and professional people. Where they found the opportunity, as in North Africa, they became farmers.

In South America, too, Italians became farmers, professional men, and also leaders in government. Before unification and during most of the nineteenth century, the great mass of Italians who chose to go overseas immigrated to South rather than to North America. Their favorite goals were Argentina and Brazil. During these years, Italian immigrants made up nearly half of all arrivals in Brazil. As a result, the Italian strain in the Brazilian population became a major one. Italian roots penetrated even deeper in Argentina. Before the end of the nineteenth century, Italians comprised about half of all the foreigners in Argentina. There the Italian farmers became pioneer settlers and, like the frontiersmen of British stock in the United States, helped in settling and building the country. In Argentina, the Italians affected the national tastes, habits, and even the language. They gained prominence in all areas of life—in law, medicine, the universities, architecture, engineering, business, and government. In no other country did Italian immigrants and their offspring come to constitute so large a part of the population. People of Italian blood came to comprise about one-third of Argentina's population.

Most of those immigrants who settled in South America came from northern Italy. Before unification, emigration from southern Italy had been slight, mainly because of laws prohibiting the people from leaving. Laws against emigration were most severe in the Kingdom of the Two Sicilies. With unification, these restrictions either disappeared or became ineffective, and southern Italians began an exodus, much of it to the United States. Rooted in his native soil, the Italian peasant, according to sociologists, was not by temperament inclined to be a wanderer. The pressure of poverty, a remorseless decline on a harsh soil, however, forced him to abandon conservative habits. "We should have eaten each other had we stayed," Italian immigrants in the United States would say.

In 1871, a population of 27 million people placed an almost unbearable strain on the limited resources of the new Italian nation. The country was not truly overpopulated; it just had too many people trying to make a living off the land. Italy lagged behind the other countries of Western Europe in commerce and industry, even though the opening of the Suez Canal two years earlier had ended the backwater nature of the Mediterranean and had permitted Italy to begin placing her ships and goods within reach of almost every major port in the world. Everywhere in the industrial countries, where technology had broken down old patterns of living, people were moving from the farms to the cities for jobs, higher incomes, a better life. In Italy, too, this movement from the land swelled the growth of cities; but unlike the cities in the more advanced industrial nations, those in Italy could not absorb the peasants who, like hungry locusts, were swarming from the countryside.

Contadini birth rates rose so rapidly that social planners did not even have time to think intelligently about how to use their country's meager resources to meet at least a few of the people's needs. Within a century, or since the time of the American Revolution, Italy's population had doubled itself, producing unemployment and widespread unrest. Emigration worked as a kind of social safety valve for the new Italian nation. Italy became an exporter of strong human bodies to

other regions that needed labor and could offer food. New, relatively
cheap, easy to obtain, and what was then considered swift transportation also stimulated a mass migration, approaching in numbers that
of the English-speaking peoples, overseas to South and North America. In the sixties, following a decade of feverish building, the comple-
tion of railroads in Italy changed the nature of travel on the peninsula.
Railways connected inland areas with port cities and joined the peninsula, more effectively than in the past, to the countries of Western
and Northern Europe, facilitating emigration.

In its way, the steamship revolutionized ocean travel almost as
much as the railroad changed land travel. Before the Civil War, a
crossing of the Atlantic in a packet took a month or more and was always perilous. In the postwar decades, a fast steamship could make
the crossing in ten days and could carry more passengers than the
sailing ships and the older steamers. The Atlantic journey became
faster and more comfortable than in the past. The competition between rival steamship companies also resulted in more comforts for
emigrants, who usually traveled in the steerage, the cheapest
passenger area of a ship. In addition, American laws helped eliminate
some of the worst evils of steerage travel.

Despite these improvements, for most Italian peasants the voyage
was still an agonizing experience. Ignorance and superstition added to
the terror of a rough passage. Most peasants had never before been
on a ship. When a ship rolled in a rough sea sending passengers,
dishes, and other gear crashing to the deck, the frightened emigrants
thought they would never survive. From Naples the voyage through
the Mediterranean and across the Atlantic to New York usually took
from two to three weeks. During the crossing, emigrants often found
themselves packed in dirty bunks, like herring in a barrel. As many as
300 people slept and lived in the steerage in rows and rows of
double-decker bunks, 6 feet long, 2 feet wide, and 2½ feet apart. Into
30 cubic feet of space, the emigrant had to stuff himself, his hand
luggage, his toilet necessities, and the eating utensils the ship furnished him.

These miserable conditions became worse when the weather turned
foul, a not unusual circumstance in the turbulent Atlantic. Then the
emigrants could not use the small open deck allotted to them. Hundreds of steerage passengers would have to spend day and night in
their berths, with the hatches above shut tight. Often, because of insufficient bedding, they slept in their clothes. The stench from unwashed
clothes and bodies permeated the steerage quarters, a sickening atmos-

phere. More nauseating was the smell from the vomit of seasick passengers that littered the decks. Time and again emigrants complained
of maltreatment by the crew. Rough seamen frequently molested the
women. They freely entered the women's dormitory and tried to drag
girls into the crew's quarters.

During the crossing, the *contadini* found no intimation of the
sweeter life they were expecting to live in the United States. "Passage
across the Atlantic," one such emigrant recollected, "seemed to have
been so calculated as to inflict upon us the last, full measure of suffering and indignity, and to impress upon us for the last time that we
were the 'wretched refuse' of the earth; to exact from us a final price
for the privileges we hoped to enjoy in America." When the immigrants landed in the United States, exhausted from their fearful voyage, small armies of exploiters would swarm around them. Runners
who spoke Italian, or one of its various dialects, piloted the newcomers to boarding houses where greedy creatures detained them until
they ran out of what little money they had. Employment agents and
bogus railroad representatives sometimes robbed and misdirected the
immigrants, selling them counterfeit or worthless railroad tickets.
Conditions such as these lasted through the nineteenth and into the
twentieth century.

Aware of the indignities and hardships suffered by the emigrants,
some of the leaders of the new Italy deplored what was happening. It
also pained them to see their people stream out of the countryside
and lose identification with the homeland. In some provinces, the
government became so concerned that it urged the people not to emigrate. In more than one instance the *contadini* answered, explaining
why they were forced to abandon their country. "We plant and we
reap, but never do we taste white bread," they said. "We cultivate the
grape but we drink no wine. We raise animals for food but we eat no
meat. We are clothed in rags. . . ."

Millions of other European peasants suffered, more or less, under
similar conditions. As though part of a world on the move, they were
now pouring into the underpopulated areas and industrial cities of
North and South America, Australia, and South Africa. Although
larger than most, the Italian migration made up only a part of this
world movement. Likewise, the immigration to the United States was
only one phase of this larger movement.

The improved transportation also stimulated tourism. As had others, Italian travelers wrote books about what they saw and experienced in the New World, and those accounts kindled the interest in

Italy in emigration. During the Civil War years, few Italians had come as tourists; but by 1870, after conditions in Italy attained some stability and faster vessels speeded the Atlantic crossing, more and more Italian travelers could be seen in the United States. A number of them were attracted to the International Centennial Exposition of 1876 in Philadelphia honoring the first hundred years of American independence. By this time Italians realized, as did other Europeans, that the United States had a vigorous, booming industrial economy. The Italian travelers, usually well-educated and perceptive, were dazzled by the prosperity in the young giant of a nation they were visiting. The affluence seemed especially striking when contrasted with the depressed conditions in their homeland. Even though the travelers could not account for the amazing prosperity they saw, they hailed the United States as a land of plenty.

These visitors did not consider everything they saw worthy of praise; some criticized social conditions. Before the Civil War, the few tourists who came had shown an interest in the Negro as a slave, and those who came later were curious over his condition as a free citizen. The reactions of the Italian visitors, depending on their own social status and racial sensitivity, were mixed. Most had deplored slavery; but, for example, after the Civil War, Ferdinando Fontana, a journalist, expressed disgust over seeing an Italian immigrant shining the shoes of a Negro. Ernesto Rossi, a Shakespearean actor of some stature who came in the eighties, was appalled by the discrimination against Negroes. During a performance, he saw a black admirer thrown bodily from a theater and other Negroes ejected from seats after they had paid for them. He also saw a black congressman denied a room in a hotel used by his white colleagues. These experiences gave Rossi a distaste for democracy as he saw it in the United States.

Almost all the Italian visitors, in one way or another, remarked on American democracy and its institutions. Many were particularly impressed by the freedom of the press, praising it as an institution natural and basic to a democracy. In articles and books, they expressed amazement over the importance of the newspaper in the everyday life of Americans. Dario Papa, a journalist who made a study of the press in the United States, praised it and castigated the newspapers of Italy. One reason, he felt, for the affluence of the American press in comparison with the poverty of Italian newspapers was simply that many Americans had the money to buy papers; whereas most Italians did not. In any case, to the visitor, American newspapers seemed rich, powerful, and influential to an extent unknown and unexpected in Italy.

Like the tourist, the Italian immigrant was also dazzled by the abundance in American life. Throughout the seventies, as before the Civil War, most of those who settled in the United States came from Italy's northern provinces and brought with them a little capital and some skills. They joined the scattered groups of earlier settlers who had laid the basis for Italian culture in the United States. These earlier immigrants had started Italian clubs, such as the *Società di Unione e Frattellanza Italiana* of New York City that in 1863 had founded an evening school for adults, making available instruction in languages and other disciplines. In these years, benevolent societies and various Italian schools got their start. In New York City, in 1871, Italians established their own Bureau of Immigration and also a *Circolo Italiano* to discuss things Italian. New York papers frequently described Italian outings and picnics; and in the Five Points area, Italians had already begun to organize to gain some political recognition. Already, too, Italian workers had begun to clash with Irishmen over jobs. Across the continent, in San Francisco and surrounding areas, many Italians found prosperity. They were in command of fishing and selling fish, owned farms, and ran businesses.

Most of the Italian immigrants who stepped off the trans-Atlantic steamers in the seventies did not go West; they settled in the large industrial centers of the East and Middle West. Their first homes were in the oldest sections, or slums, of those cities. There, as around Mulberry Street in New York City, they formed the nuclei for what came to be called "Little Italies." In Philadelphia and elsewhere, newspapers were already carrying stories of squalor, drunken brawls, and crime in the Italian neighborhoods, a theme that would soon become common in American journalism.

As these Italian settlements expanded, the people in them demanded services to fit their own tastes and customs, such as special bakeries, lawyers, doctors, and newspapers. In 1871, in New York City, Cesare Orsini and Giuseppe Norton tried to anticipate these needs and to influence the newcomers with the first regular daily newspaper to be published in Italian in the United States, *L'unione dei popoli*. The effort proved premature; the paper lasted no more than six or seven months. Nine years later, after a significant increase in Italian immigration, Carlo Barsotti, an ambitious young Tuscan businessman, started a new Italian daily in New York City, *Il progresso Italo-Americano*. Even though he had difficulty finding good newspapermen, or even Italians who could write their own language properly, he came out with a paper of four pages, two of them filled with advertising. But the enterprise prospered, becoming in time the foremost Italian newspaper in the nation. In this same year, Italians in Chicago founded their first newspaper, a daily called simply *L'italia*. These and later Italian-language papers filled a need, publishing items of community interest to Italian-Americans and news from the home country.

By this time, the end of the seventies, ironically, more and more of the Italians who were arriving were incapable of reading any newspaper. They were mostly swarthy, illiterate *contadini* from southern Italy. To most Americans they seemed particularly strange because Italians of this kind had not previously been encountered in large numbers. Earlier Italian immigrants had experienced prejudice, but these newcomers met almost instant hostility and suspicion. As early as 1872, the *New York Times* reported that in the city's "business community there is an almost unanimous refusal to hire Italians." In 1874, the Armstrong Coal Works in western Pennsylvania brought in a group of Italian laborers to break a strike. Immediately, hatred of strikebreakers and prejudice against Italians produced violence; the other workers rioted, attacked, and killed several of the Italians. Even the earlier northern Italian immigrants looked with contempt on the Sicilians, Neopolitans, and other southerners.

With the increased flow of Italians came something that seemed new in immigration, the worker who took advantage of the seasonal employment in American industry to earn a little money and then return to Italy, "as a bird in springtime repairs to its old nest." Although others, such as Irishmen, Poles, and French Canadians, migrated seasonally, and migratory workers had become familiar to every part of Europe, no previous immigrant groups had come with as many temporary settlers as did the Italians. These "birds of passage," as the temporary immigrants were called, angered old-stock Americans who considered their actions evidence of weakness in the Italian character. Actually, the relative swiftness of the steamship and the cheapness of steerage accommodations did more to stimulate temporary immigration than did the traits of Italians.

Disliking the seasonal job hunter and other aspects of Italian immigration, native Americans grumbled that a large ethnic group was appearing on the nation's shores which could not be fitted into what they considered the desirable pattern of American life. Now some of these nativists began talking about an unpleasant change from "old" to the less-desirable "new" immigration and to concern themselves with the nation's "unguarded" gates. From the beginning of the nineteenth century, state and local authorities, particularly at the main ports of entry, had enforced local laws designed to discourage paupers from immigrating and to provide money to help sick and needy newcomers. The courts now held that the government could regulate immigration as it did commerce and that Congress, not the states, should control it. President Ulysses S. Grant repeatedly stressed the need for federal laws to regulate immigration.

By 1880, when the concern for regulation started rising, the formative years of Italian immigration had ended. The main characteristics of that immigration, and also of the mounting Italian population in the United States, were now fairly clear. Most of the early settlers had emigrated from northern Italy, but beginning in the seventies, the majority of immigrants were coming from southern Italy. Like virtually all immigrants, these poor *contadini* came looking for a better, sweeter life than they had known. Some found it, others did not, but still the southern Italian kept coming.

Flood
Tide
5

If any one year can mark the turning point in the massive movement of a people, 1880 is the one for Italians entering the United States. Census figures for that year show 44,000 Italians in the country, 12,000 of them in New York, the area of heaviest concentration. Tens of thousands crowded themselves into America's cities each year thereafter, at least 100,000 pouring off the immigrant ships in 1900. In that year, there were more than 480,000 Italians in the United States, or nearly three times as many as there had been ten years earlier.

Now the peasant tide from the Mediterranean swelled to huge proportions. From 1900 to 1910, well over 2 million Italians hustled through American ports. Nearly three times as many arrived in this decade as had in the preceding ten years. In 1907 alone, as many as 285,000 flooded the shore, and they kept coming. In 1900, Italians comprised less than 5 per cent of the foreign-born population. At the end of the decade, they made up about 10 per cent of the foreigners, even though the census enumerated slightly more than 1,300,000, or just about 60 per cent of those who had arrived in that decade alone. In these ten years, when European immigration into the United States rose to its highest level, the Italian inundation reached a crest higher than that from any other nation. The flood from Italy turned into one of mankind's great voluntary movements of population.

Many more Italians came to the United States than stayed permanently, and more came than official sources indicate; thousands entered the country clandestinely and illegally. Throughout the eighties and nineties, a third or more of those who came returned to Italy. In the eighties, the new distribution of Italian emigration was becoming clear. As many Italians were migrating overseas as were going to countries nearer home, such as France or Germany. In the nineties, the Unites States became their favorite goal.

During these years, the massive migration from southern Italy, like that from other countries, followed a pattern. The first immigrants were young men, usually between the ages of fourteen and forty-five. Italy sent a higher proportion of males in relation to females than did any other European country. The average Italian immigrant was, therefore, a young, robust male, uneducated and unskilled, but in the most productive years of his life. When he became reasonably settled in the United States and could get his hands on enough money for the passage of his family still in Italy, the women and children would follow. In the first years of the twentieth century, fewer immigrants returned to Italy than in the past. Many would visit their old homes for a month or two, but few stayed. Most returned to America and to what they now regarded as their new home. More and more Italians realized, especially after reaching the United States, that they could not easily use emigration as a device for temporary relief of distress in the old homeland. By this time, Italian immigrants were becoming permanent settlers, building a bridge of bone and flesh between Italy and the United States.

This great influx of peasants from the Mediterranean surprised Americans. These Italians, the sociologist Edward A. Ross said, had "shot up like Jonah's gourd." Since their arrival noticeably changed the nature of the immigration to the United States and of the ethnic composition of the population, but not as abruptly as nativists maintained, old-stock Americans became increasingly critical. Why, they asked, did Italians keep coming to a land that was to them strange and often hostile?

Italians kept coming in far greater numbers than anyone anticipated for the same reasons that caused other peoples to emigrate, and for their own special reasons also. The United States had the reputation of a land of plenty with an expanding economy that required manpower. Technology eliminated the need for industrial skill in many factories and mines, giving the inexperienced and unlettered a chance to find jobs quickly. Emigration from Italy, as from other countries at this time, throve under such conditions; it boomed in periods of feverish industrial activity in the United States. In times such as these, foreign workmen such as the Italians, ignorant of the country, its language, and its customs, could most easily be absorbed into its industrial life.

This economic attraction, as well as the improvements in travel, was not enough in itself to force conservative *contadini* to leave the soil. All students of emigration agree that few people leave home by true free choice. Italians put this observation into an old proverb, *Chi sta bene non si muove*, or "he who is well off doesn't move." The Italians also came, and most stayed, because, as in the seventies, their homeland virtually expelled them; they left in a mass act of protest against intolerable conditions. For southern Italy, the last decades of the nineteenth century were a time of economic collapse, or nearly so. Agriculture, the nation's main economic activity, suffered a severe depression, much of it resulting from competition with other countries.

In the late eighties, the precariously balanced economy of Italy's south received two jarring blows. Owing to quick increases in the production of citrus fruits in California and Florida, the United States cut its imports of Italian oranges and lemons. The American growers also improved their fruit, built aggressive sales organizations, and worked out efficient methods of transportation. Unable to compete, thousands of citrus farmers in Calabria, Basilicata, and Sicily found themselves with unsalable surpluses and a ruined export economy. At the same time, phylloxera (plant lice) invaded Italian vineyards, leaving thousands of acres destroyed. In addition, France built a high tariff wall against Italian wines, depriving the grape growers of Apulia, Calabria, and Sicily of their chief export market. Prices dropped precipitously and winemakers all over southern Italy went into bankruptcy.

These developments stimulated a rebellion in Sicily in 1892–1893 and marked the start of a period of terrible hardship for already poor peasants all over the Italian south. *Contadini* who could no longer squeeze a living from the land also could not find jobs, which were nonexistent in Italian industries. More peasants than ever from Calabria, the Abruzzi, or Sicily, came to feel that other lands could not treat them more harshly than did their own. Even though in their lifetime they may never have wandered beyond the bounds of their native village, more and more of them became desperate and responded to the posters of emigration agents telling the prices and dates of voyages to America and became willing to encounter the perils of a new land. They borrowed money for the voyage, sometimes paying a rate of interest as high as 50 per cent; by the thousands and tens of thousands, they streamed into the United States.

Since the peasants reacted sensitively to economic changes in the countries they desired to immigrate to, chance also had a hand in bringing them to the United States. In the seventies and eighties, many thousands were already on the move from northern Italy to South America. Most of the emigration from southern Italy might have followed the same route except that conditions in South America, temporarily at least, seemed uninviting to those who might go there. An outbreak of yellow fever in Brazil had claimed some 9,000 Italian victims and had led the Italian government temporarily to ban immigration to that country. In Argentina, political disturbances, financial crises, and a war with Paraguay brought economic life almost to a standstill and caused prospective immigrants to think twice about going there. Why, *contadini* reasoned, should we go to a land where circumstances are not much better than those at home?

Once the south Italian emigration had set its course for the United States, it rapidly gained momentum. Periodic crises at home also maintained its flow. Between 1884 and 1887, cholera epidemics that killed 55,000 people set many on the move; and ten years later, a poor harvest deepened the unrest in the Italian countryside. The price of bread climbed, nearly doubling in some southern areas. In the *Mezzogiorno,* Italy's south, peasants rioted and raided bakeries, the shops of local merchants, and grain elevators. By March, 1898, the riots had spread from the original centers in Sicily, Puglia, and Calabria into Naples, and then to Tuscany and to other northern provinces. By May, Italy from south to north appeared ready to explode. The major drama took place in Milan, not the place struck hardest by the economic crisis but the most politically conscious of Italian cities. These turbulent times, known as the May Days of 1898, brought violent death to many. When workers rioted, soldiers, in enforcing martial law in Milan with cannon and grapeshot, and later in Florence and Naples, killed anywhere from 80 to 180 people and arrested hundreds.

At first the government of the new Italy had deplored, been indifferent to, or had ignored the exodus from its countryside. Slowly, despite the influence of landowners in parliament who opposed emigration, the attitude of the government changed. Seeing positive advantages in emigration, Italian officials even encouraged it. A law of December, 1888, designed to control emigration, also declared that Italians could freely emigrate from the kingdom. In immigrating to a richer land, such as the United States, Italians often helped themselves and their country by relieving the economic pressure at home. The mere act of leaving helped because it reduced the number of mouths to be fed in Italy. They continued to help by sending home some of the money they earned abroad. These emigrant remittances gave the Italian government badly needed cash and became important in Italy's effort to balance her economy. Immigrants in the United States, like those in South America, bought Italian foods and other products, so by creating a demand for Italian goods, they also helped in building Italy's foreign markets.

Emigration also brought some losses. Italy may have lost effective leaders, especially from among the bold and adventurous who often were the first to leave. In the south, emigration did what the Black Death had once done in England. It thinned out the population, emptying whole villages of able-bodied men, and leaving streets choked with grass and weeds. The cry *Ci manca la mano d'opera* ("We lack the working hand"), could be heard in many villages. "The young men have all gone to America," one villager explained in 1908. "We are rearing good strong men to spend their strength in America." Large tracts of land went uncultivated; military quotas became difficult to fill; women and children replaced the male providers, working at times almost beyond endurance to support families; and young women also faced a shortage of eligible men to marry. Suitable men who remained at home frequently asked for dowries that girls could not obtain.

At times the Italian government tried to reduce losses from emigration by encouraging internal migrations, but as always, there were not enough jobs to support such a movement. When Prime Minister Giuseppe Zanardelli, at the beginning of the twentieth century, traveled south to see conditions there for himself, he was shocked when the mayor of one town, Moliterno, greeted him "on behalf of the eight thousand people of this commune, three thousand of whom are in America and the other five thousand preparing to follow them."

Letters from relatives and friends who had immigrated to the United States, and who could write or had someone write for them, broke up the monotony of village life and in other ways affected the country. Often the "America letters" awakened desires in *contadini* for a better life and led them, and the women too, to ask for higher wages. Even though frequently stained with tears, these letters told those who had stayed behind of the plenty available in the New World for those who were prepared to bend and strain in a strange land. If you are willing to sweat, the America letters said, come and join us. These letters, like this song, showed a duality in the peasant attitude toward the United States.

Here's America for you:
Hard work and money,
A cross of gold, but all the same a cross. . . .

This kind of concrete language appealed to the *contadini* whose main assets were strong arms and a willingness to work. On the average, southern Italians brought with them about half as much money as did northern Italians, who carried with them into the United States slightly more cash than the average immigrant of any nationality. The southerner usually had so little capital and so little education that he could work only with pick and shovel, or at some other job requiring no skills, such as hod carrier or mortar mixer. "Here I am," he seemed to say, "use me where you will, only give me my daily bread."

Bit by bit, barriers rose that made emigration for these most backward of peasants difficult. In the nineteenth century, the Italian government had not required passports, so many emigrants had left the country without them. In 1901, in an effort to control emigration and its abuses, Italy made passports obligatory. This law also prohibited artificial stimulation of emigration, placed a tax on every prospective emigrant, and denied passports to those convicted of a moral crime. If an Italian with a criminal record did manage to obtain a passport, his record went with it.

Italy cooperated with the American government in keeping criminals from immigrating to the United States, and she tried to maintain a high level of health for her emigrants. She permitted American officials to give emigrants medical examinations at their port of departure. Yet some people in poor health entered the United States because American law called for the exclusion of only those aliens with notably infectious or contagious diseases. Some criminals evaded Italian passport law by going to other European countries and then making their way to the United States. Italy wanted to keep criminals from emigrating because they injured her image everywhere in the world. This concern over the quality of her emigrants brought her some benefit. In comparison to nationals from any immigrant group, Italians had the lowest percentage of rejections upon landing in the United States. The Italian government also tried to protect emigrants against exploiters. Under the law of 1901, it established a General Emigration Office, giving this agency authority to deal with everything concerning emigration. This office granted licenses to agents who transported emigrants, fixed the prices for travel, ensured some protection aboard ship, aided workers in foreign countries, and supervised institutions for helping emigrants. These agencies, public and private, published information in the press and elsewhere, and distributed guides, handbills, and bulletins on matters useful to emigrants. They usually offered these services free of charge.

A number of publications in Italy devoted themselves entirely to questions of emigration. Some organizations instructed emigrants in evening classes to prepare them for conditions they might encounter in foreign lands. The curriculum varied, depending on where they were going, what conditions they might expect to find, their own trade, and their intellectual capacity. For years the Society for the Protection of Italian Immigration, organized in 1901 by American philanthropists, looked after Italians arriving at New York and Boston and those returning to Italy. Operating with funds from the Italian government and with money contributed by people in New York, the society performed varied services, such as providing room and board at moderate prices for arriving immigrants. Through a labor bureau, it placed immigrants in jobs; and in camp schools, it taught them English and the essentials of American citizenship. Such assistance, although useful, was brief and limited to a small proportion of the arriving Italians; it did not work as effectively as self-help.

Two characteristics that Italians brought with them, although often criticized, helped them to face life in the brutal sections of strange cities—tightly knit family ties and loyalty to their *paese,* or "home village." "Italy for me," immigrants would say, "is the little village where I was raised." In New York, Boston, Chicago, and elsewhere, Italians congregated in neighborhoods with their *paesani* (others from the same region) recreating what sociologists call urban villages, or the Italian country town in a city environment. Large settlements in the cities would often be divided into almost as many groups as there were sections of Italy represented. Few were exclusively Italian in make-up, and all were in a state of flux.

It was logical for immigrants who could speak no English to want to be near relatives or those whose tongue and customs they understood. Established relatives or *paesani* could assist the newcomer to get a job or a place to live and could help in emergencies. By custom and tradition Italians expected aid from relatives. The family cohesiveness and provincial clannishness of the Italians was not unusual. Earlier immigrants—the English, the Irish, the Germans, and others—had also settled among their relatives or countrymen from the same village, and they too had created urban villages in big-city neighborhoods. But the Italian, who often continued to think of himself as a Calabrese, a Veneziano, an Abruzzese, or a Siciliano, seemed stranger, more conspicuous, less capable of national feeling, and more clannish than the earlier immigrants. Whether or not he was, many Americans thought so, and that belief colored the relationship between Italian immigrants and Americans.

Density of population was usually greater in the Little Italies than in other parts of the cities, and slum living was the general condition. In 1904, a tenement-house inspector described Philadelphia's Little Italy as thirty-five blocks of tightly packed humanity. "One can walk the streets for considerable distances," she said, "without hearing a word of English." Under such crowded conditions, life could be tolerable only when people appreciated each other's customs. In California, social conditions differed from those in the East. Little Italies were less crowded there, less provincial, and more prosperous.

The narrow loyalties of the Italians also brought disadvantages. Along with illiteracy, they hampered the development of the Italians in the settlements into a cohesive ethnic group capable of exerting social and political pressure for the advantage of all. Italians did not work together as effectively as immigrants in other ethnic groups; differences in dialect and the lack of widespread written communication kept them apart. Italian newspapers in the United States could not reach illiterates and those who spoke only one dialect; the gap between the written Italian and the spoken dialects was often too great. In the middle eighties, for example, Adolfo Rossi, an immigrant journalist, tried to find a job on an Italian newspaper, and in doing so met with vexing problems. It was impossible, he said, to find in New York City an Italian, not to speak of a professional journalist, who could write his own language with accuracy. Later Rossi became editor of *Il progresso Italo-Americano,* New York's leading Italian newspaper, and a Commissioner of Italian Emigration; he also wrote an account of the Italian immigrant.

Like the Poles, Ukrainians, Jews, and other immigrants, Italians banded together in fraternal organizations, and especially in mutual-aid societies similar to those they had known in Italy. These societies provided a kind of group-benefit insurance for workmen, small shopkeepers, and others. In these organizations Italians showed a capacity to help each other in meeting the problems of America's industrial society. In New York City alone, in 1910, there were more than 2,000 Italian mutual-benefit societies. But Italians failed to use these groups or the social strength of their neighborhoods to build an effective national pressure group. Although many of the societies and fraternal groups came together in 1906 in the National Order of the Sons of

Italy in America, this organization had strength only in fragments; it was strong at the city and state levels, but weak nationally.

In time, out of the common experience of living in the United States, immigrants discovered the larger ethnic bond—that they were Italians, not just *paesani,* with a common heritage and common interests. The Italian newspapers, magazines, and other publications that appeared in their communities by the first decade of the twentieth century contributed to the growth of this ethnic identity. So did the books on life in the United States written by Italian visitors. Italian-language newspapers published stories on Italian history and literature, and even reprinted literary classics. They often provided immigrants with a means of communication with the larger American community. In Chicago, for example, when the establishment wanted to reach Italian groups, it did so through the Italian-language press. But the quality of the Italian-American press was often low. "The majority of Italo-American editors," Luigi Villari wrote critically in 1912, "is composed of pseudo-intellectual failures, ex-barbers, ex-pharmacists, ex-bank clerks, ex-tailors, who take to the pen because they have failed at other trades." Despite their shortcomings, the various publications, whether the general cultural newspaper or the specialized magazine dealing with music and art, reflected at least some intellectual growth in the Italian immigrant.

So concerned were most immigrants with the steady pressure of earning their daily bread that at first they had little interest in, or time for, even the most meager of cultural pursuits. Contrary to his reputation for being hot-tempered and pleasure-loving, the average Italian was sober, frugal, and hard-working. He usually drank less alcohol and worked longer hours and harder than immigrants of other nationalities. When he drank, it was usually wine in the home, not hard liquor in the saloon. He was so eager to save that he frequently injured his health to do so. He skipped meals, worked in perilous, congested, and unsanitary plants, and exposed himself to all kinds of harsh weather to earn a little money. Employers used great numbers of Italians because they were readily available and in many kinds of work they produced good results. Even though the percentage of skilled workers among them was lower than among immigrants from Western Europe (but higher than those from Eastern Europe), the skilled Italians ranked high as stonecutters, mechanics, mariners, barbers, seamstresses, shoemakers, and as blue-collar workers in general.

Italian workers, like Greeks, Austrians, Syrians, Mexicans, and other new immigrants, made use of a form of bossism called the *pa-*

drone system. It really did not exist as a formal system, but rather as a unique pattern of adjustment to American conditions for Italian workers. A *padrone* could be all kinds of things, but was frequently a leader, a boss who recruited and too often exploited laborers. In the seventies, *padroni* had gone to Italy to recruit unskilled laborers on contract at a fixed wage, usually paying the fare of those they engaged. In the United States, *padroni* supplied *contadini* in gangs to employers at rates that gave them a solid profit. In this form, as in the earlier form that exploited children, the *padrone* system flourished only in the formative stage of Italian immigration, or until the eighties. In 1885, the Contract Labor Act prohibited the importation of laborers under contract, and by this time the movement from southeastern Europe had reached such proportions that American contractors had no need to go abroad to import laborers. So the padrone shifted from being a recruiter to acting as a special kind of employment agent. Newly arrived Italians, ignorant of American conditions, were pleased to be able to place themselves in the hands of a *padrone,* often a leader from their own *paese* or someone who could speak their dialect as well as English. They could rely on him not only to find them jobs but also to provide them with food and lodging; in a land of strangers he provided an anchor, a sense of security. He would also take the pay of his labor squads and divide it among the workers, a simple but necessary function when employers and employees could not speak each other's language.

Few could deny that the *padrone* system had built-in evils, but it was not, as critics maintained, a "system of practical slavery." The *padrone*'s contracts with employers often gave him too much of the workers' money. *Padroni* sometimes lied in describing jobs, and the workers who were deceived had no redress. Fearful of men of authority and of losing even poor jobs, most Italian laborers seldom thought of trying to bring the *padroni* to justice. In one instance when some Italians were told that their *padrone* was cheating them, they merely shrugged. "Signorino," they replied, "we are ignorant and do not know English. Our boss brought us here, knows where to find work, makes contracts with the companies. What should we do without him?" At another time an Italian spokesman explained, "The *padrone* can get plenty more workers, and these fellows far from home or friends don't know where to look for other work."

Aware of the evils in the system, the Italian government created independent agencies that would arrange jobs for Italian workmen in the United States. To keep petty bankers, who had been or were still *padroni,* from exploiting immigrants, it established an agency of the Bank of Naples in New York City; through it, those who wished to send money home to Italy could do so safely. In its efforts to curb the exploiters, the Italian government received little support from the *prominenti* ("leaders"), in the Italian communities, many of whom were, or had been, *padroni.*

In 1897, according to one estimate, *padroni* controlled about two-thirds of the Italian labor in New York. At the time, Italians made up about three-fourths of the building force in the city and within three years comprised almost all the workers used in building the subways. As elsewhere, they largely succeeded the Irish in the rough labor required to build and maintain subways, railroads, and other construction projects. In time, as immigrants became better acquainted with American conditions and learned how they could make their own way, they dispensed with the services of the *padroni.* As the Italian communities developed a new class of tradesmen of various kinds, and professional men, these men took over some of the functions formerly performed by the *padroni,* and the institution faded away. As Humbert S. Nelli has pointed out, the institution was a temporary one, having its heyday in the nineties. Few could deny its evils, but by bringing together Italian labor and American capital, it performed a useful function in the nation's economy. Italian immigrants improved themselves by slowly expanding their economic activities.

In these years they established themselves in a number of industrial and business enterprises. In New York City, they were particularly active in the manufacture of men's and women's clothing. Until about 1890, Jews had dominated that industry; but at that time, Italians invaded the garment district, and within a few years, they were second only to the Jews in the numbers employed there. Despite their peasant background and educational limitations, Italian immigrants showed an impressive business ability. Even though they had to start on shoestrings, often as pushcart peddlers, they owned thousands of stores, restaurants, wholesale food concerns, small contracting businesses, trucking and moving companies, brickmaking firms, and the like. The business spirit, according to some sociologists, appeared stronger among Italians than among other immigrants such as the Irish.

Italians found success mostly in small businesses. Rarely did immigrants, or their sons, claw their way to the top in the world of big business. One of them who did, Amadeo Obici, made it the hard way, living the old rags-to-riches myth, something the maudlin used to praise as being uniquely American. He came to the United States at twelve, went into business for himself at seventeen with a fruit stand, specialized in the sale of roasted peanuts, and in 1906 incorporated the Planter Peanut Company, becoming known as America's "peanut king."

In California, where economic opportunities for Italians were greater than in the ghettos of the East, Amadeo Peter Giannini, born in San Jose of immigrant parents from Genoa, fought his way into the highest circles of the tight world of finance with new and unorthodox tactics. He got his start by catering to the needs of Italian immigrants who distrusted American banks or who could not obtain services or loans from them. In his Bank of Italy, which opened in North Beach, San Francisco's Italian quarter, in October 1904, he brought branch banking to Italians in California, gave them Italian-speaking tellers, and performed services such as helping with naturalization papers free of charge, a service that *padroni* had been giving for a fee. Unlike other bankers in the various Little Italies, Giannini did not restrict his patronage to *paesani*; he sought out all Italians, regardless of their provincial ties, and tried to make them feel a sense of pride in the growth of an Italian bank. From him and his bank they gained a feeling of group identity that went well beyond the village or neighborhood.

In these business ventures, whether big or small, many Italians enjoyed a feeling of independence that they had not known in Italy. Under the depressing social and economic conditions of the *Mezzogiorno*, the *contadino* seldom if ever had a chance to assert himself. Having been brought up in a tradition of subserviency, he usually had not dared to question those of higher station for fear of losing his means of subsistence. In the United States, even simple peasants learned that if they worked faithfully and behaved themselves, they need fear no man. This idea, even if the reality often eluded them, appealed to their manhood. So despite slum living and discrimination, immigrants often found American life an improvement over the existence they had known in Italy.

Italians most often discovered the better life in America's cities rather than on her farms. Although Italian farmers could be found throughout the country, with a considerable number of them on the West Coast, the immigrants who became independent farmers were few, especially in relation to their numbers. Only scattered groups of Italians settled in the farm states of the Middle West and South. The

immigrants at flood tide made their homes mostly in the cities of the
Middle Atlantic states and New England, with large groups in Illinois
(mainly around Chicago) and in California. The census of 1910
classed about 80 per cent of all Italians as urban, a percentage of city
dwellers about twice that of the population as a whole. Only in New
Orleans did Italians exceed all other foreigners. In no other large city,
except New York, did they rank either first or second among immigrant groups.

Critics deplored the urban concentration of Italians, one of them
saying in 1906, for example, that "the demand for laborers is great
outside of the cities, but the gregarious Italian prefers to increase our
menacing urban congestion." Yet at the end of the decade, students
of population distribution could find no statistical "evidence of a
tendency to city life distinguishing the Italians either from the native
population or from other classes of the foreign-born." Italian immigrants, in other words, showed no greater fondness for urban life than
any one else did. When the Italians started arriving in the United
States in great numbers, the nation's cities were exploding, not just
growing. Everywhere native Americans were deserting farms for jobs
and bright lights in the cities. These same attractions, not love for the
crowded tenement, lured the Italians to the cities.

Italians also had other reasons for packing themselves into cities
and avoiding farms. Most important of all, they, and anyone else who
took the trouble to investigate, knew they needed capital to buy land
and farm equipment; they usually had none. In Italy, moreover, most
of them had been *giornalieri* who had worked as farm laborers, or
contadini who had owned tiny strips of land that they themselves had
tilled merely to eke out a living. They had not been true landowners
or farmers in the American sense. In the United States, these former
farm laborers could earn more money as industrial or railroad workers than as farm hands. Even if the Italian worked first as a laborer,
with the intention of saving money to buy land, his chances of succeeding as a farmer were poor. He came too late; the free, or cheap
farmland was gone. By 1890, the frontier had practically disappeared. Land became expensive; capital was scarce; and competition among farmers, tough. Under the circumstances, even though
most of them preferred rural communities, Italians acted logically in
shunning the farms. Moreover, their difficulty in the use of English
and their old-country ways handicapped them more on the farm than
in the factory.

Italians did not appear to take easily to the single-family isolated farm, where loneliness was the rule, as found in the United States. They often became truck or vegetable farmers because, observers said, in this form of agriculture they could as a rule have neighbors. When they did turn to the soil, they took up truck farming in New York and New Jersey, vine-growing in California, and cotton growing and fruit-growing in Louisiana and Texas. These farmers, often skillful and successful, were usually northern Italians who had enough money to buy land.

Success in agriculture came most readily to Italians in California. They flocked to that state in the eighties, when they could get steerage accommodations from eastern ports for only $40. Within a few decades, Italians came to comprise the second-largest foreign group in the state, second only to the Mexicans. At the beginning of the twentieth century, when Italians elsewhere were hustling for jobs in industry, about half or more of those in California worked in agriculture. California's clear blue skies, olive trees, cliffs jutting into the sea, stark mountains, lush valleys, climate, and soil, all were reminiscent of Italy and led many to call the state the "Italy of America." All this not only attracted Italians, but also kept them in California, where many owned fruit orchards, dairies, and vineyards, as well as truck farms. One of California's early Italian agricultural successes got its start in 1881 when Andrea Sbarbaro, a banker of Genoese origin interested in cooperatives for rootless *contadini,* took the lead in founding the Italian-Swiss Agricultural Colony at Asti, named after an ancient town in Piedmont where the wine had long been a source of local pride. He concerned himself first with settling immigrants on the land and secondly with growing grapes and making wine. After a few lean years, these vineyards prospered, as did others planted by Italians in California.

Elsewhere, despite the obstacles to farm ownership, critics and friends alike came up with various schemes to distribute Italians more widely in rural areas. If more Italians could be put on farms, these people maintained, then they could avoid such evils as slum living. "The philanthropists, Italian or American, who will direct the Italian to his proper place in the rural districts," one critic wrote, "will do a grand job for the Italian immigrant, for the states to which he will contribute his skill and labor, and for humanity in general." Some people, including such diverse individuals as Jane Addams, the social worker of Hull House in Chicago, and Gustavo Tosti, Italian consul general in New York City, urged the formation of Italian agricultural colonies. State governments sometimes encouraged these schemes. As late as 1910, a Board of Immigration in Colorado worked to entice Italian farmers to the state. Some southern states even offered passage money to *contadini* who would come to work on their cotton plantations. Many critics wished merely to transport Italian laborers from the cities to the areas of the South where landowners wanted white labor. Tosti, however, wanted his countrymen to go to the South not as farm hands but as farmers with landholdings of their own.

A few small groups of Italians did set up a number of isolated agricultural settlements in the South. All suffered hardships. A colony established by Waldensians at Valdese, North Carolina, in 1893, managed to survive not through general farming as planned but by turning to industrial activity as well as the growing of grapes. A few years after the beginning of the Valdese experiment, a plan to settle Italians from congested cities on land along the lower Mississippi River in Sunnyside, Arkansas, where they competed directly with Negroes in the growing of cotton, failed. Out of the Sunnyside venture came another plan, led by Pietro Bandini, a priest from Italy, for an agricultural colony farther north at Tontitown, Arkansas, named after an explorer of the Old West, Enrico Tonti, the first Italian to set foot in Arkansas. In order to survive, the Italian farmers had to overcome cyclones and droughts and fight off raids by nativists. Young farmers and others from nearby towns baited the "Dagoes," tried to destroy their schoolhouse, and burned two of their churches. But most difficulties stemmed from insufficient capital. Nonetheless, by the end of the twentieth century's first decade, Italians had tried agriculture in the South in at least thirty-five settlements.

In general, though, immigrants avoided the South, mainly because of low wages, the plantation-tenant system, and the religious and ethnic bigotry common there. Stories of lynchings and nativist hostility became known in Italy and in Italian communities of the North, deterring prospective settlers from going to southern states. In a Mississippi town in 1904, for example, the people wrecked an Italian restaurant because the proprietor had served a meal to a Negro. The restaurateur appealed to the governor for help, but he refused to act, even when the white supremacists ran the Italian out of town. At the same time, Negroes feared the Italians, mainly as competitors for jobs. Ironically, Booker T. Washington warned that immigrants from southern Europe might create "a racial problem in the South more difficult and more dangerous than that which is caused by the presence of the Negro."

The southern experience was unusual only because it was extreme;

almost everywhere, Italians found themselves culturally isolated. Even in their teeming Little Italies, many, especially the unmarried males, were overcome by dreadful loneliness. The long separation of the sexes produced an unwholesome situation, but the Italians were probably no worse off than other immigrants, many of whom had also come as single men. Loneliness did not seem to spur assimilation; Italians and old-stock Americans, or descendants of earlier immigrants, seldom intermarried. Since Italian women were relatively scarce, the male was the one who usually married outside his ethnic group.

Outsiders considered Italian women passive. Surface mannerisms deceived them; the women always played an important role in immigrant life. When men could not get jobs or earned wages too low to maintain the family, the wives worked. Some took jobs even when they had an adequate family income; they wanted to acquire money, just as native Americans did. So eager were Italian women to earn that at the turn of the century, they gained the reputation of working for the lowest wages paid to any women in the United States. Few "birds of passage" could be found among them; once settled with husband and family, they usually had no intention of returning to Italy. The women were the churchgoers; and far more than the men, they kept alive the traditional Italian adherence to the Catholic faith. This clinging to the church had deep significance, for one of the striking changes in the Italian experience in the United States occurred in religion.

Contadini, particularly from southern Italy, were as ignorant in religion as in other matters. They found the Catholic churches in the United States different from anything they had known in the old country. "The fact is," an Irish Catholic observed, "the Catholic Church in America is to the mass of the Italians almost like a new religion." Italians considered the American Catholic church uncongenial mainly because the Irish dominated it and infused it with a fierce, even harsh, militancy. These qualities repelled Italians. Other Catholic immigrants—Poles, Germans, and French-Canadians—also resented the Irish control of the church. Immigrants could not speak intimately with Irish priests as they did with their own priests in Italy. At first they had little choice; they had to use the Irish priests or dispense with religion. Some chose to abandon Catholicism, but most remained loyal, or nominally so, but in their own way. The religious dilemma of the Italians was aggravated by the fact that they were the first Catholic people to come to the United States in large numbers without bringing their own religious leaders with them.

Even though Franciscans and Servites, or Servants of Mary, had been ministering to Italians in the United States since the Civil War, they did not have to deal with large numbers of unlettered *contadini*. The Franciscans opened the first Catholic church dedicated to the service of Italians in New York City, but not until 1867. Other churches of that kind followed, but slowly. In the eighties, as Italian immigration reached flood stage, American Catholic leaders became concerned about the shortage of churches for the newcomers. The hierarchy spent a lot of time discussing the "Italian problem" within the church, mainly that it had few Italian priests, and these were often of poor quality, that Italians did not observe the sacraments, and that too many were seemingly leaving the church. In 1883, in a conference in Rome, American archbishops suggested that Italian priests be sent to the United States to minister to their countrymen. Five years later, in November, 1887, the Catholic hierarchy established an Apostolic College of Priests in Piacenza to prepare priests to take over Italian parishes in America. Pope Leo XIII hoped that the children of Italian immigrants who wished to become priests would attend the college. In the following year, with the arrival of Scalabrinian Fathers, immigrants finally got priests of their own from Italy who came with the sole purpose of taking care of their spiritual needs. In 1897, the first Salesian priests arrived in San Francisco from Italy, and in the next year in New York City, also to minister to the local Italians.

In these years, several orders of Italian nuns also settled in the United States. Most widely known was the Congregation of the Missionary Sisters of the Sacred Heart, founded by Frances Xavier Cabrini. Born in Italy, Sister Cabrini always emphasized the Italian origin and spirit of her work. She founded schools, hospitals, and homes for poor Italians and their children in the United States and in Latin America. The first American citizen elevated to sainthood, she became known as the saint of the immigrants. In time, teaching orders, such as Jesuits, Franciscans, and Ursulines, provided teachers who spoke both English and Italian for parochial schools in Italian neighborhoods.

American Catholic leaders used these priests and nuns to stem the drift to atheism or Protestantism. Beginning in the nineties, when several denominations established mission churches in Italian neighborhoods of eastern cities, Protestantism made headway among immigrants. Men with social concerns, such as Norman Thomas, the Socialist leader, served as pastors of these missionary churches. During the first decade of the twentieth century, almost 300 Protestant missionaries were working full-time in Italian communities. By 1916, more than 50,000 Italians had joined American Protestant churches.

As soon as finances permitted, those Italians who took their Catholicism seriously, also helped in stopping the flow of their countrymen to Protestantism. These laymen set up their own parishes and built churches like those in Italy. Although such efforts to make immigrants feel comfortable in American Catholicism brought Italian control of a number of neighborhood churches, they made no dent in the Irish dominance of the hierarchy. Moreover, most of the churches in Italian neighborhoods remained under Irish priests, carryovers from the time when these neighborhoods had been Irish. As in Boston's North End and Milwaukee's Third Ward, Italians moved into neighborhoods that the Irish had vacated; in many instances they had to fight the Irish parish by parish to take over the churches in their own neighborhoods. This religious rivalry paralleled that in the streets, where Italian and Irish boys frequently battled.

Conflict did not always mar the relationship; more often than not the Irish helped Italian newcomers. Knowing English well and having arrived earlier, the Irish built a powerful church hierarchy; Italians used this institution to make a place for themselves in American life. In 1891, an Irish archbishop, Michael A. Corrigan, organized the Society of St. Raphael to aid Italian immigrants. Under the care of nuns, it set up a home in New York City for the temporary shelter of women and children, and its chaplain and agents met immigrants at Ellis Island, offering the men friendly advice, meals, and lodging. Assistance of this kind, laying the basis for cooperation between an older and a newer ethnic group, continued into the twentieth century. In politics, too, the Italian found himself dependent on Irish leadership, mainly on the network of Irish political machines in the cities. Since Italians arrived later and were slower than members of other ethnic groups, such as the Jews, to become naturalized Americans, they lagged in political activity, and needed Irish help. Many Italians seem to have preferred the Republican party, but like other ghetto immigrants, most of them became Democrats. By 1892, Chicago had an Italian alderman, and two years later Italians were sitting in the Illinois legislature. New York elected its first Italian to public office in 1897.

Some Italians, as they gained a measure of economic stability, also made time for leisure and for cultural activities, as well as for politics. Before the arrival of the new immigrants, Italian opera had gained a respectable place in American cultural life. But now, in the eighties, and later, it gave Italy a cultural link with her emigrants in the United States as well as with other Americans. Italian opera took a great stride forward in October, 1883, when the Metropolitan Opera House opened in New York City. Much of the acclaim it and other opera companies won could be attributed to a stream of Italian performers trained abroad who sang with them each season. American opera houses had to rely on Italians and other foreigners because they had no permanent companies of their own.

Most Italians contributed no more to the refined cultural life of their adopted land than they had to that of their old country, which was little. They were usually so backward that they could not even appreciate what meager culture the big cities offered the poor. As Jane Addams has pointed out, in Chicago they rarely knew of the existence of public art galleries. They made their most immediate contribution to American life with backbreaking labor, something too often unappreciated in both the United States and Italy. Few also appreciated, or even understood, the bond they and their children were forming between the two countries.

Since many immigrants returned to Italy for visits and for other reasons, they formed part of a two-way stream between Italy and the United States. In general, according to investigations sponsored by the Italian government, those Italians who returned, usually called *Americani*, were better off financially than when they had left or than their old neighbors who had stayed at home. If taken at face value, this conclusion suggests greater benefits for Italy from emigration than often she actually received. Those who returned represented the most successful of immigrants and therefore were usually part of a select group. Others were less fortunate. Every year charitable organizations repatriated thousands of Italians who, for various reasons such as ruined health or maiming from industrial accidents, could not adjust to life in America's cities. South Italians seemed more prone to have pneumonia than native Americans. The impact of these unfortunate repatriates on Italy (where often they lived on charity) and on American relations with Italy was bad. Sometimes crime in Italy increased because the returned emigrant had acquired new habits, such as the use of the revolver. Those who returned sometimes brought diseases, such as tuberculosis and syphilis, to regions that previously

had been free of them. Few, moreover, realized the suffering of thousands of Italians in the United States who just managed to escape becoming wards of charity.

Few also understood the mentality of the immigrant who returned
to Italy on his own, for opinions on him varied widely. "It must be
confessed," one Italian observer wrote, "that the great majority of
emigrants depart illiterate and return so, and at home have no influence on the spirit of the country, the course of public opinion, and
so forth." Other observers took a different view, saying that even the
"birds of passage" had a beneficial influence on Italian life. Some of
them brought home advanced social ideas, such as an appreciation of
education for their children and a revulsion against violence and
crime, as well as the money they had earned. At times, it was said,
these returned workers led demands for better working conditions
and higher wage scales. By improving their own way of living, in their
homes and elsewhere, they also set examples for other *contadini* to
follow. Such examples were usually fewer in Italy's south than in the
north. Southern Italians customarily returned home in smaller numbers than those from the north did, mainly because the south Italian,
being poorer than the northerner, could seldom bring together enough
money to make his way back to his native village. For the southerner,
emigration usually amounted to a renunciation of Italy.

Some Italians recalled with bitterness the low esteem in which they
had been held in the United States. They could not shed this harsh
feeling when they returned to Italy to friends and relatives. They
spoke of America as "half a dreamland of easy wealth, half a place of
bitter disappointment."

When the immigrant who had become a naturalized American
visited Italy, the people there refused to accept him as an Italian; to
them he had become an *Americano*. Some of these returned Italians,
strutting about with pockets full of dollars, aroused hostility by giving
an impression of cockiness or arrogance that contrasted sharply with
their former servility. Monotonously, they seemed to talk only about
the money they had made. More often than not, the peasants admired
or looked in awe upon the returned emigrant. His money, his white
shirt, his coat, his cigar, his new house all advertised his success and
the prosperity in America. He aroused envy and the desire in others
to leave Italy and risk their future in the land that could supply such
plenty. "They come back arrayed like *signori*," was a comment common among the *contadini* who had stayed behind.

Angelo M. Pellegrini, a professor of English at the University of

Washington who had emigrated as a small boy, recalled the attitude of an *Americano* who returned to his native Tuscany with enough money to realize every peasant's dream—his own home and a bit of land. In 1911, this *Americano* told Pellegrini's father impressive stories about life in the United States and urged him to emigrate. "In three years," the neighbor said, "you can save enough money to do what I have done. Steerage passage across the Atlantic costs very little. When you arrive in New York the employment agents of the railroad companies will take you to the job at their own expense. If you need money for the steamship ticket I will be glad to lend it to you." The *Americano* lent the money, and in 1912 the elder Pellegrini packed up and emigrated. He had, like thousands of others, embarked on a desperate venture. He knew no one in the United States and had no assurance of a job, yet on the basis of what appeared to be the dazzling affluence of an *Americano* neighbor, he left a wife and five children (all of whom he later brought over) to seek a better life than he had known.

Francesco Nitti, the statesman and economist, was one of many who saw advantages for Italy in emigration, calling it a distribution of scholarships. Emigration may have been that in the sense that the gains in knowledge which the emigrants brought back were real but, like education, could not easily be measured. Emigrants sometimes returned with new skills in business, industry, or agriculture, and even with new social attitudes and a quickened interest in politics. If many returned as ignorant and unquestioning as they had been before they left, others were no longer so. The experience in a new culture often awakened a spirit that had been dormant, not dead. This spirit showed itself in one of the distinguishing characteristics of the Italian immigrant—his adaptability. Wherever these peasants went, to North or South America, or elsewhere, they made the best of their new situation, no matter how onerous, and adjusted fairly rapidly. They reconciled themselves to the customs of their country of settlement and worked for its welfare as well as for their own. They did not fester as a disaffected minority. This adaptability amounted to a considerable achievement in a country such as the United States, where Italians met persistent discrimination and the problems of adjustment were enormous.

Discrimination

6

The flood of southern Italians coincided with the rise of a reborn nativism in the United States. Their coming intensified this nativism, leading to demands by old-stock Americans for some kind of federal control over immigration. In response to a recommendation by President Chester A. Arthur in 1882, Congress passed the first general federal immigration law, one that placed a head tax on arriving aliens and that excluded convicts, lunatics, idiots, and those likely to become public charges. Three years later, acting on the theory that employers signed up foreign workers, such as Italians, at low wages and brought them to the United States to replace more highly paid American workers, Congress passed a law prohibiting the importation of contract labor. In May of the following year, the Haymarket Massacre, a bombing of police in Chicago attributed to foreign radicals, gave new strength to nativism and antiforeignism. Their prejudices aroused by fear, many Americans now took quite seriously the idea of tightly restricting immigration, particularly from places such as southern Italy. Ironically, at this time, October, 1886, Americans unveiled the Statue of Liberty, with its dedication to the United States as a refuge for Europe's "huddled masses."

Within a year of the dedication, there came into existence in Clinton, Iowa, the most vicious and powerful of the nativist organizations, the American Protective Association. Antiforeign and anti-Catholic, it stressed the alleged dangers of immigration to American institutions, urged selective immigration, and demanded drastic restrictions against newcomers such as Italians. These nativists wanted to deny employment to unnaturalized foreigners and to force them to use the "American language." Particularly strong in the "Bible belt" of the Middle West, where hatred of the Catholic church was widespread, the association also gained members from the working classes in other parts of the country. Those engaged in the struggles of organized labor against industry in the late eighties nursed bitter feelings toward what they considered unfair competition from Italian laborers and other immigrants from southeastern Europe. These emotions, when combined with hard times, political turmoil, and social unrest, led many workers and others into the ranks of the association.

Responding to the concerns of the nativists, Congress began investigating immigration. In 1891, it passed an act that barred polygamists and those with dangerous diseases from entering the country. This law also forbade employers to advertise for workers in foreign countries, prohibited transportation companies from encouraging immigration, provided for medical inspection of immigrants, and placed enforcement in the hands of federal officials. Federal control of immigration had now become a reality. In the following year, Congress voted the Quarantine Act giving the President authority to stop all immigration in case of an epidemic. These laws represented small victories for the nativists, who now expanded their goals. As they did so, the restrictionist movement mushroomed, accompanied by a growth in the ideology of race. By the end of 1893, the membership of the American Protective Association reached a peak; and in the following year in Boston, a new restrictionist organization, the Immigration Restriction League, came into existence.

Intellectual nativists of old New England stock founded the Restriction League to arouse people against the alleged dangers from immigration. Gaining influence rapidly in other parts of the country as well as in New England, the league espoused Anglo-Saxon racism as a credo and advocated a literacy test, an idea concocted by a bigoted New England economist, Edward W. Bemis, as a means of barring newcomers such as the Italians. The antiforeign feelings of the New England restrictionists could be seen in their whole program, but it was especially clear in their attitudes toward Italian immigrants. Since the seventies, there had been a small settlement of Italians in Boston. The warmth intellectuals had felt for the Italy of their travels had given their view of these early immigrants a pleasant coloring. Later, by the middle nineties, the Italian immigrant evoked the worst reaction of the Yankees. In their thinking, they now separated the Italian from the glamor of ancient and Renaissance Italy; he, especially the southern Italian, became the type of immigrant they particularly wanted to bar.

Earlier, William Dean Howells had distinguished between northern and southern Italians. The northerner, he said, had an appealing "lightness of temper"; whereas the southerner came from "half-civilized stock," though that stock produced "real artists and men of genius." Other Americans agreed, maintaining that the northerners were more intelligent and less susceptible to crime than were the southerners, particularly the Sicilians. Even northern Italians already in the United States, such as Luigi Palma di Cesnola, disliked the new immigrants. Cesnola, who had married into an aristocratic American family, accepted the argument that the newcomers threatened democratic institutions.

In 1891, Henry Cabot Lodge, a Republican senator from Massachusetts and a restrictionist, discussed the different classes of Italians. He, like others, directed his harshest criticism against southerners, arguing that northerners had Germanic blood and belonged to "a people of Western civilization." These "Teutonic" Italians, with their higher standard of living and capacity for skilled work, he felt, should not be confused with their undesirable relatives from the south. Three years later, he sponsored a bill calling for a literacy test that would exclude southern Italians and similar immigrants by keeping out aliens over sixteen who could neither read nor write. "The illiteracy test," he said in explaining Bemis's idea, "will bear most heavily upon the Italians, Russians, Poles, Hungarians, Greeks, and Asiatics, and very lightly, or not at all, upon English-speaking emigrants or Germans, Scandinavians, and French." Using the language from Thomas Bailey Aldrich's nativist poem "The Unguarded Gates," the senator insisted that the gates of "the great Republic should no longer be left unguarded."

Lodge appeared to be in tune with public sentiment. In 1896, at a time when an influx of Italians that nearly overwhelmed Ellis Island gave new impetus to the restrictionist movement, a federal official asked the state governments what immigrant groups they preferred to have. Only two states were interested in Italians. These feelings and the organized agitation of the restrictionists proved to have considerable political appeal. In 1897, Congress passed its first Literacy Test Act. Seeing clearly the discriminatory intent in the bill, President Grover Cleveland vetoed it. He denied that the new immigrants were "undesirable," saying that "the time is quite within recent memory when the same thing was said of immigrants who, with their descendants . . . now numbered among our best citizens."

Although Cleveland's veto blocked the literacy test, his words, no matter how true, had no effect on the restrictionists. The nativists stepped up their agitation and with it their propaganda that justified, at least in their view, the discrimination against the newcomers from southern and eastern Europe. Americans simply had to distinguish, the restrictionists argued, between desirable and undesirable immigrants. Restrictionists sometimes filled the newspapers with vile denunciations, saying for example, that "the sewer is unchoked. Europe is vomiting. She is pouring her scum on the American shore." Time and again, they held up the Italian as an example of the "undesirable." Critics considered Italians undesirable for many reasons, pointing out especially that they were not "pioneers" and therefore lacked the stamina, vigor, and other virtues of those who opened the country to settlement. Since the Italians came late and found a closed frontier, even if they had wanted to they could not benefit from the mystically cleansing experience of Americanization on the Western frontier.

Even qualities such as strength, overflowing energy, endurance in hard labor, obedience to the orders of a boss or employer, sobriety, and a willingness to work at menial tasks for low wages rather than accept charity—which in others might have been considered pioneer virtues of self-reliance—were in Italians derided. People often scorned them because they seemed not as clean-shaven or as well-kept as American workers. Many nativists condemned Italians as the most contemptible of the newcomers, calling them "the Chinese of Europe." Woodrow Wilson, in his five-volume *History of the American People,* published in 1902, gave this view the status of a scholar's judgment. These immigrants, he wrote, came from the "lowest class from the south of Italy." They had neither skill, nor energy, nor initiative, nor quick intelligence. "The Chinese were more to be desired."

Bigots, of course, saw the southern Italian in terms of an ethnic stereotype, but so did many other Americans. For example, Jack London, the novelist, picked up his antagonism from his mother. "I had heard her state," he wrote, "that if one offended an Italian, no matter how slightly and unintentionally, he was certain to retaliate by stabbing one in the back. That was her particular phrase—'stab you in the back.' " Nativists, and just ordinary people, pictured the Italian as ignorant, priest-ridden, dishonest, hot-blooded, and vengeful, a bias firmly embedded in popular literature. About all that many Americans heard concerning Italians on their shore were stories of crime, violence, and strange customs practiced in ethnic ghettos. To them the word "Italian" quickly brought to mind "the stiletto, the Mafia, the deed of impassioned violence." When an unlettered *contadino* resorted to the knife, newspapers noted his nationality and called the violence an "Italian vendetta."

This ethnic stereotype, which served as an excuse for discrimination against all Italians, stemmed less from fact than from an emotional reaction to the strange and unknown. Yet the image also developed out of some truth. Southern Italy at the beginning of the twentieth century had the highest rate of homicides in Europe, a condition growing out of a primitive code of personal vengeance, a code that Sicilians and others brought to America. From the beginning, Americans despaired over the violence of the southern Italians. "It is perhaps hopeless to think of civilizing them, or of keeping them in order," the *New York Times* had commented in November, 1875, "except by the arm of the law."

Most Americans knew little about the Italian immigrants or how they lived. To many, these newcomers huddled in their depressing ghettos were part of another culture, strange, distant, and virtually invisible. To restrictionists, these Italians were the "beaten men from beaten races, the worst failures in the struggle for existence." In common with Jews, Poles, Mexicans, and others, Italians were pilloried by insulting nicknames—such as wop, Dago, and guinea—abused in public, isolated socially, cheated of their wages, pelted in the streets, cuffed at work, fined and jailed on the smallest pretenses, lynched by nativist mobs, and crowded into slums and reeking tenements.

Racists condemned Italians and others from southeastern Europe because they were allegedly kindred to the "brownish" races and would mean as much trouble to white, Anglo-Saxon, Protestant America as the Negro. Critics sometimes lumped Italians and blacks together in their alleged propensity for crime. As one prosecutor put it, "the Dagoes are just as bad as the Negroes." Some Americans, particularly in the South, denied southern Italians their whiteness and, in one Louisiana locality, even barred them from white schools. Because Italians frequently did the same kind of work as blacks, nativists tended to treat them as they did Negroes. So some Italian officials advised their countrymen to avoid the American South.

Northerners showed a similar bigotry. In 1890, a member of a Congressional committee in the course of questioning a West Coast railroad construction boss exclaimed, "You don't call . . . an Italian a white man?" The boss reacted as though surprised that a member of Congress should ask such a silly question. "No, Sir," the construction man replied, "an Italian is a Dago."

Even intellectuals, such as Henry James, who liked the people in Italy, reacted unfavorably, in terms of the stereotype, to the immigrant when they saw him in the United States. The Italian appeared to them to symbolize all the recent immigrants who spoke no English and contaminated New England's landscape. Once the Italian peasant shed his old-world "manners" and came to the United States, according to one New Englander, he lost "that element of agreeable address . . . which has, from far back, so enhanced for the stranger the interest and pleasure of a visit" to Italy. The Yankee intellectuals who took an aristocratic delight in the Italian in Italy often looked down on the Italian in America as a ditchdigger, a man without charm or other attractions. Like all other newcomers from southeastern Europe, he appeared "crude" and "gross." As Madison Grant, Yale graduate, lawyer, and restrictionist, warned in his racial diatribe, *The Passing of the Great Race,* the old colonial stock had to protect itself against the Italians, Slovaks, Jews, and others. In their gross way, the newcomers could outbreed the Yankee stock.

For some New Englanders, the old affection for the Italy of art, monuments, and music was strong enough to survive the animus against the immigrant. In 1901, a number of them even got together to organize and support in New York the Society for the Protection of Italian Immigrants, with Eliot Norton, the son of Charles Eliot Norton, as its first president. But even these friends of the immigrants regretted that the Italian in the United States had become "the unthinking wielder of pick and shovel." Another New Englander, Charles W. Eliot, a descendant of Puritans and a president of Harvard College, became a friend of the immigrants and a foe of the restrictionists. Early in 1907, he stated his position to Ernesto G. Fabri, the president of the Society for Italian Immigration, saying that "the more Italian immigrants that come to the United States the better . . . the only way I can help you is to state these opinions wherever and whenever I can appropriately do so. That help I propose to give steadily."

As others, such as social workers, came to know the immigrant, they, too, spoke well of him. They pointed out that when he was given opportunities equal to those provided others, the Italian showed himself worthy of respect. He proved himself one of the hardest-working men ever to land on the American shore. With industry and frugality, he bettered his condition as rapidly as did immigrants of his class in other ethnic groups. Being willing to work at almost any kind of labor, the Italian was seldom a public charge. Italians applied for and received less charity than did other immigrants. The Italian, like people of other immigrant groups, had faults and virtues. Neither the best nor the worst of those who came, he faced the problem of adjustment to a new society under especially difficult circumstances, but he was capable of making a place for himself in American life. What often upset the nativist were the attitudes of the children of immigrants. They refused to accept a subservient place in American society; they tried to compete with the sons of established families for jobs, education, and whatever else Americans considered important and desirable.

Sometimes when a sensitive Italian looked closely at the ghetto confining him and his children, he questioned his ability to survive in such an environment; sometimes he wondered why he had exchanged his earlier misery for his present one. Many immigrants walked into a "one-way street" of unhappiness. "The number of those who are unhappier than I is great," one buffeted Italian cried out in his diary, "and unluckily for many of them there is no hope for better days." Slum living, with its dirt, disease, and overcrowding, demoralized the Italian, made danger a constant companion, and spawned despair and crime.

The crime in the ghettos affected mostly Italians. According to various sociological studies, most immigrants were peaceful and law-abiding. In general, police records did not show the Italians as being outstanding in criminality. Yet reputable observers could report that in some Sicilian neighborhoods, for example in Chicago, violence and crime at times became so prevalent as to constitute a reign of terror. Understandably, such conditions made it easy for xenophobic Americans to condemn all Italians for the crimes of the few. In the first years of the twentieth century, all Italians, but particularly Sicilians, suffered from the stigma of criminality because of murders, robbery, extortion, and blackmail attributed to the Mafia, then often called the Black Hand Society and considered by some a special Americanized form of the Mafia. So widespread did crime seem among Italians that, in 1904, the detective bureau in New York City's police department organized a special Italian squad to combat it.

The idea of organized Italian criminality quickly aroused controversy. In 1908, an Italian writer, Gaetano D'Amato, argued, as did others, that the Black Hand Society in the United States was a myth. That myth became notorious, he said, because of sensational stories in the yellow press and the ignorance and recklessness of the police in recording arrests. While admitting that some criminals had slipped into the country and had victimized fellow Italians, he ridiculed the idea that every Italian was a Black Hand conspirator. Giuseppe Petrosino, a lieutenant on the New York Italian squad, agreed. He investigated and concluded that no central Black Hand organization existed, only thugs who terrorized gullible immigrants. Yet police often acted as though they could fight the amorphous Black Hand most effectively by arresting Italians on meager evidence. In Chicago, over a period of seven months in 1913, police charged forty-five murders to the Black Hand, even though they had no proof. In one neighborhood, following several outrages, they arrested fifty Italians at random. When brought to jail, the men were all fined one dollar and costs for disorderly conduct. The inspector who imposed the punishment assumed that the entire Italian community in Chicago was somehow implicated in the crimes and that the fines would frighten the Italians into good behavior. Actually, the arrest and conviction of men known to be innocent stimulated distrust rather than respect for law.

Unlike D'Amato and Petrosino, some other prominent Italians and leading newspapers who interested themselves in crime and police tactics concluded that a Black Hand organization existed but that its members committed few of the crimes charged to the society. Italian leaders in Chicago even organized a White Hand Society to eliminate Black Hand crime, an idea that spread to other cities. For a time, the Italian consulate in Chicago employed a man to investigate every crime the newspapers reported as coming from the Black Hand. Out of the first thirty cases investigated, only one could not be explained by some theory other than that a Black Hand criminal had a part in it. Concerned Italians in New York City felt that their own newspapers brought the Black Hand much of the power it enjoyed. These Italian journals often romanticized the young hoodlums involved in crime and violence. But newspapers in general played up Italian violence; it seemed to make good copy. "One thing is certain," a social critic observed, "the American press gives more space to the vices of Italians than to their virtues." Some Italians in New York therefore organized the Italian-American Civic League to counter the sensational journalism.

As a result of Italian crimes whether or not by a Black Hand, of police discrimination, and of newspaper sensationalism, the innocent as well as the guilty suffered. Italians had no real protection against the criminal within or outside their community. Yet the public, growing indignant over crime, blamed them, the main victims, for its existence.

Nothing seemed to arouse deeper emotions among Americans than stories of crime among Italian immigrants. Yet at times nativists seemed as fearful of the spread of Catholicism through the Italians as they did of criminality. When Italians persisted in clinging to their faith, critics called them clannish and denounced them as unwilling to become Americanized. This criticism implied that Catholicism, when taken with Italianism, stood almost as an insuperable obstacle to true Americanism. Yet even when Italians joined a Protestant church, as many did, they did not free themselves from prejudice.

All forms of discrimination hurt, but to the *contadini* the economic proved the most crippling. When hard times came, Italian laborers suffered more than did most others. They lost their jobs more quickly and remained unemployed longer than did their American neighbors. It was in such times of difficulty that those laborers who could manage, or could afford to do so, scampered back to Italy. But most stayed, enduring their lot mutely and learning from bitter experience the meaning of the maxim, "last hired, first fired."

Ironically, organized labor in these years of struggle for the interests of workingmen often showed more prejudice against Italian workers than did employers. Native American laborers were convinced that they had good reasons for being hostile toward the *contadini*. Italians, they believed, competed for their jobs and threatened their security by being willing to take low wages. This charge held some truth. Since the average Italian immigrant arrived with only a few dollars in his pocket, he had to find work quickly or starve. He could not bargain over wages; necessity forced him to take what he could get, and at once. Often employers would hire Italians only if they would accept bargain wages or when no one else was available. Italians had little choice; to work they had to take lower wages than would others. This attitude came out clearly in Harold Frederic's novel *The Damnation of Theron Ware* (1896). A tight-fisted employer had just gotten rid of his Irish workers because they wanted higher wages. "I've got Eyetalians in the quarries now," he explained. "They're sensible fellows: they know when they're well off; a dollar a day, an' they're satisfied, an' everything goes smooth."

Such displacements, of course, infuriated American workers. So, to avoid open hostility, the Italian would frequently enter trades where he would not compete directly with native workers or earlier immigrants. This timidity came from experience. Time and again, native workers, Irish and others, rioted, and gangs of them attacked Italians and drove the newcomers from their jobs. In New York City, the Bricklayer's Union even demanded the discharge of all unnaturalized Italians who labored in the building of subways. Some of this antagonism also derived from the feeling of union members that Italians too often acted as strikebreakers. Employers did use Italians as strikebreakers, as in the strike of the shirtwaist makers in New York City in 1909-1910, when Italian girls scabbed. But Italians usually did not deliberately act against fellow workers; they just needed a job and knew nothing about trade unionism.

At first only a small number of Italians joined unions. Many did not wish to risk the loss of wages in a strike or become involved in a union battle for long-term gains. Their conservative traditions and heritage of subservience, but most of all their exclusion from various unions by the Irish and nativists who dominated the unions kept Italians out of the labor movement. Yet, as the historian Edwin Fenton has shown, the old concept of Italians being anti-union is not accurate. In time and under favorable, non-discriminatory conditions, Italian workers proved themselves true unionists and excellent strikers.

Liberal sociologists and others have criticized the leaders of Italian communities, as in New York, for being conservative and not helping workers to join the labor movement. These *galantuomini,* the critics pointed out, lorded it over the sweating immigrant as the gentry had done over the peasant in southern Italy. Editors and owners of Italian newspapers, liberals argued, should have taken up the workers' cause; instead, like Carlo Barsotti, the former *padrone* of New York's *Il progresso Italo-Americano,* they opposed unions. These owners were businessmen, and they acted like employers everywhere. Businessmen all over the United States disliked unions, and Italians of this class behaved no differently than others. The infant International Ladies Garment Workers Union had to work hard to overcome this kind of opposition among Italian leaders. But after 1910, with the help of such liberals as Salvatore Ninfo, Fiorello H. La Guardia, and Luigi Antonini (who as editor of the magazine *L'operaia* urged Italian garment workers to organize), it developed powerful Italian locals in New York. So did the Amalgamated Clothing Workers of America. August Bellanca, an immigrant tailor from Sicily, was one of its founders in 1914. Italians also produced a few outstanding radical labor leaders, men such as Giuseppe Ettor and Arturo Giovannitti who led a 1912 textile strike in Lawrence, Massachusetts, for the International Workers of the World, and Carlo Tresca, who was for many years a leading anarchist editor. As in other American communities at the time, the influence of the radical labor leaders in the Italian settlements was small.

Just as labor leaders believed that Italians opposed unionization, others felt they resisted Americanization. In comparison with other immigrants, at least in the eyes of restrictionists, Italians seemed slow in becoming naturalized citizens. So preoccupied were they with earning a living that few had time to educate themselves, immerse themselves in American ways, and become citizens. Sensitive to the prejudices against them, most hesitated to intrude where they felt they might not be wanted. Having brought with them strong traditions of localism, Italians also acted logically in moving slowly toward a new and more intense national patriotism than they had ever before known. Nonetheless, even the conservative leaders of the Italian communities, sensitive to the hostility of the larger American society, as well as Italy's own Emigration Department, urged immigrants to become American citizens as soon as possible. Sympathetic observers noted that no immigrant people, once they broke their ties to their homeland, were more anxious to adopt American ways. Italians usually turned into enthusiastic Americans.

One of the severest handicaps Italians had in trying to make a place for themselves in American life was their widespread illiteracy. "If I could read," one peasant said in explanation of his difficulties, "I should have four eyes, but now I see naught." The Italian of the immigrant generation seldom overcame his crushing burden. Out of every ten illiterates, not more than two succeeded in making just moderate educational gains. This illiteracy, when coupled with a language barrier, made it particularly difficult for many Italians to compete, except on beggars' terms, in America's industrial society. Yet these, the poorest and most socially isolated of workers, were the ones most often condemned by the nativists, the ones least capable of defending themselves, the ones who suffered most from discrimination and exploitation. One of the amazing things about these immigrants is that despite the odds against them, they did compete; they survived, and with less bitterness than most other minority peoples.

Like other immigrants, Italians wanted their children to go to school and break loose from the illiteracy that chained them to a life of poverty. "Send our children to school," they would write to their wives left behind in Italy. To the more perceptive immigrants, education seemed an obvious means of moving upward in status. "Go to school. Even if it kills you," the immigrant father of Leonard Covello, the educator, used to tell him. With an education "you have a chance to live like a man and not like a beast of burden." Yet in order to get ahead, as others around them were doing, many immigrants wanted a quicker change from their stifling living conditions than education could provide. In pursuit of betterment, immigrants sometimes exploited their children.

As soon as some Italian boys and girls reached the legal working age, parents pulled them out of school to take whatever jobs were available. Truancy, abetted by parents, as social workers reported, was a problem in the schools in Italian neighborhoods of various cities. Children of immigrants also avoided school because of discrimination. Yet their general rate of school attendance was as good as or better than that of native-born children. In the schools, these children faced language difficulties, insults, ethnic slurs, and contempt, not only from students but also from teachers and administrators. Teachers too often made them feel inferior, ashamed of being Italian. "The school," one child wrote in New York, ". . . never suggested respect for my parents." Nor did it build respect for their cultural tradition, or for Italy. Yet the fundamental reason why some Italians used their children for immediate economic gain at the expense of education remained their overwhelming concern with the harsh struggle to earn a living, a battle made doubly difficult by the prejudice they encountered. To feed everyone in a family, immigrant parents frequently had little choice; they had to put their children to work.

On this basis, critics charged Italians with another undesirable quality, that of placing a low value on education. Often enough the charge was true, for the *contadini* from Italy's south had a tradition of viewing the school as an alien institution. In the United States, it appeared more alien than ever, and attendance frequently conflicted with family requirements. Yet census statistics suggested that Italians, like other immigrant peoples who suffered from similar criticism, usually desired an education for their children when obtainable within their means. According to figures from the federal census of 1910, in every region the percentage of children of foreign parents, or where one parent was of foreign birth, enrolled in schools closely approximated the percentage of children of native-born Americans who were enrolled.

Since the children of immigrants faced greater handicaps in acquiring an education than did those of native Americans, these statistics suggest a deep desire for education among the new immigrants. Italians often surrounded education with a kind of glamor because it brought a prestige they had never known. In addition, in statistics dealing with the literacy of adults, the offspring of immigrants uniformly outranked the others. They did so even in the populous Middle Atlantic and North Central states where Italians were many and the traditions of public education in the older population were strong.

Yet few of the Italian immigrants, even those who could afford to do so, sent their children to college. In general, they did not because the *contadini* who had made their way to the United States were motivated by a strong desire for material, not cultural, improvement. Like other self-made men, those who succeeded in accumulating material goods through heavy labor, self-denial, and thrift disdained education from books. This attitude, in shutting off Italian children from the refinements of higher education, denied them one of America's richer experiences. Italians showed no antagonism to higher learning. Indeed, like peasants everywhere, they respected education and the educated man. *Contadini* simply knew no other tradition of improvement than the material one; so even when they were able to give their sons and daughters the educational advantages they could not have, it never occurred to them to do so. For example, when Angelo M. Pellegrini told his father he wanted to go to the university, the father reacted as though stunned. "Tell me, my son," he asked, "are you insane?" Before this time, young Pellegrini had not at any time even heard the word "university" spoken in his home. In another instance in later years, an Italian-American truck driver commented bitterly, "I had only a grammar-school education. My parents made me get out and work. They wanted me to be a Wop with all the other Wops, I guess."

Yet in their attitude toward education and cultural improvement, Italian immigrants did not differ notably from millions of other Americans. At the turn of the century, business criteria dominated American culture; most businessmen attained prominence without much formal education. As the late historian Richard Hofstadter has shown, academic schooling was often said to be useless and anti-intellectualism pervaded American life. While the Italian was often anti-intellectual for reasons of his own, the worship of material success and the anti-intellectualism in the United States did not foster in him an appreciation for higher education.

Regardless of the causes and extent of anti-intellectualism among Italians, their children made up a powerful force in linking them to the culture of their new home. In most instances, merely the acquired ability to read and write in English gave the child of immigrant parents an instrument for getting along in American society that his parents did not have. Since the children became citizens by birth and could vote, the act of voting set apart the second generation from the immigrant generation. Often, especially when the immigrant did not become naturalized, this matter of citizenship and Americanization drove a wedge between parent and child.

Even when an Italian immigrant became a naturalized citizen, discrimination did not disappear; other Americans seldom accepted him as an equal. They even kept him out of decent housing by restrictive covenants. In Milwaukee, earlier German immigrants who had themselves suffered discrimination raised the old complaint that Italians gave a neighborhood a bad name and lowered property values. This discrimination was quite enough to assure the immigrant that, regardless of naturalization, he was still some kind of an Italian in outlook, traits, and even manner. But in many characteristics he had also become an American. Often he came to consider himself neither an Italian nor an American, but a denizen of a third world. Even when naturalized citizens, capable of reading and writing English, earned the right to vote, critics condemned them. The Italian-Americans, nativists argued, remained political illiterates who threatened the stability of democratic politics by voting as a bloc for their own kind. What the nativists overlooked were the examples of political behavior the Italian immigrants and their children saw all around them.

Why should the Italian-Americans be expected to vote for candidates on the basis of qualifications and political principle when they saw other Americans consistently vote on the same ethnic, religious, or other emotional basis that was in them allegedly an evil? Why, it could be asked, should any immigrant group be expected to adhere to a higher standard of political conduct than the nativists themselves? The answer was simple. In judging immigrants, such as the Italians, the nativists used a double standard of morality.

These harsh attitudes of the nativists impressed on the Italian that American society exacted much for what it gave. This society of the New World applied tests, imposed conventions, demanded compromises, and forced concessions to its practical ways. To meet these demands, the Italian, with his stubborn provincial attachments and his unique emotional traits, had to undergo deep psychological change. "To be happy in America," one of them observed, "one must have a certain mechanical ability, a practical and opportunist spirit, a nature that is sharp in business but in other things narrow and matter-of-fact, with a tendency to conventionalism and the literal following of approved standards, a great interest in whatever is American and a high disdain of all that is Latin or that glorifies the Latin life."

About as well as anyone, the rootless poet of two worlds, Emanuel Carnevali, captured the ambivalent feelings in a few words. In the United States, he wrote, everything—

> Is bigger, but less majestic. . . .
> Italy is a little family;
> America is an orphan
> Independent and arrogant,
> Crazy and sublime,
> Without tradition to guide her,
> Rushing headlong in a mad run which she calls progress.
> . . . .
> And hunger is the patrimony of the emigrant;
> Hunger, desolate and squalid—
> For the fatherland,
> For bread and for women, both dear.
> America, you gather the hungry people
> And give them new hungers for the old ones.

One aspect of Italian life that quickly came into conflict with American ways was the power of the father over his family. The children of immigrants who most easily fell in with the demands of American life found a serious gap between themselves and their fathers. In seeking the promise of American life that eluded their parents, the children of immigrants often created groups of their own, with something of their own values, code, and morality. Some did not use their new values to rise any higher than the social circles of their own Italian neighborhood. To many of these children, as to their parents, life in the United States brought unhappiness, deplorable poverty, and cultural degradation on some crowded street in the slum of a great city. Others, as they became adults, never could, or would, move out of their ghettos into safer districts of higher status, but few were content to remain at the economic levels of their fathers. Like their contemporaries from old American stock, the second-generation Italians wanted to get ahead.

In seeking advancement, the children became active outside the home, and outside the ethnic group. Then communication between them and their immigrant parents dwindled to little beyond the simplest verbalizations. The Italian parents and their children lived together, each generation puzzled by the other, but each often incapable of finding the means for the appreciation of the other. Fearful of the outside world, the immigrants clung together in their ethnic enclaves where they attempted to perpetuate the life they had known in their *paesi* in Italy. Americanized, developing interests and habits their parents did not understand, the children often wanted to break out of such cultural isolation. These children refused to learn Italian, or when they did, they later forgot it. The second generation became increasingly hostile or indifferent to all—occasionally even to the food—that parents held dear.

Too often the acquisition of American ways bred in the second generation a contempt for Italian origins that brought sadness to parents. Sometimes the children came to despise the ways of their fathers, to lose any love of Italy they might have had, and to abandon their pride in being Italian. This attitude stands out in the following dialect poem by T. A. Daly, though in this instance the father shows pride in the naïve, brutal Americanization of his son.

Da Younga 'Merican*

I mysal', I feela strange
    Een dees countra. I can no
Mak' mysal' agen an' change
    Eento 'Merican, an' so
I am w'at you calla me,
    Justa "dumb ole Dago man."
Alla same my boy ees be
    Smarta younga 'Merican.
Twalv' year ole! but alla same
    He ees learna soocha lot
He can read an' write hees name—
    Smarta keed? I tal you w'at!

He no talk Italian;
    He say: "Dat's for Dagoes speak,
I am younga 'Merican,
    Dago langwadge mak' me seeck."
Eef you gona tal heem, too,
    He ees "leetla Dago," my!
He ees gat so mad weeth you
    He gon' ponch you een da eye.
Mebbe so you gona mak'
    Fool weeth heem—an' mebbe not.
Queeck as flash he sass you back;
    Smarta keed? I tal you w'at!

* Thomas A. Daly, *Canzoni and Songs of Wedlock,* New York, 1906.

He ees moocha 'shame' for be
  Meexa weeth Italian;
He ees moocha 'shame' of me—
  I am dumb ole Dago man.
Evra time w'en I go out
  Weetha heem I no can speak
To som'body. "Shut your mout',"
  He weell tal me pretta queeck,
"You weell geeve yoursal' away
  Talkin' Dago lika dat;
Try be 'Merican," he say—
  Smarta keed? I tal you w'at!

I am w'at you calla me,
  Justa "dumb ole Dago man";
Alla same my boy ees be
  Smarta younga 'Merican.

The second-generation Italians, in trying to repudiate their old-country heritage, avoid discrimination, and gain acceptance in the larger American community, sometimes anglicized their names. So much a part of the New World did they become that they were seldom willing to go to Italy when their parents wished to return. Usually the parents and children drifted apart gradually, often on a friendly basis but frequently enough with lasting bitterness. Although the tensions between generations were seldom disastrous, they seemed always to cloud the life of the immigrant family. When these tensions, coupled with pressures of vile life in the tenement neighborhoods, led Italian children to repudiate their parents or into crime, the immigrants became bewildered. The pain of the parents became so great that they regretted the day they had set foot on American soil. Time and again they complained *qui non c'è piacere nella vita* ("life had no pleasure here").

Despite such grief, discrimination, and the conflict between generations, the children often found in the United States the better life their parents never knew. Sociologists and others who, by 1904, were studying the development of second-generation Italians found their adjustment to American society strikingly successful. These immigrant offspring generally took assimilation for granted, seldom dwelling on its difficulties. "Italian children, whether born in Italy or here," Lilian Brandt, a social investigator, wrote, "find America much to their taste. They are prompt to adapt themselves to the freedom of the new country and use all the facilities at their disposal for rising to a higher economic level than their parents."

Of course, the parents disliked seeing the disintegration of their families. Like men everywhere, they derived strength from family, religious, and social ties to the group they had known all their lives. So in the maelstrom of a strange new land, where dangers of all kinds jeopardized this moral connection, the immigrants tried tenaciously to maintain their family ties. Many also turned with unaccustomed affection to their connections in Italy because the new life in the United States, with its alienation within the family, brought loneliness, disappointment, and demoralization. Sometimes this feeling was transitional; often it endured. For some, the new life turned out rich, profitable, and full, but even of them it made imperious demands. Although insisting on assimilation, American society made no large effort to aid the immigrants in this always difficult process. Unless someone reached out to the Italian and helped him to understand, Americanization meant little to him. Yet he was as capable of assimilation as most other immigrants were. What those who insisted on rapid Americanization did not see was the prodigious conflict it, like discrimination, produced within the immigrants; it strengthened some and broke others.

Not all who suffered from discrimination or appeared to resist Americanization were docile laborers or uncomprehending peasants. The few Italians from the professional ranks—doctors, lawyers, and teachers—who immigrated to the United States also encountered hostility, and even more frustration than did the *contadini*. When the educated Italians came, they had little choice of how they would live or earn a living. If they wished to put their education or professional training to use, they had to settle in some Little Italy. Otherwise, since they were usually unacceptable elsewhere as professional men, or unless they had a manual trade, they would sink into the mass of unskilled workers. When they did this, their talent was lost to both Italy and the United States, a dreadful waste.

Officials in the Italian government, aware of their special problems, discouraged professional people from immigrating to the United States. In 1893, for example, the Italian consul general in New York City urged them to stay home. "Hardly have they landed," he wrote, "when they discover that America is not for them. Wanting knowledge of the language, and every other resource, they come to the consulate to ask succor in repatriation. How many think themselves lucky if they can find employment as waiters on board a vessel bound for Italy!"

Social workers, such as Vida D. Scudder, who sought out the small number of educated Italians in Boston and tried to stir in them some appreciation for the life of cultured America, never understood them. She was disheartened because the urban Italian in the slums found Americanization vulgar and degrading. So she, like others, had misgivings about him as well as about the peasant. Some critics, such as Owen Wister, the novelist and New England restrictionist, were vicious in attacking even the Americanized intellectual Italian. In his story *Philosophy 4: A Story of Harvard University,* Wister ridiculed and vilified Oscar Maironi, whose parents "had come over in steerage," who was himself working his way through Harvard as a tutor. Wister's Maironi, "who was not a specimen of first rank," had no redeeming qualities. Not even a Harvard education could overcome his racial heritage, explained in clichés, and make him acceptable to bigots.

To sensitive Italians, most of whom did not ask for cordiality of reception and seldom received it, the discrimination against them appeared incomprehensible. They did not beg to be loved; all they sought was toleration. Yet the depth of the hostility they sometimes encountered astonished them and shook their determination to endure humiliation as long as they could earn food and shelter. "We had come to America in search of bread," one of them wrote in later years, "and so felt the inferiority of beggars. Everything was different about us—our behavior, our diet, our groping, uncertain speech—we were interpreted in terms of that inferiority."

The prejudice against migrating Italians was not unique among Americans. In other countries where Italians went as laborers, France and Germany for example, they were held in contempt. Discrimination against newcomers, particularly when they arrived in droves, could be found in almost every society. Most civilized societies, anthropologists maintain, take a tribal or parochial attitude toward cultural diversity; they refuse to accept it.

Since nativists and other Americans were accustomed to a narrow, homogeneous society priding itself on its harmonious manners and political cohesion, a society that had been isolated, even insulated, from the mainstream of world culture, their refusal to accept the Italian newcomers, although brutal, is understandable. Like all men, the old-stock Americans tended to idealize the pioneer hardships of the past and to assume that by going through them they and their parents had acquired qualities that other men of other cultures could not duplicate. Their beliefs and expectations largely determined what they thought of the Italian immigrant and how they behaved toward him.

Consciously or unconsciously, they expected him to be strange, and the expectation shaped the reality.

Acting in terms of their own reality, nativists continued to put pressure on the government to change its immigration policies. So beginning in 1902, the American government tightened its administrative control over immigration. In 1907, Congress further strengthened the government's hand in immigration by permitting deportation for illegal entry within a period of five years, and by passing laws to stop the use of fraudulent passports by aliens to gain admission to the United States from its insular possessions. Congress also authorized the President to take up the whole problem of the migration of populations in conferences with foreign powers. In this same year, President Theodore Roosevelt appointed a commission of senators, representatives, and economic experts to study the problem of immigration. Headed by Senator William P. Dillingham of Vermont, himself a restrictionist, this special United States Immigration Commission was weighted with men who favored the restriction of the new immigrants.

In Italy, news of the hostility toward Italians in the United States and the rise of restrictionist sentiment created confusion among prospective immigrants. It also frustrated the hopes of leaders in the government who wished to use emigration to relieve the pressure of a depressed population on the economy. "I pray to God," the writer and politician Giustino Fortunato said in 1908, "that nothing induces the United States to close its doors." In the Italian legislative chambers, politicians frequently denounced the discrimination against their countrymen in the United States and demanded that their government do something about it. Travelers, such as Ernesto Rossi, the actor, and Giuseppe Giacosa, the dramatist, wrote about the miserable lot of Italians in the United States and deplored the discrimination they suffered. These travelers also criticized the anti-Semitism they encountered in the United States. When the journalist Ferdinando Fortana saw in hotels signs saying "No Jews Allowed," he could hardly believe his eyes.

For years, Italian officials attempted to remove the basis for American hostility toward Italians. Through the Society for Italian Immigration, for example, they tried to discourage temporary workers from going to the United States. This society favored strict American laws against "birds of passage" and laws that would help the permanent immigrants. Government officials and other leaders in Italy made it clear to the American government that they would favor any program for a better selection of emigrants from their country, also of distributing them once they arrived in the United States. The Italian government merely wanted a policy that accorded Italians treatment equal to that given other immigrants. It opposed any "big stick" policy that would institutionalize the discrimination against Italians.

These hopes were not to be realized. In December, 1910, the Dillingham Commission made its report to Congress. Claiming to be "objective and scientific," the commission announced that since 1880, the character of immigration had undergone a fundamental change, and for the worse. It classified all immigrant groups by race, implying that old-stock Anglo-Saxon Americans were superior to others and that newcomers, such as the Italians, were basically inferior, opportunists prone to crime and pauperism who should be excluded. It favored restriction of immigration and recommended the literacy test as the means of keeping the alleged undesirables out.

The Italian government, Italian newspapers and societies in the United States, and various other immigrant papers and organizations all opposed the literacy test, pointing out its discriminatory intent. Since Italian newspapers were weak editorially and seldom exerted influence outside their own communities, their opposition did not have much effect on the lawmakers. Nor did the efforts of the few Italians who organized themselves to oppose the restrictionists. At this time, Italians had no real political muscle. The few who entered politics, mostly from the second generation, never got much beyond minor local offices; they had little or no influence in national politics. Italians, in general, did not yet show as much initiative as some other recent immigrants, such as Jews, in political affairs.

So determined were the restrictionists to curb the new immigration that neither politics nor reason based on sound scholarship could dissuade them. In 1911, Franz Boas, a distinguished professor of anthropology at Columbia University, at the request of the United States Immigration Commission, came out with a massive study of immigrants. Beneath his layers of statistics and heavy prose lay a basic finding, that those groups generally considered most hopelessly "non-Anglo-Saxon," such as Jews and Sicilians, could readily assimilate into American society. Boas's scholarship exploded the myth that the new immigrants were incapable of adapting themselves to democracy.

By 1912, those who believed in free immigration were such an ineffective minority that the findings of Boas had little impact on the politicians. Congress passed its second bill calling for a literacy test. In February, 1913, President William H. Taft vetoed the bill, saying that the immigrants were illiterate because they had been denied the opportunity for education, the very opportunity they sought in the United States. Italian newspapers praised Taft's action, but Italians had little cause for rejoicing. Restrictionist sentiment was deeper and more widespread than ever. Woodrow Wilson, a restrictionist and a man whom most of them had opposed, had just won election to the Presidency.

In 1912, Prescott Hall, the son of a Boston merchant, and one of the founders of the Restriction League, claimed in the *North American Review* that the southern Italian was by race partly Negroid and therefore undesirable. He implied that race and color of skin determined a people's quality, and that his own kind were of the most desirable quality. Although intelligent people could dismiss such slurs as the rantings of an emotional restrictionist, they could not deny that on the eve of a world war that would change the relationship between Italians and Americans, the bias against Italians could be found almost everywhere, in social attitudes, in fictional stereotypes, and in folklore. The unfavorable image of the Italian was ascendant in the United States.

Nationalist Manifestations

7

In the two decades following Italy's unification, official relations between Rome and Washington were correct and amicable, but not close. A small difference that ruffled the diplomatic calm grew out of a revolution in Colombia, where, in 1884, authorities arrested Ernesto Cerutti, an Italian national, for taking part in the insurrection. When the Italian government, in the ensuing quarrel, threatened to use warships, the United States intervened as a protector, by right of treaty, of Colombia. The affair ended amicably in March, 1897, when Grover Cleveland, as arbitrator, handed down an award in favor of Cerutti for injuries suffered.

In unofficial relations Italians and Americans got along reasonably well, but aside from tourism and immigration, they shared no vital interests. Many of Italy's intellectuals, like those elsewhere in Europe, admired the United States: its energy, its power, its wealth; some also feared it. They realized that while America was booming their own economy was languishing, especially their commerce and industry. Some of them studied American methods. In 1873, for example, the Marchese Francesco Carega di Muricce, a Florentine agronomist, compared Italian and American use of agricultural land. In the eighties, students in Bologna and Milan also brought out studies on American agriculture and industry, usually in praise of American methods. Yet the very growth of the American economy led some writers, such as Egisto Rossi, to express alarm over the rise of an "American peril."

Despite these concerns, Italy's government watched emigrants stream from its ports to American factories. It tried, in limited ways, to stimulate Italian nationalism overseas, mainly by subsidizing philanthropic societies. Policy makers did not tamper with the loyalty of Italians in the United States; they just wanted them to retain cultural ties with their homeland, to preserve their *italianità* ("Italian consciousness"). Such activity encountered no official obstacles, for the American government did not object to the spread of Italian culture.

The most important of these organizations, the Dante Alighieri Society, was founded in 1889 with headquarters in Rome. It quickly set up branches in the United States. Taking a broad view of *italianità*, the society tried to stimulate overseas nationalism by encouraging the use of the Italian language, sponsoring cultural and artistic institutes, and disseminating information on the history and literature of Italy. Yet it gave the impression of being a neutral vehicle for cultural information, one without political or religious goals. The society relied heavily on annual congresses, usually held in Italy, to advance its work. It also dabbled in Italian politics, keeping alive the question of schooling for Italians overseas. In the United States, it arranged celebrations, provided lectures, and supported various other Italian activities. Although it may have enhanced Italy's image among educated Americans, it failed to arouse nationalism, mainly because it did little or nothing for unskilled immigrants. The society's message seldom reached them.

This failure worried Italian nationalists. They urged subsidies for Italian schools in immigrant communities. These men also wanted Italy's government to use the cultural societies to build solidarity between Italians at home and those in America. Given the provincial loyalties of the immigrants who, even in Italy, had not known deep feelings of nationalism, the task of the societies was difficult. They never succeeded in promoting strong sentiments for the mother country among the mass of immigrants. But discrimination and mob violence against Italians in the United States, as in the lynching of an Italian by an armed gang in 1890 in the mining town of Gunnison, Colorado, aroused in the immigrants an awareness of their *italianità* that the societies had failed to stimulate. Similar violence in New Orleans brought about the first serious clash between Rome and Washington.

Sicilians, a people who aroused in nativists a more intense hatred than other Italian immigrants, made up much of a big Italian settlement in New Orleans. In and around the city, there had long been the usual grumblings about the Sicilians, their alleged predilection for crime, and their connections with a supposedly well-organized Mafia. This hostility came to a head in October, 1890, when five men ambushed and killed the popular young superintendent of police, David C. Hennessey, who had been investigating two rival Italian dock-working gangs. Before dying, Hennessey supposedly muttered, "The Dagoes did it."

Whether or not Hennessey had blamed the right people, public prejudice was already so heated that practically any scrap of damaging evidence would most likely have been pinned on the Italians. Immediately orders went out to the police "to arrest every Italian you come across." People became convinced that the murderers had come from and had slipped back into the local Sicilian ghetto. The police systematically combed the Italian neighborhoods, rounding up and arresting more than one hundred suspects, all Italians. The authorities released all but nineteen, accusing ten of plotting Hennessey's murder and nine of committing it. The mayor, Joseph A. Shakespeare, announced that "the evidence collected by the police department shows beyond a doubt that he [Hennessey] was the victim of Sicilian vengeance. . . ." Jail guards beat the prisoners, which led Pasquale Corte, the Italian consul, to protest, but to no effect.

While the prisoners awaited trial, Italian-American groups raised funds for their defense and employed capable lawyers. All this further angered the people of New Orleans. When the nine went to court, the jury, because of the flimsy evidence, found six not guilty and voted no convictions for the other three. Inflamed by prejudice and convinced that the accused were guilty and should be punished, citizens reacted angrily to the verdict. Many believed that the Italians had escaped justice by bribing several of the jurors. Dissatisfied townspeople immediately formed a vigilance committee, called a mass meeting, and planned a lynching. On the next morning, March 14, 1891, a mob of 6,000 to 8,000 people, led by prominent citizens, descended on the parish jail to get the "Dagoes." While state and local law officers, as well as the governor, who was in the city at the time, stood by and did nothing, the mob hanged two of the suspects from lampposts, and lined nine of them up in front of the prison wall and blasted their bodies with rifles, pistols, and shotguns, taking less than twenty minutes for the grim work. Of those murdered, three were Italian subjects and the others were immigrants who had become naturalized Americans or had declared their intentions of becoming citizens. Some of the lynchers also hurled threats at the Italian consulate and molested other Italians in the city.

News of the slaughter horrified Italians everywhere, and brought condemnation on New Orleans from all over the world, but newspapers in Louisiana and throughout the South condoned the violence. Since New Orleans approved, one paper said, the murders "should not be measured by the strict rule of legal forms in that community." Even a future president, Theodore Roosevelt, considered the mob's action "rather a good thing," and said so at a dinner party with "various dago diplomats . . . all much wrought up by the lynching."

Baron Francesco Saverio Fava, the Italian minister in Washington, immediately protested to Secretary of State James G. Blaine, denouncing the authorities in New Orleans for acquiescing in the murders, and asked him to take precautions against future attacks. Blaine expressed regret, maintaining incorrectly that the killings had no ethnic significance. He telegraphed the governor asking him to protect Italian subjects from further violence and to investigate the lynchings. Then the Secretary of State put the matter aside. Blaine's attitude did not satisfy the Italian government. It wanted official assurance that authorities would bring the guilty parties to trial and indemnify the families of the victims. By the accepted standards of international conduct, the Italians had a strong case. "Italy's indignation," the *Times* of London said, "is shared by the whole civilized world."

International law obligated the federal government to protect aliens, but under the Constitution, the states had the main responsibility for public order, including the protection of aliens and their property against mob violence. The federal government, therefore, found itself responsible for the action of state authorities without the power to control what they did. Yet Italy had to gain satisfaction from the United States, not Louisiana, something Blaine refused to give. "It is a matter of indifference what persons in Italy think of our institutions," he said. "I cannot change them, still less violate them."

After several weeks of fruitless negotiation, the Italian government recalled Fava and the United States called home its minister from Rome. Fava's recall kept the controversy on the nation's front pages. As he left, newspapers truculently spoke of war, carried rumors of an Italian fleet heading for American shores, and published derisive comments about Italians. Many Americans now began viewing Italians not only with the usual nativist prejudice but also as potential enemy aliens. Life for numerous immigrants became more miserable than ever. In Wheeling, West Virginia, miners struck because their employer refused to fire Italian workers. They would not, the miners said, work with men "allied to a nation that was trying to bring about war with the United States." In Boston, restrictionists denounced the lynched Italians as sinister *mafiosi* representing "two thousand years of Southern Italian and Sicilian civilization." One of the restrictionists, the Episcopalian clergyman Phillips Brooks, said "the fiery folk" should learn to behave or else not come to the United States "to murder and be murdered."

Restrictionists were pleased with at least one result of the New Orleans massacre; like the Haymarket riot, it strengthened popular anti-foreignism. They now demanded an end to immigration from Sicily and other parts of the Mediterranean. Despite this distrust of Italians, and the pugnacious nationalism of much of the press, level-headed commentators urged a policy of moderation toward Italy. In Italy, people everywhere heard and talked about the lynchings, reacting with passion. Newspapers attacked the United States; and in town after town, speakers at mass meetings demanded satisfaction for the slayings.

Nonetheless, neither Italian nor American leaders saw any real danger of war. The Italian government had left a *chargé d'affaires* in Washington and so did not break off diplomatic relations. The prime minister, Marchese Antonio Starabba di Rudini, had recalled Fava mainly to placate his people and not to threaten Americans with force. He had to do something; inaction could have brought down his coalition government. The attitude of the grand jury in New Orleans added to his difficulties. After investigating the lynchings for two months it failed to indict any of the leaders of the mob. It even exonerated those who had participated.

In time, tempers cooled and both governments sought an amicable settlement. President Benjamin Harrison and Secretary of State Blaine tried to find constitutional means of prosecuting the leaders of the mob, but uncovered no law empowering the federal courts to take jurisdiction. Finally, they worked out an indirect means of meeting demands for indemnity. In his annual message in December, 1891, Harrison called the slaughter "a most deplorable and discreditable incident, an offense against law and humanity," and offered Italy an apology. In the following April, Blaine announced that the "lamentable massacre at New Orleans" obligated the United States to pay a satisfactory indemnity. The President offered $25,000 to be divided among the families of the victims. Accepting the indemnity, the Italian government, as Blaine desired, restored full diplomatic relations.

Since Congress was reluctant to vote funds for indemnities, Harrison did not ask it for an appropriation. He took the money from an emergency fund earmarked for diplomatic expenses. The St. Paul *Pioneer-Press* commended Harrison's action as "proper and wise." If the question of an appropriation had gone to Congress, the paper pointed out, it "would have been fought and delayed and haggled over until all the graciousness was taken out of the act." Italian papers in the United States, such as Chicago's *L'italia*, expressed shock over the Italian government's acceptance of "a small indemnity" without gaining condemnation of the lynchers.

Even though deplored by the government, the violence against Italians continued. In West Virginia, in 1891, rumors that drunken immigrants had slit the throats of an American family led to the lynching of a number of Italians. Two years later, lynchers killed Italians in Denver. In March, 1895, a time of labor strife in Walsenberg, a town near the coal fields in southern Colorado, a group of miners slaughtered six Italian laborers who had been implicated in the murder of a saloonkeeper. In the following year, in the small Louisiana town of Hahnville, a mob dragged six Italians from a jail and hanged three of them.

For several years, nativists in Tallulah, Louisiana, had resented five Sicilian storekeepers because they dealt mainly with Negroes and associated with them almost on terms of equality. So in July, 1899, after a quarrel over a goat, the townspeople tore three of the Italians from jail, captured the other two, and lynched all five. Similar violence burst out in Erwin, Mississippi, in July, 1901, and in the coal fields of West Virginia, in 1906, where native miners mobbed, maimed, and killed Italian laborers. Elsewhere in Mississippi, nativists beat up Italian agricultural workers and even launched a movement to keep their children out of white schools. When the people of Sumrall whipped an Italian, the Italian government sent out an investigator, but could do nothing to stem the violence. Anti-Italian sentiment became so strong in the state that in 1907, Jeff Truly, a candidate for governor, made discrimination against Italians an issue in his campaign. "Italians," he said, "are a threat and a danger to our racial, industrial, and commercial supremacy. Mississippi needs no such immigration."

Mob violence continued well into the twentieth century, with attacks against Italians in Colorado mining settlements; in Tampa, Florida, in 1910; and in Willisville, in southern Illinois, in 1914. There, authorities arrested Albert Piazza for suspicion of murder in a brawl. A mob wrenched him from the jail and shot him to death. Authorities did bring the lynching suspects to trial, but they got off without punishment. In the following year, in nearby Johnson City, a mob lynched another immigrant, Joe Speranza, suspected of being a murderer and a member of the Black Hand.

These cases followed a pattern. The Italian government would protest, but authorities seldom did anything about the lynchers. When they did bring anyone to trial, no conviction followed. Local sentiment against Italians made it impossible to convict offenders.

Even though the mob murders and the lax enforcements of law established the idea in Italy that lynchings of foreigners and blacks were daily occurrences in the United States and caused hard feelings against American justice, Italy did not sever diplomatic relations. Each time a mob killed or injured an Italian national, the American government, as a matter of policy, paid an indemnity, but as an act of grace, without admitting liability. This attitude helped preserve reasonably cordial relations, even though the federal government's failure to prosecute the lynchers violated the commercial treaty of 1871 with Italy. That agreement entitled Italian immigrants to the same rights and protection enjoyed by Americans.

Such protection was usually impossible to obtain. Anti-Italian sentiment, particularly in sections where nativism had deep roots, was too strong for tolerance to prevail. By condoning mob violence and feeding public prejudices with inflammatory denunciations of Italians, restrictionists made a mockery of justice. In March, 1900, for example, Henry Cabot Lodge told an audience, "We have seen a murderous assault by an alien immigrant upon the Chief of Police of a great city, not to avenge any personal wrong, but because he represented law and order. Every day we read in the newspapers of savage murders by members of secret societies [Mafia and Camorra] composed of alien immigrants. Can we doubt, in the presence of such horrible facts as these, the need of stringent laws and rigid enforcement, to exclude the criminals and the anarchists of foreign countries from the United States?"

Despite such prejudice, Italian immigrants were usually eager to gain acceptance as patriotic Americans. In 1898, during the hysteria over the rebellion against Spain in Cuba, Italians in Missouri and Alabama offered to raise volunteers for war against Spain. One of them remarked that "every Italian who had made America his home is only waiting a call to arms in order to prove his loyalty to this country." In Italy, public sentiment generally favored the Cubans in their struggle against Spain. But as tension between the United States and Spain mounted, opinion divided. Recalling American sympathy for the *Risorgimento* and swayed by the knowledge that the United States now sheltered masses of their countrymen, many Italians sided with the United States. Some even argued that Americans would perform a noble deed in liberating the Cubans.

Various Italian journals, on the other hand, spoke of an American menace, sympathized with Spain, and suggested that Europe should go to Spain's defense. Regardless of the state of opinion, the Italian government would not join in an international appeal on behalf of Spain unless all the other powers cooperated. It would do nothing alone that might anger Americans. Finally, in April, 1898, just before war broke out, Italy joined five other European powers in a collective note appealing "to the feelings of humanity and moderation of the President and of the American people in their existing difference with Spain." Several days later the European foreign ministers considered a second note, one much more critical of the United States than the first. Although he disapproved of American behavior, Marchese Emilio Visconti Venosta, the foreign minister of Italy, took a skeptical attitude toward another communication to President William McKinley. Visconti Venosta thought the note would serve no purpose, but he also felt that Italy could not refuse to go along with it. Fortunately, the powers never sent this second note, so Italy was saved from joining a protest that could not prevent war but could have antagonized the United States.

In Italy, the Spanish-American War sharpened the image of Americans as materialists and aggressors. Nationalists saw in the war a lesson for Italy; she could use the American imperial experience as a model. In the United States, Italians caught the martial spirit, taking pride in the American victories. When the naval hero George Dewey returned to New York after the war, the Italian settlements celebrated his triumph, observers noted, "in a way they had hitherto reserved for their saints."

Educated Italians who were now visiting America, like other tourists, wrote about what they saw. They pictured the United States as a cultural desert, describing Americans as being so immersed in the making of money that they ignored the esthetic side of life. In the arts, the visitors maintained, Americans had not progressed as they had in the more practical fields. Even though Americans studied foreign masters, they lagged behind Italians and other Europeans. Even where opera flourished, critics argued, it did so mainly because upper-class Americans considered it fashionable, not because they appreciated it.

Italians also pointed out that many towns had theaters and opera houses where some of Europe's finest artists performed. The theater, the travelers seemed to agree, was one cultural institution that had developed well. Tommaso Salvini, a Shakespearean actor who made five trips to America in the seventies and eighties, considered the United States ahead of Italy, and of most of Europe, in drama. Yet the noted Italian actress, Eleanora Duse, who first came to the United States in the nineties, disliked American culture, calling it barbarous. A few visitors confessed that they were impressed by the arts in America, considering them superior to those in Italy where creativity, they felt, was declining.

For education, particularly in the elementary and secondary schools, the Italian visitors offered mostly praise. Vincenzo Botta, a discerning journalist, considered the American school system the best institution the early settlers had brought with them from Europe. Almost all the travelers agreed that Americans had shaped a democratic citizenry through their educational system, ascribing much of the impressive development of American society to education. A sociologist, Nicola Gaetani-Tamburini, was so impressed that he pointed to the American educational system as a model for Italy to follow; he assumed that good citizens are the products of a nation's schools. Angelo Mosso, a psychologist, also urged the adoption of the American primary and secondary educational system in Italy. In Italy, too, reformers followed developments in American schools closely, translating a number of books on American education into Italian. Mosso and others offered little praise and considerable criticism of American higher education. In comparison with European universities, they maintained, those in the United States were backward. Harvard stood out as the exception. Carlo Gardini, a visiting businessman, praised that institution as the best of its kind in the world.

Italian travelers took special note of the training of women, observing that in educational matters American women had outdistanced their European sisters and were more independent. One writer, Antonio Gallenga, noted that in "Cairo, a woman is an idealized slave; at Milan, or Florence, a cherished article of domestic chattel; in London, a reasoning, perhaps sometimes even an arguing, associate; in New York, she is an equal, and more often an aggravating, overbearing confederate." Frequently, the visitors felt that the women had used their education well. But Dario Papa, a journalist, disagreed. The American woman, he believed, was overeducated, too obviously aware of her powers, and generally idle.

The Italian visitors paid most attention to democracy and its institutions. They wanted to know what made democracy tick and Americans prosperous and happy. In 1886, Federico Garlanda, an authority on Anglo-American literary relations, found in practice all the liberties—such as freedom of press, worship, and education—that Europeans knew mainly in theory. Like others, he thought Italians could profit from the American example. By this time the attitudes of Italians toward the American form of government had crystallized. Most of them praised American democracy as it functioned through the political system.

A perceptive journalist, Ugo Ojetti, and a successful playwright, Giuseppe Giacosa, observed closely and tried to capture the main currents of American culture in the nineties in books and articles. Like others, they criticized the materialism they saw, but admired the ability of Americans to get things done, to work together. Ojetti, too, held America up as a model for Italians whose backwardness he flayed. His book *L'America vittoriosa* and Giacosa's *Impressioni d' America* reached a large public. Several years later, in 1913, the appetite for information on the United States led to the publication in Italian translation of James Bryce's *The American Commonwealth.*

Educated Italians in general, not just the visitors, were curious about the practical operation of democracy and searched out American authors to learn about it. Italians also showed a keen interest in American philosophy, especially in men such as Josiah Royce and John Dewey, whose works they read in translations. Reflecting the thirst for knowledge of democracy, Italian periodicals gave considerable space to American books. Travelers in Italy noticed the interest in American literature. William Dean Howells, whose own writings showed a sympathetic understanding of Italy, noted that intelligent Italians knew four American writers well: James Fenimore Cooper, Harriet Beecher Stowe, Henry Wadsworth Longfellow, and Washington Irving.

Visitors like Howells, who had returned for a year in 1882, were still charmed by Italy. He said of the Italians that "it was their lovely ways, far more than their monuments of history and art, that made a return to the Florentines delightful." Unlike the restrictionists at home, he found in Italians a humanity that deeply touched him, observing in them a "quality of courtesy" that made them "still easily the first of all men." Howells remained a warm friend of Italy all his life, an "inveterate Italophile."

In the eighties, Francis Marion Crawford, the nephew of Julia Ward Howe, made Italy his adopted country. He maintained that to know Italy one had to live among her people as he did, trudging the mountains and valleys where no highways penetrated. His novels about Italy, as a consequence, reveal a knowledge of Italians that few

Americans ever acquired. Another American writer who knew Italy well, living there as a child and an adult, was Edith Wharton. She spoke Italian naturally and easily, and steeped herself in Italian culture. Her book *Italian Villas and Their Gardens*, one of the first serious works on the subject, became a manual for gardeners and architects. For her, Italy always had a special charm. William Roscoe Thayer, the historian, also considered Italy a second homeland, a "country beyond time, where one roams the immense and majestic past." He had fallen in love with Italy and Italians in his youth, acquiring also a passionate sympathy for the *Risorgimento*. He became the first methodical student of that movement and spent nearly thirty years on a biography of Cavour.

While these and other writers carried on the old love affair with Italy, in the last decades of the nineteenth century a new breed of Americans searched the peninsula for her art treasures. For years, tourists had been accustomed to purchasing a few paintings, but mainly copies of old masters. Now the big collectors, millionaires who had made their money in railroads, steel, oil, and banking, entered the scene. They bought whole Renaissance palaces, but mostly original old masters—Raphaels, Titians, and Botticellis—as a means of displaying their wealth.

Stanford White, the architect who had first gone to Italy in 1878 with plans to become a painter, in later years traveled through the country buying frescoed ceilings, paneled walls, marble statuary, and other pieces for the "Italian Renaissance" buildings he was designing in the United States. Known as the American Benvenuto Cellini, White claimed that buildings in the Renaissance style were better suited to American needs than were those in either the Gothic or the classic style. His partner, Charles F. McKim, was also an eclectic attracted by Italian examples. Often called an American Bramante, McKim modeled his buildings, such as the Pennsylvania Station in New York City and the Boston Public Library, on old Italian or Roman themes. His interest in Italian architecture led him to organize the American School of Architecture in Rome in January, 1895. In three years it became the American Academy, an institution that grew into one of the finest centers for the training of Americans in the fine arts and classical scholarship.

The activities of these wealthy collectors contributed to the building of an American appreciation of Italian culture. Mrs. Jack Gardner, one of the first collectors, bought capitals, columns, and balconies from Italian buildings and imported Italian workmen to erect her own Venetian *palazzo* in Boston, thereby bringing Italian skill as well as art to the United States. Bernard Berenson, the man who chose her most important pictures, beginning with a Botticelli in 1894, became the outstanding American expert on the art of the Renaissance. His wanderings through Italy began in 1888. Twelve years later he settled in a villa, *I Tatti,* on a Tuscan hillside overlooking Florence; and he lived there for sixty years.

Except for the art and monuments, most Americans saw little in Italy to emulate. Frankly skeptical about her political future, they did not hold the Italian nation in high esteem. Her large-scale emigration, they felt, was evidence of weakness, of unrest that constantly threatened the stability of the government. Yet, they observed, the government strained the nation's limited resources by maintaining a large army and navy. The critics had a point; the armed forces reflected an unrealistic element in Italian nationalism. Italy was too poor to play the role of great power in international politics, yet her leaders insisted that she try.

This lack of realism also showed up in Italy's efforts to build a colonial empire. Her colonial problems began in Tunisia, where for years Italians had migrated and settled, outnumbering all other Europeans. Italian statesmen hoped to annex Tunis, but in 1881, the French invaded and occupied the country So in May of the following year, in resentment against France, Italy joined the Triple Alliance as a junior partner of Germany and Austria.

In that year the Italian government also took its first step in the building of a colonial empire. Italy bought a small region in east Africa around Assab on the Red Sea from a private concern, the Rubattino Navigation Company, which had secured a concession there from the local sultan. In 1885, Italians established themselves at Massawa, up the coast from Assab. These acquisitions laid the foundation for the colony of Eritrea. Pushing inland from Massawa, Italians extended their influence into the Tigrine uplands of Ethiopia. They quickly involved themselves in local political feuds, becoming particularly friendly with Menelek, a young prince whom they expected to accept their tutelage.

In 1887, Francesco Crispi, an imperialist, became prime minister. Taking over the foreign office himself, he worked to acquire much of Ethiopia and surrounding coastal lands. Two years later, in treaties with local rulers, Italy laid the basis for a colony in Somaliland, fronting on the Indian Ocean and touching inland the ill-defined limits of Ethiopian control. In this same year, Menelek, with Italian support, claimed Ethiopia's throne.

Italy quickly concluded an agreement, the Treaty of Uccialli, with the new emperor, Menelek II. According to the Italian copy, he had to use Italy as his channel in the conduct of foreign relations; the Ethiopian, or Amharic, version left such usage optional. No one had compared the two texts against each other. Since the Italian version would have made Ethiopia virtually a protectorate, early in 1893 Menelek denounced the treaty and prepared for war. Border clashes and an undeclared war followed. At first Italian forces won a number of victories, conquering the province of Tigre. In 1896, Menelek took to the field with an army of some 100,000 men and occupied a strong position near Adowa. Underestimating both the difficulties of the terrain and the strength of the enemy, General Oreste Baratieri, the Italian commander, goaded on by Crispi, on March 1 attacked with a force of less than 18,000. Masses of well-armed Ethiopians surrounded the Italian divisions caught in narrow mountain passes and cut them to pieces, killing or wounding more than 4,000 Italians and nearly 3,000 African auxiliaries and taking almost 3,000 prisoners.

Even though the Italians inflicted greater casualties than they received, Italy could not take her losses; Adowa became for her a national disaster. Humiliated by the defeat, the people forced Crispi to resign. His successor, giving up the imperial pursuit of *grandezza,* came to terms with Menelek. In Addis Ababa, in October, 1896, Italians and Ethiopians signed a provisional treaty of peace that annulled the Treaty of Uccialli and recognized the independence of Ethiopia.

The African war attracted attention everywhere. Italy's defeat seemed to confirm American estimates of her power. So, as far as her relations with the United States were concerned, she emerged from the conflict subdued, tarnished, and low in prestige. Despite Italy's weakness, knowledgeable American observers realized that had she been determined to do so she had the power in the end to defeat the backward Ethiopians. But the Italians lacked the will to make the necessary sustained effort. They were wrapped up in their pressing internal problems and did not, as American critics realized, choose to commit the resources necessary for the pursuit of a costly colonial policy.

Yet within a few years, as though prodded by demons, Italy experienced a striking revival of nationalism that affected politics, literature, the arts, and other aspects of life. The generation of intellectuals that came to manhood with the turn of the century disliked the attitude of inferiority evident among Italians, a feeling stemming from military defeats as at Adowa, from the ill treatment of Italian laborers abroad as in the United States, and from Italy's obvious backwardness in comparison with other great powers.

These young Italians championed a bellicose nationalism linked to the ideas of Alfredo Oriani, who preached that only through war and conquest could Italy become great. Using the European settlement of America as a model, he urged a bold expansion into Africa. Many of the nationalists were middle-class graduates from universities who could not find jobs. Unlike the peasants, they did not emigrate; they stayed home and agitated, reacting violently against the foreign image of Italy as "a nation of mandolin players." They attributed Italy's low reputation mainly to the absence of a militant patriotism among the people.

Since this new nationalism was based on ideas and emotions rather than on realities of political power, it often expressed itself in cultural terms, mainly through literature. Its ideas first turned up in 1903 in the pages of a small Florentine review, *Il regno.* Its guiding lights were two novelists, Giovanni Papini and Enrico Corradini, the editor. Corradini, considered the founder of modern Italian nationalism, was a former high school teacher who had turned to journalism. *Il regno* tried to arouse a more intense patriotism, but did not last long.

Among others who took up the cause of this new nationalism, the most articulate spokesman was Gabriele D'Annunzio, a poet, dramatist, and aesthete who glorified violence. Italy, he suggested, had to act like a lion; like other great nations, she had to plunge into the main stream of international politics. He taught a whole generation to despise *Italietta,* the intelligentsia's term of contempt for the idea of Italy as "the art museum and servile boarding-house keeper for the spendthrifts of Europe," and to dream of a new, masterful, imperial Italy. In 1908, D'Annunzio came out with a play, *La nave* (The Ship), that exalted the glory that had once belonged to Venice. The prologue supplied the vague motto of Italian imperialism, "Arm the prow and set sail toward the world." D'Annunzio's imperial message caused the young nationalists to take pride in the greatness of the Italian past; they yearned somehow to revive it. To achieve true greatness, they believed, Italy had to create an empire. Corradini and the young lions of the *Regno* wanted to build it through war.

This imperalistic urge had in it nothing original or uniquely Italian.

It was part of the European jingoism of the time. These Italian nationalists were merely urging their country to follow a pattern that others, such as England, France, Germany, and the United States, had set. When D'Annunzio held up imperial Venice as a model, he seemed almost to be aping Rudyard Kipling's preachings on the imperial mission of Britain. Despite its appeal to youth and to intellectuals, this fusing of nationalism and imperialism did not arouse a sustained response from Italy's masses. Unlike imperialism elsewhere, as in the United States for example, the Italian movement lacked a strong economic motive. Since industry had been expanding only moderately, Italy had no industrialists demanding colonies as sources for raw materials and markets for their goods. Yet some imperalists deluded themselves by believing that the conquest of colonies could make Italy rich.

Italian imperialism also had a weak political base. The nationalists relied more on emotional appeal than on votes in parliament to get their movement going. Yet Corradini, his fellow journalist Luigi Federzoni, and the writer Giuseppe Prezzolini were activists, as well as thinkers, who tried to build a political following. In 1908, they formed small nationalist groups with the idea of using them for political purposes. Even though politically weak, this movement did influence the Italian government's policy toward emigration and thereby affected the relations of Italians and Americans. These nationalistic intellectuals, as well as government leaders, saw a place for emigration in the Imperial creed and therefore looked upon emigration as a positive good. If Italy could control her emigrants more effectively than in the past, then she could use emigration as an instrument for overseas expansion.

This idea of political use of emigration was also bound up with the development of a special conception of citizenship, that no Italian anywhere could foreswear allegiance to Italy, that emigrants were merely citizens residing abroad. The theory went, "once an Italian, always an Italian." The government would not recognize the right of expatriation. The imperial theorists assumed that most emigrants expected some day to return to Italy, if only to visit friends and relatives, and that they would undergo no basic changes in their new environment. When the emigrant returned, either as a permanent resident or as a visitor, the nationalists argued, he should be welcomed as an Italian subject. Italy, according to this theory, would give affection and in return would receive it from her sons everywhere. She should also be strong and back up her subjects abroad, as in the United States, who suffered from lynchings and other abuses, with force if necessary. They would love the mother country, would be loyal to her, and would help to build a greater Italy while abroad as other Italians were doing at home.

Various nationalistic groups tried to make the theory a working reality, mainly by striving to construct a lasting connection between Italian immigrants overseas and the mother country. One of these organizations, the *Istituto Coloniale*, founded in 1906 to develop colonial action, tried to bind overseas Italians to the mother country by representing their collective interests. In an exhibition in Milan at this time, a special section was devoted to the work of Italians abroad; and in 1904 and 1911, Italian immigrants held national congresses in the United States.

Some of the nationalist intellectuals approached the problem of emigration from a different perspective. At a congress in the Palazzo Vecchio in Florence in December, 1910, where they formed the Nationalist Association, a political party of their own, they demanded a bold foreign policy, and even urged war to win land where emigrants might settle under the Italian flag. Corradini, the most vocal leader of this movement, had studied immigration, having visited Italian communities in Tunis, South America, and the United States. He had returned disillusioned, convinced that in foreign lands Italians suffered from exploitation, discrimination, and pressure for assimilation. So, taking over the language of Marxism, he transferred the idea of the class struggle to international relations. To the theory of nationalism he added the concept of the "proletarian nation." Italy, he believed, must build her power, her future, on labor, the only resource she had in abundance; in respect to the rest of the world, he maintained, Italians were a proletarian people. Emigration, these nationalists argued, was the imperialism of the poor.

Even though the nationalist party attracted few recruits and never gained significant strength in the Chamber of Deputies, Corradini's ideas won considerable attention. On March 1, 1911, on the fifteenth anniversary of the defeat at Adowa, the nationalists launched a weekly—soon changed to a daily—journal, *L'idea nazionale*, in Rome to spread their ideas over a wider area than in the past. It deplored permanent emigration. "Let us boast of the fecundity of our women," Corradini wrote, "but not of the dispersion of their children." Emigration and imperialism, through the conquest of colonies, would use Italian labor to enhance the power and prestige of Italy, not of foreign nationals. Using such arguments, *L'idea nazionale* called on Italians to take Tripoli from Turkey and make it a colonial home for emigrants. Critics of this bellicose attitude, less-extreme nationalists such as Prezzolini, opposed such an adventure. Imperialism, they argued, actually endangered Italy by luring her into undertakings beyond her capabilities.

In other European countries, nationalism and the desire for colonies were as strong as in Italy. These nationalists also argued that their countries needed colonies for a surplus population, but elsewhere such reasoning did not count as heavily as in Italy. To Italian nationalists, the imperial argument had a solid, practical ring. "Whither shall we send our sons and daughters," they asked, "who have no place at home?" To them, Turkey's lands in North Africa seemed most easily within reach for an imperialist adventure that would be cheap. But the nationalists were fooling themselves. The provinces of Tripoli and Cyrenaica, the centers of some wealth and culture in the days of ancient Rome, were at this time little more than miles of desert stretching into the heart of Africa. Only nominally under Turkish control, these provinces then had no known resources of consequence and a sparse population of about 1 million, mostly Arab nomads. Only those with wild imaginations could, at the time, assume that those deserts could support millions of peasants from Italy.

For several years Italy's designs on Tripoli had roiled relations with Turkey. In January, 1911, an incident involving a South American resident at Tripoli, accused of promoting anti-Italian propaganda, brought on a squabble between Turks and Italians. Feeling that Italy had legitimate complaints against Turkey, her allies and the other powers allowed her a relatively free hand in Tripoli. Yet the powers also feared that war might have dangerous consequences in the Ottoman Empire and in the Balkans. So they cautioned the Italians against extreme action. The warnings had no effect. On September 29, 1911, after Turkey rejected an ultimatum demanding the surrender of Tripoli, Italy declared war. Nationalists saw the conflict as that "test of arms and blood" that would erase the blot of Adowa, but Socialists and others opposed the war; some Italians even tore up railroad tracks to block troop movements.

Some observers predicted a disaster. They were wrong. Although the war required a far greater effort than Italy's leaders had envisaged, its outcome was never truly in doubt. The Italians won a series of victories, but all were on the coast of Tripoli, causing Turkey herself no real damage. Italy quickly proclaimed annexation of Tripoli, but Turkey refused to recognize it. So the war dragged on through the winter, confined in its operations to the coastal lands of Tripoli. In January and February, 1912, Italian warships bombarded coastal cities in Syria, and in April, destroyers penetrated the Dardanelles in a fruitless effort to cripple units of the Turkish fleet. In May, Italian forces took Rhodes and other nearby Dodecanese Islands. Then Italy threatened to enlarge the conflict by moving into Asia Minor and Albania. Since the powers did not want the war to spread to the continent, they exerted pressure on Turkey to come to terms.

In July and August, the belligerents discussed peace, with Italy insisting on sovereignty over all of Tripoli and Cyrenaica, and Turkey refusing to give in. Anxious to take advantage of Turkey before the war closed, Bulgaria, Serbia, and Greece in October attacked her. As soon as this, the First Balkan War, broke out, Italy informed the powers she would also assault European Turkey. Since the Balkans were more important to her than the deserts of Tripoli, Turkey yielded to Italy's demands without further haggling. In the Treaty of Lausanne, signed on October 18, 1912, Turkey ceded the last of her African possessions and allowed the Italians to occupy the Dodecanese Islands "temporarily," pending fulfillment of the terms of the peace. Italy proclaimed annexation of Turkey's African territory by royal decree in the following month and renamed it Libya.

The Italian people showed little enthusiasm for the war, but not many had opposed it or had spoken openly against it. Most had accepted it passively and were pleased with the results. Many Italians also reacted sensitively to what foreigners thought of the war. Americans followed the fighting and diplomacy of the war in their newspapers. Most of them, if the newspapers reflected their views accurately, did not consider the war important, but nonetheless felt hostility toward Italy and sympathy for Turkey. Italy's grievances, they believed, were pretexts for her desire to grab Tripoli. Some Americans could see irony in this attitude. When the Italian foreign minister asked the American ambassador what he thought of the invasion, the ambassador, with fingers on his lips, said "Ssh! I'm so afraid somebody will say 'Panama.' "

A few people, such as the publisher William Randolph Hearst, praised the Italian invaders as civilizers in Tripoli. Others called the

Italian action "the sheerest brigandage." One of these, Oscar S. Strauss, a former ambassador to Turkey, suggested, as did the Turkish foreign minister, Assim Bey, that the United States mediate the conflict. The American government acknowledged the suggestion, but would not or could not carry it out. Yet President William H. Taft expressed willingness to work for peace, and perhaps could have done so through a treaty of arbitration that Secretary of State Elihu Root had made with Italy in 1908. Such action would have run counter to the views of most American policy makers who felt that the war and the problems of the Middle East belonged to the international politics of Europe, so the United States should keep hands off. Italians in the United States were moved by the war, and of course sided with Italy. Corradini and the nationalists hoped the conflict would stimulate nationalism among them and other overseas Italians. In 1913, he even wrote a play dealing with the trials of an emigrant whose patriotism had been fired by the events in Tripoli.

Aside from boosting the national ego and enhancing her status as a colonial power, the possession of Libya brought Italy none of the benefits the nationalists claimed it would, and certainly no economic advantages. The Arabs in the interior resisted Italian rule and the campaign to pacify them dragged on until 1916, requiring a force in the field of some 80,000 to 100,000 men. Prime Minister Giovanni Giolitti explained to the Chamber of Deputies that guerrilla resistance characterized all colonial wars. True enough, but this excuse hardly satisfied those who had expected the smashing victory the imperialists had talked about. Those Italians who had thought Libya would siphon surplus population from the homeland, thereby reducing emigration to foreign lands, were quickly disappointed. Those who had lamented that their people had gone to the United States and elsewhere, to take up the lowliest of jobs, found in Libya no frontier suitable for those who would become respected pioneers. So Italian immigrants continued to go to the United States and to suffer humiliation. What they created, according to the young nationalists, brought no immediate benefit to themselves or to Italy.

Yet most students of emigration argue that Italy gained by exporting surplus population to the United States. Although early in the twentieth century Italy's birth rate fell as a whole, in the south it dropped only slightly. There the birth rate ranked with the highest in Europe. So expatriated Italians, the argument went, not only helped relieve pressure on the land, they also, with the remittances they sent home, helped to make poverty endurable and to sustain a weak economy.

Even though the money from Italians in the United States arrived irregularly and never became a reliable source of income, the total amount that came in each year was large. According to the researches of Professor Luciano J. Iorizzo, by 1914, immigrants in America sent home, in total, close to three-quarters of a billion dollars. For this reason, if for no other, economists and politicians looked upon emigrants as commodities that had a clear economic value. Some economists thought of emigration in simple terms as an industry; Italy exported laborers and received goods or money in exchange. This conviction that Italy needed and had become dependent on money from her emigrants in the United States, the source of more remittances than all other countries combined, was one reason why various congressional proposals to restrict immigration appeared to Italy as a serious threat to her economy. Yet in areas of heavy emigration, the remittances did not always bring permanent improvement. As in the past, poverty and crushing labor remained the way of life for the *contadini*. The remittances, although of considerable aid to Italy's economy, seldom meant clear profit to those who received them. When a husband emigrated and left his family, for instance, that family, no matter how hard it strove, could seldom earn the equivalent of his wages. The money he sent from the United States would pay for daily expenses, such as food and clothing, but was rarely enough for capital expenditures, such as land or education for children.

Still, the supporters of emigration argued, those who stayed at home benefited in other ways from Italy's export of labor. In areas of heavy emigration, wages rose. This argument also had weaknesses, for only a part of the rise stemmed from emigration. In these years, prices as well as wages rose all over Italy. Regardless of the theoretical benefits of emigration, therefore, those who stayed at home gained only slightly, if at all, from it. Mainly in areas such as Tuscany, where the shrinkage in population was slight, emigration brought a sense of relief and no outward injury to society.

As for the immigrant in the United States, he found himself the target of two nationalisms. Italian nationalists wanted to use him as a tool of imperialism and American nationalists wanted to bar him, even to drive him out. These pressures, when added to the experience of associating with immigrants from all parts of Italy and being discriminated against as an Italian, stimulated a consciousness of kind, a previously unheard-of solidarity, a new nationalism, even a patriotism for the old homeland, in the immigrants. Many of them, for the first time, came to consider themselves Italians instead of *paesani* knowing no patriotism beyond village or province.

Partnership
and Rift

8

Despite the strained relations with her allies during the Turkish war, Italy in 1912 signed another version of the Triple Alliance. Two years later, when war threatened to engulf Europe, this treaty, on paper at least, found her committed to Austria and Germany. Italy also retained ambiguous connections with France and Great Britain, the rival powers of an *Entente Cordiale*. In addition, Italy had a special agreement with the United States on matters affecting war and peace. In May, 1914, Secretary of State William Jennings Bryan had concluded a conciliation pact with Italy that obligated her to submit any dispute failing of diplomatic adjustment to an international commission for settlement. For at least a year, while the commission weighed the case, she technically could not resort to war. As did the other powers in the crisis of 1914, Italy ignored the conciliation obligation. She concentrated on her status within the Triple Alliance.

The seventh article called for consultation among the three allies before any one of them took warlike action. But Leopold von Berchtold, Austria's foreign minister, distrusted Italy. So he kept her in the dark about his activities during the crisis in June that arose out of a Serbian student's assassination of Archduke Franz Ferdinand, consulting only his German ally. In dealing with Serbia, von Berchtold intended to confront Italy with a *fait accompli*.

Austria did not give Rome advance notice of her ultimatum of July 23 holding Serbia responsible for the assassination. On the next day, therefore, when Italy's leaders learned of the demands, they considered themselves justified in taking Austria's action as a breach of the Triple Alliance. When war threatened to spread over Europe, leading Austria to invoke the *casus foederis* of the alliance, Italy held back. Nonetheless, the involvement of all Europe's great powers altered the nature of the crisis. When war broke out in August, with Austria pouncing on Serbia and Germany attacking France and Russia, Italy refused to join her allies, calling the Triple Alliance a defensive instrument and arguing that war had resulted from their own aggression. Legally, Italy behaved correctly. Yet she chose neutrality not on the basis of legality but because her own interests demanded it. She was unprepared for war. Her people, moreover, disliked Austria and would not willingly fight on her side.

Within a month, Italy's foreign minister, Marchese Antonio Di San Giuliano, died. In November, 1914, Baron Sidney Sonnino became the new foreign minister, a post he came to hold for four years. The son of a wealthy Italian Jew and an English mother, Sonnino was a unique figure on the Italian political scene. People reacted strongly to him; most recognized his abilities, but some felt he was too withdrawn and taciturn. The German ambassador in Rome reputedly said of him, "In a country of chatterboxes I have to deal with the only man who does not speak!"

The belligerents now wooed Italy. Sonnino bargained with both sides, attempting to derive as much as possible for Italy. American diplomats in Rome, for example, reported that France, England, and Russia were secretly offering to cede parts of Austria to Italy if she would enter the war on the side of the *Entente*. Americans also wrote that Austria was trying to buy Italy's nonentanglement by offering her the Trentino, or Italian Tyrol. Finally, in December, 1914, Italy set down what she wanted, which was essentially *terre irredente,* the unredeemed lands that Austria had held since 1866. Although the Italians considered these demands as moderate, the Austrians scorned them as blackmail. Yet ultimately, in an effort to keep the Triple Alliance alive, the Austrians came close to meeting the Italian terms, but their concessions came too late.

The Allied powers viewed Italian bargaining in much the same way Austria did. They felt Italy had an inflated view of her value, but were willing to pay her price to bring her into the war, believing she had enough power to break the military stalemate that now characterized the conflict. Moreover, the Allies could more easily promise her Austrian territory than could the Central Powers. So Italy agreed to enter the war on the Allied side. The Allies outlined the terms in the secret Pact of London signed on April 26, 1915.

This treaty committed Italy to taking the field within a month. In Europe she would acquire territory inhabited by Italians that still remained under Austrian rule, mainly Trentino and Trieste, and enough land to give her a strategic frontier against Austria. The Allies also promised her territory in Dalmatia on the eastern shore of the Adriatic. If Turkey were partitioned, Italy would receive "a just share" of Turkish lands in the Mediterranean. If Britain and France took Germany's colonies in Africa, then Italy might "claim some adequate compensation," or colonial spoils.

Within a few days of its signing, journalists and others in Paris, London, and Vienna knew the pact's terms. One of these men, Henry Wickham Steed, the foreign editor of the *Times* of London, disliked the surrender of Serbian lands on the Adriatic to Italy. Knowing that Americans believed in the idea of national self-determination, he passed on his information to Walter Hines Page, the American ambassador in London, who forwarded it to Washington. The Allies had no love for the Pact of London; they felt Italy had exacted the highest price they could willingly pay. Sonnino's impersonal manner and Salandra's remark that Italy chose war on the grounds of *sacro egoismo* ("the sacred right of self-interest"), strengthened their unfavorable impression of Italian diplomacy which, ironically, was no worse than their own. By the standards of the time Italy's demands were not exorbitant. Sonnino and other Italian statesmen did not, for example, seek large-scale colonial spoils.

Italy denounced the Triple Alliance on May 3, 1915, and on May 23 declared war on Austria-Hungary. Although the Pact of London called for Italy to fight both of her former allies, she merely severed diplomatic relations with Germany. She declared war on Turkey in August, but took a whole year before acceding to Allied demands to declare war on Germany. Both Italy and Austria asked the United States to look after their diplomatic interests in the other's country.

Despite the bargain Sonnino struck, the intervention had no popular backing. For months, outside observers had reported on this attitude. "No where in Europe," E. J. Dillon, an English journalist in Milan wrote in February, 1915, "is there a people more averse to war than the subjects of Victor Emmanuel." A minority brought Italy into the conflict. Unwisely, the policy makers banked on a short war.

In making its decision for war, Salandra's government did not take the United States into consideration, though the previous Prime Minister, Giovanni Giolitti, had been interested in the course of American diplomacy. Sonnino did explain to Walter Hines Page that he wanted "to secure the liberation of unredeemed Italian territory and Italians, and secondly, to secure to Italy defensible frontiers." Italians were either indifferent to, or ignorant of, the American attitude toward the war. Sonnino knew little of the United States and made no effort to learn much about it. Benito Mussolini's newspaper, *Popolo d'Italia,* seemed to regard American opinion as leaning toward Germany. In January, one of its contributors, Giuseppe Prezzolini, wrote that Italians should not accept an American offer of earthquake relief because Italy should not be obligated to a nation which might become an enemy. In the following month, a report to that paper from the United States emphasized the strength of German-American opinion. Yet, even though he considered the United States hostile to the Allies, Mussolini urged intervention on their side.

Italy's leaders tried to build up public support by portraying the nation as engaged in a separate war alongside but on the margin of the main conflict, a status expressed in the phrase *la nostra guerra.* They assumed that in the stalemate of 1915 the weight of Italy's power would be enough to end the war. They were wrong; her intervention merely created a new static front from Switzerland to the Adriatic. This line of battle, much of it winding through the high Alps, turned out to be one of the most difficult in all Europe. There the Italian armies, poorly led and inadequately supported, fought under conditions of intense hardship; when they took one stronghold, it only led to another stronger one. At home Italians suffered from a social unrest, discontent, and disaffection that produced grumbling, protests, and riots.

Isolated from the main battle zones, Italy's front seemed hardly to affect the course of the war. Her position in world affairs had a similar status. Americans, for example, followed the conflict closely, but knew only vaguely of what was happening in Italy. Italian policy makers did little to overcome their country's isolation, or to influence American attitudes. Maintaining that they did not want neutrals poking into their affairs, they unwisely barred American newspapermen from their front. So American reporters picked up what information they could from behind the lines of combat and sent it home. Much of what they reported was erroneous, harmful, and even hostile to Italy. From the outset, as a result, Italian leaders forfeited the chance at least of making a favorable impression on American public opinion.

At first the most important effect of Italy's belligerency on relations with the United States centered on immigration; it cut off the flow of Italians to America. The immigrant tide had actually begun to reverse itself immediately following the war crisis. Between July, 1914, and December, 1915, for every 100 emigrants who left Italian ports, 412 returned to Italy. In 1915, some 90,000 immigrants in America returned to Italy to fight. Some returned fearfully. "I don't know why I am going to Italy," one young man said, "for I don't know Italy and do not speak its language, and my parents and friends are in America. . . ."

Italy's entrance into the war also aggravated an old problem in relations with the United States, that of dual citizenship. Italian law, unchanged in its essentials since 1863, held that any man born in Italy, even though he became an American citizen, still retained Italian nationality and was subject to service in the army. An amendment to the citizenship law in June, 1912, made the problem even more difficult. The revision stated that the foreign born son of an Italian would be considered an Italian subject and would be liable for military duty. Only when he attained his majority could he renounce his Italian allegiance.

The United States did not recognize dual citizenship. When naturalized Americans of Italian origin visited Italy and were forced into the army, the American government demanded their release. When the Italians inducted the sons of naturalized parents, it protested more vehemently. Although annoying, this matter of dual citizenship caused no deep injury to Italian-American relations. In comparison with its clashes with other belligerents, the United States had only minor problems with Italy.

While the United States was clashing with Germany, Italy continued her independent diplomacy. In April, 1917, in the agreement of St. Jean de Maurienne with England and France, subject to consent from Moscow which never came, Sonnino rounded out Italy's war aims. This agreement ratified the division of the Near East by the Allies and defined Italy's zone of interest there, roughly the southwestern third of Anatolia, including the port of Smyrna.

Earlier in that same month, the American declaration of war against Germany pleased many Italians. In Rome, some of them even marched to the American embassy in a rigged demonstration of sympathy; and D'Annunzio, at the request of an American officer, later celebrated the event with an ode, *All 'America in armi* (To America in arms). Others, not understanding why, greeted the American intervention with skepticism. Since the United States did not go to war against Austria, their major enemy, Italians saw in the intervention little of importance for them. For most Americans, Italy's role in the war, even though she had now become a military partner, still remained distant and minor. In their attitudes toward the war, the two countries had little in common. Thomas Nelson Page, the American ambassador in Rome, recognized this. "Ships go back and forth between Italy and America," he said at this time, "but there is no bridge over the waters upon which two peoples may walk and meet."

Late in May, mainly because Britain and France had done so, Italy sent a special mission to the United States. It did not accomplish much. Italy still remained on the periphery of American and Allied concerns. Even when the Allies worked out a unified command, it applied mainly to the French front and never did include Italy. As for the Italian masses, the outside event that aroused their enthusiasm far more than the American intervention was the Russian Revolution in November, 1917. To war-weary workers, the events in Russia were especially welcome because they offered hope for revolutionary change in their own situation in a time of despair. The news from Russia came on the heels of a great military setback.

In October, Austrian and German troops, in a well-planned surprise attack, broke through the Italian lines at Caporetto, a small town in the Alps; inflicted losses in killed, wounded, or missing of more than 300,000; captured 4,000 large-caliber guns and quantities of ammunition; destroyed Italy's Second Army; and for a time, threatened the entire front with collapse. This defeat achieved greater notoriety than comparable Russian, British, and French setbacks because it tended to confirm the low esteem in which Italian military ability was held by many. The bad effect also derived from Italy's emphasis on the separate nature of her war.

Repercussions from Caporetto affected American policy. Italian leaders had repeatedly urged President Woodrow Wilson to enlarge America's participation in the war by fighting Austria as well as Germany. Now Ambassador Thomas Nelson Page cabled Washington asking for a declaration of war against Austria, arguing that it would have a beneficial effect on Italian morale. Colonel Edward M. House, a political adviser then in Europe as the President's own representative, telegraphed Wilson that "the Italian situation is desperate," and discussed the Italian request with British and French leaders. Caporetto forced them to place a new importance on the Italian front. If Italy collapsed, then the Austrians and Germans could transfer troops to the French front and possibly achieve victory. The Allies, therefore, urged an American declaration of war against Austria which Congress voted on December 7, 1917. Wilson signed the declaration on the same day. This belated action against Italy's major enemy inspired spontaneous demonstrations throughout the peninsula. "It went," Page reported from Rome, "straight to the heart of the Italian people," producing "an extraordinary inspiriting effect."

The American action boosted not only Italian morale but also that of the other Allied peoples. For all of them, but especially for the Italians, 1917 had been a bad year. Like the revolution in Russia, the disaster at Caporetto reflected the exhaustion and despair of common people over the war. Unlike the Russians, the Italians did not turn against their government. Britain and France rushed troops to help the Italians hold their front; but Italy's own efforts, largely by holding off the enemy at the Piave River just north of Venice, sealed the gap made at Caporetto.

In the east, the front collapsed and Germany knocked Russia out of the war. All the major belligerents except Italy then concentrated their strength on the western front in France. Although 50,000 Italians fought in France, the front against Austria, except for the British and French divisions diverted there after Caporetto, remained an Italian concern. As before, the Allies considered it secondary in the larger strategy of the war. Americans shared this view. Although some of them may have believed that England and France were fighting to defend democracy, few saw Italy in this role. She seemed callously concerned only with her own interests, a view that Italian policy makers did little to dispel. Sonnino made no effort to gain American good will, or even to sway American public opinion. From the beginning, the British and the French, in an effort to show their cause in a favorable light, maintained propaganda missions in the United States. The Italians, who needed a good image even more than they, did little of this beyond sending an occasional army officer to tour American towns and universities spreading propaganda and acquainting people with Italy's part in the war.

After Caporetto, George Creel, the head of America's propaganda organization, the Committee on Public Information, sent a group of propagandists to Italy to help bolster morale there, but did not open an office in Rome until April, 1918. Under Captain Charles E. Merriam, a political scientist from the University of Chicago, these Americans tried to convince Italians that they were not isolated in the war, that they were friends and valued allies.

American actions did not fit the propaganda. When the United States got its troops to Europe, it rushed them to the French front. When Italians saw American soldiers land in large numbers in France, their leaders asked for some to reinforce their front. But the

United States turned aside the request, causing bitter disappointment. It sent only a token regiment of infantrymen to Italy, 10 per cent of whom were Italian-Americans, and it did not arrive until July, 1918. In the following month, Assistant Secretary of the Navy Franklin D. Roosevelt visited Italy, urging the people to renew their will to fight. In Rome, as arranged by Merriam in an effort to boost pro-American feeling, he spoke to Italian newspapermen. "I can tell you," Roosevelt announced reassuringly, "that fresh American troops will be sent to Italy, for henceforward the unity of our single front is as it should be, recognized as complete, solid, and indivisible." That promise, like others, was never kept. Italians saw American soldiers, but not as fighting men. The token regiment toured the country for purposes of propaganda, seeing action only in the last days of the war. American troops in Italy, including 1,200 ambulance men, never amounted to more than 6,000. They fought in one major battle, suffering 1 killed and 7 wounded.

Only a handful of other Americans saw action on the Italian front, mainly workers in the American Red Cross, part of a commission sent there even before Caporetto, military ambulance drivers such as those Ernest Hemingway described in *A Farewell to Arms*, and some army and navy aviators and cadets trained at the Italian Royal Flying School outside Foggia. Fiorello H. La Guardia served as an officer there and also traveled up and down the peninsula urging Italians to fight and assuring them of the American help that never came in the way desired. Yet Americans gave Italy assistance through various charitable organizations, especially the Italian War Relief Fund of America. American loans, shipping, and raw materials, along with those supplied by the British, also did much to keep Italy going.

If Italians were disillusioned by America's help, most Americans who thought at all about Italy's part in the war were disappointed in her contribution. Even though Italians fought well in the battles of the Piave and Vittorio Veneto, finally knocking Austria out of the war, Americans concluded that soldiering just did not fit the Italian character. This attitude affected the peacemaking, where American statesmen could not disregard Italy as they had during the war. From the beginning, Italian and American policy makers took differing positions on the nature of the peace settlement.

One difficulty grew out of the events of November, 1917, when the Russian front collapsed. At that time, the Soviet commissar for foreign affairs, Leon Trotsky, began publishing the texts of "secret treaties" the Bolsheviks had found in the official Russian files, among them the Pact of London, which they denounced as imperialistic. The Bolsheviks also appealed for peace on the basis of "no annexations or indemnities." Since Soviet propaganda appeared to be influencing liberal opinion everywhere, President Wilson issued a program for peace on January 8, 1918, that could counter the Bolshevik appeal, making the core of it a recital of Fourteen Points. Point Nine dealt with Italy, saying that "a readjustment of the frontiers of Italy should be effected along clearly recognizable lines of nationality." This point summarized the main theme of Wilson's war aims, the principle of national self-determination, a concept that conflicted with Italy's war aims as embodied in the Pact of London.

Although pleased with the Fourteen Points as counterpropaganda against the Bolsheviks, Italian statesmen were openly skeptical about the practical application of Wilson's principles. Some Italians telegraphed the White House in protest. They objected to Wilson's emphasis on nationality as the basis for establishing new frontiers in Europe, saying that if that principle were applied to Italy's northern frontier she would be unable to defend herself against future Austrian aggression. Some criticized the President's effort to solve specifically European problems on his own, and objected to his tampering with Italy's objectives without, it seemed, understanding her needs. Most of all, they were disappointed over the slight attention he gave to Italy's desires. Regardless of the Italian reaction, the Fourteen Points, with additions, became Allied war aims. In September, 1918, as a result, the German and Austrian governments appealed directly to Wilson for peace on the basis of those points, a move Italians viewed with suspicion. Wilson then sent Colonel House to Europe to gain Allied approval of his peace program. During October, House talked to the various Allied leaders.

Well aware of the inconsistency between the Fourteen Points and their Pact of London, the Italians in their conversations with House tried to protect their interests, mainly by introducing a reservation to Point Nine that would safeguard their territorial aspirations in the north and in the Adriatic. At this juncture the isolated nature of Italy's war placed her at a disadvantage in the rapidly moving diplomacy. Italy considered Austria-Hungary the main enemy, but the other Allies looked on Germany as virtually the only enemy. Since Austria-Hungary was falling apart and Germany still seemed strong, Germany more than ever dominated Allied thinking as the sole enemy. House therefore brushed aside the Italian reservation, saying that Point Nine did not bear on the conditions of the German armistice. As far as Italian aspirations were concerned, Italy's new prime minister, Vittorio Emanuele Orlando, at this time may have made a tactical error. Going along with House, he did not insist upon American public recognition of Italy's reservation to Point Nine, and House did not inform Wilson of the reservation.

Finally, the Allied nations accepted the Fourteen Points as the basis for peace with only two publicized exceptions, one British and one French. So as peace approached, Italy's commitment to the Fourteen Points was ambiguous.

During the armistice maneuvering, the Allied armies maintained their pressure against the enemy, and Austria's Habsburg empire disintegrated. Desperately anxious to stop the fighting and unable to wait for Wilson's peacemaking, Austria-Hungary negotiated directly with Italy. Representing the Allied powers, Italy signed an armistice with Austria on November 3, 1918, at Villa Giusti, near Padua. The Austrian surrender, as a result, was not based on the Fourteen Points. Germany signed an armistice eight days later, and with regard to Germany, except for Orlando's weak reservation to Point Nine, Italy officially bound herself to the Fourteen Points.

For Italy, costs of the war were high. Her dead counted more than 600,000, about two-thirds as many as the British dead and approximately two-fifths as many as the French. Italian soil suffered devastation, but much less than had the French lands. Italy also spent less on the war than did Britain or France. But Italy's poverty and meager resources made her losses less bearable than those of her wealthier allies. So Italy, drained of resources she could not afford to lose, faced a difficult readjustment to the ways of peace. These difficulties became evident at the peace conference scheduled to open in Paris on January 18, 1919.

Two weeks before the opening, Wilson visited Italy for four days. Everywhere, in Rome, Genoa, Milan, and Turin, crowds greeted him with affection and enthusiasm. In Milan, newspapers reported, "the balconies, roofs, and every vantage point were black with people" and his route through the city "was plastered" with pictures and posters of him and "quotations from his speeches which could be applied to Italy's position." The people cheered him as though he were a savior, "the American Saint" who would bring lasting peace to the world; they showered him with flowers. The warmth of the Italians toward him gave Wilson the impression that he represented the aspirations of the masses more than did their own government. He responded emotionally to their cheers. At times, as in Milan, he threw kisses to the crowds with both hands. Putting aside old prejudices, he spoke admiringly of Italian immigrants in the United States. "I have rejoiced personally," he said in Rome, "in the partnership of the Italian and American peoples" in an enterprise dedicated to liberty.

Wilson left for Paris on January 6, mistakenly taking Italian good will toward the United States as representing solid support for his ideas on peacemaking. During his visit, he had not reached any understanding with top Italian policy makers over their peace objectives, especially those in conflict with his own. Italy's two chief negotiators at Paris, Orlando and Sonnino, on the other hand, had done nothing to avoid a clash with Wilson. Orlando, an amiable lawyer from Sicily, had a tendency to conciliate and even to avoid hard decisions. But Sonnino was no compromiser. Even though the Italian ambassador in Washington, Count Vincenzo Macchi di Cellere, had for about a year sent him dispatches on Wilson's views with respect to Italy's claims in the Adriatic, Sonnino felt that Wilson would give in to his point of view. Sonnino also realized that the President's "tenets" would make the peace negotiations complicated.

Sonnino's atitude reflected the outlook of the other Italian delegates. They went to Paris divided in outlook but confident that the Allied leaders would recognize Italy's wartime sacrifices by satisfying her territorial aspirations. Instead, in the peacemaking they found Italy as isolated as she had been during the war. Without powerful friends, the Italians operated on the periphery of the chief topics of discussion. This continuing isolation grew out of Italy's own weakness and accidentally out of the way the leaders of the great powers, or the "Big Four," conducted business at the peace conference. Neither Wilson nor the British Prime Minister, David Lloyd George, could speak French well, whereas Georges Clemenceau, France's premier, had a good command of English. As a result, much of the discussion went on in English. Orlando knew French and no English, but Sonnino spoke English with "a perfect Oxford accent." Even though one of the Big Four at the conference, Orlando had less influence than the other statesmen; he seemed excluded from important issues, particularly because most of them dealt with Germany. On these German matters, he deferred to the decisions of his colleagues.

Before the conference began, even before Wilson's visit to Italy, Italian diplomats had informed the Department of State of their claims on the Adriatic and elsewhere and had discussed them with members of the American peace commission. Exalted by their final victories, the Italians had decided to bring all Italy behind secure frontiers and to expand as permitted in the Pact of London. Wilson quickly conceded Italy's claim to Trentino, up to the Brenner Pass. Even though this boundary, by placing about 200,000 Austrians of German blood under Italian rule, violated the principle of self-determination, he did not balk. Here, he said, the demands of strategy exceeded those of nationality; Italy should have a defensible northern frontier. He also agreed that she should have three of the keys to the Adriatic: the ports of Pola, Valona, and Lissa. Arguing that the dissolution of Austria-Hungary had changed the situation envisaged by the treaty-makers at London, Italian nationalists wanted more, particularly the port city of Fiume. They desired Fiume in order to give Italy unchallengeable economic domination of the Adriatic.

Wilson's advisers, many of them scholars but not experts on Italy's difficult problems, studied her claims. Although divided in their views, the academics, on January 21, submitted a majority report. It denied Italy's right to Dalmatia, to a number of islands she claimed off that coast, and to Fiume. Taking into account nationality, strategic, economic, and political factors, the academic advisers traced a frontier for Italy running from Switzerland eastward down to its farthest point on the eastern shore of the Adriatic and urged the President not to yield territory beyond it. Since Wilson accepted this advice, making it the basic American position, that frontier became known as the "American" or "Wilson" line. Some of his other advisers, such as Colonel House, disagreed with the majority experts, arguing that he needed Italy's support for his League of Nations. These political advisers, feeling that Italy should be treated with the dignity due a great power, urged concessions.

On March 15, 1919, the very day Wilson returned to Paris after spending several weeks in the United States, Orlando conferred with him and put forward Italy's claim to Fiume. Wilson replied that before acting he must consult his experts who, as the historian Lawrence E. Gelfand has pointed out, differed on Fiume. Three days later, and again in the middle of April, the majority experts and several members of the peace commission reiterated that Fiume and all Dalmatia should go to the new state of Yugoslavia.

The Supreme Council, or Big Four, did not itself take up Italy's claims until April. Then those demands became the outstanding issue of the conference, sparking hostility between the American and Italian delegates. Even though England and France were willing to stand by their commitments, Wilson refused even to recognize the Pact of London. Following the advice of his academic experts, he opposed

Italy's claims to Dalmatia. No one blocked the claims of the other Allied powers based on similar secret arrangements, but he made himself the main obstacle to territorial rewards the Allies had promised Italy. As the chief figure at the conference and head of the most powerful nation there, Wilson was a formidable opponent. Orlando, therefore, tried to work out what he considered a compromise. He indicated willingness to give up claims under the Pact of London to the extent of yielding on the northern half of Dalmatia. In return he asked for Fiume, which had been promised to Croatia, now a part of Yugoslavia. In December, Italian troops as part of an Allied force, to the consternation of American statesmen, had occupied Fiume; and Italian public opinion, aroused by nationalist agitation, demanded retention of the city.

Fiume, which since 1868 had had the special status of a free city under the Hungarian crown, held a mixture of Italian and Slavic peoples in the ratio of about 2 Italians to 1 Slav. But its suburb of Susak contained mostly Slavs. Taken as a whole, the urban agglomeration of some 50,000 people divided itself about equally between Italian and Slavic elements. The surrounding countryside was solidly Slav. On much of the Dalmatian coast, the Italian element was dominant culturally as it had been for a long time, owing to urban concentration of Italians and to tradition descended from the days of Venetian supremacy. Italian had been the language of the Austro-Hungarian navy. The frontier promised Italy in the Pact of London included the whole Istrian peninsula, reaching the Adriatic at the head of the gulf of Fiume, within a few miles of the city. The Allies had not offered Fiume to Italy because it was the chief port of Croatia and of Hungary proper.

Orlando presented the case for Fiume in terms of self-determination, an illogical approach, for it was a mere island of Italian population. This tactic antagonized Wilson, as did the argument that the city had become a necessity of domestic politics. He realized that Fiume was a political issue because the Italian government had fostered the agitation for it. If Italy could apply the principle of self-determination to Fiume apart from the Slav countryside, then Wilson felt, she could just as well use it in Trentino with its Germans. The Italians demanded the terms of the Pact of London, partly on the strength of respect for treaty obligations, and Fiume on the basis of self-determination. Orlando did not seem upset by the inconsistencies in the case; he wanted to bargain and reach a politically acceptable compromise.

Wilson held firmly to self-determination, viewing the Italian position as part of a contest between right and wrong, with the Italians wrong and himself right. He told Orlando that Italy should make peace with Austria on the same principles as those applied to Germany, but Orlando reminded him that Italy was not bound by the Fourteen Points in the Austrian settlement. Yet Wilson argued wisely, saying that the annexation of Fiume would create a "fatal error of making Italy's neighbors on the east her enemies." This argument changed no one's mind. Wilson then offered to go along with the idea of Fiume as an international free port, but stood fast against annexation. Ethically, he was right. Nonetheless, the Italians felt they were being singled out for the strict enforcement of dubious justice mainly because they were weaker than the other major Allies. "Why does he," the historian Gaetano Salvemini wrote, "want to impose what he considers absolute justice on the Italian people alone?" Wilson made concessions to Lloyd George and Clemenceau that violated asserted principles.

At times, discussions between Wilson and the Italians got so heated that they communicated through Lloyd George and Clemenceau. Rumors floated through the corridors that Wilson would not sign the peace treaty if Italy got her way. Finally he decided to cut through the tangle of controversy, resorting to a device he had threatened to use against Britain and France on other tense occasions. On the evening of April 23, 1919, the President issued a statement rejecting the terms of the Pact of London and denouncing Italy's stand on Fiume. He also assured Italians that "America is Italy's friend. She is linked in blood and affection with the Italian people. Such ties can never be broken." He thought the Italian people would see his point and force Orlando and Sonnino to give way. Wilson guessed wrongly. His outburst created a sensation, but settled nothing. Orlando replied immediately with a defense of Italy's position. "This great free nation" he said, would not submit to the offensive views of a foreign leader. Then he, along with his delegation, went home to consult the legislature and through it seek a verdict from the people who greeted him as a hero.

The Italian legislators viewed Wilson's appeal as an attempt to tamper with their domestic politics. Newspapers throughout Italy attacked Wilson, and troops guarded the American embassy in Rome, but anti-American feeling did not sweep the country. Italians seemed more hurt than angry. Since the Italian government came from the Chamber of Deputies and the people elected the deputies, Wilson had challenged its authority in representing the people's views. On that issue the Chamber had little choice; it had to assert its own power by giving the government a vote of confidence.

With both sides taking public positions, the Italian and American leaders found themselves unable to retreat or to compromise. Neither the torrent of nationalist emotion nor the threat that Italy might fall prey to bolshevism if her aspirations were not met made any obvious impression on Wilson. He also turned aside the plea of the American ambassador in Rome, who pointed out that "the friendship between the United States and Italy is profoundly imperiled." The withdrawal of the Italians from the conference, therefore, failed to bring them any concessions.

Although bitter, Italian leaders quickly realized that Italy could not afford to cut herself off from the United States for the sake of Fiume. She needed American credit and loans. The American government, moreover, did exert economic pressure, holding back a loan of $50 million that Italy desired. Wilson himself took the attitude that "if they [the Italians] did not come back they would be out of it altogether." After several days, the Italian delegates decided that they stood to lose more by protesting from Rome than by arguing in Paris. On May 6, Orlando and Sonnino returned to the conference with nothing to show for their absence and with their position weaker than it had been before their departure. They searched in vain for a compromise.

Unwilling to cross Wilson on an issue that could bring no benefit to them, the British and French did nothing to comfort the Italians. Their attitude came out clearly in response to Italian moves in the Near East. On April 29, on the pretense of maintaining order, Italy landed troops at Adalia in Turkey; she sent a warship to Fiume and a naval squadron to Smyrna, Turkey. The Supreme Council discussed the problem, and Wilson suggested that the Big Three send ships of their own to the two ports. They agreed. The United States ordered the battleship *Arizona* and a squadron of destroyers to Smyrna and destroyers to Fiume. The British and French also sent warships to watch the Italians. Later the Council received news that the Italians were landing fresh troops and expanding their zone of occupation in southern Anatolia. Wilson then permitted the Greeks to land an army at Smyrna, which they did on May 14, to forestall the Italians, who seemed to be preparing to put troops ashore there. Even though the Allies had earlier apportioned Smyrna and Adalia to Italy, the Greeks now became the spearhead of Allied policy in Turkey.

The Big Three's opposition to Italian claims was also evident in the distribution of the former German colonies. While the Italian delegates were still gone from the conference, the Big Three decided to parcel out colonies. As punishment for Italy's walkout, they disregarded her modest claims to enemy colonies such as Togoland, or compensatory territory under the Pact of London from French and British possessions in Africa. While the Big Three gave themselves, and others, former German colonies and Turkish territory, Italy got practically nothing, merely a ratification of Libya's frontiers. This punitive action of their wartime allies further embittered the Italians, but Orlando only mildly protested Italy's exclusion from the colonies and mandates.

At the time, Italians did not realize that their failure to obtain colonies was actually a blessing. Colonies seldom brought profit; usually they were liabilities. Yet every country aspiring to greatness seemed to need colonies or suffer humiliation, and Italy, reaching beyond her means, was especially sensitive on this issue. "How could statesmen, when distributing colonial mandates," an Italian diplomat, Dino Grandi, asked in later years, "have seen fit to entrust these to Great Britain, France, Japan, Belgium, South Africa, New Zealand and Australia—and none to Italy?" Why, Grandi asked, "should Italy, who had been a loyal member of the victorious alliance in the war, have deliberately been thwarted and made discontented?"

On June 19, as a result of his failure to achieve more at Paris, Orlando's cabinet fell. Francesco Nitti replaced him as Prime Minister, and Tommaso Tittoni took over from Sonnino as Foreign Minister. Nitti was anxious to get along with the Americans, recognizing that they had the means of providing Italy with the food, coal, and loans she needed. He considered the question of Fiume secondary to Italy's economic needs and to friendship with the United States. Yet the break over Fiume remained unhealed. On June 28, 1919, the peacemakers, despite their differences, signed the Treaty of Versailles, an event that inspired no celebration in Italy, and then Wilson returned to the United States. There he found that his opposition to Italy's claims on the Adriatic had embittered Italian-Americans. Although less influential than other ethnic groups, the Italian element in the United States was just beginning to become vocal politically. Politicians, particularly in the big eastern cities, could no longer easily ignore it.

During the war, the Italian press in America had pointed with pride to Italy's contribution, to the estimated 300,000 Italian-Ameri-

cans who fought in the American armies, and to some 20,000 who
had given their lives as soldiers under the Stars-and-Stripes. Italian-
Americans responded enthusiastically to Liberty Bond drives, and no
other group of immigrants exceeded them in their admiration for Wilson. When he declared May 24, 1918, "Italian Day," Italian-Americans everywhere saluted him as the "great champion of Liberty." They
endorsed his peace program and expected him to accept Italy's claims
at the Paris conference.

Virtually the entire Italian-American community also supported
Italy's demand for Fiume. So did most of the American press.
Italian-American societies, newspapers, and others all exerted what-
ever pressure they could on politicians, on the American delegation at
Paris, and on the President himself, urging them to come out openly
for *Fiume Italiana.* In New York's legislature, for example, Senator
Salvatore Cotillo introduced a resolution asking "Wilson . . . to sup-
port Italy's claims to Fiume and Dalmatia."

The first sign of trouble between Wilson and the Italian-Americans
showed up late in February, 1919, when the President landed at Boston for a brief stay in the United States to attend to pressing domestic
duties before returning to Paris. At the time he spoke glowingly of the
new Yugoslavia's aspirations but said nothing about Italy's claims.
The *Gazzetta del Massachusetts* quickly noted this omission and, as
though speaking for all Italian-Americans, declared, "We are disappointed, Mr. President." Deep disenchantment came with Wilson's
appeal over the heads of the Italian peace delegation. Then the
Italian-Americans, who had previously shown little political solidarity, turned against him. But among other Americans, support for
Italy's position at Paris declined, blunting the effect of Italian-
American pressure. In May, nonetheless, this pressure led the Massachusetts legislature, with only one dissenting vote, to adopt a resolution asking Wilson to back Italy's position.

La Guardia, now president of New York City's Board of Alder-
men, claimed that Fiume was "Italian in spirit, blood, language, and
in every way." He organized a nationwide opposition to Wilson and
to the Treaty of Versailles. "Any Italo-American who votes the
Democratic ticket this year," this Republican would tell ghetto audiences, "is an Austrian bastard." Elsewhere angry Italian-American
editors stressed Wilson's old prejudice against Italians, reprinting the
passage denigrating Italians from his *History of the American People*
as evidence.

Isolationist enemies of the League of Nations moved quickly to take advantage of the Italian-American disenchantment with Wilson. Men such as Henry Cabot Lodge, who had a large Italian-American constituency, now became champions of *Fiume Italiana*. He told the Italians of Boston that Italy should have control of the Adriatic and that she could regard Fiume as the Founding Fathers had looked on New Orleans, a city essential to the well being of the United States. Forgetting Lodge's villification for more than twenty years against Italians and other new immigrants, many of the Italian-American community supported his position on the League and opposed Wilson's. In September, 1919, while on a western tour to arouse support for the League, Wilson stuck to his position on Fiume, arguing that if Italians were going "to claim every place where there was a large Italian population, we would have to cede New York to them, because there are more Italians in New York than any Italian city." This attitude further embittered Italian-Americans.

In Italy, Nitti pleaded for closer economic ties with the United States. In April, 1919, the American government had extended a credit of $25 million, but he wanted more help to recoup Italy's wartime losses. Americans, he felt, could guide Italy in developing her own resources. So he sought American assistance in acquiring territory in the Near East where Italy could obtain raw materials. Tittoni, meanwhile, carried on the weary negotiations for Fiume. Secretary of State Robert Lansing pointed out that Wilson would not yield because, among other reasons, he felt the Yugoslavs "should have a seaport on the Adriatic sufficient for their needs and that Italy should not control the approaches to that port." Early in September, Wilson told Nitti "that it would be as harmful to Italy herself as it would be to peace . . . to make settlements in the Adriatic which could not be squared with the principles elsewhere applied."

Fiume now became the scene of considerable agitation; critics accused the Italian occupiers of trying to Italianize the city. In August, a commission charged with investigating clashes there between Italians and others recommended that the Allies move in with an American and British police force and maintain public order. Since the United States refused to become involved, the British made arrangements to take control from the Italian force there. At this point, on September 3, 1919, Nitti again pleaded with Wilson to give way on Fiume and thereby prevent revolution in Italy. "I have searched my heart and conscience," the President replied, "and have always been forced to the conclusion that I could not acquiesce in the extension of Italian sovereignty to Fiume"; it would "precipitate war in the Balkans." Wilson then instructed the *chargé* in Rome to ignore the pressure from the Italian government. "It is all part of a desperate endeavor to get me to yield to claims which, if allowed, would destroy the peace of Europe," he explained. "You cannot make the impression too definite and final that I cannot and will not yield; that they must work out their crisis for themselves." Two days later, while speaking in Pueblo, Colorado, in support of the League of Nations, the President collapsed and later suffered a paralyzing stroke that left him bedridden.

Nitti and Tittoni then appealed to Lansing to save Italy from civil strife by yielding on Fiume. "I may not be able much longer to maintain order," Nitti wrote. The responsibility for the revolution, he added, "will rest entirely with the President." Others, too, such as Clemenceau, felt that the issue of Fiume would topple Nitti's government; then chaos would engulf Italy. Lansing rejected the Italian entreaties. The Treaty of St. Germain of September 10, whereby Italy made peace with Austria, therefore, left Italy's claims on the Adriatic unsettled.

Two days later, before the British force moved in, Gabriele D'Annunzio led a private army made up of about 1,000 volunteers and some regular soldiers wearing black shirts into Fiume. Taking possession of the city in the name of Italy, he made himself dictator. No one stopped him; the commander of the Italian forces of occupation even wished him well; Italians everywhere applauded D'Annunzio's violent seizure. Italian-Americans praised him and even raised a million lire in support of his regime. His coup, or rather its condemnation by Wilson, reinvigorated Italian-American animosity toward the President.

Infuriated by D'Annunzio's action, Wilson, on November 13, wrote directly to Nitti. "Any solution of the problem of Fiume at variance with the one I have advocated," the President said, "would run counter to the foreign policy which I have pursued." At the end of the month, the impasse over Fiume forced Tittoni to resign. Vittorio Scialoja now became Italy's Foreign Minister.

A few months later, in February, 1920, Wilson threatened to abandon the peace structure erected at Paris if the Italians did not give way in their demands. He insisted on retaining a power of veto on the issue of Fiume. Later in the month he yielded somewhat, suggesting direct negotiations between Italy and Yugoslavia to resolve the dispute. They accepted the suggestion and worked toward a settlement. D'Annunzio's rule, which lasted slightly more than fifteen months, spurred the negotiators. Finally, in November, 1920, the Italian-Yugoslav negotiations led to the signing of the Treaty of Rapallo. It gave Italy the frontier promised in the Pact of London, slightly modified, from Austria to the Adriatic, the town of Zara, and some islands off the coast of Dalmatia. In comparison with Italy's demands, these were small compensations, for she renounced any other claims to the Dalmatian mainland. As for Fiume, the treaty made it (but not its Slavic outskirts) a free state with a strip of coast connecting it to Italy. A short time later, D'Annunzio left the city.

To the last, Wilson blocked Italian aims in the Adriatic, but in doing so he bore no animosity toward Italy as a nation. By holding fast to his convictions, he thought he was promoting the interests of Italy as well as those of peace. Italians viewed Wilson's stand differently. Regardless of how others looked at it, to them Italy's contribution to the war seemed important, and they expected rewards for it. When the benefits did not come, many felt frustrated. They resented Wilson's favors to Yugoslavia, part of a recent and bitter enemy state. So Italy emerged from the peacemaking not with the pride of a victorious nation but with a sense of grievance. The Allies and Wilson, Gaetano Salvemini wrote, "after conquering Germany in war, . . . conquered Italy in peace."

Out of this bitter feeling arose the myth of a "mutilated victory" —that Wilson and the others at Paris had denied Italy what she had wrenched from Austria at great sacrifice. This idea had its roots more in an exaggerated nationalism than in reality. In the destruction of Austria-Hungary, Italy had achieved an important long-range objective: the removal of a powerful, hostile neighbor from her eastern frontier. Victory had brought her an immeasurable profit, the chance to live in unaccustomed security. In ignoring this benefit and in reaching out for Fiume, the Italian leaders blundered. Yet they could point to inconsistencies in the American position. Wilson had accommodated himself to the claims of the British, French, and others even when their demands conflicted with self-determination. He seemed most intractable when dealing with the less influential Italians. As Sonnino quipped, "he provoked among Italians the impression that he wanted to retrieve his virginity at our expense."

In the clash of wills, the Italians did not have the power to force the Americans to accept their demands or even to compromise. Yet even those Italians who shared Wilson's ideals felt he had treated Italy unfairly mainly because she was the weakest of the great powers. Whether or not justified, this bitterness hurt Italy more than it did the

United States. She required American economic assistance, both for long-range reconstruction and immediately for basic commodities such as food, clothing, and shelter. She needed American friendship, not hostility.

Wilson did not emerge unscathed from the struggle over Fiume. In the election of 1920, his attitude drove thousands of Italians into the camp of Warren G. Harding. In New Jersey, for example, Republicans asked Italian voters to "choose between the Democratic party with Wilson and the Republican party with D'Annunzio." As New York's *Bolletino della sera* explained it, many such voters turned Republican simply to "rebuff the insults to Italy of Woodrow Wilson." The Democratic candidate, James M. Cox, did not help matters much with the Italian-Americans. Instead of trying to reach them, he denounced the great "racial alignment" behind Harding, part of it being "the Italian party whose members place a futile Italian imperialism over the interests of our nation." Nor did his running mate, Franklin D. Roosevelt, do much better; he called Italian-Americans "fifty-fifty citizens." These citizens joined disgruntled Irish and German voters and later claimed a share in the Democratic defeat. They may have exaggerated their influence, but a study of voting patterns showed that in centers of Italian-American population, Democratic votes declined.

After Wilson left the White House, Italy attained her foremost Adriatic objective. In a treaty signed in 1924, Yugoslavia recognized Fiume as belonging to Italy in return for a fifty-year lease on part of its harbor and the harbor at Port Barros. This victory, coming after the long quarrel with the United States, seemed hollow. As G. A. Borgese, an Italian Liberal, pointed out, the United States, not Fiume, had what Italy needed and what really counted—the means of assuring a form of collective security and economic growth. As a province, Fiume contained little of economic and strategic value for Italy. The territory was not worth the rift that damaged the first real partnership that Italy, for a short time during the war, had enjoyed with the United States.

Restriction

9

Within the United States, the coming of the First World War stimulated an awesome revival of nationalism. Fearing divided loyalties among immigrants, such as Italian-Americans, nationalists attacked the foreign born, or what they called "hyphenated Americans." Nativists demanded a unified nation where people would conform to their notions of what Americanism should be. Americanization of the immigrant, as well as restriction of immigration, became a popular cause. These superpatriots wanted to compel foreigners to master the English language, to take out citizenship papers, and to conform in dress, manners, and mode of living to the standard set by native Americans. "We ought," these nationalists announced, "to get the immigrants into our evening schools and teach them American ideals."

At this time, the patriots were particularly suspicious of German- and Irish-Americans. But the uncompromising spirit of conformity also struck with special force at the Italian-Americans because as a group they were considered slow in assimilating. Even at best the Italian immigrant could not shed his old country ways as rapidly as the Americanizers demanded. So, as the war hysteria mounted and the intensified nationalism made the naturalized American an issue in national politics, the Italians suffered. Many understood the threat: either to give up their separateness or stand condemned to live as outsiders.

Speaking to the Knights of Columbus in New York's Carnegie Hall in October, 1915, an audience that included Italian-Americans, former President Theodore Roosevelt, for example, took a harsh stand. "There is no room in this country for hyphenated Americans," he said. "There is no such thing as a hyphenated American who is a good American." In the same year, President Woodrow Wilson also expressed distaste for the "hyphenates" "who have poured the poison of disloyalty into the very arteries of our national life. . . ." In his view "such creatures of passion, disloyalty, and anarchy must be crushed out."

Despite this attitude and his earlier dislike of Italians and other immigrants, Wilson opposed enactment into law of a literacy test for immigrants. In the election campaign of 1912, he had tried to explain away the remarks he had permitted himself to make in his history of the United States, and in 1914 he said he would veto a proposed immigration bill unless its sponsors omitted its literacy clause. To conciliate the Italian government, he also forced the softening of a clause requiring medical doctors on board emigrant ships. In January of the following year, when a literacy bill came before him he vetoed it. Two years later, Wilson vetoed another immigration bill with a literacy clause, saying it "would operate in most cases merely as a penalty for lack of opportunity in the country from which the alien seeking admission came."

Despite the President's argument, Congress enacted the bill into law over his veto. This act of 1917 prohibited the admission of adult aliens into the United States who failed to pass a simple reading test in English or some other language. As intended by its sponsors, the new law affected southern Italians more than any other important immigrant group; it barred thousands of them who wanted to come. It also convinced numerous *contadini* of the value of education. They thronged into country schools so that they could learn to read and write well enough to secure admission to the United States.

In December, 1917, Congress adopted another measure that had Italians as one of its main targets and opponents: an amendment to the Constitution prohibiting the manufacture, sale, or transportation of alcoholic beverages. In January, 1919, after the requisite number of states had approved, it became law as the Eighteenth Amendment, going into operation a year later. The "drys," mostly Anglo-Saxon and Protestant, identified their crusade for prohibition with the preservation of the American way of life. So the wine-drinking Italians who dared to oppose the law found themselves once again denounced as un-American. They came to regard prohibition as a class law, an unfair restriction they could justifiably evade. Jo Pagano, in the novel *The Paesanos*, caught the Italian attitude. "By God, what a country!" the father of a family said. "Make a goddam criminal out of you joost to take a glass of good healthy wine!"

Italians also suffered because wartime nationalism gave impetus to racism, especially to a "Nordic cult," viciously manifested in the revival of the Ku Klux Klan. The new Klan, founded in 1915 near Atlanta, stood for native, white, Protestant supremacy. It opposed foreigners, as well as Negroes, Catholics, and Jews, and equated Nordic "superiority" with "real patriotism and true Americanism." Tradesmen, small businessmen, and many middle-class Americans became convinced that foreigners and Catholics menaced American institutions. Nativists and intellectual racists such as Madison Grant and Lothrop Stoddard sounded the alarm against eastern and southern Europeans who were "storming the Nordic ramparts of the United States and mongrelizing the good old American stock." In his widely read volume, *The Passing of the Great Race,* Grant explained the alleged inferiority of Italians by claiming that the ancient Romans had died out as a race leaving their slaves as survivors. Immigrants, such as the Italians, even though they might try, could hardly escape the impact of a stepped-up Americanization movement. Even social workers adopted the condescension of the Americanizers, an attitude that came out clearly in one of their reports. "Not yet Americanized; still eating Italian food," it said. Many Italians, as a result, became sensitive to their own peculiarities and decided to resist any forcible efforts to change them. "Americanization," an Italian-American editor wrote, "is an ugly word."

This attitude infuriated the nativists, who became more determined to cut off immigration. When the war ended, they gained wider support, mainly from the disillusioned who wanted to turn their backs on Europe's problems and return to isolationism. Alarmists predicted that 25 million foreigners, many of them destitute, would rush to America's shore. Fearing that these aliens would lower the standard of living, organizations such as the American Legion, the American Federation of Labor, and the National Grange, as well as countless individual Americans, came out for exclusion.

The Literacy Test law was not proving as effective as restrictionists had assumed it would be. To their astonishment, many of the newcomers proved capable of learning English, reading and writing the language as well as speaking it. Also, a fear of Bolshevism disturbed many Americans in the immediate post-war period; in their opinion, the republic needed protection from "Reds," "foreigners," and "hyphenates" who carped at the established order. This sentiment had led Congress, in October, 1918, to pass as a war measure a law excluding alien anarchists and others who advocated the overthrow of the government. In May, 1920, it enacted another law that provided for the deportation of enemy aliens and anarchists. Ironically, Anthony Caminetti, the first Italian-American elected to Congress, a California restrictionist whom Wilson had made Commissioner General of Immigration to placate immigrants, directed the carrying out of the repressive measures.

Wilson's Attorney General, A. Mitchell Palmer, made extensive use of these laws in the early twenties. During this "Red Scare," he and other superpatriots regarded almost anyone of foreign origin with suspicion. Their crusade against the genuine Reds also became a drive for Americanization of immigrants and for conformity to a bigoted standard of "one hundred per cent Americanism." The Red Scare brought misery and humiliation to all immigrants, but especially to Italians and Jews, for the German- and Irish Americans no longer bore the brunt of the antiforiegn hysteria. The laws against anarchists, for example, although directed against all aliens, struck Italians with special severity. For a time in the 1890's, exiled radicals made Paterson, New Jersey, the center of the Italian anarchist movement. One of these Paterson anarchists, Gaetano Bresci, a silk worker, returned to Italy. In July, 1900, he assassinated King Umberto I. Such violence had contributed to the popular fear of Italian radicals.

Nowhere did the prejudice against Red agitators, Italians, Jews, and other immigrants seem greater than around Brockton, Massachusetts. For years the people in this area had been reading in their newspapers that the newcomers were the scum of Europe. When a citizen smelled garlic on a man's breath, observers reported, he usually walked by quickly for fear of being knifed. In the wake of the Red Scare, some fearful citizens became convinced that foreigners were plotting to revolutionize the country as the Bolsheviks had done to Russia.

A series of holdups and burglaries added to the atmosphere of suspicion. One of the ugliest of these crimes was committed on the afternoon of April 15, 1920, in South Braintree, an industrial town twelve miles south of Boston. Two dark, squat men, who had been loitering in the center of town, shot the paymaster of a shoe manufacturing company and his guard and escaped in a touring car, firing their guns as it careened out of sight. The murderers got away with more than $15,000 in cash. The police could unearth no clue to the identity of the bandits, but according to rumors, they were Italian. On the evening of May 5, in a streetcar in Brockton, the police arrested Nicola Sacco, an immigrant born in the mountains of Puglia, the "heel" of Italy, and Bartolomeo Vanzetti, another alien who had been born in the north, in the remote village of Villa Faletto in Piedmont. Both acted suspiciously; both were armed; both were draft dodgers; both were anarchists; both had reputations as radicals, and both were active in Italian working-class organizations. At the time, Sacco was working in the Three K's Shoe Factory, and Vanzetti earned his living as a fish peddler, selling mainly to Italian and Portuguese families.

Deep emotions over the crime, intense antiforeignism, fear of radicalism, and prejudice against Italians all came to focus on Sacco and Vanzetti. They were "wops" who could barely speak more than pidgin English, the nativists pointed out, anarchists who did not believe in God, slackers and agitators, charged with a brutal crime. But they were not ordinary peasants; they could think, read, and write. Vanzetti, a philosophical anarchist, had read works of philosophers and revolutionaries such as St. Augustine, Karl Marx, Peter Kropotkin, Leo Tolstoy, Enrico Malatesta, and Ernest Renan. Philosophical anarchists ordinarily would not act violently to carry out their doctrines, but the public lumped all anarchists together as foul-smelling foreigners who carried bombs, as implacable malcontents waiting only for the opportunity to destroy the society that had welcomed them. Sacco's mind did not range as widely as did Vanzetti's. He read little beyond the daily paper and anarchist tracts, preferring to spend whatever free time he had working in his vegetable garden.

Anarchism had no widespread following among Italians in the United States, but it appealed to a small number of sensitive immigrants who resented the humiliation they were forced to endure and seemed unable to do anything about. As in any oppressed group, there were a few terrorists, but they had little influence. In general, Italian immigrants were too concerned with gaining a stake in society and too much awed by authority to become doctrinaire terrorists. Nonetheless, established citizens in the Brockton area suspected a Boston Italian club, called the Italian Naturalization Society, of sheltering subversives. Workingmen from the nearby industrial towns used to meet there to play *boccie,* a game similar to lawn bowling, and to discuss common problems. The group included a sprinkling of anarchists, syndicalists, socialists, and other leftists who had been stimulated by the success of the Russian Revolution. Some of them believed they could fight discrimination against Italians in the United States through a program of mutual help. Sacco and Vanzetti belonged to this club, and because of this, some nativists considered them capable of resorting to murder.

In May 1921, after a number of delays and considerable publicity,

Sacco and Vanzetti were brought to trial before Judge Webster Thayer of Worcester, an old-line Yankee nativist who claimed that Vanzetti's ideals were "cognate with crime." The jury, consisting of real estate men, storekeepers, a mason, a farmer, a millworker, a shoemaker, a machinist, a clothing salesman, and a last maker, was "one hundred per cent American." Taking advantage of this circumstance, the district attorney, Frederick G. Katzmann, a small-town lawyer, treated Italian witnesses with contempt and appealed to the conscious Americanism of the jury.

In the long and stormy trial, clouded by the prevalent Bolshevik hysteria and nativist hatred of Italians, it was easy for the jury to be impressed by the circumstantial evidence against the defendants. Distrust of foreigners seemed so normal that the court refused to believe the testimony of eighteen Italian-born witnesses; it considered them perjurers. Moreover, Sacco and Vanzetti's inept testimony, given in broken English, did nothing for them. On July 14, this Norfolk County jury found them guilty of murder in the first degree. When Thayer sentenced them to death, both men claimed innocence and pictured themselves as victims of prejudice. "I am suffering," the more articulate Vanzetti told the court, "because I am a radical and indeed I am a radical; I have suffered because I was an Italian, and indeed I am an Italian."

Italians everywhere agreed with Vanzetti's indictment of American justice. But Italian support for Sacco and Vanzetti was based mainly on the fact they were *paesani* rather than on any belief in abstract justice. Italian-Americans by the hundreds contributed large and small sums to a Sacco-Vanzetti Defense Committee, organized an Italian Defense Committee for them, and published a news sheet, *Agitazione,* devoted to maintaining the interests of the convicted men. In Italy, masses demonstrated against the decision and denounced the American courts as unfair; secret service agents had to protect the American ambassador against possible assault.

On the ground that the verdict ran against the weight of evidence, the defense set in motion a series of moves for a new trial, and sentence was stayed. These motions went to Thayer who could decide whether or not there would be another trial. In November, 1924, after denying a motion for a new trial, the judge allegedly told a professor at Dartmouth College, "Did you see what I did to those anarchistic bastards the other day? I guess that will hold them for a while. . . ."

Protests against the decision and the denial of the appeal became world-wide, causing postponement of the execution and making the Sacco and Vanzetti case the *cause célèbre* of the twenties. When every legal path to another trial seemed closed, intellectuals, liberals, humanitarians, and others implored the governor of Massachusetts to grant a pardon, or at least to commute the sentences. Governor Alvan T. Fuller avoided a direct handling of the issue by appointing a commission of prominent men, presumably impartial, to review the case and to advise him. A. Lawrence Lowell, the president of Harvard University, an early supporter of the Restriction League, headed the committee. In August, 1927, the report of the Lowell Committee became public. It justified the trial, and concluded that there had been no prejudice in the treatment of the two Italians. Regardless of the defendants' guilt or innocence, radicals and liberals everywhere denounced the committee's report. Italian newspapers assailed the prejudice surrounding the case and the "mechanical justice" of American courts. Under pressure from public opinion, Italy's Prime Minister, Benito Mussolini, appealed for mercy as "an act of humanity," but with no effect. On August 23, two weeks after Lowell's committee had reported, Sacco and Vanzetti were electrocuted in Charlestown jail.

The execution set off demonstrations throughout the world. Mobs stoned American embassies, assaulted American diplomats, spat on the American flag, and chanted anti-American epithets. Men everywhere felt that Sacco and Vanzetti had died martyrs, victims of prejudice. In Italy, their execution became part of the consciousness not only of intellectuals but also of peasants who although they could not read a newspaper heard of the case through word of mouth. It convinced many Italians that the poor and the foreign born could expect only harsh justice in the United States.

This belief also had roots in other anti-Italian violence, such as the incident that occurred in West Frankfort, Illinois, in August, 1920, while Sacco and Vanzetti were awaiting trial. A series of bank robberies in this mining town, attributed to a Black Hand Society, followed by the kidnapping and murder of two boys, brought on a spasm of antiforeignism. People surged into the streets beating every foreigner they saw. Bursting into the Italian district time and again, the mobs dragged hysterical residents from their homes, clubbing and stoning them, wrecking and setting fire to their houses. Even though 500 state troopers rushed to the town, the frenzy went on for three days, leaving hundreds homeless. Many of the victims streamed from

the town, like refugees in a war, carrying anything they could salvage
—clothing, furniture, food.

Although disgusted by such brutal anti-Italianism, Italy's upper
classes also felt shame over the low reputation of Italians in the
United States. It pained aristocrats that Italy's lowest element, mainly
the illiterate southern masses, represented Italian life in America. To
many upper-class Italians, culture meant rhetoric, music, social poise,
art, and classical literature. The immigrants brought little of this with
them, so the aristocrats assumed they could contribute nothing significant to the culture of their adopted country or to a cultural link between Italy and the United States. Upper-class immigrants also had
little feeling or compassion for their peasant *paesani*. Yet affluent
Italian-Americans were becoming concerned about the mounting
prejudice against all Italians. In various ways, such as urging fellow
immigrants to adopt American practices and to become patriots, they
tried to improve the reputation of all Italians, but well-to-do Italians
did not perform many good works for the less-fortunate immigrants.
Lacking an Italian tradition of philanthropy, they set up fewer institutions to aid their own kind than did the wealthy of other ethnic
groups.

Nonetheless, through hard work, Italian immigrants slowly acquired
education and by their own skills started to get ahead and even make
noteworthy contributions to American life. In New York City in
May, 1920, Italian-Americans gained acceptance of another Italian
Day in an effort to remind other Americans that Italians, too, had a
stake in the nation's heritage. Although feeble because it did not extend beyond the New York area, this gesture showed at least that
Italians desired broad recognition of the fact that they, too, deserved
a decent place in American life. Another Italian-American bid for
recognition, this one political, came from Fiorello H. La Guardia. In
1921, he ran in the city's Republican primary, seeking the nomination for mayor. The Republican boss, Sam Koenig, had tried to dissuade him. "Don't do it, Fiorello," Koenig said. "The town isn't ready
for an Italian mayor." The boss was right. Derided by the press as
"the little Garibaldi," La Guardia failed to carry a single borough.

Regardless of these Italian-American setbacks, cultural links between Italy and the United States increased. As in the past, opera and
music provided a main link. For years, the Metropolitan Opera Company of New York City followed a policy of picking the best of Italy's
singers and starring them at its own opera house. In 1903, Enrico

Caruso, the tenor from Naples, made his American debut. His matchless voice, magnetic stage presence, and colorful life quickly endeared him to the public as well as to the music critics. Seeing in him the image of Italy, Italian-Americans worshipped him.

During the eighteen years of Caruso's tenure with it, the Metropolitan Opera Association enjoyed a golden age. Since few American cities had opera companies of their own, the Metropolitan traveled, sharing its Italian artists such as Caruso with various parts of the country. Giulio Gatti-Casazza, the head of the Teatro alla Scala in Milan, who took over as general manager of the Metropolitan in 1908, did as much as any other one person to make the Metropolitan's achievement possible. Through his efforts, covering twenty-seven years, the Metropolitan along with the Chicago Civic Opera Company, gained recognition as one of the finest opera companies in the world. An immigrant, Fortune Gallo, in 1910 founded what became the San Carlo Opera Company. Charging low prices and presenting only the best-known Italian operas all over the country for more than forty seasons, it catered to popular tastes and prospered. Gallo "was widely credited with having done more than any other man to popularize grand opera in America." In 1923, when Gaetano Merola, a conductor from Naples, organized the San Francisco Opera Association, Italians were also prominent in launching what would become the nation's third major opera company.

Despite the support of Italian-Americans for opera, these imported impresarios frequently had difficulties. Even so talented a man as Gatti-Casazza had to overcome the problem of bias encountered by many Italians in the United States. He saw in the American press, at first at least, evidence of prejudice against him. It portrayed him, he recalled, as "a narrow biased Italian who had come to the United States to favor the work of my countrymen."

Gatti-Casazza brought with him another Italian who became prominent in American musical life, Arturo Toscanini, the conductor at La Scala who took over the orchestra at the Metropolitan. As much as Caruso or Gatti-Casazza, Toscanini, considered by many the greatest conductor of his time, contributed to the eminence of the Metropolitan through six of its golden years. Over a long lifetime, Toscanini traveled back and forth between Italy and the United States conducting symphony orchestras. The people of both countries acclaimed him.

With far less recognition than that given to the music-makers, a few intellectuals among Italian immigrants added other links to the chain of culture binding Italy and the United States. The war had given birth to a literature, much of it ephemeral and scattered through newspapers and magazines, on Italian-American friendship. Some of this material could be found in *Il caroccio,* a monthly bilingual magazine founded by Agostino De Biosi in 1915. Devoted to literature and political affairs, it later became a propaganda organ for Mussolini. In 1915, Vincenzo Campora published *Columbus,* a magazine dedicated explicitly to the building of a bridge of culture between Italy and the United States. Two years later, those interested in cultural cooperation between the two countries established an Italian-American Society in Rome and New York. These efforts improved the quality of the Italian press in the United States, and also of the cultural programs sponsored by magazines. After the war, men on both sides of the Atlantic tried to broaden the cultural exchange. In 1920, Harry Nelson Gay, a well-to-do historian, together with some other Americans, founded a self-supporting "Library for American Studies in Italy" in Rome.

In the United States, sensitive Italians such as the clergyman Enrico C. Sartorio, realized that prejudice prevented Americans from appreciating the culture of the immigrants in their midst. Even though he could not overcome nativist hostility, he tried to do something of cultural value for the Italians. He wanted the schools to make available to the children of immigrants courses in Italian history and culture, hoping to instill in the offspring an appreciation for the United States "without their acquiring a feeling of contempt for their fathers' country." In this Sartorio failed. "When I discuss the matter with teachers in the public schools," he explained in 1918, "I become aware that they possess a holy horror of teaching children the language and history of Italy."

Later, in New York City, Leonard Covello took up Sartorio's cause. Covello was a teacher of immigrant background from southern Italy who escaped the tenements of East Harlem to attend Columbia University. Since American schools seldom mentioned Italy, her culture, or distinguished Italians, Covello felt that they gave Italian children the feeling that they came from inferior stock and created a barrier between children and parents. "This was the accepted process of Americanization," he recalled of his childhood. "We were becoming Americans by learning to be ashamed of our parents." When he became one of the first Italian-Americans to teach foreign languages in New York's high schools, he considered it wrong for Italian to have no place in the language program. He thought it should be offered because it was a major language, had a widespread cultural importance, and when taught along with Italian history and literature might help to enhance the self-image of Italian boys and girls. He and Salvatore Cotillo, the first Italian to win election as assemblyman in New York, battled for their cause, persuading the Board of Education in 1922 to admit the study of Italian into the city's high school curriculum.

In the following year, some intellectuals in Rome approached the cultural problem from another angle. To interpret Italy to Americans they founded a magazine, the *Revista d'Italia e d'America*, but reached virtually no native American readers. So in 1928, when Filippo Cassola took over the journal in New York City, publishing it under the title *Atlantica*, he turned to Italian-Americans for support. He hoped to promote knowledge of Italy's intellectual heritage among the children of immigrants. This journal, like some others, showed pro-Fascist sympathies. Italian intellectuals in higher education sometimes shared this attitude, especially in the *Casa Italiana*, a center for Italian cultural activities donated to Columbia University by the Italian community of New York. Members of the university's romance language department had launched the campaign for the *Casa* and Italian-Americans had provided the funds. Although the *Casa Italiana* served as a cultural link between Italians in the old world and Italian-Americans, it could not divorce culture from politics.

Other Italians in the United States became more interested in the practicalities of American life than in the generalities of cultural exchange. Awkward but determined, Italian-American leaders in the twenties turned to politics as a means of social and economic advancement. In large cities, such as New York and Chicago, more than a score of Italian political clubs sprang up attached to the two major parties. Italian-language newspapers encouraged the turn to politics, urging their readers to vote for Italian candidates wherever they could. "For a long time," New York's *Il pubilo* said in an editorial in 1922, "the Italian soul has been misunderstood in the United States, resulting in a lack of sympathy for the vast body of Italian-American citizens." Italian legislators, the newspapers pointed out, could help overcome this handicap.

No one stirred up more action than La Guardia, a politician defensively proud of his Italian ancestry. Despite his own rebuffs and failures, he prodded politically lethargic Italians, telling them they would make no impact on the political life of their state until they organized themselves in disciplined strength. Edward Corsi, an immigrant from the Abruzzi who was active in Italian-American life, preached a similar message. In 1925 in New York, in an effort to create a place within the Republican party for Italian-Americans, he helped establish the Italian Republican League.

In November of that year, in another effort to stimulate political action among Italian-Americans, La Guardia published a profusely illustrated Italian-language weekly magazine called *L'Americolo*. It had only one purpose, he explained, "the protection, the well-being, the happiness of the great mass of Italians in the United States." Designed to reach across the nation, from New York to San Francisco, the magazine would, La Guardia thought, became the voice for all Italian-Americans scrambling for a respected place in American life. It never became that. Critics said it fell between two stools, being too Italian for the second generation and too American for the semi-literate first generation. Educated Italian-Americans considered it shallow. Pleasing so few, *L'Americolo* lost money from the start. It collapsed in October, 1926.

Other journals, such as the weekly *United America*, published in English in New York City for the Italian community, also decried Italians for not being as alert politically as other ethnic peoples. It urged them to join political campaigns, insisting in November, 1927, "that Italians should no longer be used as pawns by the political bosses." Although admitting that "racial blocks [*sic*] are inconsistent with the democratic ideal of amalgamation," it contended that only through such blocs could ethnic groups gain recognition. To many Italian-American leaders, intensified political activity seemed urgent because of the viciousness of the revived nativism of the twenties. In these years Americans became accustomed to the ideology of race applied to ethnic groups and they supported the restrictive immigration measures the nativists had long desired.

This restrictive philosophy gained strength from the persistent fear that impoverished *contadini* would swarm into America. It gained credence from the pressing nature of Italy's population problem. Unlike other European countries, Italy had not declined in population during the war. Instead, her birth rate had risen to a slightly higher level than in some of the prewar years. Since at the same time her death rate was declining she could not absorb the thousands of new workers coming into her economy each year. People seeking work crowded into the cities and strained finances by compelling Italy to import quantities of cereals, mostly from the United States, to feed them. Italy looked upon emigration as an answer to her problem of surplus labor. In December, 1920, the *New York Times* reported that some 70,000 Italians were waiting to sail to America, with only 15,000 able to gain passage each month. Sicily in particular was congested with eager emigrants. These reports alarmed restrictionists, who were aware that Italians were already more numerous than any other group of foreign-born whites and wanted no more of them. In 1920 there were more than 1,600,000 persons of Italian birth in the United States.

In the previous year, Congress had given in to the pressure of nativists by considering various plans to exclude immigrants such as the waiting Italians. The stopgap measure that Congress enacted, the Emergency Quota Law of 1921, was signed by President Warren G. Harding after Wilson had vetoed it in his last days of office. This law, the first one specifically to restrict European immigration, introduced the principle of ethnic quotas. It limited the number of immigrants of each nationality allowed to come into the United States in any one year to 3 per cent of the number of that nationality resident in the country according to the census of 1910, and it cut the total number of immigrants for each year to 357,000. These provisions drastically reduced the flow of "new" immigrants such as the Italians. With the ethnic quotas the law discriminated between northern Europeans and Europeans from the south and east. It deliberately intended to bar those from the south and east of Europe so that the so-called Teutonic composition of the American people would be preserved in its nineteenth-century proportions.

Italians, for example, were limited to a yearly quota of slightly more than 42,000. The quota system, economically and socially, affected Italy more than any other country. Italians everywhere, as a result were unhappy with the new law and its extension in 1922. In Italy officials denounced American immigration policy as insulting to national honor, which it was. Yet it did not stand out as unique. Brazil, Uruguay, Argentina, and Australia also passed discriminatory immigration legislation.

So eager were Italians to get into the United States, despite its hostility to them, that thousands rushed across the Atlantic before the new quotas went into effect. In 1921, more than one-fourth of the 800,000 or so aliens who entered the United States were Italians. This number exceeded the Italian total of the previous year by more than 127,000. In the following year, the number who came amounted to less than the total of departures, so that the United States actually lost Italians.

The Italian government protested the low quota of 3 per cent, as well as the quota system itself. When it learned that congressional committees were working on new immigration legislation which would be "more or less a repetition" of the emergency law, it objected not only to the Italian quota but also to the 1910 census as the basis for it. Between 1910 and 1914 well over 1 million Italian immigrants had entered the United States, so Italy preferred the census of 1920 as the hinge for any quota system. In January, 1922, the Italian ambassador in Washington, V. Roland Ricci, made this point to Secretary of State Charles Evans Hughes. He complained, too, that use of the 1910 census violated the most-favored-nation clause in the Italian-American commercial treaty of 1871. The Italian government also objected to the concept of nationality behind the quota system. American officials used an immigrant's place of birth to determine his nationality, charging him against the quota of the nation of his origin. Italians considered this wrong; they believed that each newcomer should be counted against the quota of the nation from which he emigrated. In this way Italians who entered the United States from another country, say Argentina, would not be charged against Italy's quota.

Hughes answered Ricci in May, claiming that the immigration law did not violate the treaty, saying what everyone else knew was not true, that it did "not appear discriminatory against Italy or any other country." Italian authorities then tried to demonstrate that both countries would benefit from a more liberal American immigration policy. They suggested replacing the quota with a plan that would select Italian workingmen according to the needs of American employers. In this way the immigrant would take no one's job; he would simply fill vacancies. Although designed not to injure American workers, this scheme was unrealistic. Organized labor, as led by Samuel Gompers of the American Federation of Labor, considered all immigrants a threat to high wages and opposed any form of open immigration.

Labor, like the nativists, wanted tighter, not looser, restrictions. Congressman Albert Johnson, a nativist from the state of Washington, headed a committee charged with gathering data for a permanent policy of immigration restriction. Racist arguments that the country needed stringent restriction because ethnic intermixture would lead to mongrelization gained popular support from nativist interpretations of the intelligence examinations psychologists had given Army recruits during the war. The statistics compiled from these tests showed that southern and eastern Europeans scored lower than did those from northern countries, and that Italians, along with Poles and Ne-

groes, were close to the bottom of the list. Administered and interpreted crudely, the psychological tests ignored differences in language and environment between various groups. Restrictionists,
mixing this data with naïve racial theories, advanced it as scientific
proof that new immigrants, such as the south Italians, were "inferior
minded." Such immigrants had to be excluded or they would debase
the higher American intelligence through intermarriage with the native stock.

Gino Speranza, a lawyer born in the United States of Italian parents, added to the racist frenzy with a series of popular magazine articles on immigration, later brought together and published in a book
called *Race or Nation*. He argued that national unity, dependent on
racial and cultural homogeneity, was being transformed by ethnic in-
termixing. If Americans wanted to preserve their way of life, he
wrote, they must halt the alien invasion, Americanize the immigrants,
and have "complete American conformity." He wanted "to keep
America as it was," and put forward a racial theory in favor of an
Anglo-Saxon, Protestant America that restrictionists in Congress reiterated constantly.

At about this time, in March, 1923, the Italian government
announced a program of selective emigration to try to persuade
Washington to accept more immigrants. Italy's Commissioner General of Immigration, Giuseppe De Michelis, said that only those Italians who could meet American industrial needs would be permitted
to leave for the United States. Mussolini also went ahead with a nationalistic scheme to retain some hold on the emigrants. His plan
would extend suffrage to Italians abroad, and permit emigrants'
deputies to represent them in Italy's legislature.

In April, Italy offered to send workers to make up a 12 per cent
deficit in farm labor announced by the Department of Agriculture. In
July, Secretary of Labor James L. Davis visited Italy, where he arranged with De Michelis for the processing of emigrants before they
embarked. This procedure could eliminate the risk of their rejection
upon arrival in New York. Davis also talked to Mussolini about
American immigration policy. There would be, Davis said, bills
introduced in Congress calling for the exclusion of all Italians and
others that would bar only southern Italians. Mussolini opposed exclusion of any kind. He was also against the American inspection of
emigrants before they sailed, regarding it as an infringement of Italian
sovereignty. Knowledgeable Italians knew they had no way of persuading the United States to lift its barriers against immigrants. News-

papers reported that 90 per cent of the American people were against easing those restrictions.

Other countries were also concerned over the barriers to immigration. Earlier, the International Organization of Labor had appointed a committee to study the problem, but the committee had dissolved after a few meetings. Mussolini's government said it wanted to see the end of the shameful spectacle of hundreds of thousands of Italians wandering all over the world because they might otherwise die of hunger at home. So it called a conference in Rome of the nations "distinctly interested in either emigration or immigration," and invited the United States to send representatives. A month later, in May, 1923, the Department of State accepted but said that the American representatives would be permitted to talk only about technical problems. Under no circumstances could they dicsuss the "reception of immigrants into the United States," a wholly "domestic matter" wherein "the exclusive authority of Congress must be recognized." Basically, the American government wanted to avoid debate of any kind over its immigration laws. Although unhappy about this attitude, the Italian government went ahead anyway; it wanted most of all to secure American participation in the conference. Later, outside the agenda, the Italians hoped, they could discuss common immigration problems informally with the American representatives.

Meanwhile Congressman Johnson had gone ahead with work on a new immigration law. In December, 1923, when the Italian government learned that the legislation being considered would reduce national quotas to 2 per cent and use the census of 1890 as the basis, it protested, saying the bill would be "an unjustified discrimination" against a "friendly nation." It would make Italy "the less favored of all the most-interested nations." The Italians did not question the right of the United States to manage its internal affairs to suit its interests. Nor did they challenge the right of Americans to raise or lower their immigration quota as long as they did it impartially, but Johnson's bill was neither just nor impartial. It would restrict Italian immigration more than that of any other European nation. Please, the Italians pleaded, deal with immigration in a manner "that will not affect so harshly the interests and the pride of the Italian nation, which has always had toward the American people feelings of true friendship and esteem."

These objections had some effect on Secretary of State Hughes, who in February, 1924, wrote to Johnson protesting the planned exclusion of Japanese and referring to the Italian concerns. He asked

Johnson to find some way of handling immigration which would be "proof against the charge of discrimination." Rejecting Hughes' plea, the House Immigration Committee sent the Johnson bill to the floor with its discriminatory features intact. Still the Italian government did not give up. On April 5, it again urged the Department of State to do something about the pending immigration act. The protests reflected hurt, hostility, and bitter disappointment. An editorial in Rome's *Corriere d'Italia* expressed the feeling of many Italians. It denounced American immigration policy as "unjust, one-sided and advantageous to Anglo-Saxon, German and Scandinavian immigrants to the injury of the Slavs and Italians as well as to the yellow and black races." America's "curious nationalistic theories," it said, resulted "in a hostility toward Italians" which it hoped was more noisy than substantial.

The Italian protests had no effect on the lawmakers. By this time both they and the American public took for granted the idea that immigration policy should be based on racial considerations, regardless of how scientifically weak such concepts were. Congress therefore readily accepted and passed the Johnson bill.

While President Calvin Coolidge had the bill before him, the Conference on Emigration and Immigration convened in Rome. Mussolini opened it on May 15, 1924. He attacked immigration restriction, but observed that "the conditions on the world market preponderantly favored restrictionist tendencies." Since the Johnson bill embodied the very evils he denounced, the American delegation felt out of place. It did little more than go through the formalities of the various section meetings, making few contributions to the debates. The Italian delegation provided the conference with whatever momentum it had, offering recommendations for most of the resolutions that came to a vote.

Since the proposals usually dealt with technicalities, most of them were passed by overwhelming majorities. Yet the American delegation conspicuously abstained. Disliking contract labor, for example, the Americans could not accept the Italian view that anyone who entered a country for any but official reasons should be considered an immigrant. The Americans believed that some foreigners should be classed as immigrants and some as alien workers. It all depended on whether or not a person entering the United States intended to stay permanently. Italy had few colonies. So her nationalistic government looked upon Italian immigrants everywhere as colonizers who retained their ties to the homeland. Understandably, American policy makers would not accept this concept.

On the last day of the conference, Edward J. Henning, the Undersecretary of Labor who headed the American delegation, felt compelled to explain his country's position. Since the United States was entirely an immigrant-receiving nation, he pointed out, it had to pass immigration laws reflecting its attitudes and needs. His delegation agreed with most of the conference's decisions, he said, but often abstained during the voting because the resolutions conflicted with the bill Congress had recently passed. Aware of the anti-American feeling the bill had stimulated in Rome, Henning tried in this way to bow out of an embarrassing situation as politely as possible.

Coolidge had made Henning's position in Rome an impossible one. As he had shown in an article in *Good Housekeeping* magazine in 1921 and in his State of the Union message in 1923, Coolidge himself favored tighter restrictions on immigration. On May 26, 1924, despite the pleas of Italians and others to veto it, he signed the Johnson act into law. He agreed wholeheartedly with its main features, such as the discrimination against Italians and other southeastern Europeans, but he deplored its provision excluding Asians.

The new law halved the quota of 1921, allowing only 164,000 immigrants to enter the country each year. It limited immigration from any country in any one year to 2 per cent of that nationality in the United States according to the census of 1890. This quota would be replaced in 1927 by a "national origins" scheme that would serve as the basis for a maximum quota of 150,000 immigrants a year, chosen according to the composition of the American population, by nationality groups, in the year 1920. Based on the theory that laws could preserve the existing ethnic composition of the United States by cutting off southeastern Europeans and others, the quota system ended centuries of free migration for those who dreamed of a new start in a new world. Americans had made an unsound racial ideology a legal part of their lives. Demographers and sociologists pointed out that the law's thinly veiled bigotry could only insult, humiliate, and anger those people it excluded, or virtually excluded, such as Italians.

On June 30, a Presidential proclamation, in keeping with the law, reduced the Italian quota for each year from slightly more than 42,000 to just over 3,800. The new quota cut off Italian immigration when it was again rising. During the twenties, 455,000 Italians entered. By the end of the decade, or in 1930, there were 1,790,000 persons of Italian birth in the country, the largest number shown in any census, but Italians never reached this peak again. The quota did its work. Yet Italians still yearned to come, and as many as the stringent quota allowed continued to do so each year.

Among Italians in the United States, the new law left a bitterness that caused many of them to approve Mussolini's bombastic nationalism. His posturing seemed to compensate for the wounds it inflicted. Even though it hurt Italy's national pride, Mussolini himself appeared to accept the American law as something he could not change. Trying to make a virtue of necessity, he said Italy did not need the United States as an outlet for surplus population; she would direct emigrants to colonies in Africa. This plan never succeeded. Nonetheless, his government's protests against American immigration policy practically stopped.

Mussolini, of course, resented the American policy, expressing an increasing dislike of what he called the "Anglo-Saxon World." He recalled the opposition of the United States and of England too, to Italy's aspirations at the Paris peace conference. He announced that Italy must wrest her fate from the "plutocratic western nations" by standing on her own feet. Yet when he considered Italy's financial needs, his resentment against the United States lessened, for Americans had the economic power to help Italy. Political troubles at home also kept Mussolini from taking a stronger stand against American immigration policy. In the summer of 1924, he was more concerned over a political crisis arising out of the murder by Fascists of one of his enemies, the Socialist deputy Giacomo Matteotti, than with emigration. They are, he said of the naturalized immigrants in the United States, "foreigners to us. We only hope that they are proud of their origins."

Later in the year, Mussolini used the American law as an excuse for preaching imperialism. "Italy," he asserted, "poor in raw materials, has been hit hard by the American immigration quota law. We must have an outlet, and our main aim must be to provide raw materials; otherwise peace will be peace under constraint and in 1925 we would have decay." Fascists argued that because of overpopulation, other nations must eventually supply Italy with colonies or arrange to let her emigrants live and work in foreign lands as Italian citizens. The *New York Times* agreed that Italy "has several hundred thousand surplus population to dispose of every year—good laborers all —" and that since she "can no longer send this surplus to the United States," it said, "she must have colonies." But the United States should discourage foreigners who retained political loyalty to the home country from settling within its borders; it should prevent the growth of racial blocs. To New Yorkers, this concern over immigrants retaining Italian citizenship appeared logical, for at the time their city had more unnaturalized Italians than aliens from any other country.

The Fascists reiterated that they would discourage Italians from emigrating. "We must have courage to affirm that the emigration of our citizens to countries other than those under the direct sovereignty of Italy is an evil," Foreign Minister Dino Grandi announced in April, 1927. "Why should our race still constitute a sort of human storehouse to feed other nations?" Two years later, in July, 1929, when President Herbert Hoover put into effect the final quota provisions of the Immigration Act of 1924, Mussolini said that Italian-Americans were the best link between Italy and the United States. By now the stream of peasants from Italy had been reduced to a trickle; an era in Italian-American relations had ended.

Regardless of the discrimination and bitterness of the past, the impact of America on the Italian mind persisted. In remote villages of the *Mezzogiorno* people who could not read or write and who had never been to the United States followed closely the course of American politics. According to the anti-Fascist novelist Ignazio Silone in his tragedy *Bread and Wine*, peasants from the Abruzzi sang emigrant songs such as this one in taverns for years after the United States had closed its gates to immigrants:

> After thirty days in the steamship
> We got to America;
> We slept on the bare earth;
> We ate bread and sausages. . . .
>
> . . . .
>
> We ate bread and sausages,
> But the industry of us Italians
> Founded towns and cities. . . .

Fascism
and Isolationism
10

Italy emerged from the First World War with the attitudes and economic problems of a defeated country rather than those of a victor. She was burdened with a debt she could not pay, a depression, and widespread unemployment.

In June, 1920, in the first postwar elections, Giovanni Giolitti became Prime Minister for the fifth time. "The foreign policy of Italy," he assured the American ambassador in Rome, "is a policy of complete agreement with the United States." Her bitterness against Wilsonian America had disappeared. In the summer of 1921, the Italian government even proposed an alliance. It would, in case of war with another great power, the Italians said, give the United States control of the Mediterranean, easy access to the markets of the Near East and southern Russia, and influence in the Balkans. Italy would gain influence and the protection of a powerful ally.

Nothing came of the proposal except astonishment in the Department of State. The Italian leaders showed an amazing lack of knowledge of American attitudes toward foreign policy. This naïveté persisted. Later, in May, 1922, the Italians appealed for American good offices in their quarrel with Yugoslavia over the frontier near Fiume. The American government refused to become involved.

Within Italy bands of young men wearing black shirts brawled in the streets with workingmen and Communists. Benito Mussolini, who had organized these *fascisti,* was formerly a Socialist revolutionary. At one time, in 1909, when he was out of work, he had made plans for immigrating to the United States, where he was not wanted. Authorities at Ellis Island, learning of his desire from informants, waited to detain him.

During the war, Mussolini became a passionate nationalist; and in

Milan in 1919, he organized his first gang of street fighters, calling them *Fascio di Combattimento*. These groups became the basis of a political movement: Fascism. In October, 1922, when conservatives feared that the government might crumble before a Bolshevist coup Mussolini acted as the preserver of order. Mobilizing his blackshirts, he sent them converging on Rome. When the cabinet resigned, King Vittorio Emmanuele III gave Mussolini a mandate to organize a government. On October 30, 1922, at age thirty-nine, Mussolini became Prime Minister of Italy.

Mussolini took over legally, or nearly so. In form Italy remained a parliamentary nation. As for the people, Edgar Ansel Mowrer, an American correspondent then in Rome, recalled that most of them "acted as though neither the strikes, violence, local insurrections, and killings by the Communists and Socialists nor the Fascist 'counter action,' 'punitive expeditions,' arson, beatings and murders, concerned them." Italians went about their affairs at the end of October unaware that great changes had begun in their lives.

Americans showed even less concern about the developments in Italy, although a few of their newspapers, especially in the East, regularly carried stories, many of them critical, about the rise of Fascism. "The Italian Fascismo movement and Ku Kluxism in America have more than one point of similarity," the Boston *Evening Transcript* explained. "Under the mask of a false patriotism, both organizations seek power through terror and intimidation."

When the Fascists took power, the American ambassador in Rome reported that the "King, Ministry, and Parliament have capitulated with a surrender of constitutional prerogatives to a menace of force." Yet most Americans who followed events in Italy hailed the advent of Fascism as a victory against Bolshevism. Anne McCormick wrote in exaggerated prose for the *New York Times* that "A nation that thrilled to the Vigilantes and Rough Riders rises to Mussolini and his Black Shirt Army." Another writer later likened the march on Rome to Christ driving the money-changers out of the temple. Few at the time imagined that Fascism would profoundly affect relations between Italy and the United States.

If most Americans were unconcerned about Mussolini's coming to power, many at least were interested. American newsmen in Rome were particularly anxious to ascertain his views on foreign affairs. On the day Mussolini took office, he spoke to them, explaining that he hoped to "achieve a policy of *rapprochement* and close relations, and an economic entente between Italy and the United States." He also sent a message to Secretary of State Charles Evans Hughes expressing friendship for the United States. Hughes responded cordially.

Augusto Rosso, the Italian *chargé d'affaires* in Washington, informed Mussolini that Americans were reacting favorably to the formation of the Fascist government. Although reports described the new regime as "ultra nationalistic and expansionistic," interested Americans, particularly businessmen, according to Rosso, "considered the situation with relative optimism, seeing the elimination of the communist danger." Rosso also observed that the American government seemed concerned over the reported aggressiveness of the new regime's foreign policy. But the Harding administration retained confidence in Italy's economic stability and in the future of Italo-American diplomatic relations.

Several days later, on November 10, 1922, Mussolini again spoke to American correspondents about the two most serious problems in Italy's relations with the United States—war debts and emigration. The "debts of money are debts of honor," he said, and Italy when she could, would pay. As for emigration, he felt that "the United States must open its doors." "Italy can supply manpower," he said "and America can supply capital—an excellent combination."

In December, *chargé* Frederick M. Gunther noted Mussolini's attitude as "distinctly friendly" but said that immigration required attention; it could become the "most important subject between Italy and the United States." He asked the Secretary of State to send the Prime Minister a note expressing concern over the problem. Hughes curtly refused to do so. As far as he was concerned, Italy's worry over emigration was hardly a vital problem in American foreign policy. Most Americans, in fact, heard little about Italy that affected their country's foreign relations. Nor did they show anxiety over Mussolini's strong-arm politics.

Many in the United States admired Mussolini. The ambassador in Rome, Richard Washburn Child, who helped him with his autobiography, contributed to Mussolini's American popularity. Child often praised the Fascist leader for restoring order, discipline, and stability to Italian society. The ambassador publicly congratulated him for saving Italy from "impractical humanitarianism and whining weakness . . . worse than war." American businessmen saw Mussolini as the savior of capitalism.

Mussolini sought to convey this kind of image to Americans. He also wanted to appear as Italy's number one patriot. Since Fascism absorbed Italy's nationalist movement, he had little difficulty in reaching patriots everywhere, even in the United States. Soon after he came to power, Italian-Americans on their own created Fascist clubs, or *Fasci,* as a means of showing their *italianità.* Even though Italian officials were divided over supporting the *Fasci,* Fascist propagandists in the United States said that Mussolini would bring new warmth to Italian-American relations. Even the ambassador in Washington, Prince Gelasio Caetani, a member of the old Roman aristocracy who was not himself a Fascist and who opposed use of the *Fasci* for spreading "national Fascist doctrine," urged this idea. In January, 1923, he claimed that Italy had been "born again" and through Mussolini much could be achieved for the mutual benefit of Italy and the United States.

In this same month, Caetani asked if the Prime Minister wanted him to say anything special in a speech to bankers in New York City. Mussolini immediately told Caetani to emphasize that Fascism, while restoring order, had not established a dictatorship. The ambassador spoke as instructed and invited Americans to Italy to see for themselves that tranquility reigned. The bankers liked what they heard. More and more Americans were impressed by Mussolini. Those who visited Italy spoke of his uncommon intelligence, common sense, and charm. In April, 1923, Hiram Johnson, an isolationist senator from California, visited Rome. ". . . after having admired the grandeur of Rome," he said, "I have seen the marvel of modern Italy, Premier Mussolini." Johnson expressed confidence in Italy's ability to progress under Mussolini's leadership.

At the very least, many Americans asserted, Mussolini had set Italians on the path to stability and cleanliness. Now and then, a visiting scholar, through discreet investigation, would come up with a fairly sound impression of what the Fascists were doing. Sometimes such men reported their findings on the growth of a brutal dictatorship, but their warnings hardly made a ripple in American thinking about Italy.

Yet from the beginning, a vocal minority, made up largely of Italian-American labor leaders and liberal intellectuals, protested the Fascist regime. In April, 1923, they organized the Anti-Fascist Alliance of North America to publicize Fascist oppression and to help prevent Fascism's spread to the United States. This opposition had little effect on the growth of the *Fasci.* By the middle of the year, they numbered nearly forty in North America. At that time Giuseppe Bastianini, secretary-general in Rome of Fascists abroad, made a significant policy decision. He decided to use the American *Fasci* to disseminate propaganda.

Mussolini's agents also struck at anti-Fascists in the United States, securing the cooperation of the government in their efforts. In May, 1923, they asked American officials to prosecute "the notorious Italian labor agitators Carlo Tresca, Arturo Giovannitti, the Amalgamated Clothing Workers of America and other social-communist elements in New York" for defaming the Italian government, allegedly on orders from Moscow. Federal authorities then charged Tresca with a technical crime, the transmitting through the mails of an advertisement in his anti-Fascist newspaper, *Il Martello,* advocating birth control. Finding him guilty, the court sentenced Tresca to a year in the Atlanta federal penitentiary, but he gained his release in four months.

Mussolini tried to stifle critics such as Tresca because he wanted American good will. For this reason he went along with Child's idea of sending Vittorio Emmanuele to the United States. The Prime Minister told the King in June, 1923, that Italians should be on good terms with Americans because they had great influence in the world. The King agreed to make the trip.

Secretary of State Hughes reacted coolly to the idea, but Child and Mussolini persisted. So the American government made arrangements for the King to visit late in September. Harding died on August 3. Since Coolidge had to keep Washington officially in a state of mourning until December, the King had to postpone his trip. In October, Child returned to the United States for two months. He said, "Mussolini had the most ardent admiration for the United States," and urged the Department of State to arrange another time for the King's visit. Mussolini then delayed the trip. He wanted the King to remain in Italy until after elections in December.

Finally, American and Italian officials decided on early January, 1924, for the monarch's visit. Again events conspired to thwart Mussolini's efforts. Early in December, in his first message to Congress, Coolidge stated bluntly that he thought it "necessary to continue a policy of restricted immigration." His remarks offended Italians and clouded the King's trip. Child explained that Mussolini, regarding the immigration laws as "unfriendly, discriminatory, and anti-Italian," wished assurance that there would be no "unpleasant coincidence" between the King's visit and the introduction of restrictive legislation in Congress.

The Secretary of State then asked Henry Cabot Lodge, now chairman of the Senate Committee on Foreign Relations, if he could add his good offices to the Prime Minister's request. The veteran restrictionist refused. So Hughes told Child that he saw no way to relieve "the very natural apprehension that Mussolini entertains." Two days later the Prime Minister canceled the King's trip and with it the most striking aspect of his campaign to build friendship in the United States.

During the discussions over the King's visit, Mussolini launched his first violent adventure in foreign affairs in Albania, a small, backward country he considered an Italian satellite. For years Greece and Albania had disputed the status of the southern portion of Albania, also known as Northern Epirus. In 1921, a Conference of Ambassadors decided that a commission representing interested powers should delimit the frontier. On August 23, 1923, General Enrico Tellini, the Italian chairman of the commission, and his staff were murdered in Greek territory. Two days later, Mussolini presented Greece with a harsh ultimatum. While accepting most of the Italian demands, Greece took exception to two she deemed injurious to her sovereignty. Dissatisfied, Mussolini sent a naval squadron to Corfu, a Greek island in the Adriatic, and needlessly bombarded it. On August 31, Italian troops occupied the island.

The next day the Greek government brought the case before the Council of the League of Nations. Simultaneously the Conference of Ambassadors demanded the right to inquire into the affair. The Greeks agreed, saying they would accept any decision reached by the ambassadors. Determined not to tolerate any interference by the League, Mussolini threatened to occupy Corfu permanently.

Despite this confusion, the diplomats came up with a peaceful compromise. The Conference of Ambassadors decided that Greece should make available 50 million lire—the amount of the indemnity Italy demanded pending final adjudication. Then the ambassadors alleged Greek negligence and ordered the money paid to Italy. With this award, even though the Greeks did not meet his other demands, Mussolini declared himself satisfied. By the end of September, he evacuated all troops from Corfu.

In the United States, Mussolini's highhanded action brought a sharp revulsion against his policies. He found the comments of the American press so unpleasant that he forbade Italian papers to reprint them. Many Americans now took a closer look at Fascism, viewing it with alarm and seeing its leader as a brutal vigilante. Italian-American opinion on the incident split. Anti-Fascists condemned Mussolini as an imperialist, but others, the majority, sided with Italy as a matter of national pride, and conservatives among them defiantly defended Mussolini. Almost everywhere else, except in Italy, Mussolini's Corfu adventure left a bad taste. The Fascists created the impression that to gain their ends they were willing to use violence in disregard of international opinion and the League.

America's revulsion against Mussolini did not last long. On a number of minor issues the government even found him accommodating, especially in its effort to enforce Prohibition. To prevent the smuggling of liquor on to American shores, the government concluded sixteen conventions with foreign countries, the one with Italy in June, 1924. This agreement gave Americans the right to search Italian ships suspected of rumrunning beyond the three-mile limit. Authorities could also take into custody vessels caught violating the Volstead Act, the law supporting Prohibition, for adjudication in accordance with American laws. The treaty gave Italian ships the right to carry liquor under seal through American territorial waters. In case of dispute over the treaty rights, there would be arbitration.

Italy, meanwhile, was clearly succumbing to a dictatorship. After sweeping gains in the elections of 1924, Mussolini reduced parliament to a nonentity, curtailed the suffrage, placed the press under censorship, abolished all political parties but the Fascist, and established a secret police. Since these tactics constituted something new in their political experience, most Americans were slow to understand what was happening in Italy. Some liberals even excused Fascist violence. The editors of the *New Republic* argued that Fascists had to resort to force against opponents to save Italy from anarchy in the same way Northerners had used force in the Civil War to save the Union.

With the approval of many Americans, Mussolini delivered long speeches denouncing democracy as historically outmoded, preached the need for vigorous action under a strong leader, and took for himself the title of leader, or *Duce*. By November, 1926, *Il Duce* had organized a totalitarian state, the antithesis of America's capitalistic democracy. Despite Mussolini's high-sounding words, Fascism, unlike Communism, lacked a consistent ideological foundation. Yet various American liberals saw in it the consistency of the pragmatism expounded by two of their own philosophers, William James and John Dewey. A congressman, Milford W. Howard, called Mussolini's Fascism "the highest expression of a pragmatic philosophy of government whose invariable formula is: 'Does it work?' " Whether in practice or in theory, Fascism never had even this pragmatic consistency. We know that Fascism worked, especially through the use of factious power politics, but action without accomplishment indicated an unsound, even dangerous, political experiment.

As the repressive nature of Fascism became clearer, more and more critics in the United States spoke out. Among these the earliest were Italian political refugees, the *fuorusciti* or *emigranti*. Radical Italian-language newspapers regularly denounced Fascism. *Il nuovo mondo* of New York, sprang into existence in 1925 with the sole purpose of exposing Fascism. Even in Congress, a few critics spoke out. "We want no centers in the United States where Fascism can be promoted, either directly or indirectly   ," Representative Hamilton Fish of New York announced in December of 1925. "We want none of it," he said. Victor Berger, a Socialist representative from Wisconsin, drafted a resolution directing the President to notify the Fascist government that the United States "views with concern and alarm" its aspirations for world domination. He also asked that "a more humane policy be adopted by the Mussolini government."

Although such isolated criticism made no real impression on the American government, Mussolini's activities aroused strong feeling in Italian-American communities throughout the country. Their divided attitudes over the merits of Fascism became so bitter that Italian-language newspapers had to use whatever influence they could muster to prevent riots and street fights between the friends of Mussolini and his enemies. Clashes usually occurred on holidays, such as Columbus Day, when Italian-Americans marched and celebrated their ties to Italy.

Representing a minority in the Italian communities, the anti-Fascists found their situation difficult. They could not attack Mussolini without being stigmatized as "un-Italian." Most Italian-Americans were impressed by Fascism's pomp and propaganda and were annoyed by the anti-Fascist critics. In 1925, Mussolini's friends, aided by Count Ignazio Thaon di Revel, a prominent Fascist functionary, tried to shape the *Fasci* into a national organization, the Fascist League of North America. The League planted propaganda and worked to coordinate Fascist activity in the United States. Through it and through less-obvious centers of propaganda such as the Dante Alighieri Society, the Sons of Italy, the Italian Historical Society, and the Italian Chamber of Commerce, Mussolini tried to build up and retain the support of Italian-Americans.

Most of the Italian-language newspapers and radio stations, some of them subsidized with Fascist funds, praised Fascism. They took pride in what *Il Duce* seemed to be accomplishing—keeping beggars off the streets, running trains on time, making Italy efficient, and restoring the glories of ancient Rome. These things impressed numerous other Americans too.

What anti-Fascist Italian-Americans denounced most vehemently were Mussolini's ruthless politics, his denial of personal liberties. Distinguished exiles such as Arturo Toscanini, Carlo Sforza, and others recalled the *fuorusciti* of former days and attested to the reality of Fascism's oppressions. These men founded or worked in anti-Fascist organizations such as the Friends of Italian Freedom and the socialist Anti-Fascist League for the Freedom of Italy. In Italy, scholars critical of Fascism were reduced to undercover activity. Even Bernard Berenson, an American who stood for humanistic values, found himself forced to go into hiding and conceal his name.

While tightening his hold on Italy, Mussolini still desired American friendship. In July, 1926, he announced that Italy's imperialism presented no threat to world peace. The United States, whose economic empire stretched over the whole world, he said, should sympathize with her need to expand. America, he explained, resembled the Fascist state more than did any of Europe's liberal democracies. The historian Charles A. Beard made a similar comparison. Fascism, he wrote three years later, "is far from the frozen dictatorship of the Russian Tsardom; it is more like the American check and balance system. . . ." Other well-known American intellectuals, as well as businessmen, praised Mussolini as a pragmatic statesman. Although *Il Duce* liked this praise and frequently told Americans that he considered William James one of his principal intellectual mentors, he had no real grasp of pragmatic philosophy.

Understandably, a conservative thinker such as Lothrop Stoddard could admire Mussolini for his "hard-headed practicality," but so could liberals and former muckrakers such as Lincoln Steffens (who claimed that God had "formed Mussolini out of a rib of Italy"), S. S. McClure, and Ida Tarbell. Beard thrust aside the anti-democratic nature of Fascism, pointing out that some of America's own Founding Fathers—Alexander Hamilton, James Madison, and John Adams—had all come out with ideas as anti-democratic as those of any Fascist. Like Theodore Roosevelt, Beard wrote, Mussolini not only preached but also practiced the "American gospel of action, action, action."

American literary men, such as Kenneth Roberts, George Santayana, Henry Miller, and Ezra Pound, were also attracted to Fascism.

Pound saw in Mussolini the reincarnation of what he believed to be Jeffersonian agrarianism and Jacksonian anticapitalism, something far better than America's contemporary bourgeois ethos which he considered grubby. American magazine writers, too, continued to picture *Il Duce* favorably. So did foreign statesmen such as Britain's David Lloyd George and Winston Churchill. In 1926, Will Rogers, the cowboy humorist, interviewed Mussolini. In a magazine article, he told the folks back home that the "Dictator form of government is the greatest form of government, that is, if you have the right Dictator." *Il Duce,* Rogers felt, was right for Italy. According to another American writer, Fascism had found the successful solution to the twentieth century's weightiest problem, that of conflict between capital and labor. At this time, the Foreign Policy Association also viewed Mussolini's aspirations favorably. One of its reports in 1927 explained his expansionist foreign policy as stemming from Italy's frustrations at the Paris peace conference.

Despite this good will, Mussolini's critics were increasing in number. In New York and elsewhere the *fuorusciti* accused Italy's Fascists of establishing a tyranny. Dr. Charles Fama, an anti-Fascist Presbyterian pastor, charged that Mussolini was spending $1 million each year in the United States on secret political activities. The Fascists hired detectives to locate political refugees, denounced them to immigration authorities for various crimes, and demanded their return to Italy. To deport these people, Fama argued, would amount to nothing less than turning over to the hangman. Others too, such as the chairman of the Anti-Fascist Alliance of North America, protested the deportation of these anti-Fascist Italians, some of whom had entered the United States without passports.

To make their views known beyond their own circles, the anti-Fascists in Boston in 1927 published the *Lantern,* a magazine printed in English. In addition to *fuorusciti* such as Gaetano Salvemini and Max Salvadori, its contributors included well-known Americans, among them the lawyer Clarence Darrow and the novelist John Dos Passos. Its activities, as well as those of *Il nuovo mondo,* alarmed *Il Duce* enough to cause him to have his agents report in detail on what these journals said.

Although the anti-Fascist refugees were few and had only meager resources, they were supported by American liberals such as Carleton Beals and Louis Adamic and journals of opinion such as the *Nation.* In November, 1929, Marcus Duffield in a sensational article in *Harper's Magazine* accused the *Fasci* of tampering with the rights of

Italian-Americans. This article, along with the activities of anti-Fascist Italians and petitions from liberals, persuaded Congress to investigate the activities of the Fascist League of North America. Before the investigation could begin, Count Thaon di Revel, the head of the organization, disbanded it. Mussolini tried to get something in return, mainly a curb on "the activities of American Masons stirring up propaganda against Italy," but failed. At the time, in December, 1929, the League reported a membership of 12,500 scattered throughout the country in eighty branches.

Although clearing the *Fasci* of blame for subversive activity, Secretary of State Henry L. Stimson commended the breakup of the Fascist League as removing a source of misunderstanding and "being in the interest of better relations between this country and Italy." But a vociferous Fascist newspaper in New York City, *Il grido della stirpe* (The Cry of the Race), declared that the disbanding of the League did not destroy Fascism in America. Its ideas still lived.

Pro-Fascist Italian-Americans, like the Fascist press, made a lot of noise and attracted considerable attention, especially when they marched wearing blackshirts in military parades, brawled in the streets, or smashed the presses of anti-Fascist newspapers. Despite such antics, the genuinely pro-Fascist Italian-Americans were few. "The usual Fascist group," an observer wrote in the late twenties, "consisted of a president, a secretary, and a second-hand typewriter." Even though the pro-Fascists amounted to more than this, that contemporary assessment of their worth hit close to the mark.

During the twenties, Mussolini also tried to capitalize on American good will to resolve the most pressing economic problem in Italian-American relations, that of war debts. Upon taking power, he explained his friendliness toward Americans by telling newspapermen that "one must always speak well of his creditors, and we owe the United States money."

The problem had its roots in wartime finances. The United States had loaned Italy money, essentially in the form of credits running from May, 1917, to April, 1919, and amounting to more than $1.5 billion. Italy spent this money in the United States for war materiel and for goods needed in postwar reconstruction. After the war, her leaders wanted Americans to cancel the debts, arguing she had incurred them to buy goods for the defeat of the common enemy. Neither the American government nor the American people would accept the argument; they insisted on payment. In May, 1921, the Harding administration and leading bankers worked out a plan to force debtors to meet their obligations. It was agreed that the Department of State should block private loans to countries which did not pay their debts. Since Italy needed American financial help, such a policy could have a crippling effect on her economy.

Italians then maintained that they could not possibly pay off their debt within twenty-five years, the time limit set by Congress. High tariffs, Prohibition (which destroyed the American market for Italian wines), and restrictions on immigration, they argued, did not permit Italy to earn enough money from the United States to pay her debts. Regardless, in February, 1922, Congress created a World War Debt Funding Commission to work out a system of payment. In April, Secretary of State Hughes asked the debtor governments to negotiate means of settlement. In July, Italy responded with plans to send a delegation to Washington in October. But the Fascist march on Rome disrupted the arrangements. In November, Mussolini stated, "We wish to pay our debts." But, he added, if Americans understood the real nature of conditions in Italy, they would not press for immediate payment.

Mussolini's government, nonetheless, did nothing that could lead to a direct settlement. As American policy makers made known their impatience with his procrastination, he pleaded for leniency. He instructed his new ambassador, Nobile Giacomo de Martino, scheduled to arrive in Washington late in February, 1925, to do something about the American pressure. He was also to explore the problems of immigration and dual nationality. The American government considered immigration a dead issue, but looked upon nationality as very much a live one.

The Fascist government irritated members of Congress by forcing into its army Italian-Americans who had returned to Italy to visit friends and relatives. These "military cases" were occurring often enough to cause anxiety in the Department of State, especially when congressmen forwarded complaints from naturalized constituents who were being detained in Italy. As in the past, the difficulty grew out of differing concepts of nationality. In 1907, the United States had tried to resolve the conflict through a naturalization treaty. Nothing came of this effort. But, except during the war, successive Italian governments, although theoretically retaining their concept of inalienable allegiance, did not usually challenge the American naturalization laws.

Fascist authorities revived the enforcement of inalienable allegiance. From 1924 onward, they regularly arrested "returning Italians" from the United States for evading military service. Ambassador Henry P. Fletcher protested this "systematic impressment," and tried to revive the old idea of a naturalization treaty, but got nowhere. In January, 1925, the Fascists decided to link the naturalization problem to debts, hoping in this way to gain leverage in any bargaining over payments.

De Martino began to bargain shortly after arriving in Washington, but Secretary of State Frank B. Kellogg insisted that the Italian government do what it had promised three years earlier—send a delegation to Washington to negotiate with the Debt Funding Commission. Mussolini did not appoint such a commission, but he told his senate in May, 1925, that "the Italian government recognizes its war debts and intends [to] make good its liabilities to the last cent permitted by its present and future economic situation." Because of meager resources, he felt, however, Italy should be given a long moratorium that would permit her to strengthen finances and ultimately meet her payments. "It would indeed be painful," he concluded, "if we should find our former allies wishing to place us in conditions of inferiority with respect to conquered nations."

Nonetheless, the American government tightened its policy of blocking private loans to debtor countries. This new firmness brought an immediate response from Mussolini's government. In informal conversations with Secretary of the Treasury Andrew P. Mellon, chairman of the Debt Commission, de Martino asked for a moratorium and a favorable rate of amortization allowing Italy to reduce her debt in annual installments. Mellon replied that his commission would be lenient and would assist "in working out an agreement on the basis of Italy's capacity to pay." This principle was important because, unlike Britain and France, Italy was not a creditor as well as a debtor. Payments had to come from her own resources.

Kellogg, however, did not ease his pressure. When Thomas W. Lamont of the New York banking house of J. P. Morgan and Company inquired about giving a credit of $50 million for six months to several "friendly banking correspondents" in Italy, the Secretary of State objected. He demanded that the Italian government take suitable steps toward the settling of its debt before he would approve. Since Lamont proposed a credit and not truly a loan, he went ahead anyway. Kellogg at least had removed any lingering uncertainty about his government's position.

A few weeks later, the Italian government accepted the demand to negotiate, announcing that de Martino and others would meet in

June, with the Debt Commission. In greeting the Italian negotiators, Mellon praised Mussolini, saying he had acted with "characteristic decision." Mellon explained that he had "watched Italy emerge from the chaos of war, straighten out her industrial troubles, cut her expenditures and put her budget into equilibrium, all under the direction of one strong man with sound ideas and the force to make these ideas effective. . . ." He was "sure" Mussolini would have "the sympathetic consideration of the Debt Commission, and of the American people."

De Martino offered to settle Italy's debt on the basis of a ten-year moratorium, during which the Americans would remit all interest. She would stretch payment of the principal over ninety years. The Americans refused even to discuss these proposals. So the negotiations broke down almost immediately. Both sides then decided to meet again in August and to continue negotiations until they reached a settlement. Mellon and de Martino agreed that the negotiators should collect "full information describing Italy's capacity to pay." Upset by the breakdown, Mussolini jested that from now on he would make no one an honorary Fascist unless he could "find means to cancel our debts to the Anglo-Saxons."

While the negotiations were in recess, the Italians, as if unmindful of the policy of "no settlement, no loans," began talking once again with American bankers. Kellogg stuck to his policy, telling the Italians that "once the debt is funded it will be far easier to get money in America." This firmness left Mussolini in an awkward position. To continue in power, he needed a sound economy. Loans from the United States could help him in creating economic stability. But because he felt insecure, he could not immediately resume debt negotiations that could lead to loans for fear they would fail or produce a settlement not favorable enough to insure solid support at home. The lira, moreover, was declining. So *Il Duce* faced a delicate task. He had to avoid the impression of making a settlement only to get enough dollars to prop up his government, yet he had to get the dollars.

Since some kind of a settlement seemed inevitable, Mussolini called de Martino home and, with the prompting of Ambassador Fletcher, appointed a leading Fascist industrialist and politician, Giuseppe Volpi, as his Minister of Finance. *Il Duce* also created a debt bureau composed of financial experts to gather the information the Americans requested. With Volpi as its new head, the Italian delegation, made up of bankers, economics professors, and diplomats, returned to Washington. Fletcher also went to Washington to be on hand during the negotiations, doing all he could to insure a "realistic" settlement. The Italians arrived in November, 1925. Volpi immediately explained that Italy was the first major power to offer to settle the knotty problem of war debts. She now accepted the American conditions as a basis for negotiation.

The commissioners submitted "24 monographs composed of material gathered along scientific lines by the most prominent Italian statisticians and economists." Those studies showed that Italy's burden in the war equaled 30 per cent of her wealth. With immense sacrifices, Volpi said, she had balanced her budget, reduced government expenditures, and was the only great power which now spent less on its army and navy than before the war. The burden of taxation, he continued, was heavier than in any other country—38 per cent of Italy's net income after deducting a minimum of subsistence. Since she possessed no important raw materials, he pointed out, her industrial development could not keep pace with the stepped-up demands of her constantly increasing population. Her balance of trade had always been adverse. She imported four times as much as she exported to the United States. Volpi painted an essentially accurate picture of Italy's gloomy financial status. In summary, while national wealth and income in the United States were rising, in Italy they were decreasing. According to Volpi's figures, Italy's economic growth in 1925 was barely one-seventeenth that of the United States, whereas it had been one-tenth in 1914. Prior to the war, moreover, the per capita wealth of the average Italian had stood at one-third of that of the average American. By the middle of 1925, it had dropped to about one-sixth. If the minimum subsistence necessary to maintain life were deducted, the average net income of an Italian became 10 per cent of that of an American. So from these reports emerged the profile of a poor country struggling courageously for her existence in the face of seemingly insurmountable odds.

The Italian and American commissions held three meetings early in November, but their experts met in smaller groups at other times. On November 14, after ten days of discussion, the negotiators agreed on a settlement based on Italy's capacity to pay. The Italian Debt Funding Agreement, or Volpi-Mellon settlement, fixed the principal of Italy's debt at slightly more than $1 billion 640 million as of June 25, with interest on this amount calculated at 4½ per cent a year to December, 1922. From then to June, 1925, the rate of interest was 3 per cent, making the total debt to be funded a little over $2 billion.

Italy agreed to repay the principal on a schedule of sixty-two annual installments. During the first five years, she would pay no interest and only $5 million. Then for ten years, the average rate of interest would amount to .4 per cent; the United States in effect granted Italy a cancellation of about four-fifths of the total amount she owed, a treatment more generous than that accorded any of the other debtor nations. Critics argued that the settlemenet amounted to a gift of hundreds of millions of dollars. As Christian A. Herter wrote, "the American taxpayer will carry 75 per cent of the burden of the loans made to Italy, while the Italian taxpayer carries but 25 per cent."

In a dramatic gesture intended to show good faith, Volpi concluded the negotiations by giving Mellon a check for $5 million in payment of the first installment. Then Volpi expressed appreciation for the "good will shown by the American Commission" toward the Italian people. *Il Duce* hailed the Volpi-Mellon agreement as a stimulus to better economic relations.

Four days later, Volpi negotiated a loan with Thomas W. Lamont that would help stabilize Italy's currency. J. P. Morgan and Company immediately asked Kellogg's approval. Within five days, the Department of State announced it no longer objected to the Italian government's borrowing in the American market. The Morgan loan, for $100 million, absorbed the credit of $50 million extended to a banking group in Italy in the spring of 1925. A syndicate of American bankers purchased the loan at $90 million and offered bonds to the public for $94.5 million, leaving a margin of $4.5 million for distribution to the various members of the syndicate for expenses and commissions, a hefty profit.

Since the outcome of the debt and loan negotiations extricated them from a difficult position, the Fascists were jubilant. "November 14, 1925," Mussolini reportedly said, "must be marked with letters of gold in the Fascist calendar." He rallied his people to make great sacrifices through a voluntary subscription campaign so that he could meet what he now called Italy's "international obligations" instead of "Anglo-Saxon larceny." It resulted in collections above the amount needed to pay the next installment of the debt due in 1927.

Mussolini also used the Volpi-Mellon agreement in strengthening his dictatorship. On November 25, he gained overwhelming approval from his senate for the outlawing of secret societies. He aimed this, the first of what were called ultra-Fascist reforms, at Freemasonry. Some senators feared that this action would isolate Italy from other nations. Belittling this fear, *Il Duce* said that "while this assembly is meeting here, 900 bankers in the United States are preparing to offer to the 110 million inhabitants of America an Italian loan for $100 million. Nations which are isolated in the civilized world can find nobody to lend them $100 million." On December 8 and 17, Mussolini himself pushed the debt and loan agreements through his senate and chamber of deputies, respectively. On each occasion, he used Volpi to explain that the Americans had granted Italy preferential treatment, implying they did so only because of *Il Duce*.

In the United States, even though the press generally praised the Italian debt settlement, approval did not come so easily. When the agreement reached Congress, it set off a hot debate, a surprise to President Coolidge who endorsed it as "fair and just," urging its immediate approval. Open protest broke out on December 16, when Reed Smoot, a Republican from Utah, asked the Senate for a quick endorsement. Former Progressives, such as William Borah of Idaho, Hiram Johnson of California, and George Norris of Nebraska, and anti-Fascist Democrats, led by James A. Reed of Missouri and Kenneth D. McKellar of Tennessee, forced Smoot to withdraw his request. Critics charged that J. P. Morgan and Company and other firms had urged debt agreements in order to overcome State Department opposition to loans to supposedly bankrupt governments at high rates of interest. This attack forced the Republicans in the Senate to retreat and to turn the Italian agreement over to the House for initial disposal.

On January 4, 1926, Mellon defended the Italian settlement before the House Ways and Means Committee. He refuted charges that he gave the Fascists a lenient settlement, pointing out that insistence on a funding agreement in excess of a nation's capacity to pay justified a refusal by the debtor to negotiate. "If the debtor is to be able to pay and if the creditor is to receive anything," he said, "a settlement fair to both countries is essential." He claimed that the settlement benefited the United States.

At a second meeting of the committee, Henry J. Rainey, a Democrat from Illinois, denounced Mussolini's government as "the most dangerous, the most pronounced despotism that we have in any other section of all the world." He criticized investment companies in New York for putting pressure on Italian newspapers in the city, forcing them to stop attacks on Mussolini and on the debt and loan settlements. Other congressmen defended the agreements as fair and just. Some argued that Italy's politics had nothing to do with her capacity to pay. Politics, they said, should not color the judgment of the issues at hand.

Cordell Hull, a Democrat from Tennessee, also contended that the settlement was too lenient, saying that taxpayers should not be asked to assume approximately three-fourths of the Italian debt. He also accused the administration of being "absurdly impractical" and "hypocritical" in claiming that the agreement would stimulate trade with Italy. These were, he said, "weasel words." Italy could develop no trade with the United States, he pointed out, when Americans remained determined to "sit snugly behind a tariff wall against her [Italy] ranging as high as 99 per cent." Then the debate divided along party lines. The Democrats supported Hull's stand. The Republican majority urged endorsement to show that the United States would do its share in the economic rehabilitation of Europe. On January 15, 1926, by a vote of 257 to 133, the House approved the Italian debt settlement. The vote followed party lines.

Shortly after, several incidents across the Atlantic made doubtful an early approval by the Senate. On January 21, Mussolini announced that a government committee would supervise all loans obtained by private industries and would lay down the conditions for spending the money. This move appeared to substantiate Democratic charges that *Il Duce* was planning to destroy individual enterprise in Italy by creating a corporate state.

The President, pressing for approval, took the position that a nonpartisan commission had worked out the agreement and that the Senate should now approach it without partisan feelings. If the Senate did not approve, he maintained, Italian finances would become so unstable that the United States would probably obtain no agreement at all. Moreover, American exports would be affected adversely. He also expressed puzzlement over why the Democrats, who had always supported a lenient policy toward the debtor nations, would now want to strike down such a generous arrangement.

When the treaty reached the floor of the Senate, critics who were stimulated by anti-Fascist Italians who labeled the settlement "an endorsement of Fascism by the United States," attacked Mussolini. Senator McKellar called him "perhaps the greatest evil that has befallen the Italian people in 100 years. There is no use camouflaging the situation. Does free America, liberty-loving America, justice-loving America want to uphold and defend, furnish the sinews of war, and make secure for all time, this dictator-bandit, or would we help the Italian people?" On the afternoon of April 21, 1926, while packed galleries looked on, the Senate, by a vote of 54 to 33, approved the Volpi-Mellon agreement. Most of the negative votes came from Democrats.

Then, along with Coolidge's signing of the measure, Mellon tried to smooth the effect of the harsh things said about Mussolini, claiming they did not reflect the true feelings of the American people. *Il Duce* gave Mellon's statements wide publicity. In the following month, when movie idols Douglas Fairbanks and Mary Pickford visited him, Mussolini expressed special friendship for the United States, "especially after the debt accord." He topped this announcement with a show of appreciation for Mellon, who in August made a "purely vacation type visit" to the Eternal City. In the following year, assisted by Thomas Lamont and Martin Egan of the J. P. Morgan Company, Mussolini's government organized a press service in the United States to show itself off most favorably.

Regardless of all the publicity, the Volpi-Mellon agreement only alleviated the problem of the war debts; it brought no solution. Since it called for large and "impossible payments" later in the century, critics said, Italy could not possibly carry it out. Mussolini knew that he could not bind future Italian governments to balloon payments at the end of sixty years. He made the agreement not with the intention of paying, but with the desire of borrowing more money. As foreseen, within a decade Italy's payments dwindled until they became mere gestures.

These debts were linked to another problem of the twenties and thirties that troubled Italy's relations with the United States, that of armaments. Americans who knew something of Italy's financial difficulties considered her stubbornly foolish in maintaining armed forces, particularly a navy, larger than she could afford. Since unification, about one-third of the Italian government's expenditures had gone to military preparations. Differing Italian and American postwar attitudes toward armaments first came to the surface at the Washington Naval Conference of 1921-1922.

Fearing that the United States and England would dominate the conference to her disadvantage, Italy participated reluctantly. But the real clash came with France. The French and Italian delegates fought over the ratios in a Five Power Naval Treaty of February, 1922. According to this pact, Italy and France could each build 1.67 battleships for every 5 allowed the United States and Great Britain. Since

Italy concentrated her naval interest in the Mediterranean and could not really afford to build up to her allotted tonnage, that ratio satisfied her. But France, with a coastline on the Atlantic as well as in the Mediterranean, and with overseas colonies to protect, demanded a higher ratio than Italy. American leaders usually favored the French position. Moreover, unlike the Americans, Mussolini did not view the Washington treaties as furthering the cause of peace. To him they meant "breathing space, a respite" from tension. As predicted, the Five Power Treaty did not halt the armaments race. The powers merely shifted their competition from capital ships to the construction of categories of warships not covered by treaty restrictions. Coolidge therefore decided to call another conference on naval limitation.

Coolidge knew that the other signatories of the Five Power Treaty —Britain, Japan, France, and Italy—were sending delegates to a session of a Preparatory Commission on Disarmament sponsored by the League of Nations at Geneva. Later there would be a general disarmament conference. So in February, 1927, he invited the four naval powers to join the United States in separate discussions at Geneva concerning land, sea, and naval disarmament.

At first, Mussolini said nothing about Coolidge's proposal. Yet his controlled press made his views clear, essentially that he did not like the President's idea. The only thing a poor country such as Italy could do in competing with richer nations such as the United States, the Italians pointed out, was to build small naval craft whose cost was within her means. Furthermore, they argued, if the principle of the Washington treaties were extended as Coolidge desired, the world would be divided into top dogs and underdogs, with the underdog nations having no hope of getting on top. On February 21, both Italy and France rejected Coolidge's invitation. Georgraphic isolation, *Il Duce* said, enabled the United States to reduce its land forces, but Italy's "unfavorable geographic position exposed it to grave risks by the binding limitations of its maritime armaments" which were "already insufficient to the needs of its defense."

Warned that Americans would view him as militaristic, Mussolini softened his rejection by playing up the rivalry between Italy and France, and by asking pointedly if the President's phrase "far reaching building program" applied to Italy. Since *Il Duce* really did not want to be left out and the Americans said that Coolidge's phrase did not apply to Italy, he agreed to send at least an unofficial observer to Geneva. He now saw nothing in the American proposals that would compromise parity between Italy and France. Then in June, 1927, what had become a three-power naval conference opened. When it collapsed, Americans blamed British intransigence, along with negative pressure from arms manufacturers, for the failure. Mussolini escaped criticism. He also regained a favorable standing with the American government by siding with it in rejecting a compromise plan on naval limitation proposed by the British and French after the conference had broken up.

Before the failure of the Geneva conference, peace advocates in the United States had taken up the idea of eliminating war by outlawing it. Aristide Briand, France's Foreign Minister, and Secretary of State Kellogg accepted the idea and worked out a plan for a multinational treaty. The statesmen invited Italy, among other nations, to adhere. This invitation to sign the Kellogg-Briand Pact, a simple agreement that pledged the signers to renounce war "as an instrument of national policy" and to try to solve their disputes by "pacific means," placed Mussolini in a dilemma. If he accepted, he might have to curtail some of his jingoistic utterances and give up his drive for revision of the Treaty of Versailles. If he refused, he might find himself isolated internationally as an opponent of peace. Reluctantly, he adhered to the pact, but made it clear that he considered it foolhardy.

Since Mussolini was Foreign Minister as well as Prime Minister, Ambassador Fletcher asked him if he would go to the ceremony in Paris on August 27, 1928, and sign for Italy. *Il Duce* said no. Then instead of sending Dino Grandi, his Undersecretary for Foreign Affairs, he had Gaetano Manzini, his ambassador in France, sign for Italy. This gesture, reflecting the Fascists' low opinion of the treaty, annoyed Kellogg, but he found himself unable to do anything about it. Italian newspapers called the signers of the Kellogg Pact "an association" of "have" nations getting together an agreement "to the prejudice of the nations which are rising." Later, in a cynical speech, Mussolini called the treaty "so sublime that it might also be defined as transcendental," a vague attack whose meaning many were unable to grasp.

The making of the Kellogg-Briand Pact led American policy makers to negotiate a number of arbitration and conciliation treaties with several countries. The arbitration treaties drawn up by Kellogg were based on the ideas of former Secretary of State Elihu Root; they pledged the signatories to renounce war as an instrument of national policy. But, unlike the Pact of Paris, they took a narrow approach, excluding basic international disputes from arbitration; they really could do little for keeping peace. Italy, nonetheless, wanted such a treaty. She had signed one of the Root treaties in 1908, renewed it in 1913 and in 1918, but had allowed it to expire in 1924. In April, 1928, in response to Italian initiative, Kellogg therefore concluded one of his arbitration treaties with Italy. Like the other Kellogg pacts, the Italian arbitration agreement basically renewed the old Root formula. Even though the two countries did not exchange ratifications for nearly three years, the mere signing of the treaty gave the impression they shared a similar concern for world peace.

Coolidge's successor, Herbert Hoover, went along with these peace ideas of the twenties, particularly that of outlawing war. In 1929, he agreed to American participation in a naval conference to be held in London. The British government then invited Japan, France, and Italy. All accepted, and the London Naval Conference opened on January 17, 1930. French security stood out as the central issue. Without assurances of protection against Germany and an increasingly hostile Italy, France insisted, she would not adhere to any new plan for naval limitation. Italy demanded parity with France. These problems affected no vital American interest, but Secretary of State Henry L. Stimson tried to save the conference by "constantly offering his services as an honest broker to both sides. . . ." The London Naval Treaty, signed on April 22, extended the Washington formula of a "holiday" in the construction of capital ships for another five years with an "escalator clause" allowing each signatory to exceed the established limits if it believed an outside power endangered its security.

France and Italy, whose delegates wrangled all through the conference, did not accept Part III of the treaty, the vital section containing the naval ratios, but signed the other parts. The American leaders took the view that France rightfully needed a navy larger than Italy's and that the Italians could not really afford a big navy. There were rumors at this time, denied by Stimson, that the United States would refuse loans to Italy to pressure her into a reduction of armaments. Regardless of such pressure, France and Italy were so dissatisfied with the treaty that they battled over it, with Americans and Englishmen as interested mediators, for nearly two more years, and then did not ratify it.

Despite these problems of armaments, peace agreements, and debts, Mussolini, who constantly assessed American opinion, pictured himself as a friend of the United States. But when crossed, he could be petty. When the American government protested Fascist attacks on Americans traveling in Italy or Fascist activities in the United

States, he was surly and uncooperative. He defended his policies and denounced his accusers. He also persisted in his refusal to negotiate a naturalization treaty. The Fascists were now inducting about 1,200 young Americans of Italian parentage into their army each year. Suddenly in 1929, *Il Duce's* ambassador in Washington announced that Italians "who reside on the other side of the ocean" would no longer be impressed into the Italian army "in time of peace." Although pleased with the concession, the American government did not like the way it was done. As a unilateral arrangement decided solely by the Fascists, who could revoke it at any time, it placed Americans at their whim. American policy makers, therefore, kept trying to negotiate a nationality treaty; they even furnished drafts for one, but to no avail.

In these years, Mussolini also denounced democracy as a way of life. Yet he seemed careful to exempt the United States from his attacks. He often stated that the goals and values of Fascist Italy and the United States were compatible. Most Americans, including government leaders and newspaper commentators, did not take Mussolini's diatribes seriously, dismissing them as rhetoric for home consumption. They also felt that his military preparations and imperialistic utterances were Europe's concern; he posed neither threat nor danger to the United States.

These Americans had a false image of the new Italy under Mussolini. They considered it a land transformed, a utopia where the people were hard-working, thrifty, and self-sufficient. Through unofficial ambassadors, publicists, and others, *Il Duce* kept this image bright. This Fascist Italy had great appeal for Republican conservatives such as Coolidge and Mellon.

Those Americans and anti-Fascist Italians critical of Mussolini's Italy found their views offset by praise from ambassadors Fletcher and de Martino, former ambassador Child, Mellon, Thomas Lamont, Mayor James Walker of New York City, and a host of other "nonpartisan" tourists and newspapermen. As far as the policy makers of the Coolidge and early Hoover administrations were concerned, Mussolini had not only brought stability to Italy but had also stood as a bulwark against Bolshevism. Various attempts against his life, followed usually by waves of Fascist violence, received banner headlines in American newspapers. Invariably the journalists condemned the attempted assassins while praising Mussolini's courage. Despite the good press *Il Duce* received in the United States, he regarded the basic American policies of the twenties on debts, armaments, and peace treaties as hypocritical schemes to perpetuate a *status quo* favorable to wealthy nations and detrimental to Italy.

Given the conservative and isolationist temper of the twenties, the generally favorable attitude of most Americans toward Mussolini developed logically. In the first decade of Fascist rule, except for his seizure of Corfu and violent words, *Il Duce* did not appear to be an international menace. He spent most of his time consolidating his power at home. By 1930, though, American liberals, even the pragmatic liberals who had flirted with Fascism, were anti-Fascist. Other Americans, especially the businessmen and most Italian-Americans, however, continued to be enchanted by Mussolini. In these years, according to the investigations of the historian John P. Diggins, Americans admired Mussolini and his Fascist dictatorship more than did the people of any other Western nation.

The Depression
and Ethiopia

11

Armaments and war debts continued to be important international concerns well into the 1930's. On these issues, Italy and the United States usually took different positions, their attitudes being influenced by the Great Depression. For Italy, the twenties had been years of despair which spawned Fascism. For the United States, on the surface at least, they had been years of delirious prosperity as well as of ethnic intolerance. The prosperity ended in October, 1929, with a crash on Wall Street that marked the beginning of an economic breakdown, the most severe depression yet experienced by the modern world.

Both Italy and the United States attempted to fight the depression with government resources, but chose different ways. The Fascists resorted to a project of economic independence, or self-sufficiency, called "autarchy." A large program of public works and expanded military expenditures gave the appearance of success. The world-wide depression thereby strengthened rather than weakened the kind of economic nationalism that the Fascists preached. Outwardly they accomplished a great deal. They reclaimed land and expanded the production of wheat, making the country almost self-sufficient in at least one area, cereals. But the standard of living did not rise, nor did finances improve. Various costly efforts and much sacrifice failed to bring Italians within sight of economic self-sufficiency.

Americans who knew of Italy's desperate position were upset by Mussolini's substitution of saber rattling for social and economic accomplishment. Economists and others felt that he was spending money on armaments that he could better use on food, schools, and assistance for the needy common people. *Il Duce* condemned the critics but did nothing to remove the cause for criticism. To be a major power, he argued, Italy had to be well armed. While extolling force, he also continued to speak of a special bond between Italians and

Americans. "The friendship felt by Italy for the United States," he said in a message to the American people in January, 1931, "has its roots in history. It is the result of the large emigration to your country, of which several million Italians have become citizens, and has been fostered by the American tourists who come in large numbers to Italy. . . ."

Such words could not gloss over the realities of Italy's financial weakness, especially in her relations with the United States. The Great Depression spread over Europe like a plague, affecting Italy's payment of war debts as it did others. With banks failing in central Europe, Germany appeared on the verge of bankruptcy. Since the Germans could not pay reparations, countries like Italy, which relied on reparations to meet their debts, found themselves unable to continue paying. Alarmed by the crisis, President Hoover thought that a temporary suspension of reparations and debt payments might help ease the strain on Germany. On June 20, 1931, therefore, he announced that the United States would waive all intergovernmental payments for one year beginning on July 1, if other governments would do the same. Italy became the first country to accept the proposed moratorium. *Il Duce* wired Hoover, saying it "may mark the beginning of a period of useful cooperation between the nations. . . ."

This immediate acceptance of the Hoover Moratorium pleased American policy makers. At this time, in the view of Secretary of State Henry L. Stimson, Italy "of all the great Continental powers" was the least difficult to deal with. A visit to Europe in July, with a first stop in Rome, confirmed this opinion. There he had two interviews with Mussolini, finding him "cordial, frank and satisfactory." *Il Duce* took him and Mrs. Stimson for a motorboat ride, showing them "his attractive side"; they "both liked him very much." Trying to soften his image as a saber rattler, Mussolini told Stimson "emphatically that Italy stood for disarmament and peace." As he left Rome, Stimson issued a statement acknowledging "the kindness expressed to us not only by the Italian Government but by her people everywhere which has convinced us of the essential sympathy which exists between the people of Italy and America. This common understanding augurs well for the future relations of the two countries."

In the following November, Foreign Minister Dino Grandi visited the United States, mainly to explore American views on Europe's politics and on armaments. He met with Hoover for three hours. At a White House dinner, Grandi, who wore a neatly trimmed beard and exuded old-world charm, impressed the guests by kissing the hands of the ladies. He also conferred with Stimson, saying "we had relations of real friendship much beyond mere official contact." That December, Congress took action that both pleased and displeased Italian policy makers. It approved the President's moratorium but refused his request to revive the World War Foreign Debt Commission with authority to examine the debt situation. Congress announced it would not permit the debts to be "in any manner canceled or reduced."

Although aware of Italy's poverty, many Americans felt that she might be capable of handling her debts if she gave up her senseless armaments race with France. Some policy makers even hoped she might resolve this rivalry before the opening of a Conference for the Reduction and Limitation of Armaments, known also as the World Disarmament Conference, in February, 1932, in Geneva. Otherwise, it was thought, "Italy will be a serious stumbling block in the way of anything in the nature of reduction or even agreement." Representatives from fifty-nine nations attended the conference. Although Hoover sent a delegation, he regarded the gathering as essentially a European affair. The conference, which quickly deadlocked over the nature of disarmament, did nothing to ease Italian and American differences over armaments.

All the while, the question of inter-governmental debts festered. Although the Hoover Moratorium brought temporary relief, it proved no substitute for international discussion of the entire problem. Germany and her creditors, including Italy, therefore met in Lausanne, Switzerland, in June and July, 1932, to discuss the status of reparations after the expiration of the moratorium. Even though invited to the conference, the United States refused to participate. At Lausanne, Germany's creditors agreed to forgive about 90 per cent of her reparations bill due under a plan worked out in 1929 by Owen D. Young, an American businessman. This reduction would come immediately if the European nations could obtain corresponding relief from their creditors. With this Lausanne "gentlemen's agreement," America's debtors tried to shift the burden of canceling the reparations to the United States, the country to which all the Europeans were indebted.

To Mussolini the maneuver appeared logical. He assumed that at last Americans were ready to recognize the connection between reparations and war debts. In October, 1932, therefore, he appealed to the United States to cancel the debts. He spoke of the tragic record of the war, insisting "that it was time to pass the sponge over this bookkeeping." *Il Duce* judged the situation wrongly. Americans had not changed; they regarded the Lausanne agreement as an anti-American conspiracy. Hoover felt compelled to announce that the United States would not cancel the war debts.

After his defeat in the election of November, 1932, Hoover met twice with President-elect Franklin D. Roosevelt in vain efforts to reach some agreement on meeting the immediate crisis of debt payments. Hoover sought Roosevelt's support in urging Congress to reconstitute the old War Debts Commission with the purpose of negotiating new settlements. Roosevelt refused, before taking office, to bind his administration to any policy on the debts. In March, 1933, as power changed hands in the United States, the old problem of debts still troubled relations with Italy. Other differences seemed less important, at least the outgoing Secretary of State thought so. Stimson left office with a warm feeling for Italy's Fascist leaders. "American relations with Italy," he felt, "were of the most cordial character."

In that same month, Mussolini spoke to his Fascist Grand Council, outlining the main points of his foreign policy. Touching on arms reduction, he predicted that the World Disarmament Conference, which was still deadlocked, would fail unless it accepted Italy's proposals, the only concrete ones submitted. He also called for the "indefatigable collaboration" of all Italians to spread the Fascist spirit throughout the world. These views alarmed many previously complacent Americans.

Meanwhile, after the end of the Hoover Moratorium, Italy paid the first installment due on her debt. France, Poland, and others defaulted. On the next installment in June, she paid $1 million in order to show her "good will" and dramatize her economic distress. With this token payment that at least acknowledged the validity of the debt, the Italians asked to discuss the possible solution of the problem. Roosevelt pointed out that the power to reduce or cancel the debt rested with Congress. In light of the token payment, he added, he did not himself regard Italy as in default. Roosevelt's view did not prevail. Italy's next installment fell due in December, 1933; she again offered a token payment and asked for negotiations. They proved impossible; the Attorney General ruled that token payments did not save a debtor government from being held in default. In April, 1934, Congress passed the Johnson Act, named after Senator Hiram Johnson of California, which prohibited loans to foreign governments in default. Along with all other European nations except Finland, which continued payments on a small postwar loan, Italy then used the Johnson Act as an excuse to stop even her token payments. Like other debtor nations, she has never made a formal settlement of her debts.

Before going out of office, Hoover had agreed to send a delegation to a monetary conference, usually known as the World Economic Conference, in London to formulate means of combating the depression. When Roosevelt took office, he postponed action for several months but finally agreed that the meeting should be held in June, 1933. Statesmen from various countries then visited him to discuss conference plans. Italy, which had long looked forward to the conference, sent her Minister of Finance to Washington. In a joint statement, he and Roosevelt announced that the London conference must succeed or there would be increased international economic warfare. They called for a truce in the international tariff war then going on and said that a means of exchange with fixed value had to be re-established and that it must be gold. Yet in May, Roosevelt took the United States off the gold standard. That is, he removed the dollar from its fixed relationship to gold so that he could manipulate the currency to force prices up.

At the London gathering, Italy sided with the "gold bloc" nations, insisting that recovery and stable currencies could come only if the countries which had abandoned the gold standard would return to it. The head of the American delegation, Secretary of State Cordell Hull, agreed to a temporary stabilization plan. Roosevelt, however, in a statement usually referred to as the "bombshell" message that destroyed the conference, rejected the idea of stabilized currencies. When the status of the war debts came up, the American delegation refused to discuss it. With no solid concessions from the United States to work with, the conference thrashed about for a few more weeks, adjourning on July 27. It accomplished nothing important.

Substantial achievement also eluded those who sought arms reduction. Mussolini did not wish to disarm. As Dino Grandi stressed, he wanted a revision of the peace settlement in 1919. This new Italy, Grandi said, merited the respect of the rest of Europe. Italy attracted special attention when *Il Duce* proposed a Four Power Pact that would establish a kind of great-power directorate for Europe composed of Great Britain, France, Germany, and Italy. The problems of the depression, the failures of disarmament, and most of all, the fear aroused by Adolf Hitler's seizure of power in Germany all seemed to point to the need for new diplomatic initiative to keep the peace. Since Mussolini spoke of his scheme as being "in the spirit of the Kellogg Pact" and also of providing means for revision of the existing treaty system, it held out something for all concerned. In June, 1933, at a fancy ceremony in Rome, the powers signed the treaty.

Fearing that American leaders would interpret the pact as an attempt to create a united front against payment of war debts, the Italians stressed its peaceful intent. They even invited the United States to adhere. When reporters asked Roosevelt if he would join the "peace club," he brushed the idea aside by asking what the dues were. Nonetheless, he welcomed the pact, sending the signatories a congratulatory telegram saying that their agreement "to work closely together for the preservation of peace should give renewed courage to all who are striving for the success of the Geneva and London Conferences." This rosy view of big-power cooperation did not last long. In October, Hitler pulled Germany out of the League of Nations and the Disarmament Conference at Geneva, shattering the pact before it came to life. Only Italy and Britain had ratified it.

The failure of the Four Power Pact denied Italy the coveted equality she sought among the great powers, but she still received considerable attention, and from the United States too, when the powers discussed issues such as arms reduction. American, British, and Japanese naval experts began disarmament talks again in June and July, 1934, as called for by the London Naval Treaty, as preliminaries to another armaments conference to be held in the following year. The discussions also included France and Italy, both of whom objected to a continuation of the ratio system. At the conference, which assembled in London in December, 1935, even though the United States worked for the inclusion of France and Italy in a new treaty, it did most of its negotiating with Britain. The main task was to frame a new pact to replace the Washington and London treaties. The Japanese and Italian representatives walked out. Italy refused to sign a new agreement because she resented sanctions the League of Nations had imposed on her for invading Ethiopia. Nonetheless, in March, 1936, the United States, Britain, and France concluded a new three-power treaty designed to preserve the principles of naval limitation among themselves. Since Italy and Japan would not adhere, the London Naval Treaty of 1936 marked the collapse of the structure of naval limitation built since 1922.

In addition to these differences, the United States and Italy in the thirties found themselves at odds over the broad issues of war and peace. Yet in the early thirties, many Americans still admired Mussolini. Breckinridge Long, Roosevelt's ambassador in Rome, was one of these. Four weeks after his arrival, he gave the President "a picture of

Italy," the usual one about clean streets and trains that "are punctual, well-equipped and fast." A few months later, he described Italy as having "the most interesting experiment in government to come above the horizon since the formulation of our Constitution 150 years ago." In July, 1934, *Fortune* magazine made a more modern comparison, saying that "the Corporate State is to Mussolini what the New Deal is to Roosevelt."

At the same time, the depression and the rise of Nazi Germany prompted American intellectuals to scrutinize Fascism with increasing sensitivity; most of them not only became far more critical of Mussolini than they had been earlier but also became open antagonists of Fascism. Along with *fuorusciti* intellectuals, they added stature to the anti-Fascist cause. Exiles such as Max Ascoli, at the New School for Social Research, and Gaetano Salvemini, at Harvard, made up a nucleus of scholars who were listened to and respected in the academic community.

These intellectuals, in time, made their views known to the government. Time and again they denounced Fascist propaganda. In January, 1934, when Mussolini sent Piero Perini, director general of *Fasci* abroad to the United States to stimulate support for Fascism among Italian-Americans, the anti-Fascist intellectuals attacked him. They exposed his mission, causing it to fall short of what *Il Duce* desired, and gained support from the larger American intellectual community. These *fuorusciti* also accused the *Casa Italiana* at Columbia University of being run by Fascists and of spreading Fascist propaganda. Nicholas Murray Butler, Columbia's president, denied the charge, but finally instructed the *Casa* to confine its activities to nonpolitical matters. As intellectuals stepped up their opposition to Fascism, so did liberal and left-wing Italian-Americans, such as Vito Marcantonio, a radical congressman from New York's East Harlem. For an Italian-American politician, this kind of open opposition required courage.

In the early thirties, Italian-Americans still stood close to the bottom in America's social and economic hierarchy, but many were finally becoming politically effective. They resented their status, feeling that they were not receiving recognition in proportion to their numbers. This sense of suffering from injustice led many to defend Mussolini as an Italian who at least was doing something. They reacted against politicians who attacked him.

The political awakening of Italian-Americans was an issue in New York City's mayoral campaign in 1933. La Guardia, a Republican, sought office as a Fusion party candidate. The nomination went to him because he was the best man available, but still people opposed him because he was Italian. "What do you think would happen if we turned La Guardia down on the ground that we do not want an Italian for Mayor at this particular time when the Italians have such a big chest?" a Fusion leader asked. "You can imagine what Generoso Pope [a powerful Italian-American politician] would do with his three Italian newspapers screaming about La Guardia being turned down because he was an italian [sic]."

La Guardia ran on an ethnically balanced ticket. On it, for the first time, an Italian, an Irishman, a Jew, and a white Anglo-Saxon Protestant campaigned for the city's four top posts. Exploiting what had by now become the most famous Italian name in politics, La Guardia, according to the tabulations of Arthur Mann, his biographer, received about 90 per cent of New York's Italian vote. When La Guardia won, Italian-Americans were overjoyed; from South Brooklyn to the North Bronx they danced in the streets. "Finally," Pope's *Il progresso Italo-Americano* announced, "the greatest city in the world has an Italian Mayor." Everywhere, it seemed, Italian-Americans identified their own painful struggle for recognition with La Guardia's hard-won success. He privately loathed Fascism but, like most other Italian-American politicians, did not openly attack Mussolini. La Guardia did not wish to destroy his own value as a symbol of success or to weaken his political base.

Intellectuals, without political constituencies to worry about, faced no such problems. So in 1935, largely as a result of agitation by intellectuals, the Department of State complained to the Italian government of obnoxious activity by its consular officials and by propagandists such as Perini. At first the Fascist leaders resented the implication that their representatives were behaving improperly. Then they agreed that what Americans objected to, mainly propaganda, did not fall within the normal functions of consuls. So the Italian government promised to eliminate propaganda activities from the duties of its consular representatives.

One thing that gave Fascist propaganda a particularly alarming aspect was Mussolini's increasingly bellicose speeches. "Though words are beautiful things," he said, for example, "rifles, machine guns, planes, and cannon are still more beautiful." Yet most Americans continued to believe he would not live up to his wild pronouncements. They were surprised, therefore, when he pounced on Ethiopia.

For many Italians, the defeat at Adowa in 1896 still rankled. As early as 1932, Mussolini decided not only to settle scores with the Ethiopians but also to expand Italy's colonial empire. The decision became firm in the autumn of the following year; and by the fall of 1934, the American government knew that the Italians planned to conquer Ethiopia. Although there were numerous incidents on the frontier between Ethiopia and Eritrea, nothing truly serious happened until December. For some years, Italians had occupied the region around an oasis called Wal-Wal, which was claimed by Ethiopia. At this time about 1,500 Ethiopians clashed with some 600 colonial troops at the Italian outpost there. With the aid of reinforcements the Italians finally drove off the Ethiopians, but only after suffering a number of casualties.

From the start, Mussolini refused either to discuss the issue of the sovereignty of the region or to consider Ethiopia's offer of arbitration under a treaty of 1928. Instead, he threatened armed reprisal, demanding an apology and an indemnity of $100,000. In January, 1935, the Ethiopians appealed to the League of Nations for assistance. Although the United States had no tangible interest in remote Ethiopia, within a few weeks it became involved in the dispute. Emperor Haile Selassie sought American mediation. Secretary of State Hull discouraged him, saying that since he had asked aid from the League, American intervention would only confuse the issue. The Emperor then explained that he merely wanted the United States to remind Italy of her obligations under the Kellogg-Briand Pact. In March, Italy accepted Ethiopia's offer of arbitration under that treaty. Selassie then withdrew his protest to the League. Meanwhile, the effort at arbitration produced a deadlock, and Italy went ahead with military preparations.

Ethiopia again appealed to the League; but in May, the Council put off dealing with the issue for three months. On July 3, as chances for compromise faded, Selassie again asked the United States to remind Italy of her "engagements as a signatory of the Kellogg Pact." Assuming an attitude of detachment, Roosevelt turned the Emperor down. Mussolini's propagandists distorted this refusal into "evidence of the United States' friendliness toward Italy." Americans realized, the Fascists implied, that Italy was justified in her stand. Concerned over what he considered misrepresentation, Hull decided to clarify the record. He told Augusto Rosso, the Italian ambassador in Washington, that the United States had a deep interest in preserving peace in Ethiopia. A few days later, in a press conference, Hull insisted that his government supported the Kellogg Pact, and implied a partiality for Selassie's position. On July 26, 1935, Roosevelt himself added to the confusion. He told newsmen he hoped the United States would avoid involvement in this situation, as not directly affecting its interests. Yet he supported Hull's stand, saying that Americans were concerned over the general problem of peace, and that the Ethiopian quarrel endangered peace.

The threat of war, brought closer by the breakup of the arbitral commission investigating the Wal-Wal clash, spurred the League to appoint a commission of inquiry to investigate the incident. Then Italy agreed to discuss the crisis with the other two European powers most concerned, Britain and France. On August 18, after Hull sounded out the British and French, Roosevelt sent Mussolini a note asking for a peaceful settlement of the controversy. A failure, he warned, "would be a world calamity the consequences of which would adversely affect the interests of all nations." Before the note could be delivered, the French and British search for a compromise failed.

In replying to Roosevelt's message, *Il Duce* explained that "It was now too late to avoid an armed conflict"; his plans had advanced too far. Italy had mobilized 1 million men and had spent 2 billion lire in preparations for war. Mussolini feared, according to American observers, that if he disbanded his army, he would add so many men to the ranks of the unemployed that economic chaos would follow. Roosevelt commented that "it is never too late to avoid an armed conflict," and said later that Mussolini told him "to go to hell."

Late in August, Haile Selassie tried to forestall an invasion by involving Americans in his country's development. He granted a seventy-five-year concession with oil rights to an Anglo-American subsidiary of the Standard Vacuum Oil Company. Hull then pressured Standard Oil to withdraw from the concession, which it did. This action, Roosevelt said on September 4, was another proof that "dollar diplomacy is no longer recognized by the American Government."

On the previous day, after being prodded into action, the League's commission of inquiry had returned a finding on the Wal-Wal incident. Since each country regarded the place as its own, the commission exonerated both sides. Seven days later, Selassie again asked "whether, in order to prevent a catastrophe," the United States would mediate. Hull turned him down, still feeling that the League should handle the problem.

Some people talked about sanctions against Italy. "If sanctions are invoked at Geneva," Breckinridge Long wrote from Rome on September 18, "I sincerely hope the American Government will not associate itself with them. There would be many unfortunate grave repercussions at home and unnecessary complications here." The ambassador was right about repercussions in the United States; the controversy had aroused strong feelings. Most Americans disliked Mussolini's bullying tactics and sympathized with underdog Ethiopia. American "public opinion," Galeazzo Ciano, Mussolini's son-in-law, admitted privately, "is dead against us in the Abyssinian question." But Italian-Americans, as a matter of ethnic pride, generally approved of the Fascist campaign for empire.

From the beginning of the crisis, American Negroes, also on the basis of ethnic identification, rallied to Ethiopia's support, demanding that the American government take a strong stand against Italy. In April, 1935, the National Association for the Advancement of Colored People telegraphed the League on behalf of "12,000,000 American Negroes and many white Americans" urging measures to restrain Mussolini. In some places, Negroes, who saw the conflict as another effort by whites to subjugate blacks, boycotted Italian peddlers and smashed the windows of Italian shopkeepers. In eastern cities, where Italian and Negro neighborhoods joined, riots erupted. Lester Taylor, the chairman of a New African International League, telegraphed Hull from New York on September 18: "Black citizens are surprised and filled with misgivings at the lukewarm attitude of this government. Does State Department intend invoke Kellogg-Briand Pact only in behalf of white European nations . . . ?" The intensity of the black reaction was important in arousing American sympathy for Ethiopia.

Two days later, Hull told Ambassador Long that the American government "would not join in the imposition of sanctions upon any nation in the impending controversy between Italy and Ethiopia." Within a week, Hull had to act on this policy. Feeling that Mussolini could not carry on war for long unless he could obtain foreign exchange through the sale of Italian products to other countries, the British wished to restrain him through sanctions. They asked if the American government would cooperate in applying economic pressure on Italy in case of war. Although against sanctions, Hull did not oppose other forms of economic pressure. In his reply, he cited as one of these the Johnson Act prohibiting loans "by private American citizens or corporations to the Italian government or to any organization on its behalf." He also said that the American government would block credit through the Export-Import Bank, an international agency, for shipment of goods to Italy, and that private lenders were restricting money to Italian borrowers. Moreover, a recent neutrality law would require an embargo on arms intended for Italy and Ethiopia.

All this pressure had no effect on Mussolini. Insisting that the quarrel with Ethiopia was "a colonial and local matter," and no one else's business, he spurned compromise. On October 3, 1935, without a declaration of war, he opened hostilities by thrusting troops into Ethiopia from the Eritrean frontier and by bombing Adowa.

"They are dropping bombs on Ethiopia," Roosevelt told Hull, "and that is war." Within two days, the President proclaimed a state of war between Italy and Ethiopia and embargoed arms for both countries in keeping with the provisions of the first Neutrality Act of August, 1935. Roosevelt then went beyond the law by warning Americans against trading with the belligerents. In effect, he asked them to stop doing business with Italy, for few goods moved from the United States to Ethiopia. This voluntary curtailment of raw materials was called a "moral embargo." To Roosevelt and Hull, anxious to register their disapproval of Mussolini's invasion, the term "belligerent" applied only to Italy.

A few days later, the League's Council declared that Italy had violated the Covenant by committing an act of aggression. The Assembly upheld the Council's action, and on October 11, under British leadership, voted sanctions against Italy. Only three nations—Austria, Hungary, and Albania (all Italian satellites)—dissented.

At first Italy suffered little, if at all, from the American embargo because neither she nor Ethiopia normally acquired arms from the United States. Italians also accepted at face value a White House announcement "that American neutrality policy would be rigorously maintained with respect to all belligerent countries." They quickly learned differently. On October 16, Ambassador Rosso complained to the economic adviser in the Department of State that the moral embargo actually applied only to Italian trade. The United States was trying to cripple Italy's war effort; it was, Rosso said, responding to the appeals of the League rather than maintaining a position of neutrality. Italian-Americans, too, resented Roosevelt's hostility toward Italy. Why, *La libera parola* of Philadelphia asked, has the head of the Democratic party, which has benefited from Italian votes, not been impartial?

In November, the League's sanctions against Italy went into effect.

They required member nations, over fifty of them, to refuse loans, to halt exports of certain raw materials, to stop buying Italian goods, and to give each other mutual economic help to offset the losses from imposing sanctions. But the sanctions had loopholes. Italy's most vital import was oil; her forces in East Africa, for example, went into battle with only a two-month supply. But Britain and France would not embargo oil, fearing that if it were included in tighter sanctions, Mussolini might be provoked into enlarging the war or be driven into the arms of Hitler. So the League did not class oil, coal, or steel as implements of war. Britain and France were more concerned with what the more powerful Hitler might do than with Mussolini's invasion of an African province remote from the vital centers of their interests.

What had started as a minor colonial adventure turned the world against Italy. Mussolini became a symbol of international lawlessness. Yet, at home he grew in stature; he appeared to be the proud challenger of fifty nations. His controlled press magnified the dispute and compared it with British, French, and other colonial conquests, as in India and Morocco. National pride and a sense of discrimination made the Ethiopian war a popular undertaking in Italy. Italian-Americans generally shared these sentiments. Many sent money to aid Italy's war effort; hundreds of their women gave Mussolini their gold wedding rings.

Italian-Americans were free to help their mother country as best they could because the United States, not being a member, did not participate in the League's sanctions. Yet the American government incurred increasing Italian and Italian-American resentment because of its moral embargo. Roosevelt used it because, he felt, the neutrality law worked to the disadvantage of Ethiopia, the victim of aggression. Hull boasted that the moral embargo was taken "in advance of action by other governments." On November 15, three days before sanctions went into effect, he anticipated and exceeded the League's action; he included oil in the moral embargo. Three days later, Breckinridge Long, who feared that a unilateral oil embargo would draw the United States into the conflict, reported from Rome "that a noticeable change had come over the Italian Government's attitude toward us and that Mussolini was interpreting our policy of discouraging trade with either belligerent as placing us in the same category as the sanctionist countries." Italian diplomats also expressed unhappiness over "the hostile attitude of American public opinion and the American press."

On November 22, Ambassador Rosso again protested the moral

embargo, calling it a sanction and therefore "an unfriendly act" against Italy. He said it violated the commercial treaty of 1871. Hull liked Rosso, but this did not keep him from lashing back. Saying first that "the people of this country today do not feel personally unfriendly towards the people of Italy," he lectured the Italian on the "infamous" nature of the Fascist war. The outburst left the ambassador "very much flushed." Roosevelt himself commented that Italy's violation of the Kellogg-Briand Pact "made strict compliance with the old treaty [of 1871] impossible."

Roosevelt and Hull favored strong international measures against Italy, but feared that public opinion would not support them. "With the isolationist sentiment so strong," Hull explained in later years, "it was impossible to join any League body considering sanctions. I preferred that any action we took should be entirely independent and not even seem to be suggested by the League." His caution grew out of an awareness of the popular appeal of isolationists such as Charles E. Coughlin, a radio priest from Detroit, who denounced the League and all it symbolized. Coughlin sided with Italy. "After all," he informed millions of listeners, "Italy has at least some slight justification for her movement into Ethiopia. At least Italy can truthfully charge that her territory already existing in Algeria [sic] has been invaded at least ninety times by the Ethiopians." Emanuel Celler, a Democratic congressman from New York, told radio listeners that Italy, "in dismembering Ethiopia, may be no more guilty than England in dismembering the Boer Republic and India."

Many Americans, unimpressed by Fascism's military swagger, foresaw a long and difficult war for Italy. Then even limited sanctions might work. Roosevelt himself wondered if sanctions might be "so effective that Italy will succumb or begin to crack up within three or four months?" This view proved mistaken. Neither the League's sanctions nor America's moral embargo slowed Mussolini's war machine. Some League members urged an oil embargo to stop him. In December, the British asked if the United States, which supplied more than 6 per cent of Italy's oil imports, would cooperate in imposing such an embargo. Hull said no. From Rome, Long commented: "The potentialities of the situation suggest the possibility of our having to deal on a friendly basis in the future with a much more important Italy."

Now, more intensely than before, the League's attention switched to the United States, where Congress was considering new neutrality legislation because the arms embargo feature of the old law was about to expire. Italy watched with particular concern. If the American government showed itself even more unfriendly than in the past by extending the embargo and cooperating with the League, then the hitherto reluctant members might vote an oil sanction. *La tribuna* of Rome said that "the decision of the United States" would be a crucial one. On January 3, 1936, Roosevelt spoke to Congress, showing antipathy toward Fascist Italy. He denounced the "twin spirits of autocracy and aggression" as jeopardizing world peace and condemned reversion "to the old belief in the law of the sword." He also asked Congress to continue the arms embargo and to discourage belligerents (meaning Italy) from using American raw materials in making war. The speech understandably irritated the Italians. Italian-Americans, too, according to *La stella di Pittsburgh,* considered it offensive.

Congress immediately undertook a new neutrality act. One proposal provided opportunity for the President to impose discretionary embargoes. It led to protests from most of the Italian-American press and thousands of Italian-Americans, many of whom were far more self-conscious about their *italianità* than were their immigrant parents. In December, Italians in New England, for example, formed the League for American Neutrality, supposedly made up of Americans from all backgrounds, to oppose discretionary embargoes. Hundreds of Italian-American societies (such as the Sons of Italy and the American-Italian Union), as well as individuals, flooded the offices of influential members of Congress with letters and telegrams. In an organized campaign of letter writing, the Italian-Americans sent, within ten days, about 2,500 form letters attacking discretionary embargoes. These letters carried political weight because most of the writers were Democrats.

George H. Tinkham, an isolationist from Massachusetts (a state with a large Italian population), told colleagues on the House Foreign Affairs Committee that he disliked Mussolini and his form of government. "But the American people and the Italian people are friendly," Tinkham explained. "We should remain friendly until the Italian people show hostility to us. This provision [for discretionary embargoes] is a declaration of an unneutral policy."

Generoso Pope, whose papers ironically praised Fascism for Italy and Americanism for the United States, late in January, 1936, went to Washington where he spoke to Roosevelt, to Hull, and to various congressional leaders about the proposed law. The President said, according to Pope, "Gene, America honestly wishes to remain neutral; and I want you to tell the Italians . . . that our neutrality will in no way imply discrimination at the expense of Italy and in favor of any other nation." Roosevelt closed the interview by praising Italian-American contributions to the nation. Yet, for a while at least, the administration gave thought to a proposal to counter the political influence of the Italian-Americans with Negro pressure, mainly by asking black groups to agitate for discriminatory embargoes against Italy.

Although unaware of such schemes, most Italian-Americans, on the basis of his actions, considered Roosevelt hostile to Italy; they took offense at his continuing efforts to discourage the export of oil and other war materials to her. This attitude and their agitation on behalf of Italy did not mean they were Fascist sympathizers. Although there were Fascists among them and many Italian-American newspapers echoed Mussolini's bombastic propaganda, most remained indifferent to Fascism as such. Retaining a sentimental attachment to Italy, most of them resented criticism against her. They viewed Roosevelt's policy and the sentiment against Italy during the Ethiopian War as continuations of old prejudices, and hence they reacted with hurt pride.

Fearing defeat at the polls by their Italian constituents, a number of congressmen did not dare come out for discriminatory embargoes. Whether or not the Italian-American political pressure was the main cause, Congress rejected the proposal for such embargoes. Various Italian-American leaders regarded the result as a victory, saying that probably for the first time on an important national issue the Italian community had exerted pressure successfully. The second neutrality act that Roosevelt signed on February 29 made an impartial embargo mandatory. He denounced the new law's "inflexible provisions," but Mussolini expressed satisfaction with it, mainly because it did not extend the embargo to oil and other raw materials. Roosevelt, of course, had the last word. He called for a continuation of the moral embargo.

A week after passage of the new law, Hitler took advantage of the international crisis Mussolini had precipitated. In defiance of the Treaty of Versailles, Hitler marched his Nazi troops into the hitherto demilitarized Rhineland and occupied it. This action, for a while, shifted world attention from Mussolini and sanctions.

In Ethiopia, Marshall Pietro Badoglio, using the strategy of quick strikes at main centers, brought the Fascist campaign to a surprisingly speedy victory. He broke the back of Ethiopian military resistance early in April, 1936, and Italian forces entered Addis Ababa in the beginning of May. Italian-Americans across the country—in New York, Chicago, San Francisco—celebrated Il Duce's triumph. Italians could take pride in the work of their soldiers as civil engineers; like the ancient Romans, they built splendid roads. But Italians had little cause for pride in an unequal war between natives who fought mostly with primitive weapons and their own soldiers armed with modern explosives, planes, tanks, and mustard gas.

On May 9, in defiance of world opinion, of the League's sanctions, and of America's moral embargo, Mussolini placed Ethiopia's battered crown of the Lion of Judah on the head of Vittorio Emmanuele. With this pomp and other ceremony, Fascists decreed the annexation of Ethiopia and the birth of an Italian empire. From Rome two days later, a new ambassador, Alan Kirk, reported that "the members of the Italian Government and the people were outspoken in protestation of friendship for the United States and . . . eagerly awaited some indication of America's attitude." They did not have long to wait. Roosevelt quickly invoked the Stimson nonrecognition doctrine used against Japan's conquest of Manchuria in 1931, announcing his refusal "to recognize Mussolini's acquisition of Ethiopia by force and thereby condone recourse to arms and violation of treaties." Roosevelt considered recognition "appeasement" and hoped that nonrecognition would weaken Mussolini's regime. The United States never recognized Italy's annexation of Ethiopia, a source of constant friction in Italian-American relations.

In June, 1936, as another measure of disapproval, the American government forced a joint abrogation of the commercial treaty of 1871. If the Italians had not agreed to this action, the Americans would have abrogated the treaty unilaterally. American policy makers wanted termination for other reasons, too. The Ethiopian War had demonstrated that this treaty, guaranteeing freedom of trade, might conflict with neutrality laws. Moreover, they had long felt that Fascist Italy's restrictive trade policies, which had not existed in 1871, made the treaty no longer desirable. Those policies limited the American advantages, while the treaty assured Italy benefits from an American reciprocal trade program.

In November, after the Italian government agreed to American demands for freer trade policies, negotiations began for a new commercial treaty. In December, 1937, the old treaty expired, but the negotiators put together a temporary agreement permitting continuation of commercial relations on a smaller scale than in the past. Negotiations for the new treaty, much more desired by the Italians than by the Americans, deadlocked over Roosevelt's refusal to recognize Vittorio Emmanuele as Emperor of Ethiopia. Later, as Italy drifted closer to

Germany and Japan, Roosevelt held up treaty negotiations also as a means of exerting economic pressure on Mussolini and registering disapproval of his foreign policy. All this maneuvering produced no new treaty, only unsatisfactory commercial relations, another source of friction between Italy and the United States for the rest of the thirties and into the forties.

Unlike the United States, the League accepted the conquest of Ethiopia as an accomplished fact. On July 4, 1936, in what Galeazzo Ciano, Italy's new Minister for Foreign Affairs, called "the surrender of the besiegers," the League voted to drop the sanctions. The Roosevelt administration also ended its moral embargo. Gradually League members, but not the United States, came to accept the Italian title to Ethiopia based on the right of conquest.

Fascists and others had often exaggerated Ethiopia's uncertain resources. Nonetheless, it was the first colony with at least some economic potential that Italy acquired. Its conquest brought Mussolini to the peak of his popularity among Italians. Yet even in their hour of imperial glory many Italians were unhappy over the American attitude toward them and their country. Some Italian-Americans even tried to organize a boycott of newspapers they considered anti-Italian. Much of the pro-Fascist agitation among Italian Americans came as an effort to counteract the hostility of American newspapers toward Italy.

Regardless of Italian-American sentiment, the Ethiopian War marked a kind of turning point in American relations with Italy. It made Americans increasingly critical of and hostile toward Mussolini. He, in turn, became more openly contemptuous of democratic countries such as the United States. Some Americans, particularly those of Italian ancestry, still hoped for a reconciliation between Italy and the United States and a new warmth in their relations. In November, 1937, Mayor La Guardia, acting as a spokesman for this view, said that "relations between Italy and America had never been better." He urged greater trade between the two countries, saying "we have so many things that Italy needs and Italy has so many things that this country needs."

Yet numerous Italian-American voters who had earlier supported Roosevelt's New Deal now turned against the Democratic party because the President opposed Italy during the Ethiopian War. Many now admired Mussolini even more than before because he appeared to have earned the respect and fear of the great powers. In a country where insults to Italians had come more often than esteem, he inspired a sense of dignity. A young neighborhood leader in William Foote Whyte's *Street Corner Society*, Chick Morelli, expressed this feeling succinctly. "Whatever you fellows may think of Mussolini, you've got to admit one thing," Morelli told members of his club. "He has done more to get respect for the Italian people than anybody else. The Italians get a lot more respect now than when I started going to school. And you can thank Mussolini for that."

This new feeling among Italian-Americans could not, however, compensate for the harm Mussolini had done to Italian-American relations. Not all Americans were prejudiced against Italians. Many even considered Italians an especially cultured and civilized people. Now, however, while forgetting the brutality of their own wars of conquest (as in the Philippines), most Americans could not forget Italy's ruthless campaign in Ethiopia.

The Coming
of War
12

The anger over Ethiopia hardly had time to subside before another conflict, a civil war in Spain, added new bitterness to Italian-American relations. The rebellion began in Spanish Morocco in July, 1936, as a military coup led by the chief of staff of the army, General Francisco Franco, against the Spanish Republic's Popular Front government. Franco's conservative supporters crossed over to Spain assuming they could gain power quickly, but they miscalculated. Thousands rushed to the defense of the republic; other thousands sided with Franco. It quickly became apparent that neither the loyalists (government supporters) nor the rebels could crush the other. Spain then became a battleground that attracted foreign soldiers, adventurers, and ideologists.

On August 1, Premier Leon Blum, heading a Popular Front government in France, appealed to the powers not to intervene in Spain. Ignoring the plea, Italy and Germany went ahead with the aid they had already begun supplying to the rebel forces, while the Soviet Union, France, and others assisted the loyalists. *Il Duce* said that he intervened to keep Spain out of Communist hands. Regardless of the cause, the war took on the coloring of an ideological conflict between Fascism and Communism, with most Americans viewing the loyalists as defenders of legitimate government.

Hoping to end foreign participation while it was still small, England and France took the lead in forming a nonintervention committee representing twenty-seven nations. It sought to keep foreign war materials from going to either side. Although not a member of the committee, the United States sympathized with its objectives. Early in August the American government announced that even though it would not cooperate officially in an international embargo, it would discourage trade in arms with the rival factions in Spain. Since the

225

neutrality law did not apply to a civil war, Hull in effect called for another moral embargo.

Unlike the United States, Italy never pretended to be neutral, although at first she denied, or attempted to cover up, her intervention. As *Il Duce*'s involvement deepened, it drove Italy and the United States further and further apart. At the same time, tension with Britain and France and the common goal of a victory for Franco's nationalist forces drew Mussolini and Hitler closer and closer together. The two dictators made their partnership a formal one on October 25 when they signed an agreement pledging collaboration in various political matters, particularly against communism and in the war in Spain. This pact created what became known as the Rome-Berlin Axis.

All could now see that Italy, and even more Germany, was using Spain as a proving ground for new weapons. Of all the foreign interventions, Italy's was the most extensive, although Germany's was as important. "The war in Spain," William C. Bullitt wrote to Roosevelt from the American embassy in Paris, "as you know, has become an incognito war between the Soviet Union and Italy." Most of the Italians who fought on the nationalist side were not, as the Fascists told American policy makers, volunteers. They were soldiers who often fought under orders from their own officers in regular formations of the Italian army with no choice about whether they would or would not serve. On the other hand, more than 3,000 anti-Fascist Italians fought on the loyalist side.

On November 18, Italy and Germany formally recognized Franco's regime as Spain's legal government. A week later, in another act directed against the Soviet Union, Germany concluded an Anti-Comintern Pact with Japan, wherein each promised to combat the Communist Third International. A year later, Italy became a partner, thus creating the Rome-Berlin-Tokyo Axis.

During this time, American policy toward Italy and the civil war was changing. Roosevelt found that the voluntary embargo did not work. So he asked Congress to extend the neutrality law to the Spanish belligerents and thus make the moral embargo a legally binding one. On January 6, 1937, Congress passed a joint resolution, usually called the "third Neutrality Act," placing an embargo on arms and munitions to either side in the civil war. Socialist and Communist leaders, editors of liberal journals of opinion, and others condemned the embargo as a hostile act against an established government. They protested because the ban had the effect, unintentionally, of favoring the rebels and hurting the loyalists. Under the usual conditions of international relations, the legal Spanish government could have expected to import arms freely from abroad.

For quite different reasons, business journals criticized what Congress had done, charging that the new law represented unwarranted governmental interference with foreign trade. Representatives of the Catholic church, Italian-American organizations, and isolationist groups supported the embargo. These reactions reflected the growing divergence of opinion inside the nation toward the Spanish upheaval. The agitation also revealed a gulf between liberals and much of the Italian-American community.

The Italian, German, and Russian interventions made the wisdom of the American embargo policy questionable. Americans read accounts of Italian guns, planes, and troops reaching Franco's forces in increasing amounts, leading some Americans to demonstrate before the Italian embassy in Washington. These protests had little effect on Mussolini, who even boasted about the role of Italian arms in Spain, publicly bestowing medals on soldiers who had fought there and treating them as heroes. Beneath the surface, all was not going well for Italy. Mussolini's commitment led to a far greater investment than he had originally intended (about 40,000 troops, although outsiders estimated more) and much equipment.

Since it now appeared obvious that the efforts aimed at limiting the fighting in Spain had failed, many Americans became increasingly dissatisfied with the embargo. Some demanded that the government apply it to Italy and Germany on the theory that their troops had invaded Spain, making those countries belligerents. Claude G. Bowers, the pro-loyalist American ambassador in Spain, reported that "there are now thousands of the regular Italian army on the Guadalajara front and under the command of Italian generals, who are the real directing command." Taking such reports at face value, Senator Gerald P. Nye, a Republican isolationist from North Dakota, in March, 1937, introduced a resolution in Congress calling for an embargo against Germany and Italy.

Hull objected, but Roosevelt pursued the idea, seeking to find out from his ambassadors in Europe if the Italians or Germans had officially admitted that their soldiers were fighting in Spain. If so, Roosevelt believed, "we shall have to act under the Neutrality Act." "According to some of the newspapers," he commented, "Mussolini has personally directed participation by the regular Italian armed forces. . . ." Investigation showed that Russia, France, and England,

too (according to Italy) had at one time or another helped the loyalists. Italy argued that these interventions justified her aid to Franco's
regime. The President, therefore, dropped Nye's idea and Hull's view
prevailed. On June 2, following an announcement by Roosevelt that
policy toward the Spanish civil war remained unchanged, the Senate
Committee on Foreign Relations tabled the Nye resolution.

In July, 1937, while international tensions were still high over the
struggle in Spain, Japan launched an undeclared war against China.
Several months later, as the conflict spread, the American government began evacuating Americans stationed in China. On December
12, Japanese aviators bombed, strafed, and sank the U.S.S. *Panay*, a
gunboat assisting in the evacuation. Killed in the attack were two
American seamen and Sandro Sandi, a prominent Italian journalist.
The Japanese quickly apologized and offered reparations for the injuries inflicted. The American government accepted the apologies,
and the crisis passed. At this time Italy and Japan were courting each
other, so the Italians told the American government they would not
lodge a formal protest over Sandi's death. Yet Mussolini criticized the
United States for settling the *Panay* affair quickly. "They can only
send notes," his official newspaper, *Popolo d'Italia*, asserted.

Il Duce also found fault with Roosevelt's handling of a proposal,
sponsored by Louis Ludlow, a congressman from Indiana, for a constitutional amendment that would have required a nationwide referendum before the government could declare war, except when
American soil was attacked. Mussolini remarked in the *Popolo d'I-
talia* that "Congressman Ludlow has had the unpardonable candor of
taking democracy seriously." Those democrats who opposed the Ludlow amendment, the dictator argued, merely proved that they feared
the consequences of their own doctrines.

All the while, the Spanish civil war blazed on, with Roosevelt's
cabinet members frequently discussing the problem of Italian intervention. Then in the spring of 1938, a new attempt to repeal the embargo against the Spaniards gained momentum. Various prominent
Americans, ranging from former Secretary of State Stimson to the Socialist Norman Thomas, backed this drive. It reached a peak when
Nye introduced a resolution in the Senate that would lift the embargo
on Spain's loyalists but would continue to deny arms to her rebels.
With the most outspoken champion of neutrality legislation now leading the demand for repeal, the prospects for a change in policy suddenly appeared favorable.

The Nye resolution placed Roosevelt in a dilemma. Although public opinion polls suggested that most Americans were indifferent to the outcome of the fighting in Spain, the conflict had created intense partisanship among vocal sections of the population. In general, liberal groups sided with the loyalists. The Catholic hierarchy, as well as laymen of Irish and Italian descent, favored the nationalists. Both groups represented important segments of the political coalition behind Roosevelt's rise to power. Confronted with a choice which inevitably would alienate some of his supporters, Roosevelt hesitated.

When the Senate Foreign Relations Committee met in May, 1938, its chairman read a letter from Hull opposing repeal of the Spanish arms embargo. The committee immediately tabled the Nye resolution, killing the hopes of liberals for a change in policy. Roosevelt refused open aid to the Spanish loyalists because of domestic considerations.

Early in 1939, with Franco's armies approaching victory, pro-loyalist groups began a last desperate effort to permit the shipment of arms to the republican government. J. Pierrepont Moffat, a State Department official, reported that loyalist supporters were "pouring into Washington from all over the country" to begin the first day of "Lift the Embargo Week." Catholics immediately organized a countercampaign celebrating a "Keep the Embargo Week." In the third week of January, the Senate Foreign Relations Committee received more than 35,000 letters on the Spanish arms embargo. This pressure caused the committee to postpone consideration of neutrality revision until the agitation died down.

Meanwhile the demands of the Spanish war continued to strain Italian resources. Yet the extent of the Italian involvement made Franco, who emerged victorious early in 1939, obligated to Mussolini. This relationship pleased *Il Duce*, but his partnership with Hitler annoyed him.

Even though Mussolini and Hitler were driven together during the Ethiopian and Spanish wars, the Nazis and Fascists had no feeling of confidence toward each other; each party thought primarily of the use it could make of the other. At one time, in July, 1934, Mussolini had thwarted a Nazi attempt to take over Austria. In 1938, when Nazi troops moved into Austria in violation of the treaty structure of 1919, Hitler did not consult his Axis partner beforehand. Nonetheless, despite the Italian dislike of the German move to the Brenner Pass, this time *Il Duce* did nothing. Hitler was profuse in his gratitude. "Mussolini," he wired, "I will never forget you for this."

The *Fuehrer* next threatened Czechoslovakia, which refused to meet his demands without a fight. This crisis in May, 1938, almost brought on war. Secretary of War Henry H. Woodring commented at the time that "the democracies might some day be so angered by the acts of dictator-controlled countries that they would resort to war to stop them." Mussolini replied in a fiery speech of his own, saying that in case of war the "totalitarian States will immediately form a bloc and march together to the end."

Representative Hamilton Fish, the isolationist from New York, did not blame Mussolini for his blistering response. "We started it," he said. Speeches such as Woodring's, Fish maintained, "breed war, hatred and misunderstanding all over the world." Other Americans expressed alarm over the belligerence of the Fascists and their activities in the United States. One writer claimed that "the influence of Italian fascism is felt in every phase of Italian-American life." Such anti-Italianism in American public opinion, according to Virginio Gayda, a prominent Fascist journalist, stemmed from the propaganda against Italy by foreign agents in the United States during the Ethiopian War, from the "suicidal agitation of the Jews," from the "general lack of comprehension of Italian aims and affairs," and from "the growing aridity of ideals by which the great democracies are supposedly moved."

Gayda's scathing reference to Jews grew out of the increasingly close collaboration between Mussolini and Hitler. In the summer of 1938, the Fascist government, in a reversal of past attitudes that had disparaged anti-Semitism, issued a *Manifesto della razza* modeled on the racial laws of Nazi Germany. Because Italian officials ignored these laws or enforced them carelessly, Jews in Italy did not suffer persecution as did those in Germany. Historically, Jews in Italy had not suffered the abuse and maltreatment they did elsewhere. They were few in number and by the twentieth century so largely assimilated that they were hardly distinguishable from other Italians. Jews in Italy, Mark Twain had observed years earlier, "are treated just like human beings, instead of dogs." Italians as a people, as distinguished from their Fascist hierarchy, showed less anti-Semitism than did Americans. Jews in Italy, whether engaged in politics or in business, usually fared no worse, and no better, than did other Italians of their class. Yet the Fascist racial laws endangered the old Jewish security, and the American government protested them.

The racial laws and other apings of Hitler reflected Mussolini's increasing subordination to his more powerful partner. As German power increased, so did the probability of war. In September, 1938, continuing Nazi threats against Czechoslovakia touched off another war crisis. Demanding the Sudetenland, Hitler said his troops would march into Czechoslovakia on October 1.

Roosevelt intervened with a plea for peace. First he appealed to the German, Czech, British, and French leaders to negotiate a settlement. He urged Hitler to bring his case before an international conference and asked Mussolini to use his influence to avoid war. Pleased with the appeal, the Fascist leader telephoned Hitler and persuaded him to yield slightly by postponing the terminal date of his ultimatum and by agreeing to a conference with himself, Britain's Prime Minister Neville Chamberlain, and France's Premier Edouard Daladier on the following day in Munich. At the meeting on September 29 and 30, 1938, Britain and France persuaded Czechoslovakia to capitulate. This appeased Hitler, but Mussolini could not consider Munich much of a victory for Italy. Hitler, possibly, might next threaten to take over the Mediterranean. Nonetheless, Mussolini endorsed the results at Munich.

In December, Roosevelt appealed to *Il Duce* to persuade Hitler to treat Jews humanely. Mussolini indicated he would ask the *Fuehrer* to handle the matter in "a reasonable manner," but the intercession showed no results. A month later, Mussolini turned down another of Roosevelt's proposals, to throw open Ethiopia to Jewish immigrants.

On March 15, 1939, Hitler took over what remained of Czechoslovakia, destroying it as a nation. Again Roosevelt asked Mussolini to use his influence with Hitler in the interests of peace. On March 22, when receiving a new Italian ambassador, Prince Don Ascanio Colonna, the President told him that Mussolini had before him the chance to avert war in Europe. If *Il Duce* did so, he probably could secure desired concessions from a grateful Europe. Roosevelt's appeals had no effect.

Two weeks later, on Good Friday, April 7, Mussolini himself assaulted the peace by invading Albania. Several days later he added that backward kingdom to the Italian empire. Although unpopular in the United States, this invasion did not arouse the strong feelings of hostility that Hitler's conquests did. But Hull denounced it as an additional threat to the peace of the world. Again applying the Stimson Doctrine, the American government refused to recognize Mussolini's annexation. The insignificance of the acquisition did little to enhance Italian prestige in the United States, or anywhere else.

Concerned over the dictators' ruthless use of power, Roosevelt on April 14 asked Mussolini and Hitler to demonstrate their often-repeated desire for peace by giving thirty-one nations in Europe and the Middle East guarantees against attack for at least ten years. If they agreed, he said, the United States would join international discussions to ease the burden of armaments, to reduce the barriers to international trade, and to consider political questions that bothered them. Mussolini did not reply, but five days later called Roosevelt's suggestion an "absurd" message from a "distant spectator."

Earlier Mussolini had turned aside Hitler's suggestion for an alliance. Now several weeks after Roosevelt's message, when enraged by a report in American newspapers that a crowd in Milan had been nasty to Joachim von Ribbentrop, the Nazi Foreign Minister, *Il Duce* acted impulsively. He ordered Galeazzo Ciano, his Foreign Minister, to conclude the alliance Hitler had suggested. Signed on May 22, 1939, in Berlin, with pomp and flourish, and called the "Pact of Steel," the agreement pledged Italy to fight alongside Germany in any war. A kind of suicide pact with no time limit, it gave Hitler a blank check he could present at any time. No amount of propaganda could make this treaty, which bound Italy to Germany's destiny and further estranged her from the United States, popular with the Italian people.

During these months, Hitler also conducted a war of nerves against Poland, demanding that she surrender the city of Danzig, populated heavily by Germans. In March, England and France had promised to aid Poland if Germany attacked her. They pledged similar assistance to Greece and Rumania, in peril because of Fascist forces in Albania. As tension mounted, Roosevelt, through the Italian ambassador in Washington, proposed a meeting with Mussolini, possibly aboard a ship in the Atlantic on the occasion of American and Italian naval maneuvers, to explore what could be done to save the peace. This idea appealed to *Il Duce,* but the rush of events made it impossible to consummate. On August 21, the Nazis and Soviets shocked the world by announcing that they had agreed to sign a nonaggression pact. With this agreement, Hitler would receive assurance of Russian neutrality when he attacked Poland. This news surprised Mussolini as much as it did anyone; the *Fuehrer* had not consulted him beforehand.

Roosevelt again decided to intervene in the international politics of Europe. Only by persuading Mussolini to preserve the peace, he thought, might he prevent Hitler from plunging the world into war. "Everywhere throughout Italy," William Phillips, the American ambassador in Rome, wrote, "there is outspoken condemnation of the policy of military alliance with Germany, and nothing that Mussolini could do would be more unpopular than to drag Italy into the mael-strom with Germany. . . ."

In the light of reports such as this, on August 23, just as the Nazi negotiator and the Soviet dictator Josef Stalin were completing their treaty, Roosevelt appealed to the King of Italy, and on the following day to Hitler and Poland's President, to strive to avoid war. "It is my belief," Roosevelt said, that Americans and Italians "can greatly in-fluence the averting of an outbreak of war." He asked the King to co-operate in finding "a pacific solution of the present crisis." Vittorio Emmanuele's reply showed that he had no way of restraining Hitler. So another of Roosevelt's trans-Atlantic pleas came to nothing, although at the last minute, Ciano tried to keep the peace by calling for a high-level conference (similar to the one in Munich in the preceding year) to be held at San Remo. This effort, too, failed.

Hitler now pressed his demands on Poland. Then on September 1, 1939, after the Poles had refused to submit, his troops crashed through the Polish frontier without a declaration of war. Two days later, Britain and France declared war on Germany. The Second World War had started. A few hours later Roosevelt announced America's neutrality. For the present, at least, Mussolini decided to keep Italy on the sidelines, a policy that pleased his people. Italy's nonbelligerency appeared to justify the policy of restraint the United States had followed in dealing with Mussolini while opposing what he did.

Roosevelt spoke to the Italian ambassador in the United States, suggesting that Mussolini take the initiative and call a conference of European powers to discuss the war. He said Americans had a deep-seated opposition to any program of military domination which jeopardized the peace of the world. The President also stated that the American neutrality legislation would soon be amended. Should the war spread, he pointed out, the United States would certainly assist any country that became the victim of aggression. Germany's power, as far as Mussolini was concerned, offset the President's warning. Hit-ler quickly conquered Poland.

In January, 1940, Roosevelt again spoke to Prince Colonna, saying that American public opinion had become more friendly toward Italy than it had been in recent years because she had not gone to war. The President added that he hoped Italy would remain neutral. In the fol-lowing month, Myron C. Taylor, a Protestant and a retired chairman of the board of the United States Steel Corporation, arrived in Rome as Roosevelt's personal representative to Pope Pius XII. The President sent Taylor to Rome thinking that the Vatican's sources of information could help him in dealing with Mussolini. He also wished to gain the Pope's cooperation in efforts to keep Italy out of the war. At the same time, the President announced that he was sending Undersecretary of State Sumner Welles to Europe to talk with the leaders of the countries at war. Unofficially Welles would explore the possibilities, in four European capitals, for a negotiated peace. He also had a narrower and more specific objective: to strengthen relations with Italy in order to counter German pressure on her to become a belligerent. Welles began his mission in Rome and then visited foreign secretaries in Berlin, Paris, and London.

Since February, 1938, Mussolini had refused to see any American official, but he received Welles. Italian leaders were basically pleased to have Welles among them because usually Germany received all the attention, and now his mission placed Italy in the limelight. Welles brought Mussolini a letter from Roosevelt expressing satisfaction with Italy's neutrality and inviting him to a meeting somewhere outside their two countries. According to Welles, the President believed "that if he and Mussolini could meet in some relatively remote spot, such as the Azores, he could persuade Mussolini that the best interests of Italy could be served only if he refused to prostitute the Italian people to the greater glory of Hitler." *Il Duce* seemed to take the idea of the meeting seriously, but he never answered the letter. Later he told Ciano that "between us and the Americans any kind of understanding is impossible. . . ."

Welles then went on to Berlin. He got nowhere with the Nazis. He reported that if Hitler won some quick victories, Mussolini would probably force Italy into the war. Through personal diplomacy with *Il Duce,* Welles thought, Roosevelt might be able to keep Italy at peace. On this point Welles was wrong. He ended his mission in Rome, but on March 18, 1940, while he was there, Mussolini met Hitler at the Brenner Pass and decided on war. On the next day, Welles left for home, having achieved none of his objectives.

Within a month, Hitler launched a great offensive, shattering American illusions about the deadlock in what newspapermen and others called the "phony war" because there had previously been little fighting on the western front. Early in April, Nazi forces occupied Denmark, invaded Norway, and overcame Allied resistance there. At the time, Ambassador Phillips cabled from Rome that "Mussolini cannot make any new move until he is convinced that the Germans will come out victorious." A month later, German armies slashed through Belgium, the Netherlands, and Luxembourg and smashed their way into France.

During these weeks of *Blitzkrieg* ("lightning war"), Roosevelt tried to keep Mussolini from joining his German ally in war, from attacking Yugoslavia and Greece, and from endangering Allied routes through the Mediterranean to the East. After the German offensive began, the President appealed personally to the dictator four times to keep Italy neutral. Roosevelt first pleaded with *Il Duce* to prevent the further spread of the war on April 29. Mussolini replied that Germany could not be beaten, that Italy's position as a "prisoner within the Mediterranean" was intolerable, that her nonbelligerency had assured peace in the Mediterranean, and that Italy respected the Monroe Doctrine and expected similar respect from the United States on matters pertaining to European affairs.

Two days later, the *New York Times* reported that the coolness between Italy and the United States, dating from the Ethiopian War, had ended and that through the recent diplomatic exchanges, relations appeared to have improved. It also seemed possible that the two countries might at last agree on a new commercial treaty to replace the defunct agreement of 1871. All this appeared logical, for Italy had profited from her neutrality. Her factories and shipyards in the north did a booming business, much of it with the Allies. Actually, aside from the business boom, Italy's relations with the United States and the Allies had not improved. Mussolini ranted more loudly than ever against the democracies.

All this did not deter Roosevelt. On May 14, just after the Nazis invaded Belgium and the Netherlands, he again got in touch with Mussolini. "Reports reaching me from many sources to the effect that you may be contemplating early entry into the war," the President said, "have given me great concern. Please," he concluded, "withhold your hand, stay wholly apart from any war and refrain from any threat of attack."

The persistence of reports of Italian intervention led the American ambassador in Paris, William C. Bullitt, to demand at this moment that Pope Pius XII excommunicate Mussolini if he brought Italy into the war. Knowing that such action would look ridiculous and would have no effect, the Vatican refused even to consider the proposal.

Within four days, *Il Duce* replied to Roosevelt. Italy, he said, "intends to remain allied with Germany." She "cannot remain absent at a moment in which the fate of Europe is at stake."

Eight days later, on May 26, at the request of the British and French heads of government, Roosevelt pleaded with Mussolini for the third time. He now offered to try to meet some of *Il Duce*'s grievances by interceding as mediator with Britain and France, "if you are willing to inform me of the specific desires of Italy," he wrote. By remaining neutral, the President suggested, Italy could probably participate in "any eventual peace conference with a status equal to that of the belligerents." Mussolini could, he pointed out, quite likely gain assurance of satisfying Italy's claims merely by agreeing not to go to war. Roosevelt promised that he would himself assume responsibility for carrying out any agreement.

Mussolini rejected even this concrete proposal, maintaining that now he had to do more than realize Italy's legitimate aspirations. He was resolved to fulfill the obligations of his alliance with Germany. Foreign Minister Ciano, who relayed this message, commented that he did not know when Italy would enter the war, but said that "it will happen soon."

Roosevelt persisted. Four days later he pressured *Il Duce* with still another message, reminding him of traditional American concerns in the Mediterranean. If Italy entered the war, she would immediately affect those interests adversely, a possibility, he wrote threateningly, that "cannot be viewed with equanimity" by the American government which would at once redouble its help to the Allies. In his reply two days later, Mussolini confirmed Ciano's statement that he had already made the decision for war. He disputed the idea of a substantial American interest in the Mediterranean, arguing that it was no greater than Italy's interest in the Caribbean. Expressing a lack of concern over stepped-up American aid to the Allies, he also said he wanted Roosevelt to stop pressuring him. Nonetheless, on June 7, using an offer from France to settle Italy's territorial claims against her, Roosevelt was willing to send still another appeal to Mussolini. Saying that they had suffered enough insults from *Il Duce* already, Hull persuaded the President to hold back. The message was never sent.

Although Mussolini had long been interested in the United States and had been fascinated by American wealth, he had never visited the country, had no real understanding of American attitudes, and had no logical appreciation of American power. He was, William Phillips commented from close observation, "astonishingly ill-informed about America."

Mussolini spurned the last-minute pleas of his own high Fascist advisers, as well as those of Roosevelt, not to intervene in what was clearly Hitler's war. On June 10, 1940, as French armies were crumbling before the thrusts of German armored columns in the north, on his own, without even consulting his Fascist Grand Council, he declared war on France and Britain. Italian troops invaded France from the south. Even though Italy was not prepared and lacked the resources for a major war, he took the plunge because he assumed that a total effort would be unnecessary and that he could claim a major share of any spoils only if Italy became an active belligerent. He entered the war to triumph, not to fight. At the time, his gamble seemed safe enough.

Even though Mussolini's act came as the climax of a long development, and fitted a pattern similar to the one followed by the United States in its early history, that of taking advantage of other nations' distresses, it horrified Americans, and many Italians too. In his diary, Ciano wrote that the news "does not arouse very much enthusiasm. I am sad, very sad. The adventure begins. May God help Italy!" Pietro Nenni, an exiled Socialist, saw no reason or excuse for war, "for no real Italian interest is at stake." What Summer Welles had observed two months earlier still seemed to hold, that except for die-hard Fascists, Italians "were totally and even violently opposed to the entrance of Italy into the war." Il Duce's intervention shocked Americans because it seemed cynical and unnecessary. "No Government ever made a more sincere effort to keep another Government from going to war than the United States in the case of Italy," Cordell Hull wrote, recalling the five months of appeals to Mussolini.

Roosevelt learned of Mussolini's intervention while on his way to Charlottesville to address the graduating class of the University of Virginia. Although not surprised, he seethed with anger during the train trip because his efforts to restrain the dictator had failed. On his own, disregarding the advice that it would probably upset Italian-Americans, Roosevelt added a striking phrase to his prepared speech. "On this tenth day of June, 1940," he announced, "the hand that held the dagger has struck it into the back of its neighbor." The President also recounted his efforts to keep Mussolini from going to war. Italy has, he said "manifested disregard for the rights and security of other nations . . . and has evidenced its unwillingness to find the means through pacific negotiations for the satisfaction of what it believes are its legitimate aspirations." He also used this occasion to announce a major shift in American foreign policy. As he had told Mussolini he would do, he committed the nation's resources to the Allies.

Regardless of the deep emotions aroused by Mussolini's attack, Italy alone could not seriously threaten the United States, or even France or England. But tied to Hitler's Germany, she could potentially menace the interests of any one of them. American military leaders, for example, rated the Italian navy highly. They feared that if Hitler took over the French fleet and combined it with the German and Italian fleets, he would control a more powerful naval force than either Britain or the United States. Italy's belligerency therefore had a practical as well as an emotional impact on American policy.

Mussolini's intervention also deeply affected the emotions of Italian-Americans. Unlike the period of the First World War, they no longer suffered from uncompromising campaigns of Americanization. Gradually memories of the old country had faded and Italian-American ties to Italy, although still abundant, became weaker. The slow breakup of ethnic ghettos contributed to assimilation. More and more the children of immigrants came to live by American standards. Some also continued to live in their own Italian-American subculture, but many slipped out of their occupational and residential strait jackets to enter the mainstream of American life. In New York City alone, in the twenties, more than 90,000 Italians moved out of the congested districts of East Harlem and the lower East Side into the suburbs and into Westchester County and Long Island. Italians in Boston, Philadelphia, Chicago, San Francisco, and elsewhere moved in similar patterns. The Great Depression slowed the migration from the Little Italies; but by 1940, in New York and other cities, less than half of the Italian-born and their children lived in what could be called Italian neighborhoods.

Despite such mobility, Italians still encountered difficulty in rising socially and economically. The people of Boston's congested North End, long overwhelmingly Italian, were unable to gain political representation through one of their own until 1934, when Edward P. Bacigalupo defeated the Irish political machine to become a state representative. Not until 1939 did the Italian-Americans of this neighborhood place a representative of their own—Joseph Russo—on the city council. In Utica, New York, a city with some 35,000 Italians, no one of Italian extraction, at least until 1940, had ever served on the Oneida County Grand Jury or gained other important posts in local government. Since by numbers alone Italians deserved better representation, prejudice and rigged county politics accounted for the discrimination, according to George Schiro, a local Italian-American lawyer.

Hampered by inadequate education, by social and ethnic background, and by lack of truly powerful political connections, some Italian-Americans rejected the standards of America's majority as criteria they distrusted and refused to recognize. They tried to elevate themselves by whatever means were available—crime, gambling, and smalltime politics. Others found in the fields of entertainment and professional sports the closest approximation of the American model of achievement open to minority people like themselves. In these areas of endeavor, pedigree, origin, or education were less important than talent. In no other way, it seemed, could the children of Italian immigrants, like those of other newcomers, so readily earn the appreciation of the whole society.

Although crime brought no social recognition, it also imposed no artificial barriers to wealth, requiring mainly ruthless ambition. Before 1920, most Italian criminals worked within their own communities. With Prohibition, the marketing of illegal liquor offered more chance of gain, smaller risk of punishment, and less social opprobrium than did robbery and larceny. So young Italians in the twenties and thirties moved into organized crime in a big way. This activity, some called it success, in organized crime reinforced the prejudices of those Americans who considered Italians undesirable or incapable of noteworthy social achievement.

The investigations of social scientists suggest that although they were not unusually noteworthy, the accomplishments of Italians were not as negligible as their detractors claimed. In San Francisco, a city where people came from every region of Italy, the achievements and failures of Italian-Americans can be seen with some clarity. From the Italian population in the mid-thirties came the city's greatest banker, Amadeo P. Giannini; the mayor, Angelo Rossi; and the national head of the American Legion. But it did not yet produce noteworthy scholars, scientists, or intellectuals. Nor did these Italian-Americans produce any significant leaders of public opinion. With considerable skill they identified themselves with the ways and attitudes, bad as well as good, of the majority. As with Italians elsewhere, only a small percentage of their children, smaller than from other minority groups, went on to college and the professions. Too many of these children, it seemed, did not advance much beyond the status of their parents.

Whether in San Francisco or elsewhere, Italians of the second generation in the late thirties, unlike their parents, usually knew little or nothing of the old country. To them the ethnic tie often seemed artificial or lacking in real meaning. They concerned themselves mainly with life in the United States, doing what they hoped would gain them acceptance as full-fledged Americans. The old prejudices, the stigma of crime, and Mussolini's actions all made the task difficult. A public opinion poll of November, 1939, suggested that Americans gave first place to Italians as undesirable citizens. Understandably, some Italian-Americans deliberately tried to break connections with their Italian heritage. Like descendants of other immigrant groups, and often with more reason, they repudiated their antecedents as a means of elevating their status. As a result, Italian-American organizations, like those of other immigrant groups, lost membership, vitality, and purpose. So did the immigrant press. Although a number of Italian newspapers switched to English in efforts to attract the second generation, their decline continued.

Yet in 1940, Italian-Americans generally retained enough feeling for their heritage to dislike the idea of going to war against Italy. They also feared that in time of war they would suffer from a new wave of hatred generated by superpatriotic Americans. So Italian-Americans, like Irish-Americans and German-Americans, contributed significantly to isolationist and antiwar sentiment. They wanted Roosevelt to follow a policy of "strict neutrality" toward the warring powers. Since Italian-Americans had not yet become fully articulate politically and did not make up a powerful national pressure group, they usually did not get far with their views on foreign policy. Historians and political scientists have tended to exaggerate their influence during the Ethiopian and Spanish Wars. Italian-Americans probably felt less concern over affairs in Italy than did others of immigrant stock about their homelands. Yet when they were aroused by what they considered defamation of their national character, Italian-Americans could become a significant political force. Roosevelt's use of the "stab in the back" image at Charlottesville provided such a stimulus.

Although Roosevelt's indignant words may have reflected the sentiments of millions of Americans, they offended Italian-Americans, many of whom themselves felt shame over Mussolini's deed but who were also sensitive about their own status. As one of them pointed out, for years they had been trying to live down the popular prejudice that linked them to the stiletto, and many felt they were succeeding. Now the President seemingly had dipped into the vocabulary of bigotry to enliven the old prejudices. Even though many Italian-Americans wrote to him in approval of his speech, Roosevelt later expressed regret over the harm it might have caused any loyal citizen or alien; on Columbus Day, he tried to salve the feelings of Italian-Americans with especially kind words.

Roosevelt acted wisely, for in the presidential campaign of 1940 when he ran for a third term against Wendell L. Willkie, he needed all the support he could get, including the votes of alienated Italian-Americans. Aware of this, Willkie in the last days of the campaign challenged him to repeat his "stab in the back" reference. Roosevelt never took up the challenge. Nevertheless, Willkie carried with large majorities many Italian neighborhoods that had previously voted Democratic.

During these months, the United States became the sanctuary of the last wave of *fuorusciti* which included Carlo Sforza, Don Luigi Sturzo, Alberto Tarchiani, and Randolfo Pacciardi, and nuclear physicists Enrico Fermi, Bruno Rossi, and Emilio Segré. Fermi and Segré later won the Nobel Prize. These and earlier exiles now brought to life the Mazzini Society, with Max Ascoli as first president. This organization was dedicated to the principles of the *Risorgimento,* to inspiring an underground resistance to Mussolini, combating Fascist propaganda, and educating Italian-Americans about Fascism. Now Americans no longer regarded the anti-Fascist exiles in their midst as troublemakers, but as fighters for freedom.

Many former friends of Mussolini, Italian-Americans and others, and virtually the entire Italian-language press, shed their connections with Fascism and announced an undivided loyalty to the United States. Some Italian-Americans disliked Roosevelt's policy of aid to Britain and actions like Lend-Lease that made the United States a semibelligerent. But their opposition never became as intense as that of the German and Irish minorities. In 1941, the Fight for Freedom Committee, an organization devoted to bringing the United States into the war against Germany and Italy, had a relatively heavy Italian-American labor representation. In April, Judge Ferdinand Pecora, a prominent Italian American, formed the Legion for American Unity to rally "foreign-born elements in defense of the U.S. and in opposition to the totalitarian Axis."

Sometimes anti-Axis interventionists went to extremes in trying to pin the tag of "Axis sympathizer" on Italian-Americans. An attack on Generoso Pope, the millionaire New York construction executive, publisher, and Tammany Hall leader, was out of proportion to his behavior. In the thirties, Pope, like Mellon and Stimson, had admired Mussolini. He had even been photographed giving the Fascist salute at *Il Duce*'s side, and his newspapers had received special privileges from Fascist authorities. Like many other Italian-Americans, Pope also interpreted Roosevelt's allusion to the "stab in the back" as a slur on all Italians, not merely an angry condemnation of Fascists. "Americans of Italian origin," Pope announced, "cannot stretch their profound devotion to their adopted fatherland to the point of tolerating systematic insolences against their original fatherland." In the presidential campaign, he straddled parties. His newspapers supported Willkie while he preserved his local power by remaining within Tammany Hall.

In May, 1941, shortly after the founding of the Fight for Freedom Committee, Pope applied for membership and offered a large contribution. The interventionists interpreted Pope's attitude, including attacks in his newspaper on Mussolini, not as a change of heart but as another attempt to play on two teams at once. Ulric Bell, one of the committee's leaders, denounced him as a "pro-Fascist" and a "political bigamist" trying to "jump on the bandwagon." The committee publicly rejected Pope's application and gift. Pope and the Fight for Freedom dueled throughout the summer, with the committee seeking, unsuccessfully, to have the Attorney General revoke his citizenship, saying he had not fulfilled the oath of citizenship by "absolutely and entirely renounc [ing] and adjur [ing] all allegiance and fidelity to any foreign . . . power."

The denunciation of Pope's seeming duplicity may have been justified, but the attack on his citizenship was another matter. Few of these interventionists were motivated solely by their concern for America's safety. The historian of their movement, Mark Chadwin, has pointed out that they too had fraternal sympathy for the land of their ancestors, usually for England or for Europe's Jews.

Meanwhile, the war was going badly for the Allies, but not as a result of Italian actions. Italy's unreadiness for war and her inability to deal with a major enemy became evident in the brief fighting against crippled France. Her air force raided cities in the interior, but these attacks had little military significance. As for the Italian army, it did not advance more than several miles in a few places along the French border. Yet France's government sued for an armistice from both Germany and Italy.

After consultation in Munich, Hitler and Mussolini granted the request. *Il Duce* had little to say about the armistice; Hitler dictated the terms. Even though associated in the victory, Italy found those terms almost as humiliating for herself as for France. Whereas Germany took over more than half of defeated France, including all the coastline on the Atlantic, Italy occupied only a narrow strip of territory along the frontier that did not even include the former Italian city of Nice. In Africa, Italy had long demanded Tunisia and Jibuti, but the Germans left these territories under French control. These disappointing results in the hour of victory showed the limitations of Italian power and how negligible was German respect for it.

Mussolini's empty victory also reflected demoralization at home. Since he had rushed into a war that had no meaning for the mass of the Italian people, the soldiers fought half-heartedly, plodding into battle ill-equipped and inadequately supported. Italy's meager resources, strained by the Ethiopian and Spanish Wars, by corruption and plain inefficiency in the Fascist regime, could not sustain the war. Understandably, the average Italian fighting man quickly lost confidence in his country's war leadership. Nonetheless, at first the Italians won a few small victories. In August, 1940, their forces overran British Somaliland and crossed into the Sudan. In September, an army under Marshal Rodolfo Graziani attacked Egypt and met with initial success. Graziani then decided to consolidate his lines around Sidi Barrani, a village some sixty miles beyond the Libyan frontier.

Italy was now drifting toward war with the United States also. Early in September when Roosevelt gave the British fifty old destroyers in exchange for bases in the Western Hemisphere, Mussolini concluded that the United States would intervene in the war. On September 27, in Berlin, Italian, German, and Japanese statesmen signed a formal military alliance called the "Tripartite Pact," whereby Japan recognized Hitler and Mussolini's "new order" in Europe, and Germany and Italy accepted Japan's ascendancy in East Asia. The crucial part of the treaty, Article Three, was directed against the United States. If the United States went to war against any one of the signatories, it said, then the other two were obligated to assist the third party.

While Graziani's army was still halted at Sidi Barrani, Mussolini decided to stake out a claim in Greece, thereby diverting Italy's main war effort from Africa. On October 28, in an act condemned by Americans (but also one that did not arouse them particularly because they were preoccupied with events at home) Fascist troops invaded Greece. Not only did they fail to gain the prestige *Il Duce* sought, but the Italians also fared nowhere near as well as the Nazis had done elsewhere. They were pushed back into Albania, a development that amazed and pleased most Americans. Again, Fascist incompetence contributed to the defeats inflicted by far-from-powerful Greek forces.

In December, having reinforced their troops in Egypt, the British attacked Graziani's army, routed it, bagged some 100,000 prisoners, and within two months were deep in Libya at the gates of Bengazi. These setbacks, Ambassador Phillips reported from Rome, deepened Italian discontent over the war. Even members of the foreign office, he said, hoped that Roosevelt would mediate or would in some other way help Italy make a separate peace before the Nazis became her masters.

Roosevelt could not help Italy, but Hitler could. With Mussolini floundering in Africa and Europe, the *Fuehrer* decided to take charge and rescue him from further defeat. In the spring of 1941, German forces invaded the Balkans. The Nazis swiftly conquered Yugoslavia, and Bulgaria entered the war against both Yugoslavia and Greece. Within a few weeks in April, the Germans overran Greece, forcing the collapse of the Greek armies fighting the Italians on the Albanian front.

During these months, Roosevelt took strong measures against Italy. In February, 1941, the Fascists asked the American government to transfer its consulates in Naples and Palermo to Rome, away from the coast. The President retaliated by closing Italian consulates in Detroit and Newark, an act the Italian ambassador thought would be followed by a breach in diplomatic relations. On March 30, following disclosures that Italians had damaged twenty-five out of twenty-seven of their ships interned in American ports, Roosevelt took the vessels into "protective custody." On June 14, through an executive order, he froze Italian economic assets in the United States. Two days later, he ordered the Italian, as well as the German, government to close all its consulates, tourist agencies, and information bureaus in the United States. Mussolini immediately retaliated by shutting American consulates in Italian territory. The American government took these steps not just to injure Italy, but more to accompany similar measures against Germany. Italy, American policy makers felt, could not harm the United States, but her powerful ally had the potential to do so.

Italy's war in Africa now ranged far and wide. Italian forces fought the British, who attacked Ethiopia from both Kenya and the Sudan, reached Addis Ababa at the beginning of April, and returned Haile Selassie to his throne. By June, they had cleared the Italians from their short-lived empire in East Africa. In spite of these defeats, this campaign in East Africa marked one of the few occasions when Italian soldiers gave a good account of themselves.

In Libya, weakened British forces fell back before a slashing attack by German and Italian troops led by General Erwin Rommel, the brilliant German tank commander who had taken control of Axis forces there. Now, even in their own African colony, the Italians became virtual puppets who moved when the Germans pulled the strings. In November, the British resumed the attack in North Africa, reaching El Agheila by the end of the year. Early in the following year, Rommel's Italian-German forces again pushed the British back, this time to within sixty miles of Alexandria. Meanwhile events in Asia had changed the complexion of the war and the nature of the Italian-American relationship.

Early Sunday morning, December 7, 1941, airplanes from a Japanese carrier task force bombed Pearl Harbor in a surprise attack. The next day, Congress passed and the President signed a declaration of war against Japan. At noon on the following day, Japan, under the terms of the Tripartite Pact, asked Germany and Italy to join her war. So, on December 11, Italy and Germany declared war on the United States. On that same afternoon, Congress unanimously declared war on Germany and Italy. "The long known and the long expected," the President told Congress, "has thus taken place." American policy makers had expected Germany to declare war and had "fully anticipated that Italy would obediently follow along." So concerned were Roosevelt and his advisers with the fight against Nazi Germany that the declaration of war against Italy seemed almost an afterthought.

In Italy, on the other hand, the American entrance into the war had a tremendous impact. According to Ciano, Mussolini had long "been in favor of clarifying the position between America and the Axis." Il Duce said that since the United States had been helping England for a long time, its new status as an open enemy would not change the nature of the war. Not only was he wrong, but he was also out of step with his own people. Despite the mounting tension between the United States and Italy, most Italians retained a friendly attitude toward Americans. "The friendliness was palpable and the unpopularity of the war and the Fascist regime was so great," Herbert L. Matthews, an American newspaperman in Rome at the time, recalled, "that when the blow was struck at Pearl Harbor it almost seemed possible that Mussolini would stall again."

Now most knowledgeable Italians had become more convinced than ever that their country could not possibly win the war and that she did not deserve victory. It seemed to them almost beyond credibility that they had earned as an enemy the powerful nation where millions of Italians had made a new life, the nation that millions of others had always especially admired. Never had the relationship with Americans been so cruel and bitter.

"The Bitter Test
of Hostilities"

13

America's entrance into the war marked the beginning of a long period of torment and suffering for Italy. But the declarations of war did not bring an immediate clash between Italian and American troops. At first the Americans merely increased their supplies to the British in North Africa, rushed a few troops there, and sent planes on raids over Italian territory. Italian and American soldiers faced each other in battle in large numbers for only a brief period of about five months. American writers, and many of the soldiers, ridiculed the poor showing of the Italians in battle, although at times American troops found the Italian units they encountered tough opponents. By 1943, most Italians had become indifferent to the glories of the warrior; they often responded to pleas for courage and sacrifice by shrugging their shoulders and asking why they should show bravery in a pointless war. As Saville R. Davis, the Rome correspondent of the *Christian Science Monitor,* observed, "It is not possible to fight modern battles with an army of conscientious objectors."

Italian-Americans also thought that Mussolini had committed his country to a worthless cause. After Italy became a declared enemy, most of them lost whatever sympathy they may have had for it. Yet the American government immediately classified Italians, who comprised the largest alien group in the country, as enemy aliens and compelled them to register as such. Emotional patriots mistakenly believed that the inhabitants of the Little Italies might be more devoted to Fascist Italy than to the United States. Employers in war industries, fearing sabotage, for a while did not want to use unnaturalized Italians; some employers just discriminated against all with Italian names. In California, Attorney General Earl Warren "evacuated" several prominent Italians and about forty members of the *Fasci di Combattimento,* or Italian veterans of the First World War, from the

247

state, but government agencies prosecuted few Italian aliens. Later, California abandoned the idea of banning them from restricted areas. In New York, a number of labor unions, including the International Longshoremen's Association, which had an especially large Italian membership, segregated Italians in special work gangs. For a time, therefore, the war disrupted the pattern of adjustment of Italians and their children to American life.

As a group, Italian-Americans quickly declared their loyalty to the United States. Even those who had flirted with Fascism switched in sentiment. "Fascism may have been all right for a time over there," the editor of an Italian-language paper commented, "but we are through with it." Two days after the attack on Pearl Harbor, one of their organizations, the United Italian-American League, telegraphed the President urging defeat of all enemy forces. The Mazzini Society, Italian newspapers, and various Italian-American groups also announced their support of the war. Later, Italians in the United States formed an American Committee for Italian Democracy to persuade Italians in Europe to abandon the Axis cause.

In August, 1942, the American government made use of Italian exiles by promoting an anti-Fascist congress in Montevideo, Uruguay. This group, composed largely of *fuorusciti,* planned a provisional government in exile, and an Italian legion to help free Italy from Fascism, but nothing ever came of this effort. Prominent Italian-Americans and anti-Fascist exiles, however, did join a propaganda assault on Italy. In short-wave radio broadcasts, they urged the people to renounce Fascism and to cooperate with Americans, saying that the United States wanted to destroy Fascism but not the Italian people, that the United States desired their friendship.

So seriously did Italians in the United States take their loyalty to their adopted land that out of the more than 600,000 classed as enemy aliens, the Federal Bureau of Investigation apprehended only 400. In October, 1942, on Columbus Day, Attorney General Francis Biddle announced that the Italians designated as enemy aliens were only technically so. His department considered the Italian-American community completely loyal. After ten months of vigilance and investigation, he explained, the government had found it necessary to intern slightly more than 200, or less than one-twentieth of one per cent of the nation's Italian population. So the policy makers decided to remove the wartime disabilities from Italians, or no longer treat them as enemy aliens. On the following day, Assistant Secretary of State Adolf A. Berle addressed the Italian-American community, assuring it that the government planned no punitive peace for Italy. These announcements pleased Italian-Americans everywhere.

The concern over Italian aliens reflected an unusual attitude on the part of Americans at war. As public opinion polls in 1942 indicated, they may have held Italians in contempt as fighters, but they never looked upon them as bitter enemies. Italian-Americans profited from this attitude and especially from the special view of policy makers toward Italy. These leaders spread the idea that the United States was fighting Italy to free her; Italians were not truly enemies, but imprisoned friends.

In some instances, feelings of friendship transcended the bitterness of war. In the summer of 1942, when Gordon Sproul, president of the University of California, invited Carlo Sforza to Berkeley to fill a chair of Italian culture, he explained the circumstances. Even though the United States and Italy are at war, Sproul wrote, "We want to preserve, so far as possible, our intellectual relations with Italy; for it must not be taken that there is war between our two peoples."

Regardless of old feelings, Italians and Americans did fight each other. Americans began encountering Italians in battle on a large scale after November 8, 1942, when American and British troops stormed French beaches at Oran, Algiers, and Casablanca. The Allied forces spreading out over North Africa reached Tunis where ultimately they crushed Italian and German resistance, destroyed or captured much of Italy's war materiel and trained fighting force, and placed all North Africa under Anglo-American control. From bases there, American planes bombed cities in Italy where the Italians, lacking searchlights, antiaircraft guns, and an adequate air force, offered only slight resistance.

In January, 1943, just before the moment of final victory in North Africa, President Roosevelt and various advisers journeyed to Casablanca to confer with Prime Minister Winston Churchill and other British leaders. Although the United States was the senior partner in the Anglo-American alliance, American policy makers recognized British leadership in the Mediterranean. As Undersecretary of State Sumner Welles put it, "The general scheme was frankly based upon the preponderance of British interests in the Italian theater."

At Casablanca, as the British desired, the Allied leaders decided to concentrate their next offensive against Italy, the Axis partner most likely to collapse. They went ahead with a British plan to invade Sicily. At the close of the meeting, Roosevelt announced a policy of "unconditional surrender" toward the Axis enemies. "It does not mean the destruction of the population of Germany, Italy, or Japan," he told a press conference, "but it does mean the destruction of the philosophies in those countries which are based on conquest and the subjugation of other people." This idea disturbed even anti-Fascist Italians, prompting *fuorusciti* such as the high-minded priest, Don Luigi Sturzo, to denounce it. Churchill wanted to exclude Italy from the policy to "encourage a breakup there," but he gave in to Roosevelt. Italy therefore became the first of the Axis powers to feel the impact of the unconditional surrender policy.

The immediate events that would move Italy toward surrender began on May 11, 1943, when Churchill and his advisers arrived in the United States for two weeks of conversation and war planning. Overcoming the resistance of the American chiefs of staff, who wished to halt major operations in the Mediterranean after the capture of Sicily, the Prime Minister persuaded Roosevelt to make the Italian mainland the next Anglo-American objective. The Russians reacted coolly to the idea of an Italian campaign, seeing the peninsula as a minor area in the war. An invasion of Italy, they believed, would delay the opening of a major second front in France without drawing off much German strength from their own hard-pressed front.

Yet, as the British insisted, the chances for knocking Italy out of the war were good. "The backbone of the Italian armed forces was broken," the German military *attaché* in Rome, Enno von Rintelen, wrote, "The best divisions had been lost or routed in Africa and Russia. . . . The long coastline of the peninsula and of the big islands was unprotected." In such circumstances, a people committed to a war they believe in often stiffen their resolve and fight on, but not the Italians. They were demoralized, lacking even a will to fight. So General Dwight D. Eisenhower, the Supreme Commander of the Allied Armies in the Mediterranean, received orders to prepare for an invasion of the Italian mainland as soon as Sicily fell.

Then on June 11, Roosevelt played on the Italian dislike of the war. "I think it is fair to say that all of us—I think I speak for all the United Nations—are agreed that when the Fascist regime is thrown out," he announced, "we can assure the Italian people of their freedom to choose the non-Fascist, non-Nazi kind of Government they wish to establish." A month later, on July 10, Anglo-American forces invaded the southeastern corner of Sicily. They met no resistance from the Italian navy, whose admirals realistically did not want to risk their remaining ships without air cover, and encountered only light fighting from outgunned Italian soldiers. But German tank troops, which had been rushed to the island, put up a stiff fight.

This invasion of Sicily came at a time when the discussion of a possible Italian surrender, based on evidence of strikes and increasing opposition to Fascism within the country, was heard in Allied governmental circles. In the spring and early summer of 1943, a few Italian generals even considered overthrowing Mussolini, but the King equivocated. On July 16, as part of a stepped-up propaganda offensive designed to take advantage of popular discontent, Roosevelt and Churchill urged the Italians to capitulate. "We take no satisfaction in invading Italian soil and bringing the tragic devastation of war home to the Italian people," the two leaders announced, "but we shall destroy Fascism. The time has come for you to decide whether Italians shall die for Mussolini and Hitler—or live for Italy, and for civilization."

Although demanding surrender, American policy makers did not place the Italian people in the same category of guilt as the Germans. "President Roosevelt and I," Hull explained later, "believed almost from the time of Mussolini's declaration of war against the United States . . . that we should draw a distinction between the Italians on one hand and the Germans and Japanese on the other." Even during their intense opposition to Fascism, he said, Americans "had always been friendly with Italians." That July, while visiting England, Secretary of War Henry L. Stimson told Churchill his version of the American attitude, saying "the American people did not hate the Italians but took them rather as a joke as fighters."

In desperation, Mussolini turned to Hitler, asking for a discussion of the Anglo-American invasion of Sicily. On July 19, the two dictators met for the thirteenth time at Villa Gaggia, near Feltre, in northern Italy, with the *Fuehrer* doing most of the talking. Mussolini asked for planes and other help, but "he could not," according to one of his generals, "bring himself to admit that Italy could not fight any longer." Owing to the pressures of the war in Russia, the Germans said, they could give no further assistance. Italy's situation appeared desperate. British and American planes were bombing her at will and made a massive first attack on Rome of nearly 600 planes while Mussolini and Hitler were conferring. Now even Fascist leaders felt compelled to turn against *Il Duce*.

On July 24, the Fascist Grand Council demanded Mussolini's resignation. The next day, Vittorio Emmanuele dismissed him and ordered a small band of loyal *carabinieri* ("national police") to arrest the fallen dictator, who was carted away in an ambulance, and thereby terminated almost twenty-one years of Fascist rule. For Prime Minister, the King chose Marshal Pietro Badoglio, a conservative friend.

That evening the Italian radio announced Mussolini's overthrow and broadcast a proclamation by Badoglio saying "the war continues." At the same time, Badoglio planned secret approaches to the Allies, hoping to obtain better terms than an unconditional surrender. He also decreed the dissolution of the Fascist party, an act that no one openly opposed; most Italians rejoiced. In Sorrento, the anti-Fascist political philosopher and historian Benedetto Croce expressed privately what many Italians felt. "Fascism seems already a thing of the past to me," he wrote in his diary, "a cycle that is closed. . . ." Fascism collapsed quietly, detested by a people weary of war and anxious to escape the consequences of the defeat brought on by a Mussolini they had earlier supported.

American policy makers, surprised by the swiftness of Mussolini's fall, interpreted the transfer of power as the first step toward an Italian appeal for peace, a sound analysis. Yet on the day after it happened, Samuel Grafton, of the Office of War Information, broadcast that "there is no reason to believe that the essential nature of the Fascist regime in Italy has changed"; it survives, presided over by a "moronic little king" and a "high ranking Fascist." This comment triggered a hostile reaction in various American newspapers. Arthur Krock, a conservative political columnist for the *New York Times,* and another writer for the Chicago *Daily Tribune,* accused the men in the Office of War Information of trying to "foment a Communist revolution in Italy." Some members of Congress also grumbled about the attack on the King. Finally, Roosevelt himself quieted the furor by disavowing the broadcast.

Although exultant over Mussolini's downfall, Roosevelt did not wish to ease the pressure on the Italians. On July 26, he told Churchill he hoped to get an arrangement "as close to unconditional surrender as possible." Two days later, he warned that the Fascists could not escape punishment by the expedient of resigning. "Our terms to Italy are still the same as our terms to Germany and Japan—," he announced, "unconditional surrender."

Militant anti-Fascist Italians in the United States opposed Badoglio and the King, while others supported the idea of American cooperation with Badoglio's regime. But Italian-Americans showed no division in their feelings over Mussolini's fall. All those queried expressed pleasure. La Guardia called him "the betrayer of Italy." *Il progresso Italo-Americano,* a former admirer, came out with a similar view. Giuseppe A. Borgese also cautioned the Allies against a new dictatorship, saying that "Marshal Badoglio was responsible for the Ethiopian campaign and can be held responsible for many of the terrors of Fascism." Luigi Criscuolo, a conservative banker, on the other hand, described the King to Roosevelt as a "heroic figure" and a "man of high principle," and denounced anti-Fascists as "fifth columnists" and Marxist "mercenaries."

Eisenhower, meanwhile, tried to speed up Italy's surrender. "You want peace," he told the Italians in a radio broadcast on July 30; "you can have peace immediately under the honorable conditions which our Governments have already offered you. We are coming as liberators." On the following day, Badoglio and his advisers decided to put out feelers for an armistice. They secretly ordered envoys to Lisbon and Tangier, where they talked with American and British representatives. Insisting upon unconditional surrender, the Allies refused to negotiate as the Italians proposed.

These developments led Roosevelt and Churchill to move quickly for another meeting. First, on August 13, Churchill went to Roosevelt's home at Hyde Park, New York, for some preliminary talks with the President alone. Four days later, the leaders and their advisers plunged into full-scale discussions in Quebec concerning Italy's fate. At first, they differed concerning the treatment of Italy. Roosevelt still desired unconditional surrender; Churchill wanted to knock Italy out of the war, regardless of the terms of surrender, as quickly as possible. Unlike the American leaders, many of whom looked upon the King and Badoglio as still representing some of the worst elements of the Fascist regime and disliked having to deal with them, Churchill was willing to use them to gain his ends. "Now that Mussolini is gone," he told Roosevelt, "I would deal with any non-Fascist government which can deliver the goods." As for Badoglio's regime, it desired an armistice without surrender based on Italy's getting out of the war without further injury. Badoglio and the King were willing to change sides to save what they could, and if they could switch without provoking a German seizure of the peninsula. All this proved difficult because both the Germans and the Allies distrusted them.

Harry Hopkins, Roosevelt's personal adviser, put the American attitude in plain language. "I surely don't like the idea," he said, "that these former enemies can change their minds when they know that they are going to get licked and come over to our side and get help in maintaining political power." What Hopkins felt was true enough; but no matter how tainted Badoglio's government was and no matter how much the Italians merited defeat, they were acting as many people have done under similar circumstances. They turned against the regime that had brought them grief and tried to avoid more disaster. Badoglio therefore felt he could not openly seek peace until the Allies assured him they could protect Italy from the Germans. Lacking sufficient troops, Eisenhower could make no such promise. Knowing that the Italian armies faced extinction if they fought the Germans alone, Badoglio hesitated. The Italians were dependent on the Germans even for such essentials as ammunition and gasoline.

Regardless of Badoglio's wavering, American policy makers finally concluded that he really wanted to end the war. At Quebec, Roosevelt gave in to Churchill over negotiating with Badoglio. Since they wished to secure Italian cooperation, the terms they drew up were unconditional mainly in theory. They outlined Allied policy toward Italy in two instruments of surrender, one called the "short terms" and the other the "long terms." The short terms dealt with military matters and the long terms with economic and political affairs. The Italians were not to see the long terms until after they signed the short ones. Basically, the Allies promised to mitigate unconditional surrender and to treat the Italians humanely if they worked their passage by helping in the war against Germany.

In the middle of August, while Roosevelt and Churchill were in Quebec, Brigadier General Giuseppe Castellano, assistant to the chief of the Italian general staff and one of those who had turned against Mussolini, secretly got in touch with Allied representatives in Madrid. An accredited peace emissary, he went on to Lisbon, where on August 19, he discussed an armistice with Major General Walter Bedell Smith, Eisenhower's representative, and tried to switch Italy to the Allied side. Promising nothing, Smith insisted that Italy must surrender unconditionally, trusting the Allies' sense of justice concerning her fate. He gave Castellano the short terms for surrender, which the Italian government could either accept or reject. The Italian reaction, repeated several times, came in a question, "Are you strong enough to protect us against the Germans?" Castellano then returned to Rome.

By this time, Hitler knew that Badoglio was negotiating with the Americans. The *Fuehrer* wasted no time. Even though Italy had been a liability, he would not let her loose. By controlling her, he could retain access to her food and industries and keep the Allies away from Germany. While the American generals and Badoglio fumbled over the surrender, therefore, Hitler poured more troops and equipment into Italy and ordered the German forces already there to take over what they could.

By this time, too, on August 16, five weeks after their landing in Sicily, Allied armies had captured Messina and controlled the whole island. American and British forces now stood poised for a thrust into the Italian mainland. Preparations for this invasion and negotiations for Italy's surrender went hand in hand. Castellano made his way from Rome to Cassibile, Sicily, where he told the Allies that his government, because of the German occupation, could not go ahead with the armistice unless the British and Americans landed large forces near Rome to protect it. Smith refused to change the terms; nonetheless, late on September 1, Badoglio's government accepted them. On the next day, Anglo-American forces crossed the Straits of Messina and, meeting no opposition, pushed their way along the Italian boot. On the day after, in an army tent at Cassibile, Eisenhower's representatives and Badoglio's signed the armistice.

These short terms, which omitted the phrase "unconditional surrender," placed Italy under Allied domination. Eisenhower himself considered them "unduly harsh." They also committed Badoglio's government to keeping the armistice secret until it suited the Allies to make it public. Several days later, owing to the build-up of German forces around Rome, Badoglio decided that the Allies could not save the city and his regime. He tried to call off the armistice, but Eisenhower refused to do so, telling Badoglio that his failure to carry out the agreement would be "followed by the dissolution of your government and of your nation." As Robert Murphy, a diplomat, wrote to Roosevelt, the Italians did not have a palatable choice. "It is a nice balance in their minds whether we or the Germans will work the most damage in Italy. They are between the hammer and the anvil."

On September 8, 1943, to coincide with an assault on Salerno, Eisenhower announced the armistice. That evening a fearful Badoglio broadcast the news to the Italian people. "All hostilities by the Italian armed forces against the British and American forces," he said, "must now cease. They [the Italian forces] will, however, repel attacks from whatever quarter they may come," meaning from the Germans. This announcement assured the Allies that Italian troops would not support the Germans at Salerno, the scene of the first major Allied attack on the European continent. Since the battle was touch and go, the British and Americans profited immediately from the absence of Italian forces, according to the armistice.

A few hours after the broadcast, Badoglio and the King fled Rome to avoid capture by the Nazis. They made their way south to Brindisi, where they set up what remained of their government. Also, right after the armistice announcement, which confused Italian troops everywhere, the waiting Germans destroyed or disarmed some ninety divisions of the Italian army. German forces moved into the two-thirds of Italy that had been held by the Italian army as well as into those parts of the Balkans that had been held by Italian garrisons. A few isolated units resisted, but most Italian soldiers, finding themselves without their generals, many of whom had disappeared without leaving orders, just surrendered as a matter of policy, or drifted back to their homes. Most Italian naval units managed to elude the Germans and surrendered to the Americans and British at Malta and elsewhere.

From Allied headquarters in North Africa, Eisenhower wired Badoglio to defend Rome, but the flight to Brindisi precluded organized Italian resistance to the Germans, a collapse that disappointed the Allies. Four days after the announced surrender, Roosevelt and Churchill urged "every Italian to strike his blow" to aid in driving the Germans out of Italy. By helping "in this great surge of liberation," they told the Italians, you "will place yourselves once more among the true and long-proved friends of your country. . . ."

Roosevelt could logically make such a statement because Allied troops were now fighting as forces of liberation and occupation; yet American soldiers were told that Italy was an enemy country. Stunned by the surrender, the Italian people did not easily understand their relationship to the Anglo-American forces. In particular, they felt discouraged and resentful over the way the armistice had come about, and over what followed. From their point of view, with Italy divided and a battleground for foreign armies, their situation turned out far worse than they had ever thought it would be.

On September 12, German paratroop commandos, landing in the Abruzzi mountains, rescued Mussolini from captivity in Campo Imperatore, a resort hotel there. Three days later, he announced the formation of an Italian Social Republic headed by himself but controlled by the Germans. Most Italians could not take the new Fascist regime seriously. They called it the *Repubblica di Salò,* taking the name from a resort on the western shore of Lake Garda where Mussolini established headquarters.

During these days, American radio broadcasts were promising Italy help in postwar reconstruction and treatment according to the principles of the Atlantic Charter, the broad goals agreed upon by America and Britain. These announcements, by giving some hope for the future, mitigated the Italians' despair over their plight. Roosevelt himself also looked to the future. After overriding objections from Churchill and from his own advisers, he permitted several *fuorusciti* to return to Italy. He argued that sooner or later the Italians would become free to choose their own form of government, therefore he wanted the leading exiles to return and take part in reviving Italy's political life.

Wishing to invigorate Italian resistance to the Germans, Eisenhower wanted to do more in the present. He urged the President to give Italy belligerent status. Roosevelt agreed. On September 21, with considerable difficulty, he persuaded Churchill to recognize Badoglio's Italy as a co-belligerent if she would declare war on Germany. On the following day, Hull informed Eisenhower of this decision. Hull, too, hoped that a declaration of war would instill new vigor into the southern Italians and would encourage those in the north to boycott Mussolini's republic. He wanted to use Italians to fight the Germans. Badoglio, Croce, and other leaders in the south all favored greater Italian participation in the war, mainly through a combatant legion under the Italian flag fighting by the side of the Allies. "We did not," Badoglio explained in his memoirs, "wish the Allies to free our country without our help." American liberals disliked both the idea of co-belligerency and of an Italian armed force. Harry Hopkins told Roosevelt so, saying he saw not "enough evidence that Badoglio and the King can be trusted for us to arm any of their divisions." Roosevelt still went ahead with his plans.

On September 29, on a British warship off Malta, Badoglio and Eisenhower signed the armistice with the long terms that cleared the way for Italy to become a co-belligerent. This document in its signed version contained the words "unconditional surrender," which Badoglio protested as humiliating. Two days later, Allied forces entered Naples, where for four days the populace had been carrying on a guerrilla campaign against the Germany army. After the capture of this city, the Anglo-American Allies met increasingly stiff German resistance, particularly along the line of the Volturno River. From this stabilized front, the Allied campaign in Italy became a slow, disheartening struggle against a skillfully entrenched foe. "The *Fuehrer* is firmly determined to wipe the slate clean in Italy . . . ," Dr. Josef Goebbels, the Nazi propagandist, noted. "The only thing certain in this war is that Italy will lose it."

Now Roosevelt and his advisers wanted the Italians to act quickly against the Germans. On October 2, he told Churchill that "an immediate declaration of war by the Italian Government on Germany is necessary if Italy is to be given the status of a co-belligerent." The Prime Minister agreed, replying it was high time the Italians worked their passage. The King reluctantly consented, but not soon enough to get the declaration of war out on Columbus Day in order to assure it favorable publicity in the United States, especially among Italian-Americans, as American policy makers desired.

On the following day, October 13, 1943, Badoglio's government, shielded by Allied armies, formally joined the struggle. The Allies then accepted "the active cooperation of the Italian nation and armed forces as a co-belligerent in the war against Germany," but said that co-belligerency would not affect the terms of the armistice. In this way, southern Italy, although still an enemy state, became a limited partner of the Allies. In the north, the majority of Italians contributed to the Allied war effort through an anti-Fascist partisan movement called the *Resistenza Armata.* Americans and other Allies gave the partisans money, supplies, arms, and other help. Since some Italians remained loyal to Mussolini and fought for his Social Republic, Italians battled Italians in a brutal civil war.

Co-belligerency—*parola bruttisima* (the ugliest word) Italians called it—conferred an uncertain status. It implied a role of increasing military cooperation for Italy with her former enemies, but barred her from going to any peace conference as one of the victors. "Allied Italy," an American officer explained, "is a co-belligerent enemy. As enemies, the Italians are permitted to die for the Allies. Get it?"

As soon as Italy became a co-belligerent, the Allies treated her surrendered navy as part of their fleet. Along with other Italian shipping, it operated against the Germans in the Mediterranean. Elsewhere the process of military cooperation never went far enough to suit the Italians. Badoglio and his followers assumed that co-belligerency meant the Anglo-American leaders felt graciously disposed toward Italy. So he tried for more, essentially an alliance. Seeing their objective in Italy mainly in military terms, Americans refused even to consider such an arrangement.

At about this time, Cordell Hull flew from Washington to Moscow for a conference of Allied foreign ministers. There the Soviets complained that they had no effective part in Italian occupation policy and protested their exclusion. Vyacheslav Molotov, the Russian Foreign Minister, gave Anthony Eden, the British Foreign Secretary, a list of measures the Soviets wished to carry out in Italy to rid her of Fascist influences. Eden argued that the American and British occupiers were already putting many of the suggestions into effect. As a concession to the Soviets, the ministers agreed to establish an Advisory Control Council for Italy made up of French, Yugoslav, and Greek representatives as well as those of the United States, Britain, and Russia. It had little power in enforcing the terms of surrender because it could only advise; the Supreme Commander of the Allied Forces, an American, made the vital decisions. Stalin also demanded a part of the Italian fleet. Not wanting the Soviets in the Mediterranean, Hull balked. For a while at least, nothing came of the request.

The Allied ministers worked out a "Declaration Regarding Italy," announced on October 30. It stated that "Allied policy towards Italy must be based upon the fundamental principle that Fascism . . . shall be utterly destroyed and that the Italian people shall be given every opportunity to establish governmental and other institutions based upon democratic principles." The Anglo-American combined chiefs of staff instructed Eisenhower on the declaration's meaning and left him to carry it out. This arrangement, since it prevented the Soviet Union from playing too active a role in Italy, satisfied American policy makers.

In accordance with another decision at Moscow and with Italy's terms of surrender, Eisenhower early in November, 1943, created an Allied Control Commission, half British and half American, with authority to deal with "day to day questions, other than military operations." The commission functioned in the area to the rear of the battle front and an Allied Military Government, which was established in Algeria in the summer as the Allied Military Government of Occupied Territory but changed in title when Italy became a co-belligerent, administered the forward zones. With the exception of four small districts in the southwestern section of the peninsula, the Allied command governed all parts of Italy not in German hands. Even there Badoglio's government had no real power; it could act only under Allied supervision.

As the Allies laboriously fought their way northward, the Allied Control Commission merged with or replaced Allied Military Government and the Commission turned over direct control of Italy's southernmost provinces to the royal government. Even though the Allied Commission in 1944 eliminated the word "control" from its title, it retained power over Italy's government until the peace settlement. In most of the problems it faced, the Commission functioned reasonably well, but critics considered its governing procedures unwieldy and inadequate for conquered Italy's needs.

Italy had little or no freedom under the Allies not only because Mussolini had brought the country virtually to ruin but also because his successors in their blundered surrender had incurred the distrust of the conquerors. Also the disruption of the economy and all forms of organization, especially the disintegration of the army, made Italy's part in the Allied war effort a small one. Italians furnished supply columns that carried munitions and food to the front lines and guarded channels of communication; but except for the impressive northern resistance movement, Americans, Englishmen, and Germans did most of the fighting. Italy, as the battleground, suffered. Yet Croce, Badoglio, and others kept insisting that Italians should make a substantial formal military contribution to the war with a volunteer corps fighting under the Italian flag. Such a force, they were convinced, could revive Italian dignity and help to ease the peace terms. They also felt that the Anglo-American conquerors wanted no such army. Badoglio complained that the Allies prodded the Italians to earn their way but prevented them from "taking any share in the fighting."

The difficulties of the Italian campaign and the demands of other theaters of action led Roosevelt and his military advisers at this point to think of restricting the effort in Italy. In conferences with Roosevelt at Cairo, and with Roosevelt and Stalin in Teheran in November and December, 1943, Churchill insisted on pushing ahead in Italy; Roosevelt reluctantly went along. Nonetheless, American policy makers now were no longer willing to accept British leadership in defining policy for Italy. They claimed and exercised at least equal power. In December, after his trip to Teheran, the President visited American troops in Sicily.

In the following month, January, 1944, Badoglio again brought up the matter of Italy's contribution to the war by asking Roosevelt for allied status. The President replied that Italy would have to wait until she established a broadly democratic government. Badoglio was unable to form such a government because anti-Fascist political leaders refused to serve as ministers of Vittorio Emmanuele. They wanted to

get rid of the King but felt that Roosevelt and Churchill wished to
keep him in power. Late in February, the King gave in slightly to political pressure. He accepted a formula whereby he would not
formally abdicate, but when the Allies captured Rome he would turn
over his powers to his son Umberto.

Now the Soviets again demanded a voice in the decisions concerning Italy's future. In March, without consulting the United States
or Britain, the royal Italian government announced the resumption of
diplomatic relations with the Soviet Union. Although angered, the
Americans did not block this move, but they persuaded the Russians
to reduce recognition from *de jure* to *de facto*. In April, the Americans followed suit by appointing a High Commissioner, Alexander C.
Kirk, to Italy, but did not accredit him to the royal government nor
did they permit it to send a representative to the United States.

The fate of the Italian navy and merchant marine, too, now became an explosive issue among the Allied leaders. From the beginning, the Soviets had demanded one-third of these spoils of war.
Churchill had agreed, but Roosevelt had initially opposed any share
for Russia. He went along with the reasoning of his chiefs of staff,
who maintained that a transfer of ships to the Soviets would have a
bad effect on Italian public opinion. The chiefs argued from military
expediency rather than from a concern for Italians; they wanted maximum Italian cooperation against the Germans.

At Teheran, Roosevelt learned that the Russians felt strongly
about sharing Italian shipping. So he relented, agreeing to give them
some ships while postponing final disposition of all the vessels until
the peace conference. But concern for Italian reactions, as well as the
difficulty of transferring ships from the Mediterranean to Russian
ports, delayed action on this decision. Not until March, 1944, after
Stalin complained about the failure of his allies to act on what had
been agreed in principle, did the Americans and British meet the
problem. They gave some of their own ships to the Soviets to use in
place of Italian tonnage. The Russians were to return the British and
American vessels later when they received their portion of the Italian
ships.

Early in April, another sudden change on the Italian political scene
suggested increasing Soviet concern over Italy's future. Palmiro Togliatti, a bespectacled Italian Communist who had spent years of exile
in Russia, arrived in Naples using the name "Ercole Ercoli" (both
first and last names mean Hercules in Italian). He urged the Italian
Communists, especially active in the northern resistance, to cooperate

with Badoglio's government. Croce saw Togliatti's arrival from Russia and his exhortation to the Communists as "an able shot aimed by the Soviet Republic against the Anglo-Americans." By cooperating with Badoglio, the philosopher said, the Communists would enter the government. American policy makers understood enough of what was happening to speed up, despite British resistance, the plan to give Umberto his father's powers. Churchill wanted to keep Vittorio Emmanuele on the throne, but Roosevelt, under pressure from Italian-Americans, urged his prompt abdication. The King managed to hang on, but on April 21, Badoglio announced the formation of a party government.

Badoglio now reminded Roosevelt of his promise to consider allied status for Italy. The Americans were willing to make Italy an ally, in name at least, but not the British and other Allies. This opposition in an election year placed the President in a difficult position. La Guardia and various Italian-American groups were urging him to recognize Italy as an ally and to give her lend-lease aid. In May, Vito Marcantonio introduced a resolution in Congress calling for the revival of normal diplomatic relations with Italy. Under pressure from his European allies, Roosevelt could not go along.

Italy also met disappointment in her attempts to get back her prisoners of war in Allied hands. Badoglio wanted them for an Italian armed force; the Allies needed them as laborers. The Geneva convention on rules of war prohibited the use of prisoners for work contributing to war. In November, 1943, when the American government tried to use Italian prisoners in the United States for war work, the protests of the senior Italian general had prevented it. The Americans were willing to change the status of the Italians from prisoners to laborers, or to combatants commanded by their own officers, but the British objected. In January, 1944, the Americans asked the Italian government to renounce the rights and protection of the Geneva convention. Badoglio refused, saying he would rather go to prison himself. The Italian government was willing to have the men work, but not as prisoners. Nonetheless, beginning in May, despite Italian protests, the United States put the prisoners as such into war work, violating the laws of war. This situation, like others, showed the anomaly of Italy's half-enemy, half-ally status.

This status became more frustrating as Italians gained more political freedom. In June, 1944, Allied armies finally marched into Rome, hailed as liberators. The victory made available for government service a number of experienced political leaders. One who stood out as a popular choice to head a new government was Ivanoe Bonomi, a former Prime Minister and anti-Fascist democrat, then seventy-one years old. Despite British protests, the Americans supported him; and in Rome, Bonomi organized Italy's first anti-Fascist government. Churchill exploded over Badoglio's replacement by "a cluster of aged and hungry politicians", but Bonomi's government, as Americans realized, represented the drift of popular sentiment far more than did Badoglio's.

Once in office, Bonomi wrote to Roosevelt questioning excessive controls in occupation policy, saying they hampered the development of democratic life in Italy. He also complained of Allied resistance to any Italian armed force; they had dissolved even the small Corps of Italian Liberation. Later he asked the American government to keep promises given in the armistice, namely to end Italy's tutelage, to bring her back into the stream of international affairs, and to release Italians still being held as prisoners of war.

Interested at this point mainly in permitting the Italians a representative anti-Fascist government, the Americans did not wish to change their wartime policies. Hull therefore explained that the Allies were using the armistice terms mainly to prosecute the war against Germany. To the United States, Italy's technical status as a free country remained second to her actual position as an occupied nation. Concerning Italian participation in the war, Hull reminded Bonomi that the Allies faced practical limitations in trying to supply and equip a large armed force. Also the Italians had to overcome the crimes committed by the Fascists in the name of Italy. So Italy could not too soon expect to circulate freely in international organizations.

Others, such as Luigi Sturzo, also urged Americans to define Italy's anomalous status. They wanted the United Sates to make some sort of arrangement for feeding civilians. Although many difficulties stemmed from Fascism and from the Italians' own faults, other problems were the result of Allied policy. When the Americans occupied the country, Italians had expected them to make food, clothing, and other basic goods available in quantity. Instead, with the Allied liberation, the standard of living deteriorated abruptly. With goods in short supply, inflation followed, causing misery everywhere. The biggest factor in the runaway inflation was the spending by American troops. The soldiers did not use American money but a special currency called Allied Military lire, or AM lire. The conquerors issued this money with little restraint and with no backing in gold or securities; they used it as a simple means of making Italy pay the costs of the occupation. Italian governments, present and future, had to assume this cost as a part of the burden of defeat.

Most of the AM lire bought goods and services denied to Italians, many of whom were starving. American soldiers were paid at a level unknown to Italians. A private could draw and spend as much money as a top offiicial in the Italian government. To the average Italian, a private looked like a millionaire. In addition, American soldiers made huge profits at the expense of poor Italians in black markets, most of them filled with American merchandise—canned goods, wheat, sugar, cigarettes, meat, clothing, razor blades, and various luxuries—far beyond the reach of ordinary Italians. Even though operations in the black market were illegal, the army looked on American soldiers' participation in this traffic with equanimity.

As part of Allied policy until late in December, 1943, the civilian population had to fend for itself. At that time, the Anglo-American occupation leaders agreed that military considerations, if nothing else, required them to provide food, and they did in a limited way. Although they were grateful for this help in the essentials of survival, Italian leaders complained about American policy because, for one thing, some Italians were still starving. When Italian-Americans read letters from Italy telling of the misery there, they received the impression that the American government was holding back even its limited economic aid. Many of them felt helpless because they could not send packages of food and clothing to Italy. Since it was short of transport facilities, the army would not distribute the packages.

"Hunger," Marcantonio explained in Congress in June, 1944, "has already reached the famine stage in Italy. Children are dying. . . . 4,000 girls of adolescent age have been treated for venereal disease." Like other Italian-Americans, he sought effective aid for Italy, her acceptance as an ally, and rearmament so that she could fight the "common enemy." Although these demands got nowhere, the Foreign Affairs Committee of the House did hold hearings on his resolution calling for recognition of Italy as an ally.

Private agencies now stepped in to aid the Italians. From Rome, Myron Taylor helped establish "American Relief for Italy," an organization financed by contributions in the United States. With the assistance of the American Red Cross, he also revived the Italian Red Cross. This help, along with packages of food, clothing, and medicines from friends and relatives in the United States, now managed somehow to reach Italians, and relieved some of their misery.

Early in September, Pope Pius XII added his voice to those appealing for more aid to Italy. Later that month, when Roosevelt again conferred with Churchill in Quebec, they and their staffs discussed Italian affairs once more. The Americans insisted on concessions for Italy, something they could make public that would meet some of the demands of Italian-Americans and others. So the British reluctantly agreed to a joint statement issued on September 26, 1944, from the President's home at Hyde Park. This Hyde Park Declaration announced that since in the past twelve months the Italian people had demonstrated their willingness "to fight on the side of the democracies," the Allies would allow them greater scope in the battle against Germany. Gradually, too, they would turn over more power to the Italian government and give it the privilege of sending representatives to London and Washington.

The declaration also outlined measures for improving economic conditions in Italy. To relieve the hunger and sickness, the United Nations Relief and Rehabilitation Administration, known as UNRRA, financed mainly by American dollars and staffed largely by American personnel, would send medical aid and other supplies. To gain as much as possible from Italian resources in fighting the war, the occupation forces would help the Italians in reconstituting their wrecked economy, especially through the repair of electric power systems, railways, and other utilities. In addition, the American government would modify its laws on trading with enemies in order to enable Italians to carry on business with Americans and others. Journalists immediately hailed the Hyde Park Declaration as a new deal for Italy, publicity that pleased Roosevelt as he sought re-election to a fourth term. It indeed initiated a new deal in Italian-American relations, for it committed the United States to a responsibility for Italy's stability as a nation, the beginning of a continuing political and strategic American interest in Italy.

The economic concessions looked better on paper than they were in reality, for Italy did not quickly get anything concrete. The European members of UNRRA, for example, stubbornly resisted Italy's inclusion in the program. Finally, after considerable pressure from the United States, the council of UNRRA authorized $50 million for a plan of limited relief. Although this amounted to a mere gesture because UNRRA had no supplies to spare, Italy did in this way move out of at least one category of enemy status. Later she signed an agreement with UNRRA and obtained relief supplies.

Although the Hyde Park announcement, which pleased Italian-Americans, came in time to attract their votes, Roosevelt felt that he had to keep bidding, especially since his opponent, Governor Thomas E. Dewey of New York, also appealed to them. On October 10, 1944, the President announced that the government would now allow Americans to send dollar remittances to friends and relatives in Italy. It would also repay the Italian government in dollars for the AM lire American troops spent. Two days later, in a Columbus Day proclamation, Dewey said Italy must be considered a "friend and ally." On October 26, despite objections from the British, Roosevelt's government announced that it would, with the appointment of Alexander Kirk as ambassador, resume formal diplomatic relations with Italy. The Latin American countries and the Soviet Union immediately followed suit. On the eve of the elections, the Department of State released a letter to the Mazzini Society listing all American aid to Italy. Roosevelt himself promised to do better in the future.

The Allies also quickly moved to carry out the military promise in the Hyde Park Declaration. They set up an Italian armed force of six small divisions, or combat groups, of 9,000 men each. These new units, larger than the previous ones, were trained by the British and equipped with up-to-date weapons; they contributed modestly to the final advance into northern Italy.

Yet the Italians were still the losers, and by nature the feeling between conqueror and conquered is unpleasant. So it turned out in Italy, but there the Anglo-American military campaign and occupation got mixed up with old American prejudices, going beyond the usual difficulties between victor and vanquished. So the occupation had a profound effect on the attitudes of Americans and Italians toward each other.

As the historian H. Stuart Hughes has pointed out, the fact that the Anglo-American armies assaulted Italy from Sicily rather than from the north played a critical part in the American attitude toward the conquered. American troops received their first impressions of Italians from the most backward part of the country. Their observations of a degraded people who stole, cheated, and clawed for food from army garbage cans merely to survive, when added to the poor military record of the Italians, seemed to confirm the American prejudices that Italians were a dark, dirty, and ignorant people, corrupt, thieving, and cowardly. Polls of American soldiers indicated that many disliked Italians, mainly because they considered Italian living conditions filthy.

These soldiers often viewed the Italians as their inferiors and took an arrogant, tactless, and sometimes brutal, attitude toward the conquered. "I don't know why," John Horne Burns, a sensitive American soldier observed in his book *The Gallery,* "but most Americans had a blanket hatred of all Italians." Although this was an exaggeration, rarely did military government officers, such as the hero of John Hersey's book *A Bell for Adano,* conscientiously try to understand the plight of the people under their supervision. American soldiers often reacted cynically, even bitterly, toward their former enemy, and understandably the defeated Italians felt discouraged. Italians existed in squalor while Americans lived extravagantly, some of them exploiting half-starved women who sold themselves for food or cigarettes. The American behavior was not unusual; soldiers have always acted this way toward the civilians among whom they have been quartered.

In the *Mezzogiorno,* this relationship took a puzzling and particularly sad turn because of the twisted friendship of Italians and Americans. Numerous southern Italians were related to the Italian-Americans in the conquering army; yet American soldiers often treated the conquered as though they belonged to another civilization. The American occupiers had about them an air of superiority that made Italians feel strange and distant. Nonetheless, thousands of Americans of Italian origin discovered relatives or old friends in the villages of southern Italy. These soldiers formed a shaky bridge between two worlds; when they spoke some kind of Italian, they and the conquered stumbled toward mutual sympathy. In any case Americans, regardless of ethnic background, never took on the aloofness of the British, many of whom found it difficult to forget the wounds that Fascism had inflicted on their empire. "The bloody bastards tried for years to do us in," a high British officer said of the Italians as though speaking for all Englishmen; "now let them suffer."

Among the Americans, scorn sometimes disappeared and they made friends among the Italians. The Italians responded warmly to any small sign of sympathy. "Because I was an *americano,*" John Horne Burns wrote, "the Neapolitans treated me with a strange pudding of respect, dismay, and bewilderment." Some soldiers married Italian girls and brought them home. Before the war ended, many Americans, who like Burns had been cynical at first, fell in love with Italy. Some planned to return as students, writers, importers, or just visitors. Out of the conquest came a mass American rediscovery of Italy. The capture of Rome and later of northern Italy deepened the pleasure. As American soldiers fought their way up the peninsula, they encountered for the first time the major centers of Italian cultural and economic life; they saw the Italy that had long been an ornament of Western civilization, that had thrilled the nineteenth-century travelers, and that stood in the mainstream of Western culture.

Ironically, this rediscovery came after a neglect in the study of Italian history and culture in the United States. When the government sought specialists for use in intelligence work or in military administration, it found that few Americans had any expert knowledge of modern Italy. The government therefore frequently turned to second generation Italian-Americans for work in occupied Italy; they comprised the only large group within the United States with at least some knowledge of Italian and of contemporary Italy. By adopting the superior attitude of other Americans toward the conquered, these Italian-Americans sometimes hurt and puzzled the Italians who experienced it. They viewed Americans of Italian extraction as uncultured because they frequently spoke only a dialect and showed little appreciation for the traditions of the land of their ancestors. Perhaps, as some observers remarked, the failings of the Italian-Americans in Italy were ordinary human weaknesses. Their parents had been driven from the peninsula by poverty. Now a few of the children and grandchildren were returning as conquerors, and among them were those who exulted in the reversals of fortune.

This situation caused some concern in the United States. Early in January, 1945, Clare Boothe Luce, a congresswoman from Connecticut, protested American administration in Italy. She charged that the Allied governor, Charles Poletti, a lawyer and politician who had been lieutenant governor of New York, was failing to meet the needs of the people and that the Italian administration was no better. Both authorities, she said, were becoming symbols of "broken promises." Perhaps some starvation was inevitable, yet she believed "more relief could be brought in from the outside if the internal situation were better handled." She wanted to find some way of helping the Italians "to feed themselves by freeing trucks and railroad cars." Later that same month, Luigi Antonini, a prewar anti-Fascist and vice-president of the International Ladies Garment Workers Union, presented a resolution adopted by the Italian-American Labor Party Council to the Department of State. It called for "American political intervention in Italy to facilitate her restoration to her full place among the nations." Assistant Secretary of State James C. Dunn replied that the Roosevelt administration and the American people were both sympathetic to Italy.

Antonini felt that American interest in the military campaign overshadowed all else. True enough, for no one could ignore the gruelling struggle on the Italian peninsula. It contined to involve thousands of American, British, and German soldiers as well as thousands of partisans, often led by former officers from the Italian army. Italians considered their *Resistenza Armata* their finest contribution to the war, a kind of second *Risorgimento*. The resistance movement, although unwilling to give allegiance to the king's government, worked in liaison with the Allies, taking over many of the cities in the Po Valley from the Germans and the Italian Fascists before American and British troops arrived.

Even though the partisans themselves numbered only a small part of Italy's total population, this second *Risorgimento* had a broader base than the nineteenth-century movement. The *Resistenza Armata* even changed the views of American military leaders, who had at first scoffed at Italian fighting abilities, believing the old clichés about Italians being fine artists but poor fighters. As Americans slogged northward, they saw the partisans in action and were impressed. When armored troops "entered cities full of Italian patriots," the Army newspaper *Stars and Stripes* reported, the soldiers "finally felt they were liberating a people who wanted to be free. After long months of winter war, in the mud and the rain and the ruins, finally the Allied soldiers have seen another Italy."

Late in February, 1945, with Allied armies closing in on northern Italy, the German leaders there made contact with agents of America's Office of Strategic Services for discussion of the surrender of Nazi forces in Italy. General Karl Wolff, a high-ranking German commander in Italy, told Allen W. Dulles, the top American intelligence representative in Switzerland, that he hoped to work out a surrender without needless bloodshed and destruction. In March, without Hitler's knowledge, Wolff agreed not to destroy Italian industries, to spare the lives of hostages in German hands, to stop attacks on the Italian partisans, and to prepare the surrender of the German forces in northern Italy. In the following month, on April 29, at Allied headquarters at Caserta, after Anglo-American and partisan forces had already defeated the Germans in the field, Wolff's representatives signed an instrument of unconditional surrender effective in three days. On that same night, Marshal Rodolfo Graziani signed a document of surrender for the forces of the Italian Social Republic.

During these last days of the war, the United States and Italy took the final steps in resuming normal diplomatic relations. On March 9, Alberto Tarchiani, an anti-Fascist journalist, presented his credentials to Roosevelt as the first Italian ambassador to the United States since the declaration of war. The President used the occasion to offer words of encouragement to the Italian people. "The friendship between our two peoples," Roosevelt said, "has passed the bitter test of hostilities between us. With good-will and understanding, that friendship can find more solid bases than ever before. I know that this is the sincere desire of the people and Government of the United States."

The last act in the brutal drama of hostilities took place in a remote section of northern Italy at Dongo, near Lake Como, where partisans captured Mussolini wearing a German corporal's overcoat and helmet, after he had tried and failed to escape to Switzerland. They shot him on April 28, 1945, took his body to Milan where, with the bodies of his mistress, Claretta Petacci, and two aides, they hung it by the heels from the roof of a gas station in Piazzale Loreto. With Mussolini's death, with the collapse of the Germans, and with the Anglo-American conquest of all Italy, the Italian Social Republic, the last refuge of Fascism, disappeared. With the end of Fascism and of the war, a sad and most bitter chapter in Italian-American relations was closed.

The Peace
Settlement

14

Italy emerged from five years of foreign war, civil strife, invasion, and military occupation battered, bankrupt, and hungry. Since achieving unity as a nation, she had experienced no period of greater trial or deeper humiliation. Her military dead numbered more than 600,000 and the civilian toll, too, was high. Those Italians who had lived through it all were exhausted and starving.

Air raids, cannonadings, and fire bombings had damaged installations everywhere, leaving heaps of rubble where there had been factories or houses, and ripped concrete where there had been roads. A quarter of the railway tracks, nearly two-thirds of the locomotives and rolling stock, and a third of the bridges were destroyed. Farmers had been unable to get fertilizers, so that much of the soil was exhausted; livestock was depleted; thousands of acres of olive groves, vineyards, and orchards were useless; and hundreds of thousands of acres of farming land were sown with mines. In central and southern Italy, industrial plants were so badly damaged that their capital value had fallen 37 per cent, although in the north partisans had saved industry from destruction. Injury to national territory and property as a whole had reduced their capital value by at least a third of what it had been before the war.

Germany suffered greater wartime devastation, but in Italy the privations endured by the civilian population were more severe. The plight of the Italians became even worse in 1945, when they experienced one of the worst droughts within living memory. In 1945, as in 1919, Italy appeared to be on the verge of revolution. But revolutions do not occur just through desire. Italians lacked the means for rebellion. Revolutionaries could talk, but they were unable to act effectively because the American and British armies held the real power in the country. Desiring stability, the occupation forces would not allow a revolution. The Allied military government acted as a conservative force more interested in order than in fundamental social change. From Rome, in January, 1945, Myron Taylor urged a conservative policy toward Italy. He warned of growing Communist strength and recommended support for the monarchy because it was "traditional, definite and more dependable than any vague or untried group or system."

The British, even more than the Americans, desired such a policy. Although they were no longer able to maintain their predominant position in Italy, their views were still important enough to carry weight. During the postwar years, as British power waned, the United States exerted its own power in the Mediterranean and became the most important country in Italy's foreign policy; Italy became a dependent, a kind of distant American protectorate. This was something new in American foreign policy, for Italy was still a major European power, more considerable than any unstable Caribbean republic that had experienced American tutelage; and she could not be treated like one. A change in Italian thinking accompanied this shift in power. Before the war, Italian liberal intellectuals, anti-Fascists, and others had looked to England for democratic leadership. During and after the occupation, as Alberto Tarchiani explained in simplified terms, "America became the great symbol of democracy to the Italian people."

To ordinary Italians, the reality of American power was visible in the Sixth Fleet based at Naples and in the food and medicines that kept many of them alive. These were more effective reminders of their new relationship to the United States than were the ideas of democracy. For many who did not like their dependent status, the admiration for democratic government took the edge off resentment. Most Italians, realizing they could not do much about it, accepted their new relationship to America philosophically and tried to make the best of it. *Contadini* in Sicily, however, not only refused to be complacent about this American power in their lives but also tried to exploit it. Among some of them, enthusiasm for close ties to the United States became so strong that a wild scheme for making Sicily the forty-ninth state gained prominence. For a while, after the fall of Fascism, landowners and politicians also backed separatist movements in Sicily. Separatists even created a flag for their cause. It showed maps of Italy and the United States and two American soldiers, one of them cutting a chain linking Sicily to Italy proper and the other binding Sicily to the United States.

Giuliano

Sicily's most famous bandit of the forties, Salvatore Giuliano, issued manifestoes urging American statehood for his island. Years earlier, his parents had immigrated to the United States; but failing to make good, they had returned to Sicily. Instead of embittering him toward America, his parents' experience apparently inspired in him a desire to gain American admiration. When American officialdom ignored both him and his scheme for statehood, he petulantly denounced American foreign policy. This action caused no great alarm in Washington, but the American government did publicly disclaim support for any Sicilian separatists.

Regardless of separatist fantasies and American tutelage, Italians slowly regained control over their country. At the end of 1944, the Allied Military Government, after having placed conservative non-Fascist politicians in power, withdrew control from all parts of Italy except provinces bordering on Yugoslavia. Although the Allied Commission still remained, a few months later it relaxed most controls over domestic political decisions. These developments left the King's government on its own in many internal areas. Its most pressing problems were those of bringing order to the ruined countryside and shattered cities and finding some way to stop inflation.

Externally most of what Italy was able to do depended on relations with the United States. Early in 1945, the Allies permitted the new Italian government to send envoys to friendly countries and to carry on uncensored diplomatic correspondence. This marked an important step in an Italian post-armistice policy of trying to gain stature with the United States in order to lose as little as possible in the peace settlement. As part of this policy, Foreign Minister Alcide De Gasperi, early in February, asked the Big Three to give Italy the status of an ally. As with similar requests in the past, the Allies turned it down. This question of alliance, as well as others concerning Italy, such as economic aid, her frontiers with Austria and Yugoslavia, and her place in a new postwar international organization—the United Nations—were on the agenda of a Big Three conference in February at Yalta in the Russian Crimea.

Believing that Allied conduct toward Italy already conformed to a statement of principles they issued called the "Declaration on Liberated Europe," the Big Three made no change in policy toward Italy. Their official communiqué from Yalta did not even mention her. They refused, also to give her a seat in a conference to be held in San Francisco in April to frame a charter for the United Nations. Roosevelt supported Italy's desire to participate, but he encountered opposition from Stalin even to Italy's sending an unofficial observer. "The rebirth of Italy," Luigi Sturzo remarked in reference to these rebuffs, "is hard in itself but is harder because of the incomprehension of the Allies and their uncertain and incoherent policy." Yet at this very time (April, 1945) in Naples, UNRRA was distributing its first supplies to Italy; and the packages from private relief, which had been collecting in American warehouses since the spring of 1944, began reaching the Italian people in quantity.

Regardless of the attitudes of the other Allies toward Italy, that of the United States was clear. Although not ignoring her ambiguous enemy status, the United States now acted as Italy's best friend wanting to see her emerge from the wartime chaos as an independent nation with a democratic government. This good will stemmed from an appreciation of Italian contributions in the war, and even more from the pressure on the American government of various Italian-American groups urging lenient treatment for their old homeland.

Never before had the influence of Italian-Americans been so important to Italy. Her leaders knew that the peace terms would be hard and beyond their own power to modify in any important way. In the peacemaking, Prime Minister Ferrucio Parri, who had come to power in June, 1945, told Italians they must have confidence in the Allies; it would bring "bread, coal and credit." In an effort to enhance Italy's chances for a generous peace settlement, he asked the Allies for permission to declare war on Japan. Although the British had blocked earlier requests, the Allies now reluctantly agreed. But nothing helped Italy so much as the exertions of the American government, stimulated by Italian-Americans, on her behalf. The importance of American influence became apparent at another meeting of the Big Three, this time made up of President Harry S. Truman, Churchill (replaced during the conference by a new Prime Minister, Clement R. Attlee), and Stalin, in late July, at Potsdam, Germany.

At the first full session, Truman asked his allies to replace Italy's terms of surrender with a voluntary accord that would free her of occupation restrictions while the peace settlement was being negotiated. "I thought," he wrote, "the time had come to admit Italy into the United Nations," to recognize her as a reformed and friendly associate. Since the other Allies resisted this pressure, out of the Potsdam talks Italy gained only the assurance of becoming eligible for membership in the United Nations after she signed a treaty of peace.

The Big Three also decided on the procedure for the peacemaking with Italy. They felt that to construct a treaty at a large peace conference as had been done at Versailles in 1919 would produce lengthy discussions and little accomplishment. They agreed, therefore, to draft the treaty with Italy before convening a peace conference. So, as suggested by the United States, the Big Three created a council of foreign ministers composed of policy makers from each of the victorious great powers—Russia, Britain, the United States, France, and China—to frame the peace treaties for Italy, Finland, Hungary, Rumania, and Bulgaria, all of whom had fought on the Axis side. Stalin insisted that the peacemakers in each case should be men representing governments which had made the armistices with the former enemy states. Since the Big Three accepted this policy, the United States, Britain, Russia, and France, whom they agreed to regard as a signatory of the Italian armistice, assumed the responsibility for drafting the treaty for Italy.

At Potsdam, the Soviets centered their bargaining effort on Italy. They insisted that she must pay reparations, whereas the United States waived its own rights and tried to exempt her from any payments. As Truman explained, "the United States could not spend money to rehabilitate Italy just to enable her to pay reparations to other countries." Finally, at the end of the conference, he won an agreement that placed the Italian peace treaty first on the agenda of the council of foreign ministers. He argued that Italy deserved at least this consideration because she "was the first of the Axis powers to break with Germany, to whose defeat she has made a material contribution, and has now joined with the Allies in the struggle against Japan."

By this time, too, Italy had not only resumed diplomatic relations with other nations but had also regained the power to negotiate foreign agreements on her own. After August 1, when the Allied Commission permitted her to trade with other than Allied nations, Italy regained considerable control over her foreign commerce. For a while she traded with the countries of the Americas at the expense of commerce with her European neighbors. This practice, proving unprofitable, did not last long.

Despite the benign American attitude toward Italy, the usual friction between the conquered and the conquerors continued to roil the feelings of Italians and Americans. Some Americans wanted "to dismember Italy and treat her as the lowliest of the vanquished countries," believing that Italians still retained delusions of grandeur. This attitude was off the mark on several points. Few knowledgeable Italians now had any illusions about the power of their own country.

After the shattering blows of the Second World War, they knew that Italy could not even pretend to the status of a great power. The making of the peace treaty confirmed this knowledge.

This peacemaking began in September, 1945, when the four-power council of foreign ministers held its first meeting in London. Using a draft prepared by the British, the Allies discussed the Italian treaty in detail for the first time. As expected, the Soviets urged the harshest conditions. Their Foreign Minister, Vyacheslav M. Molotov, demanded a trusteeship of ten years over Tripolitania, or some other colony in the Mediterranean. He asked for $600 million in reparations, but insisted on $100 million. As Truman had done at Potsdam, Secretary of State James F. Byrnes argued that the impoverished Italians could not pay so large a sum unless it came from the United States. America would not, he said, permit huge reparations to be exacted from a country she was supporting. At the very time the peace council was meeting, the American government gave Italy a credit of $100 million to buy food and other essential supplies she could not obtain on her own. The Americans also resisted the attempted Soviet thrust into the Mediterranean, viewing it as a challenge to their position there. Some American policy makers now began to consider using Italy as a dike against Communist expansion.

Italy had no part in the treaty discussions, but the peacemakers did invite Foreign Minister De Gasperi to London. In a frigid atmosphere, they permitted him to state Italy's case, but nothing more. After argument and counterargument over the peace terms, the conference broke up in failure. It accomplished little beyond exposing deep differences between the Allies. Of the four powers, only the United States assumed a generous attitude toward Italy, but it alone could not settle Italy's fate. After the collapse of the conference in November, the Italian government asked the Allies for a provisional peace settlement and a revision of the armistice. American and British policy makers then considered canceling the armistice and replacing it with an interim document that would permit Italy to function as an independent nation until the Allies worked out a peace settlement. The English and Americans did not put this idea into effect, but they did promise to make changes.

At this time, Parri's government fell, a change, it was said, brought about in part by American meddling. In November, Amadeo Giannini, the California banker, was in Rome investigating the possibility of private loans to the Italian government. During a newspaper interview there, he gave his conservative views on Italian economics and politics, saying that no loans would go to Italy as long as partisans, who were largely leftists, controlled the factories in the north. To manage her problems, he added, Italy needed a new strong government, one led by pre-Fascist conservatives rather than the militant anti-Fascists of the left. Whether or not by design, the new government that came into power in December, 1945, with De Gasperi as Prime Minister fitted the Giannini formula. It represented a modest shift to the right. So eager were the English and Americans to have De Gasperi's government succeed and keep the extreme left out of power, that, the day after he formed his cabinet, they announced that at the end of the month the northern provinces still controlled by the Allied Military Government would revert to the Italian government. In an exchange of notes, the United States also agreed to open a normal commercial relationship with Italy. These measures gave the new government a good start. But its main asset was De Gasperi.

An anti-Fascist who had once been imprisoned by Mussolini, De Gasperi, in 1943, started a new political party called *Democrazia cristiana*. This Christian Democratic party fitted into the center or moderate right of the Italian political spectrum. De Gasperi served in the cabinets of post-Fascist governments, mainly as Foreign Minister. Thus, when he came to power at sixty-four years of age, he was a tested politician with strong convictions. He soon showed himself to be an astute and courageous statesman, a man whom Americans such as Dean Acheson looked upon with "great respect and deep affection." De Gasperi gave the new, dejected Italy what political analysts called a "sense of state," a revived feeling for the nation.

Much of what De Gasperi could do would depend on the Allies and on the peace settlement, so he went ahead immediately with negotiations for a revision of the armistice terms. He could not, however, do much until the Allies decided on Italy's peace conditions. Secretary of State Byrnes tried to break the deadlock at the London meeting by suggesting a special meeting of the foreign ministers of the Big Three powers. The others agreed. In December, Byrnes, Ernest Bevin of England, and Molotov met for ten days in Moscow, where they got the peacemaking started again. Basically, they decided that after they drafted the peace treaties, they would convene a general peace conference to consider them.

Then in April, 1946, the council of foreign ministers, holding its second conference in Paris, took up the Italian situation in earnest. What amazed one participant in these proceedings, Senator Arthur H. Vandenberg of Michigan, was "the way in which the Western democracies look out for a 'square deal' for defeated Italy . . ." The Allied leaders removed most of the military controls over Italy, abolished the Allied Commission, replacing it with a small supervisory committee over the armed forces, and promised to repatriate prisoners of war immediately. These terms permitted Italy to negotiate the costs of the occupation directly with the occupying powers and superseded those of the long armistice. Aside from this agreement, the foreign ministers made little headway. In May, they returned the draft of the Italian peace treaty to their deputies, called a recess, and agreed to meet again within a month.

During this time, the Italians went ahead with preparations for their first free national elections in a quarter of a century, elections that American officials were anxious to see held. These elections had a twofold character. First of all, they would give the people a chance to decide the "institutional question," that is whether Italy should remain a monarchy or become a republic. Second, they would require Italians to select deputies for a constituent assembly that would draw up a new constitution. Although the English and the Americans took a position of official neutrality, both favored the monarchy, the British more so than the Americans. On May 10, less than a month before the voting, the royalists persuaded Vittorio Emmanuele to do what he had long opposed: he abdicated in favor of his son Umberto. The new "King of May," as Italians called Umberto II because of his reign of less than a month, was a more popular figure. His accession to the throne, along with a general revival of conservative sentiment and a vigorous campaign by the clergy for the crown, swung many voters to the monarchy.

On June 2, the Italians went to the polls. The results were close. About 13 million people, or 55 per cent of the voters, favored the republic; and almost 11 million, or 45 per cent voted for the monarchy. The example of the United States and the widespread admiration for its republican institutions, according to the social critic Carlo Levi, had the effect of offsetting American policy; it swung votes away from the monarchy. In the contest for deputies to the constituent assembly, the Christian Democrats gained more seats than any of the other parties but failed to win a majority. De Gasperi, therefore, reorganized his government on a "tripartite" basis, meaning a ministry made up of three of Italy's largest parties. On June 18, 1946, Italy was officially proclaimed a republic. Now a deposed monarch, Umberto left the country to live in exile in Portugal. Italy made the shift from monarchy to republic smoothly, giving the newly elected constituent assembly all the power in the state, once the senate had been abolished.

While Italy was undergoing this change, the council of foreign ministers was holding its second session, opening on June 15, in Paris. Byrnes told Secretary of Defense James Forrestal that the Russians were dragging their feet. "We want to make a peace treaty with Italy—," Byrnes said, "Russia wants delay." Nonetheless the ministers worked out an agreement on reparations that gave the Soviets most of what they wanted from Italy. The council also finally agreed on drafts for five treaties, including Italy's, and decided to hold their general peace conference in Paris on July 29. Twenty-one nations—the Big Five and sixteen of the smaller Allied powers which had fought in the European war—sent delegates. Few of the powers liked the treaties the foreign ministers had prepared, but they could only recommend amendments and vote on their acceptance or rejection; they did not have the power to shape the treaties into final form. Italy and the small defeated states, even though allowed to state their cases, did not have even this limited authority; they could only suggest changes. The power of final decision rested with the foreign ministers of the Big Four powers.

De Gasperi appeared for thirty-five minutes at one of the first plenary sessions to present Italy's case. Since the conference treated him and his delegation as representatives of an enemy state, no one greeted him or spoke to him, even after he spoke, asking the peacemakers "within the framework of a stable general peace . . . to give breathing space and credit to the Italian Republic," and walked down a long aisle to his seat. "It impressed me as unnecessarily cruel," Byrnes wrote. "So, when he approached the United States delegation I stood and shook hands with him."

Earlier the House Appropriations Committee had not allowed the army to pay for supplies it purchased in Italy because it too considered Italy an enemy state. Before leaving for Paris, Byrnes had persuaded the committee to withdraw its objection by pointing out that the Italians had furnished the goods after they had joined the fight on the Allied side. Knowing that the reception at the peace conference had humiliated De Gasperi, Byrnes invited him to his apartment and told the Prime Minister of the American government's decision to pay for the supplies. "But I warned him our decision would not be announced until agreement was reached on the Italian treaty," Byrnes reported. "Otherwise, I explained, the claimants for reparations from Italy might increase their claims."

Byrnes's cautious attitude reflected the growing tension between the Soviets and the Western Allies and the way in which that mutual distrust affected Italy. Molotov looked suspiciously on every suggested concession for Italy, arguing that America's real objective in supporting Italy was to insure her status as an economic vassal. On October 15, in an atmosphere of rancor between the Eastern and Western Allies, the conference adjourned. Its recommendations went to the council of foreign ministers, scheduled to hold its third session in the following month.

Right after the Paris peace conference, the American government transferred $50 million to the Italian government. These dollars reimbursed the Italians for the AM lire spent in Italy. The payment came and was accepted as a gesture of good will at a moment when Italy was faced with serious financial difficulties heightened by the reparations the Paris conference had placed on her. The American government also took other steps to help. It waived its right to Italian assets in the United States and to compensation in excess of 25 per cent for damage to the property of American nationals committed by Italians, even though the treaty provided for payments of up to 75 per cent.

Despite these concessions, Italy's peace settlement now became a political issue in the United States. Thomas Dewey of New York, who was still aspiring to the Presidency, referred to the treaty in making a bid for the good will of his state's large Italian-American population. "We have pledged our active help to the liberated Italians in the great task of reorganization," he announced in October, 1946. "Our influence and whatever lies within our power, will be disposed in the cause of restoring Italy to its rightful place in the family of nations." Although significant in American politics, these maneuvers had little effect on the peace settlement. In November, as scheduled, the third session of the second meeting of the council of foreign ministers resumed the peacemaking in the Waldorf-Astoria Hotel in New York City. Now, after more than a year of heated, often bitter, discussion, the ministers agreed on the final terms of Italy's treaty. Under pressure, the Soviets made some concessions, but they did not change the basic terms adopted at the Paris conference. Although the ministers had listened to Italian opinion, they gave it virtually no consideration in framing the treaty. All that remained was the drawing up of the final text, a task the ministers left to their deputies.

When the peace terms became known in Italy, even Christian Democrats criticized De Gasperi for not obtaining a better settlement; many threatened to vote against ratification when the treaty came before them in the constituent assembly. Italians of various political persuasions seemed united on this point: that the government should not accept the treaty. Almost naïvely the anti-Fascist politicians, even De Gasperi, had hoped that Italy's limited contribution as a co-belligerent would cleanse her record of three years of aggressive warfare at the side of Nazi Germany. Aside from the United States, the Allies were unwilling to forget the sins of Fascist Italy. Americans did not share their hostility; they had defeated Italy more in sorrow than in anger. They could feel this way because Fascism had not endangered any of America's vital interests. This attitude, as well as the desire to encourage Italian friendliness within any postwar Western European system that would emerge, made it easier for the United States to be generous toward Italy than were the other Allies.

Despite American generosity, De Gasperi found that the economic distress throughout Italy, as well as the terms of the peace settlement, made his political life precarious. Aid from UNRRA had sustained Italians through the first eighteen months of the postwar era, but this help was scheduled to end the following June. Italy desperately needed foreign exchange for everyday requirements, but now she also had to prepare for the day when she, herself, would have to pay for essential imports. When Byrnes invited De Gasperi to visit Washington, therefore, the Prime Minister snapped at the chance as a hungry man would at the offer of food. De Gasperi arrived early in January, 1947, the first Italian Prime Minister since the war to visit an Allied country on a footing, at least technically, of equality with his host. Although opinions differed, many Italians hoped he would obtain a sizeable loan to finance the importation of foodstuffs and raw materials. By emphasizing the importance of the Mediterranean area in international politics, the Prime Minister also wished to commit the United States to lasting political and economic ties with Italy.

The effects of De Gasperi's negotiations were far-reaching. First of all, he received the desired assurance of aid. The American government offered wheat to tide the Italians over until their harvest in June. It also promised a loan of $100 million through the Export-Import Bank, and short-term credits if they were needed. American policy makers hinted that De Gasperi would enjoy still greater favor in Washington if he excluded Communists from his government. Regardless of the Communist issue, the United States indicated it would waive claims for payment of relief supplies the American army had furnished Italy. Truman and Byrnes offered to free the Italian assets in the United States that were blocked, and to include Italy in a relief program being recommended to Congress. The two countries agreed to negotiate a new commercial treaty to replace the prewar agreement. Italy, in turn, promised to support the United States in efforts to liberalize world trade through reduction of trade barriers.

De Gasperi felt that he had achieved the principal aim of his journey in the "restoration of confidence and active cooperation between our two countries." He spoke with considerable truth because his talks with Truman, Byrnes, and others did strengthen the foundations of the special interest the United States continued to take in Italy's welfare. De Gasperi's skillful analysis of his country's plight within a crippled Europe was important in convincing the American authorities of the need for continued aid to war-torn European countries after UNRRA ended. An editorial of January 16 in the *New York Times* praised the results of his visit, saying that if aid at this time provided Italy with a measure of economic stability and stimulated her industrial development, the United States had won a victory as important as any on the battlefield.

Four days later, Italy sent a note to the Big Four protesting the peace treaty, especially the territorial clauses. She made it clear that she would seek revision in bilateral negotiations with the interested powers, arguing that the treaty as it stood hurt the "Italian national conscience." In this instance the protest seemed logical, and the Americans and British recognized it as justifiable. They had said officially that the Italians had earned their way back to respectability by fighting the Nazis. These two Allies tried, as a result, to modify the punitive terms; but Stalin and Molotov insisted that Italy should receive no consideration not accorded to Hungary, Rumania, and Bulgaria. So the peacemakers, to the end, treated her as an unredeemed enemy state.

The punitive intent came out clearly in the final version of the peace treaty signed in the Luxembourg Palace, in Paris, on February 10, 1947, by representatives of Italy and the states which had participated in the general peace conference, except the United States. Byrnes had signed for the United States on January 20, the day before he left office, in Washington. The treaty stripped Italy of all her colonies and other possessions. Rhodes and the Dodecanese Islands in the Aegean went to Greece, and some islands in the Adriatic went to Yugoslavia. Ethiopia regained her independence. The disposition of the three older African colonies of Libya, Eritrea, and Italian Somaliland, to which Italy renounced title, proved difficult. So the treaty simply declared the intention of the Big Four to settle the problem within a year. Ultimately those powers turned over the issue of the colonies to the United Nations.

As everyone expected, the peacemakers found the European territorial issues even more sensitive. It had been clear from the start that Italy could not retain her prewar frontiers. On the Alpine border with France, the territorial adjustments were minor, but of strategic and economic importance. Over Italian objections, France gained four small Alpine areas that guarded the invasion routes into the Po Valley.

In April, 1945, in the closing days of the war, French ambitions in one of these border areas, in the Val d'Aosta, a part of Piedmont where the people spoke French, involved the United States in a minor crisis as a kind of protector of Italian territory. French troops, under orders from General Charles de Gaulle, crossed the Alps into the Val d'Aosta, occupied it, and took steps to annex the valley. Although Allied agreements permitted the French to occupy some Italian soil, nothing allowed the French a free hand to keep it. Truman, therefore, ordered the French troops out. De Gaulle hesitated, and for a while a clash between French and American soldiers seemed likely. The President then took a tough stand. "I notified de Gaulle," Truman explained later, "that no more supplies would be issued to the French Army until its withdrawal from Aosta Valley." Since de Gaulle needed American equipment, he pulled out his troops, ending an episode that worried Italy. Truman's action, showing that Italy still had a friend across the sea, was reassuring to the Italians. In the peace settlement, France did not claim the Val d'Aosta.

The peacemakers relied on local autonomy in dealing with the fate of the *Alto Adige* (or South Tyrol, as the Austrians called it). While officially at war with the King's Italy, although still allied to Mussolini's republic, Germany had occupied the region and incorporated its provinces of Bolzano, Trento, and Belluno into the Reich. Hitler's officials also introduced measures for the Germanization of the whole area, controlling it with rabid Austrian Nazis. When the war ended, Italy's rival claimant for the *Alto Adige* was Austria, technically a former enemy of Italy and of the Allies. These circumstances convinced the peacemakers they should leave the frontiers of the *Alto Adige* unchanged. Realizing she could not regain the South Tyrol, Austria signed an agreement with Italy in September, 1946, that insured the cultural rights and a degree of local autonomy for the German-speaking population there. The negotiators made this agreement an annex to the Italian peace treaty.

The most perplexing problem, and the most dangerous, concerned Italy's new frontier with Yugoslavia. Headed by the tough Communist Marshal Tito, Yugoslavia claimed all the province of Venezia Giulia, including the city of Trieste, whose population was more than 80 per cent Italian. The Soviets stood foursquare behind Tito's demands. In May, 1945, during the last days of the war, American planners anticipated Tito's desire to occupy Trieste. The Allied generals rushed a contingent of New Zealand troops into the city, and five days later American forces followed. But Yugoslavs took over the rest of Venezia Giulia, and Italy's Foreign Minister wired an immediate protest to Washington and London. The English and Americans claimed the right to occupy all Italian territory within the prewar frontiers, a right they refused to abandon. So British, American, and Communist soldiers in Venezia Giulia faced each other in an atmosphere filled with tension.

Finally Truman threatened Tito with an ultimatum backed up with combat-ready American forces. In June, after an occupation of about a month and a half, the Yugoslavs reluctantly pulled back; the Allies then took over about half of Venezia Giulia and retained control of Trieste. This Allied occupation resulted from an agreement with the Yugoslavs that divided Venezia Giulia into two zones: Zone A in the west, held by Anglo-American forces, and Zone B in the east, occupied by the Yugoslavs. The Allies proposed successively a number of boundaries intended to follow the ethnic frontier between Italians and Yugoslavs. It proved difficult to draw such a line because although Slavs populated most of the Istrian Peninsula, Italians comprised the great majority along the coast, including Trieste.

When the council of foreign ministers first approached the issue of Trieste, wide divergencies appeared among them. In March, 1946, the council sent a commission to Trieste to investigate the issue on the spot. The investigators recommended four different lines. What the Americans proposed turned out to be most favorable to Italy, leaving her not only Trieste but also about half of the Istrian Peninsula. The other peacemakers refused to accept the American line. Instead, they agreed on a compromise frontier that gave most of Venezia Giulia to Yugoslavia. Although this line approximated the ethnic border for the inland area, it gave Yugoslavia a number of coastal cities and towns that were Italian. Italy thus lost 3,000 square miles to Yugoslavia, land that included timber, cereals, coal mines, iron plants, shipyards, and refineries. American policy makers disliked this solution enhancing a Communist state, but they accepted it because they felt that only bayonets could enforce a different one.

For Trieste itself, the peacemakers could work out no agreement. Both sides were adamant. "The American government," Truman wrote, "never for a moment considered that Trieste should go to Yugoslavia." The peace treaty made the city, with a small bordering region, a free territory under the supervision of the Security Council of the United Nations. This arrangement emerged as a concession to the Soviet Union, but it proved a compromise without substance. It greatly disappointed the leaders of the Italian republic, who were political realists but who nonetheless hoped for a far more favorable frontier. Trieste's problem stemmed from its geographic situation. Ethnographically it belonged to Italy, but economically it served and was tied to central Europe, not just to Yugoslavia. Austria, Czechoslovakia, and Hungary all had an interest in the city.

While leaving the fate of Trieste unsettled, the treaty dealt decisively with military matters. It disarmed Italy. She had to demilitarize her French and Yugoslav frontiers. She gave up most of her navy, reduced her army to 250,000 soldiers and her air force, like her navy, to 25,000 men, and she renounced the possession of offensive weapons such as submarines and bombers.

To gain a peace settlement, the United States reluctantly agreed to reparations of $100 million for the Soviet Union. The treaty also provided for reparations of $260 million to be divided among Yugoslavia, Greece, Ethiopia, and Albania. The Soviets obtained a number of Italian ships, including a battleship. As had been predicted, much of the money for reparations came from the United States because Italy had to pay from the dollars she received to keep her afloat, or from their equivalent in Italian goods. Italy undertook in advance to recognize the peace treaties and the various arrangements between the Allies and the other enemy countries. Her treaty also called for withdrawal of American and British occupying forces within ninety days of its signature.

In considering all aspects of the settlement, the peacemakers could rightly conclude that it was tough and reasonable, but that they had not treated Italy with undue harshness. Even the total reparations bill, when one took into account a two-year moratorium allowed before payments began, did not stand out as truly exorbitant. The Western Allies were willing to act leniently because they did not fear Italian power, even potential power, when Italy recovered fully from the effects of war.

Yet, critics argued, the treaty turned out harsher than it could have been, in part because American negotiators based their diplomacy on premises that were obsolete almost as soon as the ink of the treaty's signatures became dry. The first of these premises held that the Allies should treat Italy as an enemy state meriting punishment; the second assumed that the leaders of the Big Four would continue their wartime cooperation in the years of peace. By the beginning of 1947, American policy makers had just about lost hope for such cooperation and had begun lining up anti-Communist friends in Europe. Among these stood Italy, a country they were now looking upon as a potentially useful ally. The signing of the Italian peace treaty preceded by just one month a major shift in American foreign policy toward Europe, a policy that would take shape as tension mounted in a "cold war" with nations of the Communist bloc.

About a week before the signing, Carlo Sforza became Italy's Minister of Foreign Affairs. Although haughty, a man "with a consciousness of effortless superiority," he was also a statesman of ability who wanted to make Italy a respected contributor to a larger European community. His first major problem was to persuade the constituent assembly to ratify the peace treaty. On the day of signature, he informed former enemy states that they should hold neither the Italian people nor the Italian republic responsible for a war launched by a Fascist dictatorship. Italy's legislature would approve the treaty, he predicted, but the government would also engage in a relentless effort to revise it.

While Sforza and De Gasperi were working to build up domestic political support for acceptance of the peace treaty, across the sea the Senate Foreign Relations Committee took it under consideration and held hearings. Viewing the treaty as severe and unfair, Italian-American leaders went to Washington to testify against it, and various Italian-American groups exerted pressure to delay Senate action on it. They wanted the treaty defeated, or at least revised, so that it could be renegotiated. This attitude led to considerable debate among the lawmakers. Senator Arthur H. Vandenberg, chairman of the committee, even urged his Republican colleagues to resist pressure from constituents of Italian origin. The pressure did not have much effect. On June 5, 1947, by a vote of 79 to 10, the Senate approved the treaty without change.

In Italy, the constituent assembly reflected the widespread dislike of the treaty; many members felt it punished postwar Italy for the crimes of Fascism and should be rejected. Former Prime Minister

Francesco S. Nitti called it a "humiliating and odious *diktat*." Arguments in favor of ratification were stronger. First of all, the United States made it clear that it would cut off economic aid if Italy did not approve, a threat that hurt American prestige among Italians. Whether or not Italy ratified the treaty, it would go into effect after the Big Four approved. They would then impose its terms upon her. Failure to ratify, therefore, would keep Italy under occupation. Moreover, her technical status as an enemy state would most likely exclude her from the planning under way for Western Europe's economic recovery. "The dilemma is this," Sforza told the assembly, "either ratify to reacquire sovereignty over our territory . . . or else do not ratify" and face "international dangers."

Sforza convinced the majority that only after ratification and recovery of full sovereignty could Italy work openly to remove the treaty's objectionable features. The Italian republic itself, he pointed out, had to prove to the victors that it had nothing in common with the Fascist dictatorship. If Italy could offer such proof, and she needed freedom to do it, the Big Four would be willing, he felt, to revise the peace settlement. Finally, on July 31, while protesting and saying in sorrow that "this is not the peace it [the Italian Republic] deserved," the constituent assembly authorized ratification. On September 15, 1947, after ratifications had been exchanged, the treaty went into force.

Meanwhile, international developments showed that in large part Sforza's arguments were sound. When the constituent assembly ratified the treaty, Secretary of State George C. Marshall sent Sforza a special message expressing sympathy for Italy's desire for revision, particularly of those terms pertaining to Trieste, colonies, reparations, and the surrender of naval units. A short time later, the United States, followed by Britain, renounced its share of the Italian navy. Those two countries also returned ships they had already taken so that Italy could use them for scrap, a gesture the Italians deeply appreciated. The Soviets repatriated prisoners they had captured from Italian units that had fought with the Germans in Eastern Europe. The various Allies returned Italian property from abroad to its owners: thirty tons of Italian gold the Germans had taken and other stolen material such as machinery and valuable works of art. In September, the United States concluded an agreement with De Gasperi's government that ended all aspects of American military government. Italy was now on her own, once again governed fully by Italians.

As Sforza had predicted, Italy entered a new phase in foreign policy. For the first time in more than four years, she became able to assume the initiative in dealing with other countries, acting once more as an equal in the family of nations. For Italy, the new freedom did not mean neutrality in the cold war; it meant a policy of alignment with the United States, for Italy's welfare depended heavily on American friendship. At the time, the United States stood virtually alone in bolstering Italy, whether against communism or against hunger. At first, few Americans realized how much the basis of power in the Mediterranean had shifted from the hands of the British to those of their own policy makers. Yet events in the Mediterranean were already making clear to the world the extent of America's involvement not only in the power politics of the Mediterranean but also in Italy's own affairs.

Cold War
Ally
15

Shortly after the signing of the Italian peace treaty, British statesmen concluded that their country could no longer afford even the pretense that she was still the dominant power in the Mediterranean. Beset by financial crises, the British decided to withdraw troops stationed in Greece and to relinquish commitments to Turkey. Britain had been giving both countries subsidies to help them withstand pressure from Communists who sought to overthrow the governments there. The British hoped the Americans would now openly assume the burden they had borne in the Mediterranean. If the United States did not take over, it seemed likely that communism would triumph in Greece, that Communists would gain strength in Italy or engulf her, that Turkey would give in to Soviet pressure, and that the Soviets could become masters of the eastern Mediterranean. If the Communists were successful in dominating Italy, Undersecretary of State Dean Acheson pointed out, they could probably take over Greece, Turkey, and the Middle East without great difficulty.

President Truman and his advisers decided that intervention in the Mediterranean with financial and military aid offered the only alternative to Soviet control. The President then asked Congress for authority to intervene in Greece. "I believe," he told Congress on March 12, 1947, "that it must be the policy of the United States to support free peoples who are resisting attempted subjugation by armed minorites or by outside pressures." This policy became known as the Truman Doctrine. The administration drew up a bill embodying the doctrine and provided the appropriation to carry it out. On May 22, after approval by both Senate and House, the President signed the bill into law.

The Truman Doctrine heralded a new departure in American foreign policy with long-range implications for relations with Italy. It openly moved the United States into Britain's old role in the Mediterranean and made that sea and Italy herself strategically more important than ever to American military planners. It marked the beginning of the cold war and determined a larger strategy of containment that committed the United States to countering Soviet expansion and to "containing" communism in Europe, especially if it threatened to spread over a country such as Italy.

Although Italy shared no frontier with the Soviet Union, she immediately became a major prize in the cold war, one that could go to either side. Owing to her geographical situation, she became crucial in American Mediterranean strategy, a country that John J. McCloy, a War Department official, described to Congress as "one of the keys to peace in Europe as a whole." Because she had the largest Communist party in Western Europe, Italy's internal stability also became a special concern of American strategists. They considered her to be an exposed outpost where Communists might come to power by *coup d'état*, by gradual infiltration, or by constitutional means. Right after the announcement of the Truman Doctrine, former Secretary of State Byrnes wrote that if "the Soviets tomorrow should take control of the Italian government, we certainly would do more than protest. . . ." Military planners discussed how they would react if the Communists used force to take over northern Italy. To keep the Communists out of power became a foremost objective of American policy toward Italy.

Staunch anti-Communists friendly to the United States, De Gasperi and Sforza were willing to guide Italian foreign policy within the strategy of containment. After his trip to Washington early in 1947, De Gasperi, with American encouragement, expelled left-wingers from his government, turning to the right with a frankly conservative ministry. With this government, Sforza and De Gasperi moved Italy ideologically closer to the United States. Then ratification of the peace treaty removed the last obstacle to full peacetime relations between the two countries and to their cooperation in the cold war.

Such cooperation did not come easily. It aroused considerable opposition, especially among Italy's left-wing parties and intellectuals. In the name of anti-communism, they felt, the United States was throwing its support to the landowning classes and to the democratic right, the groups which defended the privileges of the church and censored free expression, especially in the arts. Even ordinary Italians with no sympathy for communism leaned toward some form of neutrality in the cold war. Still numbed by their wartime experience, they feared that collaboration with the United States might lead to military commitments Italy could not afford. Italians were now more than ever opposed to war. Their still-devastated countryside constantly reminded them of war's dreadful cost and intensified their horror of it.

Nonetheless, the emergence of the United States as the paramount external influence in Italy with a long-term interest in the stability of her economy, gave American policy an importance in the daily lives of Italians that not even disillusioned left-wing intellectuals could deny. Italy's military helplessness forced her to rely on American protection, and her economic situation dictated dependence on American aid for a long time. In 1946, the United States provided about 60 per cent of Italy's imports, as well as a market of 18 per cent of her exports; whereas eight years earlier, it had supplied only 12 per cent of Italy's imports and had taken 8 per cent of her exports. Italians survived through the importation from the United States of essential foodstuffs, raw materials, and equipment to patch up plants for peacetime production. Such massive assistance to a former enemy had no historical precedent; moreover, no other major country in Europe depended so heavily on American aid.

Countless Italian families still had relatives in the United States who sent them remittances This kind of money, as in the past, represented a considerable item in Italy's balance of payments. To many Italians, therefore, American generosity and their acceptance of it was nothing new; it seemed almost natural. Yet although American aid made postwar suffering bearable, it did not remove the misery. In the winter of 1946-1947, production in Italy and elsewhere in Europe was stalled. In Italy, a continuing inflation that saw prices rise to more than sixty times the prewar level caused widespread hardship. People everywhere faced the possibility of starvation. "Our foreign exchange resources were exhausted," an Italian banker recalled. "The agricultural crop was unfavorable, and we had need for big importations of wheat, coal and raw materials." Seeking an alternative to poverty and misery, many Italians turned to the Communist party.

Even during the Greek and Turkish crisis, American statesmen realized they would be obliged to go beyond the Truman Doctrine in order to counter communism in Italy and elsewhere in Europe. They concluded that only broad economic aid could prevent disintegration in Western Europe. A program making food, fuel, raw materials, and machinery available for lasting economic recovery, not just relief, many felt, would check the growth of communism. American policy makers, as a result, worked out a plan that would replace assistance to individual countries, such as Italy, with aid for Europe as a whole. Truman and Secretary of State Marshall adopted the idea. On June 5, 1947, the same day the Senate approved the Italian peace treaty, Marshall announced the plan. He suggested, as the key to his offer of economic aid, that the Europeans themselves should take the initiative in drafting a joint recovery program.

Although Italy, as Sforza explained, "greeted the Marshall Plan with unconditional approval from the first moment," Britain and France took the lead in organizing the European response. With wartime grievances still fresh, the British at first tried to exclude Italy, pointing out that she was technically still an enemy state. American and French leaders insisted on Italian participation, as American planners had decided from the beginning, leading the British to abandon their opposition. Then the Italian government asked American policy makers not to restrict discussion of the Marshall Plan to the Big Three, as the British and French had suggested, but to allow all the European states concerned to participate.

Italy got her chance to take part in the planning and emerge from her political isolation when the British and French invited her, along with the other nations of Western Europe, to Paris in July to discuss the American offer. Sixteen countries, including Italy, sent representatives to this Marshall Plan conference. These planners quickly set up a Committee of European Economic Cooperation to gather information on what they needed for recovery. This committee's report, presented to Secretary Marshall in September, called for a four-year program of recovery supported by nearly $22.5 billion in American aid.

In Italy, the Communists opposed the Marshall Plan, saying it required subservience to America; they denounced close ties to the United States in general and attacked De Gasperi's effort to govern without them. The Communist and allied parties, according to election results, appeared to have the support of one-third of the nation. It would be impossible, Communist leaders warned, for De Gasperi's government to stay in power without their support. These tactics worried American policy makers. In October, in urging Congress to approve the Marshall aid program, Truman stressed that "the most imminent danger exists in France and Italy." Without American help, Italy's economy might collapse, giving the Communists what they sought: the chance to take over the country. In December, on the occasion of the withdrawal of the last American occupation troops from Italy, Truman reiterated his intention to help her resist communism, particularly if the Communists resorted to coercion. "If . . . it becomes apparent," he said, "that the freedom and independence of Italy . . . are being threatened directly or indirectly, the United States . . . will be obliged to consider what measures would be appropriate."

As the Marshall Plan took shape during the summer and autumn of 1947, it gradually became clear that the Communists were wrong, that De Gasperi's gamble was succeeding. Most important, Italy's economic situation began to improve. Between August and November, prices dropped by 20 per cent. She achieved a measure of financial stability, improved her industrial production, and built up foreign trade. Italy's purchase of wartime freighters from the United States helped considerably in the revival of her commerce. These Liberty ships formed the nucleus of the new Italian merchant marine, which by the end of 1947 had reached about half of its prewar tonnage.

American aid in all its forms proved indispensable in revitalizing the Italian economy. It brought not only food but also raw materials and machinery. Fortunately, Italians were able to put this equipment to use quickly because the northern factories, the heart of Italy's industrial potential, were intact. Aid under the European Recovery Program, or Marshall Plan, would not begin until the summer of 1948, but Italy received help until then from the United States in order to bridge the gap widened with the cessation of UNRRA. Communists inspired a number of strikes to prevent Italy from accepting Marshall Plan aid; but in the autumn of 1947 these strikes collapsed before blunt police action.

During this time of confrontation, in fact for nine months, Italy's constituent assembly in Rome debated article by article a new constitution drafted by a parliamentary committee and approved by the assembly on December 22. This constitution went into force on January 1, 1948, and called for a new Chamber of Deputies and Senate. Consequently, Italians spent most of the early part of the year campaigning for a general election to be held on April 18 to determine the make-up of the new legislature. Although openly committed to a policy of friendship with the United States, De Gasperi argued that his government stood as the sole democratic alternative to communism. Leaders within the Catholic church and American policy makers accepted this argument at face value. They and the great majority of Italian anti-Communists campaigned in support of De Gasperi, insisting that the issue was a clear-cut one between democracy and communism. Italian political parties and the people, in effect, found themselves forced to take sides for or against alignment with the United States.

On February 2, as if to show its solid support of the Christian Democrats, the United States concluded a new Treaty of Friendship, Commerce, and Navigation with Italy, her first trade agreement since the fall of Fascism. Although the treaty was based on the principles of reciprocity and unconditional most-favored-nation treatment, the United States permitted Italy to take some temporary measures, such as exchange controls and import restrictions, for the defense of her economy. An innovation provided for freedom of the press and information in both countries. In all, this agreement went well beyond the previous trade treaty between the two countries.

L'unità, the organ of the Italian Communist party, predicted that parliament would refuse to ratify the new treaty, saying it left Italy's door open to "American trusts." * Since Italy was small and weak and the United States big and strong, the Communists argued, reciprocity was a myth. Because the pact allowed American capitalists an opportunity to expand their activities in Italy and to exploit her, the Communist newspaper insisted, it would injure Italian interests. Other newspapers welcomed the treaty as evidence of American friendship for Italy. So did the *New York Times*, asserting also, on February 5, that without the Marshall Plan, "it is doubtful whether we would now have this treaty." Marshall aid, it said, created in Italy an "atmosphere in which resistance to the Communists is steadily strengthened."

Several other factors reinforced this resistance. In February, Communists in Czechoslovakia openly seized power in a brutal *coup d'état* that shocked Italian public opinion into an awareness of what might happen in Italy too if the Communist party captured the government. At the same time, the Truman administration expedited the delivery of surplus arms to Italy to help the government defend itself against a possible Communist coup. In addition, the Americans threatened, on March 15, to cut off all economic aid to Italy if the Communists gained power. Five days later, Marshall announced that if the people voted a Communist regime into power, they would thereby automatically disassociate Italy "from all benefits of the European Recovery Program."

Developments concerning Trieste also undoubtedly influenced Ital-

* Both countries ratified the treaty in June, 1949.

ian voters. Communist Yugoslavia followed a policy of gradually assimilating the zone of the free territory she administered. On March 20, in opposition to this policy, the United States, Britain, and France issued a declaration recommending the return of the whole free territory to Italy. The Soviets blocked such a return, but the declaration at least pointed the way to a revision of Trieste's status. American policy makers timed the statement to strengthen De Gasperi's hand in the elections. The strategy worked; Italians greeted the announcement with tremendous enthusiasm. The Christian Democrats gained prestige as upholders of Italian Trieste and as astute statesmen able to profit from their close alignment with the United States. By this time, most Italians had abandoned their early postwar dream of neutrality between East and West. By accepting Marshall Plan aid, Italy chose the West. To show the Italians they had made the right choice and to help the Christian Democrats, the American government stepped up its economic aid and set aside one of the largest shares of Marshall Plan funds,—largest in relation to the size of the national economy—for Italy.

Congress approved the Economic Cooperation Act, or Marshall Plan legislation, late in March, 1948. Truman signed the law on April 3, and on that same day, his government completed an agreement to assist Italy in industry, agriculture, and finances. Both actions came in time to have a favorable effect on the Italian elections. The Marshall Plan also gave Italy her first opportunity to rejoin the Western European family of nations as an equal. On April 16, just two days before the elections, the sixteen nations participating in the European Recovery Program signed a convention that created the Organization for European Economic Cooperation, the central body for the operation of the Marshall Plan and the first postwar international organization that admitted Italy as a member.

As the campaign in Italy reached its climax, Americans subjected De Gasperi to considerable pressure to outlaw the Communist party, but he resisted, thereby demonstrating an independence that pleased many Italians. The American government also encouraged Italian-Americans to write to relatives and friends in Italy urging them to vote for the Christian Democrats and against the Communists. Italian-Americans then flooded Italy's post offices with letters of all kinds pleading for an anti-Communist victory.

Although unusual for Italian politics, this direct participation of Italian-Americans in the election campaign stressed, as nothing had before, the close peacetime relationship between Italians and Americans. This active campaigning by foreigners and by the Catholic priesthood seemed bewildering to the ordinary voter. Anticlerical intellectuals and left-wing politicians were alarmed. They saw the Vatican, in their view a reactionary institution, acting as a liaison between Italian and American policy makers and between the two peoples, something new and frightening. For centuries the Vatican had been predominantly an Italian power; it still was. Now, to survive and grow, the Catholic church had to adjust to a new kind of political world; it found strength in the prosperous countries overseas, the most important of these being the United States. American Catholics, it was estimated, contributed more than half of the Pope's income. This support enabled the church to become, through the Christian Democratic party, the leading force in Italian political life. Many Italians were cynical about this clerical influence. One man put it this way: *Ieri ci commandava Mussolini; oggi ci commando i preti.* ("Yesterday we were ruled by Mussolini; today we are ruled by priests.")

Regardless, the results of the anti-Communist election campaign exceeded all expectations, either of American policy makers or Italian politicians. Italians went to the polls in record numbers; in the north, more than 90 per cent voted. The Christian Democrats took 48½ per cent of the vote, and the Communist Popular Front won 31 per cent. For the first time in Italy's modern parliamentary history, a single party obtained an absolute majority of the seats in the Chamber of Deputies, although not in the Senate. Believing that De Gasperi and other Christian Democratic leaders would keep Italy friendly to the United States and committed to democracy, Americans were delighted with the results. They were aware that the solid hope offered by their Marshall Plan had contributed as much as any other external factor to the anti-communist victory. But few realized that the American intervention also had a countereffect; it made De Gasperi appear almost a pawn of American cold war strategists.

Those Italians who followed the convolutions of American politics found support for this view. In his underdog campaign for re-election in 1948, Harry Truman reminded the voters of what he had done for Italy and anti-communism. His supporters saturated Italian-American communities with leaflets explaining how he had "saved Italy from communism." Although crude, the strategy apparently worked. Truman won back many of the Italian voters who had abandoned the Democratic party during the Roosevelt years.

Not all Americans were concerned solely with anti-communism in

Italy. Many saw in Christian Democracy ideals similar to those in the American political experience. What they did not see clearly was that it had also attracted some of the conservative groups that had accommodated themselves to Fascism. Nonetheless, those Americans who believed that the nature of Italian political life had changed were correct. For the first time, through the right to vote, women made their way into public life. *Contadini* and poor workers of all kinds were acquiring a political and class consciousness they had previously lacked. Now, as never before, the Italian people were becoming politically active and socially aware, something that truly democratic Americans desired.

What disturbed even liberal Americans was that none were more active in Italian political life than the Communists and left-wing Socialists. After the elections, these left-wingers set out to sabotage the government's program in every way they could. They bombarded the people with anti-American propaganda, fomented unrest, and through strikes tried to block Marshall Plan aid. They failed; Italy signed her bilateral agreement with the United States for the European Recovery Program on June 28, 1948. For the first fifteen months of the program, she received an allocation fixed at $601 million.

Italy's inclusion in the Organization for European Economic Cooperation brought her other benefits. Now, for the first time, she could participate in an international organization alongside former enemies. Elsewhere it was different. The Soviet Union repeatedly vetoed her application for membership in the United Nations. Italian statesmen came to feel like political lepers, men who lacked the opportunity for the wide international contacts that were especially important to them after Italy's long period outside the mainstream of international politics. For a while, it was mainly in the Organization for European Economic Cooperation that her leading economists found a meeting ground for discussions with colleagues from other countries. Later, Italy gained admittance into most of the organizations connected with the United Nations, such as the Food and Agricultural Organization.

Meanwhile, Italian Communists stepped up their opposition to De Gasperi and the Marshall Plan. In July, 1948, a Sicilian student shot Palmiro Togliatti, the head of Italy's Communist party, severely wounding him. Blaming the government, the trade unions, dominated by the Communists, called a nationwide strike. In some northern cities, such as Genoa and Turin, workers rushed into the streets, mounted barricades, and brought out weapons hidden since the days of partisan warfare; a left-wing insurrection seemed to be in the making. After almost two days of tension, De Gasperi's government threatened military action and dissolved the strike. Similarly, in the autumn, the Christian Democrats broke a number of strikes directed against the European Recovery Program, which was being launched with considerable fanfare. The government's firmness had a long-term effect. After this, the Communists did not seriously threaten public order or arouse fear of a revolution from below.

De Gasperi's consolidation of government authority coincided with two years of relative economic stability, level prices, and mounting production. Trade rose steadily and contributed to a gradual reduction of Italy's deficits to other countries. The Marshall Plan made possible much of this economic improvement. Fear that the Communists might gain strength had prompted the United States to extend lavish assistance to Italy, though not as much in actual dollars as to England and France, throughout the four years of the Marshall Plan's operation. Various American agencies in Italy publicized the program. In 1950, they set up special European Recovery Program exhibits in Turin and other cities which were well attended. Italy received over $1 billion in American aid and Trieste, $33 million. Between 1948 and 1952, Marshall Plan assistance to Italy amounted to more than $1 billion 500 million. Between 1945 and 1952, various American programs gave Italy a total of over $2 billion.

The Italian who did more than anyone else to spur recovery was Luigi Einaudi, a respected economist who became De Gasperi's minister of the budget. Believing in financial orthodoxy, Einaudi followed an easily understood program. He discarded the economic controls that had continued from the war period and stabilized the currency. American planners looked upon the European Recovery Program as a means of stepping up production and of giving a lift to the Italian economy. So did Einaudi, but at a slower pace. The promise of American aid was an essential element in his success; it gave the Italian public the confidence it needed to face the future. When Marshall Plan help came, it contributed directly to the raising of Italy's standard of living by increasing her production, an indispensable supplement to economic stabilization. So, in brief, the United States supplied the raw materials and the capital equipment that enabled Italian industry to expand production far above prewar levels.

By the middle of 1952, or the end of the European Recovery Program, Italy's index of industrial production stood at 140 per cent of the 1938 level. This encouraging figure suggested that she had virtually completed her economic recovery. Still American assistance did not stop. Point Four, a program of industrial and scientific aid inaugurated by Truman, the Mutual Security Agency that replaced the Marshall Plan, and government agencies that purchased goods for American troops in Europe from Italy, all gave Italy economic assistance.

Despite Italy's remarkable recovery, the program of industrial expansion did not go as far as the architects of the Marshall Plan desired. Relative to the increase of population since the outbreak of the war, the level of production actually went up about 25 per cent above the level of 1938, not a prosperous year. Basically, American experts argued, Italy had too many people; overpopulation hampered her solid economic redevelopment. Italians studied the problem and estimated that by 1955 the growth in population would end. They also stressed the need for emigration, saying it would cut down permanent unemployment and reduce the political tension inherent in the existence of a mass of unemployed or visibly underemployed people.

Regardless of the population problem, Marshall Plan economists complained that their program did not result in as high a level of Italian investment as they had originally intended. In 1949, Americans criticized the way Italians spent aid funds, or rather how they refused to spend them. The Americans said the Italians used too much of the money to swell foreign exchange reserves instead of investing it in capital equipment. Marshall Plan administrators ran into other obstacles, such as trying to raise the standard of agriculture by urging farmers to use chemical fertilizers. These were too expensive for peasants because Italian manufacturers made fertilizers with outdated processes in obsolete plants. Also, Italy's chemical cartel blocked the building of new plants that would turn out cheap fertilizers, fearing the loss of investments in the old plants.

Marshall Plan aid and the opportunity of obtaining equipment from abroad nonetheless permitted the Italian government to intervene in the economy on a broad scale. Previously, such state intervention concerned itself mainly with repairing the ravages of war. Between 1948 and 1951, the government, through the European Recovery Program, sponsored the extension of irrigation in the south, land reclamation and improvement, reforestation, and mountain river conservation. It stimulated antipest and antimalaria campaigns and revived work on agricultural experiment stations. The government also granted credit to farmers undertaking improvements.

Despite its flaws of execution, the European Recovery Program received praise from even a harsh critic of American policy, Luigi Villari. He said that "no Italian can forget the generous manner in which the American Government and people came forward to try to enable Italy to get on her feet again . . . ," saving her from economic deterioration, deeper social unrest, and perhaps Communist rule. Although Communists sometimes succeeded in identifying American aid with a kind of imperialism, they lost voting strength. But the Marshall Plan did not alter the basic structure of the Italian economy or bring solutions to old economic and social practices that hampered progress. The Italians themselves were far more responsible for the persistence of those problems than were their American advisers. The Italians, rather than the Americans, insisted on maintaining financial stability as against increasing the rate of capital investment. Yet Americans both encouraged and discouraged economic reform, saying they favored De Gasperi's redistribution of land while warning of the need to avoid damage to production. If production slowed down, then the American taxpayer would have to put up more money to keep Italy afloat.

In addition to economic aid, Italians accepted with enthusiasm many of the outward signs of the American way of life. American popular culture struck Italy with as strong a force as it did anywhere else in Western Europe. Although most Italians could not afford the luxuries of the affluent society, they admired them—big glossy cars, neon signs, movies, jazz and rock-and-roll music blaring from jukeboxes, the countless gadgets and technical competence of American life. Most of all, the Italians envied the success for which these items stood.

English, American-style, replaced French as the dominant second language, and American idioms peppered the everyday speech of Italians. People debated the virtues and weaknesses of American society; professors became seriously interested in what their counterparts in American universities were doing and began probing all aspects of American life as important areas of scholarly investigation. American policy makers moved swiftly to take advantage of this interest by promoting a program of cultural exchange with Italy. They established a network of American information libraries in Italian cities, invited students and professors to the United States, and facilitated the visits of American professors to Italian universities.

Technological progress and social change, more than academic exchanges, made Italians more willing than at any time in the past to accept doses of American popular culture. Italy's young people wanted a slice of affluence and now saw opportunities at least to work toward that goal. Even in the backward regions, they sensed that somehow they might have a chance to taste a better life than their parents had known, a kind of life that they knew existed in America. This sense of hope, especially among the young, accompanied the readiness of Italians to accept things American.

Intellectuals also admired the products of American society, but they pointed out disadvantages that went with too ready an acceptance of American cultural trappings along with economic aid. Like men in government and business, the intellectuals were grateful for the help Americans were giving, but they wanted to keep the cultural invasion small. Herbert Kubly, a playwright in Italy on a government grant, frequently encountered this sentiment expressed usually as a fear that "Americans and their money" would erode Italian culture.

Yet in other areas of contact, Italians hoped for concessions that American policy makers found difficult, if not impossible, to grant. Italian leaders resented the continuing discrimination against their emigrants, and wanted it stopped. At the very least, they desired a higher quota for their people. They also objected to tariff barriers that prevented some of Italy's characteristic products, such as cheese and olive oil, from freely entering the United States. At the same time, these tariffs hampered the operation of Italy's own policy of liberalizing trade, making it difficult for her to pay her own way. She had a constant dollar deficit.

This deficit represented a dependence on the United States that many Italians questioned, especially as conditions improved. They began to wonder if De Gasperi's government had gone too far in adopting American suggestions for the country's improvement. Such acceptance brought with it irksome controls, such as supervision over and criticism of the spending of aid money, and general American "interference" in Italy's own affairs. Left-wing propaganda, often with distortion, exploited these doubts. It was against this background that Italy embarked on the uphill task of regaining full admission to the Western European family of nations.

Wanting Italy to become strong and effective in an integrated Western Europe, American policy makers encouraged her emergence in international affairs. Even before the Marshall Plan went into effect, they began efforts to weld Europe into a military and political coalition against the Soviet Union; they wanted Italy to become a part of it. After the failure of the conference of foreign ministers in London, in December, 1947, Britain's Foreign Minister, Ernest

Bevin, publicly launched the idea of a union of Western European countries. As a beginning, he suggested an alliance linking Britain, France, Belgium, the Netherlands, and Luxembourg. He said that Britain's and France's existing Treaty of Dunkirk of March, 1947, which was directed against Germany, could serve as a nucleus. Later, he added, the alliance could be enlarged to include "other historic members of European civilization." His proposal became the basis for the Brussels Pact, a fifty-year treaty of alliance signed in March, 1948, that tied together the five European nations.

The next step toward a western union, the inclusion of Western Germany, touched off the most dangerous European crisis of the immediate postwar era. It led the Soviets, in the spring of 1948, to blockade West Berlin, 110 miles within East Germany, an area still occupied by Russian troops. Soviet resistance to the Marshall Plan and the Berlin blockade increased the desire of Western Europe for closer military ties to the United States. So President Truman began negotiations with the signers of the Brussels Pact and with Canada for a regional defense arrangement covering the North Atlantic area.

Italian leaders watched the movement toward the consolidation of Western Europe, and its alliance with the United States, with a deep concern for Italy's place in the new arrangements. Italy, they knew, had been in the forefront of a movement to bring about a political and constitutional federation of Europe with a truly European parliament. A number of leaders, such as Einaudi and Sforza, had studied American constitutional history and read *The Federalist*; they were impressed by the American example of federal government and wanted to follow it. They urged their fellow Europeans to form a United States of Europe, but they and other perceptive politicians realized that true federation lay in the future. For the present, Italy had no real choice; she had to cooperate with the other European nations and the United States or remain outside the mainstream of European politics, let alone world affairs.

In a note in August, 1948, to the French government, Sforza came up with the idea of making the Organization for European Economic Cooperation the basis for a European federation. He suggested that the nations of the western union, most of them already loosely united in the Brussels Pact, could take the lead in forming the new group. Two months later, he sent a similar memorandum to all the countries belonging to the Organization for European Economic Cooperation. Sforza's idea of using an existing supranational institution, formed originally for economic ends, on which to build a broader combination fitted the desires of American statesmen.

De Gasperi, like Sforza, saw a better future for Italy if she were part of a larger European community than if she stood alone, but he made it clear that he wanted close ties with the United States as well as with the nations of Western Europe. As for Italy's place, he explained in an interview, she "would sooner see the Organization for European Economic Cooperation expanded into a federation of European states that gave her adhesion to the Brussels Defense Pact." Italy, in other words, wanted to be included in any new developments involving Western Europe.

At the time, the most important developments concerning Western Europe were taking place in Washington. As part of their cold war strategy, American policy makers encouraged the military integration of Western Europe and went ahead with plans for the alliance with the European nations. At first, plans called for a North Atlantic Alliance that would have excluded Italy and the Mediterranean. The French insisted on Italy's inclusion. After some debate, the Americans accepted the idea. As one of them, George F. Kennan, put it, they found it difficult to exclude Italy "without this having misleading implications that could affect in unfortunate ways the delicate balance of the domestic-political struggle within that country." If Italy were left out, she might turn to communism, join the Soviet bloc, and as Dean Acheson felt, become "a source of danger" to the Allies. American policy makers, therefore, pressured the other Allies to support Italian membership. The British, who at first objected, gave in. In March, 1949, as a result, the North Atlantic planners invited Italy to join the alliance as an original member.

Within Italy, politicians of the right and left opposed membership. The right-wingers, some of them Anglophobes, still considered England and the United States enemies. Left-wingers denounced the alliance because it was anti-Soviet. Other Italians wanted to stay out of the cold war alignments. They favored a policy of neutralism which required a refusal of membership in the alliance. Italian policy makers, especially Sforza, felt that American aid depended on Italy's joining the alliance and remaining committed to an anti-Communist policy. Italy, they argued, could not expect Americans to continue to finance her economic recovery and receive nothing in return except neutrality. Still, prominent Christian Democrats, even De Gasperi himself, hesitated to commit Italy to a military pact, hoping somehow to keep her out of the cold war confrontations. Finally, they accepted the argument that military integration within a larger European community was as vital as economic and political cooperation, and that Italy could not isolate herself from Western Europe.

The hard-core opposition remained unconvinced. Togliatti accused the government of abandoning the nation's true interests. Pietro Nenni, the Socialist leader, said that "by signing the Atlantic Pact you, gentlemen of the government, will surrender the independence of the nation. You will make of us vassals of other states." Sforza countered that the arrangement was defensive and fitted Italy's commitment to "all the ideas that strengthened European solidarity." On March 18, after more than fifty hours of consecutive debate, the Chamber of Deputies approved the treaty by a vote of more than 2 to 1. This action paved the way for Italy to become one of the twelve nations that signed the North Atlantic Treaty in Washington on April 4, 1949. Since all the countries of the western union were signatories, Italy became their ally as well as that of the United States. The key commitment, Article Five, stated that the allies would consider an attack on one or more of the signatories an attack against all. Each would assist the ally under attack. To this commitment Italy could bring no real strength. She joined the alliance mainly for domestic reasons, to get economic aid, and the United States included her primarily to keep her from going Communist. Under the terms of the peace treaty, Italy could have no armed forces of consequence, so even if she desired, she could not assume the necessary responsibilities of a military ally.

Regardless, the North Atlantic Treaty gave Italy the opportunity to participate actively in the international politics of Western Europe. In May, 1949, when the Soviets lifted their Berlin blockade, representatives from Italy and nine other nations of Western Europe signed a treaty in London creating a Council of Europe. Since the Council had no legislative or military powers, it served mainly as a forum for the discussion of the European idea. In those discussions, Italy often took the lead, with Sforza and De Gasperi pressing for a bolder initiative toward European unification. American policy makers were pleased with Italy's role in this first postwar European institution.

Sforza and De Gasperi thus committed Italian foreign policy to close connections with the United States and the other nations of Western Europe. This policy reflected an intelligent appraisal of Italy's history and of her present needs. They realized that in the rivalries of independent prestige politics she could never rank higher than fourth among the powers of Western Europe. Competition in power politics, along with an exaggerated view of Italy's stature, had led Crispi and Mussolini to disaster. Political reality demanded that Italy accept a modest role in international politics. By taking the lead in renouncing some of the formal aspects of national sovereignty, she might also persuade the larger powers similarly to limit their pursuit of independent adventures. Other Europeans were not so eager to curb sovereignty as were the Italians; European political unity therefore made little progress.

Meanwhile Italy promptly ratified the North Atlantic Treaty; the United States did so in July. On August 25, 1949, after a sufficient number of other signatories had ratified it, the treaty went into effect, becoming a central part of De Gasperi's foreign policy. In the middle of September, the foreign ministers of the twelve treaty powers held their first meeting in Washington, where they set up the administrative machinery for the North Atlantic Treaty Organization, or NATO. A few months later, Italians who were acutely aware of the military helplessness of their country became alarmed by reports that the Atlantic powers might abandon Italy in case of an attack from the East. In May, 1950, therefore, Sforza informed the cabinet that the NATO powers had affirmed their alliance's provision for the defense of the territorial integrity of all signatories from the very outset of hostilities. Since American officials supported this interpretation, the Italian people welcomed Sforza's news.

At this time, France's Foreign Minister, Robert Schuman, advanced a scheme in line with the idea Sforza had urged earlier. Schuman called for a supranational organization for control of iron and steel, Europe's basic industries. Americans were enthusiastic; so were the Italians. The Schuman Plan would keep the Italian economy free of old wartime controls, would require some surrender of national sovereignty, and hence would be a step toward the kind of Europe Italians wanted. So in March, 1951, in a "treaty that would run for fifty years," Italy joined Belgium, France, Luxembourg, the Netherlands, and West Germany in planning a European Community for Coal and Steel. These countries adhering to the Schuman Plan came to be known as "Little Europe."

The United States and the other allies now recognized more clearly than ever a disarmed Italy's anomalous position in relation to her obligations as a member of NATO. Several months earlier, Sforza had raised the question of treaty revision, asking for public recognition that the peace settlement was now "out of date on a moral plane." In

September, De Gasperi attended a meeting of the Council of NATO in Ottawa; then he visited Washington, where for three days he talked with President Truman and Secretary of State Dean Acheson and addressed the Congress. De Gasperi asked the Americans to support Italy's claim to Trieste, saying it would solidify the Western coalition. He also requested more aid and treaty revision, discussed economic problems, Italy's place in international politics, the unity of Europe, and NATO. Truman praised Italy's progress and called for her admission into the United Nations, saying that "if the Soviet Union keeps on vetoing Italy's membership, other ways must be found" to get her in.

Truman, Acheson, and De Gasperi issued a joint communiqué that called the Mediterranean area "essential to the common defense" and announced the willingness of Britain, France, and the United States to remove treaty restrictions on Italy. But Truman and Acheson refused to back Italy against Yugoslavia in the Trieste dispute. "Nothing," Acheson explained later, "could have done more to heal the breach in Communist ranks." They also turned aside De Gasperi's request for an easing of American immigration laws to help relieve the pressure of population on the Italian economy. A better remedy they felt, was birth control. On September 26, the Italian and American leaders signed a supplement to their commercial treaty of 1948 providing for special loans to help Italy industrialize the *Mezzogiorno*.

Newspapers praised the visit. The *New York Times* stated that De Gasperi had now restored Italy "morally and substantially to a position of equality with the states of the West," a view shared by Acheson and other policy makers. If the Western powers deserved any criticism for what they have just done, the *Times* said, it was that they had waited too long before acting. Most of the Italian press, especially the journals of the center and of independent background, also saw impressive benefits for Italy in De Gasperi's diplomacy, but Communist papers called his mission a dismal failure.

Even though De Gasperi did not obtain all that he desired, he accomplished a great deal; but none of the pleasantries of his visit could hide the attitude of many Americans toward Italy as an ally. They considered her one of the weakest links in Western Europe's line of defense against the Soviet Union. Political unrest, a large Communist party, and a shaky economy all diminished her value. This very weakness, if nothing else, made De Gasperi's accomplishments significant.

Within the next few months, eleven of the signatory powers, including the United States but not Russia, agreed to a revision of Italy's peace treaty so that she could rearm. Then in December, 1951, Italy said that she no longer considered the restrictive clauses binding, thereby denouncing the treaty. In February, 1952, she announced her intention to rearm beyond treaty limitations. Since she could not rearm on her own, she relied on the United States to equip her military forces. Gradually, with the help of an American Military Aid Program, she reconstructed naval and air bases and other military installations. Naples became the headquarters of NATO's South European Command, and NATO placed orders for its forces with Italian industry. Within the decade, the United States poured almost $2 billion for military aid into Italy. Italian commitments under NATO also required her to increase greatly her own expenditures for arms.

Italy's effort to get into the United Nations, despite American support, did not fare as well as her treaty revision and integration into NATO. Even though in December, 1951, the General Assembly voted overwhelmingly to admit her, the Soviet Union vetoed the approval. The Soviets insisted on making Italy's admission conditional on that of twelve other countries, including Communist satellite states.

In Europe itself, Italy now stood in the center of affairs. In June, 1952, the treaty creating the European Coal and Steel Community came into force; and in the autumn, De Gasperi, now Foreign Minister as well as Prime Minister, played an important part with French leaders in putting forward proposals for a European political community for which the Coal and Steel Community was to prepare a draft constitution. In September, the six states established the formal organization for the merger of their coal and steel industries. They created common institutions and a customs union that abolished tariffs and quotas in coal and steel throughout Little Europe. Since the community was the first supranational organization in postwar Europe with real authority, both the United States and Italy hoped it would become the basis for a political confederation.

In these years, despite her new independence and economic recovery, Italy still seemed to many observers practically an American satellite. At Verona and near Pisa, they could see American air bases; at Naples, the Sixth Fleet still maintained headquarters; and elsewhere, Americans staffed guided missile bases. Italy's foreign policy, and even her politics, appeared to respond to American desires, or to what policy makers assumed would please Americans. Although not a great power, Italy was nonetheless too important for any country, even the United States, to manipulate at will. If Italian policy usually followed the wishes of American leaders, it was because Italian and American views coincided. Both wished to keep Soviet power out of Western Europe and the Mediterranean. For this reason, as well as for others, Italian statesmen had succeeded, within a few years, in transforming their country from that of a former enemy to an ally and friend of the United States.

In the Mainstream
16

During the 1950's, Italian cultural life again entered the mainstream of
the Western tradition. Again Italians showed themselves to be as re-
silient, talented, and civilized as any people in the world, going
through a cultural revival as impressive as their economic reconstruction. When Fascism crumbled, the creativity, either held in check or
unappreciated for more than twenty years, spilled out in a torrent.

No people responded more appreciatively to the burgeoning of
Italian art, literature, industry, and social and intellectual life than the
Americans. More than at any time in the past, millions of Americans
became aware of Italians as contemporaries of considerable intellectual and social vigor. Americans read Italian novels, viewed Italian
films, wore Italian clothes as a mark of taste and style, and drove Italian cars. Never had they paid so much attention to so many aspects
of contemporary Italian culture. Ordinary Americans rediscovered
the Italy that their soldiers had found in the forties. Tourists by the
thousands traveled to Rome, Florence, Venice, and other parts of the
peninsula. In fact, Italy was visited by more foreigners than any other
country in the world. Students, artists, writers, former soldiers who
had fought there, economists and military men working with the various aid programs all spent some time in Italy. Rome, Florence, and
the islands in the Bay of Naples became cultural centers radiating an
international influence.

As in the past, American writers—men like John Hersey, Alfred
Hayes, John Horne Burns, and Tennessee Williams—found in Italy
themes they wove into their own work. Unlike their predecessors of
the nineteenth century, they usually viewed Italian life realistically,
concerning themselves with social issues, human feelings, and cultural
conflicts, not merely with ruins, scenery, and art. Many of the books
by Americans, though, were more popular than profound, dealing

with atmosphere and art. Most of these faded quickly; but a few, such as Eleanor Clark's sensitive commentary on Italians, *Rome and a Villa,* could be read and reread and still bring pleasure.

American scholars, such as H. Stuart Hughes, Joseph L. Palombara, Norman Kogan, and Charles Delzell, worked on important studies of Italian political and social life. Others studied the works of social critics such as the Marxist thinker Antonio Gramsci and the Catholic historian Carlo Jemolo. Nothing stirred a greater American interest in Italian social conditions than the novels and movies depicting the suffering and heartbreak in wartime and postwar Italy. The writers and film directors who showed Italian life as it was in these years were often called, imprecisely but conveniently, "neorealists." Although neorealism dealt with contemporary problems, it had its roots in the Fascist era and took inspiration from the American literary tradition.

Before the war, Americans had usually disregarded Italian writers, assuming that Fascism corrupted whatever literary talent Italy produced. Actually, in the thirties, a group of young Italian novelists and poets were writing and finding in American literature models to admire. Although these writers had their own school of *verismo* ("realism") established in the nineteenth century by the Sicilian novelist Giovanni Verga, they were influenced by the bold, fast pace of American narrative. Naturalists such as John Steinbeck, Erskine Caldwell, Ernest Hemingway, and William Faulkner were widely read in Italy in the thirties. "They had," said Carlo Levi, speaking for Italian writers, "an enormous influence on us."

The young writers—Alberto Moravia, Cesare Pavese, and Elio Vittorini—who expressed in their works the feelings and emotions of ordinary people found more than just a model in the American novel. They used it as a means of breaking through Fascism's cultural isolation and of experiencing something of the artistic upheaval taking place elsewhere in the world. So concerned were Pavese and Vittorini with American literature that they and others like them came to be called *"Americanisti."* In 1932, Pavese translated Herman Melville's *Moby Dick* into Italian. Pavese also introduced a vernacular, or American, element into Italian literature, and probably did more than any other one person to stimulate among his countrymen an interest in American literature. Vittorini, too, brought the works of Americans to the attention of Italians. In addition to writing his own fiction, he wrote critical studies of American literature and translated various novels such as *Tortilla Flat* and *God's Little Acre*, as well as American poems, into Italian.

Men like these kept alive the legendary Italian view of America as a free, wealthy, and dynamic land. They permitted Italians in the thirties to experience this legend through American literature. As literary critic Leslie Fiedler has pointed out with some exaggeration, there took place "in Italy one of the most extraordinary feats of translation and assimilation in the history of culture; hundreds of American books have been turned into Italian, provided with prefaces, critically discussed, and most important of all, read with fantastic eagerness."

The young writers who made the translations, analyzed the American works, and gathered in Roman cafes and elsewhere to exchange ideas and discuss literature had little difficulty in obtaining American books through the mails. In the later thirties, when a tightened censorship made such works difficult to get, some of these writers published *Americana,* an underground anthology that Fascist authorities confiscated in 1942. In the Italy of the thirties, the interest in American intellectual life was an act of protest against Fascism. The mere reading of an American book was, to some, a symbolic revolutionary act, a form of personal resistance against the established order.

Italy's outstanding poets—Giuseppe Ungaretti, Eugenio Montale, and Salvatore Quasimodo—who also served as models for the neorealists, resisted the Fascist establishment in another way, mainly through a difficult, withdrawn, although rigorous and intense style called "hermetic." These men tried to isolate the poetic tradition from the vulgarity of Fascist politics, and in doing so, sealed themselves from the general public. Their works were hardly known in the United States. The novelists who had an American following, like the anti-Fascist exile Ignazio Silone, frequently wrote about emigration, taking a half-bitter, half-sweet view of the United States. They mixed the dream of the *contadini,* who pictured America as a land of easy wealth, with the attitude of intellectuals, who had lived there and remembered it as a place of galling disappointment.

The legend of America influenced the development of neorealism, particularly as it acquired a tone of social urgency with the experience of Italy's wartime resistance. Many of the young intellectuals who fought as partisans had read the American novels translated in the thirties, had viewed the cowboy movies from across the sea with their crude but clear distinctions between good and bad, and had nurtured a faith in the legendary America of Walt Whitman and Herman Melville. One of them, Giaime Pintor, expressed this view in "Americana," an essay that the literary historian Donald Heiney considers "one of the most remarkable tributes ever paid to America by a European."

The wartime experience, although not destroying this faith, brought shock. With the occupation and the coming of American soldiers, the myth collided with grim reality. This confrontation is what the young writers saw. When they wrote their first postwar novels, therefore, they reflected the American legend of the thirties, the degrading reality of their wartime experience, and the American presence of the forties.

It was this new writing that dealt with Italian reality more candidly than had anyone since Verga. In simple language, unadorned for literary effect, this literature expressed concern for the poor and the oppressed. Although impersonal on one level, this neorealism was political and passionate on another; it exposed evil and thereby implicitly called for change. Some neorealists merely imitated the American naturalists, but the better ones were original and deeply Italian. They wore American influence gracefully, producing a literature different from any that Italy had known before.

If any one book marked the beginning of this new era in Italian literature, it was *Cristo si e fermato a Eboli* (1947), by the left-wing intellectual, Carlo Levi. It dealt with *contadini* in the *Mezzogiorno* and the brutal existence they led. Translated as *Christ Stopped at Eboli*, it, more than any other book, brought Italian neorealism to the attention of a large reading public in America. In its success, Levi's book was an exception. Americans did not read many of the works of other neorealists, but they did experience neorealism through motion pictures.

In the postwar decade, creative directors tried to stir the conscience of all who viewed their films with stark but humane depictions of the misery of the war-torn Italian people. Far more effectively than the neorealist literature, these films brought to Americans a feeling for contemporary Italy, her sorrow and her problems. Like the writers, these directors got their start in the Fascist era. In 1933, in Rome, Mussolini established a *Centro Sperimentale della Cinematografia,* or experimental center for moviemaking where talented men who would become noteworthy neorealists received their training. These directors knew how to film the impact of the war on those who suffered; it was something they themselves had experienced. They mirrored Italian life in the countryside, roads, piazzas, and houses of the people.

Poor and lacking studios, these directors had no technical refinements; they often worked outdoors, in fields, streets, and cafes; they shot scenes haphazardly and cut their grainy films amateurishly. Some, such as Roberto Rosellini, did not even use scripts; they improvised dialogue as they shot their scenes. Rosellini's *Open City* (1945) marked the beginning of the impressive neorealist era of the Italian cinema. In the following year, he came out with *Paisá*, which also had a wartime theme. Luigi Zampa's *To Live in Peace* (1946), Vittorio de Sica's moving *Shoe Shine* (1946) and his simple but beautiful *Bicycle Thief* (1949), and other neorealist films brought the Italian cinema world-wide acclaim. These directors expanded the motion picture into a medium of mature and artful communication. One of the movie writers of this era, Ennio Flaiano, recalled: "To make movies was an urgent need for all of us. We could not help it."

American audiences recognized the quality of the Italian film accomplishment. The prestige of these movies helped create another facet of the Italian image in the United States. Such talent, many Americans assumed, could not be dismissed; it merited admiration. American film makers even imitated the Italian example, and some experimented with the production of movies in Italy.

Regardless of their prestige, the neorealist films never went over with the Italian movie public. With their exposures of the seamier side of Italian life, of corruption in government and church, they offended reviving national pride. Italians preferred flashier films put out by Hollywood and by their own bread-and-butter producers of cheap costume spectacles and imitations of American cowboy epics cynically called "spaghetti westerns." The cult of the Wild West was as popular in Italy as in the United States—earlier it had inspired Puccini's opera *The Girl of the Golden West*. Unable to compete with the westerns, many of the prestige films lost money; all were risky financial ventures. By 1950, the era of the neorealist film had just about ended.

Yet Italian film making as a whole did not decline. Talented new directors polished their techniques and produced some great pictures. They experimented anew and frequently failed, but they kept Italy in the forefront of the motion picture world. The influence of Italian films on Americans became evident in October, 1952, when a "Salute to Italian Films Week" was held in New York City. This festival, the first of its kind in the United States, showed seven Italian pictures produced since the end of the war. It also highlighted the importance of the films as vehicles of cultural exchange.

The older directors were still producing a few films on the old theme: the dignified suffering of Italians whipsawed by war. In 1952, de Sica brought out *Umberto D*, and in 1960, *La ciociara* (Two Women), based on a novel by Alberto Moravia about a Roman widow. American critics praised it, and the Motion Picture Academy awarded its star, Sophia Loren, an Oscar for her performance. Rosellini's most impressive film in these years, in the view of American critics, was *General della Rovere*.

In the fifties and sixties, two fresh film innovators, Federico Fellini and Michelangelo Antonioni, won considerable acclaim in the United States. Both men experimented with subjective and impressionistic interpretations of life in the twentieth century. Fellini's outstanding films were *La strada* (1954); *Nights of Cabiria* (1966); *La dolce vita* (1960), a picture which featured several American actors and which attained considerable success in the United States, *8½* (1963), and *Giulietta degli spiriti* (1966). Antonioni gained international recognition for *L'avventura* (1959), *La notte* (1961), *Deserto rosso* (1964), and *Blow-Up*(1969).

Several other directors made films that American critics acclaimed, notably Luchino Visconti, with *Rocco e i suoi fratelli* (1960) and *The Damned* (1969), a spectacle of greed and passion in Hitler's Germany; also Gillo Pontecorvo with *La battaglia di Algeria* (1966). Pier Paolo Pasolini, a Marxist whose films often deal with Christian themes, won acclaim from serious moviegoers in the United States for *The Gospel According to St. Matthew* (1964), *Uccellacci e uccellini* (The Hawks and the Sparrows) in 1966, a fable; and *Teorema* (1968), a Christian allegory.

Those Americans who knew Italy's new cultural renaissance well, saw an unusual merit in her painting and architecture, especially in the work of Pier Luigi Nervi, an architect "in the truly great tradition of Italian design," a superb practitioner in the contemporary use of reinforced concrete, who designed several buildings in the United States. Italian literature, mainly the novel and poetry, continued to command attention. Writers, turning out plays, short stories, and movie, radio, and television scripts, as well as novels, seemed driven by creative energy. In 1959, Salvatore Quasimodo won a Nobel Prize in literature for his poetry; Alberto Moravia was elected president of P.E.N., the international writers organization; and a novel by Giuseppe Tomasi, Prince of Lampedusa, became probably the most discussed piece of Italian fiction since Manzoni's *The Betrothed.*

Some called Tomasi's *Il gattopardo* (The Leopard) (1958), a masterpiece. This story about the hopes, illusions, failures, and ultimate ruin of a noble family in Sicily during the *Risorgimento* had an old-fashioned quality about it, but it was an immediate success, going through forty printings in ten months. American critics hailed it as magnificent literature and as a much finer work than anything done by the neorealists. *Il gattopardo* immediately gained a prominent place in world literature. Italy, it seemed, through the creativity of her intellectuals, had forced her way into the front ranks of contemporary Western cultural life.

In this revival, Americans, even though indirectly, had a part; their aid programs, reforms, and examples brought ferment to the Italian mind. For a while in the postwar years, it seemed as though Italians read only American books, saw mainly American films, and listened primarily to American records. According to the literary critic Agostino Lombardo, in the fifties "the influence of twentieth-century American literature on Italian writing, especially Italian literature, reached its height. . . ." More than any other people, the journalist Giorgio Soavi claimed, Italians wanted to imitate Americans. In 1954, the editors of the Mondadori publishing house asked some fifteen young Italian writers about the influence of American writing on Italian literature and on their own work. Even though a few were hostile to American literature, none denied its influence. The prestige of American literature remained high, gaining a place in the course structure of Italian universities. In the fifties, the first regular courses in American studies began to appear.

This academic interest in American studies did not emerge suddenly. It, too, went back to the Fascist era. In 1925, a group of Romans interested in American life and culture founded the Italo-American Association, but it languished. In 1934, while still interested in promoting close relations with the United States, Mussolini took up the cultural connection and established a *Centro Italiano di Studi Americani* in Turin. Two years later, the center moved to Rome, where it obtained the Library for American Studies, renamed the Nelson Gay Memorial Library, in honor of an American historian of Italy's past. The government housed the center, with its library, in Palazzo Antici-Mattei, a lovely old building in the heart of the city, gave it a staff and an annual allocation. After the war, the Italo-

American Association was revived and became part of the center for American studies in Palazzo Antici-Mattei.

Finally, in 1949, the various groups interested in American culture got together and formed the Council of American Studies in Rome. Its supporters sought to exploit the newly established Fulbright program for American and foreign scholars, wanting to make the expanding cultural exchange between the United States and Italy effective and penetrating. So seriously did the Italians take the new work in American literature and history that in 1955, they began publication of an annual review, *Studi Americani*, the first European periodical devoted entirely to American studies. The interest in American cultural life reflected a view held by many knowledgeable Italians: that in their troubled postwar years, Americans were their best and most powerful friends, a people worthy of study and understanding. Despite this warmth toward Americans, however, Italians could still get upset by an old grievance, the discrimination implicit in American immigration laws.

Even though Italy experienced considerable economic and social improvement in the postwar decade, old problems, such as massive unemployment in the *Mezzogiorno*, persisted. The Italian government tried, among other means, to reduce the jobless by reviving emigration. Even though Italy now had one of the lowest birth rates in Europe, lower even than that of the United States, she was still overpopulated for her limited resources. From 1948 onward, Italy made bilateral agreements with a number of countries willing to take emigrants. But the United States still offered little hope to Italian workers. Italy's annual quota remained less than 6,000. Nonetheless, in the late fifties, because of special openings in the immigration laws, mainly the acts of 1948 and 1950 for Europeans displaced from their homes by the war, more than twice that number of Italians entered the United States each year, most of them following old patterns by settling in the eastern cities.

In 1947, when Congress began studying the immigration and naturalization systems in preparation for a revision, Italians hoped for better treatment than in the past, or at least for a higher quota. They were doomed to disappointment. Years of study and hearings produced in April, 1950, a piece of omnibus legislation, the McCarran-Walter Bill, that gave new life to restrictionist ideas. Retaining the national origins formula as its main feature, it alloted approximately 85 per cent of the quotas to the countries of northwestern Europe. Italy found herself with a quota of 5,645 immigrants a year, a figure lower than she had ever been allocated.

Italian and Jewish groups within the country led the organized opposition to the bill. Abroad, various countries, especially Italy, protested. Throughout Italy, the bill produced shocked reactions; it perpetuated, one leader pointed out, "an unscientific and dangerous racialist doctrine." The protests and the pressures, whether foreign or domestic, had no real effect on Congress. The House, in May, 1952, gave the bill a majority of 206 votes to 68, and the Senate followed with a quick approval by a voice vote.

President Truman took a different stand. In June, despite support for the legislation from his own Department of State and immigration service, he vetoed it, saying it discriminated against important cold war allies. It would, for example, needlessly injure relations with Italy. Truman could not make his veto stick. With majorities of better than 2 to 1 in both houses, Congress quickly overrode it; and in December, the Immigration and Nationality Act of 1952 went into effect. This complex statute improved the administration of immigration regulations and, in the case of Asians, eliminated race as a barrier to admittance, but these features did not balance the law's damage to relations with many countries that felt its sting. For Italy, it stood as a reminder that in American society, the old discrimination against her people still persisted. As the President's Commission on Immigration reported in the following year, "Our immigration restrictions work against our foreign policy in Italy."

Another law, the Internal Security Act of 1950 (also known as the McCarran Act), whose provisions were carried over into the Immigration Act, also hurt American policy in Italy. Designed to strike at Communists and Fascists, the security law prevented anyone from entering the United States who had been a member of a totalitarian organization. It tried also to eliminate the "subversive alien" by permitting the deporting of those who advocated totalitarian doctrines. Italian officials maintained that the law, as enforced, violated the Italian-American treaty of friendship of 1948. This agreement permitted the exercise of "reasonable surveillance over the movement and sojourn of aliens." But, Foreign Minister Sforza insisted, its meaning should not be stretched to permit "indiscriminate detention of all Italians arriving in America." When America's anti-Communist hysteria of the fifties spent itself, this problem virtually disappeared.

Concurrently, the American government eased some of its immigration restrictions, essentially by diluting the national origins formula. Under the Refugee Relief Act of December, 1953, the United States decided to admit, for a limited time, special quotas of immigrants, mainly political refugees and those with close relatives already in the country. Italy received a quota of 60,000 persons a year, with an additional 10,000 allocated for Trieste. Owing to stipulations concerning the classes of immigrants that could enter under the McCarran-Walter Act, Italy found herself unable to utilize fully either one of the new emergency quotas. Yet 30 per cent of the persons admitted under the Refugee Relief Act were Italians. In 1955, nearly 32,000 Italians entered the country. They comprised the largest number to come under the act's provisions and the biggest foreign-born group in the country. Still, in relation to the applications for entry that poured into American agencies, the Italians who now reached the United States were few.

Although De Gasperi disliked the persisting anti-Italian aspects of the immigration legislation, he never faltered in his policy of close friendship with the United States. Ever aware of Italy's limitations, he acted on the assumption that she could make important contributions to world affairs only as a member of a political and economic unit larger than herself. He usually insisted that Italy support the interests of Western Europe as a whole. He and other Christian Democrats also stressed that the Atlantic alliance, with its dependence on the United States, stood as a shield against subversion at home.

Other Italians, and other Europeans as well, although favorable to the Atlantic idea, were reluctant to make substantial sacrifices for their own defense through NATO. Some, like the French, distrusted a rearmed Germany. Nonetheless, in 1952, while the six countries of Little Europe were working together economically, they began to consider cooperation for purposes of defense as well. The French envisaged an international force containing German elements commanded by Allied military men. In May, France, Germany, Italy, Belgium, Holland, and Luxembourg signed a treaty creating a European Defense Community designed to be "supranational in character, consisting of common institutions, common armed forces, and a common budget."

This plan immediately encountered fierce opposition from Italian leftists and others who saw in it a military commitment to the American position in the cold war even more specific than in NATO. It would, they felt, solidify the breach between East and West. Commitment to the European Defense Community and to De Gasperi's "Atlantic" policy became targets for recrimination during Italy's election campaign of 1953. Early in that year, many Italians were thinking of the possibility of an international *détente*. Should this happen, they argued, there would be no real need for intensive rearmament or for close military association with the United States and the other Western powers. Why then should De Gasperi insist on a speedy ratification of the treaty for the European Defense Community? Such thinking coincided with that of the Communist party. The European Defense Community was not made more popular by the speeches on its behalf by Clare Boothe Luce, the American ambassador to Italy. Mrs. Luce referred to the "grave consequences" to Italian-American cooperation if Italians fell victim to "totalitarianisms of Right or Left." Even Italians noted for their friendliness to the United States resented this use of threat.

Experience had seemingly convinced most Italians of the wisdom of collaboration with the major powers of Western Europe. De Gasperi's carefully nurtured alliance with the West had brought Italy the benefits of the Marshall Plan. Yet familiarity had bred a mistrust of close association with the United States, since the relationship carried with it the obligation of rearmament and gave Americans the opportunity to interfere in Italian affairs. In their impatience with American tutelage, many Italians were overly critical, tending to overlook the invaluable assistance they had accepted. To the parties of the left, De Gasperi's seeming subservience to America made his government distasteful. The parties of the right, too, while paying lip service to the Atlantic alliance, reproached the government for showing a lack of independence in its foreign policy, pointing out as an example the still-unsettled question of Trieste.

Italy held her national elections in June, 1953. As in 1948, various American spokesmen, in addition to Ambassador Luce, intervened, warning that aid would continue only if the coalition led by the Christian Democrats won. This time the American tampering, which stimulated a strong negative reaction, and the orientation of foreign policy itself did not weigh as heavily with the voters as did domestic issues. The Christian Democrats and the center democratic parties allied with them failed to obtain a clear majority in the Chamber of Deputies. Nonetheless, De Gasperi tried to organize his eighth ministry. In introducing his government's program, he stressed that Italy intended to fulfill her commitments under the Atlantic pact. His effort failed. On July 28, parliament voted against his government, and De Gasperi fell.

Since De Gasperi had involved himself in every foreign policy decision of any importance since the end of the war and had brought Italy closer to the United States than at any time in the past, his fall marked a turning point in the history of Italian-American relations. Italians and Americans reacted to his defeat quite differently. American policy makers looked toward the future with gloom. Uncertain about how faithful Italy would be in a crisis, they speculated on her status within the Atlantic alliance. They concluded that the elections showed an increase among Italians who preferred communism to democracy. Apart from acting originally on an impulse of generosity, Americans had based their policy toward Italy on the idea of keeping her within the Western orbit and of checking the growth of communism among underprivileged Italians. Some critics now thought that the United States had spent its money in Italy in vain. They blamed the Italian government for not putting into effect more rapidly plans for improving conditions among the masses and thereby countering the appeal of communism.

Viewing this criticism as simplifying the admittedly difficult but not alarming situation, Italians were resentful. Although as loyal as ever to the Atlantic alliance and to close ties with the United States, they were far less worried about communism than were their American critics. Numerous Italians expressed pleasure over De Gasperi's departure, believing that Italian democracy would show itself strong enough to function without a father figure to guide it. Italy would fail or succeed, they argued, because of her own actions; her national life would no longer be excessively dependent on the attitude of a powerful ally. American tutelage, but not friendship, would end.

De Gasperi's fall brought no answer to the question of Italy's ratification of the treaty for the European Defense Community. Various attempts to form a government foundered on that issue. Neither the Christian Democratic party, still capable of commanding over 40 per cent of the popular vote, nor the country as a whole immediately found a political formula to replace De Gasperi's policies. Before the year ended, the European Defense Community became linked with negotiations with the United States for placing NATO bases on Italian soil and with the future of the free territory of Trieste. All these issues involved American diplomacy.

Only ten weeks after the Italian elections of 1948, an event occurred that upset American calculations concerning Trieste. Marshal Tito broke with the Soviet Union. Yugoslavia's defection from the Communist bloc placed in doubt the unilateral return, as Americans had proposed in 1948, of the British and American zone of the free territory to Italy. Now Tito became a potential friend, and American policy makers did not wish in any way to offend him. "Wanting to keep Tito split from the Soviet Union," President Dwight D. Eisenhower explained, "the United States could no longer, as in 1948, back Italy to the hilt in its claim to everything."

The astute Yugoslav quickly measured the drift of American policy and used his bargaining position to entrench himself in Trieste. Italian leaders came to feel that the United States was actually throwing its support to Yugoslavia. De Gasperi's successor as Prime Minister, Giuseppe Pella, felt himself politically unable to ignore this sentiment. Pella, therefore, refused to go ahead with the treaty for the European Defense Community until the United States assured him it would protect Italian rights in Trieste, meaning Italian control of all the free territory as proposed in 1948.

Ambassador Luce then urged Eisenhower and Secretary of State John Foster Dulles to do something about the Trieste problem, fearing that Italy's pro-American policy would be jeopardized by inaction in Washington. She supported her plea with her own version of an old English verse, "For want of a nail":

> For the want of Trieste, an Issue was lost.
> For the want of an Issue, the Election was lost.
> For the want of an Election, De Gasperi was lost.
> For the want of De Gasperi, his NATO policies were lost.
> For the want of his NATO policies, Italy was lost.
> For the want of Italy, Europe was lost.
> For the want of Europe, America . . . ?

Having political influence of her own as well as direct access to the President, Mrs. Luce made her argument felt. "We need both nations [Italy and Yugoslavia] as friends," Eisenhower wrote in his diary, "and we had therefore to try for some solution." Under pressure from Luce and the President, Dulles worked out a plan. Early in October, 1953, Mrs. Luce informed Pella that the United States would shortly propose a solution that would change the whole complexion of the Trieste dispute. On October 8, the American and British governments announced that they viewed "with concern the recent deterioration of Italo-Yugoslav relations." They decided, therefore, to terminate Allied Military Government in their area of responsibility, Zone A, and relinquish its administration to Italy. This action would place Italy in effective control of Zone A in the same way that Yugoslavia controlled Zone B, south of the city on the Istrian Peninsula.

In Italy, the Anglo-American announcement had an electric effect. It offered what Italians had sought for almost two years, the prospect of a position of equality in negotiations with Yugoslavia over Trieste. Italians were jubilant. Since the wording of the declaration was ambiguous, Pella inferred that in obtaining Zone A, Italy would not forfeit any chance of also acquiring Zone B. In other words, he assumed that the English and Americans considered the Tripartite Declaration of 1948 still valid.

Tito remained immovable; he opposed the American and British solution, threatening to order troops into Zone A. The United States sent warships into the Adriatic, and in November, Italian nationalists in Trieste rioted. In helping to suppress the demonstrators, six of whom were killed and many more wounded, American troops incurred the wrath of the nationalists. Now Italians in Rome as well as in Trieste demonstrated against their American ally. Then, after tempers cooled off somewhat, Italians and Yugoslavs indicated a willingness to discuss Trieste's status. Early in December, Italy and Yugoslavia agreed to simultaneous withdrawal of troops from Zones A and B, an operation completed in about two weeks. All the while, American policy makers were searching for a new approach to the impasse. Early in 1954, American and British leaders sounded out the Italian and Yugoslav governments on the possibility of discovering a basis for agreement. Secret negotiations began in London in January, conducted by Llewellyn Thompson, the American ambassador and high commissioner in Vienna, and Geoffrey Harrison, the British undersecretary for Foreign Affairs. The Italian and Yugoslav ambassadors in London, Manlio Brosio and Dr. Vladimir Velebit, represented the two main parties.

While these negotiations were going on, the question of ratification of the treaty for the European Defense Community became pressing. Italy and France were the only countries of Little Europe which had not ratified. On August 30, 1954, before the debate in Italy's parliament on ratification could take place, the French Chamber of Deputies rejected the treaty. Italy then welcomed proposals made at conferences in London and Paris in September and October for the creation of a Western European Union, an alliance composed of Little Europe and Britain. The Paris agreements contained a special clause providing for Italy's accession to the Brussels Pact, out of which the agreements had developed.

Meanwhile the negotiations over Trieste's fate entered a final phase. In the middle of September, Robert Murphy, American Undersecretary of State visited Belgrade and Rome, where he obtained concessions from both sides. Then on October 5, the negotiators in London met for the last time and initialed a "Memorandum of Understanding" and annexes providing for the settlement of the Trieste dispute. The memorandum called for the transfer of Zone A, after a minor border rectification, to Italy. Yugoslavia would take over Zone B. The Italian government would maintain the free port of Trieste in accordance with the provisions of the peace treaty. Italy and Yugoslavia thus agreed on a practical solution somewhat as the United States proposed.

Although the United States used the desire of the Yugoslavs for wheat and long term loans as leverage in bringing about the agreement, it appeared to come out of free negotiation among all the powers concerned. On an official level, therefore, both Italy and Yugoslavia welcomed the settlement. Unofficially, most Italians deplored their country's renunciation of Zone B and the handing over to Yugoslavia of more of their nationals through the addition of a fresh strip of territory to Zone B. Despite the popular dissatisfaction, Italian policy makers considered the settlement the best they could obtain. It did have the virtue of returning the city of Trieste to their jurisdiction, of placing Italians in full control of their own area, and of thereby according Italy an independent status in the region equal to that of Yugoslavia.

The Trieste settlement also had the important side effects that American statesmen hoped it would have. It helped pave the way for Italy's acceptance of NATO bases and of the Paris agreements on Western European Union. The Chamber of Deputies approved the agreements in December, 1954, and the Senate in March, 1955, making Italy the first nation on the European continent to commit herself fully to the seven-nation alliance. As for Trieste itself, it disappeared as an international issue. Within the next few years, relations between Italy and Yugoslavia improved to such an extent that more than one American scholar called the change a minor miracle.

During this time, Italy's economy spurted forward to bring many of her people an unaccustomed prosperity. Gradually her dependence on the United States decreased, although she still counted on remittances from Italian-Americans to help bolster her economic life. Between 1948 and 1958, they sent more than $1 billion 600 million to relatives and friends. Slowly, too, the nature of trade with the United States and the considerable dollar deficit that went with it changed. Until 1952, the huge imports from America under the Marshall Plan and other aid programs were the most important feature of Italian trade. From that year onward, these imports fell and Italy's trade reverted to its prewar pattern, mainly to an exchange of goods with European neighbors. In 1953-1954, as exports to the United States increased, Italy's dollar deficit fell to about 15 per cent. The lira, in relation to the dollar, now became stabilized. As prosperity spread, Italy expanded all her exports. In 1955, for instance, her export of woolen cloth jumped 50 per cent, placing her second to England in this field.

Italy's boom formed part of a larger European economic resurgence that began in West Germany. Burdened by the underdevelopment of the *Mezzogiorno,* Italy lagged behind other Western European countries, so the wave of general prosperity that swept over Western Europe struck her last. What surprised everyone was not the lag, which they expected, but the pace and scale of Italy's industrial expansion, permitting her to compete effectively with her richer neighbors. When Italy joined the European Community for Coal and Steel, Americans and others assumed that her industries, dependent on imported coking coal, iron ore, and steel scrap, would suffer in competition with stronger German and French producers. Instead, Italy's industries—automotive, shipbuilding, and others—expanded faster than those in any of the other five countries in the community.

In the series of economic surges, that many called "miracles," in the Europe of the 1950's, the Italian example was the most dramatic. Since Italy needed improvement (more than did her neighbors), the contrast between her old situation and the new was especially striking. Aware that she still had a long climb upward, Americans continued to offer assistance. In June, 1954, in agreement with Italian policy makers, they set up a revolving fund of $20 million, 90 per cent of it earmarked for industrial development, technology, and small businesses in the *Mezzogiorno.* This long-term American aid and the lack of expensive armed forces and colonies helped make possible much of Italy's progress.

Gains in human happiness and dignity, as well as financial statistics, made the Italian economic achievement impressive. What the Italians were accomplishing, given the low base from which they started, did indeed seem more miraculous than elsewhere. From 1950 to 1960, Italy's economy grew at an annual rate of almost 6 per cent, as compared with an average growth of 4½ per cent for all Western Europe. In 1960, after a small recession during the previous two years, industrial production rose by an unprecedented 11 per cent.

Similarly, during the decade, imports more than doubled, while exports nearly trebled. For the first time, the Italian nation became a major exporter of manufactured goods, and to all parts of the world. With a vastly expanded production geared both for export and for the domestic market, industry led the boom and freed Italy from her dependence on American aid. In 1956, Vittorio Valletta, president of FIAT, Italy's giant automotive corporation, explained the new situation in these words: "Italy is grateful for all the United States has done to help us. From now on we do not want any more handouts, but hard-headed business loans which we will repay before they are due."

Yet some of Italy's internal problems, particularly unemployment, were still urgent and affected relations with the United States. Unemployment remained high even though emigration increased. In the first seven months of 1955, the number of emigrants exceeded by 175,000 the total of those returning to Italy. Emigration would have been even heavier and the pressure of the unemployed lighter if more workers could have entered the United States, as many desired, but the McCarran-Walter Act kept them out. In subsequent years, Italy's prosperity cut down but did not eliminate unemployment. Many Italians found work in the other countries of Western Europe. This mobility of workers, although not a new phenomenon in itself, was new as an aspect of Italy's acceptance in the European community. Her miracle went hand in hand with the growth of Western European cooperation.

American policy makers continually encouraged this European cooperation and Italy's participation in the movement. In March, 1955, Prime Minister Mario Scelba and Foreign Minister Gaetano Martino visited Washington, where they talked with Eisenhower and Dulles; they all stressed support for Europe's economic and political unity, especially through Western European Union. Scelba addressed the Senate, saying, as had his predecessors, that cooperation with the United States stood at the center of Italy's foreign policy. He also began negotiations for cooperation in the peaceful use of atomic energy, with the United States making nuclear research materials available to Italy.

Russia, meantime, did her best to block the treaty of Western European Union, yet the Soviets made a conciliatory gesture by finally agreeing to independence for Austria. Russia's price for the Austrian State Treaty of May, 1955, was a related memorandum pledging Austria to "perpetual neutrality." This agreement raised new problems for Italy. With the evacuation of Allied troops from Austria, with the neutralization of the northeastern Alps, and with the Brenner Pass again becoming one of the strategic frontiers of Europe, Italy found herself placed in the front line of Western European defense. Left-wing politicians lost no time in protesting against the possible transfer of American and British troops from Austria to Italy, and in reviving ideas of Italian neutrality. Foreign Minister Martino emphasized that the deployment of troops would be the concern of NATO. Italy herself, he said, was "neither big enough nor small enough to consider the idea of neutrality."

Another event that jarred Italy's political structure with repercussions felt in Washington was the election, late in April, 1955, of Giovanni Gronchi as President of the Italian Republic. A veteran leader of the Christian Democratic left, he had a reputation for neutralist leanings and for friendliness toward communism. Some American policy makers, a number of whom had tried to prevent Gronchi's election, were alarmed when he took office. They knew that he felt that Italy was becoming too subservient to the United States and should have a more independent foreign policy. Gronchi's dislike of NATO, along with the changed situation on Italy's northern frontier, made American military authorities uneasy; they wanted to reassess Italy's tie to the alliance. Yet important policy makers saw the Italian dissensions over NATO as trivial, not affecting "the large issues of international politics." Believing that Gronchi would not fundamentally change the political situation, the Department of State, unlike the military planners, saw no need for a review of American policy toward Italy.

Prime Minister Scelba offered assurances that Gronchi as president would not lessen Italy's commitments to the Western coalition. The Atlantic alliance, Scelba stressed, was one of the "pillars" of her foreign policy, supported by all the political groups except the Communist and left-wing Socialist parties. Dulles, who agreed with these sentiments, announced in November that he found "Italy to be as firmly linked to the Atlantic Community as ever."

In February, 1956, Gronchi visited the United States. In conferring with Eisenhower, he urged the development of NATO along economic lines. Dulles countered that the European Committee for Economic Cooperation was better suited to deal with economic problems. In addressing a joint session of Congress, Gronchi praised NATO for helping to remove the fear of aggression in Europe and urged its expansion into imaginative nonmilitary areas of cooperation. Although expressing gratitude for American aid and pointing to the improvement in Italy's economy, he asked for economic cooperation with the United States through mutual agreements. He also voiced appreciation for what the Refugee Relief Act had done for Italian workers, hoping that when the law lapsed in 1956, Congress would be equally generous in new legislation on immigration.

While Gronchi pacified American leaders, Italy became more deeply involved in plans for European unity, spurred on by events in the Middle East and in Eastern Europe in October, 1956. France and Britain tried to wrench the Suez Canal from Egypt's control and suffered a humiliating setback when both the United States and the Soviet Union opposed them. The Soviets brutally crushed a rebellion against Communist rule in Hungary. No one, neither NATO nor the United States alone, could do much to help the Hungarians except offer sympathy. Italy felt frustrated and helpless in both crises. Hungary's fate had important political repercussions in Italy; it disgusted the Socialists led by Pietro Nenni, who had been cooperating with the Communists. Nenni and his followers now began to move away from the Communist party. They and other political leaders hoped that a united Europe would become a third force independent of either the Soviet Union or the United States, an attitude that the Eisenhower administration distrusted.

Early in the following year, on March 25, 1957, Italians and other Europeans took their most important step toward economic unification. At the Conservatori Palace in Rome, the six states of Little Europe signed two treaties that created a European Economic Community, or Common Market, of 160 million people, and a European Atomic Energy Community, or Euratom. By eliminating tariffs, equalizing taxes, and removing other national restrictions among member countries, the Common Market would try to achieve economic union within twelve to fifteen years. Then, like a single nation, the union would have free trade among its members and a common tariff against outside countries. Euratom would foster cooperation in the development of atomic energy for peaceful purposes among member nations. Italians hoped that these plans would also lead to political union, perhaps to a United States of Europe.

Within a month of the signing of the Treaty of Rome, and while it was being debated in the Chamber of Deputies, Gronchi became the center of a small crisis concerning relations with the United States. In a reply to a message from Eisenhower, Gronchi criticized American foreign policy. He expressed concern over Italy's being excluded from important committees in NATO, his dislike of Eisenhower's doctrine for containing communism in the Middle East, unfavorable opinions of Dulles, and support for a cold war neutral zone running north and south across Europe. Foreign Minister Gaetano Martino refused to forward Gronchi's letter to Eisenhower, saying the President of the Italian Republic could not in sensitive areas express opinions contrary to government policy. The government stood behind Martino, and Gronchi lost influence. This episode revealed the continuing determination of Italian policy makers to adhere to a foreign policy of cooperation with the United States. "Italy is the most pro-American country in the world," an Italian editor explained in 1958. "There is absolutely no hostility toward the United States. . . ." But there were plenty of critics who agreed with Gronchi's views.

In July, Amintore Fanfani, a left-of-center Christian Democrat who shared some of Gronchi's views for a wider role for Italy in world affairs, took over as Prime Minister. He too wanted close ties with the United States, and pledged his government "to strict observance of the Atlantic Alliance and everything it implies." This policy was put to a test in negotiations with Americans over the construction of missile bases in Italy. These bases, for the launching of intermediate range ballistic missiles with atomic warheads aimed toward the Soviet Union, would be under Italian control, but the crucial items— the warheads—would be under the exclusive jurisdiction of Americans. This issue divided Italian leaders so that negotiators did not reach a final agreement until late in March, 1959. Then a communiqué from Washington announced that Italy was the first NATO ally on the continent to accept the missile bases. As expected, the Soviets protested. Their Prime Minister, Nikita Khrushchev, warned that Italy would be among the first targets for destruction if a nuclear war came. Nevertheless, Italy and the United States went ahead with their agreement.

Meanwhile, Italy and the other signatories ratified the Treaty of Rome and on January 1, 1959, launched the Common Market. The American government pledged cooperation with the new European Economic Community, praising the political motive behind it, and supporting Italy's place in the arrangement. In September, when Prime Minister Antonio Segni was visiting Washington, Eisenhower stressed this point. The joining of the Common Market as a founding member marked a high point in Italy's modern history. Now, in the institutions of the European Economic Community, she sat as an equal of France and Germany, ranking as one of a Big Three. For Italy, the least developed member, the launching of the Common

Market promised other important benefits. Her *Mezzogiorno* possessed the only unused pool of manpower within the six-nation community. This labor force could now be transformed from a burden to an asset. The unemployed acquired hope and a future, a sense of being wanted. These and other benefits came quickly to Italy, even before the Common Market (on January 1, 1960) began lowering tariffs and liberalizing trade quotas. She strengthened her commercial connections with the nations north of the Alps, becoming at last a full participant in the advanced European society of the twentieth century.

Italy's new status, many felt, also called for a change in her relations with the United States, an attitude Eisenhower discovered when he visited Italy early in December, 1959. Gronchi and Segni told the President that Italy now deserved more recognition in the councils of the Western allies than she had received in the past. This view surprised Eisenhower. "I had not realized that Italy felt neglected," he replied, "but the right of Italy to be represented at international conferences involving her interests is axiomatic."

Although Italians of the fifties were often puzzled by aspects of American foreign policy, they retained a favorable view of Americans as a people. According to a survey made by the *Istituto per le ricerche statische e l'analisi dell'opinione pubblica* earlier in the decade, Italians found Americans generous, practical-minded and more likeable than other foreigners, such as Englishmen, Frenchmen, or Germans. This friendly attitude elicited a sympathetic response from Americans and continued into the sixties.

The Blurred
Image

17

In the fifties and sixties, the pressures of upward mobility could be noted in the continued shrinking of the Little Italies. While most Italian-Americans had joined the middle-class trek from cities to suburbs, some of them, in New York, Boston, Philadelphia, New Haven, and elsewhere, clung to their old neighborhoods with remarkable endurance. Several Little Italies even gained renewed vitality from enlarged immigration under a new law of 1965. Where they survived, as in the North End of Boston, New York's Bleecker and Mulberry Streets and East Harlem, or in parts of Brooklyn, sociologists were able to peer through a window into the past.

Boston's North End still had the reputation of a slum, yet its rates of delinquency, disease, and infant mortality were among the lowest in the city. Its streets were remarkably free of violence, and as urban critic Jane Jacobs points out, are "probably as safe as any place on earth in this respect." Some observers attributed this to old-world traits, to the Sicilians' suspicion of governmental authority, leading them to enforce justice in their own way to keep out the law. Jacobs disagrees. She argues that the North End is safe simply because there are people on the streets all the time who know each other, and that the "unslumming" of the area "has nothing to do with Sicily," but stems from the vigor of the urban economy. Regardless of the cause, the North End was uniquely stable while retaining much of its old Italian element.

In the Williamsburg section of Brooklyn, as in Italy, the people still hold a neighborhood religious *festa*. Every July, the Italians there honor St. Paulinus, the patron saint of Nola, an ancient town near Mount Vesuvius. Many from Nola, or their descendants, continue to live in Williamsburg. This persistence of customs from the old country seems unusual because there has been no heavy immigration into the Little Italies for nearly fifty years. The older generation here, as along Mulberry Street, where for ten days and nights each year Italian-Americans celebrate the Feast of San Gennaro, the patron saint of Naples, values this link with the past and perpetuates the ceremonies. But the second and third generations, as the sociologist Herbert J. Gans has shown, usually lose their identification with Italian culture, particularly as exemplified by street celebrations.

Italian-Americans who remained in the old neighborhoods sometimes became involved in racial tensions. Often when whites moved from the city to the suburbs, colored minorities took over the tenements they vacated. At times this shift sparked violence. In the East New York-Brownsville section of Brooklyn, beginning with the end of the Second World War, the heavily Jewish portion of the population moved out steadily. Italian-Americans stayed on, determined, it seemed, to put up what they considered a defense of their homes against a massive influx of blacks and Puerto Ricans. One neighborhood, Brownsville, was virtually all black by the sixties; and adjoining East New York was racially mixed, with many Italians and other whites holding out in peripheral blocks close to the neighboring borough of Queens. In 1966, new whites, mainly Polish refugees, began trickling into East New York. Similarly, relatives from Palermo and Catanzaro, finally able to enter the country after years of waiting, reinforced some of the Italian families.

Like the newcomers, most of the Italians in East New York either came from or were descendants of residents from Sicily and Calabria. As in the past, these people had little communication with those in other Little Italies in Brooklyn, like the community in Williamsburg. Most of these Italian-Americans continued to earn their living as manual laborers, skilled workers, and small entrepreneurs in the building, trucking, and chemical industries. Some remembered vividly having, as immigrants, competed directly with Negro labor. Quite a few were still not far removed economically from unskilled blacks, and their relatively low pay was a source of resentment. Racial difficulties sometimes started over a trivial incident. "Some Puerto Rican boy whistles at a Sicilian girl, she smiles back and a rumble is on," a Catholic nun explained after an outbreak in Brooklyn in July, 1966, involving Italian-American youths. Frequently enough, minor incidents set off violence, but the distrust between Italian-Americans and colored Americans has deeper causes. Like the descendants of other immigrants, Italian-Americans adopted the values of the dominant society. One of these was an anti-Negro racism that ironically went back to a time when Italian immigrants themselves were suffering from discrimination.

During race riots in Chicago in 1921, for example, residents of an Italian neighborhood lynched a Negro. Jane Addams, the social worker, asked some professional men prominent in the community why this shocking violence occurred when southern Italians at the time had a reputation for friendliness toward blacks. "Of course this would never have happened in Italy," one of the men replied; "they [the Italians in Chicago] are becoming Americanized." This observation fits the results of sociological studies showing that, initially at least, Italians offered less resistance to residential encroachments by blacks than did people of other ethnic groups. Frequently, Italians and Negroes have lived side by side in big city neighborhoods without serious friction. Prejudice against blacks appeared to grow at about the same rate as did the assimilation of Italians into the dominant culture. Italian-Americans, it seemed, could no more escape the racism of American society than could other whites.

What made the prejudices of some Italian-Americans particularly noticeable was that more of them continued to live in crowded neighborhoods on the edge of sprawling black slums than did other whites, many of them too poor to uproot their families and migrate to suburbia. Unlike most other whites, they confronted on a basic level the new militancy of the blacks. So, these Italian-Americans, along with people from other low-income ethnic groups such as the Poles, gained a reputation for being prominent in a white backlash against the black civil rights crusade. They could be found among the enthusiastic crowds that greeted George C. Wallace, the racist third-party candidate for President in 1968, when he traveled north. Ironically, they sometimes condemned Negroes in language similar to that used against Italian immigrants earlier in the century. Anthony Imperiali, the son of immigrants, who organized a kind of white neighborhood vigilance committee in Newark, New Jersey, to defend "law and order" against black rioters, spoke this way. Negroes who moved into his neighborhood, he claimed, were dirty and incapable of dignified living. "They don't know how to live here," he said, "they have no pride."

Yet other Italian-Americans, such as Geno C. Baroni, a Catholic priest who worked for years in black communities, and James E. Groppi, another priest who led blacks in Milwaukee in a militant campaign against segregated housing, did not forget their people's bitter heritage of prejudice. Groppi walked in the forefront of the civil rights crusade. Recognizing this, the National Association for the Advancement of Colored People, in January, 1968, honored the thirty-six-year-old Groppi for his "steadfast commitment to the doctrine of equality for all mankind." Many Italian-Americans resented being called white racists, pointing out that they were not the employers in the executive suites who for years had refused to hire blacks.

The crusading blacks and the second generation in the surviving Little Italies often suffered from the same disabilities. Both were members of underprivileged minorities that had produced few men of prominence or wealth in business or the professions. From the ranks of both came a disproportionate share of blue-collar workers, though the Italian Americans held more of the skilled or semiskilled jobs and had risen higher professionally and economically. By the standards of the time, both were poor, but, as in Boston's North End, the Italian-Americans led a more comfortable existence. They were often semi-educated, clean, hard-working, and well-fed. According to sociological and economic studies in the fifties, the differences in income and occupations of first- and second-generation Italians were smaller than between first and second generations in other major immigrant groups. Differences in familial, residential, social, and economic mobility became much more important between second- and third-generation Italian-Americans. The improvements did not emerge clearly until after the Second World War. Even in the thirties and forties, most professional men came either from the small north Italian groups or from among those few southerners of nonpeasant background. Not until the fifties and sixties, did the grandchildren of immigrants move in significant numbers into the more prestigious white-collar fields.

Italians followed a pattern set by earlier immigrants. The children of second-generation small businessmen frequently acquired college educations and became professional people. Italians moved ahead on a smaller scale and a generation later than members of other significant ethnic groups, particularly the Jews. Italian-Americans frequently admired the achievements of the Jewish minority, feeling it had pulled itself up quickly while retaining its cultural identity. They took longer than the Jews to acquire large capital and make their way in America's competitive business world. Some of this backwardness doubtless stemmed from the later arrival and greater poverty and illiteracy of Italians. Despite these handicaps, they produced a few self-made men who succeeded in large businesses outside their own ethnic communities.

Probably the best known of these men was Amadeo P. Giannini, who started with the Bank of Italy in California, expanded it beyond his ethnic group, and built it into the Bank of America, the largest financial institution of its kind in the world. Equally striking was the rise of Giuseppe Di Giorgio, who at fourteen, in 1888, came over from Sicily and worked in New York City as a fruit jobber at $8 a week. Moving to Baltimore, he launched his own jobbing business and, in 1904, founded the Baltimore Fruit Exchange. In 1919, he started buying land in California, eventually acquiring extensive acreage in the San Joaquin Valley. At its peak operation, in 1959, this business, Di Giorgio Farms, spanned almost 11,000 acres, and the Di Giorgios were the largest shippers of fresh fruit in the world. In the sixties, the farming empire, hit by strikes and boycotts, began to break up. But the larger business, the Di Giorgio Corporation, survived, expanding into other fields, mainly the processing, distributing, and marketing of foods and other consumer goods.

The Gianninis and the Di Giorgios were exceptions among Italian-Americans, who, in comparison to people of other white minorities, were slow in moving into corporate and governmental bureaucracies. This slowness, in part at least, may have resulted from the prejudice against them in corporations and in the social and country clubs that big business executives dominate. Studies of prejudice suggest that in the thirties and forties, other Americans placed Italian-Americans near the bottom of the list among minorities they tolerated. Jerry Della Femina, the head of a New York advertising agency in the late sixties, put the problem of the Italian-American in another way. In the forties, a few Jews broke into the Ivy League, white, Anglo-Saxon, Protestant world of advertising on Madison Avenue with their own firms. "The Italians, they didn't even have this, they were nowhere," he said. "We were all working for the Sicilian Asphalt Paving Company. It wasn't that the WASP's hated us, they didn't even know we existed."

The situation changed in the fifties; doors were opened to men of talent from various ethnic groups. So Italian-Americans found it easier than in the past to get jobs on Madison Avenue or Wall Street, in Detroit, and in Washington, D. C., and to fit into executive positions. Some of these men like Lido (Lee) A. Iacocca, president of the Ford Motor Company, John J. Riccardo, president of the Chrysler Corporation, Pietro Belluschi, dean of the School of Architecture at the Massachusetts Institute of Technology, and Ralph D. DeNunzio, vice-chairman of the New York Stock Exchange rose to the top. Now when Italian-Americans sought corporate or professional careers, perhaps because they were still few in comparison to applicants of different origins, employers treated them as individuals rather than as representatives of an undesirable minority. Others, such as Negroes, Puerto Ricans, or Mexican-Americans, felt the sharpest discrimination. Indirectly, these minorities, working at the bottom of the social scale, helped raise the status of Italian-Americans and helped reduce the discrimination they could expect to encounter.

Another factor, and one of the most important, that restricted the mobility of the second generation came from the Italian-Americans themselves: their lack of appreciation of higher education. In the twenties and thirties, those children of Italians who desired college educations usually acquired them by taking the initiative themselves and overcoming family obstacles. Until the fifties, the few with professional degrees generally came from north Italian stock or from south Italian families not of peasant background. This situation illustrates what educators have long known, that it is more difficult for the children of the poor and uneducated to reach the universities than it is for those of educated parents.

Enrollments in New York's city colleges reflect, in rough terms, the attitude of Italians toward higher education and the failure of society and educators to meet the needs of immigrant children who could use special compensatory assistance. In 1960, 11 per cent of the graduates of Hunter College and 6 per cent of the graduates of New York City College had Italian names. For a city with a huge population of Italian origin, these proportions were low. In the sixties, a period of intense concern over higher education, less than 5 per cent of the native-born Italian-Americans were completing college.

According to sociologists Nathan Glazer and Daniel Moynihan, most of City College's Italian-American graduates took degrees in engineering because their south Italian background gave them no appreciation for courses in the more intellectual and speculative disciplines. When these young people finally saw value in an advanced education, they went into it mainly to prepare themselves for a practical career, often teaching or nursing for girls, engineering or medicine for boys. The implication here is that the Italian-Americans were more concerned with material gain and less with intellectual accomplishment than were other segments of society. Ironically, as Italian and other visitors to the United States had noted time after time, a distinguishing feature of American culture is its materialistic anti-intellectualism, an attitude probably more important in shaping Italian-American attitudes than were old-country folkways.

Catholicism in the United States, sociologists claim, also nurtured a practical approach to education. Although Catholicism was always the major religion of the Italians and their children, they were not noted as strong supporters of the American Catholic church. They did not take easily to a nationalistic church dominated by American Irish. The Irish hierarchy was not only alien, it also reflected the Catholic hostility toward the secular Italian state, a situation that troubled simple immigrants. Despite the potentially large Italian-American constituency, not until after church and state in Italy made peace in the Lateran Treaty of 1929 did parochial schools in the United States take up the teaching of Italian and thereby encourage enrollment of Italian children, most of whom were going to public schools. Earlier, immigrant children were able to study the language of their parents in the parochial schools of only a few places, such as San Francisco.

In the forties, as more and more Italian-Americans moved out of the Little Italies, the children abandoned the attitudes of their parents and turned to Catholicism with vigor. In it they found a church that had at last gained an accepted place in American society. So in the fifties and sixties, the status-conscious third-generation Italian-American suburban dweller not only usually took his religion seriously, but also found in the American Catholic church, with its ethnically mixed parishes, another anchor in his newly acquired middle-class Americanism.

While making their adjustment to Catholicism, the rising Italian-Americans did what their parents had usually avoided; they embraced the parochial schools. For years these schools had fostered a cultural separateness from mainstream America. Italian-Americans either ignored or were unaware of the weakness of the parochial system, for the proportion of their children in it steadily increased. In the early sixties, children of Italian origin made up 40 per cent of the enrollment in Philadelphia's Catholic schools. At the college level at this time, Fordham University's half-Italian student body gave some indication of the new Italian-American concern for Catholic education. In New York, at least, this attraction of Catholic universities was undoubtedly a factor in keeping the proportion of Italian-Americans in the free city colleges low. Elsewhere it prevented Italian-American children from experiencing the very best that American higher education had to offer, mainly outside the Catholic system.

As third-generation Italian-Americans streamed into church schools and became integrated within the wide structure of American Catholicism, the old antagonism between them and the Irish declined. Accepting or conforming to Irish norms, Italian-Americans underwent a kind of Hibernization, becoming in their religious practices less Italian and more Irish. Their penetration of the Catholic hierarchy did not correspond to their size within the laity. The Irish retained control of the top positions. New York City's archdiocese of the early sixties, for example, had thirteen auxiliary bishops. Of these, only one, Joseph M. Pericone, came from Italian stock. He and Archbishop Celestine J. Damiano, head of the diocese of Camden, New Jersey, were among only a handful of Italian-American bishops out of more than 100 in the church. Although ethnic discrimination doubtlessly still lingered, it probably was less important in accounting for the meager Italian leadership than was the reluctance of Italian-Americans to enter the priesthood and make themselves available for advancement to high posts.

Finally, at a time when minorities were clamoring for more than merely token recognition in all areas of American life, at least two more priests of Italian extraction stepped into major church posts. In December, 1967, Joseph B. Brunini, the grandson of an immigrant, became the bishop of the diocese embracing Mississippi. Then in September, 1968, Francis Mugavero, the son of Sicilian immigrants, as the newly ordained bishop of Brooklyn, took over the leadership of the largest diocese in the United States. He became, also, the first Italian-American to head a diocese in New York. As yet, none of the ecclesiastical princes of the American church, the cardinals, came from the ranks of the Italian-Americans, a striking situation at a time when the Catholic hierarchy in Rome was itself becoming more than ever responsive to social change and thereby less Italian.

As within the church, Italian-Americans were slow in gaining positions of state and national leadership, at least in comparison with people from other large ethnic groups. In politics, as in other areas, discrimination, the fact that they comprised the last large immigrant group to arrive, their poverty, illiteracy, and the lack of leadership by men of wealth and intellectual stature, all account for their inability to gain power at the top. Even La Guardia's rise to national prominence did not signify a sustained Italian-American political surge. Although he was elected with heavy support from the Italian community, his ethnic background hurt him as much as it helped. His own intelligence and political sophistication enabled him to attain a major office at least a decade before Italian-Americans began to earn political recognition in any manner commensurate with their numbers. Until the forties, he was the only political leader of limited national stature that Italian-Americans had produced. Although Angelo Rossi, also the son of immigrants, served as mayor of another important city —San Francisco—from 1931 to 1944, he lacked La Guardia's competence and never attained a comparable influence.

With the end of the Second World War, as Italian-Americans widened their economic and educational base and improved their status, politicians could no longer placate them with small-time patronage while reserving the important offices for others. The political rise of the Italian-Americans can be seen in Rhode Island, where they made their most striking gains. There, in 1946, John O. Pastore, the thirty-nine-year-old son of a tailor, became the first man of Italian origin to be elected governor of any state. Four years later, Rhode Islanders elected him senator, making him also the first Italian-American to sit in the Senate. In New Jersey, the political breakthrough for Italian-Americans came in 1947, when they started winning control of Hoboken and other cities. By the late forties, in the heavily populated eastern states, their new political muscle often assumed pivotal importance. In New York, Boston, Newark, Providence, and other cities, where they comprised from 10 to 30 per cent of the population, they frequently held the balance of power. Even in presidential elections, because states such as New York and Pennsylvania have large electoral votes, the attitude of Italian-Americans, if the issues were such as to elicit bloc voting, could be crucial.

In New York City, in 1945, Vincent Impellitteri, born in Sicily, became president of the city council, the first Italian-American to gain a place on a city-wide Democratic ticket. A number of Italian-Americans won posts as assemblymen and judges. In 1948, eight were elected to Congress, twice as many as in any previous year. In 1949, Carmine G. De Sapio took over the leadership of New York's Tammany Hall, becoming the first Italian-American political boss with national influence. In the following year, in one of New York City's most unusual elections, four Italian-Americans ran for mayor, Impellitteri, Ferdinand Pecora, Edward Corsi, and Vito Marcantonio. Impellitteri, an independent, won. Italian-American politicians gained greater power in Massachusetts, taking various state-wide offices, including the governorship, in 1956, with a liberal Democrat, Foster Furcolo. It became almost standard practice for the Democrats in that state to offer tickets that included Irish, Yankee Protestant, and Italian politicians. In 1966, the Republicans overcame this kind of competition by choosing Italian, Negro, and Protestant candidates.

Out West, in the state of Washington, Albert D. Rosellini, another Italian-American Democrat, won the governorship in 1956. Even in sparsely populated Nevada, the votes of Italian-Americans could sometimes be decisive. From its earliest days, when Italians had been brought in as sheepherders, Nevada, for its size, possessed a significant Italian population. Early in 1966, the state's Democratic governor, Grant Sawyer, suggested that Frank Sinatra was an evil influence in state politics. Sawyer implied that the entertainer, allegedly friendly with gangsters who had infiltrated the state's gambling casinos, also had close connections with the Republican gubernatorial candidate, Paul Laxalt. Even though Sinatra was a Democrat, the Nevada Italians, who admired him, resented Sawyer's attack on him. Laxalt, who won the election, believed that Sawyer's feud with Sinatra helped "swing the Italian vote" into the Republican column.

Despite the comments of politicians such as Laxalt, political analysts differ about whether or not a true "Italian vote" exists. Except for some overriding issue that might affect all of them, Italian-Americans, even in New York or Massachusetts, have seldom been well-enough organized to be consistent bloc voters. The separateness and provincial loyalties of Italians has usually blocked large-scale political cooperation.

Although Italians and their children, like most other immigrant peoples, have generally supported the Democratic party, they have not been prominent as liberals or in any large program for social change. In his first campaigns, Franklin D. Roosevelt captured most of the Italian-American votes, as he did those from all low-income groups. But Italians did not vote Democratic for ideological or ethnic reasons. Later, in part apparently as a reaction against Roosevelt's stab-in-the-back slur, large numbers went over to the Republican party. Many Italian-Americans also found the switch logical for other reasons. In various Italian communities, the leaders were (as were civic leaders throughout America) conservative businessmen. Their views often gave a conservative tone to entire communities.

Social psychologists traced some of the conservatism of rising Italian-Americans to insecurity and a striving for status. Concerned about their public image, they—like others from recent immigrant stock—frequently became intense nationalists. Their groping for acceptance, when supported by a desire to get rid of the stigma of not being truly "American," made it easy for them to adopt the outlook of conservative nationalists, the so-called "real" Americans. Other Italian-Americans who moved upward to well-paid jobs, big houses, and fancy cars became conservative because they were satisfied with the way the American system worked and were opposed to changing it. Consequently many found the Republican party and the conservative wing of the Democratic party increasingly congenial. By 1947, more of them were voting for Republicans than were the other ethnics in the big cities. If Democratic politicians had once taken their votes for granted, they could no longer do so. By this time, Italian-Americans were able to make their own way; if they had ever been truly dependent on ward politicians, such dependence was diminishing if not vanishing.

In the fifties, as Italian-Americans were becoming more mobile and blending with other middle-class Americans, even political scientists who believed in ethnic blocs had difficulty pinning down an Italian vote as such. Big city wards that had been Italian for decades were changing their ethnic composition. Analysts did note, however, that in areas where large numbers of Italian-Americans had recently moved, the Republican vote increased, sometimes by as much as 5 per cent. Yet in New Jersey in the fifties, the typical Italian office-holder, usually native-born and college-educated, was a Democrat. A 1969 survey in New York City suggested that at least 35 per cent of that city's Republicans were of Italian descent; they comprised the dominant bloc in the party. Most seemed to vote for conservative candidates. In that year, their votes made John J. Marchi, a militant conservative, the Republican candidate for mayor. The more liberal incumbent, John V. Lindsay, alienated Italian voters by implying that they were bigots. In the runoff, both Marchi and Mario A. Procaccino, the Democratic candidate, lost to Lindsay in part because of their "law and order" conservatism. To many Italian-Americans, as to others conscious of social status, the Republican party represented the party of the middle-class stability they at last were acquiring.

This turn to conservatism has an ironic twist, for among the conservatives of the two major parties were the strongest remnants of the racial and ethnic prejudice which Italian-Americans had not entirely escaped. Ironically, too, the conservatism came at a time when Italian-Americans in various parts of the country—New York, Massachusetts, Rhode Island, Cleveland, San Francisco, and elsewhere—

were producing singularly capable political leaders. Although some were Republicans and some Democrats, none were reactionaries. Neither, however, did any one of them stand out as a national leader of farsighted liberalism.

The one Italian-American politician of the early sixties who won national recognition for liberalism, Anthony J. Celebrezze, came not from the big eastern states, but from the Middle West. Born in Italy, he was taken to Ohio as a baby, and grew up there. A Democrat, he was elected a state senator in 1951, and two years later he won the first of five consecutive terms as mayor of Cleveland, where he made a good record for work in slum clearance and urban renewal. In July, 1962, in part in appreciation for the support he had received from Italian-American voters and in part in belated recognition that the Italians had not received many political rewards, President John F. Kennedy appointed Celebrezze Secretary of Health, Education and Welfare. Celebrezze thereby became the first Italian-American to attain a post of cabinet rank.

Another first, as far as Italian-Americans were concerned, occurred during the presidential campaign of 1968. At that time, politicians considered them capable of delivering the largest nationality vote in the country. Both major parties gave serious consideration to the selection of an Italian-American for the second place on their tickets, and in both of the national conventions, an Italian-American politician had a prominent role.

The Republicans considered giving the vice-presidential nomination to John Volpe, the son of an illiterate immigrant from the Abruzzi, who had risen from hod carrier to millionaire contractor to three-term governor of Massachusetts. Even though Volpe did not get the nomination, after the convention Richard M. Nixon, the party's presidential candidate, appointed him chairman of a nationwide nationalities committee designed to transmit Republican views to the sons and daughters of immigrants. Anticipating a close election, Nixon wanted to reach the Italian-Americans and other minorities in the big eastern states, where they could possibly swing the electoral vote one way or another. The Democrats frequently mentioned Joseph L. Alioto as a vice-presidential possibility. The son of a Sicilian fisherman and restaurant owner, Alioto gained prominence as a liberal mayor of San Francisco. Like Volpe, he did not get the nomination, but Hubert H. Humphrey, the party's presidential choice, relied on Alioto to help him carry California and attract Italian-American and other ethnic votes. Volpe and Alioto came closer to nomination for national office than have any other Italian-Americans.

National political office eluded Italian-Americans for various reasons, but in public life they suffered from a special handicap. They were unable, especially in the eastern states, to shed the stigma of crime, the notion that somehow the successful Italian-American politician is linked with crime as a business, usually with the underworld of the Mafia. In the popular mind, the connecting of Italians with crime was as American as associating Jews with shady business deals, Irishmen with boss politics, or Negroes with watermelons.

Utica's first mayor of Italian ancestry, Dominick Assaro, found the image of criminality impossible to escape. From the time he first ran for office in 1967, he had to counter rumors and allegations that he was a tool of the Mafia. "It's unfortunate," he said in June, 1969, while seeking a second term, "that some people decide because a man's last name ends in a vowel he is automatically a member of the Mafia or connected with it in some way." In the following September, when Alioto again stepped into national notice while preparing to run for governor of California, *Look* magazine published an article linking him with the Mafia. He denied the allegation as "an incredible tissue of lies, half truths and false innuendos," and filed a libel suit of $12.5 million against the magazine. Despite the denial and the explanation of *Look*'s publisher on television that the article did not charge the mayor with "having taken part in any crime as such," Alioto was hurt politically. In January, 1970, he gave up the race for governor.

What injured Assaro and Alioto is the gangster image of the Italian-American, as distinct from the older stereotype of uncontrolled personal violence. It gave many other Americans the feeling that men with such brutal connections should not be entrusted with high office. Earlier, a fellow Republican, in an angry unsigned letter, expressed this feeling in denouncing La Guardia when he had the temerity to criticize Herbert Hoover in public. "You are a little out of your class in presuming to criticize the President," La Guardia was told. "It strikes me as impudence. You should go back where you belong and advise Mussolini how to make good honest citizens in Italy. The Italians are preponderantly our murderers and bootleggers."

Regardless of the moral injustice of such ranting, few could deny the prominence of Italian-Americans in organized crime. Still, such ethnic involvement was not in itself unusual in the pattern of immigrant adjustment to American life. Various ethnic groups have produced underworld leaders. According to sociologists and social historians, the place of crime in each ethnic community has varied in correlation with other sources of wealth and prominence available to its people. For a time in the nineteenth century and until the 1920's, Irish names, such as Red Rocks Farrell and Slops Connolly, figured most prominently in crime. People heard so much about Irish gangsters that they talked loosely about the Irish being "criminal by nature." Then for a while early in the twentieth century, the Jews dominated big-city crime, and men like Arnold Rothstein, the czar of New York City's underworld in the twenties, and in the thirties Louis (Lepke) Buchalter and Gurrah Shapiro, gained notoriety. Their activities embarrassed the Jewish community; it tried to eliminate the blemish of the "Jewish gangster."

During the twenties, when conditions attendant on Prohibition were especially favorable to the spread of organized crime, as has been seen, Italians moved in. They took up bootlegging and racketeering, but only a small proportion of those engaged in bootlegging were actual gangsters. Many were just out to make a few extra dollars in an activity that everybody seemed to condone. By the late twenties in New York, Chicago, and Detroit, some of the most prominent gangsters were Italian-Americans, although Irishmen and Jews remained important figures in organized crime. Newspapers regularly carried stories about Al (Alphonse) Capone, the czar of crime in Chicago in the twenties and the prototype of the Italian gangster; Frank Costello (Francesco Castiglia), the "prime minister of the underworld" in the thirties; and Lucky Luciano (Salvatore Luciania), the overlord of vice and dope rackets in the forties. Men such as these, sometimes exuding a seedy glamor, built up the criminal image of Italian-Americans. After Prohibition, they profited from illegal gambling, the sale of drugs, and loan sharking.

The continued involvement with crime led other Americans to believe the nineteenth-century idea that Italians had brought criminal organizations from the old country. Yet Italians did not introduce criminal societies to Argentina and Brazil, other countries of heavy immigration. Like others, Italians there committed violent crimes, but they did not gain a reputation as the leaders of organized crime. The nature of the American political system, some sociologists have argued, accounts for this discrepancy between the North and South American patterns in the growth of gangsterism. Group politics, the theory goes, breeds cliques which frequently develop into gangs. Each gang seeks a friend at court, at the police station, or in politics

—usually a lawyer who can wield influence if a gangster gets into trouble. At election time, the gangster delivers the votes, either through persuasion or terrorism. Knowing this, the policeman on the beat acts accordingly. Since Italians have usually lived in their own neighborhoods, and since they meet the other conditions for an ethnic group turning to crime, they have found it easier than others to use gangster influence as an ally of political power.

All those involved in the relationship between politics and organized crime want to hide it; the connection therefore, is difficult to document. Politicians always need money and crooked businessmen usually want political protection more than legitimate businessmen do. These needs keep the arrangements between crime and politics going, especially in places like New York and New Jersey, where Italian-Americans are heavily involved in both illegal enterprises and politics.

In the fifties, exposés, notably those of Senator Estes Kefauver of Tennessee, who headed a special committee to investigate crime in interstate commerce, stressed the relationship between crime and politics and revived talk of a Mafia of far-reaching power. In 1950 and 1951, he paraded Italian-American gangsters before the televised hearings of his committee and impressed the nation with the need to combat crime. He told the people that the Mafia, controlled by Italian-Americans and Italians, "is the shadowy international organization that lurks behind much of America's organized criminal activity," implying that it extended from Sicily to America's Little Italies. This and other statements alarmed Italian-American groups; they charged Kefauver with being prejudiced against Italians. Although he may not have been prejudiced, he did cause injury to Italian-Americans by making allegations he could not prove. He insisted that "the Mafia . . . is no fairy tale," that it operated as a "national crime syndicate." Yet he failed to show, with any evidence able to stand legal scrutiny, that such an organization even existed.

The existence of a widespread Mafia is controversial. Scholars who have studied the subject, notably the American and Italian sociologists Daniel Bell and Gaetano Mosca and the criminologist Gordon Hawkins, have belittled the idea that the Mafia is a nationwide or international organization. In the United States, Bell points out, "nobody has ever been able to produce specific evidence that a Mafia is functioning." In Italy, Mosca wrote, there was "never a vast association of malefactors with a hierarchy of leaders" that could be called the Mafia. Theories of the Mafia's existence, Hawkins writes, "prove on examination to consist of little more than a series of dogmatic assertions," most of them based on "myths and folktales." But many writers, politicians, and law officers believe that a Mafia of another kind composed of Italians does exist, a loose establishment of criminals who behave in a particular way following general rules of conduct of their own.

Sociologists, historians, and others have long considered Italians the least effectively organized of America's large ethnic groups, yet many people also believe them capable of organizing and running an amazingly disciplined and efficient crime cartel. Ironically, too, popular folklore places Italians among the most talkative of people and at the same time considers them capable of adhering to *omertà*, a code of silence that makes them the least expressive of people. According to popular belief, the Mafia is that rarest of secret societies, one that is truly secret. Yet it is supposed to be run by a people who cannot keep secrets. Those who insist that a tightly knit crime syndicate, composed chiefly of Italians, is a fact of life, are groups that include government agencies (especially the narcotics bureau), journalists, popular writers, and politicians seeking headlines. The attitude of the narcotics agents is understandable. They do face a drug traffic that ignores national boundaries and wide-ranging networks of international dope smugglers. Much of the drug activity they see has been in the hands of Italians with connections in both Sicily and the United States, the world's most lucrative market for dope. This idea of an Italian narcotics syndicate gained some credence in the forties when authorities expelled Lucky Luciano. From Sicily he supposedly carried on his old career of crime, directing the international narcotics traffic which sought the American market.

The deporting of Italian-American gangsters because American courts lacked the evidence necessary to imprison them has caused some bitterness in relations with Italy. Both American and Italian students of civil rights point out that Italian-born criminals are expelled not for the crimes they commit but because they are aliens. They could, according to law, be tried in American courts, but it is less embarrassing to politicians to deport them. In 1952, a spokesman for Italy's foreign office announced that his country would no longer accept Italian-American racketeers who might be deported after denaturalization proceedings in the United States. "We do not," he said, "want another Lucky Luciano. He lived in Italy a short time and then spent most of his time in the United States. Now we have to pay for him. It's not blood that makes a man delinquent; it's society. . . . They can't send them back like parcel post. . . ."

The official had a point. Sociologists point out that American society, not inherited traits or transmitted customs, shapes American criminals. But this seems to make no difference so far as Italian-Americans are concerned. They are stuck with a mark of criminality that no social theorizing or evidence can erase. Crime and the Mafia make for sensational reading and arouse public interest; vague charges against a "crime syndicate" can give a political career a big boost. In some places, Florida for example, politicians regularly run against the "Mafia," gaining votes with "wars against crime." Yet the available evidence, like the information turned up by investigations such as Kefauver's, indicates only the existence of a loose association of criminals in various cities and states, most of them active independently in limited areas. There is no proof of a central organization, even if some of these small groups, often composed of Italian-Americans, sometimes appear capable of cooperation in the terror and violence they use to enforce their will.

In the fifties, nothing dramatized more the idea of the Mafia as a sinister government-within-a-government than a meeting of some sixty Italian-Americans, all of them allegedly connected with rackets and illegal businesses, at the Apalachin, New York, home of Joseph Barbara, a distributor of beer and soft drinks, who was suspected of involvement in two murders. None of the men were armed; and only one, a parole violator, was wanted anywhere by the law. Police stumbled on this conclave accidentally in November, 1957, publicizing it as a secret gathering of Mafia leaders from all over the United States, though most came from within a radius of 175 miles. At last, it seemed, the authorities had discovered a central organization, a kind of board of directors for organized crime. After a long trial a New York court found twenty of the men guilty of conspiring to obstruct justice by refusing to explain their presence at Apalachin. Finding no conspiracy or other legal evidence for the true purpose of the meeting, a United States Court of Appeals in 1960 overturned the verdict for lack of evidence, saying that a mere meeting did not constitute a crime. The decision discredited but did not destroy the idea that the men of Apalachin were running an invisible government of crime.

In the sixties, this concept gained new vigor from the publicity given the investigations of organized crime by a Senate subcommittee headed by John L. McClellan of Arkansas. Especially melodramatic were the disclosures of Joseph M. Valachi, a convicted murderer originally committed to the federal penitentiary in Atlanta for twenty years on a narcotics sentence. In September and October, 1963, the squat, semiliterate Valachi, in his Brooklyn slang and tangled syntax, told the investigators and millions of Americans who followed the hearings on television a sensational story of a national network of crime run by Italian-Americans. He played on the old Mafia theme but gave it a new name, *Cosa Nostra* ("Our Thing"), and described the structure of the secret organization as being divided into units called "families."

Valachi's revelations shocked Italian-Americans everywhere, many of whom had assumed that the era of the Italian gangster had passed. What especially dismayed them was that the Attorney General's office stated that investigations by federal law enforcement agencies corroborated Valachi's testimony. Now, it seemed, the authorities had what they had long lacked, a blueprint of the central organization of the Mafia. Despite all this publicity on the "full" exposé of organized crime, the results disappointed the Department of Justice, mainly because the public's reaction to the disclosures was not clear-cut. Officials in the department had hoped that Valachi's story would so outrage the people that they would demand a crusade to crush the underworld. Critics blunted the effect of the testimony by attacking the concept of a *Cosa Nostra* as simplistic and pointing out that Valachi was merely a small-time hoodlum testifying upon hearsay without disclosing anything really new about the nation's organized crime.

While in prison, Valachi wrote the story of his life of crime with the aid of Justice Department personnel. In December, 1965, the government granted him permission to publish his memoirs, making him the first federal prisoner known to have received such a favor. It justified the exception on the premise that Valachi's disclosures might alert the public to the "crime syndicate's" activities, might encourage other informers to come forward, and might thereby benefit law enforcement. On February 1, 1966, twelve relatively prominent Italian-Americans, including four congressmen, asked Attorney General Nicholas de B. Katzenbach to withold publication of Valachi's book, maintaining it would unnecessarily degrade the image of Italian-Americans. On the following day, the Department of Justice announced it would review an outline of Valachi's memoirs for material offensive to Italian-Americans before granting final approval for publication. The memoirs as such did not come out, but three years later Peter Maas, the journalist who was to have assisted in editing them, published a lurid best seller called *The Valachi Papers,* based on Valachi's disclosures. To many Italian-Americans, the action of the Department of Justice in the Valachi case—the televised hearings and unusual publicity about the memoirs—reflected a pattern of prejudice based on the Mafia stereotype.

Local law enforcement agents also appeared to react according to pattern. For example, in September, 1966, police in New York City arrested thirteen alleged "Mafia leaders" in a Forest Hills restaurant, reportedly for "consorting with criminals," meaning with one another, but charged none with any crime. Critics of the raid doubted that the police had sufficient probable cause to make the arrests. All the men arrested had Italian names and prior criminal records. When questioned, the Chief Inspector of the Police Department, Sanford D. Garelik, explained the arrests as an effort "to rid the city of top hoodlums." He described the meeting as a "little Apalachin." Some lawyers concerned over civil liberties protested. "The labeling of someone as a 'Mafia leader,' " they said in a letter to the *New York Times,* "cannot justify deviation from the principles of fairness which are at the root of our legal system. There is no room in our society for standards of law enforcement unequally applied." Police officials attempted to justify what they admitted was harassment. It "keeps the directors of the criminal syndicate off balance," they argued, and makes it difficult for them to carry on unlawful operations. Concerned observers, including two Italian-American organizations, accused the Queens County District Attorney, Nat H. Hentel, of promoting these dubious police practices for political gain.

In the past, Italian-Americans unhappily accepted such tactics without much outcry, considering them a bitter part of life they could not avoid. In the sixties, they, like other minorities, became more sensitive about abusive stereotypes. "Don't even mention the word Mafia to me," a young Philadelphia Italian-American said. "The very word is a form of anti-Italianism. Each time they hear it, the bigots' hate is reinforced." He and numerous Italian-Americans resented the slurs about Italian proficiency in organized crime, the stories saying Italians dominated gambling in Las Vegas, controlled stickup gangs in the East, and masterminded the international traffic in narcotics. They also disliked the television programs, like "The Untouchables," reaching millions of homes, where children of impressionable age were the most avid viewers, showing swarthy men with Italian names regularly opposing the forces of law and order, villains dedicated to the forces of evil. Just as bad were simplistic movies, lurid novels, and crude comic strips that took up the *Cosa Nostra* theme as though it were a huge ethnic joke. Regardless of Italian-American resentment, the Mafia theme became more and more pervasive. Like the "Western," the Mafia became a part of American folklore, a source of innumerable movie, television, and book plots and of countless political and newspaper exposes.

Most of those who conducted investigations and helped perpetuate the image of Italian-Americans as kingpins of organized crime, such as Estes Kefauver and Robert F. Kennedy (as Attorney General), maintained that Italians had no monopoly on crime, and that only a small fraction of the millions of Americans of Italian origin were in any way connected with crime. Their disclaimers and apologies did no good: the headlines they sought and made kept alive the idea of Italian criminality. What appeared to make the idea virtually indestructible is the theory that the Mafia's secret rules limit membership to people of Italian ancestry and that the alleged twenty-four "families" of *Cosa Nostra* constitute the hard core of crime across the nation.

This theory was given some respectability by a 1967 report by the President's Commission on Law Enforcement and Administration of Justice. Among various allegations, it carried excerpts from J. Edgar Hoover's testimony before a congressional committee. The nation's Number One crime buster embraced the *Cosa Nostra* as a fact, calling it a "very closely organized and strictly disciplined . . . criminal fraternity whose membership is Italian either by birth or national origin. . . ." He offered no proof, only opinion. In 1969, Hoover's Federal Bureau of Investigation again tried to buttress the theory by releasing the transcripts of illegal wiretaps of conversations of small-time underworld figures, mainly by Simone R. ("Sam the Plumber") DeCavalcante and Angelo ("Gyp") DeCarlo of New Jersey, alleged *Cosa Nostra* leaders. This and other crackdowns on the Mafia produced more headlines than results. Civil liberties lawyers denounced these disclosures as trial and condemnation by accusation without evidence of real wrongdoing. As the writer Murray Kempton has pointed out, these petty Italian-American criminals "are, after all, that precious asset to journalism, men who have crossed the shadowline beyond which they can no longer sue for libel and where they can thus be blamed, with impunity, for *everything*."

Italian-Americans were particularly upset when the President himself adopted and publicized the Mafia theory. In a special message to Congress in April, 1969, Richard M. Nixon proposed a national war on crime, essentially against the *Cosa Nostra,* which he too called a "syndicate." "It is vitally important," he said, "that Americans see this alien organization for what it really is—a totalitarian and closed society operating within an open and democratic one." Some critics dismissed the message as Nixon's effort (like Don Quixote's assault on windmills) to redeem his campaign promise to fight crime in the streets by making a strong showing against the shadowy *Cosa Nostra.* Italian-Americans were hurt. Mario Biaggi, a Democratic congressman from New York, for one, assailed Nixon's remarks as insulting. Although not denying that Italian-Americans were immersed in organized crime, he considered it unfair of the President to seek out one ethnic group for undeserved notoriety. Others of varied origins, he pointed out, were similarly engaged in criminal activities.

The President's assault also brought discouragement because it appeared to blunt the efforts of Italian-American organizations to overcome the criminal stereotype. For years, groups such as the Anti-Defamation Committee of the Order of the Sons of Italy in America and the National Italian-American League to Combat Defamation have protested ethnic discrimination. Italian leaders also spoke out on their own. In 1931, La Guardia clashed with Will H. Hays, who headed the organized motion picture industry, over a gangster film called *Little Caesar,* maintaining it reflected unfavorably on Americans of Italian lineage.

Italian-American protest organizations have not been as effective as the American Jewish Committee or the National Association for the Advancement of Colored People; but in the sixties, the Italian-Americans, like other minorities, became more militant. In March, 1966, a group of them in New York formed a new aggressive organization called the Italian Anti-Defamation League, to "enhance the Italian image" and combat disparagement of Italian-Americans. In May of the following year, it chose Frank Sinatra as its national chairman and launched a program to persuade book publishers, movie and television producers, and magazine editors not to give criminal characters names ending in *i* or *o.*

In accepting the position, Sinatra said that "no American can rest easily until all vestiges of discrimination are erased from our society." He called the new league "the right step in the right direction in one area." Others disagreed with his estimate. The day after his appointment the *New York Times* called the league an "obscure group" and denounced its choice of Sinatra as a leader, mainly because he associated with underworld figures. It also noted that most of the league's other leaders were connected with Brooklyn politics. Its board of directors did not include "professors, artists, musicians, scientists," or other truly distinguished citizens of Italian descent. Mario Puzo, a novelist, made a similar observation. "With the league for a friend," he wrote, "American Italians could use another friend to explain what they are really like." Other Italian-Americans were embarrassed by the league's antics; they called it unnecessary and negative.

Almost from its beginning, the league got itself embroiled in controversy and dubious publicity. It quarreled with Mayor Lindsay of New York, charging that in his appointments he gave recognition to few men of Italian extraction, thereby discriminating against them. It found itself involved in a legal battle with the older Anti-Defamation League of B'nai B'rith over its use of the words "anti-defamation league" in its name.

Other less-controversial groups also expressed concern over the Italian image. In September, 1967, about eighty Italian-Americans met in New York's Waldorf-Astoria Hotel to make plans for a national federation of Italian organizations. Leaders of the group estimated that there existed in the United States about 26,000 such organizations, but without national connections. They wanted the proposed federation to serve as a "clearing house" for the many ethnic societies. These leaders urged Italian-Americans to demonstrate an understanding of other minority groups' problems, such as the Negroes', "at this time of urban crisis." Still, the group took no action on a commitment to the civil rights battle being waged by blacks and other minorities. Although invited, the Italian-American Anti-Defamation League did not participate in the symposium.

The league went ahead on its own. In October, it held a rally in New York's Madison Square Garden to launch a nationwide drive to raise funds and build its membership. President Lyndon B. Johnson sent the usual perfunctory telegram, for political purposes, extolling the contributions of Italian-Americans to American life. The audience of nearly 22,000 listened to three hours of speechmaking and entertainment, including six songs by Sinatra, and applauded protests against ethnic slurs.

The court, meanwhile, decided in favor of B'nai B'rith, forcing the league to change its name to Americans of Italian Descent, Inc. (AID). In April, 1968, it closed its campaign against ethic slander and adopted a more positive means of endeavor. Claiming thousands of members throughout the country, it now stressed the contributions of Italian-Americans and sponsored programs for self-improvement in Italian-American communities, particularly with jobs and legal services for youth, cooperation with colleges and universities, fund raising for scholarships and hospitals, and efforts to improve inter-group relations. Mrs. Mary Sansone, president of the Congress of Italian-American Organizations, Inc., expressed skepticism over AID's change of policy. "It's going to take them quite a while," she said, "to clean up the mess of the group's first two years of existence."

Just about as messy were some of the controversies that self-appointed spokesmen for Italians and chauvinistic Italian-American groups got themselves into. One of the silliest was the furor over a map and who really discovered America. The commotion began on October 12, 1965, when Yale University Press announced publication of a new book, *The Vinland Map and the Tartar Relation*, the fac-simile edition of an old map and manuscript, together with essays by three scholars who had worked on their identification. Drawn fifty-two years before Columbus had sailed for the New World, the Vinland map was supposed to show that Leif Ericson had reached North America somewhere in the vicinity of the Gulf of the St. Law-rence around the year 1000 and thereby had "discovered" America before Columbus. As anyone could have expected, this claim infuriated some Italian-Americans and delighted a number of Scandi-navian-Americans. Various Italians questioned the authenticity of the map, and especially the conclusions drawn from it, because it tended to diminish the glory of their folk hero, Columbus.

The controversy erupted and gained national attention, in good part because of the timing. Yale University Press announced publica-tion just when Italian-Americans in New York and elsewhere were celebrating Columbus Day with their yearly parade and speechmak-ing and were most likely to react quickly to anything that might lessen the significance of the occasion. "Yale University scholars," the Associated Press announced, "sliced the frosting off Christopher Co-lumbus's birthday cake today." The furor and publicity, obviously, would help sell books. Later, Italy's Amintore Fanfani, at the time President of the United Nations General Assembly, was drawn into the controversy. In December, he spoke on the subject before an au-dience in New York. An outspoken Italian-American lawyer and writer, Justice Michael A. Musmanno of the Pennsylvania Supreme Court, traveled to New Haven to examine the Vinland map. He called it "spurious" and an "anachronistic fraud," and later published a passionate book, *Columbus Was First,* to support his partisan views, for which he was honored by the Boston Italian-American League.

Episodes like the Vinland map controversy and the early antics of Americans of Italian Descent, Inc., made Italian-Americans look foolish and kept other Americans from taking the work of their organizations seriously. Ridicule, however, did not dampen the militancy of AID, or obscure the essential soundness of some of its activities. In October, 1968, its program coordinator, Joseph Jordan, sent a letter to the three principal presidential candidates—Humphrey, Nixon, and Wallace—pointing out that Italian-Americans had not been represented fairly within the executive branch of the government. It called the attention of the candidates "to the glaring fact that out of 372 major appointive positions in the various categories of the Federal Government, only six members are Americans of Italian descent."

The organization's tabulation showed that no one of Italian origin held a cabinet post or seat on the Supreme Court and that among 120 ambassadors, only 1 was an Italian-American. Claiming that Italian-Americans made up 11 per cent of the population but held only 1½ per cent of the high federal posts, Jordan wrote: "We do not subscribe to the idea that there should be an exact ethnic, racial or religious group representation, but we cannot see reasons for such a wide gap in the percentages relating to American-Italians, among whom there is a wealth of talent and ability."

Aware that Italian-Americans now had about 8 million votes and that if they voted as an ethnic bloc they could swing crucial states, each of the candidates assured Jordan that if elected he would appoint Americans of Italian origin to major governmental posts. Humphrey conceded that the nation had not "made full potential use of the abilities of Americans of Italian descent." Nixon found Jordan's figures "striking and disturbing." After winning the election, Nixon kept his word; in an important token gesture, he brought John Volpe into his cabinet as Secretary of Transportation.

Such tokenism did not lessen the sense of grievance Italian-Americans felt over the activities of government agencies. On April 30, 1970, hundreds of Italian-Americans, sometimes as many as 2,000, began nightly picketing of the New York City headquarters of the Federal Bureau of Investigation to protest harassment and defamation by its agents. A new group, the Italian-American Civil Rights League, organized the picketing. Its leaders claimed that the government and the newspapers "create the fantasies of this *Cosa Nostra.*"

One of them, Anthony Colombo, the son of an alleged Mafia chieftain, pointed out that "The F.B.I. has infiltrated the Black Panthers and student radical groups. If there's a Mafia, why haven't they been able to infiltrate that?"

Even though critics found some of those who sponsored the league distasteful because of criminal records, its protest and call for an Italian Unity Day evoked sympathy among minority groups, especially among Italian-Americans deeply outraged by the carelessness of the news media, police officials, and politicians in continually associating Italians with organized crime. On that day, June 29, between 40,000 and 50,000 of them poured into Columbus Circle waving the red, white, and green Italian tricolor and American flags, dancing, singing, and cheering more than two hours of speechmaking. "This thing just snowballed," Natale Marcone, the coordinator and president of the league explained. The size and intensity of the protest made previous Italian-American demonstrations seem pale. The *New York Times*, itself an object of protest by Italian-Americans because they felt it did not pay enough attention to the discrimination they suffered, sympathized with the demonstrators, saying they had "a long ignored and genuine grievance."

In July, Attorney General John N. Mitchell, in a public reversal of the Nixon administration's position on organized crime, ordered the Department of Justice to stop using the words "Mafia" and *Cosa Nostra,* explaining that "there is nothing to be gained by those terms except to give gratuitous offense." In the following month, New York's governor, Nelson A. Rockefeller, also directed state law enforcement agencies to avoid their use, calling them "easy vivid catchwords that unjustly slander" Americans of Italian lineage. Despite these directives and the admission of some law enforcement agents that "because of the heavy publicity given Joseph Valachi . . . a misleading impression of organized crime has been left with the public," these agents underwent no change of heart. They still insisted, without offering more than opinion as evidence, that Italians controlled organized crime, and they continued to use "Mafia" and *Cosa Nostra* freely except when speaking for quotation. The executive directives appeared as little more than palliatives issued by politicians seeking votes in an election year.

The militant protest organizations, something new in the Italian-American experience, at least brought some positive responses. Just as the Italian-Americans followed the examples of Jewish and Negro groups because militancy paid off, Germans, Poles, Mexicans, and others took up the Italian model. The Germans formed a German-American Anti-Defamation League; the Mexicans formed a Mexican-American Anti-Defamation Committee; and the Poles worked through the Polish-American Guardian Society. All dedicated themselves to fighting ethnic slurs. In contrast with the past, when ethnic groups distrusted one another, the Italian organization cooperated with the other national societies in the new atmosphere of ethnic sensitivity.

Such activities seemed necessary, for traces of prejudice remained. At Mardi Gras in New Orleans in 1968, naval officers reportedly received instructions to keep party invitations out of the hands of Negroes, Jews, and Italians, minorities the carnival leaders have always discriminated against. Nonetheless, Italian-Americans have risen steadily, if slowly, in status. Those who were status-conscious no longer sought to deny their now-distant immigrant background or to evade prejudice and improve their social position by changing names or claiming connection to some old or noble Italian family. With a resurgence of white as well as colored ethnicity, many were not as eager as in the past to merge their identities in America's mythical melting pot. They could break down old social barriers on their own.

The Comfortable
Relationship

18

During the sixties, Italy gradually emerged from under American tutelage. The French, under Charles de Gaulle, led the European revolt against American predominance, and the Italians went along with him. Italy took advantage of the new independence from American leadership made possible by prosperity in Western Europe, relaxation of cold war tensions, and a war in Vietnam. The change in her attitude came with such little friction that both Americans and Italians accepted their altered relationship as a logical development.

In Italy, one of the most striking changes was political, beginning with the country-wide municipal elections of November, 1960. The parties of the left, especially the Communist, made substantial gains. In the campaigns for municipal offices, the two major parties of the left, the Communist and Socialist, had usually cooperated. As a result, the Communists gained and kept control of a number of northern and north central cities. After the 1960 elections, the Socialists, who had been dissatisfied with their Communist allies for several years, began backing out of the arrangement with the Communists to make overtures to the Christian Democrats who favored a leftward movement of their party. In Milan, Genoa, Florence, and Palermo, Socialists managed to form new *giunte* ("city governments"), in partnership with Christian Democrats.

Early in 1961, the effectiveness of the new arrangement showed that the partnership of Christian Democrats and Socialists offered an alternative to Communist control of municipal governments. Men in both parties wanted to extend the political cooperation to the national level with an *apertura a sinistra* (a national "opening to the left"), meaning a government coalition composed of Christian Democrats and various Socialists. But this extension proved more difficult to achieve than the local coalitions.

Up to this point, the American government had generally opposed the *apertura a sinistra*. President John F. Kennedy, who knew something of Italian developments, decided to change that policy, mainly by showing a discreet sympathy for a government committed to cooperating with the left. For several years, Kennedy had known Amintore Fanfani, Italy's Prime Minister. In June, 1961, when Fanfani visited Washington, the President told him privately that if he, Fanfani, wanted to move toward an *apertura,* American policy makers would follow developments sympathetically. Kennedy's policy had no immediate effect, in part at least because Italian experts within the Department of State blocked it. They distrusted the Socialists led by a tough old politician, Pietro Nenni, fearing that if these Socialists came to share power, they would weaken Italy's commitment to NATO.

Within the Christian Democratic party, there had risen to local leadership a new generation of politicians who did not share the fears of the State Department officials. They were committed to reform and economic planning, and formed the faction favoring the opening to the left. Even though they comprised the strongest single element within the party, they were lacking in experience and had no well-known leaders; their views could not easily gain influence. The turning point for these politicians came in January, 1962, at a congress of Christian Democrats in Naples. There Aldo Moro, one of the reformers, persuaded the party's center to align itself with the left. By the time of adjournment, Christian Democracy had declared itself in favor of a modest approach to the Nenni Socialists for cooperation.

In March, Prime Minister Fanfani formed Italy's first center-left government, one that gained support from the Socialists and also from Pope John XXIII. In the past, the Vatican had opposed any approaches to the left; now it accepted the idea of a dialogue between Catholics and Socialists. In the following year, when the Christian Democrats brought their program to the people for endorsement, it became evident that virtually everyone, including American policy makers, would take the results as a verdict on the *apertura a sinistra.* The parliamentary elections would be analyzed for what they might reveal about the changes that were modifying the structure of Italian society and of the Catholic church. Scheduled for late April, 1963, at the high tide of John's pontificate, these elections came at a time when leaders were ready for an appraisal of Italy's recent past.

During the preceding two years, the Pope had challenged the Italian episcopate, generally conservative in religious and political attitudes, with a number of radical changes. In May, 1961, with the social encyclical *Mater et Magistra,* he announced a concern for poverty all over the world, suggesting that Catholicism would help meet this persisting problem by cooperating with civil authorities, even when they were Communists. In the following year, he convened the second Ecumenical Vatican Council to take a new look at the church and its place in the world. Then on April 10, 1963, less than three weeks before the elections, he gave the world his second and last major encyclical, *Pacem in Terris.* It pleaded for peace and social justice everywhere, even between men of differing ideologies, thereby cutting across the animosities of the cold war.

Pope John's attitude conveyed the message that the unbending hostility between Catholicism and Marxism, as well as the world-wide ideological battles of the cold war, belonged to the past and should not be carried into the future. He offered an example of the new trend by lifting the Catholic injunction against voting Socialist. The changes he urged and instituted alarm conservatives in Italy, who labeled him the "Red" Pope. Conservative Catholics in the United States also disliked his liberalizing actions, especially his endorsement of the *apertura a sinistra.* Italian and American conservatives both stressed the dangers rather than the hoped-for gains in Italy's new course as approved by Pope John. They feared it would bring Communist dominance of Italy, a shackling of the church, and the destruction of Italy's alliance with the United States. Yet change could not be ignored; men of various persuasions were moving away from old dogmas toward a more flexible political position. Expediency, if nothing else, made it logical for the Catholic church and the Christian Democratic party to test the winds of change.

Recognizing this need for a new approach to Italy's problems, the Department of State had by this time come around to supporting the idea of the *apertura a sinistra.* For a while, it looked as though the conservatives within the department had been right. In the elections for Italy's fourth republican legislature, in April, 1963, the left made gains, the right lost heavily, and the center Christian Democrats suffered a drop in support. Critics blamed Fanfani's center-left policy for the losses. Actually, the Communists and others of the left had been more adept at exploiting discontent than had the Christian Democrats, who for this reason did not abandon the center-left idea.

That summer, Kennedy visited Italy, and the question of the *apertura a sinistra* immediately came up. He had planned his trip so that he could see Pope John. But the pontiff died on June 3, four weeks before the President could get to Rome. On June 21, Cardinal Giovanni Battista Montini, an old friend of the Kennedy family, succeeded as Pope Paul VI. Kennedy arrived in Rome on August 1 and at a reception in the evening met Italy's political leaders. "So far as I could see," he later told the historian Arthur Schlesinger, Jr., "everyone in Italy is for the opening to the left. I was told that they were blaming it all on Fanfani and on us; but I couldn't find anyone there who was against us."

Kennedy's assessment appeared correct. Under Aldo Moro, who became Prime Minister in December, the Christian Democrats continued the *apertura a sinistra.* With this program, the Italian state experienced a strength and a political stability that surprised even its liberal American friends. In the late sixties, American observers came to believe that the center-left coalition that governed Italy for much of the decade was finally attaining many of its objectives. Her Communist party, although still the largest in the Western world, was no longer able to exploit the social ferment and gain votes from the center. It faced troubles of its own, especially after August, 1968, when the Russians invaded Czechoslovakia. The tough Soviet action horrified even old-line Communists.

In December, 1968, when Mariano Rumor, another Christian Democratic politician, formed a new center-left government, Italy's opening to the left became wider. Even though this government expressed more openly than its predecessors the Italian dislike for America's war in Vietnam, it continued the old foreign policy of support for NATO and close friendship with the United States, thereby arousing no real concern among American policy makers. Later, in the winter of 1969-1970, as political squabbles upset the ruling coalition, Americans expressed concern over the revival of governmental instability in Italy.

During these years, the economic life of the Italian Republic continued its healthy transformation. Much of this change was linked to the growth of the Common Market. At first, industrial leaders feared that their businesses would be unable to compete against the more advanced industries of Germany and France. Their fears proved groundless. As the Common Market went into operation, Italy reaped all kinds of benefits and her businessmen became increasingly confident about their ability to hold their own.

By the end of 1961, within a period of just three years, Italy's trade within the European Economic Community rose by 80 per cent, giving her a larger increase than any other member. She also received more in loans for economic development from the community's investment bank than any of her fellow members. Since the Common Market made iron ore available to industry at cheaper rates than ever before, Italy at this time achieved the world's highest rate of growth in steel production. By 1962, when the Common Market reduced custom duties by half on industrial products, Italy's industries had become some of the most efficient in the world and were able to compete against many others, within and without the Common Market.

Italy now completed much of her transformation from a backward agrarian society to a modern industrial state; in six years, her economy grew more than 71 per cent. With this growth came a great change in the distribution of her work force. At the end of the Second World War, about half her workers labored in agriculture; a decade later, less than 40 per cent did so. In 1963, 27 per cent gained their livelihood from agriculture; in 1967, about 24 per cent did. Almost 76 per cent of the workers had jobs in some form of industry or business. This shift from agriculture to industry brought material gain to the entire nation because the output of each person employed in agriculture usually amounted to slightly more than half the productivity of an individual engaged in some other economic activity. National income rose steadily. It went up 5.9 per cent in 1967 and again in 1968.

Progress in commerce, based on the philosophy of free trade adopted from the United States, contributed heavily to Italy's rapid economic growth. In the early sixties, she virtually quadrupled her imports and exports. In 1968, her foreign trade was almost in balance, an unusual achievement for a country that in the past imported more than she exported, and had paid for foreign goods with money from emigrant remittances and tourism. These sources had not dried up; they gave Italy a favorable balance of payments; she now kept some of the money received from tourism. In the late sixties, nearly 12 per cent of her foreign trade was with the United States. In 1968, a year in which Italian exports rose by more than 15 per cent, the exchange of goods between the two countries, divided about equally between them, amounted to two-and-a-third billion dollars, an amount that testified to Italy's growing prosperity.

Still, Italy's economy did not catch up with those of other countries in Western Europe; they had entered the sixties with greater strength and had grown at a similar pace. Growth was uneven because of the continuing existence of two Italies, the north, where income and living standards were roughly equal to those in other Western European countries, and the south, where income was low and agriculture still formed the basis for livelihood. Italy's prosperity, her place in the Common Market, a falling birth rate, expansion in education, and economic planning nonetheless gave hope for substantial improvement in the lot of the southern *contadini*. Now, for the first time, Italian politicians and economists were able to think in terms of an agriculture capable of providing more than a bare livelihood for an underemployed population. As workers streamed from the farmlands, the planners saw the opportunity for raising productivity with modern techniques and for directing agriculture, as in other advanced Western nations, toward the goal of maintaining the food supply of a predominantly urban population.

This hope grew out of a decade of economic planning, much of it for the benefit of the *Mezzogiorno*. In 1962, the *Mezzogiorno,* with new industry and other projects sponsored by the government, was richer than all Italy had been in 1950. Still its economy lagged behind that of the north. In 1967, therefore, the government launched a five-year economic plan for industrial growth, especially in the south, and for better education and health. Even though the lag persisted, by the end of 1969, the south was approaching a viable economy.

Despite the disparity between north and south and other problems, the Italian economy proved itself capable of high rates of expansion. In the summer of 1967, despite a recession in most other countries of the Common Market, Italy forged ahead with another wave of prosperity, this one accompanied by stability in prices. Her rate of economic growth, about 6 per cent, became one of the highest in the industrialized world. American capital, more than $300 million of it invested in Italian corporations, had a part in this growth.

Italy's main problem at the end of the sixties, according to economists, was insufficient domestic investment accompanied by a flight of capital abroad. Government planners sought in various ways to overcome this weakness. They wanted to keep capital in Italy and use it to attain a steady high level of investment that would turn the recent gains into long-lasting development. In other respects, the Italian economy exuded health until 1969-1970, when strikes and inflation slowed the rate of growth. Italy's remarkable achievement appeared to justify the aid and friendship Americans had given her over the years.

As Italy became prosperous, her relationship with the United States became more comfortable than in the past. Gradually, Italians gained respect as self-sustaining friends and acquired influence in

NATO. By July, 1962, Italy paid back all her Marshall Plan loans and, in September, the American government asked her to take on a bigger share of the financing of the alliance. It urged Italians to buy military supplies from American producers to ease the flow of dollars from the United States. American policy makers also asked Italy to make long-term loans and step up technical aid to underdeveloped countries in Africa and elsewhere.

Cooperation increased in other ways as well. When Vice President Lyndon B. Johnson visited Italy in September, 1962, he and Foreign Minister Attilio Piccioni signed an agreement calling for collaboration between their countries in research in outer space. Italy, in effect, gained a limited access to American technical and scientific knowledge that would eventually enable her to launch a space satellite. Soon afterwards, questions of technology and defense became entangled in the difficulties of European unification and the special relationship between the United States and Britain. These problems, in turn, affected relations between the United States and Italy.

In December, President Kennedy met Britain's Prime Minister, Harold Macmillan, at Nassau, where they agreed on procedures for the use of nuclear weapons by their countries that would affect the future of NATO and of European unification. In January, Prime Minister Fanfani asked Kennedy about the Nassau agreements, especially how they would affect Italy's status in the alliance. The President assured Fanfani that the American proposal to share weapons with Britain would not lead to a "restricted directorate" within NATO that excluded Italy.

Like other Europeans, Italians were now sensitive about America's exclusive control over the use of nuclear weapons. Intellectuals, most of them leftist in their politics, criticized American foreign policy and opposed the planting of missile bases on Italian soil. After the crisis of October, 1962, when Kennedy forced the Soviets to pull missiles out of Cuba and the world narrowly averted a nuclear war, their distrust increased. During this crisis, Italian intellectuals of the left formed a "Solidarity with Castro Committee" to show their support for Fidel Castro, Cuba's dictator, in his conflict with the United States. Alberto Moravia, Carlo Levi, Luchino Visconti, Michelangelo Antonioni, Pier Paolo Pasolini, and others marched in the streets of Rome to protest what they called American imperialism. After the crisis, the intellectuals—including writers Salvatore Quasimodo, Mario Soldati, and Elio Vittorini and the artist Giacomo Manzu—issued a manifesto calling for the speedy removal of all American missile bases from Italy. A few months later, the Americans did take their missiles out, saying they had become obsolete. This action pleased all kinds of Italians, not just the leftist intellectuals.

When Kennedy visited Italy in 1963, the question of which nations in the Western alliance should have a voice in the use, and even manufacture, of nuclear weapons was still a troublesome one. It was driving a wedge between European leaders, in particular de Gaulle, and American policy makers. Like the French, the Italians felt as though Americans, by barring them from atomic secrets, were treating them as second-class allies. Nonetheless, unlike the French, the Italians continued to affirm their undiminished allegiance to NATO and were willing to follow the American lead in matters of nuclear diplomacy. When Kennedy returned home, for instance, he cited agreement with Italian leaders on the need for a treaty that would prohibit nuclear tests and halt the spread of nuclear weapons.

Even though Italians almost always joined with Americans in stressing the need for solidarity among the Western allies, this commitment did not prevent them from expressing publicly their own views on world affairs, something they had seldom done in the previous decade. More often than not, these views coincided with American policy. In January, 1964, for example, Prime Minister Antonio Segni announced that friendship with the United States was "the very crux of our foreign policy." He reaffirmed Italy's commitment to a united Europe, that would be "tied to America by indissoluble bonds of interdependence, of loyalty and solidarity "

Such rhetoric did not dispel an old distrust felt in Congress toward Italy in the matter of nuclear secrets. Repeatedly over a period of seven years, the Joint Congressional Committee on Atomic Energy intervened in negotiations between the Department of State and Italian officials to prevent Italy from gaining access to technology on nuclear propulsion developed by the United States in its program for building nuclear-powered submarines. The problem went back to July, 1955, when the United States and Italy signed a treaty for the exchange of information on nuclear reactors and isotopes and also for American help to Italians in adapting atomic energy for civilian uses. Two years later, an American agreement with Euratom, which included Italy, superseded the Italian treaty. Despite these agreements, the Joint Congressional Committee, in 1958 and in 1960, blocked plans approved by the Department of State whereby Americans would help Italians build a nuclear submarine.

In 1965, the committee again intervened in American and Italian negotiations. It vetoed a program permitting FIAT, the large Italian industrial concern, to build a reactor for a naval vessel through a licensing arrangement with the Westinghouse Electric Corporation, a principal manufacturer of submarine reactors for the United States navy. Under the plan, Westinghouse would not have supplied any secret technology, but members of the committee feared that some nonatomic technology, such as pump designs, could provide valuable assistance to the Italians and, perhaps through espionage, to the Russians, on submarine reactor designs. At the insistence of the congressional committee, the Departments of State and Commerce, in 1965, adopted regulations restricting the categories of maritime reactor technology that Americans could provide to foreign countries or companies.

In January, 1966, Italy tried again. She asked the United States, under a military atomic assistance agreement between the two countries, to supply enriched uranium for fuel in a nuclear-powered ship she wanted to build for her navy. The vessel was not to be a warship, but an auxiliary such as a tanker or tender. Italian industries, without American technical assistance, would build the nuclear reactor to hold the uranium.

By law, the Department of State had to present Italy's request to the Joint Congressional Committee on Atomic Energy. The Committee viewed the request as an effort to bypass the objections and regulations of the past because the Italians were seeking fuel rather than technology, and for a surface ship rather than for a submarine. Committee members feared that by providing fuel, the United States would be making the first installment in the construction of a nuclear submarine for the Italian navy. Some congressmen suspected that the nuclear-powered surface ship would be an operating prototype for a submarine. In any case, the committee rejected the request. The Italians were, of course, hurt by the rebuff and especially by the evidence that even though they were now full-fledged allies, American legislators still distrusted them.

At this time, Congress counterbalanced its distrust in nuclear affairs by acting to remove one of the old Italian grievances against American lawmakers, the ethnic discrimination written into immigration policy. Four presidents—Truman, Eisenhower, Kennedy, and Johnson—had called for a revision of the McCarran-Walter Act that would eliminate its harshest features.

The successful effort began in July, 1963, when Kennedy sent a special message to Congress urging a thorough revision of the immigration legislation. Describing the national origins system as an "anachronism," he asked for a new law that would reflect "in every detail the principle of equality and human dignity to which our Nation subscribes." Struck by an assassin's bullet, Kennedy never lived to see action on his proposal, but Congress went ahead with extended hearings. Italian-Americans, eager for a revision, attacked the existing legislation. In his testimony, Anthony J. Celebrezze commented, "I think Christ would be excluded under the present law." Finally, in September, 1965, Congress went along with what Kennedy and Johnson had recommended by passing a new immigration act. Then on October 3, in a symbolic gesture at the foot of the Statue of Liberty in New York harbor, the gateway to America for millions of Italians and other immigrants, Johnson signed the act into law. The new law, he said, "corrects a cruel and enduring wrong in the conduct of the American nation." Now "those who come will come because of what they are—not because of the land from which they sprung."

These Immigration and Nationality Amendments of 1965 called for a gradual elimination, over a period of three years, of the national origins formula. During this time, the quota system remained in effect. All unused quotas from undersubscribed nations went into an international "quota pool" and became available to preferred types of immigrants from countries with oversubscribed quotas, such as Italy. In June, 1968, when the transitional period ended, the quota system was abolished. Then the law allowed each independent country outside the Western Hemisphere to send up to 20,000 immigrants annually to the United States according to categories arranged to suit American preferences. Unused visas became available to qualified immigrants from any country on a first come, first served basis.

Since some Italians were still emigrating and many still sought to reach the United States, the new law pleased the Italian government. When the first provisions went into effect in December, 1965, more than 200,000 Italians were seeking admission. The first visa issued under the amendments went to an Italian, Salvatore Esposito, a twenty-nine-year-old cook from Naples. He came to join his wife in Brooklyn as one of 400 Italian immigrants who arrived in New York on December 22.

Within the law's first year, Italy obtained 20,000 visas, or more than 14,000 beyond her old quota. More Italians than nationals of any other country were entering the United States. For Italians, it seemed, the United States had again become one of the world's chief countries of immigration, but this surface appearance was deceptive.

For, although Italians comprised the most numerous group of new immigrant stock in the United States in 1965, they ranked only fifth among aliens residing in the country. In other words, in comparison with immigration from other sources, immigration from Italy had fallen off; in comparison with the flood before the First World War, the number of Italian immigrants coming in the late sixties was small, but larger than from any other European country.

The rush under the new law reflected the inequities of the past system. The old laws had built up a reservoir of thousands of Italians like Esposito who wanted to join their families and relatives in the United States but had been unable to do so because of the quota restrictions. With the removal of the restrictions, they came, but not as part of a new wave of immigrants. Once the backlog was reduced, Italian immigration slackened. In the late sixties, Italy no longer desperately needed the United States as an outlet. Her surplus of workers had declined.Consequently, emigration ceased to be one of Italy's major problems and lost its importance in her relations with the United States.

In the forties and fifties, Italian laborers had roamed all over Europe in search of work. For the first time, also, peasants from the south trudged north in large numbers to take jobs in the industrial cities. Some of them eventually moved on to take over the farms of northerners who were selling out and themselves seeking urban employment. All in all, almost 3 million southerners moved north from the end of the Second World War until 1963. In that year alone, 300,000 made the trek. In the early sixties, Italian workers benefited from the policies of the Common Market which permitted them to cross national boundaries without great difficulty and to take jobs offered in any of the member states, particularly West Germany or France.

The enlarged employment opportunities within Italy and within the European Economic Community brought ordinary Italians notable social gains. To the surprise of almost everyone, even optimistic economic planners, Italy's rate of unemployment in the middle sixties fell to around 3 per cent, a rate comparable to that of other advanced industrial nations. Italy had at last arrived at the major social turning point her leaders had long desired. Now, like Americans, Germans, Englishmen, and Frenchmen, the majority of Italians were living in modern industrial conditions and earning a living from urban pursuits rather than from a hostile soil.

In their lives of relative affluence, Italians continued to reflect American influence. Like prosperous Americans, they bought cars, trailers, boats, and gadgets, often on the installment plan. The economic booms even produced a new breed of Italian businessmen who had traits in common with the aggressive American tycoons of earlier decades. American practices also influenced the management of Italian industry. During the late forties and early fifties, when industry was working to revive and then expand, hundreds of young Italians were sent to the United States to study techniques of factory organization, production, and marketing. Italians also modeled their management training courses on those given in the United States. Italy's first school of business administration, *Istituto post-universitario per lo studio dell-organizzazione aziendale* (IPSOA), established in Turin in 1952 by the Olivetti Company (manufacturers of business machines), FIAT, and the Turin manufacturers' association, was for years staffed by American professors of business administration.

American social planners had helped Italy in her transition from a rural to an urban economy. The great migration from farm villages to industrial cities led not only to a rise in the general standard of living, as had been the experience in other Western countries, but also produced widespread cultural benefits. The rapid spread of television, the rising standard of living, the economic and social mobility, and improvements in education helped reduce provincialism and increase the number of those who spoke and read a standard Italian in preference to a dialect. These developments and an impressive network of superhighways gave the country a greater unity than it had ever known.

Educational policy, also influenced by American techniques, affected economic growth, as did the birth rate, the labor force, and emigration. In the sixties, Italy's birth rates were not only among the lowest in Europe, but in all the world. Italy entered a period of social maturity; she could no longer be classed as an overpopulated, underdeveloped country. She now experienced an educational as well as an economic boom. In 1952, two-thirds of her youth were without a junior high school education and nine-tenths had not completed high school. Then the educational level began to rise, and decisively so, in 1961. By 1966, there were slightly more than 7 million pupils in primary and secondary schools; and in 1969, Italy's school population reached its maximum level of about 10 million. This growth of education and of literacy spurred changes in the nature of the labor force.

Educated men were unwilling to work long hours at menial tasks for a pittance. They demanded social improvement at home instead of turning to emigration out of desperation.

Since these changes came rapidly and with little control, they brought difficulties as well as benefits. Turmoil and flux seemed to characterize much of Italian life, especially in the congested cities. Elsewhere, in dealing with various social issues, government appeared to be lacking or ineffective. So, even though the process of change and urbanization was good, expected, and long desired, many Italians suffered because of the dislocations that occur in growing societies. But with unchanging poverty they would probably have suffered more.

Gradually at first, as Italy emerged as an important industrial power, many of her workers in European countries returned home, adding momentum to the social changes taking place. In the late sixties, Italy's industrial north actually experienced a shortage of skilled workers; it readily absorbed many who returned, especially those who brought back new skills. Even while they were still in Germany or Switzerland, Italian workers often answered the "help wanted" advertisements they saw in newspapers sent to them from home. When they came back, their skills contributed to Italy's economic growth. The postwar migration that was at first European-wide in its scope was now largely confined to the Italian peninsula. Few of these workers in northern Italy sought to immigate to the United States. But in Italy's south, even though emigration as a whole had slackened, the situation differed. There the workers, despite the lessening of poverty, the heavy migration to other European countries, and a government program of industrialization, were crowding the northern factories, building a new peasant folklore that said "California begins at Milan." From the south, too, came the relatives who were eager to reach the United States and who filled the quota pools under America's new immigration policy.

The Italians who now came to the United States differed from the millions who had preceded them. By the middle of the decade, Italy's surplus rural population had clearly begun to disperse. The immigrants thus came from an Italy that was no longer hopelessly impoverished and no longer the mass exporter of human muscle to more industrial and more prosperous countries. Italy had become a cohesive political entity, a nation of more than 50 million people without festering major problems of unassimilated minorities, frontiers, and colonies—a position unusual in a troubled world. Italy had not only become widely industralized but she had also become one of the world's important trading nations, with a network of shipping and air routes and with firms engaged in construction projects on several continents. FIAT, for example, with some help from American financiers and industrialists built a huge automobile plant on the Volga River for the Soviet Union.

At this time, too, Italy and the United States cooperated in a unique way in trying to crush an international heroin-smuggling ring reputed to have been operating in France, Italy, Canada, and the United States for over a decade. In Rome in February, 1967, the Italian government placed thirty-two men on trial for working with the ring. In May, the government shifted the trial to the Italian consulate in New York City, where three Italian judges heard testimony from alleged Italian-American Mafia leaders who six years earlier had been convicted of smuggling heroin into the United States. This hearing marked the first time within recent memory that a nation held a criminal trial outside its own boundaries. International law required approval from the United States before the Italian court could hold the trial in New York. Since the American government had consented, the Italians called the trial "a revolutionary move" and the beginning of a "new chapter in international relations."

Despite the journey across the Atlantic and the publicity that accompanied its work, the Italian court found itself no more capable of proving the existence of a wide-ranging Mafia syndicate than had American courts. In Palermo, in June 1968, the Italian court cleared a group of seventeen Sicilians and various Italian-Americans of dope-smuggling charges. It ruled that there was insufficient evidence to back up the charges, and ordered all but two of the defendants freed. Earlier, in 1963, the Italian public had been outraged when a booby-trapped automobile in Sicily exploded and killed seven policemen. Since the Mafia was blamed for the crime, the Italian parliament responded to the public pressure by establishing an anti-Mafia commission and launching a drive against the Mafia in western Sicily. Finally, in July 1971, this commission published a lengthy report saying the Sicilian Mafia was not only alive but also had spread from the countryside into cities, into other parts of Italy, and had linked itself with international gangsters, especially Italian-Americans. The commission stated that Mafia leaders were hard to convict because of complicity between politicians and criminals. The social reformer Danilo Dolci had long insisted that such a politically powerful Mafia had blocked the desperately needed regeneration of Sicily.

As in the combating of organized crime, cooperation characterized most other aspects of American relations with Italy. There were some important differences, such as a dispute over airplane landing rights in the two countries that led Italy in May, 1966, to denounce the 1948 air traffic treaty with the United States and Italian dissatisfaction with America's conduct of her war in Vietnam. These differences did not impair the basic friendliness of the two countries. In June, 1970, they signed a new air transport agreement that increased the frequency of flights between Italy and the United States. Nonetheless, since students, liberals, and others everywhere in Italy so strongly disliked the bombings of North Vietnamese cities and the American war policy in general, Italy's pro-American governments found it politically risky and increasingly difficult to defend American policies effectively. While they officially supported American policy, Italian statesmen let Americans know they were unhappy with the war and opposed continued bombing of North Vietnam.

Italian leaders like Fanfani urged a negotiated settlement of the Vietnam War. In May, 1965, President Johnson encouraged Fanfani, who was then Foreign Minister, to explore the basis for some kind of peace in Vietnam. Fanfani discussed the situation with an old friend, Giorgio La Pira, a professor of law, a liberal, and a former mayor of Florence. In September, Fanfani was elected President of the United Nations General Assembly, where he warned the delegates that the United Nations would cease to be a factor in international life if it could not bring peace to the world, especially in Asia. "While it is good to deplore what is happening," he said, "It is indispensable that we should act."

Action came through La Pira, who in that month obtained an invitation from President Ho Chi Minh to visit North Vietnam. La Pira reached Hanoi early in November and returned to Rome a week later. He then cabled Fanfani in New York, summarizing purported peace feelers from North Vietnamese leaders. Fanfani then conferred with Arthur J. Goldberg, the American representative at the United Nations, sent word to President Johnson that Hanoi was willing to negotiate under certain conditions, and exchanged correspondence on the subject with Secretary of State Dean Rusk.

Although the American government had reservations about the peace feelers, it took La Pira's efforts seriously. Then when American officials made the messages public, La Pira, in an interview published in a right-wing Italian magazine, sarcastically attacked the United States. Hanoi subsequently denied having put out peace feelers. In

December, newspapers all over the world treated the affair as a fiasco. The embarrassed Italian government, stressing that Fanfani and La Pira had acted on their own, said it had no official knowledge of or part in their diplomacy. Nonetheless, Italians criticized the government for allowing the two men to meddle in international affairs not of a direct concern to Italy, and to irritate relations with the United States. The furor led Fanfani to resign from the cabinet.

That Italians, who previously had remained silent about American global policy, could become agitated over an essentially American problem was one of a number of indications that they were acquiring a deeper and more sophisticated knowledge of American affairs than in the past. Their new prosperity made it possible for more and more of them to cross the Atlantic to see American life for themselves. In the summer of 1962, for instance, more than 7,000 Italians flew to the United States as visitors. Ships sailing to and from the Mediterranean sometimes appeared to carry as many Italians as Americans—businessmen, students, tourists who were visiting relatives or just coming to the United States for a vacation.

More than ever, cultural exchange now flowed two ways. Americans no longer went to Italy mainly to absorb culture and to look for inspiration in her artistic treasures. They now brought their arts and their culture to Italians. This aspect of cultural exchange could be seen in the work of Gian Carlo Menotti, an Italian-American composer of several successful operas. In the summer of 1957, Menotti organized the Festival of Two Worlds in the medieval town of Spoleto, set among Italy's Umbrian Hills. Sponsored also by the Italian government, the festival brought together artists and performers from Italy, the United States, and other European countries to present music, drama, poetry, and the dance to international audiences. Although it started precariously and on a small scale, within ten years the Spoleto festival became a major instrument of cultural exchange.

Recognizing this growth, the Samuel Rubin Foundation of New York, in July, 1967, established a fund of $1 million to guarantee American participation in the festival for another ten years. Concurrently, the Italian government gave assurances of continued financial help. Rubin called the festival "a cultural miracle," and "a source of learning and hope and experience for students in the arts." Other Americans also worked to keep the festival alive and vital. In 1967, the well-known American architect R. Buckminster Fuller designed one of his famous geodesic domes in aluminum, called the

Spoleto Sphere, for performances at the festival. The Aluminum Company of America donated the building material, and Southern Illinois University along with the National Endowment for the Arts bore the other costs. Architectural students from six countries made up the labor force that completed the building in July, 1967.

Elsewhere in Italy, universities established new programs in American studies. Although noteworthy, in the early sixties, these efforts did not go as deep or as far as similar programs in other major European countries. Most of the academic work in Italy focused on American literature, virtually ignoring subjects such as history; Italian universities had no professors in American history. Moreover, except for the small Nelson Gay Memorial Library in Rome, which was inadequate for serious study, Italy had no important collection of materials for the study of American life and history. But the growing number of *Americanisti* were producing mature experts in American literature. With unusual warmth, Italian intellectuals were acclaiming the American theater, impressed not only by its quality and freshness but also by its relevance to contemporary life.

In the late sixties, as interest in American culture grew, the academic situation began to change. From 1967 through 1968, university chairs in American literature increased from two to six; and in 1968, Italian universities offered twelve courses in American literature for degree credit. Now, too, Italian academicians were becoming seriously interested in American history as a field of scholarship, but only two universities, Genoa and Florence, offered courses in United States history. Visiting American scholars, however, frequently supplemented these offerings with lectures and seminars. This use of Americans had drawbacks. In 1969, as Congress drastically cut funds for the Fulbright exchange program, the number of Americans studying and teaching in Italy declined. The loss of Fulbright scholarships and a cut in the State Department's annual subsidy also threatened in 1970 to shut down the Johns Hopkins University Center of Advanced Studies in Bologna, which had been in operation for fifteen years.

Political leaders on the highest level, as well as professors and intellectuals, from both countries traveled back and forth exchanging ideas and keeping Italian-American relations on a comfortable level. Vice President Hubert Humphrey visited Italy and talked to her leaders in April, 1967. He found them opposed to the multilateral treaty that the Soviet Union and the United States had prepared for halting the proliferation of nuclear weapons. This resistance to American leadership marked the first major official disagreement between Italy and the

United States in more than twenty years. Two months later, Prime Minister Moro and Foreign Minister Fanfani traveled to Washington, where they talked to President Johnson and other policy makers. Moro stressed the closeness of Italian and American views, not the differences, on most international issues.

The following September, Italy's Socialist President, Giuseppe Saragat, spent two days in Washington, where he discussed foreign policy. A strong believer in European integration, Saragat emphasized Italy's continued support of the Atlantic alliance. He also reiterated her opposition to provisions in the nonproliferation treaty. Italians, like the Germans and others in Nato who also did not possess nuclear weapons, felt that the treaty as drawn would hinder the scientific, technological, and even social progress of nonnuclear powers and prevent them from developing weapons of their own. On all other issues, even on American policy in Vietnam, the two presidents expressed agreement. Finally, in January, 1969, Italy went along with the desire of her trans-Atlantic ally and signed the nonproliferation treaty.

In December, 1967, just two days before Christmas and at the climax of a sweep around the world of nearly 28,000 miles in five days, Johnson visited Rome, where he conferred with Pope Paul for four hours and with Italian statesmen for about twenty minutes. The President avoided anti-American demonstrations in Rome by taking a helicopter and hopping from Ciampino airport to Saragat's summer home outside the city, where he had virtually summoned the Italian President and Moro for the ignominiously brief encounter. Johnson then flew to the Vatican grounds, where he renewed the acquaintance he had made in October, 1965, when Pope Paul had visited the United Nations in New York. Jack Valenti, a Texan who was an old friend, adviser, and former special assistant at the White House, had urged Johnson to talk with Pope Paul, mainly because of the Pope's unique knowledge of the diplomatic issues in the Vietnam War. The Pope and the President discussed ways of finding peace in Vietnam, the plight of prisoners of war there, and how to combat hunger in the world. Despite its drama, the meeting produced no workable peace plan.

Early in March, 1969, shortly after taking office, President Richard M. Nixon also conferred with Pope Paul at the Vatican. These talks, too, dealt largely with the search for peace in Vietnam. A few days earlier, Nixon had discussed world affairs with Italian political leaders, mainly President Saragat, Prime Minister Mariano Rumor, and

Foreign Minister Pietro Nenni. Leftist students and others used the occasion of Nixon's visit to mount anti-American demonstrations, but these events did not upset the outward cordiality between the statesmen. Both parties described their talks as a general "convergence of views" on practically all the issues they touched.

Although the Italian leaders had gone along with much of what de Gaulle had done in trying to make Europe independent of American power, they made clear their opposition to his attacks on NATO and to his anti-American actions. Earlier, on three occasions in 1963, 1967, and 1968, when de Gaulle had vetoed Britain's effort to join the Common Market, the Italians had reacted angrily. Like the United States, Italy wanted Britain as a member. More than any other large country on the continent, Italy supported the European idea and with it the hope for an Atlantic community. The Italian leaders, therefore, explained this attitude to Nixon and stressed their continuing loyalty to NATO.

This commitment to the Atlantic alliance took on added significance because of a new element in international relations: the increase of Soviet activity in the Mediterranean. The Russians built up a powerful modern fleet in the Mediterranean as a direct response and challenge to the American Sixth Fleet which had its headquarters at Naples. Italian statesmen, feeling threatened by this expanding Soviet naval power, brought up the question in a meeting of the Western European Union in 1967. In November of the following year, the Soviets, arguing that they belonged by right in the Mediterranean because they had a coastline on the Black Sea, a tributary, suggested that the United States navy abandon the Mediterranean and let their fleet take over. American and Italian leaders gave not the slightest consideration to such a move. Quite the contrary: American strategists considered Soviet naval power a serious threat to their Polaris submarines operating there. These undersea craft, each carrying sixteen nuclear missiles, had an advantage over missile launchers on land because they could hide easily and launch surprise attacks. This advantage, counted upon as a means of striking at the southern flank of the Soviet Union in case of a nuclear war, would be lost if the Soviets came to dominate the Mediterranean. In 1969, therefore, NATO headquarters in Naples set up a new command to keep watch on the Soviet ships.

In view of the threat posed by the largest Russian force ever assembled in the Mediterranean, the United States and Italy needed each other. Italy wanted American protection against Soviet power, and the United States required Italian bases for its ships and planes in the Mediterranean, as well as the assistance of the modern, specialized Italian navy. Furthermore, with turmoil in the Middle East and Soviet naval power active there, the United States needed a reliable friend, such as Italy, in order to operate effectively in the Mediterranean and to carry out its commitments in the Middle East.

With the Soviet threat continuing unabated, the situation that existed since the end of the Second World War for Italy's defense retained its basic feature; she still relied on the United States. Earlier, many Italians felt that this dependence detracted from their country's dignity and independence. In the late sixties, this attitude changed, although there was in Italy, as elsewhere in Europe, a latent anti-Americanism, much of it fueled by disgust over the war in Vietnam. In most matters of foreign policy, Italy now acted as she saw fit, without undue deference to the United States. She had, for example, worked toward official recognition of Red China and a stepped-up dialogue with the Communist nations of Eastern Europe, measures that would earlier have alarmed American policy makers. Italy achieved a comfortable relationship with the United States, that of a lesser but still-important ally who acts as she wishes within the context of her alliance. Her friendship with the United States, although not as turbulent as America's relations with some other countries, had become mutually profitable. Based on mutual respect, the relationship between the United States and Italy had improved considerably over what it had been in the past.

America Dolce,
America Amara
19

In 1970, the United States was home to more people of Italian origin than any other country in the world except Italy herself. Aside from those who claimed some place in the British Isles as their ancestral home, Italians comprised one of the largest ethnic groups to have migrated voluntarily to the United States. In 1969, various estimates placed the number of first-generation Italians at about 5 million and the second generation at slightly more than that figure. If third- and fourth-generation Italian-Americans (who do not show up in official statistics) are included in a broad estimate, people of Italian stock can be numbered at more than 20 million, or about 11 per cent of the population. Since the actual number usually exceeded census figures, mainly because those who entered the country illegally did not want to be counted, the most liberal estimates say that the Italians slightly outnumber the Germans; conservative estimates indicate that people of German stock are more numerous.

Despite their numbers, only in recent years have Italian-Americans, really the young men and women of the third and fourth generations, begun to acquire a truly respected status in the United States. In wealth, status, and influence, they are still behind members of most other major ethnic groups from Europe. In part, at least, this lag has stemmed from the nature and timing of Italian immigration. Italians were the last and most backward of immigrants to arrive in large numbers before restrictive laws ended mass immigration. They have had further to go in less time than the other groups to achieve success American-style. Their status also reflects the twisted nature of relations between Italians and Americans, its half-bitter, half-sweet quality.

Basically, relations between the two peoples have often been more friendly than hostile. Theirs has usually been a relationship based on conflict and accommodation, on affection accompanied at times by contempt. To understand each other, Italians and Americans have had to build bridges between cultural structures that differed greatly and to pierce popular images distorted by prejudice, ignorance, and fear. Although they have frequently been far apart in attitude and in appreciation of each other, Italians and Americans in the twentieth century have also often been close, sometimes as intimate as strands in a rope. Their hostilities had shallow roots. Even when Italy and the United States fought each other in a great war, Italians and Americans did not come to hate each other, not even for the short time when they were engaged in head-on hostilities. Through war and peace, the basic friendship remained, although it was twisted by the repulsions and attractions of the past.

Taking at least some ingredients from reality, Italians and Americans have created a kind of mythology about each other. In the words of the crusading humanist Carlo Levi, writing in 1947, southern Italian peasants cherished many myths, but "one stands out among the rest by providing the perfect avenue of escape from grim realities. It embodies fable and fact, concrete existence and romance, necessity and imagination. It is their version, magical and real at the same time, of an earthly paradise, lost and then found again: the myth of America." This myth has lived in the minds of Italian peasants for over a century. They have pictured the United States as a land where streets are paved with gold, where the poor can become rich, where work brings real rewards, like white bread, cheese, and wine. When they finally came to America they suffered from shock; reality struck with a deep and puzzling ugliness. They toiled ceaselessly and endured exploitation only to discover that in America they were "wops" and "dagoes," members of a detested minority. Despite this stigma, some did gain rewards, even the wealth they dreamed of, especially in the West. There, as the historian Andrew F. Rolle has suggested, Italians suffered less from alienation than they did in the East. Most of them, however, experienced both sides of life, but more an America *amara* than an America *dolce*.

The American popular myth of Italy was an old one, too. The American visitors to Italy during the late eighteenth and early nineteenth centuries gave it firm roots; it flowered with the later travelers. Italy was a land cherished for the glories of her past, for tradition, for being a huge art museum and a warehouse of culture. Like their British counterparts, the American travelers had no respect for modern Italy as a nation or for contemporary Italians as a people. "Certain prejudices prevent us [Americans] from trusting Italians," Theodore Dwight wrote in 1851. "They have been regarded, for so many ages, as the bigoted and fanatical supporters of popery, and so cowardly, fickle, treacherous and blood-thirsty in their dispositions, that we cannot easily feel towards them as we do towards each other." In the 1950's, American military men visiting in Italy sometimes expressed this attitude more succinctly. "Pigs, nothing but Dago pigs," they spat. Yet many Americans accompanied their hostility or contempt with a backhanded affection. Dwight himself said that Americans were mistaken in their negative view of Italians, and a century later, America's nonmilitary visitors to Italy usually liked the people they encountered.

Contempt mixed with compassion came easily to Americans because in her relations with the United States, Italy has usually been the impoverished but distant friend grateful for favors. Even though she is the home of old and venerable societies, Italy as a nation is younger by a century and less experienced in government than the United States; for this reason some Americans take a condescending attitude toward Italian political experimentation. Until recently, Italy has been poor, unstable politically, and weak militarily, especially so in contrast to a rich, relatively stable, and strong United States.

From the beginning, the friendship has not been one of equals, or one based on mutual respect. The warmth has usually flowed more strongly in one direction than in the other, more from Italians toward the United States than from Americans toward Italy. Most educated Italians who visited the United States returned home with favorable impressions of the people, the country, and its institutions. They often came expecting to find the perfect state, politically, socially, and economically, a nation that could serve as a model for their own country. Even if the reality rarely matched the extravagant expectation, the travelers were seldom disappointed. Unlike the Americans in Italy, most Italians who visited the United States either acquired respect and admiration for the democracy across the sea or found enough good things in it to retain the favorable image they had brought with them when they arrived.

Until the 1940's, the massive immigration, more than anything else, helped to shape the attitude of ordinary Americans toward Italians. Those *contadini* from Sicily, Calabria, the Abruzzi, and elsewhere in the south were part of a pattern of mobility that continued into the sixties. They crossed the sea to a land of alien language, religion, and social customs to enter the world of the modern industrial city. Those who stayed in the new land, and their children after them, contributed significantly to its industrialization and urbanization. Although not necessarily noble or heroic, the work of Italians in the United States has about it an almost epic quality, if only because of the numbers involved. With bursting energy and amazing hardiness, the sons of Italy labored and built, but too often they strained and lived in great privation. "If the immigrant were a horse instead of a human being," Stefano Miele, an immigrant himself, wrote with noticeable bitterness in 1921, "America would be more careful of him; if it loses a horse it feels it loses something, if it loses an immigrant it feels it loses nothing."

Except for the exploited masses in the great industrial cities of Europe in the nineteenth century, these Italian peasants in the United States led lives more burdensome and degrading than did any other comparable class of modern American or European workers. No one, neither historical scholar nor novelist, has truly told their story, capturing their proud spirit, their despair, their crushing failures and small triumphs. For anyone who is concerned about America's history in depth—in the migration of peoples, in the plight of the poor, in the class structure, or in mass acculturation—the Italian experience is of great significance. It is part of the common experience of millions of European immigrants, but it is also unique. Italians made up the only truly great proletarian immigration to the United States. They themselves sometimes summed up their experience in the bitter-sweetness of their songs, such as "How many tears this America cost."

Despite the cruelty of their experience, the suffering, and the discriminations they endured, these people of Italian stock took a tenacious hold on life in the United States. Yet they came too late and were too inarticulate, without even a clear national heritage or command of a common language beyond some dialect, to impress deeply their own cultural traits upon the social structure of America. At times, out of shame for their origins or to lessen the sting of discrimination, some abandoned even the cultural identity that went with Italian names. But that practice faded as second, third, and fourth generations acquired a sense of security in their own status.

Sociologists and historians have argued convincingly that immigration—unless the emigrating group has special reasons for cultural survival, such as resistance to persecution—breeds grave problems. Ultimately in such a case, the new nationality would be absorbed without leaving much of a legacy. Italians and their descendants in the United States seem to have gone through this process, but with neither the swiftness nor the completeness the theorists have postulated. Although it is true that immigrant peoples in the second and third generations largely lose their language and culture, are transformed by the pressures for conformity in American society, are stripped of their original attributes, and are recreated as something new, some, such as the Italian-Americans, are still identifiable as distinctive groups.

Although in many parts of the country, third- and fourth-generation Italian-Americans have become virtually indistinguishable from the rest of the population, in the eastern cities, large numbers have retained their distinctiveness as American Italians. They are still identifiable as having traits popularly associated with Italy. This persistence of the old ethnic pattern, even after two or three generations, for a people who made less effort to retain it than did most other ethnic groups, is most striking in New York City, where in the late sixties at least an eighth of the population was Italian or of Italian extraction.

Nonetheless, except in a few areas like New York, with new concentrations of immigrants, the proletarian city life is disappearing. Among Italians, the old ethnic pattern has been particularly tenacious because articulate expression has usually been confined to a cultivated minority, one too often separated from and unrepresentative of the great body of immigrants. Even those who rose from the ethnic ghettos took on elitist attitudes. Listen, for example, to the strikingly "contemporary" complaint (written in 1909) of an Italian writer, Alberto Pecorini, about his countrymen in the United States: "The relatively few successful youths of Italian parentage and American birth and education are lost to the Italian population of New York; they are not interpreters of American life and American ideals, as they should be." Since the Second World War, this gulf between the cultivated elite and the laboring masses has narrowed. In most places, the old ethnic pattern is being replaced by a new middle-class style, one that pulls Italian-Americans—just as it pulls others—from working class to middle class, from cities to suburbs.

In their cultural life, politics, and social attitudes, aside from the elements of language and education, Americans of Italian descent have become absorbed into the dominant society. They have little in common with the society of contemporary Italy. They are as American as anyone else; but still, they are Americans who have managed somehow to retain at least a few unique ethnic qualities aside from their old-world names. Some of these qualities have come from something no knowledgeable Italian-American can forget, his half-bitter, half-sweet heritage. The bitterness is embedded in the knowledge that the people in the ruling circles of American society have long looked down upon Italians as among the least desirable of the immigrant peoples. Contrary to the views of many historians, discrimination against Italians did not coincide with the coming of mass immigration in the 1880's; it began much earlier, just about as soon as Italians appeared on the American scene in small, isolated groups. The bitter roots are old and deep.

The bitterness persisted well into the twentieth century, aggravated by the tainted image of criminality imposed on the Italian-Americans. As Nicholas Pileggi and others have pointed out, bad movies and worse television shows, as well as popular writers catering to simple minds, have regularly cast the Italian-American in the role of racketeer, "supplanting the American Indian as the national bad-guy" in popular folklore. In 1970, a publisher even came out with a *Mafia Cookbook,* giving "the succulent recipes of the *Cosa Nostra* chieftains." To many an Italian-American, it seemed that no matter how worthy he might be, American society would not let him forget that he bore from his origins the mark of an inferior man.

Within the Italian-American communities, this bigotry, this bitter heritage, often produced frustration covered by a veneer of ethnic chauvinism that seemed ridiculous to outside observers. To maintain his own self-respect, the Italian-American, sometimes arrogantly, sometimes pathetically, told himself and others that Italians were and are a great people, with a culture second to none and great men unsurpassed in their accomplishments. Italian-Americans, knowingly and unknowingly, frequently resorted to exaggerated and unnecessary glorification of their cultural heritage to compensate for the sneers they suffered and to balance their poor record in political life in the United States and the supposed bad soldiering of their old-world countrymen.

Like other defensive minorities, Italian-Americans frequently praised and admired extravagantly the poorly educated and sometimes coarse athletes and entertainers with Italian names merely because they had achieved a passing success in the wider dominant society. Even their protest organizations blunted their effectiveness by naïvely giving mass testimonials to such men and entrusting them with roles of leadership. Although the Sinatras, Joe DiMaggios, Rocky Marcianos, and Vince Lombardis merited the recognition they received for their talent and athletic prowess, and deserved no one's condescension, the Italian-American community could more effectively enhance its national image with a leadership respected for its social, cultural, or intellectual accomplishments. Regardless of their crude leadership and blunders, Italian-Americans have, in their protests, at last served notice that they find wholesale public denigration based on stereotypes and ethnocultural grounds unacceptable.

The sweetness in the Italian-American heritage comes in the fullness of the life the immigrant and his children and their children built in the New World, in the escape from the oppressive institutions, demeaning social structure, and miserable living conditions of their homeland. To many of them, as to peoples from other lands, America was truly the land of plenty, a place where they got more than enough to eat and where their descendants, if worthy, could eventually rise above their origins and taste the promise of the good life. To those who raised themselves from nothing, the full life was worth the price American society exacted.

This sweetness also persists in the broad cultural bond that not even a lingering bigotry and a great war could sever. Even into the late sixties, American intellectuals continued to look to Italy for inspiration. They still felt for her and her people an affection that transcended old hates and misunderstandings, a unique attachment quite unlike the stronger tie to England. This may be why, according to literary historian Nathalia Wright, "no other foreign country has figured so provocatively in American fiction." Americans, intellectual or otherwise, have found in Italy and in Italians something that made their own cultural heritage fuller and more complete than it would have been without the Italian connection.

The Italian contribution to the American heritage is sometimes intangible and obscured by sentimentality, but much of it is recorded in laws, newspapers, poems, stories, and increasingly in scholarly studies. Italian-American novelists have been among the most successful in probing aspects of this heritage, usually within the themes of the Americanization of Italian families or of the isolated man—the alien—in an established society. Among the writers who used these themes most effectively was Giovanni Fante, born in Denver, Colorado, the son of an Abruzzese father and an Italian-American mother. His noteworthy works, most of them autobiographical, include *Wait Until Spring, Bandini* (1938), *Ask the Dust* (1939), and *Dago Red* (1940). He and Jo Pagano, also born and raised in Denver and author of *The Paesanos* (1940) and *Golden Wedding*

(1943), showed the spirit and feelings of immigrant miners in Colorado, truck farmers in the field in California, and cannery workers preparing fruits and vegetables on assembly lines.

Guido D'Agostino, born of Sicilian parents in the heart of New York's Little Italy, added to this literature with two novels, *Olives on the Apple Tree* (1940) and *Hills Beyond Manhattan* (1942); both are concerned with the problem of immigrant adjustment to American society. Jerre Mangione, also the son of Sicilians, in *Mount Allegro* (1942) tells the story of a Sicilian family group living in the Italian colony in Rochester, where the author was born. Later, in *Reunion in Sicily* (1950), he describes his own journey to Sicily, expressing doubt about which world the Italian-American belongs to—the new one or the old.

Mari Tomasi, the daughter of Piedmontese parents who had settled in Vermont, moved away from the theme of alienation. In her novel, *Deep Grow the Roots* (1940), she tells the story of Italian peasants caught in the demands of the Ethiopian war. The book suggests that immigration does not mean a clean and final separation from Italy. Pietro Di Donato, the son of immigrants from the Abruzzi, and a self-educated bricklayer, wrote one of the best known of all novels dealing with Italian-American themes, *Christ in Concrete* (1939). It is a rough but moving story about his father, a hard-working construction laborer forced to raise his family in a slum.

An Italian-American writer whose work exceeded that of Di Donato's in popularity is Mario Puzo, born and educated in New York City. In *The Fortunate Pilgrim* (1965), he handles the immigrant theme as successfully as anyone. This novel about immigrant life in New York stresses the conflict between generations and the bittersweetness of the American dream for the Italian peasant. Lucca Santa, the main character, finds the cost of survival in "America, America, blasphemous dream," high—perhaps too high. Puzo's *The Godfather* (1969) also revolves around an immigrant family of several generations, but the theme is the Mafia as a way of life in America. Filled with violence, sex, and stock *Cosa Nostra* characters right out of the newspapers, it quickly soared to the top of the best-seller lists.

Several writers of mixed Italian origin, such as Bernard A. De Voto and Hamilton Basso, have also reached wide audiences. They had a deeper impact on American literary and scholarly circles than the writers of fiction who dealt with alienation. But Basso's novels and De Voto's varied writings, especially his popular histories of the

American West, do not deal with Italian-American themes and are not Italian in flavor.

A number of poets, such as Emanuel Carnevali, John Ciardi, and Lawrence Ferlinghetti, have gained wide recognition as possessing talent of the first rank. Although dynamic and captivating as a person and a poet, Carnevali, writing in the twenties, found himself consumed by a dreadful sickness. When he returned to his native Italy to die, he left only beautiful poetic fragments. Born in Boston, Ciardi acquired a university education, entered academic life, and made himself at home in literary circles, becoming poetry editor of the *Saturday Review*. As both poet and critic, he writes about the broad American scene, though sometimes he explores Italian themes. Ciardi became especially popular in college literary circles in the fifties, although critics differ concerning the quality of his work, some considering it good but pretentious, others calling it brilliant.

Ferlinghetti, born in New York and educated in various universities, where he acquired advanced degrees, has written poems of protest that deal with broad American, not Italian-American, themes. He gained fame in the fifties and sixties as a leader of the San Francisco movement in poetry. Experimenting with ideas and sounds as well as with written words, he writes earthy poems to be read aloud. Even though he is controversial, critics consider Ferlinghetti one of the nation's most important poets.

Although a few of these Italian-American writers are men of notable talent, and there are more of them than ever before, until the late sixties, the group had not contributed a great deal to the mainstream of American literary tradition. Many were or are competent craftsmen; but their output is small, and none has yet achieved distinction as a truly great writer or major literary figure.

In comparison with intellectuals from the other major ethnic groups, Italian-Americans have also lagged in other areas of cultural and social achievement. In American education, it was rare to find men like Henry Suzzallo, who became president of the University of Washington, in Seattle, in 1915 and president of the Carnegie Foundation for the Advancement of Teaching in 1930. Italian-Americans have not produced thinkers, scholars, scientists, and other leaders of national and international stature, at least not in quantities commensurate with their numbers, their growing resources, and the talent of their forebears. Some critics blame these failings on the prevalance of a basic anti-intellectualism among Italian-Americans. Others place the fault on the American Catholic community as a whole. Regardless of the source of the problem, Italian-Americans, with a few noteworthy exceptions, at the end of the sixties had not yet earned a secure place in the forefront of America's intellectual life.

Much of this intellectual backwardness has its roots in southern Italy, in the social structure and the traditions of poverty and illiteracy that most Italian immigrants tried to shake off in the new country. Given this demeaning part of their heritage and their relatively short period of acculturation in the United States, what surprises is not the crudity of Italian-Americans and their inability to measure up to rigorous standards of social and intellectual accomplishment set by other Americans, but the progress they have made in overcoming the obstacles of their past in an alien, patronizing, and often hostile society. In America, Italians have and have had obvious faults, but they have been more sinned against than sinning. They gave more than the fruit of their backbreaking labor; they fertilized American society, contributing richness to its cultural diversity. For good or bad, the Italian strain, although not yet in full cultural bloom, has already become a noteworthy element in American national character.

Italian scholars have frequently lamented the bitterness of the immigrant experience in the United States. With impressive evidence, they have argued that, on the whole, Italy has not benefited from the loss of millions of her sons and daughters through emigration. Based mainly on narrow economic considerations, such a judgment does not take into account the intangible but pervasively important cultural and political aspects of Italy's relationship to the United States. When immigrants settled in the United States, they were not truly lost to Italy. On the whole, they managed somehow to combine an unusually tenacious loyalty to their adopted country with affection for their land of origin, an attitude that was passed on to many of their offspring. They gave Italy a close connection with the most powerful nation in the world, a democracy that aided and comforted dispirited Italians even during the hostilities of a great war.

If it had not been for the presence of millions of citizens of Italian origin in the United States and the pressure they exerted on the government, Italy's occupation during the Second World War would have been more onerous and her peace terms harsher than they were. Whatever their faults, Italian-Americans helped make the United States a reasonably understanding and tolerant friend of a fallen and humiliated Italy. More than anything else, they brought Italy closer to the United States than to any other country. The ties of blood and sentiment have long kept Italians in more intimate contact with the

United States than almost any other foreigners except, possibly, the English.

In the decades after the war, as Italy became prosperous, the warmth of feeling did not pass away. Italy remained one of the few countries in Europe where Americans were regarded with genuine affection. But the old relationship, anchored on the immigrant foundation, has changed. Rather than emigrate, more and more of Italy's sons stay home, where they speak their own language, maintain their own traditions, and perpetuate their own culture as it expresses itself freely through the energy and activities of a highly civilized people. As the cultural critic Elena Croce observed in the early sixties, "The Italian of today feels his own identity more clearly than he did when Italy became a nation and nationalism was the vogue." Americans, recognizing the change, no longer think of Italy as a backward museum but rather as one of the most modern countries in the world, with a society as sophisticated and as advanced as can be found anywhere. Italian-Americans now also look upon their original homeland as a country in the ranks of the most advanced nations of the world, an ancestral home with a rich cultural heritage and a vital, dynamic present.

Regardless of the tensions, the injustices and the intellectual aridity of the past, and the traces of discrimination, Italians, their children, and their children's children have for the most part finally found a comfortable place in American society. Jerre Mangione believes that in the decades since the end of the Second World War, "Few minority groups in this country [the United States] have enjoyed as much affection and esteem as the Italian-Americans." This judgment exaggerates the sweetness of one aspect of the relationship between Italians and Americans, for although basically friendly, it has been more often bitter than sweet. By 1970, however, it had become sweeter than it had ever been before.

Bibliographical Essay

Although I hope scholars will find this book stimulating and intellectually sound, I did not write it mainly for them. I have written it for all people interested in history, ideas, and the cultural legacy of the wide world they have inherited. Because this is a wide-ranging survey and analysis stretching over more than two centuries and across half the world, I have omitted the usual documentation within the narrative. Nonetheless, I consider it a scholarly study, for it has been based on extensive research among primary and secondary sources of all kinds. A selective bibliographical essay, made up mostly of printed sources, has been added to permit the interested reader to follow in the main tracks of my research. It will also serve as a starting point and guide for anyone concerned to make a deeper exploration of the topics I have discussed.

GENERAL WORKS

In neither English nor Italian does there exist a full, solid, scholarly history of relations between Italy and the United States.[*] The best book on the subject is the brief episodic survey by H. Stuart Hughes, *The United States and Italy* (rev. ed., Cambridge, Mass., 1965). It was published originally in 1953 and is still valuable for its sophisticated insights on Italian policy and attitudes. Angelo F. Giudi, *Relazioni culturali fra Italia e Stati Uniti d'America* (Padua, 1940) begins with Columbus and attempts a broad coverage of diplomatic and political relations based on documentary sources, a basic source but dull and pedestrian. Howard R. Marraro, *Relazioni fra l'Italia e gli Stati Uniti* (Rome, 1954) contains factual essays on American relations with various Italian states, but goes only to 1870. The introduction to Marraro, ed. *Diplomatic Relations between the United States and the Kingdom of the Two Sicilies* (New York, 1951) also includes a documented but disjointed account of early relations between the United States and Italy. The documents are taken from official correspondence. Livio Chersi, *Italia e Stati Uniti: relazioni diplomatiche, 1861–1935* (Trieste, 1937) is superficial but has some in-

[*] When a work is available in both Italian and English I have usually referred to the English version or translation. I have usually not given both versions because of space limitations.

formation not easily obtained elsewhere. Two relatively broad doctoral studies offer important information and insight concerning aspects of the bittersweet relationship: James Pfau, "Economic Relations between the United States and Italy, 1919–1949," unpubl. diss. (University of Chicago, 1951), and Martin F. Hastings, "United States-Vatican Relations: Policies and Problems," unpubl. diss. (University of California, Berkeley, 1952). Another unpublished study, Harold D. Langley, "Highlights in the History of the United States Diplomatic and Consular Posts at Turin, Italy," Historical Office, Bureau of Public Affairs, Dept. of State (Washington, D.C., 1961): Research Project No. 432, rev., is an excellent summary based on archival sources but is not interpretive. Scattered references to Italian-American relations may be found in *The American Secretaries of State and Their Diplomacy*, Samuel F. Bemis, ed., 10 vols. (New York, 1927–29). In 1963 Robert H. Ferrell assumed editorship of the series and so far has expanded it to 16 volumes.

For the documentary record from the American side, the series *Foreign Relations of the United States: Diplomatic Papers* published by the Department of State under slightly different titles since 1861, is basic. It should be supplemented by the diplomatic correspondence relative to Italy and the Italian States deposited in the National Archives. Many of these documents are available on microfilm. On the Italian side the diplomatic record is more restricted and materials pertaining to relations with the United States are scattered. Important correspondence from private and royal sources, and from the *Archivo storico* can be found in Ministero degli affari esteri, Commissione per la pubblicazione dei documenti diplomatici, *I documenti diplomatici italiani,* published in various series since 1952 by the Libreria dello Stato in Rome.

Important bibliographical tools are Samuel F. Bemis and Grace G. Griffin, eds., *Guide to the Diplomatic History of the United States, 1775–1921* (Washington, D.C., 1935), Carl R. Fish, *Guide to the Materials for American History in Roman and Other Italian Archives* (Washington, D.C., 1911), and Mary L. Shay, "Italy," *Guide to the Diplomatic Archives of Western Europe,* eds., Daniel H. Thomas and Lynn M. Case (Phil., 1959), pp. 125–157.

Like the diplomatic record, the literature on Italians in America lacks a comprehensive scholarly book. The best study, Andrew F. Rolle, *The Immigrant Upraised: Italian Adventurers and Colonists in an Expanding America* (Norman, Okla., 1968) deals mainly with Italians in the West and advances a thesis inapplicable to the total Italian immigrant experience. Lawrence F. Pisani, *The Italian in America: A Social Study and History* (New York, 1957) is useful but poorly organized, defensive, and superficial, and Michael A. Musmanno, *The Story of the Italians in America* (New York, 1965) is filio-pietistic, naïve, and inadequate for any real understanding of the subject. Four works by Giovanni E. Schiavo, an immigrant journalist from Sicily, though not always accurate and lacking in coherent structure and analysis, are useful as source books. See his *The Italians in America Before the Civil War* (New York, 1934), *Italian-American History,* 2 vols. (New York, 1947–49), *Four Centuries of Italian-American History* (5th ed., New York, 1958), and *The*

Italians in Chicago: A Study in Americanization (Chicago, 1928). For a study of Italians in a unique Western situation see Frederick G. Bohme, "A History of the Italians in New Mexico," unpubl. diss. (University of New Mexico, 1958). Two important bibliographical articles are Ina Ten Eyck Firkins, "Italians in the United States," *Bulletin of Bibliography*, VIII (Jan. 1915), 129–132 and Rudolph J. Vecoli, "The Immigration Studies Collection of the University of Minnesota," *American Archivist*, XXXII (April, 1969), 139–145. The American-Italian Historical Association, with headquarters in New York City, plans a general bibliography and guide to published and unpublished materials relating to Italians in America.

Among recent studies of value are Humbert S. Nelli, *The Italians in Chicago, 1880–1930: A Study in Ethnic Mobility* (New York, 1970); and Luciano J. Iorizzo and Salvatore Mondello, *The Italian-Americans* (New York, 1971).

For all aspects of the Italian-American relationship, newspaper files and periodical literature of opinion comprise invaluable sources; they provide a sense of the period and contemporary focus on what was considered most relevant to the relationship. The American, the Italian, and the Italian-American press, whose runs of newspapers have been preserved, all contain important materials.

CHAPTER 1: EARLY ENCOUNTERS

For the Waldensians see Sophia V. Bompiani, *A Short History of the Italian Waldenses* (2nd ed., New York, 1899); George B. Watts, *The Waldenses in the New World* (Durham, N.C., 1941), a well-documented account; and Robert Baird, *Sketches of Protestantism in Italy, Past and Present, Including a Notice of the Origin, History, and Present State of the Waldenses* (Boston, 1845). For Benjamin Franklin see Antonio Pace, *Benjamin Franklin and Italy* (Phil., 1958), although uneven in quality this book is carefully researched and contains much information on Italy and the United States which goes beyond Franklin and his influence. See also Emilio Goggio, "Benjamin Franklin and Italy," *Romanic Review*, XIX (Oct.–Dec. 1928), 302–308; and Lawrence S. Mayo, *Beniamino Franklin: diplomatico-scienzato-filosofo-economista (1706–1790)* (Florence, [1922]) contains an introductory essay by Luigi Rava, "La fortuna di B. Franklin in Italia." Bruno Roselli, *The Italians in Colonial Florida* (Jacksonville, Florida, 1940) is a useful but unreliable pamphlet. E. P. Panogopoulos, *New Smyrna: An Eighteenth Century Greek Odysse* (Gainesville, Fla., 1966) provides data on Italian settlers.

For background on American cultural life containing a few scattered references to Italians and Italian influence see Louis B. Wright, *The Cultural Life of the American Colonies, 1607–1763* (New York, 1957); Carl Bode, *The Anatomy of Popular Culture, 1840–1861* (Berkeley, 1959); Lillian B. Miller, *Patrons and Patriotism: The Encouragement of the Fine Arts in the United States, 1790–1860* (Chicago, 1966) contains information on several Italian artists; Clay Lancaster, "Italianism in American Architecture before 1860," *American Quarterly*, IV (Summer 1952), 127–148 shows the influence of Palladio and Italian models, such as the dome of St. Peter's in Rome which served as the model for the White House dome. See also Gilbert Chinard, "The American Philosophical Society and the World of Science (1768–1800)," *Proceedings of the American Philosophical Society,* LXXXVII (1943), 1–11; and Merle Curti, "The Reputation of America Overseas (1776–1860)," *American Quarterly,* I (Spring 1949), 58–82.

Several articles by Howard R. Marraro trace the scant influence of Italians and Italian culture in early America. See his "Interpretation of Italy and the Italians in Eighteenth Century America," *Italica,* XXV, No. 1 (1948), 59–81; "Italian Culture in Eighteenth-Century American Magazines," *ibid.,* XXII (March 1945), 21–31; "Italian Music and Actors in America During the Eighteenth Century," *ibid.,* XXIII (June 1946), 103–117; "Italians in New York During the First Half of the Nineteenth Century," *New York History,* XXVI (July 1945), 278–305; "Italo-Americans in Eighteenth Century New York," *ibid.,* XVI (July 1940), 316–323; and "Italo-Americans in Pennsylvania in the Eighteenth Century," *Pennsylvania History,* VII (July 1940), 159–166.

Information on New York's earliest "Little Italy" can be found in Robert Ernst, *Immigrant Life in New York City, 1825–1863* (New York, 1949); Francesco Moncada, "The 'Little Italy' of 1859," *Atlantica* (Jan. 1933), pp. 160–161; and Moncada, "New York's 'Little Italy,'" *ibid.* (April 1937), pp. 14–15, 24. For information on Italians in the early West the best source is Andrew F. Rolle, *The Immigrant Upraised* (Norman, Okla., 1968), but see also Francesco M. Nicosia, *Italian Pioneers of California* ([San Francisco], 1960), a superficial but useful account; Camillo Branchi, "Gli Italiani nella storia della California," *L'universo,* XXXV (May–June 1956), 421–432; John B. McGloin, "John B. Nobili, S.J., Founder of California's Santa Clara College," *British Columbia Historical Quarterly,* XVII (July–Oct. 1953), 215–222; Helen A. Howard, "Padre Ravalli: Versatile Missionary," *The Historical Bulletin* (Jan. 1940), pp. 33–35.

Richard C. Garlick, Jr., et al., *Italy and Italians in Washington's Time* (New York, 1933) is a collection of essays by five authors. Although uneven in quality they provide a good source on early relations between Italians and Americans. For Italian reactions to America see Rosario Romeo, *Le scoperte americana nella coscienza italiana del cinquecento* (Milan, 1954); and Henry T. Tuckerman, *America and Her Commentators, with a Critical Sketch of Travel in the United States* (New York, 1864).

There is a modest literature on individual Italians who traveled in America or settled there. See Richard C. Garlick, Jr., *Philip Mazzei, Friend of Jefferson: His Life and Letters* (Baltimore, 1933), a solid account; Philip Mazzei, *Memoirs and Peregrinations of the Florentine Philip Mazzei, 1730–1816,* trans. Howard R. Marraro (New York, 1942). See also articles by Marraro, "Four Versions of Jefferson's Letter to Mazzei," *William and Mary College Quarterly Historical Magazine,* XXII, Series 2 (Jan. 1942), 18–29; "Jefferson's Letters Concerning the Settlement of Mazzei's Virginia Estate," *Mississippi Valley Historical*

Review, XXX (Sept. 1943), 235–242; "Mazzei's Correspondence with the Grand Duke of Tuscany during his American Mission," *William and Mary College Quarterly Historical Magazine,* XXII, Series 2 (July 1942), 275–301; *ibid.* (Oct. 1942), pp. 361–380, translations of some Mazzei letters; "Philip Mazzei on American Political, Social, and Economic Problems," *The Journal of Southern History,* XV (Aug. 1949), 354–378, translations from articles and essays; "Philip Mazzei, Virginia's Agent in Europe: The Story of His Mission as Related in His Own Dispatches and Other Documents," *Bulletin of the New York Public Library,* XXXVIII (March 1934), 155–175; *ibid.* (April 1934), pp. 247–274; *ibid.* (June 1934), pp. 447–474; (July 1934), pp. 541–562, a biographical sketch is included; "Unpublished Correspondence of Jefferson and Adams to Mazzei," *The Virginia Magazine of History and Biography,* LI (April 1943), 113–133; "An Unpublished Jefferson Letter to Mazzei," *Italica,* XXXV (June 1958), 83–87; "Unpublished Mazzei Correspondence during His American Mission to Europe 1780–1783," *William and Mary College Quarterly Historical Magazine,* XXIII, Series 2 (July 1943), 309–327; *ibid.* (Oct. 1934), pp. 418–434; "Unpublished Mazzei Letters to Jefferson," *The William and Mary Quarterly,* I (Oct. 1944), 374–396; *ibid.* II (Jan. 1945), 71–100. Giovanni Schiavo, *Philip Mazzei: One of America's Founding Fathers* (New York, 1951) is the reprint of a chapter from a larger work.

For Alfieri see Charles R. D. Miller, "Alfieri and America," *Philological Quarterly,* XI (April 1932), 163–166; Virginia Watson, "Alfieri and America," *The North American Review,* CXCVI (Aug. 1912), 244–253, and Gaudens Megaro, *Vittorio Alfieri: Forerunner of Italian Nationalism* (New York, 1930). For information on Vigo see Bruno Roselli, *Vigo: A Forgotten Builder of the American Republic* (Boston, 1933), a rambling, defensive work of limited scholarly value. The views of other Italians in America may be found in *Seeing America and Its Great Men: The Journal and Letters of Count Francesco dal Verme, 1783–1784,* ed. and trans., Elizabeth Cometti (Charlottesville, Va., 1969); Luigi Castiglioni, *Viaggio negli Stati Uniti dell'America settentrionale fatto negli anni 1785, 1786 e 1787 da Luigi Castiglioni . . . ,* 2 vols. (Milan, 1790); Howard R. Marraro, "Count Luigi Castiglioni: An Early Italian Traveller to Virginia (1785–1786)," *The Virginia Magazine of History and Biography,* LVIII (Oct. 1950), 473–491; Hubert G. Smith, "Count Andreani: a Forgotten Traveler," *Minnesota History,* XIX (March 1938), 34–42. Da Ponte's own writings are a good source, especially *Memoirs of Lorenzo Da Ponte: Mozart's Librettist,* trans. L. A. Sheppard (London, 1929), and Da Ponte's *Storia della lingua e letteratura italiana in New York* (New York, 1827). See also Joseph L. Russo, *Lorenzo Da Ponte: Poet and Adventurer* (New York, 1922); and pieces by Howard R. Marraro, "Da Ponte and Foresti: The Introduction of Italian at Columbia," *Columbia University Quarterly,* XXIX (March 1937), 23–32; "Unpublished Documents on Da Ponte's Italian Library," *PMLA,* LVIII (Dec. 1943), 1057–72; and "An Unpublished Letter of Lorenzo Da Ponte," *Italica,* XIX (March 1942), 26–27.

Eugene S. Scalia, "Figures of the Risorgimento in America: Ignazio

Batolo, alias Pietro Bachi and Pietro D'Alessandro," *Italica,* XLII (Dec. 1965), 311–357 throws light on the lives of two Italian intellectuals in exile. Vidua's views are analyzed in Joseph Rossi, "The American Myth in the Italian Risorgimento: The *Lettere* from America of Carlo Vidua," *Italica,* XXXVIII (Sept. 1961), 227–235; Elizabeth Cometti and Valeria Gennaro-Lerda, "The Presidential Tour of Carlo Vidua with Letters on Virginia," *Virginia Magazine of History and Biography,* LXXVII (Oct. 1969), 387–406; and see Cesare Balbo, ed., *Lettere del Conte Carlo Vidua,* 3 vols. (Turin, 1835). For Beltrami's activities see Timothy Severin, *Explorers of the Mississippi* (New York, 1967) which has a chapter on the Italian's wanderings; Theodore Christianson, "The Long and Beltrami Explorations in Minnesota One Hundred Years Ago," *Minnesota History,* V (Nov. 1923), 249–264; Eugenia Masi, *G. C. Beltrami e le sue esplorazione in America* (Florence, 1902); Giacomo C. Beltrami, *La découverte des sources du Mississippi et de la Rivière Sanglante* (New Orleans, 1824). For Arese the basic source is Romualdo Bonfadini, *Vita di Francesco Arese: con documenti inediti* (Turin, 1894). See also Francesco Arese, *A Trip to the Prairies and in the Interior of North America, 1837–1838,* trans. and ed. Andrew Evans (New York, 1934); Lynn M. Case, ed., "The Middle West in 1837: Translations from the Notes of an Italian Count, Francesco Arese," *Mississippi Valley Historical Review,* XX (Dec. 1933), 381–399; and William R. Thayer, "An Italian Nobleman's Glimpse of Boston in 1837," *Massachusetts Historical Society Proceedings,* XLII (1909–10), 88–92.

Early cultural contacts are treated in a series of articles by Emilio Goggio. See "The Dawn of Italian Culture in America," *The Romanic Review,* X (July–Sept. 1919), 250–262; "Italy and the American War of Independence," *ibid.,* XX (Jan.–March 1929), 25–34; "Italian Educators in Early American Days," *Italica,* VIII (March 1931), 5–8, "Italian Educators in Early American Days," *Atlantica,* XI (June 1931), 255–256, 281; "First Personal Contacts between American and Italian Leaders of Thought," *The Romanic Review,* XXVII (1936), 1–8. See also Howard R. Marraro, "Pioneer Italian Teachers of Italian in the United States," *The Modern Language Journal,* XXVIII (Nov. 1944), 555–582; his "The Teaching of Italian in America in the Eighteenth Century," *ibid.,* XXV (Nov. 1940), 120–125; and Bruno Roselli, *Italian Yesterday and Today: A History of Italian Teaching in the United States* (Boston, 1935).

For the Italian view of America in histories and other books, see Charles R. D. Miller, "Some Early Italian Histories of the United States," *Italica,* VII (Dec. 1930), 103–106; Vincenzio Martinelli, *Istoria del governo d'Inghilterra e della sue colonie in India, e nell'America settentrionale . . .* (Florence, 1776); Vincenzio A. Formaleoni, *Teatro della guerra . . . fra la Gran Brettagna . . .* (Venice, 1781); Carlo Botta, *Storia della guerra dell'indipendenza degli Stati Uniti d'America,* 4 vols. (Paris, 1809). In English it is published as *History of the War of the Independence of the United States of America,* trans. George A. Otis, 2 vols. (7th edition, New Haven, 1837); Carlo Dionisotti, *Vita de Carlo Botta* (Turin, 1867) contains a full account of the writing of the *History;*

Carlo G. Londonio, *Storia delle colonie inglesi in America, della loro fondazione, fino allo stabilimente della loro indipendenza* (Milan, 1812–13); Luigi Angeloni, *Dell'Italia del 1818* . . . , 2 vols. (Paris, 1818) refers to the United States as a model for a united Italy; Giovanni A. Grassi, *Notizie varie sullo stato presente della repubblica degli Stati Uniti dell'America settentrionale* (Rome, 1818); Giusèppe Compagnoni, *Storia dell'America, in continuazione del compendio della storia universale* . . . , 28 vols. (Milan, 1820–22); Francesco Ageno, *I casi della guerra per l'independenza d'America* . . . , 3 vols. (Genoa, 1879); Dante Visconti, *Le origini degli Stati Uniti d'America e l'Italia* (Padua, 1940) is a study of the influence of the American Revolution in Italy showing the impact of culture and myths such as the "noble savage." Other significant specialized travel accounts are Paolo E. Botta, *Viaggio intorno al globo, principalmente alla California ed alle isola Sandwich* (Rome, 1841) and Carlo Barinetti, *A Voyage to Mexico and Havanna, Including Some General Observations on the United States* (New York, 1841).

CHAPTER 2: WANDERERS IN ARCADIA
Some works pertinent to topics in this chapter have been cited in the bibliographic commentary for the preceding chapter. There are in print a number of good books and articles on American artists, writers, and others in Italy. For an excellent analysis of pertinent literature as well as an interesting interpretation of the cultural premises of the Risorgimento see A. William Salomone, "The Nineteenth-Century Discovery of Italy: An Essay in American Cultural History. Prolegomena to a Historiographical Problem," *American Historical Review*, LXXIII (June 1968), 1359–91. The pioneer scholarly study of travelers in Italy which delineates the American image of the country is Giuseppe Prezzolini, *Come gli Americani scoprirono l'Italia, 1750–1850* (Milan, 1933). A charming account covering a longer period is Van Wyck Brooks, *The Dream of Arcadia: American Writers and Artists in Italy, 1760–1915* (New York, 1958), but it tells us little about ordinary Italians, of Italy herself, or how Americans there generally influenced American attitudes toward Italy. Brooks's *Literature in New England*, 2 vols. (Garden City, N.Y., 1936) also deals with writers in Italy. A more penetrating study covering a shorter period is Paul R. Baker, *The Fortunate Pilgrims: Americans in Italy, 1800–1860* (Cambridge, Mass, 1964). It explains what Americans saw and did and what aspects of Italian culture particularly impressed them. Nathalia Wright, *American Novelists in Italy. The Discoverers: Allston to James* (Phil., 1965) is concerned with the influence of Italy on American writers. See also Edgar P. Richardson and Otto Wittman, Jr., *Travelers in Arcadia: American Artists in Italy, 1830–1875* (Detroit, 1951), a catalog with an introductory essay; Otto Wittman, Jr., "The Italian Experience (American Artists in Italy, 1830–1875)," *American Quarterly*, IV (Spring 1952), 3–15; Madeleine B. Stern, "New England Artists in Italy, 1835–1855," *New England Quarterly*, XIV (June 1941), 243–271; Charles Edward Lester, *The Artists of America* (New York, 1846); Henry T. Tuckerman, *Book of the Artists: American Artist Life* . . . (New York, 1870); and James T. Flex-

ner, *That Wilder Image: The Painting of America's Native School from Thomas Cole to Winslow Homer* (Boston, 1962).

A number of general studies relate Italy to the broader European experience of nineteenth century Americans. Among the best is Cushing Strout, *The American Image of the Old World* (New York, 1963). *Discovery of Europe: The Story of American Experiences in the Old World,* Philip Rahv, ed. (Boston, 1947) and *The American in Europe: A Collection of Impressions Written by Americans from the Seventeenth Century to the Present,* Frank MacShane, ed. (New York, 1965) are anthologies. Hilton Anderson, "Americans in Europe before the Civil War," *The Southern Quarterly,* V (April 1967), 273–294 and Angelina La Piana, *La Cultura Americana e l'Italia* (Turin, 1938) deal with literary figures.

Geoffrey Trease, *The Grand Tour* (New York, 1967) is a popular account that covers the American as well as the British aspects. William E. Mead, *The Grand Tour in the Eighteenth Century* (Boston, 1914) and Paul F. Kirby, *The Grand Tour in Italy (1700–1800)* (New York, 1952) treat mainly the English travelers. For an account of the general interest in Italy see Carl P. Brand, *Italy and the English Romantics: The Italianate Fashion in Early Nineteenth Century England* (Cambridge, Eng., 1957).

Works that touch on specific minor topics in the chapter or that give useful background are Whitfield J. Bell, Jr., "Philadelphia Medical Students in Europe, 1750–1800," *Pennsylvania Magazine of History and Biography,* LXVIII (Jan. 1943), 1–29; John C. Greene, "American Science Comes of Age, 1780–1820," *Journal of American History,* LV (June 1968), 22–41; Antonio Pace, "Notes on Dr. John Morgan and His Relations with Italian Men and Women of Science," *Bulletin of the History of Medicine,* XVIII (Nov. 1945), 445–453; Carl and Jessica Bridenbaugh, *Rebels and Gentlemen: Philadelphia in the Age of Franklin* (New York, 1962). See also Marcello T. Maestro, *Voltaire and Beccaria as Reformers of Criminal Law* (New York, 1942); Humbert S. Nelli, "Cesare Beccaria and Penal Reform in Pennsylvania in the 1790's," *Archivio Storico Lombardo,* IV (1964–65), 162–170; and Samuel F. B. Morse, *Imminent Dangers to the Free Institutions of the United States through Foreign Immigration* (New York, 1835).

For information on various travelers and others who helped shape the American image of Italy see Emilio Goggio, "Italy and Some of Her Early American Commentators," *Italica,* X (March 1933), 4–10; Edward Dumbauld, *Thomas Jefferson, American Tourist* (Norman, Okla., 1946); Goggio, "Washington Irving and Italy," *The Romanic Review,* XXI (Jan.–March 1930), 26–33; [Theodore Lyman], *Rambles in Italy: in the Years 1816 . . . 1817 by an American . . .* (Baltimore, 1818); William Berrian, *Travels in France and Italy in 1817 and 1818* (New York, 1821) contains a perceptive analysis of relations between American travelers and Italians; N. H. Carter, *Letters from Europe, Comprising the Journal of a Tour through Ireland, England, Scotland, France, Italy, and Switzerland in the Years 1825, '26, and '27,* 2 vols. (2nd edition, New York, 1829); George Ticknor, *Life, Letters, and Journals of George Ticknor,* 2 vols. (Boston, 1876); David B. Tyack, *George Ticknor and the Boston Brahmins* (Cambridge, Mass., 1967); James Fenimore Cooper, *Correspondence of James Fenimore Cooper*, ed. [by his grandson] James F. Cooper, 2 vols. (New Haven, 1922); and Cooper, *Excursions in Italy* (Paris, 1838) is often considered the most perceptive study of Italy by an American of this period; Goggio, "Cooper's Bravo in Italy," *Romanic Review*, XX (July–Sept. 1929), 222–230; Goggio, "Italian Influences in Longfellow's Works," *Romanic Review*, XVI (July–Sept. 1925), 208–222; *Life of Henry Wadsworth Longfellow with Extracts from His Journals and Correspondence*, Samuel Longfellow, ed., 3 vols. (Boston, 1891); Oliver W. Larkin, "Two Yankee Painters in Italy: Thomas Cole and Samuel Morse," *American Quarterly*, V (Fall 1953), 195–200; Rembrandt Peale, *Notes on Italy by Rembrandt Peale* (Phil., 1831); James Jackson Jarves, *Italian Rambles* (New York, 1833); Jarves, *Italian Sights and Papal Principles Seen Through American Spectacles* (New York, 1856); *Letters of Francis Parkman*, Wilbur R. Jacobs, ed., 2 vols. (Norman, Okla., 1960); Henry James, *William Wetmore Story and His Friends: From Letters, Diaries, and Recollections*, 2 vols. (Boston, 1903); William W. Story, *Graffiti d'Italia* (New York, 1868); Henry T. Tuckerman, *The Italian Sketch Book* (2nd. ed., Boston, 1837); William M. Gillespie, *Rome: As Seen by a New Yorker in 1843–44* (New York, 1845); Wayne Craven, "Henry Kirke Brown in Italy, 1842–1846," *The American Art Journal*, I (Spring 1969), 65–77; George S. Hillard, *Six Months in Italy* (Boston, 1853) was the most popular book of its time by an American on Italy; and Charles E. Lester, *My Consulship*, 2 vols. (New York, 1853).

CHAPTER 3 : RISORGIMENTO

A useful bibliographical article for this chapter is Donald C. McKay, "Storici americani sul Risorgimento," *Rassegna storica del Risorgimento*, XLI (1940), 404–409. Two essays by William A. Salomone, "Statecraft and Ideology in the *Risorgimento*," *Italica*, XXXVIII (Sept. 1961), 163–194 and "The Risorgimento between Ideology and History: The Political Myth of *rivoluzione mancata*," *American Historical Review*, LXVIII (Oct. 1962), 38–56 offer interpretation and bibliographical commentary. Giorgio Spini, *Risorgimento e Protestanti* (Naples, 1956) discusses American Protestant activity during the *Risorgimento*. See also Agostino Lombardo, et al., *Italia e Stati Uniti nell' età del Risorgimento e della guerra civile: atti del II symposium di studi Americani, Firenze, 27–29 maggio 1966* (Florence, 1969), a collection of essays.

The basic book for the American reaction is Howard R. Marraro, *American Opinion on the Unification of Italy, 1846–1861* (New York, 1932). Although a Ph.D. dissertation filled with too much detail, it is an excellent source. Marraro also edited American diplomatic correspondence for this period. See his *L'unificazione italiana vista dai diplomatici statunitensi (1848–1861)*, 2 vols. (Rome, 1963–64) and his essay "Il Risorgimento italiano e gli Stati Uniti," *Mondo Occidentale: Revista bimestrale di politica e di varia cultura*, VIII (April 1961), 17–23. Sexson E. Humphreys, "The Attitude Toward Moderate Liberalism Expressed by United States Envoys in Italy during the Risorgimento," *Atti del XXXVII Con-*

gresso de Storia del Risorgimento Italiano (1958), pp. 132–138 and Roy M. Peterson, "Echoes of the Italian Risorgimento in Contemporaneous American Writers," *PMLA,* XLVII (March 1932), 220–240, trace and analyze two aspects of the American reaction to the *Risorgimento,* one diplomatic and political and the other literary and intellectual. James A. Field, Jr., *America and the Mediterranean World, 1776–1882* (Princeton, 1969) concentrates on missionary and economic activity, devoting little space to Italy and much to the broad context of the eastern Mediterranean world. Louis Baker, *A View of the Commerce of the United States and the Mediterranean Sea-Ports . . .* (Phil., 1847) is based on the manuscript of John M. Baker who was for forty years an American consul in the Mediterranean area.

For the upheavals of 1848 see Priscilla Robertson, *Revolutions of 1848: A Social History* (Princeton, 1952); Antonio Caccia, *Europe ed America: scene della vita dal 1848 al 1850* (Monaco, 1850); Arthur J. May, "America and the Revolutions of the Middle of the Last Century," *The Opening of an Era, 1848: An Historical Symposium,* François Fejtö, ed. (New York, 1948), pp. 204–222; George M. Trevelyan, *Manin and the Venetian Revolution of 1848* (London, 1923); and Merle E. Curti, "Young America," *American Historical Review,* XXXII (Oct. 1926), 34–54 which deals with revolutions' impact on the United States.

Various aspects of American relations with the Two Sicilies are discussed in seven articles by Marraro. See "William Pinkney's Mission to the Kingdom of the Two Sicilies, 1816," *Maryland Historical Magazine,* XLIII (Dec. 1948), 235–265; "John James Appleton's Mission to Naples (1825–1826)," *Journal of Central European Affairs,* IX (Jan. 1950), 404–418; "John Nelson's Mission to the Kingdom of the Two Sicilies, 1831–1832," *Maryland Historical Magazine,* XLIV (Sept. 1949), 149–176; "Auguste Davezac's Mission to the Kingdom of the Two Sicilies 1833–1834," *The Louisiana Historical Quarterly,* XXXII (1949), 791–808; "William H. Polk's Mission to Naples, 1845–1847," *Tennessee Historical Quarterly,* IV (Sept. 1945), 222–231; "John Rowan's Mission to the Two Sicilies (1848–1850)," *The Register of the Kentucky Historical Society,* XLIII (July 1945), 263–271; and "Edward Jay Morris' Mission to Naples (1850–1853)," *Pennsylvania History,* XII (Oct. 1945), 270–291. See also Vincenzo Giura, *Russia, Stati Uniti d'America e Regno di Napoli nell'età del Risorgimento* (Naples, 1967); Charles Moran, "Commodore Preble's Sicilian Auxiliaries," *United States Naval Institute Proceedings* (Jan. 1939), pp. 80–82; Louis M. Sears, "Robert Dale Owen's Mission to Naples," *Indiana History Bulletin,* VI, Extra No. 2 (May 1929), 43–51; Richard W. Leopold, *Robert Dale Owen: A Biography* (Cambridge, Mass., 1940); Sexson E. Humphreys, "New Considerations on the Mission of Robert Dale Owen to the Kingdom of the Two Sicilies," *Indiana Magazine of History,* XLVI (March 1950), 1–24. Paul C. Perrotta, *The Claims of the United States against the Kingdom of Naples* (Washington, D.C., 1926) is a doctoral dissertation that gives the fullest treatment of the subject; and Samuel Eliot Morison, *"Old Bruin:" Commodore Matthew C. Perry, 1794–1858* (Boston, 1967).

Diplomatic relations with Sardinia and other Italian states are discussed in seven articles by Marraro. See his "Ambrose Baber at the Court of Sardinia (1841–43)," *The Georgia Historical Quarterly*, XXX (June 1946), 105–117; "An American Diplomat Views the Dawn of Liberalism in Piedmont (1843–1848)," *Journal of Central European Affairs*, VI (July 1946), 167–196; "Nathaniel Niles' Missions at the Court of Turin (1838, 1848–1850)," *Vermont Quarterly*, XV (Jan. 1947), 14–32; "Spezia: An American Naval Base, 1848–68," *Military Affairs*, VII (Winter 1943), 202–208; "William Burnet Kinney's Mission to the Kingdom of Sardinia (1850–1853)," *Proceedings of the New Jersey Historical Society*, LXIV (Oct. 1946), 187–215; "Relazioni ufficiali fra il Granducato di Toscano e gli Stati Uniti d'America (1848–1959)," *Rassegna storica toscana*, V (July–Dec. 1959), 303–319; "Documenti americani sul conflitto italo-austriaco del 1859," *Rassegna storica del Risorgimento*, XLI (Jan.–March 1959), 3–44; and Sexson E. Humphreys, "United States Recognition of the Kingdom of Italy," *The Historian*, XXI (May 1959), 296–312. See also Henry Wikoff, *The Reminiscences of an Idler* (New York, 1880), a man whose escapades in Piedmont caused difficulties.

For the influence and fate of Italian exiles in the United States see "Italians in America," *Putnam's Monthly*, XLIX (Jan. 1857), 1–8 provides sympathetic sketches; Angelina H. Lograsso, "Piero Maroncelli in America," *Rassegna storica del Risorgimento*, XV (1928), 894–941; Lograsso, "Piero Maroncelli in Philadelphia," *Romanic Review*, XXIV (Oct.–Dec. 1933), 323–329; Lograsso, "Poe's Piero Maroncelli," *PMLA*, LVIII (March 1943), 780–789; Lograsso, *Piero Maroncelli* (Romo, 1958) is especially useful for its discussion of Italian opera in the United States and the New England intellectuals and Italy; Pietro D'Alessandro, "Letters of an Italian Exile," *Southern Literary Messenger*, VIII (Dec. 1842), 741–748; Marraro, "Eleutario Felice Foresti," *Dictionary of American Biography*, VI, 522–523; "The Fate of the Carbonari: Memoirs of Felice Foresti," Marraro, trans., *Columbia University Quarterly*, XXIV (Dec. 1932), 441–475; Marraro, "Eleutario Felice Foresti," *ibid.*, XXV (March 1933), 34–64, the basic article on Foresti; Marraro, "Italians in New York in the Eighteen Fifties," *New York History*, XXX (April 1949), 181–203; (July 1949), pp. 276–303; Marraro, "Gli italiani negli stati uniti d'America," *Il Veltro: Rassegna di vita italiana*, V (May–June 1961), 111–132 reviews the years before 1860; Angelina H. Lograsso, "Silvio Pellico in the United States," *International Comparative Literature Association, Proceedings of the Congress*, II, No. 2 (Chapel Hill, N.C., 1959), pp. 429–443 deals mainly with the fate of *Le mie prigioni* in the United States.

For diplomatic problems see Alberto M. Ghisalberti, "Il primo rappresentante degli Stati Uniti a Roma," *Rassegna storica del Risorgimento*, XXVIII (1951), 3–20; *United States Ministers to the Papal States: Instructions and Dispatches, 1848–1868*, Leo F. Stock, ed. (Washington, D.C., 1933) and *Consular Relations between the United States and the Papal States: Instructions and Dispatches* (Washington, D.C., 1945) are two volumes of documents on official relations. Stock, "The United States at the Court of Pius IX," *Catholic Historical Review*, III (April 1923),

103–122; Stock, "The United States and the Vatican—Past Diplomatic Relations," *Carnegie Institution of Washington, News Service Bulletin,* No. 10 (1929), pp. 57–61; Joseph F. Thorning, "American Notes in Vatican Diplomacy," *United States Catholic Historical Society, Historical Records and Studies,* XX (1931), 7–27; and Loretta C. Feiertag, *American Public Opinion on the Diplomatic Relations between the United States and the Papal States (1847–1867)* (Washington, D.C., 1933).

There is an extensive literature on revolutionary leaders such as Mazzini and Garibaldi but only some of it is pertinent to Italian-American relations. One of the best studies showing Mazzini's broad influence among Americans is Joseph Rossi, *The Image of America in Mazzini's Writings* (Madison, Wis., 1954). See also Evelina Rinaldi, "Giuseppe Mazzini e gli Stati Uniti d'America," *Rassegna storica del Risorgimento,* XIX (1932), 428–433; Sexson E. Humphreys, "Mazzini e il falso nome di Brown," *ibid.,* XLVI (April–Sept. 1959), 28; H. Bolton King, *The Life of Mazzini* (New York, 1911); Gaetano Salvemini, *Mazzini,* trans. I. M. Rawson (Stanford, Calif., 1957); and Giuseppe Avezzana, *I miei ricordi* (Naples, 1881).

Garibaldi's exploits have received considerable attention. George M. Trevelyan's trilogy: *Garibaldi's Defense of the Roman Republic* (London, 1907), *Garibaldi and the Thousand* (London, 1909), and *Garibaldi and the Making of Italy: June–November 1860* (London, 1911) is virtually considered a classic. For excellent short studies see Denis Mack Smith, *Garibaldi: A Great Life in Brief* (New York, 1956) and Christopher Hibbert, *Garibaldi and His Enemies: The Clash of Arms and Personalities in the Making of Italy* (Boston, 1966). A well-written popular book is George Martin, *The Red Shirt and the Cross of Savoy: The Story of Italy's Risorgimento (1748–1871)* (New York, 1969). For specific experiences in America or involving Americans see Elsa Feraboli, "Il primo esilio di Garibaldi in America," *Rassegna storica del Risorgimento,* XIX (1932), 247–282 which deals with the South American experience; H. Nelson Gay, "Il secondo esilio di Garibaldi da documenti inediti," *Nuova antologia,* CXLVII (1910), 635–659; Marraro, "Garibaldi in New York," *New York History,* XXVII (April 1946), 179–203; Marraro, "Documenti italiani e americani sulla spedizione garibaldina in Sicilia," *Rassegna storica del Risorgimento,* XLIII (Aug.–Sept. 1956), 463–472; Gay, "Garibaldi's Sicilian Campaign as Reported by an American Diplomat," *American Historical Review,* XXVII (Jan. 1922), 234–238; Gay, "Garibaldi's American Contacts and His Claims to American Citizenship," *ibid.,* XXXVIII (Oct. 1932), 1–19; Francesco Moncada, "Incidents in Garibaldi's Life in America," *Atlantica* (Oct. 1932), 16–18; and Sexson E. Humphreys, "Two Garibaldian Incidents in American History," *Vermont History,* XXIII (April 1955), 135–143. For Cavour see William R. Thayer, *The Life and Times of Cavour,* 2 vols. (Boston, 1911) and Denis Mack Smith, *Cavour and Garibaldi, 1860: A Study in Political Conflict* (Cambridge, Eng., 1954).

The literature on Margaret Fuller is extensive. Basic are *Memoirs of Margaret Fuller Ossoli,* eds. R. W. Emerson, W. H. Channing, and J. F. Clarke, 2 vols. (Boston, 1874) and Sarah Margaret Fuller Ossoli, *Sojourn in Rome,* 2 vols. (New York, 1901). Good brief modern biographies are Mason Wade, *Margaret Fuller: Whetstone of Genius* (New York, 1940); Arthur W. Brown, *Margaret Fuller* (New York, 1964); and Joseph J. Deiss, *The Roman Years of Margaret Fuller* (New York, 1969) which stresses life in Italy. Specialized accounts touching on Italians and Americans are Leona Rostenberg, "Margaret Fuller's Roman Diary," *Journal of Modern History,* XII (Dec. 1940), 209–220; Rostenberg, "Mazzini to Margaret Fuller," *American Historical Review,* XLVII (Oct. 1941), 73–80; Anna Benedetti, "Mazzini e Margharita Fuller," *Nuova antologia,* CCLXXVII (Jan. 1918), 166–180; and Giovanni Mori, "An American Disciple of Mazzini," *Atlantica,* VII (Feb. 1929), 55–61. For background on the Roman Republic see R. M. Johnston, *The Roman Theocracy and the Republic, 1846–1849* (London, 1901); Theodore Dwight, *The Roman Republic of 1849* . . . (New York, 1851) is an angry Protestant book that discusses American attitudes toward the Italians; Marraro, "Unpublished American Documents on the Roman Republic of 1849," *The Catholic Historical Review,* XXVIII (Jan. 1943), 459–490; Sexson E. Humphreys, "Lewis Cass, Jr. and the Roman Republic of 1849," *Michigan History,* XL (March 1956), 24–50; and Humphreys, "Lewis Cass, Jr. and Pope Pius IX, 1850–1858," *ibid.,* XLI (June 1957), 129–161.

Various aspects of the Italian-American relationship pertinent to this chapter are touched upon in the following works: Marraro, "American Travellers in Rome, 1848–1850," *The Catholic Historical Review,* XXIX (Jan. 1944), 470–509; Marraro, "Viaggiatori americani in Italia durante il Risorgimento," *Rassegna storica del Risorgimento,* LIV (Oct.–Dec. 1967), 524–547; Horace Greeley, *Glances at Europe* (New York, 1851); Henry A. Brann, *Most Reverend John Hughes, First Archbishop of New York* (New York, 1892); Alessandro Gavazzi, *The Lectures Complete of Father Gavazzi* (New York, 1854), the speeches given in the United States; James B. Angell, *Reminiscences* (New York, 1912); William Cullen Bryant, *Letters of a Traveller: or, Notes of Things Seen in Europe and America* (New York, 1850); Henry Adams, *The Education of Henry Adams* (Boston, 1918); Daniel Varè, *Ghosts of the Spanish Steps* (London, 1955) has a chapter on Henry Adams as a young man in Rome, "Henry Adams and Garibaldi, 1860," [J. Franklin Jameson], ed., *American Historical Review,* XXV (Jan. 1920), 241–255; *Testimonianze americane sull'Italia del Risorgimento,* Elisabeth Mann Borgese, ed. (Milan, 1961) is an anthology; Charles Eliot Norton, *Notes of Travel and Study in Italy* (Boston, 1860); *Letters of Charles Eliot Norton,* with biographical comment by his daughter Sara Norton and M. A. DeWolfe Howe, 2 vols. (Boston, 1913); Kermit Vanderbilt, *Charles Eliot Norton: Apostle of Culture in a Democracy* (Cambridge, Mass., 1959); Joseph Rossi, *"Uncle Tom's Cabin* and Protestantism in Italy," *American Quarterly,* XI (Fall 1959), 416–424; James Woodress, *"Uncle Tom's Cabin* in Italy," *Essays on American Literature in Honor of Jay B. Hubbell,* ed. Clarence Gohdes (Durham, N.C., 1967), pp. 128–140; Nathaniel Hawthorne, *Passages from the French and Italian Note-Books* (Boston, 1872); William Arthur, *Italy in Transition: Public Scenes and Private*

Opinions in the Spring of 1860 (New York, 1860); Frederika Bremer, *Life in the Old World; or, Two Years in Switzerland and Italy,* 2 vols. (Phil., 1860); Leonetto Cipriani, *Avventura della mia vita,* 2 vols. (Bologna, 1934); Cipriani, *California and Overland Diaries from 1853 through 1871,* trans. and ed. Ernest Falbo (Portland, Ore., 1962). The bibliographies for previous chapters also contain relevant works.

CHAPTER 4: UNIFICATION AND EMIGRATION

For diplomatic and general relations between the emerging Italian nation and the United States see H. Nelson Gay, "La relazioni fra l'Italia e gli Stati Uniti (1847–1871)," *Nuova antologia,* CCXI (1907), 657–671; Mary P. Trauth, *Italo-American Diplomatic Relations, 1861–1882: The Mission of George Perkins Marsh, First American Minister to the Kingdom of Italy* (Washington, D.C., 1958); David Lowenthal, "George Perkins Marsh," unpubl. diss. (University of Wisconsin, 1954); Mrs. Caroline (Crane) Marsh, *Life and Letters of George Perkins Marsh,* 2 vols. (New York, 1888); "Young Italy and her American Allies," *United States Catholic Magazine,* IV (1845), 540–542 attacks the "politico-religious" Christian Alliance; Joseph T. Durkin, "The Early Years of Italian Unification as Seen by an American Diplomat, 1861–70," *The Catholic Historical Review,* XXX (Oct. 1944), 271–289; Howard R. Marraro, "Mazzini on American Intervention in European Affairs," *Journal of Modern History,* XXI (June 1949), 109–114; "Letters Concerning the 'Universal Republic'," W. F. Galpin, ed., *American Historical Review,* XXXIV (July 1929), 779–786; Moncure D. Conway, *Autobiography: Memories and Experiences,* 2 vols. (New York, 1904) contains firsthand observations of Mazzini; Marraro, "The Religious Problem of the Risorgimento as Seen by Americans," *Church History,* XXV (March 1956), 41–62.

Raimondo Luraghi, *Storia della guerra civile americana* (Turin, 1966), the first general history of the Civil War published in Italy, views the conflict as part of the broad nineteenth century movement of national unification and industrial revolution that swept over Italy and Europe. For other aspects of the Italian reaction to the American sectional crisis see Augusto Pau, *Abramo Lincoln e la guerra fra i federali ed i confederati negli Stati Uniti,* 2 vols. (Leghorn, 1866–68); Luigi Taparelli d'Azeglio, "La disunione negli Stati Uniti," *Civiltà Cattolica,* series IV, IX (1861), pp. 312–324; L. Bertolozzi, "La schiavitù e la guerra civile in America," *Letture serali del popolo,* I (1862–63), 378–379; II (1863–1864), 21; Augusto Bosco, "La schiavitù e la questione dei neri negli Stati Uniti," *Rivista italiana di sociologia,* II (1898), 207–224; Vincenzo Botta, "La questione americana," *Rivista contemporanea,* XXVI (1861), 141–152, 241–255; XXIX (1862), 250–267 deals with slavery, Negroes, and race; Marraro, "Italy and Lincoln," *The Abraham Lincoln Quarterly,* III (March 1944), 3–16; Marraro, "Lincoln's Italian Volunteers from New York," *New York History,* XXIV (1943), 56–67; Marraro, "Volunteers from Italy for Lincoln's Army," *The South Atlantic Quarterly,* XLIV (Oct. 1945), 384–396; Gay, "Lincoln's Offer of a Command to Garibaldi: Light on a Disputed Point of History," *Century*

Magazine, LXXV (Nov. 1907), 63–74; Marraro, "Lincoln's Offer of a Command to Garibaldi: Further Light on a Disputed Point of History," *Journal of the Illinois State Historical Society,* XXXVI (Sept. 1943), 237–270; Raimondo Luraghi, "Il mito e popolarità di Garibaldi nel sud degli Stati Uniti," *Miscellanea di storica ligura* [Milan] (March 1966), pp. 399–412; Giuseppe L. Capobianco, "L'integrale messagio di Abramo Lincoln a Macedonio Melloni, tradotto e diffuso da Giuseppe Mazzini," *Rassegna storica del Risorgimento,* XVIII (1931), 460–467; Eugenio Casanova, "A proposito della lettera de Abramo Lincoln a Macedonio Melloni," *ibid.,* pp. i–viii; Vincenzo Botta, *Resolutions on the Death of President Lincoln . . . at the Meeting of the Italian Residents of New York Held at the Cooper Institute, April 23, 1865 . . .* (New York, 1865); Ella Lonn, *Foreigners in the Confederacy* (Chapel Hill, N.C., 1940) points out that a a battalion of Italian Guards served in the Confederate army; Francesco Gallo, *Biografia del generale americane e console in Cipro, Luigi Palma de Cesnola da Rivarolo Canavese* (Vercelli, 1869); Decimus et Ultimus Barziza, *The Adventures of a Prisoner of War, 1863–1864* (Austin, Tex., 1965) provides data on an Italian-American in Texas.

For the American reaction to events in Italy see Francis J. Grund, *Thoughts and Reflections on the Present Position of Europe and Its Probable Consequences to the United States* (Phil., 1860) which contains a great deal on Italian affairs; H. Nelson Gay, *Scritti sul Risorgimento,* ed. Tomaso Sillani (Rome, 1937) is a collection of works covering various aspects of Italian-American relations; ten articles by Marraro, "American Opinion on Sardinia's Participation in the Crimean War," *South Atlantic Quarterly,* XLVI (Oct. 1947), 496–510; "American Opinion and Documents on Garibaldi's March on Rome, 1862," *Journal of Central European Affairs,* VII (July 1947), 143–161; "Unpublished American Documents on the Battle of Lissa (1866)," *Journal of Modern History,* XIV (Sept. 1942), 342–356; "American Documents on Italy's Annexation of Venetia (1866)," *Journal of Central European Affairs,* V (Jan. 1946), 354–377; "American Opinion on Italy's Annexation of Venetia in 1866," *The South Atlantic Quarterly,* XLVIII (July 1949), 384–400; "Unpublished Documents on Garibaldi's March on Rome in 1867," *The Journal of Modern History, XVI* (June 1944), 116–123; "Canadian and American Zouaves in the Papal Army, 1868–1870," *Canadian Catholic Historical Association Report* (1944–1945), pp. 83–102; "The Closing of the American Diplomatic Mission to the Vatican and Efforts to Revive It, 1868–1870," *The Catholic Historical Review,* XXXIII (Jan. 1948), 423–447; "Unpublished American Documents on Italy's Occupation of Rome," *Journal of Modern History,* XIII (March 1941), 48–64; "American Opinion on the Occupation of Rome in 1870," *South Atlantic Quarterly,* LIV (April 1955), 221–242. See also Leo F. Stock, "An American Consul Joins the Papal Zouaves," *Catholic World,* CXXXII (Oct. 1930), 145–150; Stock, "American Consuls to the Papal States, 1797–1870," *The Catholic Historical Review,* XV (Oct. 1929), 233–251; R. DeCesare, *The Last Days of Papal Rome, 1850–1870,* trans Helen Zimmern (New York, 1909); Robert W. Bohl,

"I documenti diplomatici statunitensi sulla questione veneta," *Rassegna storica del Risorgimento,* LIII (Oct.–Dec. 1966), 615–621; James L. Woodress, Jr., *Howells and Italy* (Durham, N.C., 1952) views Howells as playing "a vital part in fostering the cultural affinity which existed between the United States and Italy in his lifetime"; Edward Wagenknecht, *William Dean Howells: The Friendly Eye* (New York, 1969); Robert L. Gale, "Henry James and Italy," *Studi Americani,* III (1957), 189–203 is a perceptive and important article; Christof Wegelin, *The Image of Europe in Henry James* (Dallas, 1958); Henry James, *Italian Hours* (Boston, 1909), James, *The American Scene,* ed. W. H. Auden (New York, 1946); Leon Edel, *Henry James,* 4 vols. (Phil., 1953–1969), William J. Stillman, *The Autobiography of a Journalist,* 2 vols. (New York, 1901), Bayard Taylor, *At Home and Abroad: A Sketch-Book of Life, Scenery and Men* (New York, 1860).

For the views of Italians who visited the United States see Andrew J. Torrielli, *Italian Opinion on America as Revealed by Italian Travelers, 1850–1900* (Cambridge, Mass., 1941), a fine source based on solid scholarship; Giulio Adamoli, *Da San Martino a Mentana: Ricordi di un volontario* (Milan, 1892) has for its author a fighter for unification who visited the United States; Luigi Adamoli, "Letters from America, I and II," *The Living Age,* CCCXIII (March 1922), 582–593, 716–721 [published originally in *Nuova antologia*]; Salvatore Cognetti de Martiis, *Gli Stati Uniti d'America nel 1876* (Milan, 1877), commentaries of a journalist; Giacomo F. Airoli, *Democrazia americana* (Città di Castello, 1887) analyzes American life as a model for Italy; Elena Albana, "Corrispondenza da Boston," *Revista europea,* I (1871), 136–137, 361–364; II (1871), 160–165, 334–335, 538–540; Luigi Arditi, *My Reminiscences,* ed. Marie Antoinette Von Zeidlitz (New York, ·1896) is the collected memoirs of an Italian opera conductor who toured the United States. Also useful are three article by Vincenzo Botta, "Dell'istruzione pubblica negli Stati Uniti d'America," *Rivista contemporanea,* VI (1856), 695–727, VIII (1856), 495–519, "L'America all 'Italia," *Il mondo illustrato,* III (1860), 283; "Intorno la scuola italiana in Nuova York," *Il Politecnico,* XXII (1864), 200–207 as well as Charlotte Adams, "Italian Life in New York," *Harper's New Monthly Magazine,* LXII (April 1881), 676–684.

Works on immigration are treated extensively in the bibliographical commentary for the next chapter but these studies touch on problems discussed within this chapter. Antonio A. Arrighi, *The Story of Antonio the Galley-Slave* (New York, 1911), an account by a young soldier who served with Garibaldi before making his way to the United States; Giovanni Florenzano, *Della emigrazione italiana in America comparata alle altre emigrazione europèo* (Naples, 1874); Attilio Brunialti, *Le colonie degli italiani* (Turin, 1897); Leone Carpi, *Delle colonie e dell'emigrazione d'italiani all'estero sotto l'aspetto dell'industria, commercio, agricoltura e con trattazione d'importante questioni sociali,* 4 vols. (Milan, 1874), an early broad study of Italian emigration; Celso C. Moreno, *History of a Great Wrong: Italian Slavery in America (Schiavitù italiana in America)* ([Washington], 1895) is a pamphlet attack on the *padrone* traffic in children; and Robert H. Woody, "The Labor and Immigration Problem of South Carolina during Reconstruction," *Mississippi Valley Historical Review,* XVIII (Sept. 1931), 196–202 mentions early efforts to attract Italian labor. Also see references to the preceding chapters and the following one.

CHAPTER 5: FLOOD TIDE

The immigrant theme in American history has produced a literature that is steadily improving in quality. Much of it is discussed in Franklin D. Scott, *Emigration and Immigration* (2nd ed., Washington, D.C., 1966). Oscar Handlin, *The Uprooted: The Epic Story of the Great Migrations that Made the American People* (Boston, 1951) is a basic though impressionistic study that stresses the theme of alienation. Andrew F. Rolle, *The Immigrant Upraised* (Norman, Okla., 1968) challenges the Handlin interpretation by emphasizing accommodation and upward mobility. Handlin's work is broad while Rolle concentrates on Italians. Although the works of Marcus Lee Hansen give little space to Italians they are useful pioneer studies. See his *The Atlantic Migration, 1607–1860* (Cambridge, Mass., 1951) and *The Immigrant in American History* (Cambridge, Mass., 1940). Maldwyn A. Jones, *American Immigration* (Chicago, 1960) and Carl Wittke, *We Who Built America: The Saga of the Immigrant* (rev. ed., Cleveland, 1964) deals with Italian immigration in a broad context. For the European background see *International Migrations,* Walter F. Willcox, ed., 2 vols. (New York, 1929 31); Donald R. Taft and Richard Robbins, *International Migrations: The Immigrant in the Modern World* (New York, 1955); and Alfred Legoyt, *L'émigration européenne, son importance, ses courses, et ses effets* (Paris, 1861).

For Italian emigration see Robert F. Foerster, *The Italian Emigration of Our Times* (Cambridge, Mass., 1919), considered by scholars as one of the finest studies of the mass migration of a people. See also Renzo De Felice, "L'emigrazione e gli emigranti nell'ultimo secolo," *Terza Programma,* III (No. 3, 1964), 152–198, a broad interpretive essay; René Le Conte, *Étude sur l'émigration italienne* (Paris, 1908); Paolo E. de Luca, *Della emigrazione europea ed in particolare di quella italiana,* 4 vols. (Turin, 1909–1910); Egisto Rossi, *Del patronato degli emigranti in Italia e all estero* (Genoa, 1893); Guglielmo Godio, *L'America ne'suoi primi fattori: la colonizzazione e l'emigrazione* (Florence, 1893); Luigi Villari, *Gli Stati Uniti d'America e l'emigrazione italiana* (Milan, 1912), a treatment critical of the United States; Harry Jerome, *Migration and Business Cycles* (New York, 1926); Giovanni B. Scalabrini, *Il disegno di legge sulla'emigrazione italiana* (Piacenza, 1888); Luigi Bodio, "Dell'emigrazione italiane e dell'applicazione della legge 31 gennaio 1901," *Bollettino dell'Emigrazione* (1902), No. 8, pp. 9, 21; Gino C. Speranza, "The Italian Immigration Department in 1904," *The Survey,* XV (Oct. 21, 1905), 114–116; and Booker T. Washington, "Naples and the Land of the Emigrant," *Outlook,* XCVIII (June 10, 1911), 295–300, an interesting Negro commentary.

Among the numerous accounts of Italian immigrant life and immigration the following are especially useful and rewarding: Eugene Schuyler,

"Italian Immigration into the United States," *Political Science Quarterly,*
IV (Sept. 1889), 480–495; Pacifico Capitani, *La questione italiana negli
Stati Uniti d'America* (Cleveland, 1891); Vincenzo Grossi, "L'emigra-
zione italiana in America," *Nuova antologia,* LV (1895), 740–757;
Grossi, *Gli italiani in America* (Rome, 1902); Costantino Ottolenghi,
"La nuova fase dell'emigrazione del'lavoro agli Stati Uniti," *Giornale
degli economisti e annali di economia,* XVIII (April 1899), 332–385
shows how emigration responded to economic forces; Kate H. Claghorn,
"The Changing Character of Immigration," *Public Opinion,* XXX (Feb.
14, 1901), 205–206; Elliot Lord et al., *The Italian in America* (2nd ed.,
New York, 1905); G. E. di Palma Castiglione, "Italian Immigration into
the United States 1901–04," *American Journal of Sociology,* XI (Sept.
1905), 183–206; John F. Carr, "The Italian in the United States,"
World's Work, VIII (Oct. 1904), 5393–5404; Carr, "The Coming of the
Italian," *Outlook,* LXXXII (Feb. 24, 1906), 418–431; *Gli italiani negli
Stati Uniti d'America,* Luigi, Aldrovandi, ed. (New York, 1906); Salvatore Mondello, "Italian Migration to the U.S. as Reported in American
Magazines, 1880–1920," *Social Science,* XXXIX (June 1964), 131–142
shows that the American reaction was generally unfavorable; Mondello,
"The Magazine *Charities* and the Italian Immigrants, 1903–14," *Journal-
ism Quarterly,* XLIV (Spring 1967), 91–98 explains why the Progressives failed to reach the immigrants; William E. Davenport, "The Italian
Immigrant in America," *Outlook,* LXXIV (Jan. 3, 1903), 28–37; Ghe-
rardo Ferrari, *Gli italiani in America: impressioni di un viaggio agli Stati
Uniti* (Rome, 1907); Giovanni Preziosi, *Gl'italiani negli Stati Uniti del
Nord* (Milan, 1909) deplores the poor reputation of Italians in America,
denies the existence of a well-organized Black Hand society, and urges
education to achieve upward mobility; Alberto Pecorini, "The Italians
in the United States," *The Forum,* XLV (Jan. 1911), 15–29; Umberto
Coletti, "The Italian Immigrant," *National Conference on Social Welfare
Proceedings* (1912), pp. 249–254 tells of the work of the Society for
Italian Immigrants; Peter Roberts, *The New Immigration* (New York,
1914); De Ritis, "Italians in America," *The Living Age,* CCCXXIII
(Nov. 22, 1924), 433–36 is a perceptive essay on intellectuals and their
resistance to assimilation; Allen H. Eaton, *Immigrant Gifts to American
Life* (New York, 1932) is a sentimental commentary; Phyllis H. Williams,
South Italian Folkways in Europe and America (New Haven, 1938);
Robert E. Park and Herbert A. Miller, *Old World Traits Transplanted*
(New York, 1921); Park, *The Immigrant Press and Its Control* (New
York, 1922); Eliot G. Mears, "Financial Aspects of American Immigra-
tion," *Economic Journal,* XXXIII (Sept. 1923), 332–342; Stefano Miele,
"America as a Place to Make Money," *World's Work,* XLI (Dec. 1920),
204–206; Baldo Aquilano, *L'ordine figli d'Italia in America* (New York,
1925); and Ida L. Hull, "Special Problems in Italian Families," *National
Conference on Social Welfare Proceedings* (1924), pp. 288–291, analyzes
the conflicts between first and second generation in the United States.

Some of the best accounts of immigrant life deal with specific localities
such as a city or neighborhood. The following are good examples of such
literature: Humbert S. Nelli, "Italians in Urban America: A Study in

Ethnic Adjustment," *The International Migration Review*, I (Summer 1967), 38–55, an imporant essay that attacks old myths; Lillian W. Betts, "Italian Peasants in a New Law Tenement," *Harper's Bazaar*, XXXVIII (Aug. 8, 1904), 802–805; Betts, "The Italian in New York," *University Settlement Studies* (Oct. 1905–Jan. 1906), pp. 90–105; Antonio Mangano, "The Associated Life of the Italians in New York City," *The Survey*, XII (May 7, 1904), 476–482; Thomas J. Jones, *The Sociology of a New York City Block* (New York, 1904); Pietro Acritelli, "Il contributo degli italiani alla prosperità materiale della città di New York," *L'Italia coloniale*, I (Jan.–Feb. 1904), 36–40; Louise C. Odencrantz, *Italian Women in Industry: A Study of Conditions in New York City* (New York, 1919); David Ward, "The Emergence of Central Immigrant Ghettoes in American Cities. 1840–1920," *Annals of the Association of American Geographers*, LVIII (June 1968), 343–359 uses Boston as an example; Frederick A. Bushée, "Italian Immigrants in Boston," *Arena*, XVII (April 1897), 722–734; *Americans in Process: A Settlement Study*, Robert A. Woods, ed. (Boston, 1903) deals with Boston's North and West Ends; Woods, "Notes on Italians in Boston," *The Survey*, XII (May 7, 1904), 451–452; Vida D. Scudder, "Experiments in Fellowship: Work with Italians in Boston," *ibid.*, 47–51; Oscar Handlin, *Boston's Immigrants* (rev. ed., Cambridge, Mass., 1959); Emily W. Dinwiddie, "Some Aspects of Italian Housing and Social Conditions in Philadelphia," *The Survey*, XII (May 7, 1904), 490–493; Joan Y. Dickinson, "Aspects of Italian Immigration to Philadelphia," *Pennsylvania Magazine of History and Biography*, XC (Oct. 1966), 445–465; Grace P. Norton, "Chicago Housing Conditions, VII: Two Italian Districts," *American Journal of Sociology*, XVIII (Jan. 1913), 509–542; John R. Vecoli, "Chicago's Italians Prior to World War II: A Study of Their Social and Economic Adjustment," unpubl. diss. (University of Wisconsin, 1962); Vecoli, *"Contadini* in Chicago: A Critique of *The Uprooted,"* *Journal of American History*, LI (Dec. 1964), 404–417; Humbert S. Nelli, "The Role of the 'Colonial Press' in the Italian-American Community of Chicago, 1886–1921," unpubl. diss. (University of Chicago, 1965); Giorgio La Piana, *The Italians in Milwaukee, Wisconsin* (Milwaukee, 1915); Charles W. Coulter, *The Italians of Cleveland* (Cleveland, 1919), a pamphlet.

For the views of social and settlement house workers see Charles Loring Brace, *The Life of Charles Loring Brace* . . . , ed. Emma Brace (New York, 1894); Elizabeth Gilman, "Italian Notes of a Social Worker," *The Survey*, XXI (March 27, 1909), 1264–67; Jane Addams, *Twenty Years at Hull House* (New York, 1910); and *The Second Twenty Years at Hull House* . . . (New York, 1930); Lillian D. Wald, *The House on Henry Street* (New York, 1915); Mary K. Simkovitch, *The City Worker's World in America* (New York, 1917); and *Neighborhood: My Story of Greenwich House* (New York, 1938).

Andrew F. Rolle has recorded Italian pioneering and settlement in the West. See his "The Italian Moves Westward," *Montana: The Magazine of Western History*, XVI (Winter 1966), 13–24; "Italy in California," *The Pacific Spectator*, IX (Autumn 1955), 408–419; and "Success in the Sun: The Italians in California," *The Westerners Brand Book, Book Nine,* ed. Henry H. Clifford (Los Angeles, 1961), pp. 13–31. See also Doris M. Wright, "The Making of Cosmopolitan California: An Analysis of Immigration, 1848–1870," *California Historical Society Quarterly,* XIX (Dec. 1940), 323–43; XX (March 1941), 65–79; Marius J. Spinello, "Italians of California," *Sunset,* XIV (Jan. 1905), 256–68; Ettore Patrizi, *Gli italiani in California, Stati Uniti d'America* (San Francisco, 1911); C. Dondero, "Asti, Sonoma County, an Italian-Swiss Agricultural Colony and What It Has Grown To," *Out West,* XVII (July–Dec. 1902), 253–266; Raymond S. Dondero, "The Italian Settlement of San Francisco Bay," unpubl. M.A. thesis (University of California, Berkeley); Giovanni Perilli, *Colorado and the Italians in Colorado* (Denver, 1922); Anthony M. Turano, "An Immigrant Father," *The American Mercury,* XXVII (Oct. 1932), 221–229 is a nostalgic account about the Italian community of Pueblo, Colorado.

The best analysis of the *padrone* as an institution is Humbert S. Nelli, "The Italian Padrone System in the United States," *Labor History,* V (Spring 1964), 153–167. See also S. Merlino, "Italian Immigrants and Their Enslavement," *The Forum,* XV (April 1893), 183–190; John Koren, "The Padrone System and Padrone Banks," *Bulletin of the Department of Labor,* No. 9 (Washington, D.C., March 1897), pp. 113–129; Gino C. Speranza, "The Italian Foreman as a Social Agent," *Charities,* XI (July 4, 1903), 26–28; Charles B. Phipard, "The Philanthropist-Padrone," *ibid.,* XII (May 7, 1904), 470–72; Allan McLaughlin, "Italian and Other Latin Immigrants," *Popular Science Monthly,* LXV (Aug. 1904), 341–349; Frank J. Sheridan, "Italian, Slavic, and Hungarian Unskilled Immigrant Laborers in the United States," *Bulletin of the Bureau of Labor,* XV, No. 72 (Washington, D.C., Sept. 1907), 403–486.

For Italian religious life in the United States the best scholarly account is Rudolph J. Vecoli, "Prelates and Peasants: Italian Immigrants and the Catholic Church," *Journal of Social History,* II (Spring 1969), 217–268. Also basic is Henry J. Browne, "The 'Italian Problem' in the Catholic Church of the United States, 1880–1900," *United States Catholic Historical Society Historical Records and Studies,* XXXV (New York, 1946), 46–72. See also Raffaele Bollerini, "Delle condizioni religiose degli emigrati italiani negli Stati Uniti d'America," *Civiltà Cattolica,* IX (1885), 129–140; Bernard J. Lynch, "The Italians in New York," *Catholic World,* XLIII (April 1886); John J. McNicholas, "The Need of American Priests for the Italian Missions," *The American Ecclesiastical Review,* XXXIX (Dec. 1908), 677–687; Antonio Mangano, *Sons of Italy: A Social and Religious Study of the Italians in America* (New York, 1917); Mangano, "What America Did for Leonardo," *World Outlook,* III (Oct. 1917), 10 summarizes Protestant missionary work among Italians; Frederick H. Wright, "How to Reach Italians in America: Shall They Be Segregated, 'Missioned,' Neglected or Welcomed?" *The Missionary Review of the World,* XL (Aug. 1917), 588–594, a Protestant concern; F. Aurelio Palmieri, "Italian Protestantism in the United States," *The Catholic World,* CVII (May 1918), 177–189; Palmieri, *Il grave problema religioso italiano negli stati uniti* (Florence, 1921); Philip M. Rose, *The*

Italians in America (New York, 1922), a Protestant assessment; Gerald Shaughnessey, *Has the Immigrant Kept the Faith? A Study of Immigration and Catholic Growth in the United States, 1790–1920* (New York, 1925). For Mother Cabrini see James J. Walsh, "An Apostle of the Italians," *Catholic World*, CVII (April 1918), 64–71; Theodore Maynard, *Too Small a World* (Milwaukee, 1945); and Pietro Di Donato, *Immigrant Saint* (New York, 1960). For the work and influence of Bishop Scalabrini see Marco Caliaro and Mario Francesconi, *L'apostolo degli emigranti: Giovanni Battista Scalabrini . . .* (Milan, 1968), the basic biography; and Antonio Perotti, "La società italiana di fronte alle migrazioni di massa:—Il contributo di Mons. Scalabrini a dei suoi primi collaboratori alla tutela degli emigranti," *Studi Emigrazione*, V (Feb.–June 1968), 1–196.

There is a considerable literature, much of it controversial, on the Italian immigrant as a farmer. The following urge the settlement of Italians on farms: Gustavo Tosti, "The Agricultural Possibilities of Italian Immigration," *The Survey*, XII (May 7, 1904); Emily F. Meade, "The Italian Immigrant on the Land," *Charities*, XIII (March 4, 1905), 541–544; Alice Bennett, "The Italian as a Farmer," *ibid.*, XXI (1908), 57–60; Alberto Pecorini, "The Italian as an Agricultural Laborer," *Annals of the American Academy of Political and Social Science*, XXXIII (March 1909), 380–390; Alexander Cance, "Immigrant Rural Communities," *The Survey*, XXV (Jan. 7, 1911), 587–595; and Edmond de Schweinitz Brunner, *Immigrant Farmers and Their Children* (Garden City, N.Y., 1929) shows that Italians as farmers were more diffused throughout the country than immigrants of any other nationality.

For the Italian agricultural experience in the South see Bert James Loewenberg, "Efforts of the South to Encourage Immigration, 1865–1900," *South Atlantic Quarterly*, XXXIII (Oct. 1934), 363–385; Rowland T. Berthoff, "Southern Attitudes toward Immigration, 1865–1914," *Journal of Southern History*, XVII (Aug. 1951), 328–360; Robert L. Brandfon, "The End of Immigration to the Cotton Fields," *Mississippi Valley Historical Review*, L (March 1964), 591–611; Alfred H. Stone, "The Italian Cotton Grower: The Negro's Problem," *South Atlantic Quarterly*, IV (Jan. 1905), 42–47; Stone, "Italian Cotton Growers in Arkansas," *Review of Reviews*, XXXV (Feb. 1907), 209–213; Emily F. Meade, "Italian Immigration into the South," *South Atlantic Quarterly*, IV (July 1905), 217–223.

For various Italian agricultural colonies see John L. Mathews, "Tontitown: A Study of the Conservation of Men," *Everybody's Magazine*, XX (Jan. 1909), 3–13; Anita Moore, "A Safe Way to Get on the Soil: The Work of Father Bandini at Tontitown," *World's Work*, XXIV (June 1912), 215–219; Allen Drayer, "Italy in the Ozarks," *American Fruit Grower*, XLIII (Sept. 1923), 6, 14; Gustavo Chiesi, "La nostra emigrazione agli Stati Uniti e la colonizzazione italiana nel Texas," *Rivista Coloniale* (March–April 1908), pp. 177–194; Mina C. Ginger, "In Berry Field and Bog," *Survey*, XV (Nov. 4, 1905), 162–169 deals with the exploitation of Italian farm workers in New Jersey; H. F. Raup, "The Italian-Swiss in California," *California Historical Society Quarterly*, XXX

(Dec. 1951), 305–314; Hans C. Palmer, "Italian Immigration and the Development of California Agriculture," unpubl. diss. (University of California, Berkeley, 1965).

For the effect of emigration on Italy see Giuseppe Lo Guidice, *Agricoltura e credito nell'esperienza del Banco di Sicilia tra L'800 ed il '900* (Catania, 1966); Attilio Brunialti, "L'èsodo degli italiani e la legge sull'emigrazione," *Nuova antologia,* XVI (July 1868), 96–114; William E. Davenport, "The Exodus of a Latin People," *Charities,* XII (May 7, 1904), 464–466; Francesco Coletti, "Il costo di produzione dell'uomo e il valore economico degli emigrante," *Giornale degli economisti,* XXX (March 1905), 260–291; Pasquale Villari, "L'emigrazione e le sue consiguenze in Italia," *Nuova antologia,* CXXVII (Jan. 1, 1907), 33–56; Antonio Mangano, "The Effect of Emigration Upon Italy," *The Survey,* XIX (Jan. 4, Feb. 1, 1908), 1329–38, 1475–86; XX (April 4, May 2, June 6, 1908), 13–25, 167–179, 323–335, an excellent series of articles based on field research; Walter E. Weyl, "Italy's Exhausting Emigration," *Review of Reviews,* XXXIX (Feb. 1909), 177–182. Although a novel that deals with a later period, Carlo Levi, *Christ Stopped at Eboli* (New York, 1947) vividly describes the effect of emigration on Lucania.

The returning immigrant is treated in Dino Taruffi et al., *La questione agraria e l'emigrazione in Calabria* (Florence, 1908); Victor von Borosini, "Home-Going Italians," *The Survey,* XXX (Sept. 28, 1912), 791–793; Francesco P. Cerase, "A Study of Italian Migrants Returning from the U.S.A.," *The International Migration Review,* I (Summer 1967), 67–74 stresses the conservative influence of the returned immigrant, as does George R. Gilkey, "The United States and Italy: Migration and Repatriation," *The Journal of Developing Areas,* II (Oct. 1967), 23–35.

CHAPTER 6: DISCRIMINATION

For a useful psychological study explaining the basis of stereotypes, national character, and discrimination see Gordon W. Allport, *The Nature of Prejudice* (Boston, 1954). Thomas F. Gossett, *Race: The History of an Idea in America* (Dallas, Tex., 1963) contains much on nativism, immigration, and restriction, with specific reference to Italians. Three important books deal with nativism: Ray Allen Billington, *The Protestant Crusade, 1800–1860: A Study of the Origins of American Nativism* (New York, 1938); John Higham, *Strangers in the Land: Patterns of American Nativism, 1860–1925* (corrected edition, New York, 1963); and Barbara M. Solomon, *Ancestors and Immigrants: A Changing New England Tradition* (Cambridge, Mass., 1956). Higham points out that among European immigrants none suffered from a greater hostility than Italians. Solomon is perceptive in her treatment of Italians in New England and the antiforeignism there. See also Higham, "Origins of Immigration Restriction, 1882–1897: A Social Analysis," *Mississippi Valley Historical Review,* XXXIX (June 1952), 77–88; Robert J. Ward, "Europe in American Historical Romances, 1890–1910," *Midcontinent American Studies Journal* (Spring 1967), 90–97 shows that Italians, more than other foreigners, suffered from the persistent bias of novelists; Ray Stannard Baker, *Following the Color Line* (New York,

1908) contains several incidents touching on Italian as well as Negro discrimination in the South; and Julius Weinberg, "E. A. Ross: The Progressive as Nativist," *Wisconsin Magazine of History*, L (Spring 1967), 242–253 shows how Ross' nativist prejudice distorted his judgment and scholarship.

Examples of anti-immigrant and anti-Italian literature for this period are Edward W. Bemis, "The Distribution of Our Immigrants," *Andover Review*, IX (1888), 587–596; Richmond Mayo Smith, *Emigration and Immigration* (New York, 1890); Francis A. Walker, "Immigration and Degradation," *Forum*, XI (Aug. 1891), 634–644; Nathaniel S. Shaler, "European Peasants as Immigrants," *Atlantic Monthly*, LXXI (May 1893), 646–655; Eliot Norton, "The Diffusion of Immigration," *Annals of the American Academy of Political and Social Science*, XXIV (1904), 161–165; Prescott F. Hall, *Immigration and Its Effects on the United States* (2nd ed., New York, 1906); Anonymous, "To Keep Out Southern Italians," *The World's Work*, XXVIII (Aug. 1914), 378–379; and Edward A. Ross, *The Old World in the New* (New York, 1914).

For favorable views of the Italian immigrants see Grace Abbott, *The Immigrant and the Community* (New York, 1917) and J. H. Senner, "Immigration from Italy," *The North American Review*, CLXII (June 1896), 649–657. Napoleone Colajanni, *Latini ed anglosassoni (Razze inferiori e razze superiori)* (2nd ed., Rome, 1906) refutes allegations of Italian degeneration or inferiority. Giovanni Preziosi, "La proibizione dello sbarco agli analfabeti negli Stati Uniti dell'America del Nord," *Vita italiana all'estero* (Feb. 1913), pp. 99–114 deals with the literacy test movement and its meaning for Italy. Amy A. Bernardy wrote two books describing the torment, as well as some of the satisfactions, of Italian immigrant life, which criticize American life in general. See *America vissuta* (Turin, 1911) and *Italia randagia attraverso gli Stati Uniti* (Turin, 1913). See also Giuseppe Giacosa, *Impressioni d'America* (Milan, 1908); Edmondo Mayor des Planches, *Attraverso gli Stati Uniti. Per l'emigrazione italiana* (Turin, 1913); Jacob A. Riis, *How the Other Half Lives* (New York, 1890); and Riis, *Out of Mulberry Street* (New York, 1898). Both books provide glimpses of Italian slum life, crime, and degradation.

The alleged Italian propensity for crime and violence has a large literature. The following titles in one way or another are critical of the Italians. Giuseppe Alongi, *La Maffia: nei suoi fattori e nelle sue manifestazioni* (Turin, 1886) is useful for the Sicilian background. Charles Loring Brace, *The Dangerous Classes of New York, and Twenty Years' Work Among Them* (New York, 1872) shows that even before large-scale immigration Italians suffered from discrimination and had acquired a bad reputation. Morgan Appleton, "What Shall We Do with the 'Dago'?" *The Popular Science Monthly*, XXXVII (Dec. 1890), 172–179 and Anonymous, "The Italian Problem," *Harper's Weekly*, LIII (July 3, 1909), 5 argue that the Italian is prone to violence. Prescott F. Hall, "New Problems of Immigration," *Forum*, XXX (1901), 555–567 charges Italy with dumping criminals on the United States, as does Lindsay Denison, "The Black Hand," *Everybody's Magazine*, XIX (Sept. 1908), 291–

301. See also Arthur Woods, "The Problem of the Black Hand," *McClure's Magazine*, XXXIII (May 1909), 40–47; three articles by Frank M. White, "How the United States Fosters the Black Hand," *Outlook*, XCIII (Oct. 30, 1909), 495–500; "Against the Black Hand," *Collier's*, XLV (Sept. 3, 1910), 19; "The Black Hand in Control in Italian New York," *Outlook*, CIV (Aug. 16, 1913), 857–865; Sydney Reid, "The Death Sign," *Independent*, LXX (April 6, 1911), 711–715 deals with alleged Black Hand outrages in clichés; Arthur Train, "Imported Crime: The Story of the Camorra in America," *McClure's Magazine*, XXXIX (May 1912), 82–94; and Tommaso Sassone, "Italy's Criminals in the United States," *Current History*, XV (Oct. 1921), 23–31.

For defense of the Italians and refutations of criminal propensities see I. W. Howerth, "Are the Italians a Dangerous Class?" *Charities Review*, IV (Nov. 1894), 17–40; Cesare Lombroso, "Why Homicide Has Increased in the United States," *North American Review*, CLXV (Dec. 1897), 641–648; CLXVI (Jan. 1898), 1–11; Gino C. Speranza, "The Mafia," *The Green Bag*, XII (June 1900), 302–305 argues that the Mafia had no real organization; Napoleone Colajanni, "Homicide and the Italians," *Forum*, XXXI (March 1901), 63–68 refutes the idea that crime is linked to race; Gaetano D'Amato, "Black Hand Myth," *North American Review*, CLXXXVII (April 1908), 543–549; Anonymous, "The Black Hand Scourge," *Cosmopolitan Magazine*, XLVII (June 1909), 31–41, an analytical, unemotional piece; Kate H. Claghorn, *The Immigrants' Day in Court* (New York, 1923) contains useful commentaries on the treatment of Italians; John Landesco, *Organized Crime in Chicago: Part III of the Illinois Crime Survey, 1929* (Chicago, 1968) is a pioneer scholarly study by a Romanian immigrant which contends that no Black Hand society "of national or international proportions" has been proved to exist; and Alberto C. Melloni, "Italy Invades the Bloody Third: the Early History of Milwaukee's Italians," *Milwaukee County Historical Society Historical Messenger* (March 1969), pp. 34–46 calls the Mafia imaginary.

The attitudes of business and organized labor toward Italians and the immigrants' reaction to labor organization has been the subject of historical revision. The following literature deals with various aspects of the problem. Isaac A. Hourwich, *Immigration and Labor: The Economic Aspects of European Immigration to the United States* (New York, 1912); Morrell Heald, "Business Attitudes Toward European Immigration, 1880–1900," *Journal of Economic History*, XIII (Summer 1953), 291–304 points out that businessmen abetted nativism; Edwin Fenton, "Immigrants and Unions, a Case Study: Italians and American Labor, 1870–1920," unpubl. diss. (Harvard University, 1957); Fenton, "Italian Immigrants in the Stoneworkers Union," *Labor History*, III (Spring 1962), 188–207; Fenton, "Italians in the Labor Movement," *Pennsylvania History*, XXVI (April 1959), 133–148 all refute the idea that Italians were difficult to unionize or were poor union members; Charlotte Erickson, *American Industry and the European Immigrant, 1860–1885* (Cambridge, Mass., 1957) disproves the view that contract labor undermined the American worker and contains information on Italians as strikebreakers;

Herman Feldman, *Racial Factors in American Industry* (New York, 1931) argues that "the Italian has perhaps been the most generally abused of all the foreign born." See also Gerd Korman, *Industrialization, Immigrants, and Americanizers: The View from Milwaukee, 1866–1921* (Madison, Wis., 1967); Kate H. Claghorn, "The Italian Under Economic Stress," *Charities,* XII (May 7, 1904), 501–504; Katherine Anthony, "Mothers Who Must Earn," *West Side Studies,* ed. Pauline Goldmark (New York, 1914); Charles B. Barnes, *The Longshoremen* (New York, 1915, explains Italian-Irish rivalry for jobs). Dominic Ciolli, "The 'Wop' in the Track Gang," *Immigrants in America Review,* II (July 1916), 61–64 describes the misery and exploitation of immigrant laborers as well as the prejudice they encountered; and Samuel L. Baily, "The Italians and Organized Labor in the United States and Argentina: 1800–1910," *The International Migration Review,* I (Summer 1967), 56–66, and also Baily, "The Italians and the Development of Organized Labor in Argentina, Brazil, and the United States: 1880–1914," *Journal of Social History,* III (Winter, 1969–1970), 123–134.

For the Italian attitude toward education and intellectual life one must search out data scattered in general works. Richard Hofstadter, *Anti-Intellectualism in American Life* (New York, 1963) is valuable for background. Lawrence Franklin, "The Italian in America: What He Has Been, What He Shall Be," *Catholic World,* LXXI (April 1900), 67–80 says that Italians in America have developed a reverence for education. See also Lilian Brandt, "A Transplanted Birthright: The Development of the Second Generation of the Italians in an American Environment," *The Survey,* XII (May 7, 1904), 494–499; Enrico C. Sartorio, *Social and Religious Life of Italians in America* (Boston, 1918) is one of the best contemporary analyses, especially for insight on educational discrimination; Joseph W. Tait, *Some Aspects of the Effect of the Dominant American Culture upon Children of Italian-Born Parents* (New York, 1942); and Mary F. Matthews, "The Role of the Public School in the Assimilation of the Italian Immigrant Child in New York City, 1900–1914," unpubl. diss. (Fordham University, 1966) shows that Italian immigrants desired education for their children and were not hostile to education but the educational system was hostile to them. Timothy L. Smith, "Immigrant Social Aspirations and Education, 1880–1930," *American Quarterly,* XXI (Fall 1969), 523–543, supports a similar interpretation. Since discrimination runs through the entire Italian-American relationship, the bibliographical commentaries for other chapters also contain pertinent titles.

CHAPTER 7: NATIONALIST MANIFESTATIONS
For the Cerruti case see John Bassett Moore, *History and Digest of International Arbitrations,* 6 vols. (Washington, 1898), V, 4694 ff. Ernest R. May, *Imperial Democracy* (New York, 1961) places the Spanish-American War in a world context and takes note of Italian reaction. For Italian commentary on the war see M. Morasso, "La guerra ispano-americana e la propaganda contro il militarismo," *La riforma sociale,* VIII (1898), 563–567; Ugo Ojetti, "Note sull'America durante la

guerra," *Nuova antologia,* CLXII (1898), 146–157; Augusto Pierantoni, *Cuba e il conflitto ispano-americano* (Rome, 1898); A. V. Vecchi, "Le marine militari degli Stati Uniti e della Spagna," *Rivista d'Italia,* II (1898), 36–60; Ojetti, *L'America vittoriosa* (Milan, 1899) discusses the war, imperialism, public opinion, and anti-imperialism. For the influence of religion and politics on Italian-American affairs see two articles by Joseph P. O'Grady, "Politics and Diplomacy: The Appointment of Anthony M. Keiley to Rome in 1885," *Virginia Magazine of History and Biography,* LXXVI (April 1968), 191–209 and "The Roman Question in American Politics," *Journal of Church and State,* IX (Autumn 1968), 365–377. Paul S. Holbo, "Perilous Obscurity: Public Diplomacy and the Press in the Venezuelan Crisis, 1902–1903," *The Historian,* XXXII (May 1970), 428–448, contains a good account of Italian reaction to American pressure.

There is a considerable but scattered literature on the New Orleans incident. Robert H. Marr, Jr., "The New Orleans Mafia Case," *American Law Review,* XXV (May–June 1891), 414–431 is viciously nativist in its defense of the lynchers. Henry Cabot Lodge, "Lynch Law and Unrestricted Immigration," *North American Review,* CLII (May 1891), 602–612 also defends the mob. John E. Coxe, "New Orleans Mafia Incident," *Louisiana Historical Quarterly,* XX (Oct. 1937), 1067–1110; and John S. Kendall, "Who Killa de Chief?" *ibid.,* XXII (April 1939), 492–530 are detailed accounts showing bias against the Italians. Jules A. Karlin has written two more balanced accounts. See his "New Orleans Lynchings of 1891 and the American Press," *ibid.,* XXIV (Jan. 1941), 187–203; and "The Italo-American Incident of 1891 and the Road to Reunion," *Journal of Southern History,* VIII (May 1942), 242–246. For Italian accounts and critical appraisals of American justice see S. M. Brandi, "La legge de Lynch negli stati uniti," *La civiltà cattolica,* series XIV, vol. XII (1891), 266–277; Augusto Pierantoni, *I fatti de Nuova Orleans e il diritto internazionale* (Rome, 1891), by a senator and professor of law at the University of Rome; Pietro Nocito, "La legge di lynch ed il conflitto italo-americano," *Nuova antologia,* DLI (1891), 337–367, 551–583; Francesco Auriti, *Questioni guiridiche nella vertenza fra l'Italia e la federazione americana pei fatti di Nuova Orleans* (Rome, 1893); Pierantoni, "I linciaggi negli Stati Uniti e la emigrazione Italiana," *L'Italia coloniale,* I (April–May 1904), 423–447; II (July 1904), 37–52, traces the lynchings of Italians in the United States but stresses the New Orleans incident. James Bryce, "Legal and Constitutional Aspects of the Lynching at New Orleans," *The New Review,* IV (May 1891), 384–397 is a perceptive British analysis. Arthur Desjardins, "Le droit gens et le loi de Lynch aux Etats Unis," *Revue des deux mondes,* CV (May 15, 1891), 321–355 is critical of American justice.

For the general problem of protecting Italians and of lynchings see Angelo P. Sereni, *The Italian Conception of International Law* (New York, 1943); and Luigi Bodio, "Della protezione degli emigranti italiani in America," *Nuova antologia,* LX (1895), 628–644 which covers Argentina and Brazil as well as the United States. Augusto Pierantoni, "Italian Feeling on American Lynching," *The Independent,* LV (Aug. 27,

1903), 2040–42 calls for prevention of lynchings and punishment of lynchers. Gino C. Speranza, "How It Feels to Be a Problem," *The Survey*, XII (May 7, 1904), 456–463 explains the feelings of Italians who suffered discrimination and deplores their treatment, especially the lynchings. Also critical of the lynchings is Charles H. Watson, "Need of Federal Legislation in Respect to Mob Violence in Cases of Lynching of Aliens," *Yale Law Journal*, XXV (May 1916), 561–584. John Bassett Moore, *A Digest of International Law*, 8 vols. (Washington, 1906), VI, 837–849 contains a record of the lynching of Italians. See also Paul M. Angle, *Bloody Williamson: A Chapter in American Lawlessness* (New York, 1952) relates Ku Klux Klan violence against Italians; and George E. Cunningham, "The Italian, a Hindrance to White Solidarity in Louisiana, 1890–1898," *Journal of Negro History*, L (Jan. 1965), 22–36 shows that Italians first opposed restrictions against blacks but that lynchings and discrimination led them to adopt the ways of the white supremacists.

Various cultural and ideological influences in the Italian-American relationship of this period may be found in Francesco Ferrara, "L'americanismo economico in Italia," *Nuova antologia*, XII (1878), 300–327, 464–499; XIII (1879), 123–154; Giovanni Boglietti, "Nuove utopie americane: Il libro di Edvardo Bellamy: *Looking Backward*," *ibid.*, XXVIII (1890), 609–627; Luigi Palma di Cesnola, "L'ideale degli Stati Uniti d'Europa," *ibid.*, CXXIV (1892), 426–439; and his "A proposito della guerra e della pace fra gli Stati Uniti d'America e la Spagna," *ibid.*, CLXI (1898), 193–211 advances the idea of a united Europe modeled on the United States. Lee Benson, "Achille Loria's Influence on American Economic Thought: Including His Contribution to the Frontier Hypothesis," *Agricultural History*, XXIV (Oct. 1950), 182–199 follows the exchange of ideas. For theater, opera, art, and architecture see Hermann Klein, *The Reign of Patti* (New York, 1920); Walter Rundell, "The West as an Operatic Setting," *Probing the American West*, ed. K. Ross Toole et al. (Santa Fe, New Mexico, 1962) discusses Puccini; Giulio Piccini, *Vita aneddotica di Tommaso Salvini* (Florence, 1908); Charles Moore, *The Life and Times of Charles Follen McKim* (Boston, 1929); and Louise H. Tharp, *Mrs. Jack: A Biography of Isabella Stewart Cooper* (Boston, 1965).

The following are useful travel accounts or critiques of American life by Italian visitors: Francesco di Muricce, *In America 1871–72*, 2 vols. (Florence, 1875); Francesco Varvaro Pojero, *Una corsa nel nuovo mondo*, 2 vols. (Milan, 1876); Giovanni Vigna del Ferro, *Un viaggio nel Far West americano* (Bologna, 1881); Egisto Rossi, *Gli Stati Uniti e la concorrenza americana* (Florence, 1884); Egisto Rossi, *L'istruzione pubblica negli Stati Uniti* (Rome, 1889); Alessandro Zannini, *De l'Atlantique au Mississippi, souvenirs d'un diplomate* (Paris, 1884); Antonio Gallenga, *Episodes of My Second Life: English and American Experiences*, 2 vols. (London, 1884); Carlo Gardini, *Gli Stati Uniti: Ricordi*, 2 vols. (Bologna, 1887), one of the best memoirs concerning American life by an Italian visitor; [Gustavo Strafforello], *Greater America: Hits and Hints* (New York, 1887); Federico Garlanda, *La nuova democrazia americana* (Rome, 1891); Garlanda, *La terza Italia: lettere di un Yankee* (Rome, 1903) includes commentaries on lynchings and the Mafia; Edmondo de Amicis, *On Blue Water,* trans. J. B. Brown (New York, 1897); S. M. Brandi, "La questione scolastica negli Stati Uniti," *Civiltà Cattolica,* series XV (1892), I, 552–565; Tommaso Salvini, *Ricordi, aneddoti ed impressioni* (Milan, 1895); Guido Rossati, *Relazione di un viaggio d'istruzione negli Stati Uniti d'America* (Rome, 1900); Ugo Ojetti, *L'America e l'avvenire* (Milan, 1905); Alberto Pecorini, *Gli americani nella vita moderna osservati da un italiano* (Milan, 1909); and Alfredo Bosi, *Cinquant'anni di vita italiana in America* (New York, 1921), a detailed account of Italian-Americans.

Foreign relations, imperialism, and nationalism are dealt with in a number of books. Parker T. Moon, *Imperialism and World Politics* (New York, 1926) places Italian imperialism in a broad context. Two works by William L. Langer, *The Diplomacy of Imperialism, 1890–1902,* 2 vols. (New York, 1935) and *European Alliances and Alignments, 1871–1890* (2nd ed., New York, 1950) are basic for background, as is Federico Chabod, *Storia della politica estera italiana dal 1870 al 1896* (Bari, 1951), considered a masterpiece by some historians. See also Donald A. Limoli, "Francesco Crispi's Quest for Empire—and Victories—in Ethiopia," *The Partition of Africa Illusion or Necessity,* ed. Robert O. Collins (New York, 1969), pp. 111–136; *The Memoirs of Francesco Crispi,* compiled by Thomas Palamenghi Crispi, trans. Mary Prichard-Agnetti, 3 vols. (London, 1912); Robert L. Hess, *Italian Colonialism in Somalia* (Chicago, 1966); Luigi Villari, *The Expansion of Italy* (London, 1930); Archibald C. Coolidge, *Origins of the Triple Alliance* (2nd ed., New York, 1926); Luigi Salvatorelli, *La triplice alleanza, storia diplomatica, 1877–1912* (Milan, 1939); Francesco Tommasini, *L'Italia alla viglia della guerra; la politica estera di Tommaso Tittoni,* 3 vols. (Bologna, 1934–37); and Lloyd C. Griscom, *Diplomatically Speaking* (New York, 1940), by a former ambassador to Italy.

For works dealing specifically with Italian nationalism see Giovanni Giolitti, *Memoirs of My Life,* trans. Edward Storer (London, 1923); A. William Salamone, *Italy in the Giolittian Era* (Phil., 1960); four books and an article by Enrico Corradini, *L'ora di Tripoli* (Milan, 1911); *Il volere d'Italia* (Naples, 1911); *Sopra le vie del nuovo impero* (Milan, 1912); *La vita nazionale* (rev. ed., Siena, 1923); "Italy from Adowa to the Great War," *The Nineteenth Century,* LXXXI (May 1917), 1015–27; Scipio Sighele, *Ultime pagine nazionaliste* (Milan, 1910); Sighele, *Il nazionalismo ed i partici politici* (Milan, 1911); Mario Missiroli, "Le nationalisme italien," *L'indépendance,* I (1911), 419–435; Anonymous, "The Ethics of the Tripoli Affair," *The Outlook,* XCIX (Oct. 14, 1911), 367–368, a poll of the American and foreign press; E. J. Dillon, "The New Way of Acquiring Colonies," *The Contemporary Review,* C (Nov. 1911), 712–732; Ignotus, "Italian Nationalism and the War with Turkey," *Fortnightly Review,* XCVI (Nov. 1, 1911), 1084–96; Giuseppe Bevione, *Come siamo andati a Tripoli* (Turin, 1912); Thomas Barclay, *The Turco-Italian War and Its Problems* (London, 1912); Albert Dauzat, *L'expansion italienne* (Paris, 1914); Ezio Flori, "Nazionalismo e individualismo," *Rivista d'Italia*, XIX (March 1916), 309–350; and (April 1916), 502–536; Pier L. Orchini, *Enrico Corradini e la nuova coscienza nazionali* (2nd ed., Florence, 1925); William C. Askew, *Europe and Italy's Acquisition of Libya, 1911–1912* (Durham, N.C., 1942); Fernando Manzotti, *La polemica sull'emigrazione nell 'Italia unita* (Milan, 1962) covers the debate over emigration with a concluding chapter on the nationalists. Richard A. Webster, *The Cross and the Fasces: Christian Democracy and Fascism and Italy* (Stanford, 1960) and Jack J. Roth, "The Roots of Italian Fascism: Sorel and Sorelismo," *Journal of Modern History*, XXXIX (March 1967), 30–45 shows the links between nationalism and fascism. Also see bibliographical commentaries in preceding chapters for pertinent works.

CHAPTER 8: PARTNERSHIP AND RIFT

For a scholarly detailed account of European politics and diplomacy as general background with Italy's position explained, see Luigi Albertini, *The Origins of the War of 1914,* ed. and trans. Isabella M. Massey, 3 vols (London, 1952–57). For Italy's position see Leonida Bissolati, *La politica estera dell'Italia dal 1897 al 1920: scritti e discorsi* (Milan, 1923); Ivanoe Bonomi, *La politica italiana da Porta Pia a Vittorio Veneto, 1870–1918* (Turin, 1944); E. J. Dillon, *From the Triple Alliance to the Quadruple Alliance: Why Italy Went to War* (London, 1915); Antonio Salandra, *Italy and the Great War: From Neutrality to Intervention,* trans. Kendrick Pyne (London, 1932); William C. Askew, "The Austro-Italian Antagonism, 1896–1914," *Power, Public Opinion, and Diplomacy: Essays in Honor of Eber Malcolm Carroll . . . ,* eds. Lillian P. Wallace and William C. Askew (Durham, N.C., 1959); Mario Toscano, *Il patto di Londra* (Bologna, 1934); Toscano, "Rivelazioni nuovi documenti sul negoziato di Londra per l'ingresso dell'Italia nella prima guerra mondiale," *Nuova antologia,* (August–November, 1965), 433–457, 15–37, 150–165, 295–312; William A. Renzi, "The Russian Foreign Office and Italy's Entrance into the Great War, 1914–1915: A Study in Wartime Diplomacy," *The Historian,* XXVIII (Aug. 1966), 648–668; and Renzi, "Italy's Neutrality and Entrance into the Great War: A Re-examination," *American Historical Review,* LXXIII (June 1968), 1414–32 argues that Italy's diplomats were no more deceitful than their European counterparts.

The following accounts deal with Italy at war. Thomas Nelson Page, *Italy and the World War* (New York, 1920), by the American ambassador in Rome, 1913–1919; Luigi Cadorna, *La guerra alla fronte italiano . . .* (Milan, 1921); Cadorna, *Altre pagine sulla grande guerra* (Milan, 1925); W. W. Gottlieb, *Studies in Secret Diplomacy During the First World War* (London, 1957), a great part of which is devoted to "Italy among the Great Powers"; Edgar E. Hume, "Italy's Part in the World War," *Atlantica* (March–April 1935), 87–90, 123–126; Maffeo Pantaleoni, *Note in margine della guerra* (Bari, 1917); Henry Wickham Steed, *Through Thirty Years, 1892–1922: A Personal Narrative,* 2 vols. (New York, 1925) contains considerable information on Italy; John A. Thayer, *Italy and the Great War: Politics and Culture, 1870–1915* (Madison,

Wis., 1964); Edgar Ansel Mowrer, *Immortal Italy* (New York, 1922) and *Triumph and Turmoil: A Personal History of Our Time* (New York, 1968) contain sensitively drawn accounts of Italy and the war; and two pieces of pro-Italian propaganda, Jacques Bainville, *Italy and the War*, trans. Bernard Miall (London, 1916), An American Observer in Italy, *Italy's Contribution to the Great War* (New York, 1919). Augusto Torre, "La posizione dell' Italia tra gli alleati dal Patto di Londra a Vittorio Veneto," *Rassegna storica del Risorgimento*, LVI (Oct.–Dec. 1969), 535–545, points that divergence between Italy and the United States began with the Fourteen Points.

For other aspects of the American wartime experience in Italy see Gino C. Speranza, "The 'Americani' in Italy at War," *Outlook*, CXXII (April 12, 1916), 844, 861–864; *The Diary of Gino Speranza: Italy 1915–1919*, ed. Florence C. Speranza, 2 vols. (New York, 1941); Norval Richardson, *My Diplomatic Education* (New York, 1923), by an American diplomat in Italy, 1913–1920; Frank Freidel, *Franklin D. Roosevelt: The Apprenticeship* (Boston, 1952); Arthur S. Link, *Wilson*, 5 vols. (1947–65); Fiorello H. La Guardia, *The Making of an Insurgent, An Autobiography: 1882–1919* (New York, 1948); Howard Zinn, *La Guardia in Congress* (Ithaca, N.Y., 1959); Carlos Baker, *Ernest Hemingway: A Life Story* (New York, 1969); Charles M. Bakewell, *The Story of the American Red Cross in Italy* (New York, 1920); James R. Mock and Cedric Larson, *Words that Won the War: The Story of the Committee on Public Information, 1917–1919* (Princeton, 1939) discusses propaganda work in Italy. For more on the committee and Italy see George Creel, *The War, the World and Wilson* (New York, 1920); and Creel, *Rebel at Large: Recollections of Fifty Crowded Years* (New York, 1947). Ronald Radosh, *American Labor and United States Foreign Policy* (New York, 1969), tells of Samuel Gompers' visit to Italy in 1918 as propagandist.

There is a considerable literature on the peacemaking. General accounts which place the Italian question in a broad setting are: *A History of the Peace Conference of Paris*, Harold W. V. Temperley, ed., 6 vols. (London, 1920–24); Harold Nicolson, *Peacemaking, 1919* (Boston, 1933); James T. Shotwell, *At the Paris Peace Conference* (New York, 1937); Paul Birdsall, *Versailles Twenty Years After* (New York, 1941); Paul J. Mantoux, *Les délibérations du Conseil des quatre* (24 mars–28 juin 1919) (Paris, 1955); Arno J. Mayer, *Political Origins of the New Diplomacy, 1917–1918* (New Haven, Conn., 1959); Mayer, *Politics and Diplomacy of Peacemaking: Containment and Counterrevolution at Versailles, 1918–1919* (New York, 1967).

Works that deal mainly with Italian issues are: Giovanna Procacci, "Italy: From Interventionism to Fascism, 1917–1919," *Journal of Contemporary History*, III (Oct. 1968), 153–176; Gino C. Speranza, "An Italian Ambassador's Diary of the Peace Conference," *Political Science Quarterly*, XXXVII (June 1922), 299–309. René Albrecht-Carrié has written extensively on Italy's peacemaking. See his *Italy at the Paris Peace Conference* (New York, 1938); "Italy and Her Allies, June, 1919," *American Historical Review*, XLVI (July 1941), 837–843; "New Light on Italian Problems in 1919," *Journal of Modern History*, XIII (Dec.

1941), 493–516; "Fiume: Nationalism versus Economics," *Journal of Central European Affairs,* II (April 1942), 49–63; "Italian Colonial Problems in 1919," *Political Science Quarterly,* LVIII (Dec. 1943), 562–580; Vittorio Emmanuele Orlando, *Memorie (1915–1919),* ed. Rodolfo Mosca (Milan, 1960); Carlo Sforza, "Sonnino and His Foreign Policy," *Contemporary Review,* CXXXVI (Dec. 1929), 721–732 is critical of Italy's role at Paris; Tom Antongini, *D'Annunzio* (Boston, 1938), uncritical; Frances Winwar, *Wingless Victory: A Biography of Gabriele D'Annunzio and Eleonora Duse* (New York, 1956); G. A. Andriulli, "How We Alienated Wilson," *Living Age,* CCCVIII (Jan. 29, 1921), 266–270; and Mario Toscano, *Storia diplomatica della questione dell'Alto Adige* (Bari, 1967).

The following deal mainly with the American outlook on the peace-making and in various ways touch on the Italian issues. See Ray Stannard Baker, *What Wilson Did at Paris* (New York, 1919); Baker, *Woodrow Wilson and World Settlement,* 3 vols. (New York, 1922–23); Baker, *Woodrow Wilson: Life and Letters,* 8 vols. (New York, 1927–39); Robert Lansing, *The Peace Negotiations: A Personal Narrative* (Boston, 1921); Allan Nevins, *Henry White: Thirty Years of American Diplomacy* (New York, 1930); George B. Noble, *Policies and Opinions at Paris, 1919* (New York, 1935); Edith Wilson Bolling, *My Memoir* (Indianapolis, 1939); Charles Seymour, *Letters from the Paris Peace Conference,* ed. Harold B. Whiteman, Jr. (New Haven, Conn., 1965); Thomas A. Bailey, *Woodrow Wilson and the Lost Peace* (New York, 1944); and *Woodrow Wilson and the Great Betrayal* (New York, 1945); Lawrence E. Gelfand, *The Inquiry: American Preparations for Peace, 1917–1919* (New Haven, Conn., 1963), contains a well-balanced analysis of differences among Americans regarding Italy's claims; David F. Trask, "General Tasker Howard Bliss and the 'Sessions of the World,' 1919," *Transactions of the American Philosophical Society,* LVI, Part 8, New Series (Phil., Dec., 1966), 1–80; John P. Posey, "David Hunter Miller as an Informal Diplomat: The Fiume Question at the Paris Peace Conference, 1919," *Southern Quarterly,* V (April 1967), 251–272; Dragan R. Živojinović, "The Vatican, Woodrow Wilson, and the Dissolution of the Hapsburg Monarchy, 1914–1918," *East European Quarterly,* III (March 1969), 31–70; Ivo J. Lederer, *Yugoslavia at the Paris Peace Conference: A Study in Frontiermaking* (New Haven, Conn., 1963); Lawrence Evans, *United States Policy and the Partition of Turkey, 1914–1924* (Baltimore, 1965); David Burner, "The Breakup of the Wilson Coalition of 1916," *Mid-America,* XLV (Jan. 1963), 18–35; and John B. Duff, "The Italians," *The Immigrants' Influence on Wilson's Peace Policies,* ed. Joseph P. O'Grady (Lexington, Kentucky, 1967). See also relevant titles in references to other chapters.

CHAPTER 9: RESTRICTION
Important background material on the Red Scare and revived nativism can be found in Robert K. Murray, *Red Scare: A Study in National Hysteria, 1919–1920* (Minneapolis, 1955); Stanley Coben, "A Study in Nativism: The American Red Scare of 1919–1920," *Political Science*

Quarterly, LXXIX (March 1964), 57–75; Paul L. Murphy, "Sources and Nature of Intolerance in the 1920's," *The Journal of American History*, LI (June 1964), 60–76; William Preston, Jr., *Aliens and Dissenters: Federal Suppression of Radicals, 1903–1933* (Cambridge, Mass., 1963); Kenneth T. Jackson, *The Ku Klux Klan in the City, 1915–1930* (New York, 1967); and Gustavus Myers, *History of Bigotry in the United States* (New York, 1943). On hyphenism see Louis L. Gerson, "Immigrant Groups and American Foreign Policy," *Issues and Conflicts: Studies in Twentieth Century American Diplomacy*, ed. George L. Anderson (Lawrence, Kans., 1959), pp. 171–192; and Gerson, *The Hyphenate in Recent American Politics and Diplomacy* (Lawrence, Kans., 1964). For the reformers, reform measures, and nativism see Eric F. Goldman, *Rendezvous with Destiny* (New York, 1952); Richard Hofstadter, *The Age of Reform* (New York, 1955); Joseph J. Huthmacher, "Urban Liberalism and the Age of Reform," *Mississippi Valley Historical Review*, XLIX (Sept. 1962), 231–241; Constantine M. Panunzio, "The Foreign Born's Reaction to Prohibition," *Sociology and Social Research*, XVIII (Jan.–Feb. 1934), 223–228; and John R. Meers, "The California Wine and Grape Industry and Prohibition," *California Historical Society Quarterly*, XLVI (March 1967), 19–32.

The literature on Italian radical movements in America is sparse but see Paul Ghio, *L'anarchisme aux États-Unis* (Paris, 1903); Mario De Ciampis, "Note sul movimento socialista tra gli emigrati Italiani negli U.S.A. (1890–1921)," *Cronache meridionali*, VI (April 1959), 255–273; Luigi V. Ferraris, "L'assassino di Umberto I e gli Anarchici de Paterson," *Rassegna storica del Risorgimento*, L (March 1968), 47–64; and Sidney Fine, "Anarchism and the Assassination of McKinley," *American Historical Review*, LX (July 1955), 777–799.

Since the Sacco-Vanzetti case captured the imagination of literate liberals a great deal has been written about it, but much of the material is polemical. The following titles are worthy of perusal: Bartolomeo Vanzetti, *Non piangete la mia morte: lettere ai familiari a cura di Cesare Pillon e Vincenzo Vanzetti* ([Rome], 1962); two books by Herbert B. Ehrmann, *The Untried Case: Sacco Vanzetti and the Morelli Gang* (New York, 1933); and *The Case that Will Not Die: Commonwealth vs. Sacco and Vanzetti* (Boston, 1969), a full history; G. Louis Joughin and Edmund M. Morgan, *The Legacy of Sacco and Vanzetti* (New York, 1948); Francis Russell, *Tragedy in Dedham: The Story of the Sacco-Vanzetti Case* (New York, 1962); David Felix, *Protest: Sacco-Vanzetti and the Intellectuals* (Bloomington, Ind., 1965), which is critical of the two men and their intellectual supporters. Robert H. Montgomery, *Sacco-Vanzetti: The Murder and the Myth* (New York, 1960) considers their innocence the myth; and Martin H. Bush, *Ben Shahn: The Passion of Sacco and Vanzetti* (Syracuse, New York, 1968).

Two memoirs that tell something of transatlantic culture are Giulio Gatti-Cassazza, *Memories of the Opera* (New York, 1941); Theodore Dreiser, *A Traveler at Forty* (New York, 1923) devotes considerable space to impressions of Italy. For opera see also Donald J. Grout, *A Short History of Opera*, 2 vols. (2nd ed., New York, 1965); John

Briggs, *Requiem for a Yellow Brick Brewery: A History of the Metropolitan Opera* (Boston, 1969), a popular account; Donald L. Davis, *Opera in Chicago* (New York, 1966); and Dorothy Caruso, *Enrico Caruso: His Life and Death* (New York, 1945).

For the influence of the Army intelligence tests on the restrictionists see *Army Mental Tests,* Clarence S. Yoakum and Robert M. Yerkes, eds. (New York, 1920); Edward G. Conklin, "Some Biological Aspects of Immigration," *Scribner's Magazine,* LXIX (1921), 352–359; Arthur Sweeney, "Mental Tests for Immigrants," *North American Review,* CCXV (May 1922), 600–612. On the basis of tests, the author says, we can "strenuously object to immigration from Italy." Carl C. Brigham, *A Study of American Intelligence* (Princeton, 1923) has a similar bias. Antonio Stella, *Some Aspects of Italian Immigration to the United States* (New York, 1924) is an inadequate effort to answer critics who attacked Italians on the basis of the tests. Daniel J. Kevles, "Testing the Army's Intelligence: Psychologists and the Military in World War I," *Journal of American History,* LV (Dec. 1968), 565–581 points out flaws in the tests.

For the old argument used by restrictionists that Italians were prone to crime see William S. Bennett, "Immigrants and Crime," *Annals of the American Academy of Political and Social Science,* XXXIV (July 1909), 117–124; Gino C. Speranza, "The Alien in Relation to Our Laws," *ibid.,* LI (March 1914), 169–176; Speranza et al., "Crime and Immigration (Report of Committee G, of the Institute)", *Journal of Criminal Law, Criminology, and Police Science,* IV (Nov. 1913), 523–547; John H. Mariano, *The Italian Immigrant and Our Courts* (Boston, 1925); and Egal Feldman, "Prostitution, the Alien Woman and the Progressive Imagination, 1910–1915," *American Quarterly,* XIX (Summer 1967), 192–206.

The Americanization and restrictionist movements are linked as is their literature. See U.S. Immigration Commission, 1901–1910, *Abstracts of Reports of the Immigration Commission* (Washington, D.C., 1911); U.S. Senate, 61st Cong., 3d sess., Reports of the U.S. Immigration Commission, *The Children of Immigrants in Schools,* 5 vols. (Washington, D.C., 1911); Maurice R. Davie, *World Immigration with Special Reference to the United States* (New York, 1936); Madison Grant, *The Passing of the Great Race* (New York, 1916); John R. Commons, *Races and Immigrants in America* (New York, 1920); Calvin Coolidge, "Whose Country Is This," *Good Housekeeping,* LXXII (Feb 1921), 13 14, 106–109; Clinton S. Burr, *America's Race Heritage* (New York, 1922) is a racist diatribe arguing that Columbus probably had Teutonic blood in his veins; Madison Grant and Charles Davison, *The Alien in Our Midst* (New York, 1930); Jeremiah W. Jenks and W. Jett Lauck, *The Immigration Problem* (New York, 1917); Howard C. Hill, "The Americanization Movement," *American Journal of Sociology,* XXIV (May 1919), 609–642; Kenneth L. Roberts, *Why Europe Leaves Home* (New York, 1922); Horace M. Kallen, *Culture and Democracy in the United States* (New York, 1924) contains an analysis of Americanization; Camillo E. Branchi, *Il primoto degl'italiani nella storia civiltà americana* (Bologna, 1925) discusses anti-Italian bigotry; Speranza, *Race or Nation: A Conflict of*

Divided Loyalties (Indianapolis, 1925); Henry Pratt Fairchild, *The Melting-Pot Mistake* (Boston, 1926); Niles Carpenter, *Immigrants and Their Children* (Washington, D.C., 1927); Emory S. Bogardus, *Immigration and Race Attitudes* (Boston, 1928); Roy L. Garis, *Immigration Restriction: A Study of the Opposition to and Regulation of Immigration into the United States* (New York, 1928); Hannibal G. Duncan, *Immigration and Assimilation* (Boston, 1933); William C. Smith, *Americans in the Making: The Natural History of the Assimilation of Immigrants* (New York, 1939); Edward G. Hartmann, *The Movement to Americanize the Immigrant* (New York, 1948); Isaque Graeber, "An Examination of Theories of Race Prejudice," *Social Research,* XX (Autumn 1953), 267–281; and Milton M. Gordon, *Assimilation in American Life* (New York, 1964).

The following titles illuminate various aspects of Italian life in the United States in this period or stress the Italian contribution to American life. Winfield Scott, "Old Wine in New Bottles: When Italy Comes to California Through the Panama Canal—What Then?" *Sunset,* XXX (May 1913), 519–526; "Beams Thrown from Garibaldi's Candles," *Survey,* XXXVIII (June 30, 1917), 293–294 reports a gradual breaking down of prejudice against Italian laborers; Frank O. Beck, *The Italian in Chicago* (Chicago, 1919); Angelo Patri, *A Schoolmaster of the Great City* (New York, 1920); Albert R. Bandini, "Concerning the Italian Problem," *The Ecclesiastical Review,* LXII (1920), 278–284 calls the Italians an asset to the American Catholic church; John C. Gebhart, *The Growth and Development of Italian Children in New York City* (New York, 1924); John H. Mariano, *The Italian Contribution to American Democracy* (Boston, 1921); Pascal D'Angelo, *Pascal D'Angelo, Son of Italy* (New York, 1924); Niles Carpenter, "On Their Way: The Implacable Optimism of the Immigrant Worker," *Survey,* LVI (July 15, 1926), 453–54, 476 concerns Italians in menial jobs; Constantine Panunzio, *Immigration Crossroads* (New York, 1927); Panunzio, "The Contribution of New Immigrants," *World Tomorrow,* XIII (July 1930), 301–303; John Fante, "The Odyssey of a Wop," *The American Mercury,* XXX (Sept. 1933), 89–97; Panunzio, *The Soul of an Immigrant* (New York, 1937); Joseph J. Huthmacher, *Massachusetts People and Politics, 1919–1933* (Cambridge, Mass., 1959) analyzes Italian political influence; and Federal Writers Project, Works Program Administration, *The Italians of New York* (New York, 1938). Sources from other chapters on immigration and nativism are equally important for this topic.

CHAPTER 10: FASCISM AND ISOLATIONISM

Two important though uneven studies on Italian-American diplomatic relations during the early Fascist era are John M. Berutti, "Italo-American Diplomatic Relations, 1922–28," unpubl. diss. (Stanford University, Stanford, Calif., 1960) which covers thoroughly the problem of debts, armaments and various minor issues; and Louis A. De Santi, "United States Relations with Italy under Mussolini, 1922–1941: A Study Based on the Records of the Department of State and Documents from the Captured Files of Mussolini," unpubl. diss. (Columbia University, New York,

1951), a longer study dealing with broad issues. Two other manuscripts deal with the American and Italian-American response to fascism and Mussolini. See John B. Carter, "American Reactions to Italian Fascism, 1919–1933," unpubl. diss. (Columbia University, 1953); and John P. Diggins, "Mussolini's Italy: The View from America," unpubl. diss. (University of Southern California, Los Angeles, 1964). Diggins has expanded and published some of his findings. See his "Flirtation with Fascism: American Pragmatic Liberals and Mussolini's Italy," *American Historical Review*, LXXI (Jan. 1966), 487–506; "Mussolini and America: Hero-Worship, Charisma, and the 'Vulgar Talent'," *The Historian*, XXVIII (Aug. 1966), 559–585; "The American Writer, Fascism, and the Liberation of Italy," *American Quarterly*, XVIII (Winter 1966), 599–614; "American Catholics and Italian Fascism," *Journal of Contemporary History*, II (Oct. 1967), 51 68; and "The Italo-American Anti-Fascist Opposition," *Journal of Modern History*, LIV (Dec. 1967), 579–598.

For additonal data on Fascist activities in the United States see Alan Cassels, "Fascism for Export: Italy and the United States in the Twenties," *American Historical Review*, LXIX (April 1964), 707–712; Gaetano Salvemini, *Italian Fascist Activities In the U.S.* (Washington, D.C., 1940), a pamphlet; Anonymous, "Mussolini and the Casa Italiana," *The Nation*, CXLI (Nov. 27, 1935), 610; Giuseppe Prezzolini, *L'Italiano inutile: memorie letterarie di Francia, Italia e America* (Milan, 1953), a director of the Casa Italiana in the Fascist years gives his views on its affairs; Marcus Duffield, "Mussolini's American Empire: The Fascist Invasion of the United States," *Harper's Magazine*, CLIX (Nov. 1929), 661–672, an exposé of the Fascist League; Clarence Darrow, "The New York Fascist Frame-Up," *The Lantern*, I (Feb. 1928), 13–14; Ray J. Tucker, "Tools of Mussolini in America," *The New Republic*, LII (Sept. 14, 1927), 89–91; Arthur Livingston, "Italo-American Fascism," *Survey*, LVII (March 1, 1927), 738–740, 750; and John Herling and Morris Shapiro, *The Terzani Case: An Account of a Labor Battle Against a Fascist Frame-up* (New York, 1934), a pamphlet.

Ideas, style, and their influence are difficult to trace, but Selig Adler, *The Isolationist Impulse: Its Twentieth Century Reaction* (New York, 1957) and *Isolation and Security: Ideas and Interests in Twentieth-Century American Foreign Policy*, ed. Alexander DeConde (Durham, N.C., 1957) throw light on these problems The following items discuss such influences on both Americans and Italians: William James, "G. Papini and the Pragmatist Movement in Italy," *Journal of Philosophy, Psychology and Scientific Methods*, III (June 21, 1906), 337–341; Anonymous, "Why Mussolini Charms the American Business Man," *Literary Digest*, LXXVII (June 9, 1923), 72–74; William K. Stewart, "The Mentors of Mussolini," *American Political Science Review*, XXII (Nov. 1928), 843–869, William James is here considered a mentor; Charles A. Beard, "Making the Fascist State," *New Republic*, LVII (Jan. 23, 1929), 277–278; Ezra Pound, *Jefferson and/or Mussolini* (London, 1935); Horace Kallen, "Mussolini, William James, and the Rationalists," *Social Frontier*, IV (May 1938), 253–256; Carlo Golino, "Giovanni Papini and Amer-

ican Pragmatism," *Italica,* XXXII (March 1955), 38–48; and Giovanni
Gullace, "The Pragmatist Movement in Italy," *Journal of the History of
Ideas,* XXIII (Jan.–March 1962), 91–105.

Mussolini has attracted numerous biographers and other writers. See
Charles F. Delzell, "Benito Mussolini: Guide to the Biographical Litera-
ture," *Journal of Modern History,* XXXV (Dec. 1963), 339–353. Renzo
De Felice has written the finest scholarly biography; see his *Mussolini,*
3 vols. (Turin, 1965–68). Good one-volume studies in English are Paolo
Monelli, *Mussolini: The Intimate Life of a Demagogue,* trans. Brigid
Maxwell (New York, 1954) and Ivone Kirkpatrick, *Mussolini: A Study
in Power* (New York, 1964). See also Benito Mussolini, *My Autobiography,* foreword by Richard Washburn Child (New York, 1928); Emil
Ludwig, *Talks with Mussolini,* trans. Eden and Cedar Paul (Boston,
1933); Ludwig found Mussolini more popular in America than anywhere
else he visited; and Giuseppe Prezzolini, "Mussolini's First Year," *New
Republic,* XXXVI (Oct. 31, 1923), 251–253.

For the Italian and European background of fascism and various
assessments see Edward H. Carr, *International Relations between the
Wars (1919–1939),* (London, 1948); Christopher Seton-Watson, *Italy
from Liberation to Fascism, 1870–1925* (New York, 1967) is a splendid
political history and the best available in English; Edward R. Tannenbaum, "The Goals of Italian Fascism," *American Historical Review,*
LXXIV (April 1969), 1183–1204; F. L. Carsten, *The Rise of Fascism*
(Berkeley, Calif., 1968); Angelo Tasca, *The Rise of Italian Fascism,
1918–1922,* trans. Peter and Dorothy Wait (New York, 1966); Richard
Washburn Child, *A Diplomat Looks at Europe* (New York, 1925);
Luigi Sturzo, *Italy and Fascismo,* trans. Barbara B. Carter (London,
1926); Luigi Villari, *The Fascist Experiment* (London, 1926); Herbert
W. Schneider, *Making the Fascist State* (New York, 1928); Milford W.
Howard, *Fascism: A Challenge to Democracy* (New York, 1928); Her-
man Finer, *Mussolini's Italy* (New York, 1935); Gaetano Salvemini,
Under the Axe of Fascism (New York, 1936); Giuseppe A. Borgese,
Goliath: The March of Fascism (rev. ed., New York, 1938); Daniel A.
Binchy, *Church and State in Fascist Italy* (London, 1941) shows how
the Vatican became dependent on American money; Charles F. Delzell,
Mussolini's Enemies: The Italian Anti-Fascist Resistance (Princeton,
1961) is a fine scholarly study showing considerable insight into the
Italian-American relations it touches; Massimo Salvadori, "Nationalism
in Modern Italy: 1915 and After," *Orbis,* X (Winter 1967), 1157–75;
and Adrian Lyttelton, "Fascism in Italy: The Second Wave," *Journal of
Contemporary History,* I, No. 1 (1966), 75–100.

Various aspects of Italian foreign policy under Mussolini are dealt
with in Muriel Currey, *Italian Foreign Policy, 1918–1932* (London,
1932); Constantine E. McGuire, *Italy's International Economic Position*
(New York, 1926); James Barros, *The Corfu Incident of 1923* (Princeton, 1965); Robert Ferrari, "The Italo-American Conflict on Naturalization," *Current History,* XXXI (Nov. 1929), 306–311; Konrad H.
Jarausch, *The Four Power Pact, 1933* (Madison, Wis., 1965); René
Albrecht-Carrié, "Four Power Pacts: 1933–1945," *Journal of Central*

European Affairs, V (April 1945), 17–35; Dino Grandi, "The Foreign Policy of the Duce," *Foreign Affairs,* XII (July 1934), 553–566; *The Diplomats, 1919–1939,* Gordon Craig and Felix Gilbert, eds. (Princeton, 1953) contains two excellent essays on Fascist foreign policy, one by H. Stuart Hughes and the other by Felix Gilbert; Salvemini, *Mussolini diplomatico* (Rome, 1945); and Luigi Villari, *Italian Foreign Policy under Mussolini* (New York, 1956), a biased, revisionist account; and Alan Cassels, *Mussolini's Early Diplomacy* (Princeton, N. J., 1970), a scholarly account of the years 1922–1927.

For general accounts, from the American side, on debts, disarmament, and related issues see Harvey E. Fisk, *The Inter-Ally Debts: An Analysis of War and Post-War Public Finance* (New York, 1924); *Selected Articles on Interallied Debts and Revision of the Debt Settlements,* James T. Gerould and Laura S. Turnbull, eds. (New York, 1928); two books by Harold G. Moulton and Leo Pasvolsky, *World War Debt Settlements* (New York, 1926) and *War Debts and World Prosperity* (New York, 1932); Benjamin H. Williams, *The United States and Disarmament* (New York, 1931); Merze Tate, *The United States and Armaments* (Cambridge, Mass., 1948); Robert H. Ferrell, *Peace in Their Time: The Origins of the Kellogg-Briand Pact* (New Haven, 1952); Herbert Feis, *The Diplomacy of the Dollar: First Era, 1919–1932* (Baltimore, 1950); and Herbert Hoover, *Memoirs,* 3 vols. (New York, 1951–52).

CHAPTER 11 : THE DEPRESSION AND ETHIOPIA
Important background material for Italian and American foreign policy in this period may be found in Maxwell H. H. Macartney and Paul Cremona, *Italy's Foreign and Colonial Policy, 1914–1937* (London, 1938); Raimondo Luraghi, *Ascesa e tramonto del colonialismo* (Turin, 1963); Fulvio D'Amoja, *Declino e primi crisi dell'Europa di Versailles. Studio sulla diplomazia italiana ed Europa (1931–1933)* (Milan, 1967); Robert H. Ferrell, *American Diplomacy in the Great Depression. Hoover-Stimson Foreign Policy, 1929–1933* (New Haven, 1957); Robert A. Divine, *The Illusion of Neutrality* (Chicago, 1962); Manfred Jonas, *Isolationism in America, 1935–1941* (Ithaca, N.Y., 1966); Hugh R. Wilson, *Diplomat Between Wars* (New York, 1941); Henry L. Stimson and McGeorge Bundy, *On Active Service in Peace and War* (New York, 1948); and *Franklin D. Roosevelt and Foreign Affairs,* Edgar B. Nixon, ed., 3 vols. (Cambridge, Mass., 1969), covers Roosevelt's first administration, 1933–1937.

For the Ethiopian War and its international implications see Angelo Del Boca, *The Ethiopian War, 1935–1941,* trans. P. D. Cummins (Chicago, 1969), a full-scale history; George W. Baer, *The Coming of the Italian-Ethiopian War* (Cambridge, Mass., 1967), a sound, scholarly study; A. J. Barker, *The Civilizing Mission: A History of the Italo-Ethiopian War of 1935–1936* (New York, 1968), a popular military account; Robert G. Woolbert, "Italy in Abyssinia," *Foreign Affairs,* XIII (April 1935), 499–508; and Vera Micheles Dean, "The League and the Italo-Ethiopian Crisis," *Foreign Policy Reports,* XI (Nov. 6, 1935), 214–224; Helen Hiett, "Public Opinion and the Italo-Ethiopian Dispute: The

Activity of Private Organizations in the Crisis," *Geneva Special Studies,* VIII (Feb. 1936), 1–20; Hugh R. Wilson, Jr., *For Want of a Nail: The Failure of the League of Nations in Ethiopia* (New York, 1959); Emilio de Bono, *Anno XIII: The Conquest of an Empire* (London, 1937); Pietro Badoglio, *The War in Abyssinia* (New York, 1937); Pompeo Aloisi, *Journal (25 Juillet 1932–14 Juin 1936)* (Paris, 1957), the diary of an Italian diplomat in Geneva; and two pieces by Gaetano Salvemini, "Can Italy Live at Home?" *Foreign Affairs,* XIV (Jan. 1936), 243–258; and *Prelude to World War II* (New York, 1954).

Various aspects of the American reaction are discussed in Brice Harris, Jr., *The United States and the Italo-Ethiopian Crisis* (Stanford, Calif., 1964); John Norman, "Italo-American Opinion in the Ethiopian Crisis: A Study of Fascist Propaganda," unpubl. diss. (Clark University, Worcester, Mass., 1942); Norman, "Influence of Pro-Fascist Propaganda on American Neutrality, 1935–1936," *Essays in History and International Relations in Honor of George Hubbard Blakeslee,* Dwight E. Lee and George E. McReynolds, eds. (Worcester, Mass., 1949), pp. 193–214; Paul A. Fitzgerald, "American Neutrality and the Italo-Ethiopian Conflict," 2 vols. unpubl. diss. (Georgetown University, Washington, D.C., 1953); Lawrence H. Fuchs, "Minority Groups and Foreign Policy," *Political Science Quarterly,* LXXIV (June 1959), 161–175 is useful for background on the general problem; Luigi Criscuolo, *After Mussolini . . . What?* (New York, 1936), a pamphlet in defense of the Fascist war; Anonymous, "The Impassioned Preacher of Royal Oak," *The Living Age,* CCL (April 1936), 169–170 shows Coughlin's pro-Italian stance; Charles J. Tull, *Father Coughlin and the New Deal* (Syracuse, 1965); William E. B. DuBois, "Inter-Racial Implications of the Ethiopian Crisis: A Negro View," *Foreign Affairs,* XIV (Oct. 1935), 82–92; Herbert Feis, *Seen from E. A., Three International Episodes* (New York, 1947); Raimondo Manzini, "Le leggi di neutralità degli Stati Uniti d'America (1793–1941)," *Rivista di studi politici internazionali,* XXIII (Jan.–March 1956), 28–70; Henderson B. Braddick, "A New Look at American Policy During the Italo-Ethiopian Crisis, 1935–36," *Journal of Modern History,* XXXIV (March 1962), 64–73; Robert A. Friedlander, "New Light on the Anglo-American Reaction to the Ethiopian War, 1935–1936," *Mid-America,* XLV (April 1963), 115–125; Manfred Jonas, "Pro-Axis Sentiment and American Isolationism," *The Historian,* XXIX (Feb. 1967), 221–237; and Stuart L. Weiss, "American Foreign Policy and Presidential Power: The Neutrality Act of 1935," *Journal of Politics,* XXX (Aug. 1968), 672–695.

For some Italian reactions toward the United States in the thirties see Emilio Cecchi, *America amara* (Florence, 1939) which is a widely read critical account that influenced the attitudes of intellectuals toward America; a more favorable but still critical appraisal is Mario Soldati, *America primo amore* (Milan, 1934). See also Amerigo Ruggiero, *Italiani in America* (Milan, 1937); Luigi Villari, *Gli Italiani negli Stati Uniti* (Rome, 1939); and the anti-Fascist novel, Ignazio Silone, *Bread and Wine,* trans. Gwenda David and Eric Mosbacher (New York, 1937).

Aspects of the Italian-American experience in the thirties and earlier can be found in Edward Corsi, "My Neighborhood," *Outlook,* CXLI (Sept. 16, 1925), 90–92; Corsi, "The Voice of the Immigrant," *ibid.,* CLXVII (Sept. 21, 1927), 88–90, on foreign newspapers; and Corsi, *In the Shadows of Liberty: The Chronicle of Ellis Island* (New York, 1935); Nat J. Ferber, *A New American: From the Life Story of Salvatore A. Cotillo, Supreme Court Justice of the State of New York* (New York, 1938); Leonard Covello, "The Social Background of the Italo-American School Child: A Study of the Southern Italian Family Mores and Their Effect on the School Situation in Italy and America," unpubl. diss. (New York University, 1944), published finally in 1967 in Leyden; Leonard Covello, with Guido D'Agostino, *The Heart Is the Teacher* (New York, 1958); Robert W. Peebles, "Leonard Covello: A Study of an Immigrant's Contribution to New York City," unpubl. diss. (New York University, 1967); Ruth Teiser, *An Account of Domingo Ghirardelli and the Early Years of the Ghirardelli Company* (San Francisco, 1945); Julian Dana, *A. P. Giannini, Giant in the West* (New York, 1947); Marquis and Bessie R. James, *Biography of a Bank: The Story of Bank of America, N.T. & S.A.* (New York, 1954); Joseph Giovinco, "Democracy in Banking: The Bank of Italy and California's Italians," *California Historical Society Quarterly,* XLVII (Sept. 1968), 195–218; Russell M. Posner, "The Bank of Italy and the 1926 Campaign in California," *California Historical Society Quarterly,* XXXVII (Sept. 1958), 267–275, and (Dec. 1958), 347–358; Posner, "A. P. Giannini and the 1934 Campaign in California," *Historical Society of Southern California Quarterly,* XXXIX (June 1957), 190–201; and Theodore W. Lilienthal, "A Note on Gottardo Piazzoni, 1872–1945," *California Historical Society Quarterly,* XXXVIII (March 1959), 7–9, about a well-known California artist. Arthur Mann has written the finest study of La Guardia, which also examines how Italian-Americans came of age politically. See his *La Guardia: A Fighter Against His Times, 1882–1933* (Phil., 1959) and *La Guardia Comes to Power, 1933* (Phil., 1965). See also Paul J. Kern, "Fiorello La Guardia," *The American Politician,* John Salter, ed. (Chapel Hill, N.C., 1938), pp. 3–46; Lowell M. Limpus and Burr W. Leyson, *This Man La Guardia* (New York, 1938); Ernest Cuneo, *Life with Fiorello: A Memoir* (New York, 1955); Newbold Morris, *Let the Chips Fall: My Battles Against Corruption* (New York, 1955); Salvatore J. La Gumina, *Vito Marcantonio, The People's Politician* (Dubuque, Iowa, 1969); and Alan Schaeffer, *Vito Marcantonio, Radical in Congress* (Syracuse, N.Y., 1966). Angelo M. Pellegrini, *Americans by Choice* (New York, 1956), tells of the fortunes of six Italian immigrants.

The following are pertinent analyses or sociological studies of acculturation. Everett V. Stone, *The Marginal Man: A Study in Personality and Culture Conflict* (New York, 1937); Elin L. Anderson, *We Americans: A Study of Cleavage in an American City* (Cambridge, Mass., 1938); William F. Whyte, *Street Corner Society: The Social Structure of an Italian Slum* (Chicago, 1930); Whyte, "Race Conflicts in the North End of Boston," *The New England Quarterly,* XII (Dec. 1939), 623–642; W. Lloyd Warner, and Leo Strole, *The Social Systems of American Ethnic Groups* (New Haven, Conn., 1945); David J. O'Brien, *American*

Catholics and Social Reform: The New Deal Years (New York, 1968); also, Caroline F. Ware, *Greenwich Village, 1920–1930* (Boston, 1935) which contains an excellent essay by Archie Bronsen, "The Public School's Contribution to the Maladaptation of the Italian Boy." Paul Radin, *The Italians of San Francisco: Their Adjustment and Acculturation* (San Francisco, 1935); R. A. Schermerhorn, *These Our People: Minorities in American Culture* (Boston, 1949); E. P. Hutchinson, *Immigrants and Their Children, 1850–1950* (New York, 1956); *Children of the Uprooted,* Oscar Handlin, ed. (New York, 1966); Frank C. Hanighan, "Foreign Political Movements in the United States," *Foreign Affairs,* XVI (Oct. 1937), 1–20; Oscar Handlin, "The Immigrant and American Politics," *Foreign Influences in American Life,* ed. David F. Bowers (Princeton, 1944), pp. 87–89; Laurence H. Fuchs, "Some Political Aspects of Immigration," *Law and Contemporary Problems,* XXI (Spring 1956), 270–283; Fred I. Greenstein and Raymond Wolfinger, "The Suburbs and Shifting Party Loyalties," *Public Opinion Quarterly,* XXII (Winter 1958), 473–482; Paul F. Cressey, "Population Succession in Chicago, 1898–1930," *American Journal of Sociology,* XLIV (July 1938), 59–69; Richard C. Ford, "Population Succession in Chicago," *American Journal of Sociology,* LVI (Sept. 1950), 156–160; Leo Grebler, *Housing Market Behavior in a Declining Area: Long-Term Changes in Inventory and Utilization of Housing on New York's Lower East Side* (New York, 1952) shows Italian-Americans had no compunctions about leaving Italian neighborhoods; Albert Parry, "Good-Bye to the Immigrant Press," *American Mercury,* XXVIII (Jan. 1933), 56–63; Thorsten Sellin, "Crime and the Second Generation of Immigrant Stock," *Interpreter Releases,* XIII (May 23, 1936), 144–150; Howard L. Kingsley and Mary Carbone, "Attitudes of Italian-Americans Toward Race Prejudice," *Journal of Abnormal and Social Psychology,* XXXIII (Oct. 1938), 532–537; Ruby Jo Reeves Kennedy, "Single or Triple Melting Pot: Intermarriage in New Haven, 1870–1950," *American Journal of Sociology,* LVIII (July 1952), 55–66; Joshua A. Fishman, et al., *Language Loyalty in the United States* (The Hague, 1966); and Anthony M. Turano, "The Speech of Little Italy," *American Mercury,* XXVI (July 1932), 356–359.

Laura Fermi, *Illustrious Immigrants: The Intellectual Migration from Europe, 1930–41* (Chicago, 1968) contains some information on *fuorusciti.* See also her *Atoms in the Family, My Life with Enrico Fermi* (Chicago, 1954); and "Process of Americanization," *Mademoiselle,* XXXIX (Sept. 1954), 115 ff. Two studies by the Works Progress Administration of the thirties tell something of Italian acculturation. See *The Italian Theatre in San Francisco* (San Francisco, 1939); and *The Italians of Omaha* (Omaha, 1941). Many of the writings mentioned for the other chapters are also important for this one.

CHAPTER 12: THE COMING OF WAR

The literature on the Spanish Civil War is extensive and almost all of it, in one way or another, refers to the Fascist intervention. Solid general accounts are: Gabriel Jackson, *The Spanish Republic and the Civil War, 1931–1939* (Princeton, 1965); Hugh Thomas, *The Spanish Civil War*

(New York, 1961); Patricia A. M. van der Esch, *Prelude to War; The International Repercussions of the Spanish Civil War, 1936–1939* (The Hague, 1951); Norman J. Padelford, *International Law and Diplomacy in the Spanish Civil Strife* (New York, 1939); Dante Puzzo, *Spain and the Great Powers, 1936–1941* (New York, 1962); Luis Bolin, *Spain: The Vital Years* (Phil., 1967), a nationalist Spaniard's favorable view of the Italian intervention; Spanish Foreign Office, *The Italian Invasion of Spain* (Washington, 1937), a critical Loyalist view; and Roberto Cantalupo, *Fu la Spagna* (Milan, 1948), an Italian view.

For various aspects of the American reaction to the war and the Italian intervention see Claude G. Bowers, *My Mission to Spain* (New York, 1954); F. Jay Taylor, *The United States and the Spanish Civil War* (New York, 1956); Allen Guttmann, *The Wound in the Heart: America and the Spanish Civil War* (New York, 1962); Richard P. Traina, *American Diplomacy and the Spanish Civil War* (Bloomington, Ind., 1968); Robert A. Rosentone, "The Men of the Abraham Lincoln Battalion," *Journal of American History*, LIV (Sept. 1967), 327–338; and J. David Valaik, "Catholics, Neutrality, and the Spanish Embargo, 1937–1939," *ibid.*, LIV (June 1967), 73–85.

The most authoritative and thorough account of the coming of the Second World War to the United States is a two-volume study by William L. Langer and S. Everett Gleason, *The Challenge to Isolation, 1937–1940* (New York, 1952) and *The Undeclared War, 1937–1940* (New York, 1953). A. J. P. Taylor, *The Origins of the Second World War* (London, 1961) is a provocative general interpretation; Henry H. Adams, *Years of Deadly Peril: The Coming of the War, 1939–1940* (New York, 1969) is a descriptive military history; and Robert A. Divine, *The Reluctant Belligerent: American Entry into World War II* (New York, 1965) is a brief general account. More specialized works are: U.S. Department of State, *Peace and War: United States Foreign Policy, 1931–1941* (Washington, D.C., 1942); U.S. Department of State, *United States and Italy, 1936–1946: Documentary Record* (Washington, D.C., 1946); Charles F. Delzell, "Pius XII, Italy, and the Outbreak of War," *Journal of Contemporary History*, II (Oct. 1967), 137–161; Howard R. Marraro, "Diplomatic Relations with the Vatican," *Catholic World*, CLXIV (1946), 131–139 emphasizes Myron C. Taylor's mission; Arturo C. Jemolo, *Church and State in Italy, 1850–1950*, trans. David Moore (London, 1960) is useful for background, Mark L. Chadwin, *The Hawks of World War II* (Chapel Hill, N.C., 1968); Kathryn D. T. Bartimo, "American Opinion Toward the European War, 1939–1941," unpubl. diss. (Clark University, Worcester, Mass., 1941); George Gallup, "What We, The People, Think About Europe," *New York Times Magazine* (April 30, 1939), pp. 1–2, 16; and *Public Opinion, 1935–1946,* Hadley Cantril, ed. (Princeton, 1951).

For Fascism going to war or at war, see Charles F. Delzell, "Studi americani sul fascismo," *Nuovo osservatore*, LVI–LVII (1966), 952–962, a fine bibliographical essay; William Ebenstein, *Fascist Italy* (New York, 1939); Galeazzo Ciano, *Italy's Foreign Policy* (Rome, 1937), a speech; Barbara Ward, *Italian Foreign Policy* (Oxford, 1941), a pamphlet;

Frank M. Tamagna, *Italy's Interests and Policies in the Far East* (New York, 1941); David H. Popper, "Strategy and Diplomacy in the Mediterranean," *Foreign Policy Reports,* XIII (June 1, 1937), 66–76; Bernadotte E. Schmitt, "Italian Diplomacy, 1939–1941," *Journal of Modern History,* XXVII (June 1955), 159–168, a review article; Elizabeth Wiskemann, *Europe of the Dictators, 1919–1945* (New York, 1966), and her *Fascism in Italy* (New York, 1969) are brief, popular surveys. Two perceptive studies of Italians at war are Reynolds and Eleanor Packard, *Balcony Empire: Fascist Italy at War* (New York, 1942); and Saville R. Davis, "Morale in Fascist Italy in Wartime," *American Journal of Sociology,* XLVII (Nov. 1941), 434–438.

American memoirs or biographies that touch on the Italian relationship or are important to it are Sumner Welles, *The Time for Decision* (New York, 1944), which contains a full account of the meetings with Mussolini and Ciano; Robert E. Sherwood, *Roosevelt and Hopkins* (rev. ed., New York, 1950); James M. Burns, *Roosevelt: The Lion and the Fox* (New York, 1956); Cordell Hull, *The Memoirs of Cordell Hull,* 2 vols. (New York, 1948); *The War Diary of Breckinridge Long,* Fred L. Israel, ed. (Lincoln, Neb., 1966); William Phillips, *Ventures in Diplomacy* (North Beverly, Mass., 1952), a good part of these memoirs deal with Italy; and *The Moffat Papers: Selections from the Diplomatic Journals of Jay Pierrepont Moffat, 1919–1943,* Nancy H. Hooker, ed. (Cambridge, Mass., 1956).

For the status of Jews in Italy see: Renzo De Felice, *Storia degli ebrei italiani sotto il fascismo* (Turin, 1962); Richard Arvay, "Where Justice Is Done: Italian Repugnance to Racist Doctrine," *Commonweal* (June 8, 1945), 182–186. For the status of Italian-Americans see Edward Corsi, "Italian Immigrants and Their Children," *The Annals of the American Academy of Political and Social Science,* CCXXIII (Sept. 1942), 100–106; Irvin L. Child, *Italian or American? The Second Generation in Conflict* (New Haven, Conn., 1943); Jeanette S. Smith, "Broadcasting for Marginal Americans," *Public Opinion Quarterly,* VI (Winter 1942), 588–603 is a perceptive study showing discrimination against Italian-Americans; Constantine Panunzio, "Italian-Americans, Fascism, and the War," *The Yale Review,* XXXI (June 1942), 771–782; Alberto Cupelli, "The U.S. Italian Language Press Dances to the Nazi Tune," *Il mondo,* VII (March 1944), 3–9; and John Norman, "Repudiation of Fascism by the Italian-American Press," *Journalism Quarterly,* XXI (March 1944), 1–6, 54.

For the views of the anti-Fascist exiles see *Neither Liberty nor Bread: The Meaning and Tragedy of Fascism,* Frances Keene, ed. (New York, 1940); Anonymous, "About the Mazzini Society," *Free Italy* (Feb. 1945), p. 13; Aldo Garosci, *Storia dei fuorusciti* (Bari, 1953); and Gaetano Salvemini, *Memorie di un fuoruscito* (Milan, 1960).

CHAPTER 13: "THE BITTER TEST OF HOSTILITIES"
There is no good scholarly account of Italy and the United States at war. The literature on the subject is scattered and often part of larger studies dealing with the war against the major American enemy, Germany.

Much of it is composed of contemporary journalistic or impressionistic accounts. Charles F. Delzell, "Mussolini's Italy Twenty Years After," *Journal of Modern History,* XXXVIII (March 1966), 53–58 offers a review of a number of important works on Fascist Italy. Gordon Wright, *The Ordeal of Total War, 1939–1945* (New York, 1968) is good for its extensive background free of excessive detail. The basic book for an interpretation of Fascist Italy in this period and earlier is Luigi Salvatorelli and Giovanni Mira, *Storia d'Italia nel periodo fascista* (Turin, 1956). Also important is Federico Chabod, *A History of Italian Fascism,* trans. Muriel Grindrod (London, 1963), based on lectures given in Paris in 1950; and Carlo Sforza, *Contemporary Italy,* trans. Drake and Denise De Kay (New York, 1944), based on lectures given at the University of California, Berkeley, in 1942–43. The relationship between Mussolini and Hitler is analyzed in Dino Alfieri, *Dictators Face to Face,* trans. David Moore (New York, 1955); Frederick W. Deakin, *The Brutal Friendship* (New York, 1962), the finest scholarly account; and Elizabeth Wiskemann, *The Rome-Berlin Axis* (London, 1949). See also Enno von Rintelen, *Mussolini als Bundesgenosse* (Tubingen, 1951), memoirs by the Nazi military observer in Rome 1936–1943; and Maxwell H. H. Macartney, *One Man Alone: The History of Mussolini and the Axis* (London, 1944).

Various specialized pieces explain Italy's conduct during the war. Useful data may be found in Robert A. Graham, *Vatican Diplomacy: A Study of Church and State on the International Plane* (Princeton, 1959); Camille M. Cianfarra, *The Vatican and the War* (New York, 1944); Howard McGaw Smyth, "The Command of the Italian Armed Forces in World War II," *Military Affairs,* XV (Spring 1951), 38–52; Giuseppe Berto, *The Sky Is Red,* trans. Angus Davidson (New York, 1948) is a novel about the war in Italy which says much about Americans; Gaetano Salvemini and George La Piana, *What to Do with Italy* (New York, 1943) attacks American diplomacy; Peter Tompkins, *Italy Betrayed* (New York, 1966); Luigi Sturzo, *Italy and the Coming World* (New York, 1945); Sturzo, *La mia battaglia da New York* (Milan, 1949); Luigi Villari, *The Liberation of Italy, 1943–1947* (Appleton, Wis., 1959), a revisionist account by a former Fascist diplomat; and Maxwell H. H. Macartney, *The Rebuilding of Italy* (London, 1945). Nathaniel Weyl, *Treason: The Story of Disloyalty and Betrayal in American History* (Washington, D.C., 1950) contains a chapter on Ezra Pound's work for Fascists in Italy. See also Nemi d'Agostino, *Ezra Pound* (Rome, 1960), a literary study. Randolfo Pacciardi, "A Free Italian Legion," *Nation,* CLV (Oct. 3, 1942), 299–300 deals with the Montevideo anti-Fascist conference; and Gabrio Lombardi, *Il corpo italiano di liberazione* (Rome, 1945) covers the activities of the liberation corps. Massimo Salvadori has written a number of pieces on the partisan movement in Italy. Two of these are: *Brief History of the Patriot Movement in Italy, 1943–1945* (Chicago, 1954), and *Resistenza ed azione: ricordi di un liberale* (Rome, 1962). See also Guido Quazza, *La resistenza italiana: apprenti e documenti* (Turin, 1966); and Norman Kogan, "Gli alleati e i partiziani," *Il movimento di liberazione in Italia* (Nos. 52–53, 1958), pp. 180–183.

The only book that deals largely with American relations with wartime Italy is Norman Kogan, *Italy and the Allies* (Cambridge, Mass., 1956), a well-balanced, scholarly study. Two useful journalistic accounts are Alfred Wagg and David Brown, *No Spaghetti for Breakfast* (London, 1943); and Herbert L. Matthews, *The Education of a Correspondent* (New York, 1946). Three books that place policy toward Italy in a broad context are William H. McNeill, *America, Britain and Russia: Their Cooperation and Conflict, 1941–1946* (New York, 1953); Herbert Feis, *Churchill, Roosevelt, Stalin: The War They Waged and the Peace They Sought* (Princeton, 1957); Gabriel Kolko, *The Politics of War: The World and United States Foreign Policy, 1943–1945* (New York, 1968) is the most critical of American policy in Italy. U.S. Department of State, *Foreign Relations of the United States: The Conferences at Malta and Yalta, 1945* (Washington, D.C., 1955) contains a section on policy toward Italy. Useful military histories are J. F. C. Fuller, *The Second World War, 1939–45* (New York, 1949); Kent R. Greenfield, *American Strategy in World War II: A Reconsideration* (Baltimore, 1963); A. Russell Buchanan, *The United States and World War II*, 2 vols. (New York, 1964); W. G. F. Jackson, *The Battle for Italy* (New York, 1967); Trumbull Higgins, *Soft Underbelly: The Anglo-American Controversy over the Italian Campaign, 1939–1945* (New York, 1968); and Robert H. Adelman and George Walton, *Rome Fell Today* (Boston, 1968).

Important memoirs or accounts by leading participants that deal with Italy are: Winston S. Churchill, *The Second World War*, 6 vols. (Boston, 1948–53); *The Roosevelt Letters: Being the Personal Correspondence of Franklin Delano Roosevelt*, Elliott Roosevelt, ed., 3 vols. (London, 1949–52); Joseph C. Grew, *Turbulent Era: A Diplomatic Record of Forty Years, 1904–1945*, ed. Walter Johnson, 2 vols. (New York, 1952); William D. Leahy, *I Was There* (New York, 1950); Harry C. Butcher, *My Three Years with Eisenhower* (New York, 1946); Dwight D. Eisenhower, *Crusade in Europe* (New York, 1948); Mark W. Clark, *Calculated Risk* (New York, 1950); and Robert D. Murphy, *Diplomat Among Warriors* (New York, 1964). Important memoirs or accounts from the Italian side are: Benedetto Croce, *L'Italia nella vita internazionale* (Bari, 1944), a pamphlet; *Croce, the King and the Allies: Extracts from a Diary by Benedetto Croce, July 1943–June 1944*, trans. Sylvia Sprigge (London, 1950); Benito Mussolini, *The Fall of Mussolini*, ed. Max Ascoli (New York, 1948); Galeazzo Ciano, *L'Europa verso la catastrofe* (Milan, 1948); *The Ciano Diaries, 1939–1943*, ed. Hugh Gibson (Garden City, N.Y., 1945); Howard McGaw Smyth, "The Ciano Papers: Rose Garden," unpubl. paper written for the Dept. of State [Washington, 1969]; Mario Roatta, *Otto milioni di baionette* (Milan, 1946); Giacomo Zanussi, *Guerra e catastrofe d'Italia*, 2 vols. (Rome, 1945–46); Pietro Badoglio, *Italy in the Second World War*, trans. Muriel Curry (London, 1948); Raffaele Guariglia, *Ricordi, 1922–1946* (Naples, 1950); Albert Kesselring, *Soldat bis zum letzen Tag* (Bonn, 1953); and Marc' Antonio Bragadin, *The Italian Navy in World War II*, trans. Gale Hoffman (Annapolis, Md., 1957).

There is a considerable literature on Italy's surrender. *The New Republic,* CXI (Aug. 9, 1943) contains articles and opinions on the fall of Mussolini and Italy's defeat; Giuseppe Castellano, *Come firmai l'armistizio di Cassible* (Milan, 1945); Malbone W. Graham, "Two Armistices and a Surrender," *The American Journal of International Law,* XL (Jan. 1946), 148–158; Francesco Rossi, *Come arrivamo all'armistizio* (Milan, 1946); Howard McGaw Smyth, "The Armistice of Cassibile," *Military Affairs,* XII (Spring 1948), 12–35; Norman Kogan, "L'armistizio di Cassibile," *Il ponte,* V (1949), 1360–70; Paul Kecskemeti, *Strategic Surrender: The Politics of Victory and Defeat* (Stanford, Calif., 1958); Anne Armstrong, *Unconditional Surrender: The Impact of the Casablanca Policy upon World War II* (New Brunswick, N.J., 1961); Robert J. Quinlan, "The Italian Armistice," *American Civil-Military Decisions,* Harold Stein, ed. (University of Alabama Press, 1963), pp. 203–210; Ruggero Zangrandi, *1943: 25 Luglio–8 Settembre* (Milan, 1964); Albert N. Garland and Howard McGaw Smyth, *Sicily and the Surrender of Italy* (Washington, D.C., 1965); Allen Dulles, *The Secret Surrender* (New York, 1966) deals with the surrender in northern Italy and the end of the war; Mario Toscano, *Dal 25 Luglio all' 8 Settembre: Nuove rivelazioni sugli armistizi fra l'Italia e le nazioni unite* (Florence, 1966), Ivan Palermo, Storia di un armistizio (Milan, 1967); and John K. Wildgen, "The Liberation of the Valle d'Aosta, 1943–1945," *Journal of Modern History,* XLII (March 1970), 21–41.

Aspects of American policy in occupied Italy are discussed in Maurice F. Neufeld, "The Failure of AMG in Italy," *Public Administration Review,* VI (Spring 1946), 137–148; Hajo Holborn, *American Military Government: Its Organization and Policies* (Washington, D.C., 1947); George C. S. Benson and Maurice Neufeld, "American Military Government in Italy," *American Experiences in Military Government in World War II,* Carl J. Friedrich, ed. (New York, 1948), pp. 111–147; Robert W. Kromer, "The Establishment of Allied Control in Italy," *Military Affairs,* XIII (Spring 1949), 20–28; Thomas R. Fisher, "Allied Military Government in Italy," *The Annals of the American Academy of Political and Social Science,* CCLXVII (Jan. 1950), 114–122; Henry M. Adams, "Allied Military Government in Sicily, 1943," *Military Affairs,* XV (Fall 1951), 157–165; C. R. S. Harris, *Allied Military Administration of Italy, 1943–1945* (London, 1957); and Harry L. Coles and Albert K. Weinberg, *Civil Affairs: Soldiers Become Governors* (Washington, D.C., 1964), an excellent documentary source. The following deal with the economics of the occupation: Walter E. Spahr, *Allied Military Currency* (New York, 1943); Donald L. Kemmerer and T. Eugene Beattie, *Allied Military Currency in Italy* (New York, 1944); Frank A. Southard, Jr., *The Finances of European Liberation, with Special Reference to Italy* (New York, 1946); Walter Rundell, Jr., *Black Market Money: The Collapse of U.S. Military Currency in World War II* (Baton Rouge, La., 1964); and Vladimir Petrov, *Money and Conquest: Allied Occupation Currencies in World War II* (Baltimore, 1967).

For the Italian-American status during the war see Louis Wirth, "Morals and Minority Groups," *American Journal of Sociology,* XLVII

(Nov. 1941), 415–433; Harold B. Hoskins, "American Unity and Our Foreign-Born Citizens," *The Annals of the American Academy of Political and Social Science,* CCXX (March 1942), 153–159; Max Ascoli, "On the Italian Americans," *Common Ground,* III (Autumn 1942), 45–49; and two items by Luigi Criscuolo representing a conservative, defensive outlook, *Il Mondo and the Mercenaries of Karl Marx and Co.* (New York, 1942) and *The Rubicon: Criscuolo Newsletter,* published in New York (© Sept., 1941–Aug., 1945) for private circulation; Anonymous, "An Italian Manifesto," *Life,* XVI (June 12, 1944), 37–39; Louis H. Bean, Frederick Mosteller, and Frederick Williams, "Nationalities and 1944," *Public Opinion Quarterly,* VIII (Fall 1944), 368–375; Hugo V. Maiale, *The Italian Vote in Philadelphia between 1928 and 1946* (Phil., 1950); and Joseph S. Roucek, "Italo-Americans and World War II," *Sociology and Social Research,* XXIX (July–Aug. 1945), 465–471.

CHAPTER 14: THE PEACE SETTLEMENT
No one has yet written a full scholarly account of the peacemaking with Italy. The story comes out in documents, memoirs, and various brief accounts. A good general account of postwar diplomacy, useful for background, is William L. Neumann, *After Victory: Churchill, Roosevelt, Stalin and the Making of the Peace* (New York, 1967). See also Herbert Feis, *Between War and Peace: The Potsdam Conference* (Princeton, 1960). Ivor Thomas, *The Problem of Italy: An Economic Survey* (London, 1946) stresses poverty; and William Barrett, "Reflections on Returning from Italy," *Partisan Review,* XIII (Winter 1946), 57–67 offers impressions. Barbara B. Carter, *Italy Speaks* (London, 1947) argues against a punitive peace. For other discussions of immediate postwar problems, see Muriel Grindrod, *The New Italy: Transition from War to Peace* (London, 1947); Howard McGaw Smyth, "Italy: From Fascism to the Republic," *The Western Political Quarterly,* I (Sept. 1948), 205–222; Harriet E. Davis, "The Forgotten Italians," *Independent Woman,* XXIV (Sept. 1945), 244–246; Sumner Welles, *Where Are We Heading?* (New York, 1946); William S. Caldwell, "The Organization and Operation of American Information and Propaganda Operations in Early Postwar Italy," unpubl. diss. (University of Minnesota, Minneapolis, 1960); U.S. Congress, Senate Committee on Foreign Relations, *A Decade of American Foreign Policy: Basic Documents, 1941–1949* (Washington, D.C., 1950) contains reports on Italian peacemaking; U.S. Department of State, *Paris Peace Conference, 1946: Selected Documents* (Washington, D.C., 1948); *Il trattato di pace con l'Italia; documenti e carta,* Giuseppe Vedovato, ed. (Rome, 1947); Basilio Cialdea and Maria Vismara, eds., *Documenti della pace italiana: Tratto di pace con l'Italia,* (Rome, 1947); F. W. Pick, "Peacemaking in Perspective," *Journal of Central European Affairs,* VII (July 1947), 162–196; and F. Lee Benns, "The Two Paris Peace Conferences of the Twentieth Century," *Essays in History and International Relations . . . ,* Dwight E. Lee and George E. McReynolds, eds. (Worcester, Mass., 1949), pp. 153–170.

Important recollections by policymakers are: *Memoirs by Harry S. Truman,* 2 vols. (Garden City, N.Y., 1955–56); James F. Byrnes,

Speaking Frankly (New York, 1947); Byrnes, *All in One Lifetime* (New York, 1958); James Forrestal, *The Forrestal Diaries,* ed. Walter Millis (New York, 1951); *The Private Papers of Senator Vandenberg,* Arthur H. Vandenberg, Jr. and Joe Alex Morris, eds. (Boston, 1952); Attilio Tamaro, *La condanna dell'Italia nel trattato di pace* (Bologna, 1952); and Mario Toscano, "Ricordo della ratifica del trattato di pace," *Nuova antologia,* DI (Sept. 1967), 3–12. For the Trieste problems see Geoffrey Cox, *The Road to Trieste* (London, 1947); Mary E. Bradshaw, "Military Control of Zone A in Venezia Giulia," *Department of State Bulletin,* XVI (June 29, 1947), 1257–72; and Diego de Castro, *Il problema di Trieste* (Bologna, 1953). For the problem of Alto Adige see Mario Toscano, *Storia diplomatica della questione dell' Alto Adige* (Bari, 1967); and Dennison I. Rusinow, *Italy's Austrian Heritage* (New York, 1969). See also Benjamin Rivlin, *The United Nations and the Italian Colonies* (New York, 1950); and Ernest Hauser, "Something New in Striped Pants," *The Saturday Evening Post,* CCXXII (Nov. 12, 1949), 47, 88–99 deals with the diplomacy of Ambassador James Dunn in Rome.

CHAPTER 15: COLD WAR ALLY

William Reitzel, *The Mediterranean: Its Role in America's Foreign Policy* (New York, 1948) places Italy within the structure of American post-war strategy. For other analyses or discussions in a narrower context see U.S. Department of State, "U.S. and Italy Discuss Topics of Mutual Interest," *Department of State Bulletin,* XXIV (Oct. 8, 1951), 563–570; Ninetta S. Jucker, "Italy: East or West," *The Political Quarterly,* XXII (April–June 1951), 175–186, a British view critical of American policy; Alexander Werth, "Italy, the Vatican and U.S. Catholics," *Nation,* CLXXIV (May 10, 1952), 450–452; Shepard B. Clough, "Italy: Ideological and Strategic Ally," *Current History,* XXIV (Feb. 1953), 99–102; and Anonymous, "Italy, An Ally in Distress," *Scholastic,* LXIV (Feb. 17, 1954), 14–16.

For the Truman Doctrine and the Marshall Plan see Joseph M. Jones, *The Fifteen Weeks (February 21–June 5, 1947)* (New York, 1955); Seymour E. Harris, *The European Recovery Program* (Cambridge, Mass., 1948); Harry B. Price, *The Marshall Plan and Its Meaning* (Ithaca, N.Y., 1955); U.S. Economic Cooperation Administration, *European Recovery Program: Country Studies* (Washington, D.C., 1949) analyzes Italy in Chapter IX of this mimeographed study; Carlo Storza, "Italy, the Marshall Plan, and the 'Third Force'," *Foreign Affairs,* XXVI (April 1948), 450–456. For Italy and the Atlantic alliance see *Il patto atlantico al parlamento italiano. Le dichiarazioni del governo e i discorsi dell'opposizione (11–18 marzo 1949)* (Rome, 1949); Pietro Nenni, *Il cappio delle alleanze* (Milan, 1949); Nenni, *Dal patto atlantico alla politica di distensione* (Bologna, 1953); and Vittorio De Caprariis, *Storia di un'alleanza: Genesi e significato del patto atlantico* (Rome, 1958).

Various aspects of Italian foreign policy and relations with the United States are treated in: Norman Kogan, "Revision of the Italian Peace Treaty," *Indiana Law Journal,* XXVIII (Spring 1953), 334–353; Robert Strausz-Hupé, "Italian Foreign Policy," *Current History,* XXIV (Jan.

1953), 214–221; Charles F. Delzell, "The European Federalist Movement in Italy: First Phase, 1918–1947," *Journal of Modern History,* XXXII (Sept. 1960), 241–250; F. S. C. Northrup, *European Union and United States Foreign Policy* (New York, 1954); Clare B. Luce, "Italy in 1955," *Department of State Bulletin,* XXXII (Jan. 24, 1955), 132–136; Barbara Blair, "Italy as Mrs. Luce Sees It," *U.S. News and World Report,* XXV (Sept. 25, 1953), 46–52; and Cyrus L. Sulzberger, *A Long Row of Candles: Memoirs and Diaries [1934–1954]* (New York, 1969).

The following memoirs or biographical studies cast light on Italian-American relations for this period: Paolo Canali [Adstans], *Alcide De Gasperi nella politica estera italiana (1944–53)* (Verona, 1953); Giulio Andreotti, *De Gasperi e il suo tempo* (Milan, 1956); Maria Romana Catti De Gasperi, *De Gasperi, uomo solo* (Milan, 1964); Elisa A. Carrillo, *Alcide De Gasperi: The Long Apprenticeship* (Notre Dame, Ind., 1965); Carlo Sforza, *Cinque anni a palazzo Chigi: La politica estera italiana dal 1947 al 1951* (Rome, 1952); Dean Acheson, *Present at the Creation: My Years in the State Department* (New York, 1969); and Alberto Tarchiani, *Dieci anni tra Roma e Washington* (Verona, 1955).

For Italy's internal problems that affected American relations see Lawrence H. Battistini, "Italy's Educational Crisis," *Educational Forum,* X (March 1946), 317–325 which stresses the admiration of Italian educators for America; UNRRA, Italian Mission, *Survey of Italy's Economy* (Rome, 1947); Giulio Pietranera, "Considerations on the Dynamics of the Italian Inflation," *Banca Nazionale del Lavoro Review,* I (Rome, 1947–48), 20–60; Bruno Foa, *Monetary Reconstruction of Italy* (New York, 1949); Jacob J. Kaplan, *Economic Stagnation in Italy?* (New Haven, Conn., 1949); Panfilo Gentile, "Italy's Greatest Problem Is Lack of Hope," *New York Times Magazine* (Dec. 7, 1952); pp. 14, 55–61; and Robert E. Dickinson, *The Population Problem of Southern Italy* (Syracuse, N.Y., 1955).

Accounts by or dealing with travelers, returned immigrants, and others that are worthy of perusal are: Jerre Mangione, *Reunion in Sicily* (Boston, 1950); Angelo M. Pellegrini, *Immigrant's Return* (New York, 1951); Mary Dick, "Those *Americani,*" *New York Times Magazine* (April 20, 1962), p. 42, a collection of comments by Italians on Americans in Italy; Luigi Barzini, Jr., *Gli Americani sono soli al mondo* (Milan, 1952), an analysis of America's position in the cold war; Jacques Freymond, "America in European Eyes," *The Annals of the American Academy of Political and Social Science,* CCXCV (Sept. 1954), 33–41 points out that "Italy is one of the few countries in Europe in which Americans are regarded with genuine affection"; Andrew F. Rolle, "America Through Foreign Eyes," *Western Humanities Review,* IX (Summer 1955), 261–264; Indro Montanelli, "The Americans and Ourselves," *Ladies Home Journal,* LXXII (Jan. 1955), a favorable commentary on American life by an Italian journalist; Herbert Kubly, *American In Italy* (New York, 1955), essays by a Fulbright scholar; Ezio Bacino, *America bifronte* (Florence, 1957), an analytical travel account; and two books by Giorgio Soavi, a writer who visited the United States in 1954 and recorded his impressions in poetry and prose. See *L'America tutta d'un fiato* ([Rome], 1959) and *Fantabulous: Racconti americani* ([Rome], 1962). For other works pertinent to this chapter see the writings listed for the preceding and following chapters.

CHAPTER 16: IN THE MAINSTREAM
Cultural and social relations between peoples attract a varied literature, most of it broad and imprecise, but within it can often be found insights unavailable elsewhere. For background see *Cultural Affairs and Foreign Relations*, Robert Blum, ed. (Englewood Cliffs, N.J., 1963), composed of essays by different authors. Sigmund Skard, *American Studies in Europe*, 2 vols. (Phil., 1958) contains important information on cultural connections between Italy and the United States, as do two reports by the U.S. Foreign Scholarship Board, *Experiment in International Understanding* (Washington, D.C., 1963) and *Teacher and Scholar Abroad* (Washington, D.C., 1964); Walter Johnson and Francis J. Colligan, *The Fulbright Program: A History* (Chicago, 1965) uses the program in Italy as an example of similar programs in Europe. See also two essays by Howard R. Marraro, "American Studies in Italy," *South Atlantic Quarterly*, LVII (Spring 1958), 254–264 and "Relazioni culturali tra Italia e gli Stati Uniti," *Il veltro*, IV (1960), 103–112; and Cipriana Scelba, "The Fulbright Program in Italy," *Italian Quarterly*, III (Winter 1960), 21–39.

For wartime American fiction concerning Italy see Harry Brown, *A Walk in the Sun* (New York, 1944); John Hersey, *A Bell for Adano* (New York, 1944); Alfred Hayes, *All Thy Conquests* (New York, 1946); Hayes, *The Girl on the Via Flaminia* (New York, 1949); and John Horne Burns, *The Gallery* (New York, 1947). For postwar commentaries and fiction see Eleanor Clark, *Rome and a Villa* (New York, 1950); Tennessee Williams, *The Roman Spring of Mrs. Stone* (New York, 1950); Leslie A. Fiedler, *An End to Innocence: Essays on Culture and Politics* (Boston, 1955); Mary McCarthy, *Venice Observed* (New York, 1956); and Michael Novak, "An American in Italy," *America*, C (March 28, 1959), 740–741.

American writers and their influence on Italian thought and literature are discussed in Giame Pintor, "Americana," *The Western Humanities Review*, trans. and ed. Donald Heiney XVII (Summer 1963), 203–212; Mario Praz, "Hemingway in Italy," *Partisan Review*, XV, Part 2 (Oct. 1948), 1086–1100; Elio Vittorini, "American Influences on Contemporary Italian Literature," *American Quarterly*, I (Spring 1949), 3–8; Glauco Cambon, *Tematica e sviluppo della poesia Americana* (Rome, 1956); Richard H. Chase, "Cesare Pavese and the American Novel," *Studi Americani*, III (1957), 347–369; Agostino Lombardo, *Realismo e simbolismo: saggi di letteratura Americana contemporanea* (Rome, 1957); Elio Vittorini, *Diario in pubblico* (Milan, 1957); Lowry Nelson, "Americanisti italiani," *Italian Quarterly*, II (Summer 1958), 77–79; Donald Heiney, "American Naturalism and the New Italian Writers," *Twentieth Century Literature*, III (Oct. 1957), 135–143; Heiney, *America in Modern Italian Literature* (New Burnswick, N.J., 1964), one of the most thorough explorations of the cultural bond; Salvatore Rosati, *L'ombra dei padre: Studi sulla letteratura Americana* (Rome, 1958);

Rosati, "Gli scrittori Italiani," *Il veltro,* IV, Nos. 1–2 (1960), 29–36; Glauco Cambon, "The Italian Response to American Literature or the Second Discovery of America," *Cesare Barbieri Courier,* II, No. 2 (June 1960), 3–8; "Italian Criticism of American Literature: An Anthology," *The Sewanee Review,* Agostino Lombardo, ed. LXVIII (Summer 1960), a discussion of American literature by Italian authors; Lombardo, "Gli scrittori americani e l'Italia," *Il veltro,* IV (1960), 20–28; Lombardo, *La ricerca del vero: saggi sulla traduzione letteraria Americana* (Rome, 1961); Vito Amoruso, "Cechi, Vittorini, Pavese e la letteratura americana," *Studi Americani,* ed. Agostino Lombardo, VI (Rome, 1960); Cesare Pavese, *La letteratura americana e altri saggi* (Turin, 1962); and Carlo Izzo, *Civiltà americana,* 2 vols. (Rome, 1967).

For assessments of modern Italian literature and its impact on Americans see Vincent Luciani, "Modern Italian Fiction in America, 1929–1954: An Annotated Bibliography of Translations," *New York Public Library Bulletin,* LX (1960), 12–34; P. M. Pasinetti, "The Incredible Italians," *New World Writing,* I (1952), 183–192; Luciani, "The Vogue of Contemporary Italian Literature, 1947–58," *Italian Quarterly,* III (Spring 1959), 50–58; Leslie A. Fiedler, "The Rediscovery of Italian Literature: Chance, Chic and the Task of the Critic," *Italian Quarterly,* III (Spring 1959), 7–18; Sergio Pacifici, *A Guide to Contemporary Italian Literature* (New York, 1962); Pacifici, "La riscoperta italiana dell'America," *Quadrivio,* II (March 1962), 23–42; Pacifici, "From Engagement to Alienation: A View of Contemporary Italian Literature," *Italica,* XL (Sept. 1963), 236–258; *From Verismo to Experimentalism: Essays on the Modern Italian Novel,* Pacifici, ed. (Bloomington, Ind., 1970); Donald Heiney, *Three Italian Novelists: Moravia, Pavese, Vittorini* (Ann Arbor, Mich., 1968); and Furio Felcini, "Dieci anni del 'Gattopardo' (Bilancio e prospettive)," *Cultura e scuola,* VII (Jan.–March 1968), 55–65; H. Stuart Hughes, "Gli studi di storia moderna italiana in America," *Rassegna storica del Risorgimento,* XLV (April–June 1958), 272–277 discusses Italian studies in American universities. On the Italian cinema see Angelo Solmi, *Storia de Federico Fellini* (Milan, 1962); Fabio Carpi, *Cinema italiano del dopoguerra* (Milan, 1965); Gian Luigi Carpi, *Italian Cinema Today, 1952–1965* (New York, 1966); and Dwight Macdonald, *Dwight Macdonald on Movies* (Englewood Cliffs, N.J., 1969) which covers many of the important Italian films of the postwar years.

For analyses of the continuing problems of emigration and immigration see J. S. McDonald, "Italy's Rural Social Structure and Emigration," *Occidente,* II (Sept.–Oct. 1956), 437–455, a perceptive sociological examination; John Higham, "From Immigrants to Minorities: Some Recent Literature," *American Quarterly,* X (Spring 1958), 83–88; Higham, "American Immigration Policy in Historical Perspective," *Law and Contemporary Problems,* XXI (Spring 1956), 213–235; Marion J. Bennett, *American Immigration Policies* (Washington, D.C., 1963); Robert A. Divine, *American Immigration Policy, 1924–1952* (New Haven, Conn., 1957); Maurice R. Davie et al., *Refugees in America* (New York, 1947); William S. Bernard, *American Immigration Policy: A*

Re-appraisal (New York, 1950); U.S. President's Commission on Immigration and Naturalization, *Whom We Shall Welcome* (Washington, D.C., 1953); J. Campbell Bruce, *The Golden Door: The Irony of Our Immigration Policy* (New York, 1954); and John H. Burma, "Some Cultural Aspects of Immigration: Its Impact, Especially on Our Arts and Sciences," *Law and Contemporary Problems,* XXI (Spring 1956), 284–298.

Various other aspects of economic, social, and political conditions in Italy pertinent to American relations are discussed in Muriel Grindrod, *The Rebuilding of Italy: Politics and Economics, 1945–1955* (London, 1955); two essays by George H. Hildebrand, "The Postwar Italian Economy: Achievements, Problems and Prospects," *World Politics,* VIII (Oct. 1955), 46–70 and "Postwar Italy: A Study in Economic Contrasts," *Italian Quarterly,* I (Fall 1957), 56–74; Emiliana P. Noether, "Italy Reviews Its Fascist Past," *American Historical Review,* LXI (July 1956), 877–899; "The New Italy—A Close-up of American Aid," *U.S. News and World Report,* XL (Oct. 5, 1956), 82–83; Charles Delzell, "Italy: Opening to the Left?" *Current History,* XXXI (Nov. 1956), 282–288; *Perspective of Italy,* supplement to *The Atlantic Monthly,* Elisabeth Mann Borgese, ed. CCII (Dec. 1958), 113–196; Edward C. Banfield, *The Moral Basis of a Backward Society* (Glencoe, Ill., 1958), a study of a village in the *Mezzogiorno;* A. C., "Italy, the Common Market, and the Free Trade Area," *World Today,* XIV (April 1958), 152–162; Hadley Cantril, *Faith, Hope, and Heresy: The Psychology of the Protest Voter* (Princeton, 1958), a study of the Communist voter in Italy and France; Joseph La Palombara, "Italian Politics Since the War: A Study in Contrasts," *Italian Quarterly,* IV (Spring–Summer 1960), 79–91; Maurice F. Neufeld, *Italy: School for Awakening Countries* (New York, 1960) traces Italy's conversion from a museum to an industrial country; Louis Lister, *Europe's Coal and Steel Community* (New York, 1960); Pietro Nenni, "Where the Italian Socialists Stand," *Foreign Affairs,* L (Jan. 1962), 213–223 answers American critics. Journalist Giorgio Bocca comments on life in Italy, on the "miracle" and on American influences on it in *Miracolo all'italiana* (Milan, 1962) and *La scoperta dell'Italia* (Bari, 1963). See also Alvo Fontani, *Gli emigrati: L'altra faccia del "miracolo economico"* (Rome, 1962); James J. Divita, "The Course of the Debate on the Treaty of Rome in the Italian Chamber of Deputies, March–July, 1957," *Italian Quarterly,* XI (Fall 1967), 63–100; Bernard Berenson, *Sunset and Twilight: From the Diaries of 1947–1958,* ed. Nicky Mariano (New York, 1963); and Nicky Mariano, *Forty Years with Berenson* (New York, 1966).

For Italian views of America see Guido Piovene, *De America* (Milan, 1953), a penetrating effort by a journalist to present American life to Italians; David M. Epstein, "Two Italian Composers View the American Scene," *Musical America,* LXXVII (Jan. 1, 1957), 10; and Carlo L. Golino, "On the Italian Myth of America," *Italian Quarterly,* III (Spring 1959), 19–33. Educational influences are discussed in E. Mortimer Standing, *Maria Montessori: Her Life and Work* (Fresno, Calif., 1959); Montessori schools became popular in America of the fifties.

References to the political relationship can be found in Luigi Salvatorelli, *La guerra fredda* (Venice, 1956); Lloyd A. Free and Renzo Sereno, *Italy: Dependent Ally or Independent Partner?* (Princeton, 1956), a mimeographed essay; Lloyd A. Free, *Six Allies and a Neutral: A Study of the International Outlooks of Political Leaders in the United States, Britain, France, West Germany, Italy, Japan and India* (Glencoe, Ill., 1959); Jean-Baptiste Duroselle, *Le conflit de Trieste, 1943–1954* (Brussels, 1966); John C. Campbell, *Tito's Separate Road: Yugoslavia in World Politics* (New York, 1967); John R. Beal, *John Foster Dulles* (New York, 1957); Dwight D. Eisenhower, *The White House Years: Mandate for Change, 1953–1956* (New York, 1963); Giovanni Gronchi, *Discorsi d'America* (Milan, 1956), speeches during the visit to America in 1956; Gaetano Martino, *Per la libertà e per la pace* (Florence, 1957); Martino, *Verso l'avvenire* (Florence, 1963); "Visit of Prime Minister Scelba of Italy," *Department of State Bulletin,* XXXII (March 28, 1955), 612–615; "United States and Italy Reaffirm Their Close Ties: Visit of Prime Minister Segni and Foreign Minister Pella," *ibid.,* XLI (Oct. 19, 1959), 541–543; Robert Pell, "The Mind of Giuseppe Pella," *America,* CII (Oct. 10, 1959), 46–48; and Paul H. Frankel, *Mattei: Oil and Power Politics* (New York, 1966), which contains scattered references to American influence. See also titles on pertinent subjects cited for other chapters.

CHAPTER 17: THE BLURRED IMAGE
Earlier references for similar topics are important for this chapter. On the changing problems of immigration see Nathan Glazer, "The Integration of American Immigrants," *Law and Contemporary Problems,* XXI (Spring 1956), 256–269; Massimo Livi Bacci, *L'immigrazione e l'assimilazione degli italiani negli Stati Uniti secondo le statistiche demografiche* (Milan, 1961); Philip Gleason, "The Melting Pot: Symbol of Fusion or Confusion," *American Quarterly,* XVI (Spring 1964), 20–46; John J. Appel, "American Negro and Immigrant Experience: Similarities and Differences" *ibid.,* XVIII (Spring 1966), 95–103 explains which immigrant groups have feared their Negro neighbors; William S. Bernard, "The Integration of Immigrants in the United States," *The International Migration Review,* I (Spring 1967), 23–33; Daniel N. Gordon, "Immigrants and Urban Governmental Form in American Cities, 1933–60," *American Journal of Sociology,* LXXIV (Sept. 1968), 158–171; and Nathan Glazer, "A New Look at the Melting Pot," *The Public Interest,* No. 16 (Summer 1969), pp. 180–187.

For general background on ethnic stratification, acculturation, and social mobility see Tamotsu Shibutani and Kian M. Kwan, *Ethnic Stratification: A Comparative Approach* (New York, 1965); Gerhard Lenski, *Power and Privilege: A Theory of Social Stratification* (New York, 1966); E. Digby Baltzell, *The Protestant Establishment: Aristocracy and Caste in America* (New York, 1964); Peter Schrag, "The Decline of the WASP," *Harper's Magazine,* CCXL (April 1970), 86–91; Gerald D. Suttles, *The Social Order of a Slum: Ethnicity and Territory in the Inner City* (Chicago, 1968) is useful for insight into relations of Italians with other minorities; Melford E. Spiro, "The Acculturation of American Ethnic Groups," *American Anthropologist,* LVII (Dec. 1955), 1240–52;

and Nathan Glazer, "Ethnic Groups in America: From National Culture to Ideology," *Freedom and Control in Modern Society,* ed. Monroe Berger *et al.* (New York, 1954), pp. 158–173; and Colin B. Burke, "Cultural Change and the Ghetto," *Journal of Contemporary History,* IV (Oct. 1969), 173–187, stresses dispersal of immigrant groups.

For various views of Italian-Americans within the cultural pattern of urban America see Blake McKelvey, *The Emergence of Metropolitan America, 1915–1966* (New Brunswick, N.J., 1968); Jane Jacobs, *The Death and Life of Great American Cities* (New York, 1961); Walter Firey, *Land Use in Central Boston* (Cambridge, Mass., 1947); Herbert J. Gans, *The Urban Villagers: Group and Class in the Life of Italian-Americans* (New York, 1962); Nathan Glazer and Daniel P. Moynihan, *Beyond the Melting Pot: The Negroes, Puerto Ricans, Jews, Italians, and Irish of New York City* (Cambridge, Mass., 1963); Rudolph J. Vecoli, *The People of New Jersey* (Princeton, 1965); George Schirro, *Americans by Choice (History of the Italians in Utica)* ([Utica], N.Y., 1940); William G. O'Donnell, "Race Relations in a New England Town," *New England Quarterly,* XIV (June 1941), 235–242; Francis A. Ianni, "The Acculturation of Italo-Americans of Norristown, Pennsylvania, 1900 1950," unpubl. diss. (The Pennsylvania State University, 1952); "Proud Seattle Celebration: The Citizens Pay Tribute to Their Italian Heritage," *Life,* XLIII (Dec. 9, 1957), 169–171; Norman Thomas di Giovanni, "Tenements and Cadillacs: Boston's Italian Quarter," *Nation,* CLXXXVII (Dec. 13, 1958), 443–445; Gaeton J. Fonzi, "Philadelphia's Italians: A Bubbly Minestrone," *Greater Philadelphia Magazine* (Jan. 1961), pp. 24–28, 66–69; Richard Rogin, "How One Middle-Class Family Gets Along in New York," *The New York Times Magazine* (Aug. 17, 1969), pp. 32–48; Nathan Kantrowitz, "Ethnic and Racial Segregation in the New York Metropolis, 1960," *American Journal of Sociology,* LXXIV (May 1969), 685–695; Nicholas Pileggi, "Little Italy: Study of an Italian Ghetto," *New York,* I (Aug. 12, 1969), 14–23; Blake McKelvey, "The Italians of Rochester: An Historical Review," *Rochester History,* XXII (Oct. 1960), 1–24; and Wilbur S. Shepperson, "The Foreign-Born Response to Nevada," *Pacific Historical Review,* XXXIX (Feb. 1970), 1–18.

For Italian-Americans in general and their life styles see William Drake, "Pioneers Next Door," *The American Magazine,* CLXIV (April 1949), 21, 134–137; Idwal Jones, *Vines in the Sun: A Journey Through California Vineyards* (New York, 1949); Rose Grieco, "They Who Mourn," *The Commonweal,* LVII (March 27, 1953), 628–630; Grieco, "Wine and Fig Trees," *ibid.,* LX (June 4, 1954), 221–223; Albert Q. Maisel, "The Italians Among Us," *Reader's Digest,* LXVI (Jan. 1955), 1–6; Maisel, *They All Chose America* (New York, 1957); Mario Puzo, "The Italians, American Style," *New York Times Magazine* (Aug. 6, 1967), pp. 7, 14–30, an essay that set off a chain reaction of letters, especially by Italian-Americans. See "Letters to the Editor" in *ibid.,* Aug. 20, 27, and Sept. 10, 1967. Nicholas Pileggi, "How We Italians Discovered America and Kept It Clean and Pure While Giving It Lots of Singers, Judges, and Other Swell People," *Esquire,* LXIX (June 1968),

80–82, 174 is a derisive account of Americans of Italian descent. For examples of upward mobility see Patsy D'Agostino, "I Found $5,000,000 in a Pushcart," *American Magazine,* CLIV (Sept. 1952), 15 ff; and Charles Sopkin, "What a Tough Young Kid with *Fegataccio* Can Do On Madison Avenue," *New York Times Magazine* (Jan. 26, 1969), pp. 32–39. For the Vineland Map see G. R. Crone, "The Vineland Map Cartographically Considered," *Geographical Journal,* CXXXII (March, 1966), 75–80; and Michael A. Musmanno, *Columbus Was First* (New York, 1966).

The Italian family in America as a unique institution is a subject of controversy. See Paul J. Campisi, "Ethnic Family Patterns: The Italian Family in the United States," *American Journal of Sociology,* LIII (May 1948), 443–449; Alfonso La Falce and family, "An Italian in America," *Life,* XXXV (Oct. 5, 1953), 134–144; and discussion (Oct. 26, 1953), 12; and Leonard W. Moss and Walter H. Thomson, "The South Italian Family: Literature and Observations," *Human Organization,* XVIII (Spring 1959), 35–41. For Italian-American youth and education see Alan M. Thomas, Jr., "American Education and the Immigrant," *Teachers College Record,* LV (Feb. 1954), 253–67; Richard O. Ulin, "The Italo-American Student in the American Public School: A Description and Analysis of Differential Behavior," unpubl. diss. (Harvard University, 1958); Francis A. Ianni, "The Italo-American Teenager," *Annals of the American Academy of Social and Political Science,* CCCXXXVIII (Nov. 1961), 70–78; Andrew M. Greeley and Peter Rossi, *The Education of Catholic Americans* (Chicago, 1966); and Joseph G. Fucilla, *The Teaching of Italian in the United States* (New Brunswick, N.J., 1967). For data on religious adjustment see Will Herberg, *Protestant-Catholic-Jew: An Essay in American Religious Sociology* (New York, 1960); François Houtart, *Aspects sociologiques du catholicisme américain* (Paris, 1957); Aurelio P. Palmieri, "Il clero italiano negli Stati Uniti," *La vita italiana,* VIII (Feb. 15, 1920), 113–127; Francis X. Femminella, "The Impact of Italian Migration and American Catholicism," *The American Catholic Sociological Review,* XXII (Fall 1961), 233–241; and Nicholas J. Russo, "Three Generations of Italians in New York City: Their Religious Acculturation," *The International Migration Review,* III (Spring 1969), 3–17.

The influence of the Italian-American in politics and his political allegiances are interpreted differently by various writers. See Humbert S. Nelli, "John Powers and the Italians: Politics in A Chicago Ward, 1896–1921," *Journal of American History,* LVII (June 1970), 67–84 which deals with Italian-Irish political rivalry, as does Leo E. Carroll, "Irish and Italians in Providence, Rhode Island, 1880–1960," *Rhode Island History,* XXVIII (Aug. 1969), 67–74; Samuel Lubell, "Rhode Island's Little Firecracker," *Saturday Evening Post,* CCXXII (Nov. 12, 1949), 31, 174–178 is a sketch of John O. Pastore and Italian-Americans in politics; Vincent R. Tortosa, "Italian-Americans, Their Swing to G.O.P.," *The Nation,* CLXXVII (Oct. 24, 1953), 330–332; Samuel Lubell, *The Future of American Politics* (2nd ed., New York, 1956); *I Vote My Conscience: Debates, Speeches and Writings of Vito Marcantonio, 1935–1950,*

Annette T. Rubinstein, ed. (New York, 1956); Duane Lockard, *New England State Politics* (Princeton, 1959); Michael J. Parenti, "Ethnic and Political Attitudes: A Depth Study of Italian-Americans," unpubl. diss. (Yale University, 1962) predicts the passing of ethnic loyalties and "balanced" tickets; Parenti, "Ethnic Politics and the Persistence of Ethnic Identification," *American Political Science Review,* LXI (Sept. 1967), 717–726; Raymond E. Wolfinger, "The Development and Persistence of Ethnic Group Voting," *ibid.,* LIX (Dec. 1965), 896–908; Wolfinger, "Some Consequences of Ethnic Politics," *The Electoral Process,* ed. M. Kent Jennings and L. Harmon Zeigler (Englewood Cliffs, N.J., 1966); Patrick Anderson, "Born Hero-Worshipper Who Serves His Hero," *New York Times Magazine* (Feb. 20, 1966), pp. 28 29, 61 71, a sketch of Jack Valenti, a former adviser to President Lyndon B. Johnson; Warren Moscow, *What Have You Done For Me Lately? The Ins and Outs of New York Politics* (Englewood Cliffs, N.J., 1967); Paul Goldberger, "Tony Imperiale Stands Vigilant for Lawandorder," *New York Times Magazine* (Sept. 23, 1968), pp. 30–31, 117 ff; Salvatore J. La Gumina, "Ethnicity in American Political Life: The Italian-American Experience," *The International Migration Review,* III (Spring 1969), 78–81; Tom Buckley, "What is a Mario Procaccino?" *New York Times Magazine* (Aug. 10, 1969), pp. 7–9, 47–62 traces the rise and character of an Italian-American politician in New York; and David W. Abbott, Louis H. Gold, and Edward T. Rogowsky, *Police, Politics, and Race: The New York City Referendum on Civilian Review* (Cambridge, Mass., 1969).

There is a considerable literature on Italians and crime in postwar America. Most of it, however, amounts to little more than imaginative journalism centering on sensationalism and alleged exposés of the Mafia and *Cosa Nostra.* No one has yet written a thorough, objective, and scholarly study of Italian-Americans in crime. For the old country background see Renato Candida, *Questa Mafia* (Rome, 1956); Enzo D'Alessandro, *Brigantaggio e mafia in Sicilia* (Messina, 1959); Danilo Dolci, *Report from Palermo,* trans. P. D. Cummins (New York, 1959); Dolci, *Waste: An Eye-Witness Report on Some Aspects of Waste in Western Sicily,* trans. R. Munroe (New York, 1964); Jerre Mangione, *A Passion for Sicilians: The World Around Danilo Dolci* (New York, 1968); Eric J. Hobsbawm, *Social Bandits and Primitive Rebels* (Glencoe, Ill., 1959) is a scholarly study that points out data on the Mafia is unreliable, contradictory, and based mostly on rumor, and that even in Sicily the Mafia had no proper organization above the local level; Lewis Norman, *The Honored Society: A Searching Look at the Mafia* (New York, 1964); Michele Pantaleone, *The Mafia and Politics* (New York, 1966); and Paolo Sipala, "Napoleone Colajanni e gli studi sulla mafia," *Nord e Sud,* XIV (No. 155, 1967), 115–128. For general background in the United States see Frank Tannenbaum, *Crime and Community* (Boston, 1938); Milton R. Konvitz, *Civil Rights in Immigration* (New York, 1953); Irving A. Spergel, "Types of Delinquent Groups," unpubl. diss. (New York School of Social Work, 1960); Giuseppe Selvaggi, *La mie tomba è New York: Storie di gangsters* (Milan, 1957); and an anthology that relies heavily on opinion rather than documented historical accounts,

Organized Crime in America, Gus Tyler, ed. (Ann Arbor, Mich., 1962).

For examples of the sensational literature see Fred D. Pasley, *Al Capone: The Biography of a Self-Made Man* (New York, 1930); Estes Kefauver, *Crime in America* (New York, 1951) is based on Senate committee hearings and calls the Mafia "a shadowy international crime organization"; Burton B. Turkus and Sid Feder, *Murder, Inc.: The Story of "The Syndicate"* (New York, 1951); Ed Reid, *Mafia* (New York, 1952); Reid, *The Shame of New York* (New York, 1953); Eliot Ness and Oscar Fraley, *The Untouchables* (New York, 1957), a potboiler that became the basis for an immensely popular television series; Louis McLain, "Mafia: Secret Empire of Evil," *Coronet,* XLV (Nov. 1958), 56–64; Frederic Sondern, Jr., *Brotherhood of Evil: The Mafia* (New York, 1959); Robert F. Kennedy, *The Enemy Within* (New York, 1960); Harry J. Anslinger and Will Oursler, *The Murderers: The Story of Narcotic Gangs* (New York, 1961), by a U.S. Commissioner of Narcotics; Allen J. Edward, *Merchants of Menace—The Mafia: A Study of Organized Crime* (Springfield, Ill., 1962), by a policeman who equates the Mafia with communism; Ed Reid and Ovid De Maris, *The Green Felt Jungle* (New York, 1963); Raymond V. Martin, *Revolt in the Mafia* (New York, 1963); Fred J. Cook, *The Secret Rulers: Criminal Syndicates and How They Rule the U.S. Underworld* (New York, 1966); Nicholas Pileggi, "The Lying, Thieving, Murdering, Upper-Middle-Class Respectable Crook," *Esquire,* LXV (Jan. 1966), 50–52 ff.; Charles Siragusa, *The Trail of the Poppy: Behind the Mask of the Mafia* (New York, 1966), by a former narcotics agent; Bill Davidson, "The Mafia: How It Bleeds New England," *The Saturday Evening Post,* CCXL (Nov. 18, 1967), 27–31; Hank Messick, *The Silent Syndicate* (New York, 1967); Sandy Smith and William Lambert, "The Mob," *Life,* LX, Part I (Sept. 1, 1967), 15–22; Part II (Sept. 8, 1967), 91–104; U.S. President's Commission on Law Enforcement and Administration of Justice: Task Force on Organized Crime, *Task Force Report: Organized Crime. Annotations and Consultants' Papers* (Washington, D.C., 1967). The quality of the essays vary but the report accepts as fact Kefauver's allegation that the Mafia is a centralized international crime syndicate and alleges that it is dominated solely by men of Italian ancestry. Alvin Moscow, *Merchants of Heroin: An In-Depth Portrayal of Business in the Underworld* (New York, 1968); Richard Carlson and Lance Brisson, "The Web That Links San Francisco's Mayor Alioto and the Mafia," *Look,* XXIII (Sept. 23, 1969), 17–21; Donald R. Cressey, *Theft of the Nation: The Structure and Operations of Organized Crime in America* (New York, 1969), the fullest treatment of the theme of *Cosa Nostra* as "a nationwide illicit cartel"; Simone R. De Cavalcante, *The Discourses of Simone Rizzo De Cavalcante, 1962–1965* (New Jersey, 1969), transcripts of Federal Bureau of Investigation wiretaps on conversations of an alleged *Cosa Nostra* boss; Peter Maas, *The Valachi Papers* (New York, 1969), based on interviews. Maas calls *Cosa Nostra* "a huge, tightly knit secret criminal conspiracy . . . an entire subculture of evil." See also Ed Reid, *The Grim Reapers: The Anatomy of Organized Crime in America* (Chicago, 1969); Fred J. Cook, "The People vs. the Mob: Or, Who Rules New

Jersey?" *The New York Times Magazine* (Feb. 1, 1970), pp. 9–11, 32–36; and Nicholas Pileggi, "The Story of J," *ibid.* (March 29, 1970), pp. 12–13, 28–32, about a *Mafioso* and his activities.

One of the best scholarly analyses of the Italian involvement in crime is Humbert S. Nelli, "Italians and Crime in Chicago: The Formative Years, 1890–1920," *American Journal of Sociology,* LXXIV (Jan. 1969), 373–391. Robert T. Anderson, "From Mafia to Cosa Nostra," *ibid.,* LXI (Nov. 1965) points out that the evidence on the Mafia is "incomplete, inconsistent, and inaccurate," but takes for granted its existence as an institution; Luigi Barzini, "The Real Mafia," *Harper's Magazine,* CCVIII (June 1954), 38–46 questions the existence of the Mafia as "a tight, disciplined, centralized organization"; Giovanni Schiavo, *What Crime Statistics Show About Italians* (New York, 1931); Schiavo, *The Truth About the Mafia and Organized Crime in America* (New York, 1962) acknowledges the one-time existence of a Mafia as a network of small gangs. This is a poorly organized, defensive work but sound in many details. Reflecting the views of Virgil Peterson, a former federal agent, Joseph N. Bell, "Exploding the Mafia Myth," *Pageant Magazine* (May 1960), pp. 50–55 denies the existence of a super criminal organization. The sociologist Daniel Bell analyzes organized crime and concludes that both the Mafia and *Cosa Nostra* are myths. See his *The End of Ideology* (Glencoe, Ill., 1960) and "The Myth of the Cosa Nostra," *The New Leader,* XLVI (Dec. 23, 1963), 12–15. Earl Johnson, Jr., "Organized Crime: Challenge to the American Legal System," *Journal of Criminal Law, Criminology and Police Science,* LIII (Dec. 1962), 399–425, LIV (March and June 1963), 1–29, 127–145 suggests that the Mafia does not exist, but says that organized crime does and is the basis of a popular folklore. Murray Kempton, "The Mafia," *New York Review of Books,* XIII (Sept. 11, 1969), 5–10 examines several popular books on the Mafia and concludes that its alleged power is based on myth. Gordon Hawkins, "God and the Mafia," *The Public Interest,* XIV (Winter 1969), 24–51 is one of the most penetrating critiques of Mafia literature. He believes that theories of the Mafia's existence "prove on examination to consist of little more than a series of dogmatic assertions." See also Mark H. Haller, "Urban Crime and Criminal Justice: The Chicago Case," *Journal of American History,* LVII, and Joseph L. Albini's excellent *The American Mafia: Genesis of a Legend* (New York, 1971).

CHAPTER 18: THE COMFORTABLE RELATIONSHIP

For Italy of the sixties see Vera Lutz, *Italy: A Study in Economic Development* (London, 1962); Daniel L. Horowitz, *The Italian Labor Movement* (Cambridge, Mass., 1963); *Italy,* Ronald Steel, ed. (New York, 1963), an excellent anthology; Bruno Foa, "Italy's Stake in the Common Market," *Current History,* XLV (Nov. 1963), 289–294, 303; Margaret Carlyle, *Modern Italy* (rev. ed., New York, 1965); Gustav Schachter, *The Italian South: Economic Development in Mediterranean Europe* (New York, 1965); Norman Kogan, *A Political History of Postwar Italy* (New York, 1966) contains a great deal on Italian-American relations; Giuseppe Mammarella, *Italy After Fascism: A Political History, 1943–1965* (rev.

ed., Notre Dame, Ind., 1966); George H. Hildebrand, *Growth and Structure in the Economy of Modern Italy* (Cambridge, Mass., 1967); Serge Hughes, *The Fall and Rise of Modern Italy* (New York, 1967); Charles P. Kindleberger, *Europe's Postwar Growth: The Role of Labor Supply* (Cambridge, Mass., 1967); Muriel Grindrod, *Italy* (London, 1968); M. V. Posner and S. J. Woolf, *Italian Public Enterprise* (Cambridge, Mass., 1967); Aubrey Menen, "In Rome They Call It *Il Miracolo Italiano*," *New York Times Magazine* (July 9, 1967), pp. 6–7, 32–36, a gentle spoof of Italy's new prosperity; and Aurelio Peccei, *The Chasm Ahead* (New York, 1969) deals with the technological gap between Europe and America.

For foreign policy and other aspects of foreign relations see Ennio Di Nolfo, "Gli studi sulla politica estera italiana del secondo dopoguerra," *Cultura e scuola*, VII (Jan.–March 1968), 103–109, an important bibliographical essay; Norman Kogan, *The Politics of Italian Foreign Policy* (New York, 1963); *La politica estera della repubblica italiana*, Massimo Bonanni, ed., 3 vols. (Milan, 1967) contains essays by various authors on important aspects of postwar foreign policy; Luigi Graziani, *La politica estera italiana nel dopoguerra* (Padua, 1968), a brief account; Piero Ostellino, *L'Italia tra atlantismo e neutralismo* (Turin, 1964); David Kraslow and Stuart H. Loory, *The Secret Search for Peace in Vietnam* (New York, 1968); F. M. Murphy, "The Soviet Navy in the Mediterranean," *U.S. Naval Institute Proceedings*, XCIII (March 1967), 39–44; Ph. Mason and J. Labayle Couhat, "La présence navale sovietique en Méditerranée," *Revue de Défense Nationale*, IV (May 1968), 858–873; Walter Laquer, *The Struggle for the Middle East: The Soviet Union in the Mediterranean, 1958–1968* (New York, 1969); Vincent P. De Santis, "The United States and Italy," *American Foreign Policy in Europe*, Omer De Raeymaeker and Albert H. Bowman, eds. (Louvain, Belgium, 1969), pp. 45–55; and Arthur M. Schlesinger, Jr., *A Thousand Days: John F. Kennedy in the White House* (Boston, 1965).

Various aspects of emigration and immigration in the fifties and sixties are discussed in Grazia Dore, *La democrazia italiana e l'emigrazione in America* (Brescia, 1964); Salvatore Cafiero, *Le migrazione meridionali* (Rome, 1964); Franco Della Peruta, "Per la storia dell'emigrazione meridionale," *Nuova revista storica*, Nos. 3–4 (1965), pp. 344–356, a review article; Abba P. Schwartz, *The Open Society* (New York, 1968) deals with events leading to the law of 1965; Jethro K. Lieberman, *Are Americans Extinct?* (New York, 1968) also deals with the battles for the law of 1965; "The Italian Experience in Emigration," *International Migration Review*, Silvano Tomasi, ed., I (Summer 1967) comprises the entire issue. The articles are wide-ranging, scholarly, and perceptive. Particularly pertinent are those by Herbert J. Gans, Giuseppe L. Monticelli, Joseph Velikonja, and Antonio Perotti. See also the essays in "The New Immigration," *Annals of the American Academy of Political and Social Science*, Edward P. Hutchinson, ed., CCCLXVII (Sept. 1969); and Grazia Dore, "Some Social and Historical Aspects of Italian Emigration to America," *Journal of Social History*, II (Winter 1968), 95–122.

For Italian views of America of the fifties and sixties, see Mario

Soldati, *The Capri Letters,* trans. Archibald Colquhoun (New York, 1956), a novel that bridges two cultures; Gianfranco Corsini, *America alla specchio* (Bari, 1960), a journalistic stripping of traditional Italian stereotypes about Americans. Giorgio Spini, *America 1962: New Tendencies of the American Left* (Florence, 1962) attacks the anti-American stereotypes of Italian leftists and the ridiculous in American life; and Nantas Salvalaggio, *America a passo d'uomo* (Milan, 1962), gives impressions of a journalist.

For cross-cultural appreciation and the American view of Italy see Robert O. Mead, *The Atlantic Legacy: Essays in American-European Cultural History* (New York, 1969), broad, but useful for background and ideas; "Image of Italy," a special issue of *The Texas Quarterly,* Harry H. Ransom, ed., IV, No. 2 (Summer 1961) attempts in various articles to show the texture of Italian life; Irving R. Levine, *Main Street, Italy* (New York, 1963); John Ney, *The European Surrender: A Descriptive Study of the American Social and Economic Conquest* (Boston, 1970) contains a chapter on Italy, Ada Louise Huxtable, *Pier Luigi Nervi* (New York, 1960); Carlo Falconi, *Pope John and the Ecumenical Council* (New York, 1964); Michael Durham, "They Made a Satellite Launch Look Almost Easy," *Life,* LXII (May 26, 1967), 102–103 deals with Italian space scientists aided by American technology; Giorgio Spini, *Autobiografia della giovane America: La storiagrafia americana dai Padri Pellegrini all'independenza* (Turin, 1968) is a fine example of Italian scholarly interest in American history; "Shangri-la for Artists," *Time,* LXXI (June 23, 1958), 59–60 describes the opening of the Festival of Two Worlds; Lawrence Alloway, *The Venice Biennale 1895–1968* (Greenwich, Conn., 1968); Willi Bongard, "When Rauschenberg Won the Biennale," *Studio International,* CLXXV (June 1968), 288–89, tells how an American, Robert R. Rauschenberg, in 1964 won this most coveted prize; and "Italian Ministry of Education Creates New Chairs in American Studies: Fulbright–Hays Exchanges and Seminars Play Key Supporting Role," *American Studies News,* VII (Autumn–Winter 1968–69), 1–3.

CHAPTER 19: AMERICA DOLCE, AMERICA AMARA

All the works previously cited are in a sense pertinent to this concluding assessment, but the following are of special value because of their ideas or themes. David B. Davis, "Some Recent Directions in American Cultural History," *American Historical Review,* LXXIII (Feb. 1968), 696–707; Robert Erwin, "Civilization As a Phase of World History," *ibid.,* LXXI (July 1966), 1181–98 explains why the slum farmer became the city's slum dweller; David M. Potter, "The Quest for the National Character," *The Reconstruction of American History,* John Higham, ed. (New York, 1962), pp. 197–220; David Reisman, "Some Questions About the Study of American National Character in the Twentieth Century," *Annals of the American Academy of Political and Social Science,* CCCLXX (March 1967), 36–56; Thomas L. Hartshorne, *The Distorted Image: Changing Conceptions of the American Character Since Turner* (Cleveland, 1968); Michael De Capite, "The Story Is Yet To Be Told," *Com-*

mon Ground, I (Autumn 1940), 29–36; Timothy L. Smith, "New Approaches to the History of Immigration in Twentieth Century America," *American Historical Review,* LXXI (July 1966), 1265–79; and Carlo Levi, "Italy's Myth of America," *Life,* XXIII (July 7, 1947), 84–86, 89–95.

Giuseppe Prezzolini has written extensively on the cross-cultural theme, but in retrospect views the Italian-American relationship bitterly and pessimistically. See his "America and Italy: Myths and Realities," *Italian Quarterly,* III (Spring 1959), 3–12; *America in pantofole* (Florence, 1950); *America con gli stivali* (Florence, 1954); *Tutta L'America* (Florence, 1958); and *I trapiantati* (Milan, 1963).

The Italian-American artist and writer frequently bridges two cultures or combines them in his work. For artists see Frances Winwar, *Ruotolo: Man and Artist* (New York, 1949), a brief appreciation of Onorio Ruotolo; and Irma B. Jaffe, *Joseph Stella* (Cambridge, Mass., 1970), about the only American futurist, one who wrote poetry in Italian in addition to painting. Olga Peragallo, *Italian-American Authors and Their Contribution to American Literature,* ed. Anita Peragallo (New York, 1949) is an annotated bibliography that shows the meagerness of the Italian-American output. A more penetrating study is Rose B. Green, "The Evolution of Italian-American Fiction as a Document of the Interaction of Two Cultures," unpubl. diss. (University of Pennsylvania, 1962).

Examples of Italian-American fiction or fiction on the Italian-American theme are: Luigi Capuana, *Gli "Americani" di Ràbato* (Milan, 1912), a story about a repatriated Sicilian immigrant; Eugenio C. Branchi, *"Dagoes," Novelle Transatlantiche* (Bologna, 1927), two novellettes on immigrants; John Fante, *Wait Until Spring, Bandini* (New York, 1938); Pietro Di Donato, *Christ in Concrete* (New York, 1939); Guido D'Agostino, *Olives on the Apple Tree* (New York, 1940); D'Agostino, *My Enemy the World* (New York, 1947); Jo Pagano, *The Paesanos* (Boston, 1940); Pagano, *Golden Wedding;* Mari Tomasi, *Deep Grow the Roots* (Phil., 1940); Jerre Mangione, *Mount Allegro* (Boston, 1942); Michael De Capite, *Maria* (New York, 1943), a view of Americanization from immigrant to third generation; Lee A. Crown, *If This Be My Harvest* (New York, 1948), about Italian-Americans in California's vineyards; Pietro Di Donato, *Three Circles of Light* (New York, 1960); Octavia Waldo, *A Cup in the Sun* (New York, 1961); Joseph Caruso, *The Priest* (New York, 1956); Mario Puzo, *The Fortunate Pilgrim* (New York, 1965) stresses the conflict between generations; Puzo, *The Godfather* (New York, 1969); Arturo Giovanitti, *Arrows in the Gale* (Riverside, Conn., 1914), poems expressing some of the bitterness of the Italian-American experience; Emanuel Carnevali, *The Autobiography of Emanuel Carnevali,* compiled and prefaced by Kay Boyle (New York, 1967) gives insight on the poet's worlds of Italy and America in the nineteen twenties; and Carnevali, *A Hurried Man* (Paris [1925]), a collection of poems and essays. P. M. Pasinetti, *From the Academy Bridge* (New York, 1970) links the two worlds of Venice and Southern California in the fifties and sixties.

Index

Prepared by Joseph P. Navarro